Auntie
Charlotte,
Enjoy The trip
to Poofano!
XO Catie

Kit
Bridget
Paolo
Lassino
Lorenzo

Love
on the
Rocks

A Positano Tale

Catie Costa

This is a work of fiction. Any presumed likenesses to people or places in Positano are completely coincidental.

ISBN: 978-1-4834-2324-1 (sc)
ISBN: 978-1-4834-2326-5 (hc)
ISBN: 978-1-4834-2325-8 (e)

Library of Congress Control Number: 2014922004

Lulu Publishing Services rev. date: 3/26/2015

To the real "Queen of Seduction," Positano

And for Bunny, with me always—XO

Prologue

Bridget flipped through the photo album labeled "Positano." She and her best friend, Kit, had started the album two summers ago when they had returned from their first visit to the seaside resort. The girls conceded that the cliffside town had cast some sort of spell over them that summer. What had it been about that first summer: the lazy beach days; the hot, prosecco-downing nights at the disco? Yes, of course. But more than those things, it had been about the people they'd met there.

Bridget perused the pages of the album and sighed nostalgically. There was Tino in front of his ceramics shop; the Americans they'd met at the disco; there was bespectacled Lassino sticking his tongue out at Kit; and there was *Paolo*. Paolo, with his prominent nose, bright-blue eyes, and gorgeous white teeth. Paolo and Bridget, well, what had transpired between them during this last trip had been completely harmless, although a bit out of character for Bridget. There was nothing *wrong* with what she'd done, *per se*. Everybody did stuff like that on vacation. That's what *they* said. Whoever "they" were. Bridget remembered the night all too well …

She and Kit had been dining at Solo Tu; the reservation had been set up by Lassino. Owned by one of Lassino's friends, the restaurant was up the hill quite a bit, out of the touristy shuffle of Positano proper. Listed in *Condé Nast Traveler* magazine for its creative Italian dishes and its Californian ambience, it had become a hotspot for the locals, as well as travelers in the know. Bridget had felt the mood of the evening was somewhat dampened, though. Kit was upset with Lassino, and it was obvious. Kit was normally upbeat and sunshiney to a fault, and her irritable mood was not lost on Bridget that night. Bridget, being the more sullen and moody of the pair, never quite knew how to act when Kit got this way, it being such a rare occurance.

"You know why Lassino sent us up here to dinner, don't you?" Kit had asked Bridget suddenly.

Not sure if the question was rhetorical, Bridget guessed, "Because we always eat at his restaurant and Lassino thought it would be nice to have us try Solo Tu? Nice of him to make the reservation for us. It's pretty hard to get one, isn't it?"

"Don't give him that much credit, Bridget! Lassino is *friends* with Franco. We could get in here anytime we want. No. He sent us here because he has some 'friends'—*girls* from Australia visiting, and they'll probably be at his restaurant tonight. He just doesn't want me running into them. Does he think I'm stupid?"

Bridget decided to definitely *not* answer that question.

Kit sighed. "I don't know why he goes to such lengths. Why isn't he just honest about it? Why would I care about girls he met last summer?" Bridget shrugged as she rhythmically stirred the brown sugar at the bottom of her mojito with her straw. She would not be the one to figure out Lassino. Supposedly, he had an on-again, off-again American girlfriend, but he also seemed to have quite a few friends of the international tourist female persuasion, Kit among the lot.

They were a moment away from asking for the check when Franco sat down at their table. "So, you are friends of Lassino?" he asked cheerily.

Kit answered, "Yes, we met him and Paolo last year."

"Lassino has many friends, and any friend of his is a friend of mine. Especially if they are beautiful women like you! Don't worry, I am just joking—I have a girlfriend!" He laughed heartily.

Franco sat and talked with them for quite a while. Assuming they knew all about Lassino's girlfriend, Monica, he freely chatted about her. The girls exchanged looks. In a town like this, you never knew when interesting tidbits of information would fall into your lap. Franco continued, "Monica is a very sweet girl. You have seen Lassino's closets?"

Kit sat with her chin in her hand and said with a smile, "Actually, yes, I have." Kit had seen *and* been inside the huge walk-in closet. Bridget had listened in awe to Kit's description of it. It was three-tiered on both sides, with all hanging clothes covered in clear garment bags. Kit said it looked like the dry cleaners'. If Lassino had actually pushed a button that rotated the clothing, she wouldn't have been surprised in the least. Then there were the two shelves worth of shoes and a whole shelf devoted to all his T-shirts. Bridget felt that it was just so wrong to have a closet like this wasted on a man, but she had to admit, it sounded as if Lassino had certainly put it to good use.

Franco said, "Then you know how huge they are and how many clothes he has. When Monica was here in March, she tried to help categorize Lassino's clothing on his computer."

"That would be *quite* an accomplishment. Was she able to do it?" Kit asked.

"No, she was only here for a week and that was not long enough! When she comes back, she will finish, I guess!" Franco replied.

Bridget laughed while Kit fiddled with her bangly bracelets and then asked nonchalantly, "So, where *is* Lassino tonight?"

Franco answered, "I don't know what he is doing after he works at the restaurant." His cell phone rang and he answered it. He spoke Italian into the phone while looking at the girls. Bridget could get that he was telling whoever was on the other line that Lassino's *regazze americane* were sitting with him.

He hung up. "That was Paolo. He is at the disco. He says there is some famous American basketball player there. Would you like a ride down the hill with me?"

"Sure! Ooh, we get to ride on the scooter!" Kit sang.

Franco smiled. "Okay, you pay and then we go."

Franco jumped on the scooter and put his helmet on.

"Just hold on tight since I don't have helmets for you."

Bridget looked at the scooter skeptically and frowned. The seat looked small—no, make that miniscule. She knew that many Italians were on the trim side, but this was ridiculous. Besides, Bridget didn't even like to ride bikes, let alone anything that was motorized and required extreme balance and caution. Surely, this was an accident waiting to happen.

Bridget shook her head and said, "Kit, we are *not* all going to fit on that!"

"Yes, we are! We just squeeze in tightly. Here, you sit in the middle. I don't care about sitting on the end."

Bridget looked skeptically at the scooter and then at Kit, which caused Kit to say, "Okay, fine, I'll sit in the middle," and she hopped on and threw her arms around Franco.

"Really, I can just walk down the hill and meet you at the disco—"

Franco kick started the scooter.

"Come on, Bridget. Just get on!" shouted Kit over her shoulder.

"Oh, Lord," Bridget muttered under her breath. She quickly catapulted herself onto the back of the scooter and clung to Kit. God help her if she fell off. God help Kit too, because she'd kill her—if she were still alive.

"Is this safe?" Bridget muffled tentatively into the back of Kit's hair.

Kit turned to look over her shoulder at Bridget as she said, "Don't worry, they drive these roads all the time, and we're only going down to the hill till we get to the parking garage."

The scooter sputtered and lurched forward as they pulled away from the curb. Bridget scooched in and held onto Kit even tighter. She hoped her butt wasn't hanging off and that they didn't hit some rock (or person) that would send her flying off the end of it. That would just be her luck.

Driving Via Pasitea was comparable to maneuvering an obstacle course since you had to constantly dodge a myriad of scooters, cars, buses, pedestrians, and the occasional dog that scampered out into the road. It was a one-way road that wound its way down to where the buses stopped to drop off tourists, a place known as "the square." In reality, it wasn't a square at all, but a fork in the road (one more thing to baffle the tourists), where Via Pasitea and Via C. Colombo met.

Anybody on wheels could continue up Via C. Colombo, but it was pedestrians only on Via Pasitea after the fork split, as it descended all the way down to the beach. Of course, if you were walking to town and wanted to cut the time in half, you could always take any of the hundreds of stairs that branched off of Via Pasitea. This was a bit precarious and none too conducive for those wearing heels, since the steps were either super narrow and close together, or so far apart that you had to take two and a half steps in between each or risk going into the jazz split. Grab onto a handrail? Maybe, if you could find one. They were sporadically placed, so one never knew when they'd appear.

It would seem that safety was not a pressing issue in Positano. Of course, it was typical that the one night Bridget wore semisensible shoes was the one night she didn't have to take all the stairs. Bridget concentrated on the fact that, thankfully, scooters weren't allowed on the stairs! Even the Positanesi weren't crazy enough for that. At least, she hoped they weren't. One never knew.

Right then, Bridget would have preferred to be one of the walking pedestrian targets. She kept her eyes squeezed shut as the scooter sped up, then slowed down, then sped up again. She was quite sure that whenever Franco slowed down, it was to avoid hitting someone or something. No, she was not having fun at all, and she'd always wanted to ride on the back of some Italian's scooter in Italy, like Audrey Hepburn in *Roman Holiday*—although Audrey Hepburn looked so dainty and carefree doing it. But, if Bridget remembered correctly, Audrey certainly didn't hang off the back of a scooter while gripping her best friend in the Heimlich, and she'd have her eyes open, too.

Bridget opened one eye, just in time to see the side of a bus—much too close for comfort—as they whizzed by it. *Bad idea*, she thought and clamped her eye shut again. Just a couple more turns and they'd be at the parking garage. This had to be the longest ride of her life. The scooter slowed down to a putt and then came to an abrupt halt.

"Bridget, we're here. You can loosen up the death grip now," Kit sputtered.

Bridget exhaled as she put one foot on the ground and swung her other leg off the scooter. She hadn't realized that she'd been holding her breath for a while, and she had a kink in her neck, too. Before she could apologize, Franco smiled at them and said, "*Andiamo!* Okay, let us go!"

They followed the sound of the music to the end of the beach, strolled past the empty beach chaises, and climbed the stairs that led into the disco. The beefy bouncer in a tight, black T-shirt and a headset scowled at them and handed them their drink cards. Once they were inside, Bridget was always amazed to find that the disco really was built into the rocks. The two-story building was actually a circular tower, part of the cliff that had been hollowed out. The sparse fluorescent disco lights cast shadows on the unevenly protruding rock walls.

You might think you were in a cave—a very posh cave with sleek, white couches and ottomans that wound around mysteriously curved hallways— until you looked past the bar to the other side of the dance floor and saw the inky, black water beyond the balcony-terrace.

It was only twelve thirty, early by Positano standards, but that night, the club was already full. Bridget assumed this was due to the presence of the American basketball star, whomever he was. As they shuffled through the crowd, they bumped into Lassino and another of his restaurant friends, Mario. Bridget was slightly disappointed that Paolo was not with them. Hadn't he told Franco over the phone that he was here?

"Hi!" Kit smiled toothily at Lassino and Mario.

Lassino nodded at Kit and Bridget and said, "Hello. We came down to see the basketball player. Do you know who he is?" He squinted in the direction of the dance floor.

"Oh, yeah, what's his name? He plays for the Lakers," Bridget said.

"Wasn't he in some kids' movie too? I'm taking a picture!" Kit whipped out her camera.

"Well, you will have to use your zoom lens, because nobody is allowed near him," Mario spoke up.

The seven-foot-tall player was tightly surrounded on the dance floor by his hip-hop entourage of baggy-trousered males wearing diamond-studded earrings and huge Rolexes. Bridget assumed that the lone female allowed in that circle must be his girlfriend or fiancée. She was petite—even while wearing four-inch heels, she was still a good two feet shorter than the NBA star. She sported a huge diamond ring on her left hand that sparkled in spite of the lack of lighting.

It was clear that the sports celebrity was the main attraction at the disco. People on the dance floor tried to get as close as they could to the outer circle that surrounded him. All those sitting or standing on the outskirts simply gawked at the towering figure. Bridget laughed to herself at the pretentiousness of it all.

Kit was about to thank Lassino for the dinner reservation at Solo Tu, but before she could, he turned to her and said abruptly, "We're leaving; see you tomorrow."

They watched Lassino and Mario leave, and Kit rolled her eyes and called out, "Bye." She then shrugged her shoulders and said, "Whatever. I'm staying. I'm gonna dance."

She shimmied off to the dance floor. Usher's "Yeah" was thumping loudly. Bridget watched as the dance-floor sharks slowly circled Kit. Kit smiled and looked at no one in particular, her white teeth glowing in the fluorescent disco lighting. She jiggled her shoulders and hips seductively and paid no attention to her male admirers. Bridget pondered over whether Kit might need some protection out there or if she should just sit on one of the cushioned ottomans and watch the amusing dance-off that was occurring between the prevailing dance circles of NBA guy and her best friend.

Bridget scanned the place for Paolo, but even with his large nose, he'd be hard to spot in this crowd tonight. Bridget was disappointed, yet relieved. She was about to look for somewhere to sit when she felt someone blow on the back of her neck. She turned around sharply. Paolo stood there holding his prosecco glass in one hand and his cigarette in the other, pretending to look innocently in the other direction. Smiling devilishly, he quickly turned back to Bridget and said, "Hello, Bridget. How are you?"

How was she? Suddenly jumpy and shy. How was it that a mere twenty-four-year-old could look at her with his turquoise eyes and gorgeous set of huge, white teeth, in his ridiculous orange linen pants and reduce her to a blushing puddle of nerves? Well, there was more to it than *that*. On their nights out during this vacation, Paolo had taken it upon himself to find Bridget at the disco, dance with her, and walk her back to the girls' hotel, where they'd kiss for quite awhile on the steps until the garbage collectors would rumble by or the random roosters in the town would crow, which interrupted them and sent Paolo off with a jaunty, "*Ciao, Bella!* See you tomorrow!"

This had happened on more than several occasions, and Bridget kept reminding herself that it was all very harmless. Yet, she was quite thankful to the garbage collectors and the screeching roosters, however annoying they were, since who knew what else might've transpired, had she been left alone with Paolo for much longer. Bridget was content with the mere kissing. That was about all she could handle at this point. For the last few nights, though, Bridget had not seen Paolo at the disco and had assumed, to her mortification, that he was avoiding her, having moved onto his next tourist conquest, as was common during the height of tourist season.

Although Bridget knew it was silly, that it had just been some light summer fun—and for God's sake, she was thirty-three and Paolo was twenty-four (ouch!)—she couldn't help feeling a little let down by this international rejection. Yes, how *was* she? She chose to answer pleasantly instead. "Fine. How are you?"

"Good," he replied just as brightly. "I am back from Rome. I was there for a few days, picking up some things for the store."

If any clothing or shoe shop could compete with the high Italian couture being sold in Positano, it was Da'Stella, Paolo's family boutique. No Prada or Miu Miu, but you could get that all over Italy. Positano was a beach resort town. Every other shop sold sandals and resort wear that ranged from ultra-tacky tourist to super chic and expensive. Paolo's family boutique definitely fell into the latter category. The racks in the shop were all adorned with handmade linen clothing, ala *Moda Positano*, in unique, cutting-edge styles in whatever the "it" color of the season was. And Paolo was usually found to be sporting the latest his shop offered, either a linen shirt or linen pants in an assortment of colors; hence the orange linen pants tonight. Bridget would find it quite suspect and questionable for any man at home to be caught wearing that hue, and in baggy linen, no less, but it worked on Paolo.

"Oh." Bridget nodded her head lamely and smiled. So, he hadn't completely been avoiding her. He had been out of town! *Yes!*

"So, how much longer will you and Kit be staying in Positano?" Paolo asked as he reached over to the bar and stamped out his cigarette in an ashtray. Hmm, Bridget wondered wryly, could he not wait for her to be gone?

"We leave the day after tomorrow. I should probably start packing now, since it's going to take me a while to fit everything back in my suitcase," Bridget answered.

"When did you come into the shop to buy the sandals?" Paolo changed the subject.

You couldn't get away with anything around there. Heading home from the beach that afternoon, Bridget had stopped in Da'Stella on her way back to the hotel. She'd *only* gone in because she'd seen that Paolo wasn't there and she really had been desperately wanting to try a pair of sandals on. Now Paolo probably thought that she had been snooping around for him when truly, she'd just been in need of some retail therapy.

Bridget answered, "Oh, I stopped in today and bought them."

Paolo spoke earnestly. "I am sorry that I was not there. You should have waited so I could give you a better price."

The old "discount" line. He probably said that to all the girls once he knew they were leaving.

"Well, I just figured I'd stop in today, since I didn't know if I'd get around to it tomorrow. Tomorrow's our last day, and Kit and I have a tendency to lose track of time when we're in Positano!" Bridget laughed.

Paolo chuckled. "Yes, I know. Weren't you supposed to leave for Santorini six days ago?"

Bridget shrugged. "I know; this is a hard town to leave. It's just so relaxing and beautiful."

And, of course, her best friend had begged her to prolong their stay and forego the Santorini leg of the trip.

"Bridget, I've been to Santorini. Look, you've seen one beautiful beach, you've seen them all! Besides, we actually have friends here now!" Kit had pestered Bridget. Friends? That was one way of putting it. And it was quite true that everyone in the town seemed to know who Kit was, and therefore, they knew Bridget by association. Sometimes it was just easier to give in to Kit. Bridget really loved Positano, too. And she had to admit, a few more days of avoiding packing her suitcase was fine with her. No need to tell Paolo that.

Paolo smiled at her. "Positano is a beautiful place, but of course, I say that because it is my home. What I really like about Positano is that people always come back. I am lucky because I meet many, many people every summer, and I enjoy seeing them when they come back to Positano. Like you and Kit. You are back again this summer. I am happy that I met you."

Bridget couldn't help but wonder how many other girls Paolo was happy to have met. Positano was just so completely tourist-infested. What made one girl different from the next? Yet, she felt Paolo really was sincere. Maybe he was just being nice, but maybe he was really glad he had met her. How could you ever really know? This was a confusing town. So Bridget just smiled and nodded her head.

Paolo continued, "I want to get your e-mail address. Before you leave, okay?" He looked at her imploringly.

Bridget felt it was probably a line, but what was the harm?

"Sure," she answered gamely.

"*Benissimo*," Paolo smiled.

Usher segwayed into a remix of Mariah Carey's "It's Like That." Paolo set his glass down on the bar. "Let's dance," he said as he took Bridget's hand and led her out onto the crowded dance floor.

The NBA star and his crew had left to go sit in a dark corner and sip Dom Peringon, which opened up the dance floor to hordes of civilians. Bridget looked around for Kit and found her at the other bar across the room, talking to the gorgeous bartender with the dark-fringed bedroom eyes.

Mariah sang suggestively:

"I came to have a party.
Open up the Bacardi.

Feelin' so hot tamale;
Boy, I know you're watchin' me, so what's it gonna be?"

The dance floor was crammed with couples gyrating to the beat of the song. Groups of drunk, half-dressed girls (of the American-Australian-English variety) were wiggling around, tossing their hair and doing those Britney Spears stripper-type moves that Bridget found so stupid. The dance floor sharks sidled up beside them, hoping to infiltrate the girls' personal dance space. Bridget watched as one girl did the standard drunk-girl dance. She tossed her head, bent over, rolled and arched her back, then whipped her head back up. Bridget thought that all she was missing was her imaginary pole. The girl continued with a super-fast butt shake until she rolled off one of her four-inch platforms, which sent her into a heap in the middle of her dance circle. Her friends laughed hysterically and helped her limp off the dance floor, where they continued drinking.

There'd be none of that for Bridget. Drinking—yes, dancing like that—no. She admitted she was not above throwing out cheesy dance moves like the sprinkler or the running man if a certain song permitted, but she didn't want to contribute to the stupid American dancing that had already occurred on the dance floor. Besides, this definitely wasn't the song for that.

Paolo stood behind her, one hand on her hip, the other clasping her opposite hand, and swayed to the beat, almost sambalike. Bridget followed his lead.

Mariah crooned:

"Baby, come and get it if you're really feelin' me,
'Cause it's my life, so stress, no fights, I'm leavin' it all behind …"

It was a sexy song, and Bridget felt that *sexy* was the last word she would use to describe herself. But she went with it, all the while praying that Paolo didn't start up with that Lambada-style dirty dancing. She would just die, and she hadn't had enough alcohol for that. In fact, she didn't even have a buzz. Bridget hoped that wouldn't impair her dancing tonight.

Paolo spun himself around to face Bridget. They continued to strut around each other, Paolo grabbing her hands from time to time and pulling her in close to him so that they were chest to chest. Then he'd twirl her out and around so that when she whirled back into him, he was standing behind her, in a type of dancing embrace.

"… d.j. keeps on spinnin' the cut;
It's like that, ch'all, that ch'all, like thatta, tha-that, it's like that ch'all …"

Paolo maneuvered Bridget around so she was facing him, and before she knew it, he had planted his lips on hers firmly. She opened her eyes and realized that she must've had a surprised look on her face, because he stood there grinning at her. He pulled her in closer to him and kissed her again for much longer. What was happening? Bridget couldn't believe she was pda-ing on the dance floor. That was the ultimate of tackiness and so *not* her. And she couldn't blame this on alcohol since she was stone-cold sober. Bridget decided at that moment that she didn't care that she was kissing a way younger guy on a crowded dance floor. *In Italy.* Still, she hoped nobody was watching them, especially not Kit with her candid camera.

The Mariah Carey song ended and was replaced by an Italian song, which everyone in the disco seemed to know as raucous singing broke out. Paolo and Bridget managed to squeeze through the boisterous singers and dancers till they reached the edge of the dance floor. Bridget glanced over toward the door and saw Kit grinning at her. Kit waved good-bye, paid for her drink card, and left. *What next?* thought Bridget.

As if he had read her mind, Paolo cleared his throat and said, "My friends and I are going down to the beach to swim. Would you like to come?"

A sudden feeling of panic seized Bridget. Anything that had to do with swimming would entail bathing suits, and she did not want to be seen in one, especially by Paolo and all his friends. No, she most certainly and absolutely would *not* like to go swimming. Before she could answer, though, Paolo spoke.

"Come, I must say good-bye to one of my friends first," he said and headed toward the bar. Bridget followed, unsure of what to do next. Should she make a run for it? The surly bouncer would certainly tussle her to the ground in no time flat before he allowed her to leave without paying. What was this swimming thing all about? It could not be good.

At the bar, Paolo put his arm around Bridget and, nodding at the bartender, made introductions. "This is Emilio, one of my best friends. Emilio, this is Bridget. We're going to the beach to swim." Why did Bridget feel like she was a show-and-tell object up for scrutiny?

Emilio, attacking Bridget with his bedroom eyes, smiled saucily at her and said, "It's nice to meet you. How did *you* get to be so lucky?"

Bridget raised her eyebrows in surprise. What did he mean by *that* remark? Before she could answer, Paolo called, "Ciao, Emilio," and tugged Bridget by the hand and away from the bar. She turned around to smile at Emilio and could've sworn that he winked at her a couple of times, almost as if to imply, I know what's in store for you, you lucky thing, you!

Hmmm ... Bridget was starting to get the queasy feeling that maybe Paolo wasn't as boyishly sweet and harmless as he let on. Maybe there was *no* swimming going on at the beach at all. Could that be code for *sex* on the beach? No, noo-hoo-nooo ...

Maybe Paolo was luring her down to the beach to kill her! Oh, how she wished. She'd rather die a thousand deaths than have him see her in a bathing suit, let alone naked! Of course, nothing like murder ever happened in *this* town. But sex certainly did, at least for a lot of other people, she'd heard. Uh oh. Bridget undoubtedly felt that she just might be leaving with one of the biggest playboys in Positano. Why her? She was practically a nun!

Paolo carelessly pulled a bulging wad of bills from his pocket and laid them out on the counter. A spiky-haired, statuesque girl in a vinyl minidress counted his money without even looking, and the bouncer laughed (laughed?) and nonchalantly waved them out. Paolo clasped Bridget's hand firmly, as if he suspected she'd bolt down the stairs and up the boardwalk at any minute, and they purposefully headed down the stairs that led to the beach. Bridget soon realized with disappointment that she wasn't going to be killed after all. She could already see a group of people huddled by the lounge chairs at the water's edge. They all looked like they had their clothes on, too. There were no swimsuits or towels in sight. She didn't know whether that was a good or bad sign.

With a flicker of hope, she thought, *maybe they all swim in their clothes?* She could possibly handle doing that.

"So, do you all go home and get your swimsuits?" As soon as she asked it, though, Bridget knew what a stupid question that was.

Paolo looked at her and said plainly, "Oh, no, we just swim in our underwear. And if we're drunk enough, we swim naked!" He laughed, his huge set of teeth glistening. Had his eyeteeth always been so pointy, like Dracula's fangs? Wait a minute; she was getting herself all worked up about nothing. Probably. Besides, a moonlit swim in your underwear wasn't a *crime*.

Bridget swallowed and tried not to look petrified. "Oh," she managed to chirp as cheerily as she could, as if she always frolicked about, swimming at night in just her underwear, with a bunch of people she didn't really know, in a foreign country. Well, she *could* just sit on one of the lounge chairs. She didn't have to swim, did she?

Bridget questioned cautiously, "I don't have to swim, do I?" She quickly added, "I mean, I just don't think, you know, I'm really up for … that." Paolo stared at her, his head cocked to one side.

Bridget blundered on, "You know, I ate a big dinner … and it's, just, not … good to swim … on a full stomach, a very, very, *full* stomach." She patted her stomach (which, ironically, at the moment, she was desperately trying to suck in) and hoped she sounded believable, but she knew she wasn't fooling Paolo in the slightest.

Paolo gaped at her in surprise. Then her hidden fears dawned on him, and he answered, "Ah, *allora*, no problem. You can sit on the chair."

Crisis averted. For now.

"Ciao, regazzi!" Paolo called as they approached the group.

Of the random assortment of people there, Bridget recognized a few. Franco and his sister Chiara were there, as well as the guy from the disco who always wore True Religion jeans and had a diamond chip in his right front tooth. Bridget was startled to see the little bellboy that helped at the hotel—was his name Ricardo? In fact, she thought he might be one of Marta's grandsons, or at least some relative. What was *he* doing there? He couldn't be more than fifteen, practically a child! Well, now, there was no way Bridget was going to be responsible for visually scarring some delinquent Italian youth by stripping down to her undies. Besides, he'd probably go back and inform Marta, the hotel matron, what she had been up to.

The rest, Bridget recognized from around town, but she didn't know them. Thankfully, most were already getting undressed and didn't pay much attention to her as she settled herself onto one of the lounge chairs, hoping to become invisible. Paolo stood talking to Franco and Chiara.

Franco looked over and called to Bridget, "Ciao, Bridget! Are you coming swimming?"

"No, no, I'm fine!" she called. Bridget tried not to stare as everyone undressed, but she couldn't help it. She had to peek a little bit. Kit would want some details. Good thing Lassino wasn't there with his visiting "friends" from Australia.

From what Bridget could see without totally gawking was that everyone was very comfortable with his or her body. Of course, that was easy when you *had* a perfect body. There were no muffin tops, spare tires, or saggy, dejected boobs in sight. It appeared that stretch marks and cellulite didn't exist in Positano, either. But there was still hope, since Bridget was sitting a bit away and it *was* dark out. Everyone just seemed so ... perfect: beautifully tanned girls in their bras and bikini bottoms and men in their briefs or thigh briefs. Thank God, *nobody*—male or female—was in a thong. Bridget shuddered. You never knew; this was Italy, it *could* happen.

Unfortunately, her attempt at being one with the beach chaise was unsuccessful. Franco walked over to Bridget and said, "Come on; come swimming! It's very refreshing. You don't have to be shy!" He cajoled her, his hands on his hips.

Bridget shook her head. "Nooo, maybe later—"

Franco interjected. "Bridget, do not worry. Look at my sister, Chiara!"

Bridget looked over at Chiara, who stood ankle deep in the water and looked like a younger, taller version of Sofia Loren. "Yes, your sister is absolutely beautiful!" she commented.

Franco said, rather disgustedly, "Ah, but look, she is not even wearing a matching bra and underwear!" and walked away.

At this particular moment in time, matching underwear was not really the issue for Bridget.

"Right, well, that's because she doesn't need to since she looks a *freakin'* supermodel!" Bridget mumbled under her breath.

Paolo walked over and set his messenger bag down at the foot of the chaise. "Can you watch my bag? It has the keys to my shop."

Bridget nodded.

"Are you sure you won't swim?" Paolo asked and then pulled his shirt up over his head.

"Uhh, no ... well, maybe later," Bridget's voice trailed off as she quickly glanced sideways to get a look at Paolo. He was trim, yet had cut biceps and a well-defined and hairless chest and stomach. There couldn't possibly be one inch of fat on his tanned body. Bridget suddenly wished she had remembered to do her sit-ups this morning.

Paolo unbuttoned his pants. As he pulled them down, he pretended to pull his underwear down with them and exposed the tan line on his hipbone. Bridget's eyes widened and she turned her head quickly. Paolo laughed and said, "Bridget, just kidding!" and instead just pulled his pants down.

Bridget couldn't help it. She giggled and felt herself blushing. Paolo kicked the pants off and stood in a pair of black thigh briefs. Bridget noticed that he had a row of Asian characters tattooed down the outside of his right calf. *What could they stand for?* she wondered. Wow. He was utterly gorgeous, big nose and all. This was not good. This was trouble. How was she going to sneak away?

Bridget watched Paolo run toward the water, plunging in headfirst. She felt so completely lame just sitting there. She envied the Italians, who were all clowning around in the surf, splashing each other and doing handstands like they were at a pool party instead of right outside the disco. She really wanted to go in. She could *do* this. Bridget unbuttoned her jeans but found herself powerless to pull them off. Why did she have to be so self-conscious? Probably nobody would give her a second glance, so why should she worry? If only she hadn't eaten so much at dinner, then she'd be able to suck in her poochy little gut and not look so bad. And it was dark, so her touch of inner-thigh cellulite probably wouldn't be *too* noticeable …

"Bridddgeetttt, come in the waaattterr!" Paolo called out in a sing-songy voice as his head and shoulders bobbed up and down in the water.

Bridget called back in the same sing-songy voice, "In just a minnnuutte!"

That was it; she was leaving. The whole swimming thing was not going to happen, and she was such the oddball sitting there. Bridget stood up and grabbed her wallet. She waved at Paolo, since naturally, he happened to look over as she was trying to sneak off. He swam to shore and ran up to her.

"Why are you going?" He frowned.

"I'm not going to swim, and it's late, so I'm just going to go," she answered.

"Bridget," Paolo said and put his hands together in a prayerlike pose, "come swimming. The water is beautiful."

Bridget stood there uncertainly. Paolo sensed her wavering, took her hands, and said matter of factly, "I know you want to swim."

God, he was good.

"Okay, I *do* want to swim, but I just don't want to swim in my underwear in front of all these people." Bridget waved her hands around in the direction of the water. There, she'd said it. Now Paolo would probably think she was just a prude American and take off for the water, and she could leave.

Instead, he answered, "Don't worry; come with me. We'll go further down the beach where no one is. I know a place and no one will see us. Okay?"

Shockingly, Bridget heard herself answer without hesitation, "Okay."

What? Well, dammit, why couldn't she go swimming? She never did *anything* daring or adventuresome. Stupid, yes, and this was probably not the smartest move, since it was more than likely going to involve more than swimming.

Nobody seemed to notice as Paolo grabbed his clothes and bag and led Bridget further past the disco. They clambered over a pile of rocks and were suddenly alone in a secluded alcove. A staircase leading up its rocky terrain and beach chaises scattered about indicated that it must belong to one of the hotels situated high up in the rocks above. Off in the distance, the water was roped off to warn swimmers not to go past that point.

Bridget could no longer hear the voices of Paolo's friends. The water lapped against the rocky shore quietly, lit by the moon and the lights from far up the hill above them. Bridget had to admit that it was quite romantic.

She sarcastically joked, "So, do you come here often?"

Paolo smiled and shrugged. "Um, sometimes." As he led her past an empty beach chaise, he turned to Bridget and added in mock sternness, "By the way, *never* have sex on a beach chair—very dangerous, very dangerous!"

"I'll try to remember that," replied Bridget, but Paolo was already laying his things down on a pile of flat rocks. Bridget stood a few feet away, her hands in her front jean pockets, staring at the water. She turned and found Paolo watching her. Why didn't he go into the water? *What is he waiting for?* Bridget thought anxiously. Bridget shrugged at him as if to say, *What? What are you looking at?*

Paolo shrugged back. "Are you going to get undressed?"

Oh, that. Good Lord, he was going to *stand there* and wait for her to get undressed.

"*Yesss,*" Bridget answered and rolled her eyes.

Paolo continued to stand there, watching her. Bridget unbuttoned her jeans, hoping that would encourage him to head toward the water, but no. She stopped and waved her hand at him like she were shooing him away and said, "Paolo, you can go swim. You don't have to stand there watching me get undressed."

Paolo tapped his wrist and replied smartly, "I'm waiting. Besides, if I turn around, you may disappear and I will be all alone out here."

"Fine!" Bridget mumbled under her breath. This was possibly her worst nightmare coming true: a hot Italian watching her undress.

As she pulled her jeans off, she was suddenly thankful for the fact that, unlike Chiara, she *had* worn matching underwear, bra, and a camisole. Bridget, anal retentive about color coordinating, had decided to wear the lace boyshorts with the matching lace bra. The bra that actually made her chest look good because it pushed her breasts in and up to create sexy cleavage. Not that she had been planning to have anyone see it. Bridget then grimaced as she thought about how close she had come to wearing her Spanx girdle. For some odd reason, maybe this *was* supposed to happen tonight.

Bridget nervously fumbled around as she tried to slip her arms out of the armholes of her top, and Paolo kept his gaze steady on her. She pulled it over her head and threw it down with her jeans. All righty, she was all set. And, what luck, she had worn the matching camisole. Bridget felt a little bit safer, almost like she was wearing a bathing suit; plus, her lily-white stomach would still be covered. *Time to get this swimming thing over with,* she thought.

Bridget called out, "Okay, I'm ready."

Paolo walked over to her, touched the the strap of her camisole, and said, "You need to take *that* off."

"You *said* I could swim in my underwear! This is underwear!" sputtered Bridget.

"Your *bra* and your underwear, not that!" Paolo laughed and shook his head, like she knew nothing in the world about lingerie of any sort.

She *did not* like him anymore. This was absolute torture, and he was enjoying this.

"All right, but just turn around or something, okay?" Bridget almost shouted.

"Okay!" Paolo shouted back amusedly, but he remained staring at her with his arms folded across his chest.

Bridget sighed, semiglared at him, and turned the other way as she removed her camisole. She looked down at her white stomach and then at her golden legs. Talk about two-toned. She sucked in her gut and turned around.

"Okay, let's swim," Paolo said as he grabbed Bridget's hand and dragged her across the stony beach to the water. Paolo dove in and swam out a ways. He stopped and turned around, treading water as he waited for her. Bridget slowly waded in, taking her time. The water wasn't as cold as she had expected, since the night was still pretty balmy.

Bridget finally submerged herself completely in the water. She swam toward Paolo, but she was still a bit annoyed with him, so she continued until she was little past him. She stopped when the water was up to her chest, but she was still able to stand. Paolo backstroked until he was beside her. He stood up and ran his hands through his hair.

"The water is very nice, don't you think?" Paolo asked as he inched closer to Bridget. He was going to kiss her. Bridget knew it. He had *that* look on his face. It wasn't as if they hadn't kissed a ton of times already. But now they were hardly dressed *and* in the water, a far cry from the bottom steps of the hotel. There was no crowing rooster or passing scooter to break the mood. She'd have to do it herself, if she wanted to stall for a little longer.

"Let's swim to the rope out there!" Bridget quickly said. She turned and broke into the breaststroke as she headed in the direction of the rope.

"What?" Paolo called.

Bridget swam with full force, as if she were in the Olympics, never stopping to look back. For all she knew, Paolo could be long gone by now. At least she was getting some exercise. She wondered how many calories she was burning. When she finally reached the rope, she stopped and hung onto it. She looked back and saw what a long way it was from the shore. Uh oh, maybe she'd been a little too gung-ho with the record-breaking swimming. She just might have to rest a little while at the rope. Bridget noticed that Paolo had not given up on her and was just about there. He reached out and grabbed the rope, panting, "*Mamma mia*, Bridget ... you ... are ... a very ... fast ... swimmer!"

Bridget joked, "Bet you wish you didn't smoke now!" She let go of the rope with one hand, all set to swim back.

"Ha, ha, you are very funny." Paolo grabbed her hand that remained on the rope. He closed his eyes for a moment and then opened them and said, "Bridget, *wait*, please. You know, some crazy American girl once told me it's not so good to swim on a full stomach."

Bridget shrugged sheepishly. "Yeah, well ... it's supposedly true ... maybe ..."

Paolo pulled himself down the rope so he was closer to Bridget. He leaned in and kissed her, his large nose grazing hers.

"Sorry, my nose is so big." Paolo tilted his head and kissed her again. They would have remained there much longer, but straddling a rope in super-deep water while trying to kiss called for practically Cirque de Soleil-type acrobatic water-treading. And they still had to make it back to shore. Bridget didn't want to press her luck, either. It was a wonder in itself that Paolo hadn't tried to drown her out there for being so difficult in the first place. It was time to swim back.

"Ready?" Paolo asked.

Not really. Nervous about what might be about to happen, Bridget still answered, "*Si.*"

They swam much slower this time, Paolo managing to keep a little bit ahead of Bridget. *What* had she been thinking, swimming out to the rope? The rocky beach seemed a million miles away. For all of this, she better have worked off *some* of her dinner. While the whole undressing fiasco would have been a lot easier had she been slightly inebriated, Bridget was thankful now that she wasn't drunk-swimming this marathon. At this point, all Bridget really needed to worry about, besides making it back to where she could actually stand, was getting out of the water gracefully while keeping her gut sucked in.

Bridget sighed with relief when she saw Paolo standing chest-high in the water. She stopped next to him and placed her feet upon the stones beneath her.

"Wheww!" Bridget exhaled.

"Are you tired?" Paolo asked as he moved his arms back and forth in the water.

"Uh-huh." Bridget shook her head. Wait a minute, uh-oh, what was

Paolo doing now? He grabbed Bridget's hands and threw them over his shoulders. His arms around her, he kissed her, starting at her collarbone and working his way up her neck, till he reached her lips. Oh, okay. The soft, fluttery kisses became deeper and stronger. Paolo's hands moved up and down her back and butt. Bridget didn't mind. They continued kissing, while his hands moved up to the middle of her back, and stopped there. What was he doing with his hands back there?

Oh, shit. He'd undone her bra.

"Paolo! What are you doing?" Bridget gasped, her arms immediately flying up from Paolo's shoulders in an effort to stabilize her boobs within her unhooked bra.

She was too late. Paolo had the bra slipped off of one of her arms, saying, matter-of-factly, "I'm taking off your bra!"

Bridget floundered around in the water and exclaimed, "Yes, *I know*—"

"Here, Bridget, stop. Let me help you with your bra, okay?" Paolo said calmly.

"No, no! That's okay," replied Bridget through clenched teeth.

Paolo laughed. "*Prego*. Just stop moving. I will help you. You worry too much!"

Bridget stopped and looked down at the water. Paolo stood behind her and gently pulled her tightly folded arms down away from her chest. Bridget was mortified. One boob dangled, while her bra hung from the other shoulder, still somehow covering the remaining boob. Thank God, Paolo was standing behind her and couldn't get an eyeful of this.

"Okay, now I am going to fix this bra problem," Paolo whispered huskily into Bridget's ear as he placed his hands on her shoulders. Instead, he quickly slipped the bra off the other shoulder. Bridget's boobs were now bobbing like fluorescent buoys in the moonlit water.

"Now we don't have any more problem with your bra!" Paolo nibbled on her ear.

Bridget inhaled sharply while one hand instinctively projected out to pull her chest back in and the other arm floundered around behind her, trying to locate her bra. Paolo's arms appeared in front of her and he cupped her breasts. Bridget stood frozen like a statue while Paolo began kissing her neck. His hands slid down to her waist and he turned her so she was facing him.

Paolo kissed her and said, "Bridget, *Bella*, why are you so shy? You are *buona*."

This might have been enjoyable had Bridget not been worrying about her bra floating off somewhere in the dark Tyrrhenian Sea and having to walk back to the hotel with her boobs practically on top of her stomach.

Bridget put her hands up against Paolo's chest and gently pushed him away. "Paolo, stop for a moment. Where is my bra?" Bridget asked worriedly.

Paolo looked over his shoulder and said, "Probably somewhere out there. Bridget—"

"Please, just wait while I find it. Sorry!" Bridget said as she started doggy-paddling out a bit. It couldn't be too hard to find; it was size huge! But still, it was lacy, beige, and now wet. How would she be able to see it in the dark water? Thank God for the moonlight; there was something floating ahead of her. It was her bra! She put out her hand and grabbed it.

Unfortunately, in her giddy excitement, she took in a much-too-big mouthful of water. She sputtered, surprised, and then started choking as it went down the wrong way. She gasped and tried to cough it all up, but she continued choking.

"Bridget! Are you all right?" she heard Paolo shout.

Bridget tried to say something but couldn't stop choking. She desperately treaded water, her bra tightly in her hand. By God, she was not going to lose the damn thing again. But she was getting tired, and just as she'd try to catch a breath of air, more water would rush into her mouth, causing her to choke again. Oh, she was going to drown in Italy, and without a bra on! How could this happen? *Please, God, please, don't let me drown half naked. My mother and grandmother will be so upset!* she thought.

And then she felt Paolo's arms around her stomach, pulling her backward.

"Just kick your legs Bridget, okay?" Paolo said. Bridget thought she'd do just about anything if he got her onto land again.

"Okay, here we are; you can stand here. Can you stand? Do you want me to carry you?" Paolo asked, a look of concern on his face. Good God, she didn't want him carrying her; she probably weighed more than he did, especially now that she was wet.

"No, no." Bridget shook her head as another coughing fit began. Paolo led her up out of the water, whacking her on the back as they staggered upon the rocks.

"Here, sit," he said and pointed to an area of flat rocks. Bridget sat down as Paolo walked over to grab their clothes. While his back was to her, Bridget quickly reassembled herself into her bra, which, because it was soaking wet, was no easy task. Two brushes with death—the scooter ride and the near-drowning, as well as the de-clothing debacle—had been too much. Of course, she was slightly exaggerating, but still, it would have been a lot of drama for anyone, wouldn't it? Exhausted, Bridget laid back down on the flat rocks with one arm over her forehead. Paolo lay down on his side next to her and placed a hand on her stomach. Fantastic, now he was touching her flab. Would there be no end to the utter mortification?

"Well, at least you found your bra!" he said cheerily.

Bridget took her arm from her forehead, looked at him, and began laughing. "Yes, I did. Sorry about almost drowning out there."

"It's okay. But you know, your bra—it is very dangerous," Paolo replied seriously as he rolled in toward her and threw his leg over hers.

"I actually think *you're* a little more dangerous than my bra," laughed Bridget as she gently poked a finger into his chest.

Paolo smiled impishly. *"Allora,* well, let's take care of your bra once and for all before anyone else gets hurt. This time, when I take it off you, leave it. With your luck, you might start an avalanche in the rocks here!"

Bridget rolled her eyes, but she couldn't disagree with Paolo this time. He pulled her into him and quickly undid her bra and slipped it off her arms. He tossed it back behind them and spoke softly into her ear. "Bella," as said as he laid her back down into the rocks.

◆   ◆   ◆

The next day, Bridget and Kit made their way down the cobblestone walk. It was actually their last day, and they had managed to get up and out of the hotel before eleven. There would be no wasting good sun, and they intended to spend most of the day at the beach. Bridget planned to nap there, if she could, in this ridiculous heat. Having returned to the hotel at six a.m., Bridget was exhausted and hoped her super-dark, oversized sunglasses would help hide the obviousness of it.

"You're very quiet. Are you all right? How was last night? What happened after I left?" Kit asked Bridget.

Bridget snorted. What had happened? Hmmm … where to begin?

"Um, it was fun. I went down to the beach and went swimming with Paolo and his friends," Bridget responded blandly.

Kit stopped in the middle of the pathway and said, "You went swimming? In a *bathing suit*? In front of Paolo?"

"Well … not in a bathing suit," Bridget answered and kept walking.

Kit sped up to Bridget. "I'm sorry; were you *naked?*" A couple walking ahead of them turned around and stared. Obviously, they were English-speakers.

"*Shhh!*" Bridget hissed. "Of course not! We were in our … underwear."

It was Kit's turn to snort. "I can't believe it. This is fabulous! Bridget, the girl who practically wears a wetsuit to the beach, swimming in her underwear with a bunch of Italians! I'm shocked. This is so fantastic. Gosh, I want to go swimming like that!"

Well, of course you would, since you look like a Sports Illustrated *swimsuit model!* thought Bridget in exasperation.

"Well, we didn't swim with all the Italians, so it wasn't that big of a deal. We swam alone, where no one could see us."

Kit stared at her. "But, you just said you went swimming with all his friends …"

They were rapidly approaching Paolo's shop. Bridget mumbled, "I know, come on, I'll tell you later."

"Okay, want to stop in and see if Paolo's there?"

"No!" Bridget almost shouted, causing Kit to look at her strangely.

"I mean, he's probably not there; we can see him on the way back. Just keep walking," Bridget rattled away.

"Ooh-kay," said Kit as she shook her head. They were passing Paolo's shop and she said, "You know, he might be in there, Bridget. We should stop and say hi."

The glare from the window made it difficult to tell, but Bridget continued walking, pretending to look for something in her purse.

"Yes, just keep walking; keep walking," Bridget muttered to Kit under her breath.

"Bridget! Kit! Ciao!" Paolo called. Bridget's stomach lurched as he stepped out of Da'Stella. He stood on the steps in a U2 concert T-shirt and jeans, the most "un-Italian"-looking outfit she'd seen him in since they had arrived. Bridget was all right with that. She actually felt that she didn't want to see any type of colored linen anyway for quite a while, unless it was covering a table. He certainly looked perky, she thought, for someone who'd spent the early hours of the morning playing lifeguard and shamelessly seducing an older woman.

To call Paolo goal-oriented was putting it mildly. Smugly, Bridget thought, at least she'd made him work a bit. Little did he know that when he led her into his rock-laden shangri-la, he was going to swim laps and have to practically perform CPR and the fireman's carry. Bridget could be proud about that, but not much else. While it made for a good story, Bridget wished the whole "love on the rocks" thing hadn't happened. She knew that probably everybody would hear about Paolo's latest foreign conquest, and they'd soon forget about it. In the grand scheme of Positano life, it was no big deal. Things like this happened all the time, so who cared? Bridget did. She just wasn't like that. Ever. But maybe everybody said that when they went on vacation. Well, Bridget had been on countless vacations and *this* had never happened before. Still, she wasn't mad at Paolo. How could she really be upset when she'd known all along what was going to happen? It was a good thing they were leaving tomorrow.

"Ciao, Paolo!" gushed Kit. Bridget smiled; she was glad he couldn't see her eyes hidden behind her dark glasses.

"So, it is your last day here?" Paolo asked, shaking his head sadly.

Bridget let Kit do the talking. It was much easier than trying to be witty when she felt brain-dead.

"Yes, we are sooo sad. We love it here." Kit waved her hands around emphatically to make her point. "But, next year—we'll be back!"

Paolo grinned. "Ahh, very good. We will be waiting. I will see you tonight before you go?" He looked back and forth between the girls. Bridget, who had yet to speak, shook her head yes.

"Bridget, are you tired?" Paolo asked playfully.

Bridget managed to say, "Yes, just a little."

Kit butted in and said, "So, I heard you went swimming last night. Was it fun?" Bridget cringed. Why? Why did she have to keep talking?

Paolo turned from Kit, looked straight at Bridget, and answered seriously, "Yes, it was a very beautiful night."

Please kill me now, Bridget thought, as she cracked a weak smile and nervously cleared her throat.

"Yes, it sounds like it," Kit said as she looked from Paolo to Bridget with an amused smirk on her face. Paolo turned back to Kit and smiled at her innocently.

Bridget cut in. "Well, we better get to the beach and let you get back to work now." It had suddenly become a hundred degrees hotter and she felt herself starting to sweat.

"Ciao, Paolo!" Kit waved and started walking.

"Ciao." Bridget gave her fake Mona Lisa smile, once again glad the super-dark glasses concealed what her eyes would probably give away.

"Have a good day," Paolo said and reached the back of his hand out to touch Bridget's cheek. He smiled warmly at her. Bridget felt a little better, until he winked at her. Uh-oh.

"Thanks; you, too." Bridget backed away quickly and hurried to catch up with Kit.

As soon as they rounded the corner, Kit said, mimicking Paolo's accent, "It was a very beeyootifool night!"

"You sound like Count Dracula; stop it," Bridget snapped, thinking of Paolo's huge teeth. And his lips. And his crazy turquoise eyes. And his smooth chest, not to mention ... oh no, she was so totally distracted.

"Mary Bridget Moretti, don't change the subject—what the hell happened last night?"

Bridget winced. Unable to look at Kit, she answered, "Not now, I'll tell you later, at the beach."

The beach. She'd never look at those rocks the same way again.

"*Of course*, you're going to *tell* me. Well, come on, you're usually such a *fast* walker. Jeez, you're like dead man walking now. Pick up the pace!" Kit cried, snapping her fingers at Bridget. Bridget trudged along. Kit continued talking, turning every once in a while to make sure Bridget was keeping up.

"You know, Bridget, I just love Paolo, so whatever you did, good for you! He is so adorable and—"

"Kit, he's a little player, like all the rest of the boys here," Bridget ruefully responded.

They headed down the steps to the Spiaggia Grande. Kit said, "Well, I doubt he's as big a player as you think. Paolo really is a good person, and he genuinely likes you. At least he's respectful of you,"

Respectful. Bridget immediately thought of her bra floating out to sea and bit her lip as Kit chattered nonstop. "Unlike *jackass* Lassino, who was so rude! He barely even talked to me last night before he left the disco … probably stay in hiding until he knows I'm safely on the plane tomorrow! He so does not even care … probably at Giorgio's last night with the Australian girls … I don't need that! Am I crazy?"

They had finally reached the beach. Kit turned to Bridget. "So, you see what I'm saying?"

Bridget was not about to tell Kit that she hadn't been able to concentrate on *anything* she had been saying for the last five minutes.

She answered, "Uh-huh, sure."

She and Paolo never did exchange e-mail addresses. She thought she'd have a chance to say good-bye to him before she left, but he wasn't in his shop when they headed back from the beach. And when Kit took off with Lassino after dinner, Bridget had just decided to return to the hotel to finish packing. She wasn't about to go anywhere near the disco, water, or rock formation of any sort.

Yet as she sat alone, on the floor in her hotel room, staring at the barrage of clothing, shoes, and souvenirs that surrounded her, she felt quite sad and dejected. Not to mention overwhelmed. If her brain hadn't become so prosecco-soaked and sun-warped, she would've thought to just ship all this extra stuff back instead of dealing with it now. Bridget sighed and thought how anticlimactic it seemed sitting there, compared to what she had been doing last night at this time. The swimming, the rocks, the sneaking in at dawn, it all seemed like a million years ago, but Bridget wouldn't soon forget it. If they came back next summer—and Kit was already talking about it—she wondered, *would it start all over again?* She opened her suitcase and began to pack. They'd be back next summer.

From:	kitmcnally@yahoo.com
To:	olivia@posirentals.it
Cc:	mbridget@aol.com
Subject:	apartment rental

Dear Olivia,

Hello! My friend and I are looking to rent an apartment in Positano this summer (July to mid-August) and Francesca Leonardi told us you might be able to help us out. Do you have any two-bedroom apartments available? We don't mind being high up and away from the town center. In fact, the more stairs, the better. Thanks so much and hope to hear from you soon.

Kit McNally

From:	olivia@posirentals.it
To:	kitmcnally@yahoo.com
Subject:	re: apartment rental

Hi, Kit,

I have an apartment you might be interested in: 2 bedrooms/2 bathrooms, good-sized kitchen/eating area, washer/dryer, and large terrace with a beach view. A bit far up, and a 15-minute walk down to the town center if you take the road. Faster if you take the stairs down, but coming back up may take your breath away (literally). I won't scare you by telling you now how many steps there are. It sounds like you and your friend are already familiar with this aspect of Positano. The price is 1,100 euros per week.

Olivia

Chapter 1

Kit stood at the reservation podium near the entrance of La Bella Vita Ristorante and glanced around anxiously. The restaurant was empty, as it was only a mere 4:58 p.m., and was as quiet as it would ever be. Kit could hear the familiar clanking and clattering from the kitchen and the garbled Italian and Spanish being thrown around back there by the owners and waiters alike. She knew no one from way back in the kitchen could see her, but still, she furtively peeked over her shoulder. She had heard her cell phone buzz furiously in her purse, hidden away in the recesses of the podium stand, and she could take the suspense no more. However, if Vittorio caught her doing anything other than folding napkins or checking the Bible-sized reservation book (a.k.a. *"The Da Vinci Code"*; it was so confusing to read), he'd once again be heard swearing in Italian before shouting, "New year, new hostess! Do your job, Keett!" Seriously, why was she doing this hostessing job when she made a pretty decent salary as a teacher?

Granted, she worked in one of the wealthiest public school districts on the peninsula—Kit could take the nagging abuse from Vittorio for a while longer. She needed the extra cash for the apartment in Italy … *in Positano*. This was going to be her dream vacation. She sighed longingly, just thinking about it. Yes, she could stomach the extra late nights hostessing, the annoying leers of the busboys as they ogled her boobs, and Vittorio's temperamental ways a little longer. It would all be worth it this summer. Oh, and she *needed* this summer. Her cell phone vibrated insistently again. Kit quickly looked over her shoulder and to her relief saw that she was alone in the front of the restaurant. She fumbled quickly in her purse and yanked her phone out. Oh, she hoped it was from *him*.

Something from him, *anything* from him. It didn't matter if it was one of his vague, mysterious messages—although, *all* his messages were a bit on the cryptic side due to his spelling—but she really needed to hear from *him.* Yes! It was from *him.* It was from *Lassino.* Kit read and then reread the latest text.

> *Come stai? I not hear from you for long time. I tink you not love me no more. Ciao and kisses Lass*

Kit read the message a third time and chuckled in spite of herself. Well, Lassino's English was better spoken than written, which was a tad frightening. But aside from that, and more importantly, the game was still on …

Kit had returned from Positano that summer and was sure sure that she'd never hear from Lassino. At the very least, maybe not until March, when the Posi boys usually started making contact with their past summer flings (she assumed) in an effort to keep up the good PR with female tourists. But Lassino had sent her a message only a week after she'd been back, while she was in Spokane visiting Johnny, no less!

Since then, he'd regularly sent her messages. Of course, if Kit texted him right back, she was sure to *not* hear from him for days, which would irk her to no end. If she made him wait, he'd send her a flurry of texts and leave messages on her answering machine (most of which she could barely understand since it was like listening to the teacher in *Charlie Brown* or that odd character on *Fat Albert*), "Keet, waa-waa-waa-waa, you're very *rude!* Waa-waa-waa-waa, call me back!" At best, Lassino was annoyingly immature. Yet he was enigmatically handsome with his thick glasses, wild, blonde hair, and nearly unintelligible speech. Kit was perpetually frazzled by his hot-and-cold routine, but she was admittedly smitten. She'd tried to wholeheartedly wean herself from her Italian obsession but had been less than successful.

She'd convinced herself that once she was home, jumping back into the old routine would help get Positano out of her system. It took her less than half an hour being back, sitting around her quiet apartment, to realize she was kidding herself. So unnerved was she to be back home that she'd fled, mid-unpacking, and headed straight to La Bella Vita for a glass of prosecco to help clear her head. The prosecco had produced a lovely buzz, but not the necessary life coaching she direly needed. *What is the matter with me?* Kit wondered.

So what had she done to help herself out of this funk? Well, she'd convinced Bridget to take up Beginner's Italian at the local recreation center, and in addition to teaching all day long, she'd started hostessing at her favorite Italian restaurant four nights a week. Yes, she shamelessly admitted that it was as if Positano and Lassino had put some voodoo hex upon her that she couldn't shake. If people only knew how often she checked the Positano webcam daily, just so she could catch a glimpse of the view from Le Sirenuse Hotel of the Spiaggia Grande, the Grand Beach—well, it was kind of embarrassingly corny, or perhaps bordering upon obsessively stalkerlike. However, she preferred to think of it as wistful interest, a bonafide longing.

Yeaahhh ... all this probably was not conducive to curbing the Positano obsession. Being home had only made her miss Positano more. At the moment, Kit was still determined to stay in Positano for the whole upcoming summer, regardless of what might be going on with Lassino and Monica, his on-again, off-again girlfriend. She could certainly live there and just be *friends* with Lassino. Kit had no problem with that. It kind of sucked, since he was the only guy she'd truly been interested in for a long time, but she wasn't about to become the *amante* (lover) of some Italian playboy. She didn't need the drama.

Kit determined that it would just be a relaxing summer of lazy days at the beach and late-night dinners with friends. She must remember to send out an e-mail inviting all their friends to come visit her and Bridget. And, of course, she and her best friend would learn the ways of the locals. The apartment she and Bridget would rent would be up so high that they'd be out of all the touristy commotion.

Yes, it would be perfect. Lassino and his friends would not know what they were up to all the time, which in itself would be quite a coup since everyone knew everyone's business in the small resort town. And by the time summer came around, she and Bridget were sure to be practically fluent in Italian. Or at least least, maybe Bridget would be, since she was good with languages. Whenever Kit tried to speak any semblance of Italian, she ended up wielding what resembled a Chinese-Russian accent. You'd never know that half the blood coursing through her veins was Sicilian! Her fair complexion and blonde—albeit, salon-induced blonde—hair didn't do anything to give away her Mediterranean heritage, either.

But yes, this summer, she and Bridget were sure to assimilate into the local scene and become real Positanese, not just interchangeable, forgettable

American tourists. Ha! Take that, Lassino! Kit certainly did not want to be ignored by Lassino, but renting an apartment that far up would ensure that he would barely know Kit was even around. She was determined to show him that she could live in that town like it was her own. In her heart, she already felt it was.

Kit wanted Lassino to see that she was more than just the mere tourist who saw Positano as just another pretty face on the map. She could do it; she could! Kit swore wholeheartedly that she would not draw any unnecessary attention to herself. It might be a little difficult in such a small town like Positano—where everyone, for some reason, seemed to know her—but, well, she'd *really try* to blend. She couldn't help it if she was blonde and friendly. She could probably—no, definitely—help the blonde part, but going back to her adolescent mousy-brown mop was not ever going to happen again. She'd work on the whole unobtrusive tourist thing. Kit cringed. It wouldn't be easy.

Her cell phone buzzed again. Oooh, another text. Kit looked around again and then down at her phone. She needed to get a grip but couldn't help feeling giddy at the prospect of receiving another text from Lassino. However, she tried tricking herself into thinking it was going to be from Bridget. Yes, of course, it had to be from her best friend. No doubt it was just Bridget telling her she was skipping the restaurant tonight because of her emotionally draining session with her therapist. Kit momentarily got caught up in the supposed, yet imaginary text from Bridget.

Or *maybe* her best friend was actually in a chipper mood tonight. Perhaps the therapist had skipped making Bridget talk about that awful ex-boyfriend of hers. What else could anybody say about that creep? He was a totally maniacal sociopath that had manipulated Bridget for the last three years. Hmmm, perhaps they *would* need to continue hashing *that* unpleasantness out. Kit just couldn't imagine having to relive all of that. However, maybe that evening, they'd glossed over the ex-boyfriend debacle.

Kit hoped optimistically that they'd gone straightaway into positive self-affirmations: "Bridget, repeat after me: I am smart; I am pretty; I am lovable …" Kit really hoped so, since Bridget's moods swung like a pendulum lately and she usually holed herself up hermit-style at home a few days at a time after a therapy session. Kit sighed. The text could very well be from

Bridget. An exhausted feeling suddenly took hold of her. It wasn't always easy being the sunny, upbeat best friend.

Kit glanced down at her cell phone and then squinted at it again. Her stomach suddenly lurched unpleasantly. It was not a message from Bridget. It was from *Johnny*. She read queasily.

Hi - thinking about you. Miss and love you.

Kit read it again and felt the tight knot growing in her stomach, quite the same way she did whenever her pesky lactose intolerance flared up. This was a bad time for *that* to happen.

Why was Johnny doing this? They were so *over*. They'd been over officially for three months already. Of course, before Kit had even left for Italy that summer, she knew in her heart that she was ready to move on. Unfortunately, the transition had been less than smooth—at least for Johnny.

Upon returning home from Positano, she'd flown only a week later to Spokane to visit Johnny for the weekend, since he'd bought the plane ticket for her months earlier. Kit dreaded going because she knew she was going to tell him what had happened—well, maybe not *everything*—but she had to tell Johnny that *something* had happened.

Others might call it a slight moral breakdown, but it seemed to Kit that she had undergone some kind of epiphany in Positano—albeit, an epiphany that involved a crazy Italian man, and there was no going back—but in reality, it was so much more than that. She was not the same person. She preferred to think, though, that she was *more* herself than she had ever been. Was she coming into her own—finally? She didn't know. And no matter how painful it would be, and it had been, to tell Johnny, Kit could no longer pretend that she wanted to spend the rest of her life with him.

She'd admitted to herself that she'd been stalling with Johnny for quite some time, simply and quite honestly because she was terrified of spending the rest of her life alone. However, she was even more frightened to spend the rest of her life in boredom.

Johnny was so good and such an honorable person. And so straight and narrow. He bent over backward for her. Kit knew most girls would tell her not to complain, that they could barely get their boyfriends to glance their way without prying the remote control out of their hands, but she couldn't stand it anymore. She wanted to feel alive. Kit wanted someone to keep her on her toes. Someone who could take what she dished out and give back just as good. The only person so far who made her feel that way was a lunatic (although, a hot lunatic) who lived across the Atlantic Ocean. Typical.

Yes, Lassino was more than adept at dishing it back at her. *In fact, a little too good*, Kit thought gingerly. And half the time, she could barely understand what he was saying! Why did things have to be so complicated? She knew what her friends and family were thinking: *Here she goes again, blowing it with another perfect guy, as well as wasting her time frivolously traveling back and forth to Italy.*

Bridget seemed to be the only one who understood her, as she didn't quite fit the whole typical dating/marriage mold either. Yes, Bridget got it, but everyone else was quite disappointed in her. Kit knew she wasn't imagining her friends raising their eyebrows critically as they made their judgments about her and the choices she made. She was well aware that they were all secretly siding with Johnny—*her own friends!* No one ever seemed to care about understanding *her* side of the story. Why did everyone always hate *her*? It hardly seemed fair. Was she being a little dramatic about this? Kit didn't think so.

Yet, the one person who should've hated her didn't. The irony was too much for Kit. Maybe *that* was her punishment. When she told Johnny that she'd *met* someone in Italy (and she couldn't bring herself to reveal any more than just that), he sat there, dumbfounded. How much Johnny believed her, Kit didn't know. But of course, he then wanted to know everything.

"Who was it, Kit? That Lasso guy you met last year?"

"*Lassino*," Kit couldn't help answering icily.

Ignoring the disdain in her voice, Johnny had countered bluntly, "Did you sleep with him? Do you still love me? I need to know."

That had been the longest weekend of Kit's life. She returned to the Bay Area completely worn out and shellshocked. The "Positano situation" had indeed caused a rift between her and Johnny … but they weren't broken up. Johnny still wanted to be with her!

Kit had thought she'd never hear from him again, but he called her every day to check in. What would they talk about? Typical things like work, friends, and family ... his next visit to see her. Kit repeatedly bit her lip, knowing that she would not allow Johnny to come see her ever again.

Somehow, she just couldn't bring herself to explain this to him. Each phone conversation left Kit more irritated, frustrated, and guilt-ridden. What was the matter with Johnny? He was supposed to throw up his hands and walk away from their broken relationship. Why was he still sticking around? Kit couldn't wrap her brain around it.

She'd whimper to Bridget, "Bridget, it's so awful! He's so sad when I talk to him. It makes me want to cry. But he still wants us to be together. I don't know what to do!"

To which Bridget would reply matter-of-factly, "Kit, you *don't want* to be with Johnny. *You* know it. *We* all know it! On some level, Johnny probably even knows it. And I'm no expert on relationships, but do you really think it's a good idea to talk to each other every night, if you're trying to end it with him? It seems like mixed signals to me and ... it's just kind of ... weird."

"Yeah, but we're still friends," Kit whined.

Bridget sighed. "Well, Johnny doesn't want to be just *friends* with you. He wants to marry you! How's he ever going to get over you if you continue this? This isn't helping. Put an end to it or stop complaining about it. But that's just my opinion."

Kit had sniffed mournfully, but she silently conceded that Bridget was correct. The next night, when Johnny brought up coming to the Bay Area for a visit, Kit flat-out told him no. Amid Johnny's protests, she told him she loved him, she really did, but she needed to be on her own. And so did he, she'd added.

Apparently, in Johnny's mind, this meant that there was still hope for them because now it was December, and Kit was still getting texts and calls from him on a regular basis. Kit didn't think she could be any more obvious. It wasn't as if she was using the Jedi mind trick on him! It had been really difficult for her not to return his calls, but she was getting better at it. Maybe she'd send him a message tomorrow or the next day. She sighed sadly. She hated being mean.

Oh, her stomach. It was rumbling, and not because she was hungry. Kit reached into her purse again and found her Rolaids. She was in the midst of popping three of them when her phone buzzed yet again, causing her to almost choke on the chalky antacid tablets. Dear God, she couldn't take much more of this. Why had she ever decided to check her phone? Kit felt she was pushing her luck, but she decided she might as well check to see who it was from. *Thank God.* She exhaled. It was from Bridget.

At Mon Amis with Marren - b there soon. P. S. get the prosecco out ... X B

"Keeett! *Dai*, come on, customers are waiting!" the sound of Vittorio's irritating voice, calling from the back of the restaurant, immediately stopped Kit from her texting. She rapidly thrust the phone into the podium and looked up. Oops, how had she not seen this group of people come in? And who ate at the unheard-of hour of five thirty? *Americans, that's who*, Kit sighed to herself.

"Si, Vittorio. Ggrrrrrrr," she mumbled under her breath. She quickly glanced at the reservation book and found the first name at the top of the page. She fervently hoped she was translating the Italian version of this last name correctly. She plastered her toothiest of smiles on her face before she spoke. "*Williams*, table for four? Right this way, please."

A block away, Bridget stood outside the Mon Amis storefront as Marren locked up. She looked down at the two pink Mon Amis shopping bags in her hands and a wave of buyer's remorse came over her. What had she been thinking? She'd done it again. Maybe Donna Lynn was right. A registered therapist ought to know, she guessed. Bridget attempted reasoning with herself. The Repetto ballet flats, at $192, were a *complete* deal at Mon Amis, especially when everything there was usually $200 or more. Plus, Bridget got the 25 percent friends and family discount, so the shoes had really been ... well, she wasn't sure since she was terrible with math. *But* she knew they'd been super reasonable. And she could wear them to school too, which was clearly a bonus. That counted for something, right? The multicolored sequin Vanessa Bruno cashmere ... she had not intended to buy that. However, in her defense, she had tried it on thinking that it would most likely look terrible on her and therefore would not be even be remotely purchaseable. *Wrong.*

From the moment she'd slipped the luxurious V-neck on, Bridget knew she had to have it. The large, gem-colored sequins covered the right shoulder in an asymmetrical fashion and made the short-sleeved sweater completely retro 80s glam. And it was fitted enough to not look dowdy on Bridget's short frame, yet just loose enough to conceal her horrid midsection, which she was always desperately trying to camouflage. In Bridget's mind, that alone made this sale a done deal.

Plus, now she had something to wear to any holiday parties. Yes, and Christmas and New Year's Eve. Never mind that the vast majority of her friends were no longer single anymore and never *actually* had holiday parties, and Bridget admitted she'd *never* wear the same thing for New Year's that she'd worn on Christmas … but whatever. The holiday-wardrobe dilemma was somewhat solved now.

Her reasoning was ridiculously lame. She knew that wholeheartedly. But it was too late now anyway. Bridget knew the store's return policy more than well, since she was not only a frequent shopper there, but also close friends with Marren, who worked there. There were no returns, only exchanges and store credits within ten days. She was just going to have to suck it up and admit to the fact that she had made yet another bad choice. She had a shopping problem. *Clearly.* Donna Lynn, her therapist, was right. She was self-medicating herself through buying. God, she was a loser. An extremely well-dressed one—but what did *that* matter? Bridget wiped her tearing eyes miserably.

Marren locked the front door of Mon Amis, looked up, and said, "Okay, we're all set. Wait, are you okay?"

Bridget wiped her eyes again and answered, "Yeah … I'm just … God, I did it again! I shouldn't have bought anything. I'm just gonna go home. I don't need to go out now and eat and drink. I'll just hate myself even more."

In addition to Bridget's overspending, she constantly berated herself for her binge eating and drinking, which as of late, were also getting a bit out of hand. There was just something about being out with friends in a bar or a restaurant that made Bridget feel compelled to eat and drink as much, if not more than everyone else. Why *not* have that fifth or sixth glass of prosecco? And then another few pieces of bread from the breadbasket? Her reasoning became quite blurred from the good times-comraderie and the alcohol consumption, which made the eating and drinking always seem like a good idea at the time. Until she tried to fit into her ultra-expensive clothes the next day or the next week or the next month.

In a less dramatic state, Bridget would concede that she was honestly just a social eater and drinker. The problem was, she was quite social. Never during the week, of course, since she had to teach and teaching second graders while irritably bloated and hungover was not something she wished on herself or her young students. But the weekends, well, Bridget could tie them on with the best of her friends.

And she did, hence the self-reference to *binge* eating/drinking. Unlike most binge-eaters, though, Bridget couldn't find it in herself to purge. Even if she'd been so inclined, she'd never be able to make herself throw up. The thought of purposely inducing herself to vomit repulsed her. It'd never happen. The most she'd be able to get out of it would be some awful gagging and a bit of dry heaving. Nothing too conducive to getting rid of whatever she'd inhaled.

Yes, and now she had a wardrobe that spanned four different sizes, depending on her weight that day, week, or month. If she were to bargain shop at TJ Maxx, Ross, or even Old Navy, her yo-yoing weight wouldn't cause her such trauma. But when you only shopped in the likes of Mon Amis Boutique and your favorite department store was Neiman Marcus … well, you were inevitably screwed, on a teacher's salary. And her friends, Kit and Marren, of all people—well, they were no help. In fact, they were practically enablers!

Marren would airily blow off Bridget's complaints, saying, "Bridget, calm down. I don't know what you're talking about. You look great. You always do!"

"Oh, well, it's good to know that the Jabba the Hutt look works for me. I have ballooned to a size *six*! What am I going to do?" Bridget would fairly shriek in hysteria.

"This conversation is starting to irritate me. FYI, I'm a size six, and I don't feel I resemble Jabba the Hutt, thank you very much! Bridget you're being completely ridiculous. You have dysmorphia. Kit, are you listening to this?" Marren would call out.

Kit would answer absent-mindedly, "No, she lost me at the Jabba the Hutt analogy."

As Bridget would scowl stubbornly, Marren would chastise, "You are *fine*! Be thankful for the way you look. So, you put on a few pounds—which, by the way, none of us can see. There are people that are so obese that they can't even get out of their houses!"

Yes, of course, that made Bridget feel all the more guilty for her obscene, self-centered vanity. Marren was right. She wasn't anywhere near becoming an Oprah special … yet.

Donna Lynn had told Bridget in many a session that being upset about things was quite normal. However, Bridget's responses of overindulgence and then obsessive self-loathing were not. It had become somewhat of a vicious cycle. She would shop because she ate and drank too much. Then she would party with friends to forget how bad she felt about the money she'd blown on clothes. Yes, she'd done it again. Bridget gazed down in disgust at the Mon Amis shopping bags in her hands. Going to La Bella Vita right now was out of the question. She was sure to overdo it.

Putting the shop keys into her bag, Marren tilted her head to the side and said wryly, "Well, you hate yourself anyway, so you might as well stay out with us. If you don't want to drink, fine, but you need to eat!"

Of course Bridget wanted to drink and eat. That was the whole problem. Like everything, if she could just quit while she was ahead, she'd be fine. In fact, she'd be a size or two smaller. Bridget scowled and rolled her eyes at Marren.

Sighing, Marren said, "Okay, so you bought some things you shouldn't have, but there's nothing you can do about it now. And you're here, so just enjoy being with your friends, because we're glad you're out and not hiding out at home!"

Bridget opened her mouth to protest, but Marren took her hesitation as an opportunity to grab her hand and say, "Come on, let's go. I could use a glass of prosecco, and Kit's probably wondering what happened to us."

"All right, all right," Bridget grumbled.

Marren smiled over her shoulder. "Aha! I knew you'd come around."

Bridget and Marren walked in the front door of La Bella Vita to the usual Friday night mayhem. They crammed themselves in behind a dozen people waiting to be seated and surveyed the scene. It was even more hectic than usual. Every table downstairs was occupied. The waiters dashed about, pouring wine and bringing food to the tables, while busboys scurried around, clearing plates. Kit, trying to be heard above the din, was practically yelling into the phone. "Okay, rigatoni rustica and calamaretti alla griglia, okay, yes ..." She glanced over at the surly-looking woman waiting at the head of the reservation line. "I'm sorry. I'll be right with you."

Her eyes fell upon Marren and Bridget, and she pointed to a table for two next to the bar. "That's for you. Go sit. Cido will get you something to drink." She then spoke into the phone again.

"I'm sorry, what? Yes, of course the calamari is real! Okay, it'll be ready for pick-up in about twenty minutes. *Grazie.*" Kit hung up the phone and mumbled to herself, "Yeah, twenty minutes, my ass."

"I don't know how Kit does it—all that smiling and being pleasant all the time. Blech!" Marren shuddered before adding, "Can we please get a drink?"

Kit returned, laid a couple of menus before them, and said, "I'm assuming you want to eat something too. Hi, there! I'm glad to see you two. It's been so crazy—all these holiday parties, and of course, they overbooked. Here, let me get you some prosecco; otherwise, you could be waiting for a while."

Kit scooted behind the bar and grabbed three glasses and a bottle from the fridge. While Kit poured, Bridget asked, "Has it been like this all night?"

Kit set the glasses down on the table, shrugged, and said, "No, it's been okay, but I'm letting Vittorio deal with the crazies because *he's* the one who took the reservations and screwed most of them up. He tries to blame it on me, but I had to remind him that I actually teach during the day and am not the one who takes the reservations! And if I were, you'd be able to read my writing! Salute!" She clinked her glass against Bridget's and then Marren's and took a quick swig.

Several groups of diners finished their dinners and left, and suddenly, the restaurant hit an unexpected quiet lull. Kit sighed and pulled a barstool over to the table. She looked around and asked nonchalantly, "So, guess who I got a text message from tonight?"

Simultaneously, Marren said, "Johnny?" as Bridget said, "The pizza chef of Positano?"

Kit smiled and said, "Correct and correct. How weird is it that they always call or text at the same time?"

"Maybe there's a full moon," retorted Marren.

"What did they have to say?" asked Bridget.

Kit answered, "Well, Johnny's message was ... the usual, you know. And Lassino's was—"

Bridget cut in. "Let me guess: 'Uuhhh, waaaa, Keet, uuhhh, why you not call me, uhhhhh?'"

Kit snorted. "It's frightening how well you do that. No, it was actually a sweet text ... in fact, very unlike him! I don't know why he even bothers to call or text. He never answers any of the questions I text him."

"Yeah, such as: Do you still have a girlfriend or not?" Marren said before downing her glass.

Ignoring her, Kit spoke excitedly. "Oh, and listen, so, Olivia—you know, the English lady who rents apartments in Positano—e-mailed me back with an apartment that would be perfect for us. Two bedrooms, two bathrooms, a kitchen, and a huge terrace that looks out to the beach. What do you think?" She then added, "Oh, and it's high up, off of Via Pasitea, so we won't be under close scrutiny all the time! We'll be living where all the locals live!"

"It sounds great, but ..." Bridget paused.

"But what?" asked Kit worriedly.

"How much is it going to cost? We're going at the height of tourist season—"

"Eleven hundred euros per week, and we'll be there for five weeks, so 5,500 euros, which in dollars is about, I don't know, $8,000," Kit said in one breath. Bridget inhaled sharply.

Kit saw the distress written on Bridget's face and quickly added, "*But*, you'll be coming a week later since you're teaching summer school, so you can just pay for the weeks you're there. And I also thought," she paused dramatically, "that we could send out an e-mail to all our friends and let them know the dates we'll be there and invite them to come and stay with us. Then they can pay for the nights that they stay with us, which will be *far* cheaper than any hotel in Positano, and we'd be making the money back. Plus, with a kitchen, we'll be able to cook dinner and not eat out all the time, so we'll totally save money. What do you think?"

Bridget highly doubted she, let alone Kit, with their sparse culinary skills, would be cooking, but she decided that wasn't really the issue at hand.

"Well, do you think we'll get enough people to come visit us?" she asked skeptically.

"Bridget, how many people have we told about Positano? I think we've brainwashed enough people into being interested about visiting! Besides, some of the single girls I work with are thinking about traveling this summer. They'd definitely come."

Bridget remained silent. Kit jumped in. "*And*, before you even think about saying no, I know you're trying to watch your weight, which is *crazy*, but anyway, the apartment is so far up the hill,that we'll constantly be taking the stairs. You'll probably come home having lost weight—not that you need to!"

Marren cut in. "Well, I'm long overdue for a vacation, and I'm sick of hearing you drone on about it all the time, so I'm in. I'm coming to Positano!"

Bridget said slowly, "Well, with my tax return and summer-school money, I can probably make just enough to cover rent—"

"Remember, we'll make people pay upon their arrival *in euros*, and that'll be our spending money, since we'll have to pay Olivia up front when we get there."

Bridget was still frowning. She really wanted to go. Was this going to work? "Kit, you know I'm the last person to be frugal. I'm just so poor right now."

Kit looked down at the pink Mon Amis bags at Bridget's feet and said, "Bridget, I know you're not a cheapskate. You never have been. Just stop buying clothes. Think of all that money you'll be saving. It'll all work out."

Easy for you to say, Bridget thought testily. Why didn't Kit just ask her to stop breathing, too, while she was at it? Besides, Kit was one to talk, being a clotheshorse herself. Of course, she did make probably twice what Bridget made teaching in a Catholic school and could probably afford what she was spending. But that was beside the point, kind of. Kit could not go to Positano without Bridget … it would kill her. She'd make this work somehow. Bridget sighed and said, "Okay, okay, you know you're not going without me!"

Kit jumped up and did a little dance. "Yay! I'm so excited! And this will be perfect, because Diana and Leo get married in July in Scalea, which is only a few hours from Positano, so we'll be able to go to the wedding! I'll e-mail Olivia tonight when I get home, and then we can send out an e-mail to everyone!"

Out of the corner of her eye, Kit saw Vittorio making his way back toward the bar. She quickly downed her entire glass of prosecco, stood up, and set it on the bar. She squeezed Bridget's hand and whispered, "We're not going to regret this!"

Chapter 2

Driving home, Bridget thought about Positano with giddy excitement and an impending sense of dread. She shouldn't be doing this. But she wanted to. But she really shouldn't. She couldn't think straight; she was so stressed out about anything and everything. There was her mom, for one thing. She wasn't in the best of health and had to go to kidney dialysis three times a week, among other various doctor appointments. Even with her sister being close by to help out, Bridget knew she'd get the guilt trip about being gone for so long. She did not want to deal with that.

However, being treated like a sixteen-year-old, even though you were in your thirties, was one of the lesser joys of living at home again. And then there was the money issue. Her bills just seemed to keep multiplying—partly due, no thanks, to Seamus, who had skipped the country and gone back home to Ireland, saddling her with the BMW M3 that she had helped him finance. The car payments were killing her. And it was impossible getting a hold of Seamus, let alone getting payments from him, while he was overseas. Bridget couldn't even drive the car because it was a stick shift. Of all the rotten and unfair irony!

Although it was the last car on earth Bridget would be caught dead driving, since it so reminded her of her ex-boyfriend. So, she prayed it would sell. However, no one seemed to want a 1999 M3 that had been run into the ground, except a few teenagers interested in drag racing, and they weren't willing to pay even half of what she needed to break even. No, she couldn't hang her hat on selling the car anytime soon.

So, in the meantime, Kit was right. Bridget *should* stop buying clothes. Please, tell her something she didn't know. Bridget was trying, and she had the best of intentions, but it was so much more difficult than she'd ever expected. Was there such a thing as binge shopping, she wondered? She could definitely be the poster child for that too. Yet, she'd brought that on herself, and she'd own up to it, but thinking about it freaked her out. And didn't stress cause cortisol levels to rise, leading to extra stomach fat (which she surely had an abundance of these days)? She knew she'd read that in some reliable magazine like *Newsweek* or *Time*, or maybe it was *Allure*. Well, somewhere. Bridget had the typical "apple-shaped" body. She gained all her weight in her chest and stomach area, which, in essence, made her appear to look three months pregnant (at least to herself)—not a look she was going for.

Whenever these body-loathing episodes occurred, she'd skip the couture shopping and go for the comfy, baggy, exercise apparel—a new set of running shoes and an Adidas sweatsuit, with all the matching pieces, of course. And some new running socks, since hers got so grimy. Or a Mike & Chris hoodie—which would cost the price of the entire Adidas ensemble but would be so worth it. It was amazing how easily you could spend money.

And all because she'd *just had* to scrape that frosting off the whole side of the leftover birthday cake in the faculty room and devour it (of course, while no one else was in there. She'd be mortified if anyone knew). Because she'd *just had* to have that third prosecco, or fourth—she'd lose count sometimes, since everyone else was having another. The excuses went on and on. Yeah, the weight issue was a problem. But at least she wasn't oblivious to it. Bridget knew she was both a secret eater and a social eater. Not a good combination. There was no other way to describe it, except to say that Bridget felt like her world was spiraling out of control. What was happening to her? She had always been responsible, reliable, goal-oriented. For a long time, she'd been able to maintain a weight that had made her feel good about herself. Which was no easy task, since her mom had always kept a plethora of diet-sabotaging foods around.

And Bridget had always been pretty good with money, too—well, better at spending it than saving it, but she'd known her limit. Yes, she'd always liked to shop, but she'd never let it get that out of control. She'd never spend more that she had. She'd been able to save her money pretty well. She had actually moved into her own apartment a few years before her mother had gotten sick. Bridget looked back proudly at that time in her life, when she could say that she'd done things on her own, like a real adult. She had been completely mature and capable of budgeting for her rent money and other expenses, like any normal person.

And now look at her. What did she have to show for herself? Thirty-three, living at home (with no real possibility of moving out anytime in the near future, it seemed), hefty credit card bills. She had a decent job teaching, which she knew was something, but she didn't even enjoy that any more. Was she *really* helping children? She'd been doing this for so long, she didn't even know. Maybe it was time for her to get out, but what would she do?

When Bridget and her therapist, Donna Lynn, discussed this, Donna Lynn had asked her to name some of her other gifts and talents. Bridget hadn't been able to think of one. How she hated to be put on the spot with all the introspective questions, but this *was* therapy. "Uh, I don't know. Sorry, I don't know; I just … don't … know …" Bridget had shrugged plainly.

To which Donna Lynn had replied, "Bridget, find your words. Do you realize that you always answer 'I don't know'? But I think you *do know*." Did she? Once again, she … uh … didn't know. It was quite pathetic. She was a failure at therapy too, it seemed.

"Yeah, I guess, umm, I don't kn—oops, sorry," Bridget's voice trailed off. What *was* she good at, besides teaching, if she was even still good at that? Um, she was super-organized; she kept her obscene collection of shoes all painstakingly arranged according to color palette and style. She was *stellar* with blow-drying and flatironing her hair, so that you'd never know she had a wave in it at all. She had cooking a baked potato down to an art. Professional boozehag on weekend outings with friends? Don't forget, she had perfected the whole "dating losers" thing—or just not dating at all. Did any of these qualify? No, she didn't think so. Yeah, her self-esteem was running pretty low these days.

Donna Lynn hadn't found her to be amusing, either, when Bridget had sarcastically mentioned these so-called talents. It had prompted her to say to Bridget, "All right, then, your homework for next week is to come up with ten—and *no less* than ten—things you are good at or like about yourself."

Well, Bridget knew she was definitely good at fooling herself about many things. And no matter how pessimistic she could get at times, she was good at wishing, too—wishing for things that seemed impossible. Oh, how she wished all her problems would magically disappear.

If she had any sort of gumption, though, Bridget knew she'd get a second job. If anyone should have a second job, it should be her! She didn't understand how Kit did it, teaching all day and then working four nights a week till 11:00 p.m. at the restaurant. She was like the Energizer Bunny! When Bridget got home, all she had time to do was run on the treadmill, eat something, and fall asleep, and not necessarily in that order.

But she'd already tried the extra job thing, anyway. Working at Mon Amis on weekends hadn't gone so well. But that was a no-brainer. Of course, with her shopping problem, what had she been thinking? If she was ever going to make some extra money, she'd have to work somewhere that had things that she absolutely would not buy, like … what wouldn't she buy? Hardware or gardening tools, something like that. Yeah, she wasn't into tools or dirt. That would work. Or—maybe not.

Still, as much as she was worried about the expense of traveling this year, she really wanted to get away. *Far away.* She didn't want to worry about correcting papers or paying bills, about a life that revolved around her mother's doctor appointments. Bridget felt guilty and selfish. Was she being overly dramatic and self-centered? Her life was not that bad. She knew she was lucky to have the things she had and that there were far worse things that could happen to her. She loved her mother and family.

And as much as Bridget had complained about being burned-out lately, she really loved teaching. But she just wanted to go somewhere for a while where no one knew how pathetically messed up she was, where she appeared to be a normal adult, not someone masquerading as one, which was how she so often felt at home. It wasn't so wrong to want to go somewhere to just relax and not think about anything, was it? And a change of scenery would do her some good and maybe help her get her head together.

Bridget knew, in the end, that her worry over money troubles was definitely going to be overruled by a desire for some self-preservation. Bridget liked to believe that a longing for and a sense of adventure and self-preservation were what were truly driving her on this trip. It sounded a whole lot better than labeling herself as self-centered. Right— Kit wasn't the only one who was fun and spontaneous. Bridget admired her best friend's constantly sunny disposition and her willingness to go wherever the wind blew her at any time. She and Kit were opposites in many ways, but Bridget knew that she, too, had a certain wanderlust and spontaneity. Although, in Bridget's case, some might argue it was just plain stupidity and a problem with impulse control. And they might be right—*sometimes.*

But Bridget truly enjoyed traveling, and she loved the beauty of Italy. Traveling made her happy and gave her some sense of freedom. Right now, Positano was her answer to these needs, her escape. She'd get the money together and leave the rest to Positano, she thought as she pulled the car into the driveway and put it in park.

Later, Bridget climbed into bed and nestled down underneath the thick duvet. She hadn't been that bad in the restaurant tonight—only two pieces of bread and two proseccos. And she hadn't touched Kit's zabagnione at all; she could be proud of herself for that, at least. Of course, her old friend, Buyer's Remorse, had semiruined her appetite. And once Kit had started talking about the apartment and the cost of it, she hadn't been able to concentrate on anything the girls were saying, let alone food. In her mind, she kept going over whether she could realistically come up with the cash for this summer. Would it all work out? Would Kit's plan work?

Although she always had the best of intentions, Kit had a tendency to dream up some cockamamy schemes. Bridget, of course, was a sucker for them. And for the most part, they were always unregrettably fun. Bridget was glad she had a friend like Kit who made things happen and got her to step out of her shell. Yet, there were times when Bridget would feel remorseful about throwing caution to the wind during these adventures. Kit would always console her, though, and say, "Bridget, at the end of the day, at least you can say you've done things that many people haven't. You've lived life."

Yes, it was true. Bridget had certainly been living life, but too bad that a lot of these adventures were costly, in one way or another. She sure wouldn't be thinking about how she'd lived life to the fullest, though, when she was fifty, single, and still living at home! Well, one more summer, and then she'd have to lay off the traveling for a while—if she could even swing it this summer.

Chapter 3

From:	kitmcnally@yahoo.com
To:	jgirl@hotmail.com oneamica@aol.com,
	amyafter5@hotmail.com
	Show 23 more
Subject:	Meet us in Positano …

Ciao Amici,

So, it's February … but summer is just around the corner, and that can mean only one thing. Your immediate reaction may understandably be, "Not again! I do not want to hear one more word about that Posi place." However, as Bridget and I begin to plan our return, we thought perhaps you might like to join us so you can experience firsthand the wonders of Positano, instead of listening to us drone on incessantly about …

Dancing till dawn at the disco, soaking up the sun on the spiaggia, braving the hundreds of hazardous stairs, the cobbler who will make a pair of spiffy shoes just for you, sipping Rossini's at Mario's restaurant, our long, leisurely, delicious meals, and of course, the friends we have met there along the way.

But don't take our word for it. Even Steinbeck caught Positanoitis. To quote him: "Positano bites deep. It is a dream place that isn't quite real when you are there and becomes beckoningly real after you have gone."

We are planning to arrive in Positano at the end of June.

We will be traveling the first week of July to our friends' wedding in Calabria (Congrats, Diana and Leo!) and then returning to Positano for a month.

There is a great apartment available that sleeps 4-6 comfortably ... but there is always room for more friends. Let us know if you're interested and the dates you'd like to visit. If you'd like to check out airfares, Positano is about a 40-minute drive from Naples (if there's no traffic). We'd love to see you under the Positano sun.

Baci, Kit and Bridget

Kit read the e-mail for a fifth time. As a former English major, she couldn't stand poor grammar and spelling errors. It was rather good, she thought, pleased with herself. No, it was better than good. It sounded colorful and enticing. Who of their friends *wouldn't* want to come visit them? Well, the marrieds and those who weren't teachers wouldn't or couldn't ... which pretty much amounted to *all* their friends ... but she and Bridget should be able to get *at least* five or six of them to make the trip.

Hmmm, Kit wondered if she should add Johnny to the e-mail list. She could just hear Bridget and their other friends screaming at her, "*What are you thinking?*" But she and Johnny were still *friends*. Well, they hadn't spoken in quite some time, actually, since Kit had told him not to come visit her. Anymore. Ever. But that was okay, wasn't it? He'd finally gotten the hint. Although, he still sent text messages every once in a while, which she didn't respond to right away, but ... but you know what? She would add him to the e-mail list.

Then Johnny would see that she was returning to Positano and that her life was moving on without him. Then he could move on, too. Besides, he'd never crash their girls' holiday in Positano anyway. In his mind, Positano was like Sin City, Sodom and Gomorrah reincarnated. There, she'd added Johnny's e-mail address. There was no chance in him showing up, so she wouldn't even need to mention this to Bridget.

Kit just hoped Bridget wouldn't mind that she was sending the e-mail out to so many people, let alone Johnny, but what was the harm? It was better to have more options; otherwise, they'd pay for it dearly. Having a kitchen in the apartment was going to be great, but Kit certainly didn't want to be stuck cooking dinner every night if they couldn't afford to go out because of the rent! Well, if it came to that, with her and Bridget's next-to-nill cooking skills, Bridget would at least be assured of losing weight (of course, not that she needed to, but she *was* always going on about it).

Yes, money was going to be a little bit tighter this year. Kit sighed just thinking about the extra hours she would need to put in at the restaurant. Well, maybe she could cut back on her clothing and shoe shopping a little, instead. Kit admitted she had a way of talking Bridget into doing some things she might not do on her own. But Bridget was just as bad an influence on Kit when it came to the realm of clothing. It was Bridget who had told her she *had* to check out Mon Amis and their assortment of Majestic and Vanessa Bruno T-shirts. Kit had never even heard of Majestic or Vanessa Bruno, but she was a pushover for a good-fitting, stylish tee.

Bridget was definitely Kit's "foda," short for "fashion-Yoda," as Kit teasingly liked to call her. She could tell one designer from the next without even looking at the label. It was a little uncanny, not to mention intimidating at times. Still, if and when a clothing crisis or wardrobe malfunction occurred, it was Bridget that Kit went to. She was always so levelheaded, although a bit conservative for Kit's style. Bridget frequently had to remind her, "Kit, you need to lose the sequins *or* the sparkles. It's just too much together."

"But I like sparkly, shiny things!" Kit would pout. "Does it really look *that* tacky?" she'd laugh.

Bridget would shrug and raise her eyebrows. "Well, it's fine, I guess, if the bedazzled rodeo look is what you're going for."

Kit would then surrender. "Okay, okay, you're right, but I *am* going to wear the rhinestone belt!"

Yes, Bridget was in the know regarding fashion matters and had introduced Kit to Mon Amis, Marren, and the rest of the staff. Now Kit had a host of other *fodas* to help her put things together, should Bridget be MIA. It was great, but a bit problematic, since she was now quite accustomed to dropping a couple hundred dollars on a pair of jeans and at least $300 on a decent pair of shoes. She and Bridget didn't compare American Express bills, but Kit was sure they might be quite comparable when it came to what was inside their closets.

Well, Kit reasoned with herself, at least she got a lot of wear out of her clothes because she wore them while teaching and not just on the weekends (except for the really low-cut stuff). Whereas, poor Bridget could hardly wear any of the clothes she bought to her school, what with the strict faculty dress code there. Bridget had phoned Kit practically jumping for joy the day that her principal had abolished the mandatory "pantyhose at all times" rule (which included wearing them even with sandals or open-toed shoes—blech!). Talk about medieval!

If Kit needed another reason to shop, well, she *insisted t*o herself that it was professional and part of her job to look well groomed and coutoured when she hostessed at La Bella Vita. Everyone knew that Italians had style, and she did too, even if she sometimes overdid the bejeweled, sparkly look. All the Italians she knew were a bit flamboyant anyway. Besides, why buy beautiful and expensive pieces of clothing if you weren't going to wear them? The restaurant was the perfect place to showcase Mon Amis clothing. Heck, she even kept some of their business cards in her purse to hand out when customers complimented her on what she was wearing.

No, forget about the cutting back on shopping. She'd cut back on something else, like manicures and pedicures. Actually, no, Julianna did her nails for free already. Okay, so *good*, she was saving some money! Uh, she'd do less grocery shopping. Yes, that was it! Wait a minute; there was never anything in her fridge, since she didn't grocery shop. They always fed her at the restaurant, anyway. Hmmm, instead of monthly facials and hair appointments, schedule them for every other month? Oh, that was going too far. Dammit, she'd just have to work more days at the restaurant. Vittorio would be miserable to work for, and she would just be plain miserable.

It would all be worth it, though, when she and Bridget were sitting on their balcony overlooking the Tyrrhenian Sea and sipping their homemade espressos (Cido was helping her practice after hours), or their chilled prosecco. And she and Bridget would throw parties and invite their Italian friends. They could even have a Fourth of July party! She wondered how difficult it would be to smuggle hot dogs and sparklers into Italy. You couldn't have Fourth of July without hot dogs and sparklers. The Italians would think the hot dogs were completely foul and the sparklers amateur, but it would be a good cultural learning experience. They could also serve Twinkies and peanut butter and jelly sandwiches too! You couldn't get much more American than that. Oooh, and she'd pack some fun decorations to put up …

The ringing of her cell phone disrupted Kit's patriotic fantasy. She had forgotten she'd left the ringer on. Good thing her class was at recess. She picked it up and saw the foreign prefix. It was Lassino. Why he was calling? He should be working—she used the term loosely—at the restaurant.

"Ciao, Lassino!" Kit shouted into the phone. For some unknown reason, Kit always found herself speaking loudly when she conversed with Lassino. She hoped she would be able to understand him today. At least in Positano, she could read his lips to figure out what he was saying.

"Ciao, my love. What are you doing?" came Lassino's voice.

"I am at school, working. What are you doing?"

"What do you think? I am working. I am very beesy!" he grunted.

Then why was he calling? It was always the same conversation.

After Kit quizzed Lassino on how Paolo, Mario, and the rest were, she threw in, "So, how is Monica?" She knew it would annoy Lassino, but she felt she had a right to be nosy. After last summer, nothing was going to get by her.

"Why do you always ask about Monica? We are over. She wanted me to move to Miami! So, we are finally done." Lassino's erratic voice mumbled over the phone. Kit's stomach dropped in surprise. Before she could quiz him about what he'd just divulged, he asked, "So, how is your boyfriend in Spokane? What's his name again? Donny?"

"It's *Johnny*, and I told you months ago that we broke up when I got back from Italy, Lassino," Kit explained.

There was a pause on the other end. Then Lassino spoke. "So, you don't have a boyfriend and I don't have a girlfriend … when are you coming to Positano again?"

He seriously had to have ADD. His attention span was on par with some of her six-year-old students! Kit must've told him a dozen times already, just in case he needed to mentally prepare himself—or flee the town and country before she got there.

"The end of June, Lassino. Why? Are you planning on leaving Positano as soon as I get there?"

She could hear him laughing, and then he said, "No, I will be there. But you know, I am going to be—"

Kit interrupted. "*Very busy.* Yes, I know. Bridget and I are going to be very busy too, so don't worry about us. We have a lot of friends coming to visit us." She hoped she wasn't lying when she said this. "So, you and Monica are really not seeing each other?" Kit asked again; she wanted to make sure.

"Yes, I just told you that. You do not listen to me! I must go! Tell Bridget I said hello. Ciao!"

Kit listened to the abrupt dial tone in her ear for a moment and then set her phone down. The confusion was starting already, and they hadn't even gotten to Positano. Randomness and the occasional befuddlement here and there, she could handle. It was the heartache and drama she wanted to avoid. Everything was going to be on the up and up *this* summer. She had no boyfriend. And, Kit thought with relief and giddy excitement, Lassino did not have a girlfriend. At least, as of now, that was his story.

Kit knew what she felt for Lassino was different than what she had felt for Johnny or any other ex-boyfriend. Kit couldn't pinpoint it exactly, but she just knew. And she was certain now that living in Positano this summer would not be a mistake. Everything was going to be fine. She just couldn't let herself get too carried away about it all. Oh, but the end of June could not come soon enough. The recess bell rang. Kit clicked on *send* and watched as her screen read: "*Your e-mail has been sent.*" Now all that was left to do was wait to see who would be joining them on the Amalfi Coast. She closed her laptop and practically skipped out to pick up her class.

From:	kitmcnally@yahoo.com
To:	amyafter5@hotmail.com, jgirl@hotmail.com, oneamica@aol.com
	Show 26 more
Subject:	"Pronto!"

Pronto ...

... that's what they say when they answer the phone in Italy (see, our Italian classes weren't a complete waste). For our friends who'll be visiting us in Italy, for those who are still pondering the possibility of a Positano visit, and for those we will miss and wish we could pack in our carry-ons ...

Here's our Italian cell # 011-39 (use these five numbers only if calling from outside Italy)

329-423-4264

If you find yourself in Positano and can't get in touch with us (which would be very unusual), you can:

1. Try to find us at our apartment, which is a ways up the hill (oxygen mask not absolutely necessary, but recommended), located at the top of the steps that are next to Palazza Bianca Hotel.

2. Go to Mar Incanto Restaurant and ask Mario, Donato, or Gianna if they have any idea where we are. The restaurant is located right off of the main beach (walk down the main staircase; you can't miss it).

3. See Tino at Tutta Ceramica on Via C. Colombo.

   Travel note: Le Sirenuse Hotel is close by. This is where Marissa Tomei, star of *Only You*, stayed while on her quest to find her destined true love, Damon Bradley.

   Tino is extremely kind and helpful, and you might like to kill two birds with one stone and purchase some lovely local Italian pottery while you're there. He can ship it home for you … "No problem."

4. Go to the beach and ask Tomaso or his father if they've seen us. This is where we can often be found (roughly) between the hours of 11:00–4:00 (if not, we're more than likely snacking at one of the beachfront restaurants).

   If all else fails, just yell our names … it's such a small, everyone-knows-your-business town that chances are, you'll find us.

   Until then, ciao ciao! K & B

Kit rummaged through the massive pile of clothing, shoes, and beauty products that covered her queen-sized bed as she looked for her cell phone. She knew she'd put it down somewhere before she'd started round one of her "packing." Round one basically consisted of pulling just about everything out of her closet and throwing it on her bed. Round two was the elimination round, where she'd sift through and decide what items made the cut. Only the best of the best would make it into her suitcases. It was going to be tough.

Truly, it was going to be next to impossible *not* overpacking this time. She had to cut herself some slack, though, since she was going to be there for way more than a month. Her mom kept asking her what day she was getting back so she could come pick her up from the airport, but Kit kept telling her she'd forgotten. Gee, she'd have to check her ticket again and let her know. The truth was, she hadn't booked her flight home yet. Maybe she wouldn't be coming back. She wondered how hard it would be to sublet the condo and find a teaching replacement.

Ahh, there was her cell phone, hiding underneath a towering stack of bras and other intimates. She wondered how she had ever survived without a cell phone. She checked the time on the clock—for some reason, all the clocks in her place read different times. It was 12:05 a.m. In eight hours, she'd be on a plane to Naples. Why had she picked such an early flight? She really should've started packing yesterday. Bridget was probably already packed, and she wasn't even leaving for another five days. Well, that was Bridget, but not her. It would all get done eventually, and who needed sleep anyway? That was what the plane was for.

Before Kit could put her phone down, it suddenly rang. Who could be calling at this time? The lit phone screen read "Natalie." If Kit considered Bridget one of her oldest friends, since they'd known each other from high school, then Natalie was practically her sister. They'd met each other the first day of kindergarten at Our Lady of Sorrows and had stayed friends ever since. Something must be wrong for Natalie to be calling at this hour, and Kit had a feeling she knew what it was about.

Last week, when she'd stopped over to visit, Natalie had seemed stressed beyond the limit. When she wasn't taking care of the house, she was chasing around her precocious three year old, Joey, and her bouncy eighteen month old, Gina, who was just learning to walk. This alone would have been enough for any young mother to handle. *But then there was Madison.* Her husband Joe's thirteen-year old niece had come to live with them recently. Having Madison in the house would've been a big help to Natalie, had the girl not come with some extremely heavy-duty emotional baggage. Madison's drug-addicted mother had finally lost custody of her, and it was clear that the girl had been exposed from an early age to drug use and strange men coming in and out of her mother's apartment.

Since no one knew where Madison's father was, and Joe's parents were unwilling to take on parenting a second time around, Madison's welfare had been placed—or rather, thrust—upon Natalie and Joe. And clearly, Madison's problems exceeded the baggage weight limit. Natalie would often comment, "She's really a sweet and lovable kid when she isn't sneaking out of the house to meet boys, stealing my makeup, or getting kicked out of school." And she wasn't exaggerating. The kid was thirteen, but had the body and the attitude of an eighteen-year-old. Could you say *Lolita*?

Yes, Kit noticed that Madison was not a big help, and as much as Natalie loved Madison like her own, she was, in fact, the cause of a lot of Natalie's stress. And Joe … well, Joe was a great husband, but he was busy working, or golfing, or working. Natalie was dealing with it all, and not very well lately. Kit had been extremely alarmed when Nat casually mentioned to her that she'd taken up heavily smoking again—of course, not around the kids. She was smoking enough that she was practically not eating and was looking quite skeletal. This was serious. Kit had suggested that Natalie get away from it all. How about joining them in Positano? No, no, Natalie had said, she couldn't leave Joe to deal with all this. He wouldn't know what to do. Kit looked at at her ringing cell phone and thought maybe Natalie had changed her mind.

"Hello, Nat?" Kit spoke tentatively into the phone.

"Kit …" Natalie whimpered.

"Natalie, what's wrong?"

"I can't do this anymore," she replied in a voice that sounded as heavy as lead.

"What? What's happening? Is this about Madison?" asked Kit.

Natalie sighed. "It's *everything*. I'm trapped in this house, and when I'm not, I'm dealing with Madison's shit. I've been trying to get her into St. Anne's—or anywhere, really—but no one wants to take on a kid who's been kicked out of a couple schools already. She snuck out again last night, and this morning she asked me if she could go on birth control!"

"*What?* Does Joe know about all this?" shouted Kit.

"No, I can't tell him," Natalie answered.

"But this is his sister's kid! He should know how bad it is!"

"I know, I know, it's just hard for him to deal with all this," Natalie said, and then she began sobbing.

"Nat, this isn't easy for you, either. You're falling apart, and I'm worried. What can I do to help?" Kit said quietly.

Natalie sniffed a few times and then said, "Can I still come to Positano? It's relaxing there, right?"

"Oh, my God, yes! Come! This will be the perfect place for you to get away from everything. We'll go to the beach, go out to dinner, or just stay in the apartment, whatever you want. How soon can you fly out?" Kit said excitedly.

"Well, if I get online right away for tickets, it should be no problem. I mean, the kids already have passports from our Easter vacation in Mexico, and I can get us all packed pretty quickly. Oh, I'll bring the stroller, too. Yeah, we can probably be there a day after you!" Natalie exhaled.

Kit was baffled. For a small moment, she thought she'd heard Natalie mention bringing the kids.

"Wait, you're bringing the kids? *Whose* kids?" asked Kit.

"*My kids*—Joey and Gina. Oh, no, is this going to put a damper on you and that Italian guy? Will this annoy Bridget?" Natalie asked worriedly.

"No, not at all! I have no idea, as usual, what's going on with Lassino, and Bridget will be fine with it. She loves you and the kids. I'll just have to let Carrie—you know, the one I teach with—know, since she'll be there, but don't worry. I'm not … I mean, it's just that … well, I just thought you needed to get away—from *everything*, meaning, like, *all* the kids," Kit said quickly.

"Kit, I can't leave the babies *and* Madison with Joe or my parents. It's just too much. Both Mom and Dad *should* be able to handle just Madison, though. Oh, God, at least I hope so."

"Did you ask Joe about this?" Kit asked—she didn't want to be the one Joe blamed for his wife's sudden globe-trotting with the kids.

Natalie answered sharply, "No, I didn't ask him. I *told* him. Kit, I told him that he didn't have a choice. He doesn't understand what I go through every day, and he doesn't try to. I just need to get away, because I'm losing it!"

"Okay, then," answered Kit.

Natalie continued, "Oh, and then I told him that if he and Madison want to fly over in a week or so to join us there, that's fine. We can have a family vacation together and start dealing with our problems together! Oh, and I specifically told Joe that money was not going to be an issue, since he works so much, so by the way, we'll be paying you for two full weeks, plus some, for doing this for us."

Kit was speechless. This wasn't quite how she thought this conversation was going to proceed. But she was so excited to have Natalie come. Now she'd be in Positano with her two best friends. Bridget wouldn't mind Natalie coming. In fact, Kit knew she'd be especially sympathetic, having gone through her own turmoil this year.

Carrie, on the other hand, might not take it so well. Carrie was one of the other kindergarten teachers at Kit's school. She was fresh out of the credential program, and this was her first teaching job. But before landing the kindergarten position, she'd traveled extensively in Italy, and what a coincidence—she'd fallen in love with a boy from Positano and was all gung-ho on returning! Kit remembered fervently hoping that Carrie's Italian boy wasn't Lassino. Although it would've been completely typical, that would have been just too much. Luckily, it turned out that he was some guy named Luigi who delivered bottled water and fish around the town.

Well, Kit and Carrie had bonded quite a bit over Positano and its quirky cast of men. And while their Italian romances seemed to oddly parallel each other to a certain extent, that was about all they shared in common. After all, Carrie was a good nine years younger than Kit. Her biggest dilemmas were figuring out how many bars she and her friends could hit in the city without having to cab it, or checking her Facebook page to see how many friends she had. Kit was glad that Carrie was joining them for a few days, but she worried that maybe she was expected to be an around-the-clock party buddy for her. That wasn't how Kit and Bridget rolled in Positano. They did a lot together, but they also went their separate ways. Hopefully, Luigi the fish guy would help pick up the slack with their young houseguest.

Kit's main concern, though, was that Positano would provide Natalie with the respite she desperately needed. It was crazy to think a place possessed magical healing powers, but Kit believed in it.

However, how calming and tranquil would it be for Natalie if she was bringing Joey and Gina? Between the baby's teething, nonstop diaper changes, and lugging the stroller around, Kit couldn't imagine Natalie relaxing much. Surely, she'd be better off coming on her own. And how would the kids do there? Walking the stairs or up and down Via Pasitea, with or without heels, was bad enough, but how hard would it be while pushing a baby in a stroller? And what would Joey do—walk the stairs or have to be carried? Oh, boy. *Be careful what you wish for*—wasn't that the old saying? Well, Kit *had* wanted their friends to come to Positano, and they certainly were, so she wasn't going to complain. It appeared that Positano was going to be a refuge for all of them this summer.

"Kit, are you there? Listen, before I hang up and get online, is there anything else you can think of that I should know to get us ready for Positano?"

Where should she begin? Kit would keep it light. Better not to scare Natalie away from coming.

"Well," Kit answered slowly, "you'll see for yourself: it's very beautiful, and … did I mention there are a lot of stairs?"

Chapter 4

Kit tipped the bellboy and shouted, "Grazie!" as she shut the door behind him. She wasn't sure why she'd handed him the couple of euros since he hadn't actually carried anything for her. She'd made it safely to Naples. Her luggage had not. All she had was her bottomless pit of a leather satchel, which was crammed with anything she might need, should she be stranded on a deserted island—or in this case, Naples. No way was she going to let anybody get his hands on her bag in this city.

Kit had never actually visited Naples. Her view of it had always been confined to the window of a speeding cab that was driving her to or from Positano. What she had seen on those rides looked less than appealing, with hundreds of dirty, slumlike apartments haphazardly stacked on top of each other and endless rows of laundry hanging off and between balconies. It always looked so decrepit and ominous. "Enter if you dare!" Naples seemed to shout and shake its metaphorical fist at passerby. Well, Kit had always been somewhat of a daredevil.

Although, this time, it wasn't by choice as much as necessity. Natalie, one of her oldest friends, and her two small children were arriving tomorrow morning. "You'll be there at the airport when we get there, right?" Natalie had asked, her voice quavering nervously.

Tino, who now ran a taxi/car service in addition to running the ceramics shop, would send a completely reliable driver to pick up Natalie and the kids. But Natalie didn't know Tino and was nervous enough traveling to Italy (and Naples, no less) toting two kids. Kit decided it was best to just book a room there and have Tino send someone for all of them tomorrow. In fact, she wouldn't even call Tino to tell him she was in the country yet, until tomorrow. She had a feeling she'd get an earful for staying overnight here by herself.

Well, if anything happened to her, her mom had her itinerary. At least she would know where she was. If various tales and opinions of Naples were accurate, Kit supposed she really should be nervous, staying overnight by herself. Wasn't it Mafia Central, headquarters to the Camorra? But here she was, staying in the heart of Napoli, and she wasn't scared at all.

Instead, as they drove into the city center, she'd found herself fascinated. Once you got past the dilapidated buildings and grime, Naples was chaotically beautiful. There was style and grandiose architecture, if not in all its former Baroque and Rococo glory. Like an aging movie star past her prime, the city was a worn but regal beauty, surrounded by a knowingness, a resounding hint of what had been. And the streets were alive and teeming with outdoor markets and people—people everywhere.

And the pizza. Maybe she was delusional from being tired and hungry, but Kit swore that from her room, she could smell pizza. Oh, the food in this country. And Naples was supposed to have *the* best pizza. To be in this metropolis and not try its famed cuisine, was just so wrong.

But it was getting dark, and Kit was too exhausted to peruse a city map. If she aimlessly wandered the streets with her huge camera and her blonde hair, she wouldn't exactly blend in. In fact, she'd be seen as easy bait for some mafioso swindler. However, pizza and an ice-cold beer were necessary. The Baci candy that she'd bought at the airport was not able to silence her rumbling stomach—and she only had one left. Well, danger seemed to be her middle name these days, anyway. Kit could rationalize anything, if it had to do with really good food. She'd simply ask at the front desk and have them send a cab to take her somewhere. She'd be fine. She'd even use some of her terrible Italian to ingratiate herself to the locals.

◆   ◆   ◆

Kit grabbed her camera case and shoved a wad of euros and her lip-plumping gloss into the front pocket of it. As she tried to tug a comb through her blonde mane, there was a knock at the door. She sincerely hoped it was someone delivering her wayward luggage.

"Who is it?" she asked hopefully.

The voice on the other side of the door answered back, "Kit?"

Kit cocked her head to the side. The male voice sounded familiar, but she couldn't quite place it.

"Yes?" she asked uncertainly. Wait a minute; wait a minute. She did know this voice. But, no … it couldn't be, not *here*. Could it?

"It's me, Johnny." Oh, God, it was.

Kit swiftly unlocked the door and peeked her head out. Real and life-like, not a figment of her imagination, Johnny stood there, a backpack slung over one shoulder. Kit glanced down and noticed his suitcase—and a rather large one, at that—next to him. This did not bode well. Upon seeing her, Johnny's face lit up, leaving Kit with an overwhelming sense of dread laced with some heavy guilt.

"Ciao, Bella!" he cried brightly.

She was speechless and answered with a weak, "Hi."

"It's been about nine months, Stranger. Can I get a hug or something?" Johnny joked, but nevertheless, he held his arms out to her. He was right. This was the first time they'd seen each other since Kit had broken up with him, last September. And here they were, in a whole other country. What the hell was going on?

Kit stepped toward Johnny as if in a trance. As he squeezed her tightly to him, she stood there limply, like a wilted piece of lettuce. He went to kiss her cheek, but she pulled quickly away and said, "Um, how did you know I was here?"

"All right if I come in?" he said, oblivious to her shock.

"Oh, of course, come in." Kit stepped out of his way as Johnny rolled his suitcase in and sat on the bed. Kit remained standing and waited for him to say something.

"So!" Johnny grinned at her. Why was he grinning?

"So," Kit replied tersely.

"Here I am in … Napoli," Johnny continued, looking to Kit for some type of emotional cue or facial expression.

"Yes, here you are in *Naples*," Kit once again dryly repeated what he'd said. What was with him being all cheesy with the Italian?

Johnny stood up and took a step toward her. He looked at Kit seriously and then cleared his throat and said, "It's really good to see you, Kit."

No, no, no. This wasn't going well. Before he had a chance to come any closer, Kit asked abruptly, "It's good to see you too, but what are you doing here?"

Johnny stopped mid-step and replied cautiously, "Well, I got your e-mail."

That damn e-mail she'd sent out to, well, everyone, to come visit her in Positano. Why, why had she included him?

"And I thought, me, go to Italy? While Kit's there? Might be kinda awkward!" Johnny chuckled.

Ya think? Kit fumed inside her head. She then answered expectantly, "*Yesss* …?"

Johnny continued on. "But then I thought, that's just silly. We're still friends. Haven't used any of my vacation days, so why *not* take a trip to Italy?"

Trip to Italy? So did that mean Johnny would be traveling all over the country?

"And your first stop is Naples? How did you find out I was staying here?" This was like pulling teeth. Kit wished he'd get to the point, even though she was afraid she already knew what it was.

"Well, that's where your mom was a big help. See, I hadn't saved the e-mail, so I just called your mom to get the Positano address. She told me you were staying the first night here. So, luckily, I was able to get a flight, and here I am!"

Note to self: kill mother, if ever to return to the States. This was not luck. This was some type of voodoo hex. She was being punished for sure. What had her mom been thinking? Of course, seeing as it had taken a full six months to even tell her mother that she and Johnny were dating, it was quite possible she'd forgotten to tell her mom about their breakup. Kit just couldn't stand her mother hounding her about her love life or the potential grandchildren she wouldn't be getting anytime soon. Better to keep her in the dark about these things for as long as possible.

"You're shocked, aren't you?" Johnny reached out and squeezed her hand.

She smiled weakly. "Uh, yes; yes, I am."

"Well, I gotta be honest, Kit, after last summer and everything, the thought of Italy made me sick. I didn't want to ever hear anything about it. I mean, Positano was the last place I thought I'd ever want to visit."

Kit spoke up. "Listen, Johnny, Italy has nothing to do with what—"

Johnny held up a hand. "Wait, please. So, your e-mail pissed me off at first. You know, a real slap in the face. But then I realized, you're not like that."

Was he joking? Where was he going with this? Kit looked down at the floor studiously.

"You went out of your way to include me, and I appreciate that. If you could be a big enough person to invite me, *your ex-boyfriend*, to visit you in Positano, then I could get past all that. I mean it when I say I'm over the whole Italy thing, and I'm *really* looking forward to seeing Positano." He smiled warmly at her.

Over my dead body, Kit thought. Kit had to say something, because Johnny in Positano was not an option. Oh, God. What was she going to say? How could she tell him that he could travel anywhere in Italy—anywhere, but just not to Positano? Before she could utter anything, Johnny said, "Kit, thanks for e-mailing me."

E-mail. Ugh, how could she have been so stupid?

Johnny looked at Kit worriedly and said, "Hey, are you all right? You haven't said much, and you look a little pale."

"Can we go get something to eat? I really need to … eat." Kit grabbed her camera case and headed toward the door.

"Oh, yeah, great idea! Hey, wait up! You must be really hungry," Johnny called and closed the door behind him.

She'd tell him at dinner.

If *Dante's Inferno* had included a level in hell for jilted ex-boyfriends to mercilessly, albeit unwittingly, assault their ex-girlfriends with sickening kindness, thus inducing in the ex-girlfriends vomitous feelings of shame, guilt, and then rage to the point of wanting to kill themselves, then Kit surely would've found herself burning there.

Dinner had been tortuous, first for her, then for Johnny. Every time Kit was about to tell Johnny that the Positano leg of his trip was completely unnecessary, he'd say something like, "Can't wait to see Positano!" or "You'll be a great tour guide!" But the capper came when he'd said just a little too casually, "So, I hear there's only one disco there. I'll have to check that out. Will that Lassino guy be there?"

"Johnny!" Kit snapped. Johnny put his fork down and looked up from his seafood risotto.

"What?' he said, stunned.

Kit lowered her voice and said, "Look, there's no easy way to say this, but I don't think you coming to Positano is a good idea."

Johnny looked at her blankly. "What do you mean?"

"I just don't think you should come," Kit said and looked away.

"Don't *think* or don't *want* me to come?" Johnny's voice became icy.

Obviously, being post-breakup friends had been a bad idea. Kit was going to have to be blatant, but she guessed she'd dug herself into a hole this time. But she was not about to sacrifice her summer plans over this.

Kit sighed and said, "I don't think you should come *and* I don't want you to come." She exhaled. There, she'd said it. Kit felt a mixture of relief and that damn Catholic guilt that she never could seem to shake.

"Then why the hell did you send me that e-mail?" demanded Johnny.

"Johnny, I'm sorry. I really am. I just thought … I mean … I just thought—" Kit stammered nervously.

"You just thought what?" Johnny snarled and took a swig of his Chianti.

"I just thought you'd see the e-mail and realize it was over with us and that maybe it was a sign for you to move on."

"Right, of course, how couldn't I have seen the obviousness of that?" Johnny rolled his eyes and quickly drained the rest of his glass.

Kit continued. "Whatever. You didn't come here because you're over Italy. I just don't feel it's right for you to visit or stay with us in Positano. If you really want to come to Positano, fine, but you should come on your own."

Johnny filled his wine glass and spat out disgustedly, "Well, I certainly don't want to ruin your vacation, Kit. You think I want to be in Positano when I'm not wanted, so I can be laughed at by you and your Italian … boyfriend … gigolo?"

"He's not my boyfriend and he's not a *gigolo!*" Kit shouted a little too loudly. Was Lassino a gigolo? She hardly thought so.

"Oh, please. Do you really think I'm that stupid? Waiter, another bottle of Chianti. Gratzee!" he slurred.

It's grazie, *you moron!* Kit thought and then immediately felt ashamed of herself. This was all her fault again, wasn't it? She truly hadn't meant for this to happen. Had she? Nooo. She decided to bite her tongue and sit there while Johnny finished his second bottle of Chianti. Her stomach churned so badly that she'd been forced to leave her pizza Margherita and Peroni beer untouched. What a waste. Just add that to the list of sins she'd committed, she thought bitterly.

Somehow, Kit managed to keep Johnny from finishing a third bottle of

Chianti, paid the bill, and steered his staggering frame into a cab and back to the hotel. Then to prolong the agony, when she asked him what room he was staying in, he'd told her sheepishly that he hadn't actually booked a room.

"Oops, silly me, guess I thought I'd be staying with you. What was I *thinking*? Hey, is that the minibar?" He hiccupped.

Now he was passed out, spread eagle, on the middle of the bed, fully clothed, and snoring loudly enough to peel the paint. Kit's eyes burned with exhaustion and her stomach felt hollow with emptiness. Was it her stomach or her complete being that felt hollow, though? Why was God doing this to her? She wasn't a bad person. She really wasn't. Just so mixed-up. Why couldn't she will herself to lie down and snuggle up beside Johnny? To let him wrap his arms around her—that is, if he ever woke up from his Chianti coma. It would make life so easy, wouldn't it?

But it wasn't easy. Kit wanted desperately to love Johnny with all her heart, but she couldn't. And no matter how awful or selfish she felt, Kit knew it would be far worse to pretend to feel something that wasn't there.

Kit looked back at Johnny and thought about the last words he'd drunkenly drawled before he closed his eyes and passed out: "Sorry, Kit. I just wanted us to be together, 'cause I love you … that's … all."

With the back of her hand, she wiped away the tear trickling down her cheek and went into the bathroom to wash her face.

Chapter 5

When Johnny left early the next morning, Kit pretended she was asleep. The door closed behind him and her heart suddenly felt heavy, but she just hadn't been able to bear the prospect of another accusatory and guilt-laden discussion. She wondered where Johnny was headed now. Was he on his way home to Spokane, or would he be meandering around Italy, scornfully cursing her and throwing out badly pronounced Italian phrases? Wherever he was, though, Kit hoped he was all right and would someday forgive her.

Yet, all that was suddenly forgotten, or rather, pushed to the back of her mind, when Natalie and the kids showed up, and without their luggage either. If Kit thought it a pain to survive a few days out of *her* carry-on purse (regardless of how big it was and how much it held), it was ten times more disastrous for a mother with two small children. Natalie had a small backpack, which was stocked with some of the kids' toys and books, and her carry-on that contained her makeup and hair products, one change of clothes for the three of them, and a few spare diapers. *And that was all.* Oh, yes, and, but of course, typically, the big-ass collapsible stroller and Baby Bjorn for the kids had somehow made it to Italy just fine.

"Tino, can you help us? We have a problem ..." Kit had stopped into Tutta Ceramica after picking up the key to the apartment when they'd first arrived in town. Since then, Tino had barraged the airlines nonstop trying to find the whereabouts of the missing luggage.

Indeed, there seemed to be some Italian conspiracy against any of them having or wearing clothing on their stay, because when Carrie arrived on their second day there, she, too, came solo. She threw herself down into one of the lounge chairs on the terrace and cried, "Oh, my God, I can't believe it! This *so* totally sucks! And Luigi didn't even come to pick me up from the airport, either! Whatever!"

Kit shook her head sympathetically as she hesitatingly said into her cell phone, "Ciao, umm, Tino? We have another problem …"

"Okay, no problem. *Dimmi*, tell me, what happen now?" Tino laughed at the other end of the phone.

Kit silently said a prayer of thanks for easygoing Tino. He appeared to be their go-to guy in these types of situations.

On the third day, Kit's luggage mysteriously arrived at Tino's shop, but nobody else's did. Kit was ecstatic, but not just about her clothes arriving. The fact that she was in Positano, and for the whole summer, had finally sunken in! It was sooo unbelievably beautiful here—the rocky beach, the imposing mountainside, the crystalline water, the mouth-watering food—and there were *tons* of clothing shops and tiny markets to tide the rest over till their luggage came! Couldn't they see it was truly *la dolce vita*! But nobody else seemed to share Kit's enthusiasm. It was all *very* disappointing.

By day five, Natalie was openly irritated and frequently commented things like, "Ugh, it's just so *hot* here! I can't take the freakin' stairs anymore! Joey, stop pinching Gina, do you hear me?"

Kit felt like saying, "Of course it's hot here; we're in Southern Italy in July! And didn't I warn you about the stairs? What did you expect, when the town's built into the side of a damn cliff? And did you really need to bring the kids too?" But she didn't. Kit knew the source of Natalie's complaints was not really Positano, but the stress and inconvenience of not having their own belongings in a strange place.

Still, Kit fretted when Natalie stated accusingly, "Kit, if our bags don't get here soon, I'm changing our tickets and we're leaving early. Can I borrow the phone to call Tino and see if he's heard anything?"

"I'm sure Tino will call if there's any news, but okay, go ahead," Kit said resignedly and handed the phone over.

If only the bags would come in. Once Operation Luggage Watch was over, the real vacation could start for everyone. Until then, Kit felt her typically sunny disposition slipping away. There was no doubt that Natalie was miserable. Kit now felt guilty for talking her into coming to Positano (although, it wasn't her fault the airlines had lost the bags; she'd been a victim too) and she also felt wretched that there was nothing she could do to make Natalie feel better.

Clearly, it appeared that everyone's happiness and well-being had become dependent upon their luggage turning up and what Kit could do to make their life better in the meantime. Although, try as she might, nothing Kit did seemed to make any of them more comfortable. In doing so, Kit truly felt for Natalie and the kids, but she was losing patience with Carrie fast.

Carrie, too, had made it very clear she was less than happy—and with just about everything. In actuality, Kit wondered how she'd never noticed what a complete pill her co-worker was. It was quite difficult to muster up empathy for Carrie, especially after she had the audacity to pull Kit aside to tell her off after she had *just* arrived. Kit had just led Carrie through the master bedroom that she and Bridget would share, to the little alcove that held a twin bed. "So, here's your room!" she'd said cheerily.

To which Carrie bitchily blurted out, "You know, Kit, I really don't appreciate the fact that you just invited Natalie and her two kids without telling me first. This just totally changes the whole tone of my vacation!"

Kit fumed, thinking it quite ballsy for a twenty-three year old to attempt to chastise someone older, who also happened to be a co-worker and her teaching mentor! Kit would never in a million years have had the guts—or rather, the bad manners—to do that when she was that age.

Well, Kit wasn't twenty-three now. She was … well, a *young* thirty-four, and she wasn't going to stand for it! She'd worked two jobs for the last year, and Bridget had worked summer school, so that they could be here. Kit was not about to let some baby-head twit walk all over her.

Kit made sure her voice was calm before she spoke. "Well … Carrie, I'm not going to apologize for inviting Natalie. She's one of my best friends and is going through a lot right now. She really needed to come."

"Well, you really should have let me know ahead of time!" Carrie retorted sullenly.

"Listen." Kit felt her voice uncontrollably rising a bit. "I didn't have a chance to tell you ahead of time since I *only* found out the night before I was leaving. However, that's beside the point, since the apartment really belongs to Bridget and me. We worked our asses off so we could have this place, so quite frankly, I don't really *feel* she or I need to ask your permission about who we have staying here, since you're a guest, too."

"Well, I hope you don't expect me to do any babysitting," Carrie sniped back.

Kit snorted. "Of course not. You'll hardly have to see them at all. When you come in from the disco, they'll be long asleep. When you get up, they'll be gone to the beach already. I'll be helping Natalie with Joey and Gina, anyway. Look, if this is really a problem for you and you want to find somewhere else to stay, please, go right ahead, although you're not going to find anything cheaper than what we're asking you to pay."

Carrie blinked a couple of times in surprise before whining, "But who am I supposed to hang out with?"

Aha! Kit knew Carrie had expected her to be her BFF!

"You're twenty-three; figure it out," she answered matter-of-factly and turned to walk away.

"Huh?" Carrie's jaw dropped.

Kit felt a tinge of remorse; she looked back and added, "Look, I'll go out with you, but I just can't all the time. Natalie's going to need me until Joe gets here. Besides, you'll meet people. You met Luigi last year, didn't you? How's he doing, anyway?" Kit asked innocently, knowing fully well that Luigi was already giving Carrie the runaround.

When Carrie had called him shortly after arriving at the apartment, he wasn't too concerned about seeing her right away, and he was less than sympathetic to her luggage trauma. Kit thought perhaps this might once again be a case of typical Positano male psyche (if there was such one)—keep the long-distance romance alive enough to get a girl to come back and visit, then act like you couldn't care less once she got there. At any rate, the phone conversation had been quite short and ended with Carrie hanging up and muttering, "Can't wait to see you too. Thanks a lot, asshole!"

Carrie stood there silently scowling at the floor. Kit decided that she'd won this battle. In her opinion, the conversation was over. Whether Carrie stayed or left, she didn't care anymore, although her leaving would mean she and Bridget would have to cough up more rent money. Well, right now, she had other things to worry about.

"Just let me know whether or not you're staying, Carrie, okay?" Kit called as she walked away.

Somehow, leaving the fate of her Positano social life in the hands of Luigi, the town water/fish boy, didn't appeal to Carrie. After a day of sulking around the apartment and barely leaving her bedroom, she emerged, perky and overly accommodating. "Oh, here, Natalie, let me hold Gina for you while you eat. She's so adorable! I love kids! Kit told you I teach with her, didn't she?"

Kit rolled her eyes behind Carrie's back, while Natalie answered brightly, "Uh, yes, she did." Natalie knew all about the conversation Kit and Carrie had, but she wasn't going to be partial to who held Gina. She'd take the extra help with the kids where she could get it. So, now, here they were, on their sixth day in Positano. Hopefully, Kit thought, the knock at the door would bring some good news, or maybe …

"Lassino, hi!" Kit sang as she looked into the squinting face on the doorstep. With all the crazy mayhem surrounding the lost baggage, Tino hadn't been the only one to go out of his way to help Kit and her guests. Since they'd arrived, Lassino had stopped by the apartment every morning with a hot thermos of espresso and some cornetti from the café up in Chiesa Nuova. Not only that, but he made sure to bring a package of diapers or some type of clothing, which he borrowed from his young nephew and niece, for Joey and Gina.

"You know, Kit, I wasn't sure I was going to like Lassino, after hearing your stories about him, but he's been absolutely wonderful!" Natalie had commented after one of Lassino's morning visits. Kit beamed. Kit had been so right about Lassino, even though he was crazy at times. She had known all along what a good person he was. She loved that he cared about his family and friends and that he cared about hers too, because Natalie was family to her and so was Bridget, and he loved Bridget. Yes, Lassino was always so concerned about what Bridget thought of him, as if she was the morality parameter of the two of them.

It was quite funny, and a bit annoying at times, that everyone seemed to think of Bridget as so holy and modest. Well, she did teach in a Catholic school, and she went to church on a regular basis. And, of course, she'd absolutely go into cardiac arrest if she thought she had an ounce of cleavage showing. But she was no saint. If they only knew about "love on the rocks," Kit and Bridget had said and laughed. Kit had a feeling that Lassino did, but there was no need to tell Bridget. She'd never come back to Italy again.

And while Bridget claimed that she had a tendency to blend into the woodwork and that she "knew for a fact" that she only received special attention when she was with Kit (and especially when they were in Italy), Kit saw it differently. The Italians might not always know how to joke with

Bridget because she was so shy (by their standards), but they treated her with respect. Kit conceded to herself that Bridget was right. Kit *was* treated differently, but the thing was, she didn't always like it. Well, the whole attention thing was really nice, but she *never* took advantage of it or let any of these boys and men think anything was going to happen. She knew she had the "blonde California girl" thing going on, and true, she preferred wearing figure-hugging clothes (they certainly weren't cheap ones, at least!), but why did that seem to make men so crazy? Just once, she'd like to be treated with a little respect, and not just in regards to her boobs and whether they were real.

Lassino stepped inside and said in his usual rapid speech, "*Buon giorno.* You are looking very sexy today. Are you going to the beach already?" Lassino gave Kit's body the once-over, his eyes traveling up her legs, over her True Religion denim mini and stopping at her pushed-up breasts, which slightly bulged sexily out of her tiny, red Cosa Bella bikini top. It was always the boobs, wasn't it? Kit sighed, but she appreciated the compliment, coming from him.

Lassino didn't look so bad either. He stood in his black Umbro shorts and a white Tee-shirt. His blonde hair was pulled back into a tiny ponytail, which made him look, oddly enough, like a bespectacled David Beckham. Kit suddenly felt ravenously anxious to spend time alone with him, at his place. Except for these morning visits, she hadn't seen much of him. He would text and call her a lot, but he was mostly working, and Kit had been too preoccupied with Natalie and the others to get to the disco at all.

"Uh, yeah, we're heading down later. What are you up to?"

"I have to get the pizza dough ready at the restaurant, and then I have soccer practice. So, here is the espresso and cornetti. And no clothes for the kids today, because your luggage is here," he said and nodded to the assorted wheelies outside the door.

Carrie jumped out of the kitchen and onto the terrace, squealing, "Oh, thank God! Thanks, Lassino!" She grabbed her suitcase greedily and wheeled it off to the bedroom.

"Look, guys, all our stuff is here!" Natalie called.

"Yay, Mommy! Are we going home now?" Joey asked as he clapped his hands and danced around.

"No, Sweetie. Here, help me bring this all to our room." Natalie laughed. She placed Gina in her stroller, which had also been acting as a high chair/

porta-crib, and she and Joey dragged their bags through the double doors at the other end of the terrace that led to their room.

"Thanks, Lassino!"

"Sure. So, everything is all right now?" Lassino looked at Kit.

"Thank you, yes," Kit radiated warmly.

Lassino laughed. "Yes, everything is all right until the next person comes. Poor Tino! Who is coming next?"

Kit replied, "Bridget gets in today, and Natalie's husband and niece get here tomorrow, along with our other friend, Julianna. So, I know I'll probably be saying this again, but thank you so much, for—everything."

Oh, enough of the small talk already, Kit thought. Right this minute, all she really wanted to do was throw herself on top of Lassino, or have him throw himself on top of her. She wasn't particular. Either would be fine.

Instead, Lassino gave Kit the Italian face-shrug, which was a tilt of the head with the lips pressed together and slightly downturned. Kit and Bridget had so nicknamed this facial expression "the Italian face-shrug" since it was synonymous to shrugging one's shoulders as if to say, *Ay, whatever; Sure;* or *So?* and was often accompanied with the actual shrugging of the shoulders and the head tilt.

"It's all right. Okay, well, I must go. Maybe I will see you tonight? What are you doing?"

"Well, we're all going to dinner—not sure where yet—and I invited that really nice Australian girl, Rachel, who works at Giorgio's store, to come. Oh, and there were these other two American girls there, Georgia and Beth? Yeah, so I invited them too. They're here for a few days and seem fun. Maybe Carrie will want to hang out with them since they're around her age."

Kit thought she detected a startled look on Lassino's face, but perhaps she had imagined it? He was probably just squinting again. The poor guy *was* pretty blind. No, it had definitely been a surprised look of panic, and Kit felt more than sure she knew why. At any rate, though, she pretended not to notice. It wasn't worth getting into right now.

"Okay! Ciao, *Amor.*" Lassino quickly kissed her on the lips and stepped out the door before Kit could even try to put her arms around him.

"Ciao." Kit smiled as she watched Lassino take the steps two at a time up the staircase until he was no longer visible. She closed the door and leaned against its cool surface. Ahh, the vacation had finally begun.

Chapter 6

"Ti ricordi? You remember? There is Positano." The driver turned down the radio and smiled at Bridget expectantly as they rounded another bend on the winding Amalfi Coast. It didn't seem possible, but she was finally in Italy. The last week of summer school had seemed to drag on endlessly, each day longer than the next. She'd tried to remain focused for her poor students, but reading-comprehension skills and English grammar were the last things on her mind. There was so much else to compulsively obsess about. Like, had she taken enough euros out? Should she get more or wait till she got to Italy? Where were her color copies of her passport and driver's license? Did she have everyone's addresses written in her day planner so she could send postcards?

It was probably the least important thing in the scheme of things, but the most worrisome and stressful for Bridget was the packing. Had she packed enough shoes? Yes, she had a whole duffle bag full of varying heights of heels, flats, sandals, flip-flops, and of course, her running shoes. Was it ludicrous to bring that many shoes? Absolutely not. This would be the longest trip she'd ever taken, and if she got sick of her wardrobe, she'd end up using that as an excuse to buy more clothing. She, of all people, knew she didn't need any more. Yes, she was going to *try* to exercise some restraint with the shopping in Italy.

Bridget had carefully scrutinized her wardrobe, packed, unpacked, and repacked several times over. Big Blue, as her gargantuan, trunk-sized suitcase had been so nicknamed by her family, was filled to its monstrous capacity with shirts, jeans, shorts, Tee-shirts, and just about anything else that would fit. And she'd done it a whole three days before she was even leaving!

Yes, on the eve of her departure, Bridget had felt a sense of relief. For some unknown reason, she seemed to be on top of things. She'd lost twelve pounds since joining Weight Watchers in March and could fit back into her clothes (and of course, the new ones she'd bought to celebrate); she'd made enough money to cover her half of the apartment rent, and she'd still have money to eat; she had paid and mailed off a round of bills; and she was all packed and ready to go.

And then she'd gotten into bed and saw the cell phone blinking. How had she missed Kit calling from Italy? The message was harried and a tad cryptic. In short, *everyone's* luggage had been lost so far (Natalie's and the kids' still hadn't arrived!) and Bridget had better make sure she packed some changes of clothes in her carry-on. In her carry-on? Her carry-on had her hair dryer, flatiron, all her makeup and necessary toiletries, iPod, a few boxes of Weight Watchers Mint Cookie Bars, books to read, and her travel journal, plus a very expensive pair of black, sequined Miu Miu heels that she positively didn't want to risk losing en route. There was no room, Bridget thought in a panic.

Bridget also could've sworn she'd heard Kit mention, before hanging up, some kind of weird drama about Carrie and then something about Johnny being in Italy. *What? Johnny?* She must've heard wrong. The whole thought of repacking the carry-on had completely thrown off her concentration and apparently, her hearing. Her anal-retentive timeliness had all been for nothing, and now she would have to pull things out and rearrange them to fit into her small wheelie.

She'd gotten it done, but she had gotten no sleep at all. By the time Bridget was satisfied with the foolproof repacking of Big Blue and the side-kick carry-on, it was almost dawn. She knew it probably wouldn't make a difference at that point, but nonetheless, she hopped on the treadmill for a good hour and then showered. She'd even had time to hit Starbuck's for her nonfat, extrafoamy latte (only two points on the Weight Watchers Flex Program). Bridget hoped the latte wouldn't hinder the effects of the Ambien she was planning on downing as soon as she was airborne. As much as she loved traveling, long flights made her antsy, and if she thought about the miracle of flight too much, it really freaked her out. Oh, that reminded her. She'd better make sure she had her Rosary beads in one of her purse pockets. What? She positively needed them, especially for takeoffs and landings and any turbulence in between.

And then, suddenly, amidst the flurry of hotel shuttles, swerving taxis, and whistle-blowing traffic police, Annie pulled up and double-parked the

Chevy Tahoe at SFO's international terminal. She dragged Bridget's luggage out of the trunk and up onto the curb and said sarcastically, "Wow, I don't think you packed enough."

Bridget smirked. "You have all my flight info?"

"Yes, yes. Have fun, and make sure you come back, okay?" Annie hugged her quickly and added, "Better say bye to Mom before they start whistling at us to get moving."

Mrs. Moretti had insisted on coming to the airport and sat forlornly looking out the window at the two sisters.

"You'd think you were leaving for Iraq or something," Annie muttered as Bridget walked over to the passenger side of the Tahoe and opened the door.

"Okay, bye, Mom. Love you," Bridget reached in, put her arms around her mom, and kissed her on the cheek.

Glassy-eyed, her mom clung to her and whispered, "Bye, honey. I love you too."

Bridget thought about her mom being alone for the next six weeks. Annie would be over every morning to get on the treadmill and to drive her to dialysis during the week, but aside from that, she'd virtually be alone. While this was Bridget's longest trip by far, it was clearly going to be an even longer one for her mother.

Bridget couldn't help it, but she immediately thought of what state the house would be in when she returned. Her mother wasn't too big on housekeeping these days. If Bridget didn't clean regularly, the house would end up looking like something on one of those Oprah specials.

And Bridget could only imagine what remnants of taboo snacks she'd find hidden in her mother's chair when she got back. She suddenly felt doubtful and apprehensive about leaving her mother. Six weeks *was* a long time, wasn't it? Bridget didn't want to leave her mom; yet, she wanted to leave so desperately. But for Pete's sake, her mother was nearly sixty years old and was just going to have to be responsible for herself again. One day, Bridget would move out (God, she hoped), and her mother would have to cope.

Besides, Annie would keep a watchful eye on her. Annie would probably even be able to get their mom up and exercising a little, too, a mini-bootcamp! Sure, her mother would be okay, right? Bridget stopped herself from thinking about it any longer. If she didn't, she'd never get on that plane.

"*Mom,* you need to let Bridget go. She has to check her bags, and the traffic cop is coming back around," Annie said as she glanced in her sideview mirror.

"Okay." Their mother sniffed. She touched Bridget's cheek and said, "Be careful, now—and remember to call me."

"Okay, Mom." Bridget was déjà vu-ing to the first time she had gone away to camp.

Annie rolled her eyes as Mrs. Moretti continued. "And you and Kit stay together. You girls be safe!"

Safe, in Positano? Well, she would certainly be safe. Of course, that depended upon your definition of *safe.*

"Yes, Mom." Bridget smiled and sighed. She was too old for this.

Bridget waved and started wheeling her suitcases toward the automatic sliding-glass doors. As the Tahoe pulled away from the curb, she heard her mother call out faintly, but loud enough for anyone in close proximity to hear, "And try not to drink too much! Love you!"

Good Lord, as if drinking was the one and only reason Bridget was going to Italy! She cringed slightly, hoping no one within earshot knew the remark had been directed at her. That did it. Bridget wouldn't allow herself to feel bad about Italy anymore. She needed this trip, and she couldn't get there soon enough.

The flight had been outstanding; in fact, it was the best transatlantic flight she'd ever been on. Of course, Bridget knew her sleep deprivation, combined with the Ambien, had something to do with that. She didn't care, though. She'd been knocked out for eight hours straight. Not only did Bridget sleep soundly, but she'd been saved from having to make polite conversation with Ron, her seatmate from Fresno, from listening to the screaming two-year-old across the aisle, and from the obnoxious trio of teenagers who kept kicking the back of her seat and calling over her to their friends in the row ahead of her.

When she awoke, everyone around her was either still sleeping or just groggily waking up as the breakfast cart was being wheeled down the aisle. Only an hour or so remained before landing. Bridget discreetly wove her Rosary beads around her fingers and hoped for a safe landing as well as the good fortune of being reunited with her luggage upon Neapolitan soil.

Well, now, who'd have ever thought *her* bags would literally be the first ones to slide down the ramp onto the baggage-claim carousel? As long as she'd been traveling, Bridget guaranteed that had *never* happened. Her luggage was usually the very last to show up, if it hadn't taken some random detour along the way. It had all been too easy, she thought.

Surely, now there'd be some mix-up with the driver Tino was sending to pick her up. Bridget would probably be forced to camp out at the airport because the driver was stuck in crazy traffic or had been unable to spot her (she did blend in with the locals) and had taken off without her.

But no. Bridget had gingerly wheeled her luggage out, trying to keep from running into or over stray travelers, all of whom seemed none too concerned whether they bumped into *her* and knocked *her* purse off her shoulder as they jostled their way by. As she looked out into the sea of olive-tan faces waiting behind the waist-high metal gates, Bridget hardly knew who or what to look for. But as she scanned the crowd, she noticed a grandfatherly looking gentleman standing off a bit. In fact, he quite reminded Bridget of her own grandfather. It seemed it would be a good omen if he were to be her driver.

He had a thick and wavy head of silver hair, and he was not too tall. Yet, even so, he was very dignified-looking, lightly tanned, his navy-blue polo shirt tucked into his Gucci-belted seersucker slacks. Bridget actually wanted this stranger to be her driver. He looked so kind and peaceful. And when she looked at him, she knew he just *had* to be her driver. That, and he was a holding a huge posterboard sign that read "Breeeget Moretti."

This was a good sign. Bridget approached him and smiled. Just as she was about to introduce herself using some of her sparse Italian, he spoke first and said, "Hello, Bridget! Tino sent me. I thought I would be driving a ninety-year-old, but Tino tell me to look for a beautiful girl! He was right!"

He laughed and grasped her hand in both of his. He patted her gently on the back and then took Big Blue's handle from Bridget. *A girl? And beautiful?* Oh, no question about it, she knew she would like him.

And when he wasn't maniacally cutting off drivers and incessantly tailgating, Bruno was every bit the pleasant driving companion Bridget had thought he'd be. They spent the first half of the drive practicing their English and Italian on each other and singing along to his CD of Dean Martin Italian songs. After they'd finished a hearty rendition of "Volare,"

Bruno stated proudly, "I knew Dean Martin. I drove him many times. He stayed in Positano, in Zefferelli's Villa!"

Before Bridget could ask to hear more, he added, "Now, I take you for the best half-sandwich you ever had—better than McDonald's! By the time you done, you be ready for a cappuccino!"

Suddenly famished, Bridget couldn't argue with that, but she nervously wondered, *How many Weight Watchers points would a panini be?* Oh, to hell with it. She had to eat eventually.

When they had finished, Bruno helped her back into the sleek, black Mercedes E 320, and they hastened back onto the road. Despite the cappuccino, Bridget felt a bit drowsy after eating and laid her head back against the seat. Bruno, seemingly sensing her inevitable weariness, put on a less raucous song. A melodramatic chorus of mandolins played the intro to "Come Back to Sorrento." Bridget stared out the window at the dark-blue water, her eyelids heavy, as she tried translating the words inside her head:

> *Guarda il mare com'e bello!*
> *Spira tanto sentimento.*
> *Come il tuo soave accento, che me desto fa sognar.*

Something about "the beautiful sea" and "feeling sentimental" was about as much as Bridget could comprehend. Her mind drifted off. Yet, even lost in her near-REM-like thoughts, she kept coming back to how smoothly everything had gone thus far.

Bridget acknowledged her pessimistic tendencies, but she did wonder when the proverbial other shoe was going to drop. Maybe she'd get to Positano to find that the apartment had burned to the ground when Kit had tried cooking! Completely possible. *Or*, maybe Olivia had misquoted the rental price and Bridget wouldn't have enough money. Suddenly panic-stricken, she wondered if she still had her passport. She opened her eyes and frantically shuffled through her oversized metallic tote; she sighed with relief when she found both tucked away safely in one of the inside pockets.

Or *maybe* … she was about to die in a catastrophic Grace Kelly-type car crash on her way to Positano! All right, Bridget knew she was being so morbidly ridiculous. Although, with Bruno's Indy 500-like driving, zigzagging and dodging in and out and around cars as they sped their way along the cliff-hugging two-lane Strada Statale, the car crash would actually be the most likely scenario to happen, Bridget thought. Who said old people couldn't drive?

As nerve-racking as it was, Bridget could at least appreciate the fact that apparently age didn't affect one's driving reflexes in Italy. This still didn't stop her, though, from death-gripping the armrest and repeatedly hitting the imaginary brakes, as Bruno relentlessly shifted gears, lurched ahead of and around motorbikes, and dodged head-on traffic on the famously panoramic Nastro Azzurro, or Blue Ribbon. All the while, Dean Martin's smooth voice pleaded,

> "Smiling leave I saw you taking
> All that once you loved forsaking
> And I felt my heart was breaking
> Oh, how could you go away?"

Bruno's voice brought her back as he asked again, "*Signorina* Bridget, *ti ricordi? Ecco* Positano!" He pointed ahead. Bridget opened her eyes just as they passed the large statue of the Madonna next to a fruit stand selling lemons, a sight so common in Southern Italy. The glorious first glimpse of the pastel-colored houses dramatically tiered down the mountainside juxtaposed to the glimmering water once again astonished her and caused her heart to skip a beat. Bridget relaxed her grip on the armrest, and replied with a catch in her throat, "*Si, mi ricordi.* I remember."

With apparent ease, Bruno lifted Big Blue out of the trunk as if it were empty instead of the overstuffed, "heavy enough to possibly be storing a dead body" piece of luggage that it actually was. Before Bridget could reach for the industrial-sized, shoe-filled duffle, Bruno beat her to it. Well, she'd never again underestimate the strength of petite, Gucci-wielding, seersucker-clad septuagenarians. Bruno smiled, nodded toward the descending stairs just adjacent to them, and said, "Tino says the apartment is down here."

And with luggage in tow, he began the descent.

Bridget slung her tote over her shoulder and pulled the handle up on her carry-on. She sighed happily and took a moment to look around. This was their *street*, their *neighborhood*, and for the next *month*. Looming over the staircase leading to the apartment was the luxurious, five-star Palazza

Bianca. A navy-suited doorman held the front door open for a rather glamorous-looking couple just stepping out a chauffeured Jaguar. The bellhop scrambled behind them, lugging a large Louis Vuitton trunk. They might be high up Via Pasitea, but apparently they'd be in swanky company.

And there was no chance of them starving, since right across the narrow street was a little market. Tables loaded with colorful eggplant, tomatoes, lemons, and basil stood outside the doorway, while the front window displayed a hefty assortment of bottles, all containing the very popular and fluorescently yellow limoncello. The potently filled vessels gleamed beautifully in the afternoon sun. It was a shame Bridget couldn't stand the taste of the stuff. A streamer of triangular Italian flags hung over the doorway, as they did all over the town, in hopeful support of an Italian World Cup victory.

Bridget looked up and made direct eye contact with the balcony owner across the narrow road. An older woman, sporting dark, shortly cropped hair, a tan, calf-length shift, and slippers, stood leaning over her green wrought-iron balcony. Her downward-sloping bosom seemed to sit perfectly atop the balcony edge, almost giving Bridget the feeling it was staring at her too. The woman and her bosom eyed Bridget suspiciously. Bridget supposed she must be face-to-face with the neighborhood watch and she might as well make friends now. With a slight wave, she grinned and said, "Buon giorno!"

She quickly recoiled as the woman scowled back at her and answered in a monotone voice, "*Sera.*"

Great, her first Italian faux paus, Bridget thought. She now realized, it was too late in the afternoon to use the expression "Buon giorno." She should have used "Buona sera" or apparently, "Sera," instead. She'd try to remember next time. Bridget gulped, did a quick about-face, and headed down the stairs, before her new neighbor could put some ancient Italian hex upon her. She heard Kit calling, "Bridget, where are you?"

Bridget made her way down the first short flight of steps and turned the corner. At the bottom of this next set, Bruno and Kit stood in front of a green door, watching for her. Bridget stopped a moment, noticing that once past their doorway, the stairs seemed to continue on for miles … oh, well, not to worry about that now. She'd made it, so far.

Seeing Bridget, Kit ran up the steps, hugged her, and shouted, "You're here, you're here, and you actually have your luggage! I can't believe it. I am so happy! This has got to be the best day of the trip so far!"

Bruno laughed. "Quite a welcome for you! *Allora!* Signorina Bridget, it was a pleasure. Perhaps I will be driving you back to the airport!" He gave Bridget the Italian double kiss and headed up the steps.

"Wait, Bruno! I need to pay you!" Bridget ran after him.

He turned and said, "Ah, no, no. Tino said you no pay, okay?"

"Please, take this, Bruno, grazie!" Bridget pressed forty euros into his hand, probably almost half of what the total fare would have been. God, she was such a fool with money. But Bruno had been so good to her, what with feeding her *and* getting her here alive.

Bruno cupped her hands and said warmly, *"Prego;* enjoy your stay in Positano."

"I will," Bridget watched the seersucker pants disappear around the staircase. She turned back to Kit and said gleefully, "Okay, show me the apartment. I can't wait to see it!"

◆　　◆　　◆

Kit pushed the door open and ushered Bridget onto the terrace. "Welcome to your new home! This is the veranda ... oops, watch your step there." Kit looked back just as Bridget tripped on a bottle of blowing bubbles that had been left in the doorway. Bridget looked down at the bubbles and then quizzically at Kit. Kit explained, "We only have one key, so the bubbles are acting as our doorstopper. When we put the bubbles there, you can't even tell that the door is open. Pretty nifty, huh?"

"Very," Bridget agreed and then looked around for anything else she might trip over.

Kit continued with a sweep of her hand. "And to your left, below us, is the beautiful Tyrrhenian Sea and Fornillo Beach."

"Speaking of the beach," Bridget said, "how is Tomaso?"

Kit raised her eyebrows and said, "Yeeaahh, with the whole luggage fiasco, we've, uh, sort of been confined to the apartment. We haven't really been down to the beach more than once."

Bridget interrupted. "Does that have something to do with why the floor is covered with dirty towels?"

Kit answered in mock seriousness. "Correct, um, and I'm not sure if you noticed this, either, but," she spoke in an exaggerated whisper, "it's very *hot* here and there are a lot of stairs too! Apparently, I didn't make that clear enough. Yeah, so, hence the kiddie pool in the corner there. I think I've even jumped in it a few times myself!"

"What's with all the towels, though?" Bridget asked.

"Well, the beautiful ceramic tile that you and I have no problem walking on is evidently not clean enough for the kids to walk or crawl on, even though I am quite sure that Italian dirt is far cleaner than ours at home. But you can't tell that to a mother of two small kids."

"Oh," Bridget said as she looked at all the sopping wet, grayed towels that covered practically half of the terrace. "At least the apartment has a washer and dryer."

"Yeah, that's another thing. Those aren't really working right now," Kit added. "But there is a laundromat down the street. I have a feeling we'll be giving them a lot of business."

"So, where is everyone, anyway?" asked Bridget.

"The excitement of the luggage arriving and then the whole unpacking tired out Nat and the kids. They're all napping."

"And where's Carrie?" Bridget asked, raising her eyebrows.

"Oh, as soon as she unpacked, she took off. I think she went down to the beach to meet up with a couple of American girls that we met at Giorgio's shop. Man, I'm glad she's out of my hair. And she thought *she* would have to babysit! I feel like that's all I've been doing!"

"What?" said Bridget.

Kit pulled up the handle on the duffle bag, began wheeling it through the large, shuttered doors that lead into the kitchen, and said, "Here, let me show you to our room and I'll tell you all about it while you're unpacking."

◆　◆　◆

Bridget carefully stacked her shoes in the closet as she listened to Kit recount the happenings of the last six harrowing, luggage-less days. Every once in a while, she'd comment appropriately with, "Are you serious?", "Oh, no, she said *that*?", or "You're kidding, right?" While Bridget hung up her skirts and shorts and refolded her T-shirts, she listened as Kit talked about Lassino.

"Bridget, Lassino's been wonderful. Every morning, he stops by and brings us espresso in a mason jar, and some pastries, and things for Joey and Gina. He really does care!"

"Of course he does." Bridget nodded her head as she hung up yet another pair of jeans. Why had she decided to bring this many clothes? Was she actually going to wear all this? Well, maybe she would, now that the washer and dryer weren't working.

She turned away from the closet and asked Kit, "So, I'm going to have to ask: Besides the morning deliveries—which, by the way, *are* very sweet of him—has anything else happened with you two? Is the girlfriend really out of the picture?"

"Well ..." Kit began.

"Uh-oh," replied Bridget.

"Wait, wait. Lassino's been at the restaurant, and I've been mostly hanging out with Natalie. The one night I did make it to the disco, it was way too crowded and then Carrie had a meltdown because Luigi ignored her and then danced with some other bimbo, so we left."

"And ..." Bridget added.

"And, apparently, he and Monica *are* really broken up. At least, that's the word on the street, or in the fork in the road, or whatever they call 'the square,' where all the taxi drivers hang out."

As Bridget squeezed her camisols, underwear, and bathing suits all into a dresser drawer, Kit continued. "So, there's no Monica any more, *but* Lassino's got some girl in town visiting him."

Bridget shoved the dresser drawer closed and said, "Aha, so that's why you haven't seen him much."

Kit snorted. "Yes, it's really kind of funny, too. Lassino thinks I have no clue about her, but I actually met her!"

"You *did?*"

"It's the weirdest thing, Bridget, and I swear to you, I don't go snooping around trying to find out things about Lassino. I just happen to be in the right—or wrong—place at the right time, and people just tell me things!"

"How'd you meet the mystery girl?"

"Well, Carrie and I were in Giorgio's store, chatting with him and the Australian girl, Rachel, who's working for him. These two girls at the counter started talking with us too; they must have heard us speaking English."

Bridget reminded her with a laugh, "Everyone here speaks English, Kit."

"Well, they heard our American English, whatever. While Rachel's ringing people up, Georgia—that's her name—mentions to me that she'd been here last summer with her friend Beth and they'd met two guys."

Bridget cut in and said, "Wait, wait, let me guess: Lassino and Paolo. God, they're like a tag team, aren't they?" There, Bridget had finally uttered *his* name. She wondered when she'd finally hear about Paolo.

"But of course! So they're traveling again this summer and are here for a few days—staying at Lassino's."

Bridget shook her head in amazement. "You're kidding. Did you say anything about you and Lassino?"

"No, no." Kit shook her head, then shrugged her shoulders and said, "Lassino's not my boyfriend, so I don't want to make a big deal out of it. Plus, they're only here a short time. In fact, they leave tomorrow. And they're *really* nice girls." Kit paused. "That's why I invited them out to dinner with us tonight."

"You invited them out to dinner with us?" Bridget was somewhat puzzled, yet not surprised. Kit was always meeting random people and inviting them to join her for dinner or drinks. Traveling with her was like traveling with a US foreign correspondent or United Nations representative. Bridget sat down on the bed, suddenly exhausted. Unpacking was just as tiring as packing.

Kit nodded, "Well, why not? Listen, they're leaving tomorrow. We're here for the rest of the summer! We have a history with these boys that they don't."

Bridget held up her hand. "I think *a lot* of people have a history with these boys. Well, okay, you and Lassino have … *something*. You two have kept in touch. Paolo and I, well, there's not much, just, just—"

Kit burst into dramatic song: "Love on the rocks—ain't no surprise; pour me a drink, and I'll tell you some lies!"

"Now you've just sullied one of Neil Diamond's greatest hits. There're not going to be *any* rocks this summer. In fact, there will be no *love* this summer … *at all*," Bridget stated emphatically.

Kit laughed as she repeated, "'*There will be no love this summer?*' Oh, please! There'll be something, believe me. *What*, I don't know, but there *will* be something. Paolo will be very excited to see you. Every time I run into him, he asks about you."

Bridget rolled her eyes.

"Stop rolling your eyes. He does. And Lassino, God, he's such an enigma. Just when I think I have him figured out, he says or does something that completely baffles me. I hope this town is big enough for the both of us." Kit's eyes twinkled.

"I guess we'll find out. So, are Georgia and Beth meeting us for dinner?"

"Actually, they have plans, but they invited us to come meet them at Solo Tu when we're done. Rachel, the Australian, is joining us, though. Wait till you hear her story! She has some kind of weird romantic saga going on with a younger guy here."

Bridget responded, "That seems to be a recurring theme. Who is he?"

Kit shook her head. "I have no idea who he is. She's never mentioned his name, but apparently, he's quite a bit younger than her."

"How much younger?" Bridget asked, last summer's cradle-robbing instantly coming to mind.

"I know exactly what you're thinking about Bridget, so this should make you feel better: Rachel's forty-two, and her Italian boy-toy is only twenty-six!"

"You're right. I don't feel like such an old hag anymore. Jeez, what is it about this town and the men here, anyway?"

"I don't know, but ugh, I can't wait to get out. Tonight should be a lot of fun!"

"I have no doubt," Bridget agreed.

◆   ◆   ◆

"*Viva le donne!* Long leeevve the weemen!" the maitre'd standing in front of Casa da Renzo shouted out whenever any female between the ages of sixteen to fifty (or older—American women *were* pretty well preserved, and thus, deceiving with their ages) walked past the restaurant. This being the height of tourist season, the hordes of strolling visitors constantly making their way down Via Pasitea meant that whomever was within earshot was subjected to listening to his favorite phrase every five minutes. In fact, it spewed from his mouth so frequently that it simply became one with all the other background noises that permeated this winding, one-way road and the town itself, on a busy summer night: clanking silverware, sputtering mopeds, heaving tour buses, intimate candlelit conversations, and "*Long live the weemen!*"

In fact, Vinnie, as he was known, said it so often that the words had become synonymous with him and the curbside-dining area that Casa de Renzo occupied on Via Pasitea. He owned that phrase and no one else dared to utter it, unless it was in agreement with him after he'd shouted it out at some unsuspecting females. Other than that, no one, not the waiters, nor the busboys he worked with, not even the customers dining there after five minutes or so, paid any attention to it. Just another noise wafting into the night air. Vinnie knew people probably wondered why he kept repeating the overused expression. It was quite simple, really. For every Italian (or French, for that matter) woman who heard it and either ignored him or gave him an exasperated or disgusted look as she passed, there were hundreds of other girls and women to use it on—Australians, Irish, English, even the occasional Japanese, and of course, *Americans.*

These women would make their way up and down Via Pasitea their first night in Positano and would receive Vinnie's own personal Positano greeting. And what would he receive in return? A coy backward glance, a sweetly shy blush, a brilliantly white smile, a wave, a new customer or two, a possible kiss at the disco. Although, for some odd reason, this often seemed to work to his disadvantage there. Go figure.

Yes, "Viva le donne!" was an ode to *these* women. Vinnie lived for those first-timers. After that, he knew he'd become just a Positano caricature to them, like that fellow who walked up and down Spiaggia Grande and Fornillo Beach every day of tourist season selling fresh coconut and shouting, "*Coco bello! Coco fresco!*" Did anyone ever buy any? Maybe and maybe not. But, hey, every tourist sure knew who he was.

So, so what if his special phrase only elicited a response when heard for the first time? He had made an impression, and not like some of the other slick playboys in this town, who made their impressions, in, ahem, *other* ways. Truth be told, though, Vinnie sure wouldn't mind a little piece of that action, a little more often. But no matter. Anyway, there were some who never failed to smile at him, no matter how many times they walked by and heard, "Long live weemen!"

Ahh, and here was one now. That sexy, blonde American girl that walked by at least a few times every day. She supposedly was the lover of

Lassino. How did the crazy, blind fool have such a beautiful woman, Vinnie wondered, as did the rest of the men in the town. Apparently, she wouldn't have any other man here, but she always had a dazzling smile for everyone and a wiggle in her step, and those were enough to make any man hope, if not completely lust, for her. And there was no harm in wishing—or even trying, for that matter—was there?

Hmm, and she was with two new ones tonight. Oh, *that* was the one who was seeing Luigi, the fish boy. Vinnie didn't dare bother with her. Luigi was an incredibly jealous sort, and a touch crazier (at least by town standards) than most. And the other one? He didn't recognize the petite, dark-haired one, but she must be the friend that always traveled with the *angela bionda*, the blonde angel. It was well known that this was their third summer here (funny, he'd never seen the little one before) and they were living in an apartment close to Palazza Bianca.

Before Vinnie had a chance to shout his favorite words, the blonde smiled a fluorescent-white smile at him and, wait, appeared to be walking straight toward him. Vinnie felt himself perspire more than he normally did. They were coming to Casa da Renzo for dinner! Maybe this would be his lucky night. He smoothed his well-oiled hair back, unbuttoned another two shirt buttons, and called to the approaching trio, "*Madonna! Viva le donne!*"

"*Buona sera,*" the waiter with the slicked-back hair and incredibly furry chest standing outside Casa da Renzo purred at Kit. Of course Kit recognized him. He always managed to be standing outside the restaurant whenever she happened to walk by, no matter what time of day or night. Didn't he ever take the Italian *siesta?* Kit wondered. Well, if he didn't, he must be the hardest-working waiter—no, make that, person—in this town. And he was always shouting, "*Viva le donne!*" in his raspy voice. So completely cheesy, but Kit couldn't help but smile every time she heard him yell it. *Only* in Italy.

"*Buona sera,*" Kit smiled back. Damn, her Chinese-Russian accent was back in effect. Why couldn't she ever sound like a real Italian?

Looking from Kit to Carrie, to Bridget, and back to Kit, he asked, "A table for three?"

It never failed to impress Kit how well the Italians here (and in most of Italy, for that matter) spoke English. She racked her brain for some bit of

Italian she'd learned. She could at least try, she thought. Ahhhaa! She did remember something.

Hesitatingly, Kit answered, "Uh, *vorrei … una tavola per cuatro … per favore?*" She then quickly held up four fingers, smiling as she did so. Sign language and a smile always helped.

"*Brava!* You speak Italian! Ahh, *benissima!*" The waiter beamed and began speaking to Kit in rapid Italian. When he finished, he looked expectantly at her. Kit looked sideways at the girls. Did he say something about a street, or was that the word for swordfish? Uh-oh, bad, bad idea trying out the Italian.

Carrie flipped her long, dark hair over her shoulder and shrugged. "Don't look at me. Neapolitan dialect is like, practically African."

Bridget spoke up. "I think he wants to know if we'd like a table outside."

Kit laughed. "Oh! Si, si! Sorry, my Italian is not so good!" Street, outside—well, she hadn't been too off, had she?

The waiter looked at Kit beseechingly and answered, "Ahhh, Signorina, no problem. I will speak English for you."

He led them past the other outdoor diners and stopped at an unoccupied table.

"You like?" the waiter gestured to the table, the starched, white tablecloth glowing beneath the small, lit lantern that rested in the middle. He stared directly at Kit, as if Bridget and Carrie were not even there.

"Si, grazie," Kit nodded, breaking eye contact. Why did this guy keep staring at *her*? She wasn't even showing any cleavage tonight. She had on a simple, drapey, short-sleeved Twelfth Street sweater. Of course, it was thin, shimmery silver and hung off of one shoulder, à la the Jennifer Beals Flashdance look (but that look *was* back in), with short, cuffed black shorts offset by high, suede Loeffler Randall slingbacks, but the whole outfit was nothing too revealing, was it?

Or maybe he was someone else in this town who seemed to know who she was. This was happening more and more often. She couldn't walk more than a few feet from the apartment without someone calling from his moped, "Ciao, Kit!" as he drove by. And half the time, she had no idea who these men were. Kit was a friendly person, she knew, and the town was small, but why did all the *men* seem to know her? Kit supposed it might have a little something to do with Lassino, but why?

"Prego, please, sit." With a flourish, the waiter pulled out the chair for Kit as Bridget and Carrie were left to seat themselves. As he handed each of them a menu, he looked at Kit and asked, "So, you are the teachers?"

Bridget and Kit shot each other surprised glances, as Carrie sat there, bored. Kit said, "Yes! How did you know we were teachers? By the way, my name is Kit."

The waiter grabbed Kit's extended hand and kissed it. He looked up at her and said throatily, "*Piacere*, Kit. I am Vinnie—and the best waiter in Positano! Oh, and I work for the taxi service, if you ever need a ride anywhere!"

Kit chuckled. "Well, then, we came to the right restaurant tonight! These are my friends, Bridget and Carrie." Kit managed to pull her hand out of Vinnie's grasp so she could motion to the girls. Vinnie glanced quickly in the direction of Bridget and Carrie, smiled politely at them, and then looked adoringly back at Kit.

"So, you are the *friend* of Lassino?"

Aha, yes, of course, it always came back to Lassino. Kit was undecided if it was a good omen or a curse to be associated with him and wasn't sure how to respond. Was she Lassino's friend? *Friend* wasn't quite the appropriate word. His lover? Ughh, she hated that word. It sounded so tawdry. Or was she just nothing at all? She never could tell, but Kit was beginning to think so. She'd barely even been alone in a room with Lassino since she'd set foot in the town last week! Yet, this Vinnie seemed to be implying that she and Lassino were clearly *something*.

She cleared her throat and said, "Uh, yes. Lassino is a *friend* of mine."

Vinnie gave her the Italian face-shrug as if to imply, "Hmm, whatever are you thinking?"

Then he looked at Carrie, who was ignoring the conversation by scrutinizing the wine list, and stated, "And *you*. You are the girlfriend of Luigi." Upon hearing Luigi's name, Carrie looked up and gave a half-smile, which really wasn't a smile at all. Sarcastically, she answered, "Depends on what day it is."

He turned to Bridget and asked matter-of-factly, "And whose girlfriend are you?"

Startled, yet amused, to be included in this conversation, Bridget raised her eyebrows and replied, "I'm nobody's girlfriend."

Her response also received the Italian face-shrug, this time its implication being a cross between, "Yeah, right," and "What's the matter with you?"

Vinnie shrugged and stated assuredly, "Don't worry. You'll be able to find a boyfriend in Positano."

"Oh ... good," Bridget mumbled under her breath.

In a suddenly cheerful voice, Vinnie asked, "So! Would you like some wine, some prosecco, while you are waiting for your other friend?" Vinnie wondered who the other friend would be. Hopefully, she'd be at least half as good-looking as Kit and a lot more friendly than the other two. The blonde one was so sexy, but it was clear she was Lassino's, even though she wasn't saying much about him. And Luigi's girlfriend, or whatever she was, was a sourpuss. No fun whatsoever. And the other one ... hmmm. He couldn't figure her out. *No boyfriend in Positano?* He'd never heard of such a thing! Well, you never knew about those quiet ones. Or maybe she was lesbian.

"Oh, there she is now! Hi, Rachel!" Kit waved.

Vinnie turned, ready to pour on the charm. Oh, no, *mamma mia!* It was that blonde Australian, the *pazza*, the crazy one, the one having a fling with ...

"Hiya!" the tall, lanky blonde bent over Kit and kissed her on both cheeks. She looked up at both of the other girls and reached out her hand to shake each of theirs.

"Hi, I'm Rachel! Uh, girls, I don't know about you, but I'm *famished!* And completely parched! It's so damn hot in this bloody town!" She fanned herself with one hand and lifted her shoulder-length hair up from the back of her neck. She turned abruptly to Vinnie and practically shooed him off, and then she said, "Ciao, Vinnie, would you bring us a bottle of prosecco, per favore? Grazie!"

"Si," Vinnie answered curtly, bowing as he backed away. Well, he could kiss any chance of romance away now. Although very attractive, the Australian was known to be a bit of a nutcase when she drank, which happened to be every night. What was she doing with these girls? Maybe they were *all* crazy. Too bad, he sighed to himself. Well, he could still flirt with the blonde American. No harm in that. And the night was young. Perhaps, Vinnie thought resignedly, he'd find a happy ending with some other tourist this evening. He made his way indoors for the bottle of prosecco.

"Mind if I have a ciggie? I know you Americans don't like the whole secondhand smoke thing, but I'm dying for one. Promise I'll blow my smoke out there." Rachel smiled widely and nodded her head in the direction of the street.

"No, go ahead." Kit answered for both of them. Bridget wondered why Rachel had even bothered to ask if they minded, since she'd lit up and took her first drag before they could even reply. At home, Bridget would've been irritated, but not here. One of the mysteries of travel, she'd noted. If she didn't already have a complete migraine from the overpowering exhaust fumes of nonstop passing vehicles, then a little cigarette smoke wasn't going to kill her either.

In fact, she might even indulge in a cigarette herself. Bridget wasn't a smoker, but if she'd had enough to drink and the mood suited her, she just might. And it looked like the mood tonight was most likely going to suit her, she thought, since they'd gone through at least three bottles of prosecco and had just downed a shot of limoncello.

Bridget practically gagged as she swigged it down, then immediately chased the shot with a whole glass of fizzy water. She realized she should really stop drinking alcohol and stick to water. She couldn't remember how many points her Weight Watchers Complete Food Companion Booklet had listed for a small glass of prosecco. Something ridiculous, since the points were probably based upon a glass being the size of a thimble. All right, well, maybe a shot glass—but an amount that small was surely a setup for *overly* drinking, just so you could get even the tiniest of buzzes. Well, Bridget had stopped counting her points an hour after she'd gotten there and had her first gelato, anyway. There was no going back tonight. She'd just walk the stairs tomorrow—all day. And there must be a gym at one of the hotels around here too.

Across the table, Rachel hiked her black, linen skirt up a bit and fanned herself with the hem of it, revealing her long, tanned legs and her lace-up gladiator sandals (a summer staple in each Positano woman's dress code). She crossed her legs, took another drag on her cigarette, and exclaimed, "Oh, I'm sorry! I shouldn't assume you girls don't smoke. Would either of you care for one?"

Kit answered, "Oh, no thanks," as Bridget answered, "Sure, I'll have one."

"Right, then, I knew I'd find a smoking partner." Rachel smiled and handed Bridget a cigarette.

Kit raised her eyebrows and laughed. "Uh-oh, it's a smoking night!" She grabbed her camera and snapped a picture as Rachel flicked her lighter on for Bridget.

"Now, let's finish this bottle, girls. We've got other places to go," Rachel said as she poured a new glass for each of them. "Does Carrie want any? Where's she gone to, anyway?" Rachel held the bottle and waited.

Kit looked in the direction of the indoor dining area. Carrie had gone in to use the bathroom more than an hour ago and had never come back. Kit assumed that she had left without saying good-bye or leaving any money for her share of the bill. It was becoming somewhat of a habit for Carrie to go MIA whenever the check came. As soon as the bill had been taken care of, she'd suddenly reappear and say she'd "pick up the tab next time."

But, no, Carrie was still there, sitting at the bar, giggling and twirling her hair around her finger. Kit strained her eyes to see. Who was she talking to? Even with her less than adequate eyesight, it didn't take Kit long to figure out who Carrie's coquettish display was directed toward. Standing behind the bar was the most beautiful (in a completely manly way) man Kit had ever seen, at least in this town, no offense to Lassino. Kit racked her brain trying to figure out who he reminded her of. Ooh, yes, that guy on *Sex and the City*, the one who played Samantha's model boyfriend. What was he doing here, washing and drying glasses behind the bar? Shouldn't he be on some runway modeling underwear?

Kit watched as he refilled Carrie's wine glass. She felt her jaw drop with a tinge of envy as he stroked Carrie's hand, then leaned over the bar to murmur something into her hair. That did it. It had been so long since Kit had had any serious one-on-one male attention. Men calling to her from their mopeds and incessantly staring at her boobs did not qualify. When would she and Lassino ever be alone together?

"She doesn't need any prosecco, but I do! God, he's hot! Who is *that*?" Kit surprised herself by shouting out loud.

Bridget and Rachel sat up and craned their necks to see. "Oh, that's Jared. Gorgeous, isn't he? He's from Los Angeles, an aspiring actor of course, just working here for the summer. If I didn't have my fella here, I'd go after him myself!" Rachel voraciously tossed back her prosecco and lit up another cigarette.

"Wow," Bridget said, unable to help staring, herself, at the chiseled jawline, dark-blond, swept-back hair, and the unmistakably perfect teeth. She took a sip from her glass and thought, *Paolo who?*

"Well done, Carrie. By the looks of things in there, I'd say you'll be having another houseguest tonight!" Rachel laughed.

"Well, then, I'm gonna charge her double occupancy. She hasn't paid for a darn thing since she's been here, including her share for the apartment! She'd better not try to skip out on the check tonight, either!" Kit snapped sassily as she applied her Nars lip gloss.

Rachel smiled seductively. "Speaking of double occupancy, I better send *mi amor* a message to see what he's up to tonight." She pulled her cell out of her shoulder bag and began texting.

Bridget took a puff of her cigarette and tried to inhale, then completely choked; her seal-sounding bark caused a few diners to turn around and stare. Why was she always so uncool? She guessed she could cross off smoking from her weight-loss plan.

"You all right, there?" Rachel looked up from her phone.

Her eyes watering, Bridget shook her head yes as Kit slid the ashtray over to her. Taking the hint, Bridget stamped out her cigarette. Her buzz had suddenly kicked in and there were many stairs to climb and, of course, take a tumble down, too, if she wasn't careful. Besides, too much more and Bridget would be in danger of not remembering much of the evening at all. And the evening's dinner conversation had been anything but dull.

The girls had sat, entranced, as Rachel talked quite a bit about her entrance into Positano life: how she'd left her native Melbourne four months prior for a Positano man she'd met there. After spending a week with Salvatore, she'd impetuously quit her job in retail and moved to Positano. And just as soon as she'd found the job at Giorgio's beachfront boutique, she'd been unexpectedly and relentlessly swept off her feet by some delicious twenty-six year old.

In fact, aside from withholding the name of her young lover, Rachel gave quite possibly much more information than Bridget would've ever wanted to know, having just met her. Rachel's story was well packed with smoldering sex galore. Indeed, Bridget thought, Jackie Collins herself couldn't have written a better plotline. Bridget wondered if it was possible for anyone (porn stars excluded) to have *that* much sex. *Come on*, was it really possible? And in all those places, too? Well, living at home, she'd never know.

Rachel was finishing her story, gushing, her eyes holding a faraway look. "Oh, it was just mad passion! We spent every night together for over a month. Ahhh, complete heaven. I even met his whole family—"

"But what happened to your other guy?" Kit asked, the thought of Johnny suddenly and involuntarily popping into her head.

"Oh, Salvatore? He screamed at me, of course, called me a slut, and doesn't speak to me now. He runs his own bar on Fornillo Beach, so we only have to avoid each other every so often at the disco."

"But you were—I mean, you are—happy with *this* guy ..." Bridget began to ask.

"Oh, of course. I'd found the most perfect man—sweet, beautiful, well-connected here, and I couldn't complain one bit about the glorious, nonstop shagging! Not at all." Rachel paused and then added dryly, "And then tourist season started up."

Bridget and Kit waited for her to continue. Rachel looked at them and shrugged nonchalantly before sputtering darkly, "And he became a bloody little shithead bastard!"

With that, she smashed her cigarette violently into the ashtray, causing the glasses on the table to rattle. Before Bridget or Kit could comment, she sang, "Who's ready for dessert and a bit more prosecco?"

Bridget was dying to know who the mystery man was. She'd sure heard enough about his sexual prowess. She'd like to put a name to a face. Or not. If nothing else, to *at least* steer clear of him and his wild libido. Bridget certainly had enough liquid courage to be nosy enough to ask, but after the cigarette-smashing outburst, it might be unwise to provoke any more bitterness. Yes, Bridget had decided Rachel was a tad scary. She definitely wouldn't want to tangle with her over anything. Best to let the topic go.

However, Rachel continued to bring up the relationship. Bridget noted that whatever it was, it appeared to be a bit of the love-hate variety. It was clear, though, that one minute, Rachel seemed to be deeply in love (or lust) with nameless Posi Boy. "Ahh, girls, he just sent me a sweet text message. He says he'll be at Solo Tu."

"Oh, good, that's where we're meeting Georgia and Beth!" Kit exclaimed.

The next minute, Rachel was totally pissed off at him. "Another bloody text—he's not going out now! He's too tired. Bullshit, he's probably out with some other little bitch tourist! God, I hate that *fucker!*" This elicited another fist-pounding on the table, which made both Bridget and Kit jump slightly.

And then a half an hour later … "Well, he *has* been working a lot in his shop. He really is probably tired. Poor baby. I'll just send him another text. Maybe he'll want some company tonight."

Bridget raised her eyebrows at Kit as Rachel madly punched the phone keys. Bridget was no expert on men, but in her opinion, texting this guy appeared to be a bad move. But what did she know? Bridget always erred on the overly cautious side in regards to romance. Maybe that was why she had none in her life.

Bridget took a moment to scrutinize Rachel. She embodied that natural, beach-blonde look that Bridget always associated with Aussies. Effortlessly thin (so unfair) and just toned enough, with a deep tan, straight, blonde hair, now pulled back in a messy knot, a touch of crow's feet about her green eyes … she was a wee bit weathered in a *Survivor*-ish way, but Rachel was beautiful. *But* she was also forty-two, and while Bridget knew that wasn't old by any means, it was a lot older than *twenty-six.*

Whoever *he* was, Bridget suspected he was definitely giving Rachel the runaround. How depressing, Bridget thought. Was this what she had to look forward to one day? God help her if she began desperately texting some immature, oversexed youngster when she was forty-two! Well, it'd probably never happen since she could barely e-mail attachments without causing her laptop to crash, but *still.* How awful. And quite pitiful. Bridget suddenly felt sad for Rachel, even though she seemed a little, well, volatile—either that, or slightly bipolar. But this fellow didn't need to be such a jerk. Bridget decided that, already, she didn't like him, and if she ever met him, he'd better stay away from her.

"All right, I've sent my little text. Let's get the check. Vinnie! *Il conto, per favore!*" Rachel called, waving at him.

"Si, si," Vinnie called absentmindedly over his shoulder. He had finally cultivated some female contacts for the disco and now, *right this minute,* they wanted the bill? *Madonna!*

"Un momento." He rushed over, flung it on the table, then hurried back.

Kit looked over the bill and decided they'd better start eating at Lassino's. They'd gotten nothing for free tonight, not even the limoncello, and they hadn't even ordered that. Carrie sauntered up to the table, glassy-eyed and smiling loosely from the *free* alcohol she'd been tossing back all evening.

"Having fun?" Rachel asked, raising her eyebrows.

"Yeaahhhh. Jared's soooo freakin' hot! Listen, I'm gonna take off. Jared's going to drive me around on his scooter to show me Positano." Carrie grinned tipsily.

"I reckon that's not all he's going to show you, missy!" cooed Rachel.

"That's fine with me! I am *so* over Luigi. Just leave the bubbles in the door, Kit."

"No problem. Have a good time." Kit smiled as she pulled some euros from her wallet.

Hunky Jared walked up, put an arm around Carrie, and said, "Ready?" He noticed Rachel and added, "Oh, hey, Rachel!"

"Hi, there, Jared. Going to show our little guest here about town?" Rachel smiled coyly.

"That's the plan. See you all later," he said, and then winked and pulled Carrie's hand to go.

"Oh, wait! I don't want to forget to pay! Kit, here's money for *everything* I ordered," Carrie said as she magnanimously threw some euros onto the table. "Ciao, girls!"

She hopped onto the back of the sputtering scooter and waved as they putted away from the restaurant.

"She didn't even introduce us!" exclaimed Bridget disappointedly.

"Well, I can't believe she actually paid! Thank God, because we didn't have enough cash here at all," Kit added. Kit picked up Carrie's contribution, stared at it, and disbelievingly said, "You've got to be kidding!"

"What?" Bridget asked as she and Rachel stared at Kit.

"Carrie only left *ten* euros! The bill is one hundred and thirty!"

"Well, she did make quite a big deal about only wanting to order that small little pizza. I guess, technically, that's all 'she ordered!'" Rachel chuckled and then sucked deeply on her cigarette.

Bridget added, "Well, she may have only *ordered* a small pizza, but she drank nearly a whole bottle of prosecco and ate more than half of the antipasti platter! And the anipasti platter alone was ten euros!"

Kit was incredulous. "Yeah! *And* she ate dessert and had a limoncello too! I can't believe her! Now I'm going to have to use my Visa. Damn her!

Oops, sorry, for swearing!" Kit covered her mouth apologetically. "I'm just so irritated!"

◆　　◆　　◆

They rounded the bend in the road as they made their way to Solo Tu, and Kit asked worriedly, "Do you think Vinnie was annoyed that we asked to split the bill between our three Visas?"

Rachel answered, "Kit, I wouldn't give a thought about Vinnie. I dare say he was just glad to be rid of us so he could get himself to the disco and harass some other girls!"

"Yeah, he knew he wasn't going to get anywhere with you," Bridget agreed, catching herself before she tottered over in her tall espadrilles. When would she learn that drinking and wearing heels did not mix well in this town?

Kit rolled her eyes, but she grinned just the same.

Rachel's long legs kept her a few steps ahead of Kit and Bridget, and she turned around to ask, "Well, he's not the only one to have a thing for you. So where's *Lassino* tonight, Kit? And don't pretend you're just friends. Everyone in town knows you're far more than that!" She reached into her bag and pulled out her pack of cigarettes, and then asked, "Bridget?"

Bridget involuntarily hiccupped. Great, she was practically staggering in her heels, and now she had the hiccups. All she needed now was to run into Paolo. "No, thanks," she replied as she then tried holding her breath.

Responding to Rachel's question, Kit sighed and answered, "I have no idea where Lassino is tonight. He said he was working, but I never know whether to believe him. He usually knows where I'll be before I even do, so I'll either run into him tonight, or he's somewhere in hiding!"

"He's quite the character, isn't he?" Rachel laughed and exhaled a cloud of smoke.

Kit changed the subject, and said, "So, Rachel, you never did tell us who your guy is here. This is our third summer in Positano. Is it anyone we know?"

Glad that Kit had asked what she, too, had been so curious about, Bridget nodded her head in agreement. She could see Solo Tu just up ahead, and she decided she most certainly did not want to enter like a hiccupping drunkard; she deeply inhaled again and held her breath.

Rachel turned around and, walking backward, shouted, "Did I *never* tell you his name? Oh I can't believe it! Oh, God, of course you know him! He's one of Lassino's cousins, Paolo!" She turned around and continued walking.

Bridget exhaled sharply. Kit's eyes were wide as she hit Bridget in the arm and looked at her, mouthing, "*What?*"

Bridget shrugged. Well, her hiccups were gone, at least. Bridget stifled her laugh. Rachel's Italian squeeze was Paolo, *of course*. She should have known, but, *seriously?* Her mind drifted back to the night of "love on the rocks." And she knew she wasn't imagining it—she could actually feel goosebumps on her arms, which was quite bizarre in this incredibly hot weather, as well as a definite heat coming to her cheeks. No doubt the alcohol consumption, right? Maybe? Well, she guessed Paolo as the Positano love bandit wasn't too far-off a notion. He did have a way with ... well, maybe she shouldn't go there right now. But ... *Paolo?*

Bridget called to Rachel, "You know what? I think I'll have that cigarette."

Chapter 7

Bridget dreamed she was being chased by a large prosecco bottle. This alone would not have been so odd, given the hefty consumption of it the evening before. Yet, the bottle was covered in feathers and crowing furiously as it chased her on its creepy chicken legs. Bridget tried to escape the poultri-fied prosecco, but at every corner, she'd reach another flight of neverending stairs. She realized she was having some sort of twisted nightmare, but she couldn't wake up. So, her only escape was to clamber up the steps. Why, why, in all of Italy, did they have to pick a town with so many damn stairs? She couldn't last much longer. Whoever said they enjoyed doing the Stairmaster was absolutely insane. Of course, this had to be ten times worse.

Up, up, up, more stairs Bridget climbed, as the shrilly-squawking bot-tle followed close behind. For the love of God, where was the green door to the apartment? Bridget caught her foot on one of the unevenly spaced stone steps and felt herself hurling forward, and her immediate thought was, *Great, now I've wrecked another pair of expensive shoes!* Although, she realized, she should probably be a bit more worried about being hunted down by a bottle disguised as one of the Foster Farms chickens than about a mere shoe-scuffing.

On her hands and knees, Bridget looked quickly over her shoulder. The bottle was a short flight of steps away, its maniacal crowing getting louder by the moment. Did she have a chance to get away? And why was she being unfairly singled out as its victim? She certainly hadn't been the only one drinking last night!

Bridget swung her head around and noticed that right in front of her lay the green door. The apartment. She was saved! All she had to do was open the door. She pushed herself up on her knees and reached for the door handle. It was locked!

In a panic, Bridget looked down and saw that no one had remembered to leave the bubbles out as a doorstop. She closed her eyes tightly and waited for her impending doom. She couldn't help but think that death by that of a feathery prosecco bottle probably wouldn't be the worst way to go. Bridget heard the chicken feet stop and knew the thing was standing beside her. She opened one eye and looked up at the bottle. As soon as she did so, it let out a deafening rooster crow, "Errr-errr-err-oooooooo!"

Bridget quickly plugged her ears until the crowing had stopped. Was this all the bottle had come to do? Make her run, against her will, these damn stairs and then deafen her? How annoying. Opening its sharp, curvy beak, it cackled and then asked in a strangely familiar Australian accent, "Hiya, dearie, like another ciggie?"

Bridget's eyes flew open and she shot up. Her heart was pounding, and she realized she was sweating. In the dim light, she had no idea where she was, only that she was … outside. She heard the faint sound of a rooster crowing. It was that crazy strangled-sounding rooster. The one that always sounded like it was choking on something. *Of course.* She was in Positano, *but where?* She wasn't in her bed. Did she have her clothes on from last night? Better yet, did she have any clothes on at all? Her hand flew to her chest and she looked down. Ahh, thank God. Yes, she was in a pair of her running shorts and her Madonna concert tee.

Where the hell was she? She squinted and ran her hands over the blanket that was covering her legs. Upon doing so, she realized that it wasn't a blanket, but a beach towel. She had passed out in one of the lounge chairs on the apartment's terrace. How ridiculous of her to have forgotten.

She now somewhat remembered the hike home last night. Her heart had been racing as she and Kit trudged up the three hundred or so stairs up to the apartment. Between the gasping breaths and profanities that escaped from Bridget's mouth each time they reached another lengthy flight of steps, Kit, who, never seemed out of breath at all, could be heard calling over her shoulder encouragingly, "Just a few more, Bridge, we're almost there!" Bridget had thought she'd be quite content and perfectly safe just lying down on the cool steps and sleeping right there. She'd have absolutely no problem either, with passerby and random neighborhood dogs and cats stepping over her when morning came. Could she just, please, rest for a minute? And why were there no handrails here either, to grab onto? If she only had a handrail, the climb would be so much easier. *But no.*

"*Why* … are there … no … *goddamned* … *stupid* … handrails … in this freakin' town?" Bridget cringed as she recalled herself drunkenly shrieking.

Kit, two flights ahead of her, had stopped and whispered loudly, "Bridget, shhhh! It's late—I mean, early. People are sleeping."

"Oh, bite me; *God*, I just want *to sleep*," mumbled Bridget as she kept her head down and continued climbing.

"What?" Kit asked. Bridget looked up and saw that Kit was closer than she'd realized. Damn, she hadn't actually said that out loud, had she? She was just drunk and in a pissy mood. She hadn't really *meant* that. She looked up at Kit. Kit looked at her, puzzled, and repeated, "What did you say? I couldn't hear you. You were mumbling."

Bridget scratched her head, slurred, and sighed. "Uhh, I'm jus' sooo, sooo, sooo tired. I'm jus gon' sit right here and sleep. You go ahead, Kit. I'll be fine." She waved her hand at Kit and sat down on the stairs. She put her head in her hands and thought, *I never should've smoked those cigarettes. All two of them.* Ughh, the drunkenness had just seemed to hit her out of nowhere. Why, why, had she continued to drink?

Oh, and Paolo … and Rachel … Lassino … she was never drinking again. Everything was awful, and she was fat again—she'd probably drunk three days' worth of Weight Watchers points, and she'd be fat again within a few days—and Mom was at home alone, all because of her selfishness, and she was so *lame*, why was she so disappointed about a twenty-six year-old not being into her? How stupid could she have been to even hope! And why couldn't she ever seem to find someone? And it was so hard having a friend that was *perfect* that everyone adored. And shit, why weren't there any handrails here? Jesus, it was like a bizarre metaphor for her life, since she felt like she was drifting through life without handrails. Just when she thought she had things under control, something would happen, or she'd do something lame to mess things up again.

And now she was drunk and had probably pissed off Kit when she really didn't mean to. She was a horrible, horrible person. And oh, God, she'd be living at home forever if she didn't stop shopping … the drunken stream of conscious babbling inside her head continued. And before she knew it, she was crying. She leaned against the wall, shoulders shaking, and the complete, silent sobbing took her over.

Why was she even here? Bridget wondered. Who did she think she was?

She didn't deserve this vacation. Someone else should be here, not her. Her mom, for one. But with her health issues, she wouldn't be traveling anywhere that was more than an hour radius away. Annie should be here! Her sister worked like a dog and never spent anything on herself, and when she did, it was on groceries. Aside from their honeymoon, Bridget couldn't remember the last time Annie and her husband had taken off for a weekend getaway.

And here Bridget was, traipsing around one of the most expensive vacation spots in Italy, for the third year in a row. And in a pair of $400-plus shoes, no less! The sudden reality and absurdity of it all appalled Bridget. Yet somehow, she'd been aware of it all along, hadn't she? She'd just chosen to ignore it. When was she ever going to pull her head out?

"Bridget, Bridge, what's the matter?" Kit sat down next to her and put her hand on her shoulder.

"I don't know. I don't know. I think I want to go home." Bridget sniffed loudly and wiped her eyes with the back of her hand.

Kit said softly, "Bridget, you do not want to go home. You and I have been talking about being here since we left last year. You're just tired and—"

"And totally *wasted*! I am such a loser!" Bridget sobbed.

"Stop saying things like that! You are not a loser! You're a little bit drunk, but you're not a loser. You're one of the best people I know, and you've been through a lot this year. And now we're here, just like we planned, and everything's going to be fine. *Let* yourself have a good time, okay? Enjoy this. This is what life is about. Right?"

Bridget wondered why she couldn't be like Kit—happy all the time, even when things sucked. Well, she'd try, if she could just get over the whole "hating and feeling sorry for herself" thing. She knew it was getting old. Instead of answering, Bridget stared ahead of her at the steps below. She wondered how they'd ever made it up this far. Oh, there she went again, being negative …

Kit stood up, reached her hand out to Bridget, and said, "Look, it would really give the neighbors something interesting to talk about, but you can't sleep out here on the steps. And I'm not leaving you here, so come on."

Kit was right. She couldn't stay out here. Bridget grabbed onto Kit's hand and shakily stood up. They continued the climb, Bridget keeping her hand flat against the unevenly worn wall to steady herself, as she blithered through another round of heavy tears.

Kit grabbed onto her hand again and said, "I know; I wish there were handrails too."

When they'd finally reached the apartment, Bridget had limped into the bedroom, kicked her shoes off, and jumped out of her sweat-drenched and smoky-smelling clothes. After changing, she'd then thrown herself into the lounge chair while Kit opened another bottle of prosecco. Anything after that, well, there was no after that. And the scary thing was, she didn't have a bit of a headache now.

Bridget looked out over the balcony. In the light-gray tinge of the approaching dawn, she could see the water, serenely smooth, like a glass tabletop. This was the perfect time to run around the town, before the street cleaners and the locals started bustling about, before the town was swallowed by the Mediterrannean heat.

Although, after last night, she'd probably just stick to walking. She'd grab her running shoes and her iPod and take a stroll. It would be good to have a little alone time with Positano, since that was next to impossible once the place awakened. And of course, there'd be time to digest last night's randomness.

As Bridget tried hoisting herself quietly out of the lounge chair, she realized she wasn't the only one up in the apartment. Someone was in the kitchen. Bridget could hear the refrigerator being opened and then closed. Hoping it was Kit, since there was a lot to rehash from last night, Bridget opened the patio door that connected to the kitchen and found herself staring at the naked backside of some man. She involuntarily gasped. Was she in the right apartment? Maybe in her drunken narcolepsy, she had been sleepwalking.

The naked figure turned around, showing a front side that was just as taut and well sculpted as the backside had been. Oh, Jesus, it was Jared, the hot glass-washer from the restaurant. "Hey, morning." The beefcake grinned and took a sip of water.

"Uh … morning," Bridget repeated, making sure her eyes didn't stray far from Jared's face. So there was a naked male supermodel in the kitchen? No big deal at all. Bridget would just pretend he had clothes on. How hard could that be? *Puh-lease.*

Jared smiled again and said, "I didn't get a chance to meet you last night. I'm Jared." He walked toward her and extended his hand. Oh, jeez, how was she going to shake his hand without looking down a little? If she kept her eyes on his face when she went to shake his hand, what if she missed and accidentally grabbed something else? No, no, she mustn't think about that!

"Hi, I'm naked; I mean ... I mean, you're naked; I mean, I'm Bridget! Oh, God, sorry," she squeaked nervously as she extended her hand and looked away, blushing.

Jared laughed. "Oh, no, no, sorry, about ... this," he said and motioned to his lower body. "I didn't think anybody else was up. Oops!" He grinned seductively.

"Oh, yeah, well ... oh, no problem at all. So, you're ... naked ..."

Why had the word *naked* come out of her mouth again? Could she just get out of the kitchen already? She hastily added, "I'm off for a walk now, so, uh, it was really nice meeting you, Jared!" Bridget did an about-face and stepped out onto the patio. She heard Jared say, "See ya, Bridget," and then realized that the only way to get to the hallway was through the balcony doors and through the kitchen. She would have to go back in. Why did these things always happen to her? Well, maybe he would be gone. Bridget sheepishly peeked her head back into the kitchen. Jared stood there drinking his glass of water.

"Quick walk—forgot your shoes, huh?" He teasingly nodded at her bare feet.

"Ha, ha, yes, I forgot my shoes and apparently, how to get to my room," Bridget pointed down the hallway and then took off before she could say or do anything else remotely lame. She heard Jared go into the bathroom and shut the door, and she tied her shoes quickly and decided to forget looking for her iPod in the dark. She didn't want to risk doing some kind of accidental naked tango with Jared if he happened to come out of the bathroom while she was walking down the darkened hallway. She shook her head and breathed a sigh of relief as she left the bubbles out as a doorstop. Bridget headed up the steps that led out to Via Pasitea and she couldn't help but chuckle to herself. Definitely the only naked man she'd be seeing on this trip, and she'd barely been able to even look! That reminded her ... *Paolo.* She'd seen Paolo last night.

Solo Tu had been ... well ... quite comical and, Bridget had to admit, a tinge disappointing. Could she expect anything less from this town? Could she expect anything less from her *life*? But, of course, this time, thankfully, she had really just been a spectator to all the night's drama, and that was the way she wanted to keep it.

They had barely had time to regain their composure after hearing that Rachel's boytoy was none other than Paolo before they'd entered Solo Tu. Gnarls Barkley's "Crazy" played as patrons sat casually smoking and chatting loudly so as to be heard by those they shared a table with.

"Hmmm, no tables," Kit said as she scanned the crowded patio. "Well, hopefully, Georgia and Beth have room at their table for us. Do you see them here, Rachel?"

"Oh, I love this song. I'm, sorry, what? Uh, no, but they've got to be somewhere; it's not that big of a patio. I'm going to the bar to order us some drinks. Stick to prosecco or mojitos, girls?"

"Oooh, a mojjito, please," answered Kit.

"Mojito," repeated Bridget. Oh, good, now she was mixing alcohol. She guessed she was past the point of caring about avoiding a hangover. Bridget turned and casually surveyed the patio. She saw familiar faces, but no one she knew. That was probably a good thing. She glanced about, not really looking at anything in particular. With the exception of the candles on each table and the lighting over the bar, the patio was dim, and to Bridget, everyone at the tables appeared to blend into each other.

She turned back to Kit, who had meandered over to the bar, and her eyes lingered a bit at a table a few feet away. Bridget stared at the back of some guy in a bright-purple shirt. She hadn't worn purple since junior high. She seemed to recall a heinous pair of thick purple cords, as well as an Esprit sweatshirt and various IZOD polos. Ick. But if guys here were wearing the jewel color, Bridget supposed that within the next six months, the trend would be picked up by women and men alike in the States. She might as well get used to it.

Hmmm, could she ever wear purple again? She guessed she probably could, as she absentmindedly fixated on the back of the bepurpled male. His arm was casually slung over the shoulders of the girl sitting next to him, and smoke trailed from the cigarette perched between his fingers. A silver ring on his thumb caught her eye. It seemed to her she knew *someone* who wore a thumb ring. Who was it?

Without warning, the dark head attached to the purple shirt turned and stared at her. Embarrassed to be caught staring, even if it had only been at his shirt, Bridget looked away. *Wait a minute!* She looked back again. The purple shirt, accompanied by a huge set of smiling teeth and bright-blue eyes, was now standing up and facing her. It was Paolo, and he was walking toward her.

"Bridget! How are you?" Before she knew what to do, he'd pulled her into an embrace and kissed her on each cheek and then quickly on the lips. The girl he'd left sitting by herself stared over her shoulder with a perplexed look on her face, no doubt wondering who had taken Paolo from her side. Bridget assumed she must be an American, since she wasn't smoking and seemed far more concerned than any Italian woman would deem acceptable.

"I'm fine! How are you?" Bridget replied—overly cheerily, she felt, yet with a genuine smile upon her face.

He stepped back and looked at her appraisingly. "Your hair, it is longer. I like it." Bridget waited; she hoped he wouldn't say, "Ahh, and I see you've put on some weight since last summer too!" But Paolo smiled, then laughed and continued. "I am fine! I heard you had arrived. Please, can I get you a drink?"

"Paolo, ciao!" Kit, who'd wandered back from the bar, shouted.

"Hello, Kit. I was just going to tell Bridget to please, come join us at our table. Lassino is over there," Paolo said and motioned.

"Oh, he is? Oh, good." Kit smiled and looked at the table. "Oh! You're with Beth and Georgia. That's who we're meeting here!"

Kit waved to the girls. As they waved back to Kit, Bridget noticed a look of relief on the face of Paolo's companion. She guessed that being with Kit, who the girls had already met, she was no longer considered competition. Bridget saw Lassino squint uncomfortably around. Oh, boy, this was going to be entertaining.

Kit smiled brightly at Paolo. "Sure, we'd love to join you guys!" she said, and she headed over to the table. Paolo grabbed Bridget's hand. "It is so good to see you. So, what can I get you and Kit to drink?"

What could he get them to drink? Bridget stared at Paolo's huge teeth and could barely think. The alcohol that she was starting to feel behind her eyes wasn't helping, either.

Suddenly, Bridget remembered Rachel, who should be back from the bar at any moment. Bridget thought of what might happen when Rachel saw that "poor" Paolo had lied and was here with another girl. It was going to be ugly. Still, she better hurry to the bathroom now so she could get back in time to see it all. Bridget actually felt a little sorry for Paolo and his friend, who had no idea what might be in store for them. She knew she certainly wouldn't want to be on the receiving end of Rachel's fury. As long as Rachel never found out about *her* and Paolo, Bridget would remain safe.

Bridget hastily pulled her hand out of Paolo's grip and said, "Oh, thank you, but we already ordered some drinks. I'm going to use the bathroom, and I'll be right back."

"You remember where it is?" asked Paolo.

"Oh, yes," Bridget said and then added without thinking, "I have a very good memory." Why had she said that? It sounded like a cheesy innuendo to last year's fling.

Paolo winked at her and in a low voice, answered, "Yes, so do I."

Well, at least Paolo remembers, but—uh-oh. Bridget smiled awkwardly and hurried off.

Bridget returned, sat at the end of the table, sandwiched between Rachel and Beth, and thought what a fantastic Italian reality show the unfolding scene would make. She literally couldn't get a word in edgewise. Kit and Georgia chatted like they'd known each other for years. Apparently, they both had Sicilian grandmothers, the same birthday ("Omigod, no way! *My* birthday's Groundhog Day too!"), and had brothers who drove Harleys. Could you believe it? They chattered nonstop while Lassino squinted angrily through his thick glasses between his two paramours. As soon as Kit had come to the table, he had made it a point to immediately get up from his seat next to Georgia to reseat himself next to Kit. Bridget wondered, was this some sort of respect for the lover with the higher rank? Who knew?

In between the furtive glances he shot the two girls, Lassino would grunt Italian to Paolo. Yes, Bridget could see that Lassino was clearly perturbed to have had his game called. Bridget also noted that he most definitely seemed weirded out by the fact that Kit was so friendly and *so not upset* to be sitting and chatting with another of his romantic liasons.

While Lassino was obviously out of sorts, Paolo appeared to be without a care. He seemed oblivious to the fact that he was sitting at a table with a collection of past and present flings and that one, in particular, was without a doubt fuming about it. Every time one of the girls or Lassino said anything, Paolo laughed heartily, and every raucous guffaw caused Rachel to shoot deathly daggers at him from the other end of the table. Bridget thought if Paolo noticed at all, he most certainly couldn't care less.

While the table chatter was entertaining, it was nonstop. Even if Bridget had wanted to add something, anything, to the table conversation, she wouldn't have been able to. So she listened—and drank. As a matter of fact, the mojitos were about the only thing helping her get through the verbal assault she was getting on both sides from Rachel and Beth.

She awkwardly sat and listened as Beth droned on incessantly in her nasally Bostonian accent about how she'd met Paolo last year—he was just so cute, wasn't he? And so sweet to take huh and Georgia on a day trip to Capri today … she really wanted to get him some type of thank-you gift. Did Bridget think he'd like something classy, like a bottla kuh-loo-ahh (aka Kahlua)? And didn't she just love the shoes in his boutique, although you could the same sandals for a lot cheapah at Tawhget?

"Huh?" Bridget couldn't help but look at the girl like she was speaking another language. The alcohol was not aiding her deciphering of the East Coast lingo, either. In fact, she felt that at this very moment, Boston-speak was ranking right up there with something akin to Scottish. She knew she was hearing English but was a bit delayed in translation. *Tawhget, tawhget?* What could *tawhget* mean? "Tawhget …" Bridget stalled for time and hoped she didn't appear too special-ed.

"Yeah, yeah, Tawhget!" Her new friend smiled expectantly. "Ya know, like yuh shooes theh. Did ya get them theh at Tawhget?"

"Oh, *Target!*" Sweet mother of God, thank you!

"Yeh, yeh, Tawhget!" She squealed elatedly, like they were playing some type of language charades.

"*Target!* Yes, Target! No, I didn't get them there. I got them at—" She stopped when she noticed a sudden, puzzled look on Beth's face. "I got them at … um, Neiman … Marcus." Bridget let her voice trail off.

"Oh, *Neiman Mahwkus*," Beth replied and looked down at Bridget with what appeared to be a slightly disdainful sneer. "Anyway, so what do ya think of Paolo?"

And on and on she babbled. Bridget tried to muster up some fake enthusiasm. Would this girl never shut up? Bridget gamely nodded yes to everything anyway and sincerely hoped that the subject of Target, shoes, rocks, or the beach never came up. She'd just die.

On Bridget's other side, Rachel sat and chain-smoked. The secondhand smoke was so thick that there was no longer any need for Bridget to light one up for herself. After every other puff, Rachel would mutter into Bridget's ear some foul-mouthed comment about Paolo, usually pertaining to one of his body parts.

"That bastard! His bloody fucking nose is bigger than his prick!" This caused Bridget to choke on her ice more than once.

"Oh, awh you ahlright?" Beth paused from her monologue on Paolo for a moment to ask. Bridget shook her head yes, and before she could speak, Beth had begun again.

"Tomorrow we leave for Florence, but I think I may come back heyuh for a few days and visit Paolo before heading home. Kit mentioned you have room at the apahhtment for us. That'd be great if we could stay with you girls!"

"'That'd be great if we could stay with you girls!'" Rachel mimicked Beth under her breath. "She's going to come back here for *him?* She's pathetic!"

Bridget snorted and hoped that Rachel would just think she was laughing at her comment about Beth. *Pathetic?* Bridget decided there was no need to remind Rachel that she had done the same thing for a Positano man and then dumped him *for* Paolo. The question wasn't really *who* was pathetic, but who was the most pathetic: a delusional, *Fatal Attraction*-ist forty-two-year-old, a twittering, bubble-headed twenty-something, or, well, herself? At least *she* hadn't come back to Positano for any man, Bridget consoled herself. It was more like Paolo was an added bonus attached to the beautiful Positano vacation package. Bridget felt so foolish to have even speculatively hoped. But you couldn't blame her for wondering what *might* happen.

While Bridget was glad she could honestly laugh at the situation before her, she couldn't help feeling a little let down. She'd get over it. After all she'd been through, dealing with a twenty-six-year-old who was less than interested in her was clearly not the worst thing to ever happen to her. Bridget would just have to embrace the fact that she was just not lucky in love. *Anywhere*, since, unfortunately, this seemed to be a cross-cultural, continental thing. Hmm, was it time to order another mojito? Yes, she thought so ...

"Bridget, ready to go?" Bridget stared, wide-eyed, at Kit. Everyone at the table was standing. Was it closing time already? Bridget looked at her watch; it was 3:30 a.m.! She'd somehow managed to finally tune out Beth and Rachel. This was definitely a skill she had perfected in the classroom with her students when they were too noisy. Where was Rachel? Bridget hadn't even seen her leave. Good Lord, she hoped she hadn't been semi-passed out at the table or anything! No …

"Bridget, are you all right? You look like you're a million miles away," Kit said and patted her hand.

Well, she had been. "Yes, yes, I'm ready," Bridget said, carefully enunciating her words, lest she sound as inebriated as she felt. She stood up, making sure to keep herself steady. It was going to be a long walk back to the apartment. And hadn't she been right about that?

◆   ◆   ◆

In the dark the next morning, Kit threw her hand in the direction of the nightstand and felt around for her cell. She hadn't been able to sleep at all, and now that stupid rooster was crowing. The damn thing crowed at the most random times—day and night. Even the male *animals* in this town were bizarre!

Her mind was racing. What had happened at Solo Tu? She knew she had pissed off Lassino by sitting down at the table with them all. But Paolo had invited them! And Georgia and Beth had invited them to meet them at Solo Tu! How could she have known that the two girls were going to be *with* Lassino and Paolo? Well, she might have figured it out just a little, since the girls *were* staying at Lassino's place, but still. You never could guarantee where Lassino was going to be at any given moment anyway.

She didn't care about that, though. So what if he had some girl staying with him? It really didn't bother Kit. Georgia was a nice girl—in fact, she was too nice and wholesome for Lassino! Was she being jealous? No. Kit knew there was something more between her and Lassino that didn't exist between him and Georgia. Georgia was just another girl in Lassino's revolving Positano door. Besides, why would Lassino have gotten up and placed himself next to her at the table? He did care about her, Kit decided.

Dammit, though. The scene at Solo Tu would probably have some repercussions—the most disappointing being that Lassino probably wouldn't show up for the Fourth of July party, which was a couple days away, that

Kit had planned for the arrival of Julianna, Joe, and Madison. Of course, she had her own selfish, cheesy reasons for throwing the party. She loved theme parties, she loved planning them, and she wanted the Italians here to come and to finally see her as a real, bona fide friend, not just some tourist. So they wouldn't understand the tacky decorations and less-than-gourmet American treats. They would appreciate the hospitality and have fun, anyway. Kit just knew they would.

That is, *if* they showed up—because if Lassino didn't, then probably none of the rest would either. Why anybody listened to him, she'd never understand. She hadn't even done anything either, Kit thought defensively. All her glittery, festive Fourth of July decorations, all the Twinkies, all the fixings for s'mores, all the peanut butter she'd lugged in her suitcase so she could make peanut butter sandwiches (well, if she couldn't bring hot dogs, she had to have some other American foods) ... it was all going to be for nothing.

But maybe not. At least Tomaso would still come. He was going to take her and Bridget to some store to buy all the alcohol today. Sure, they'd still have the party, with or without Lassino. But, why, why was he being so difficult? Now another night would go by and she'd end up in bed, alone. God knew, Bridget might end up sleeping out on the patio every night with the way she'd been drinking, so she really would be alone.

And Kit was tired of being alone. She'd given up Johnny and had shied away from any type of dating whatsoever. For the last year, she'd tried focusing on herself and doing things that made her truly happy. Was it a coincidence that her happiness and enjoyment were tied to Italy?

She had worked at the restaurant and become good friends with Leo and his fiancé Diana, and now she and Bridget would be at their wedding in a few days—in Calabria! She'd loved every minute of her Italian classes (well, when she'd been able to make it to them). Everything just seemed to revolve around Italy. Wasn't that a sign of some sort? *Why* was she immersing herself in all that?

Because in the back of her mind, there was always Positano reminding her that she'd return. There was Positano, and then there was Lassino. The two were synonymous to Kit. She couldn't think of one without being reminded of the other. Truth be told, Kit had waited all year to be here and, she had to admit to herself, to be with Lassino.

And if he didn't show up for the party, she would be more than disappointed. But of course, she'd never let anyone see that. Kit was very good about putting on her happy face. So good, in fact, that if she didn't smile, people actually thought she was sick or something. It probably wasn't too healthy of a thing, holding everything inside. She had created such a sunny-side-up persona that at times, it was actually tiring being herself.

God, she just wished that every once in a while, she could be allowed to be like Bridget—possessed with depressive, gloomy thoughts that tormented her and caused her to become all reclusively hermitlike, where she could hole up for days without talking to anyone. If she could have just *one* day like that and get it all out of her system … because she didn't always feel as happy as everyone thought her to be, and this "being alone for eternity" thing was really starting to get to her … but no. She'd *never* get away with acting like that. It wouldn't do her any good to mope around Positano anyway, so it was pointless even entertaining the thought.

Kit's cell phone vibrated and hummed loudly. She quickly pulled it off the nightstand and saw that there was a text message from Lassino. He'd barely said good-bye to her, let alone two words while they were at Solo Tu. Actually, he'd uttered a whole sentence under his breath as he'd moved to sit next to her. "Do you know who *that* is?" he'd said and jerked his head in the direction of Georgia.

"Yes, of course. I told you I met Georgia and Beth at Giorgio's store, didn't I?" Kit had smiled at him. What did Lassino expect her to do? Did he expect her to tell Georgia that she had known him longer and had a relationship with him? Did he expect her to go ballistic on him? Why *wouldn't* she like Georgia? Why *couldn't* she talk to her?

After that, Lassino hadn't spoken again to her. But she had just acted like it was nothing and had talked to everyone else. So what could he want now? Kit thought. Maybe to apologize? No matter how he acted, Kit knew Lassino was a kind person.

She read his text hopefully.

Are you happy you know what I am like?

Kit sighed. Like what? What was his point? So he had a girl visiting him. Were there many others coming this summer as well? Kit wasn't sure how to respond. She knew she didn't want to be just friends, but putting pressure on Lassino was the last thing Kit wanted to do. That would send him running. She must play it cool. Without giving it any more thought, she sent a reply that she hoped would smooth things over and pacify Lassino.

Lassino, we are still friends. It is okay.

Kit stared at her phone and was about to place it back on the nightstand when it vibrated again. She hit "open" and would've laughed at Lassino's misspelled English, had the words not been these:

Live me alone.

Kit set the cell back on the nightstand and rolled over onto her side. She would not reply.

"Daddy's here! Mommy, Daddy's here!" Joey stuck his head inside the green door and hollered into the apartment. "And Madison too!"

"I know, Sweetie. We're all coming out," Natalie called as she joined him on the step, Gina on her hip, Kit and Bridget right behind her.

Kit grabbed Gina from Natalie. "Here, Nat, I'll hold Gina. Sheesh, she's getting heavy!"

"I know. All the girl wants to eat now is pasta! Ugh, you're a mess for Daddy!" Natalie flicked off a piece of rigatoni that had been stuck to Gina's chubby cheek before she ran up to meet her husband and niece. When she reached them, Joe dropped his luggage, threw his arms around Natalie, and kissed her.

"Eww, and by the way, I'm here too." Madison stood on the step behind them and rolled her eyes.

Natalie pulled herself out of Joe's embrace and then grabbed Madison and said, "Maddie, I missed you! I'm so glad you two are here!" She stopped short, looked her niece up and down, and asked, "Sweetie, what are you wearing?"

Madison wore a tight, white spaghetti-strapped tank top over an obvious push-up bra and very short, pink terry cloth shorts that read "Juicy" on the butt—clothes that barely covered her tall and lean, yet shapely stature. Her long, dark hair was swept over one shoulder, her brown eyes artfully lined, her lips heavily glossed. She tossed her hair over her other shoulder, shrugged, and said, "Uncle said I could wear this."

Natalie gave Joe a look. "You said that was *okay* to wear on the plane?"

Joe threw up his hands and said, "Believe me, I did not let her get on the plane like *that*. One minute she was in sweats, and then she went into the bathroom at the Naples airport and came out in that getup! What could I do, drag her back in there and make her change?"

Madison pouted. "It's so hot in this country! I *had* to change!"

From the bottom of the stairs, Bridget mumbled out of the side of her mouth to Kit, "She's thirteen? She looks like she's seventeen!"

"She wishes. I better make it clear to the boys around here about how *young* she is!"

"You don't think any of them would try anything with her, do you?" Bridget asked worriedly.

"I'm not worried about the men; I'm worried about *her* trying to fool *them*!" Kit retorted.

"Daddy, pick me up!" Joey tugged on Joe's jeans.

"Hey, there, Buddy!" Joe bent over and scooped up Joey. "How ya been? You havin' fun here?"

"Yeah, Daddy, we go in our pool every day 'cause it's hot here! And we eat pasta for dinner, and Mommy and Auntie K and Bridget have some wine," Joey stated matter-of-factly.

"Living the life." Joe smiled at his wife.

Joey continued, "And guess what? I saw a naked man in the apartment!"

"Oh, yeah, then there was *that* ..." Natalie's voiced trailed off sheepishly and she scowled, as if they'd been exposed to some naked, hairy ogre.

Bridget hadn't been the only one lucky enough to have run into Jared that early morning. The accidental Jared sightings and the loud moaning coming from Carrie's room had caused Natalie to tell Kit the next morning, "Kit, I'm no prude, really, but Jesus, they were screwing their brains out! And that's putting it mildly! I actually found it quite entertaining, until Joey woke up out of a deep sleep and asked, 'Mommy, why are you screaming? Are you hurt?' I had to tell him I was fine, it was just the TV in the next room! And then to bring my son to the bathroom later on and find Jared in there, naked! Although, I have to say, *I* didn't mind that so much *at all*. But still, do you think you could say something to Carrie?"

Of course she could. Kit dreaded it, though, since she and Carrie had already had it out. But they were all adults (to some degree), and there were children in the apartment. Carrie and Jared would have to be a little more discreet or take it elsewhere.

And elsewhere it would be. Kit took Carrie aside and explained the "trauma" caused to Joey and "poor Natalie," and Carrie had all but disappeared since then. She spent her day at the beach and all her evenings with Jared, only stopping in to shower and change, as well as to raid the fridge for food and to swipe some beers or prosecco.

"We might want to tack on a minibar fee to her final bill before she leaves," Kit stated dryly after one of Carrie's quick visits. The fridge needed to constantly be restocked, but at least they didn't have to worry about any more nudity or live sex shows.

Joe raised his eyebrows at Natalie and then down at Kit and Bridget and said, "A naked man in the apartment, eh? Boy, sounds like you girls have been busy." He smirked.

"We wish!" Natalie replied.

"Don't look at any of us, though." Kit chuckled.

Perplexed, Joe asked, "Then who? Ohhh, the young one—"

"Excuse me, the *younger* one!" Kit mockingly scolded.

Natalie noticed Madison listening intently and cut him off, "Joseph, we'll tell you *later*. I'm so happy to see you guys!" She stood on her tiptoes to kiss Joe again, then added, "Welcome to Positano, Honey!"

Chapter 8

"Are you sure you don't need any help getting ready for tonight?" Natalie watched as Kit draped glittery, star-spangled garland from the wrought-iron balcony.

Kit looked over her shoulder and said, "No, of course not. Go and enjoy the beach. Bridget and I have everything under control. Besides, we need to be here when Tomaso has all the bottled water and alcohol delivered, and Julianna will be here in about an hour or so, if her luggage made it in all right. Let's keep our fingers crossed on that one!"

"You don't need any help hanging the lanterns or any of the other decorations?" Natalie shifted Gina from one hip to the other.

"Joe can help with that when you guys get back," replied Kit.

"Well, what about the food?"

"Bridget's on it. She's doing the shopping now. Plus, we have all our little American treats. Not much prep work needed for Twinkies and peanut butter and jelly sandwiches."

"Well, are you sure you don't need any—"

Kit interrupted Natalie and shouted, "You are on vacation. In Italy! *Get out of here and go to the beach!*"

"Okay, okay." Natalie laughed. "I will; I will. Joe! Joey! Madison! Are you guys ready to go?"

Joe stepped out onto the patio with Joey following behind. "We're ready, Hon. Don't we need the stroller?"

Natalie shook her head. "No, no, just leave it here."

Joe scowled. "You're going to carry Gina all the way there and back?"

"Well, *no,* I thought you'd be helping me, right? Trust me, with all the steps, it's just easier to leave the stroller here."

Kit didn't know how Natalie could smile so pleasantly at her husband, when he seemed to question everything she did. Why did husbands conceive their wives to be so clueless? As if Natalie knew nothing about taking care of their two children, when she did that every day.

Joe shrugged. "All right, if you say so."

"Where's Madison? She cannot possibly still be sleeping. It's one o'clock," Natalie snapped.

Joe answered with a sigh. "I have no idea what she's been doing in the bathroom for the last hour." He poked his head in through the bedroom doorway and shouted, "*Madison!* We're leaving!"

"I'm coming!" Madison rolled her eyes and slouched out through the kitchen doors, wearing her flip-flops and an electric-blue knit bikini that resembled three very small triangles.

Joe took a look at her and asked, "You need all that makeup to go to the beach?" He paused and did a double take on the miniscule bikini, then added, "And what the hell are you wearing? You're not wearing that to the beach! Go change!"

"I don't have another suit with me!" Madison spat back.

"Well, go put on some shorts, and get your towel!"

Madison stood and glowered at Joe with her arms folded and her chin out.

"Madison, go get them now, or you're not going to the beach!" Joe shouted.

Madison tossed her head and flipped her long hair over her shoulder, and then she marched out of the room and sneered. "Fine!"

Joe looked back at Natalie quizzically and asked, "Do you let her get away with that crap?"

"Yes, of course. I actually encourage her to dress like a teen prostitute. Jesus, I am on her *all* the time, Joe!" Natalie answered bitterly and then shifted Gina to her other hip.

"Well, I'd love to know where she got that bikini from."

She opened her eyes wide and raised her eyebrows, then replied, "Your *mother* bought it for her. You might want to talk to her about that."

"*What?*" Joe said.

"Look, can we discuss her wardrobe later?" Natalie asked as she noticed that Kit was trying to appear invisible as she tiptoed around the patio, gathered dirty towels, and threw them into a pile by the door.

"Jesus Christ!" Joe cried as he angrily swiped his towel from the lounge chair.

"Jesus Christ!" Joey bellowed in his best Joelike imitation.

Kit snorted and pretended to cough.

"Joey! That's naughty! You don't say that!" Natalie shouted and glared at Joe.

"Mommy," Joey whined as he beat his plastic shovel against his mother's thigh, "can we go to the beach? I'm hot and fetty!"

"Ouch! Stop that! Mommy's hot and sweaty too, but we're waiting for Madison. *Madison!*"

As if on cue, Madison strutted out in a pair of denim Daisy Dukes with her towel slung over her shoulder. "All right, I'm ready. Can we go now?"

"Yes, we are going. Joe, grab the diaper bag, will you? Before I change my mind!" Natalie opened the green door and placed one foot out, then looked back at Kit and shook her head. "God, help me," she muttered. "Sure you don't need me to stay and help, Kit?"

"No, no, no. Look, it'll be fine, Nat; once you all get there, it'll be fine. Just go." Kit patted her back.

"All right," Natalie smiled feebly and stepped into the alleyway. "Say bye to Auntie K, guys!"

"*Bye!*" Joey screamed and charged out the door and down the steps.

"Joey, wait!" Natalie screamed down the steps and then back toward the apartment. "Joe! Would you help me? I can't chase after him. I've got my hands full with Gina here!"

"Jesus, I'm coming! Joey, listen to your mother! Bye, Kit." Joe threw the diaper bag over his shoulder, nodded in the direction of Kit, and hustled out the door. Madison followed after, rolling her eyes, with a somber, "Later."

"All right, have a good time!" Kit ran over to the door, stuck her head out, and called, "And remember to help your aunt, would you?"

She stood in the doorway and watched them clamber down the steps. She winced as she heard Joe advise Natalie, "Hon, did you remember to put sunscreen on the kids? They could get seriously burned in this sun. It's not like California, you know."

To which she heard Natalie reply wearily, "*Yes,* I put sunscreen on them."

Well, maybe there was something to be said for the single life, Kit thought as she wandered back inside and returned to her tacky Fourth of July decorating.

◆　◆　◆

"Grazie." Bridget thanked the mustachioed gentleman behind the counter as he placed some euros back into her hand.

"Prego, signorina. You needa some help?" He gestured to the five fully laden bags that sat between them. Well, there would certainly be no shortage of crostini, fruit, and vegetables at this party. Or Nutella, not that Kit had asked her to get any. Bridget thought that maybe she'd gone a little overboard by buying ten of the jars. But she just couldn't help it. They were a limited edition, the glass containers sporting the Italian World Cup soccer team on them. Besides, when all the Nutella was gone, she'd have a set of juice glasses. Yes, of course, wasn't that *just* what she needed? *What* had she been thinking? Ten jars of Nutella? As much as she loved it, how was she going to eat all that? She didn't want to even think of the Weight Watchers points value on that one. Well, maybe she and Kit could host some massive Nutella fondue party.

Needless to say, the little shop owner had looked at her a bit oddly when she'd placed them on the counter next to her overabundance of produce. She'd tried to divert his perplexed gawking at the counter by asking for a pack of paper napkins. Instead, he'd come back with toilet paper. Bridget shook her head politely and tried using some of her Italian. Although the man spoke English, the whole "paper napkins" thing obviously wasn't translating well.

"Ahh! Si, si." The man smiled and hurried to the back of the store. Well, maybe she *had* learned a few things in Italian class, Bridget thought excitedly. Then again, maybe not, she realized, since it wasn't a pack of napkins that he returned with, but a twenty-four-roll pack of toilet paper.

She really needed to brush up on her Italian.

"Oh, no, grazie, I'm okay, thank you," Bridget replied. She looked at the bulging bags on the counter. It was a *long* way up to the apartment. She didn't even want to think about the stairs. Why start now, since clearly, she had had not been thinking about the stairs a few moments ago when she impulsively bought the armada of Nutella. Maybe she *could* use some help carrying all this. She glanced around the tiny shop and noticed that she and her little friend behind the counter were the only two in it. Still, she couldn't ask him to close down his store to help carry her caravan of Nutella and toilet paper up three hundred-plus stairs. Could she? Bridget hated to admit, but it was seriously tempting.

"Signorina, I knowa you leeve up a long way, by Palazza Bianca, si? You gonna need some help," he said matter-of-factly and smiled. How did everyone around here know where they lived? Bridget looked at the tiny man and thought he couldn't be any younger than seventy-five. She did not want to be the cause of him having a massive coronary on the stairs in this heat. She'd suck it up and carry the bags herself. She needed the extra workout anyway.

"No, no, grazie. I will be all right," she answered as she started gathering the bags by the handles.

With an Italian face-shrug, the man replied, "Okay, prego." Careful not to knock over the rack holding gum and candy, Bridget dragged the bags off the counter by their plastic handles and headed toward the door. She could feel her biceps starting to ache already. Damn that Italian World Cup Soccer team. She was just about to step through the floor-length hanging beads that dangled from the open doorway when she felt her arm jerk back as one of the plastic bags caught on something. And then she heard a loud yelp. The instinctual cry of utter pain had come straight from her mouth when the ten jars of Nutella plunged from the torn bag onto her right foot before hitting the floor. Her eyes involuntarily welled with tears as she could feel her foot already starting to throb. And then she felt something wet. Oh, no, had the impact of the ten jars broken skin? Was she bleeding?

Bridget squeezed her eyes open and looked down. She breathed a sigh of relief—for a quick moment. No blood, just Nutella. *Everywhere.* Four of the jars had shattered, and the brown goo completely covered Bridget's right foot and calf, as well as the surrounding area where she stood. Bridget gingerly set the remaining bags down on a clean patch of floor. Ughh, what a mess she had made. She quickly stooped down to try picking up some of the shards of glass. It was a wonder none of the flying glass had cut her.

"Signorina! Are you okay? Are you hurt?" the little shopkeeper hurried to her side.

"No, no! I'm fine! I am so sorry!" Bridget winced at the man as she gestured to the brown mess in front of them. It seemed as if she was always apologizing for *something* in this country. Why did she have to be such so clumsy?

He waved her off and said, "Please, it's okay. Don't worry about it. Lorenzo, *vieni qua!*"

Bridget called after him, "No, please, let me clean all this!" She bent down and reached for the twenty-four-roll pack of toilet paper. She tore it open and grabbed a roll. She rolled a huge wad around her hand, bent down, and began wiping up the floor. She felt the swinging beads hit her rear end, signifying a customer entering the shop. Bridget kept her head down and continued unraveling toilet paper to wrap around her hand. She watched a pair of thick, pantyhosed ankles in black-sandaled feet walk around the Nutella explosion, past her, and then stop and turn back. Great, not only had she created a slippery mess, but she was obstructing most of the entryway. "Scusa, sorry … 'bout this," Bridget muttered as she looked up at the customer.

Bridget involuntarily winced as she recognized the familiar face staring down at her. It was scary old neighborhood-watch lady. The one who lived across the street and always assaulted Bridget with her evil eye whenever she passed beneath her balcony. What was she doing down this way? Of course, this *would* be the one day she decided to leave her second-story stoop. Bridget smiled anyway and offered a droll, "Ciao."

Not surprisingly, the woman scowled back at her and said nothing. Bridget watched her look at the gooey, Nutella-covered floor, then the toilet paper, then specifically back at Bridget's brown foot and leg. Wait a minute; she didn't think … well, squatting down in an unidentified pool of brown with a wad of toilet paper in your hand probably might give people the wrong impression at first glance. She must clear up this misunderstanding at once!

"Nutella. *Nu-tell-a!* *Mi piace* Nutella. I like … Nutella!" Bridget overgesticulated her toilet-papered hand at the woman. The woman pursed her lips in disgust and walked away. Great, now the rumor would be all over the town that the clumsy American teacher had managed to have a diarrhea attack in the middle of the neighborhood market.

"Oh, crap!" Bridget sighed and continued with her mopping. The man returned with a real mop and a bucket and said, "No, no, I take care of this. You can just … fix yourself," he smiled and gestured toward her foot and leg. "Prego, please."

Bridget slowly got up and stepped to the side to wipe herself off. By the time she managed to get her leg and foot as clean as she could using flimsy toilet paper, the man had finished cleaning the floor and placed the unharmed Nutella jars in a new bag for her. Bridget supposed there was nothing else she could do. She certainly wasn't going to ask for four more jars to replace that ones that had broken.

"I am really very sorry for all … this." Bridget apologized once more as she began gathering up her bags.

"It is no problem. Please, you needa some help carrying alla this home?" he asked again.

"Oh, really," Bridget answered, "thank you, but I will be fine. You do not have to help me with my bags. I live up, very high, and then you'd have to close the shop …"

"Oh, signorina, I am old! I'm not gonna carry your bags up all those stairs!" He chuckled and continued, "My *grandson*, he can help you. He is a young boy. Lorenzo! Lorenzo!"

Oh, no, now some poor child was going to help her with all this! It was time to get out of here. Bridget carefully backed away and peeked over her shoulder to make sure she didn't snag another bag on something else. The shopkeeper had his back turned and was shouting at the invisible grandson in Italian. Bridget caught the words *piccola, signorina, forte, l'appartamento, and Palazza Bianca*, and she knew he was explaining her ridiculous plight. She safely made it through the hanging beads and heard the shopkeeper shout one last time, "Lorenzo, *dai, dai!*"

"Nonno, che cosa? Che cosa?"

Bridget hesitated. That was not the voice of a young child. It was a deep, manly voice. Curious, Bridget hid outside the doorway and cautiously peered in to get a peek at the mysterious grandson. She raised her eyebrows in surprise and strained to inconspicuously get a better view through the hanging beads. In a white tank top and Hawaiian board shorts, the "young" grandson towered over his short grandfather and looked to be around her age. With a tanned hand, he tucked his dark, chin-length hair behind his ear and listened as his grandfather repeated the story in Italian: … blah, blah, blah, the young lady … blah, blah, blah, needed help … blah, blah, blah, where had he been?

She watched him shrug and scrunch up his long, straight nose. Bridget knew enough Italian to understand his response. *"Well, where is she?"* At that, he turned and looked toward the doorway, his green eyes scanning the entrance. Bridget sucked in her breath and spun away from the doorway, lest she be seen.

He was not bad. He was *cute*. And he was going to help her carry her *toilet paper* and *vegetables* home? Bridget looked down at herself. She could feel sweat gathering on her lip and dripping down between her boobs. There was still a faint ring of Nutella around her ankle and still some between her toes. And to make it worse, she had a piece of dirty toilet paper stuck to the bottom of her flip-flop. She looked atrocious. There was no way in hell she was going to let help her home. Despite her injured foot, she jumped off the step and hurried up the closest stairway she could find.

Bridget limped up the final step and staggered back onto the narrow, curving street. This last staircase had been a killer. Her heart was pounding, and she stopped for a moment and leaned against the wall, breathing heavily. She didn't dare put the bags down for fear she'd leave them there and plop down in exhaustion, never to get up again.

Instead, she wiped her chin on her shoulder the best she could. That would have to do for now. She was drenched with sweat and her arms and calves ached. The stairs of Positano would humble even the fittest of athletes—and she was not even close to being one of those, no matter how much she did exercise. Having a gimpy foot didn't help much either. Besides the ring of brown around her ankle that was now beginning to run, a large, swollen, purple knob had developed on the top of Bridget's foot. This was definitely not the town to be podiacally challenged in.

Funnily enough, she couldn't care less about her gargantuan-sized foot right now. She was more concerned with how she smelled. God, had she even put deodorant on before she left the apartment? Hopefully, the sweet smell of Nutella might mask any possibility of body odor.

She took a deep breath and started her death walk again. Just a few more feet and she'd veer off Via Pasitea and up the final, lengthy staircase that would take her to the apartment. She could've easily just walked the main road that wound around the town, but that would have taken much longer, and she was trying to avoid running into anyone she might know, especially now that, with one foot dragging behind her, she was positive she might be mistaken for Quasimoto. And although the stairs were brutal, forcing her to stop at the end of each round to lean against the wall and suck wind, at least the only people on them, besides herself, were unsuspecting tourists who'd mistakenly wandered off-course or some of the older locals, who didn't pay her any attention.

Bridget passed the tiny, chapellike church, then the dumpsters that stood in front of the imposing stone staircase. She paused just short of the staircase, staring in a daze at the concert posters that had been plastered on the wall. All right, she could do this; she closed her eyes and breathed in deeply. Just a few more staircases. After all, what would another couple hundred of steps be? She opened her eyes in time to see a moped heading toward her. The driver beeped the horn a few quick times and putted to a stop next to her. Bridget quickly prayed that it wasn't Paolo. Ah, there was a God. It was Lassino, and hopefully, with his bad eyesight, he wouldn't be able to see how disgusting she looked. He squinted at her, and Bridget could tell that despite his impaired vision, he was still giving her a judgmental once-over.

"Hello, Bridget," he said and nodded.

"Hi, Lassino. Where are you off to?"

He shrugged. "Work, of course. I have to get the pizza dough ready." He scrunched his nose up, sniffed at her, and said, "You smell like Nutella."

She wouldn't even try to explain this one. Instead, Bridget shrugged back, as if Nutella were the most natural thing to smell like, and replied, "Yes, I know."

Lassino shook his head at her and revved the moped as he got ready to take off.

"Wait!" Bridget called as he started to pull away from the staircase. "Are you coming to our party tonight?" Kit still hadn't heard from him since their evening at Solo Tu.

Lassino looked back and shouted, in a tone that signaled she must be ridiculous to even ask, "No, I'm very beesy! Tell Kit I cannot come!"

It was Bridget who shook her head this time as she rolled her eyes and called, "You two are such drama."

Amused, Lassino chuckled and said, "Huh, drama! Heh heh!"

The moped sputtered and sped away. Lassino was enjoying this, of course. And Kit was going to be disappointed. Would anyone else show up now? Bridget wondered. She slowly began her ascent up the steps.

"Okay, I was able to finagle a few bags of ice from the bartender at Palazza Bianca," Kit sang as she shoved the apartment door open with one hip and set the plastic bags down with a thud on the patio floor.

With the exception of Bridget and her throbbing foot, for the last two hours, they had all been scampering about the apartment, hanging up decorations and preparing the snacks. The party was to officially start in another hour or so. That is, if anyone showed up. Bridget hadn't the heart to tell Kit that she'd run into Lassino earlier and what he'd said.

Natalie poked her head out from the kitchen where she had been garnishing a platter with peanut butter and jelly sandwiches to ask, "How in God's name did you walk those steps and carry all that ice in *those* heels?"

Kit looked down at the chunky, open-toed platforms that just peeked out from beneath her cream-colored, wide-leg jeans and shrugged. They were death-defying heels, but they made the outfit. She looked good tonight. A deep-red, silky halter showed off her tan, freckled shoulders, as well as her pushed-up cleavage. Her unruly blonde mop was now sleek and slightly feathered back, thanks to Bridget's turbo professional flatiron, which she'd used to flatten the humidity-induced frizz out of. To hell with Lassino if he didn't show up. But she hoped he did. You always had to keep a little hope in your back pocket.

And although it seemed so strange to be celebrating the Fourth of July in another country, here they were, and it seemed so right to her. Kit glanced around the dim patio. Starry, patriotic Mylar draped the wrought-iron balcony, flickering tea-lights adorned the balcony ledge and the table, and they had a plethora of hard alcohol and wine (thanks to Tomaso) and a bunch of terribly terrible American snacks ready to go. What would the Italians think of peanut butter and jelly sandwiches? Or s'mores and Twinkies, for that matter? Kit wondered. Their gastronomically superior palates would automatically cringe in disbelief and disgust, she conceded. This was so ridiculously crazy. Kit smiled giddily. She couldn't think of another place she'd rather be at this moment. She just hoped people came.

Joe, who was busy hanging large, metallic red, white, and blue stars from the eaves, took a moment to glance over at the hefty bags of ice. "How'd you manage to get all that? I hear ice is a precious commodity around here," he commented.

"Well," Kit answered, "the bartender was just a really *nice* guy—"

"And?" Bridget called from the lounge chair and table where she had her foot propped.

"And ... well, I invited him to our party." She looked over to find Bridget cackling at her. Kit replied defensively, "Well, he knew where we lived anyway! Besides, maybe he can make some cool drinks. What's a really American drink?"

Joe chuckled, just as Kit caught a glimpse of Bridget's foot in the shadowy candlelight and gasped, "Oh, my gosh, Bridget! Look at your foot! It looks awful! Here, we'll put some ice on it!" Kit bent down and tore open one of the plastic bags.

"It's not that ... bad." Bridget gazed at her foot. In the candlelight, if she squinted at it, the blackish-purple color was actually quite pretty. The shape of her foot, however, was not.

"Not that bad? Jesus, she looks like she has a club foot!" Joe barked from his side of the patio.

"Oh, no, do you think it's really that bad?" Bridget asked nervously. Damn, she'd really wanted to wear her Twelfth Street slip-on platforms tonight. Probably not a good idea now, but maybe if she pushed her foot into one, it'd help keep the swelling down.

"Joe! It does not look *that* bad." Kit rolled her eyes and handed Bridget some ice wrapped in a kitchen towel. "But it is pretty bad. Do you think maybe you broke a bone or something?"

Bridget whined, "Noo! What am I going to do? How am I going to ... to ..."

Kit finished her question. "... exercise? With an injured foot, you're not! You'll make it worse. Bridget, you don't need to be working out every day here anyway. Really, I think you're overdoing it. Don't you guys think so?"

Natalie stepped out onto the patio. "Kit's right. Besides, there's nothing to you anyway! So just take this little injury, however annoying it is, as a sign to relax. I would!"

Joe walked over, looked at Bridget's propped up foot closely, and stated, "Well, they're right, but this ain't no town for the handicapped. So my advice is, pop some Advil, start drinkin', and you'll be fine!"

"Don't listen to *him*, Bridget. You'll be fine, with or without the alcohol. Just take it easy," Natalie called as she went back into the kitchen.

"I know, I know. Actually, though, maybe I will have a little glass of prosecco." Bridget winced as she shifted herself and her foot.

"Thatta girl!" Joe nodded his head at her.

"*Daddy!* I went *poo* and I need you to wipe me!" Joey's voice could be heard screaming from the bathroom. Joe sighed wearily and said to Bridget, "As soon as I deal with this, you got yourself a drinking partner." He walked off the patio and into the bedroom.

"One *big* prosecco—sorry, there's no such thing in this apartment as a 'little glass of prosecco!'" Kit smiled as she handed Bridget a fizzing champagne flute. "And a bottle of Advil coming up! Gee, where is Julianna? She was supposed to be here two hours ago!"

"Oh, I forgot to tell you. She called while you were searching for ice. She's here, just not *here*, yet. Something about her driver decided to take her for some pizza and a beer on their way from the airport? So, she should be here any time now," Bridget relayed before taking a sip.

"Oh good. Do you think she'll have time to do my nails before the party starts? They're so disgusting!" Kit scrunched her nose up as she studied her hands.

It was truly a godsend having a friend like Julianna who owned a nail salon, and one who not only owned the salon, but still did nails as well, especially since hers had a tendency to get quite mangled due to the beauty hazards of teaching. Dry hands from chalk, paint or dirt under the fingernails, and jagged cuticles were a given in this profession. It was a shame there was no worker's comp for things like that.

Thanks to Julianna, though, her nails, for the most part, almost always looked shockingly immaculate, quite a feat for a primary-school teacher. After being introduced to her at the restaurant by Leo's fiancé Diana, Kit and Bridget had become friends with her and frequented her salon on a regular basis, not only for their nails, but to hang out and chat after hours. No longer considering them as just acquaintancelike clientele, Julianna refused to let the girls pay. Try as they might to leave money somewhere in the salon or to even hide it in her purse, Julianna wouldn't hear of it. And one did not argue with Julianna.

To call Julianna tough was putting it mildly. What she lacked in height, she made up for in ferocious sass and attitude. Motioning to herself à la Vanna White, she'd say, "This is all real, but I'm not above the whole smoke and mirrors effect—or even a little Botox!"

She stood no taller than five foot two in her platforms or stilettos, and she was never without her heels. To add an extra inch or two, she'd tease her wispy, blonde-streaked hair into a messy chignon. She made it a point to never wear anything that didn't show off her petite curves. Leaving the house in baggy clothing, or God forbid, without one of her favorite Victoria's Secret push-up bras, just did not happen. Nor did she go out unless her eye makeup was perfectly applied. And it always was, from the smoldering shadows to the cat-eyed liner on her lids. She looked every bit the walking doll. That is, until she opened her mouth, one of her favorite expressions being, "*Fuucckkk*! That is sooo *jacked* up!" which she could often be heard shouting into her wireless Bluetooth, even as she worked on a customer.

Everything and anything could be "jacked up," and usually with an expletive or two attached. And being "jacked up" in any sense of the term, was not a good thing. One's hair, one's nails, one's car, one's boyfriend, one's ex-boyfriend, or one's *life*, for that matter, could be deemed "jacked up." Nothing was spared from Julianna's observational cursing.

Yes, to be sure, Kit and Bridget agreed that there was no one quite like her. A few years older than the girls, half Greek and half Puerto Rican, she'd grown up in industrial South City, a town Kit and Bridget only remembered stepping foot in to play scary rival softball teams in grammar school. In fact, most people wouldn't have placed her as being from South City at all, but rather, from the East Coast. The constant energetic vibe that flowed from her, along with her raspy, fast-talking voice, always threw people off, and she was often pegged to be a New Yorker. She didn't mind, as long as people didn't mess with her. And most people didn't.

If you asked her if she had any enemies, Julianna would laughingly answer in her Demi Moore-like voice, "No, I don't argue with people, and people don't argue with me. Why? Because I'm always fuckin' right!" Most people would have to agree. And if they didn't, it was best to keep it to themselves.

Which explained why Bridget and Kit hadn't paid for a manicure or pedicure in the last year. Instead, they'd schedule themselves as Julianna's last appointments and bring chilled prosecco and assorted cheese and crackers. Diana and Marren would often stop by to join them for the after-hours nail-and-gab session.

As Kit schlepped the ice bags into the kitchen, she decided it was much better to have Julianna as a friend. While she was one of the most unselfishly kind people Kit had ever met, Kit was still scared of her temper and more than a little fearful of ever making her mad. Although, lately, it appeared to Kit that she was afraid of making everyone mad. She always seemed to be rubbing *someone* the wrong way. Well, just so long as it wasn't Julianna.

Oh, she was probably being silly. She really needed to stop worrying about these things, Kit told herself. She should focus on how fantastic it was that Julianna would be here any moment and that the three of them would be in Calabria for Leo and Diana's wedding by tomorrow afternoon! A nice mani-pedi was just icing on the cake.

Natalie grabbed a bag of ice from Kit and commented, "Um, I think Julianna's here." There was a loud ruckus on the stairs outside the apartment and the sound of heavy luggage being either dragged or scraped along the steps, and Julianna's gravelly voice shouted, "Oh my *God*, is this it? This is it! This is it, right? Bridget, Kit, my girlies, where *are* you? I'm here!"

Before Kit could get to the door, it flew open, practically hitting her in the face as it struck the wall with an echoing boom. Julianna stood on the step in a super-snug Juicy sweatsuit, four-inch, cork-heeled wedges, and a messy updo that was slightly askew. Dramatically laying one hand atop the waist-high trunk next to her and unzipping her hoodie with the other so she could fan herself, she squealed, "*Oh, my, God!* I am finally here! Can you believe it! Ooohhh, girlies, come here; gimme a hug!"

Kit scurried over. "Julianna, how are you? How was your flight?"

"Oh, it was great. I *love, love, love* Alitalia! I don't care if that airline is *never* on time. The flight attendants are all *gorgeous*. Talk about fuckin' eye candy!"

"Daddy, what is *that*?" Joey looked wide-eyed at Julianna and then up at his father. Together with Joe and Madison, he'd come out onto the patio after hearing the commotion.

"That's Auntie K and Bridget's friend, Julianna."

"She sayed a bad word, Daddy! She sayed fuuuu—" Joe quickly clamped a hand over Joey's mouth and said sternly, "Joey, that's not a word you repeat!"

Behind Joe's back, Madison smirked then went back to staring at Julianna with a look of envious awe.

"Oh, God, so sorry!" Julianna pushed Kit out of the way. "I didn't know there were kids out here!" she squeaked as she hustled over to Natalie and Joe with an extended hand.

"Hi, I'm Julianna. It's so nice to meet you! Kit didn't tell me you had a *teenager*. You two look way too young to have a seventeen-year-old! I thought you only had a couple of little ones!" She nodded in the direction of Madison, who looked down and smiled, pleased to be mistaken for being older than she was.

"So nice to finally meet you too! This is actually my niece, Joe's sister's daughter. Madison, say hello," Natalie prompted her.

Madison gave a slight smile and said, "Hi. So, you do nails? Do you think you could do mine after you do Kit's?"

"Maddie! Julianna is on vacation. She didn't come here just to do everybody's nails! Sorry." Natalie looked apologetically at Julianna.

Julianna waved her off and said, "Oh, please, I've learned never to go anywhere without my nail equipment. Sure, Sweetie, if there's time. Kit! Get over here and let me see your nails. I *just* did them before you left!"

Kit argued, "Julianna, it can wait, really. Let's get you settled first. We haven't even gotten your suitcase in the door. Is that all your luggage?"

Julianna laughed huskily. "Oh, of course not. I have a whole other case! Oh, Jesus, my little driver was supposed to bring it down. Oh, God, what *happened* to him? I hope he didn't have a heart attack or something. He *is* kind of old! But you should see him! He is soo *hot* for a sixty-year-old! I kinda like him! Oh, God, Igor! Igor—shit, I think that's his name—are you all right?" Julianna shouted as she clomped across the patio toward the door. She poked her head out the doorway and then looked back over her shoulder at everyone and hissed in a stage whisper, "Oh, thank God, he's not dead! He's coming!"

She awkwardly dragged her trunk out of the doorway to make room for him to come in. A short, wiry man in an expensive-looking dark suit with aviator glasses perched upon his head stepped onto the patio carrying a suitcase so large that Bridget felt it made her "Big Blue" look like a mere handbag.

"How long is she staying?" Joe mumbled to Bridget.

"A couple of weeks," Bridget retorted matter-of-factly, as if packing that much for two weeks was entirely plausible and necessary. Joe raised his eyebrows and shook his head.

The square-jawed driver set the suitcase down as if it was empty and smoothed back his salt-and-pepper hair with a gracious smile. Then he took a silk handkerchief out of his inside coat pocket and elegantly wiped his brow.

"Oh, everybody, this is my driver! He is sooo nice. Can you believe he took me for pizza and beer?" Julianna squealed.

"*Piacere.* I am Gregorio." He bowed slightly at them all.

Julianna mumbled out the side of her mouth, "*Oh, my God,* I thought his name was *Igor!*"

She placed a hand on his arm and smiled sweetly. "Gregorio—you know what, I'm gonna call you Greg from now on, hope you don't mind, but I feel I can call ya that since we shared a pizza and beer together! Thank you so much; you are just so sweet! Don't go anywhere, now; hold on, let me get my money to pay you." She bent over to rummage through her purse. *Greg* gazed longingly at Julianna's curvaceous backside.

She found her money in her wallet, jumped up, and held her hand out to him to give him his money. "Okay, Greg, grazie, grazie!"

He took the money and gave her the Italian kiss. As soon as he finished, he grabbed her hand, kissed it, and looked up at her adoringly. "Grazie, bella Julianna. I have *never* met a woman like you before! You are amazing!"

Julianna giggled and said, "You are so sweet! Well, Greg, maybe you can be my driver when I go back to the airport." She batted her eyelashes flirtatiously at him.

"I would like that very much. Have Tino call me. Ciao!" He bowed again and waved to the gawking audience on the patio. He winked at Julianna and headed out the door.

Julianna turned to them all and shrieked, "Can you believe it? He's so cute! He's kinda old, don'tcha think, but he's fine!"

"Wow, and I thought Kit would have a monopoly on the men around here!" Joe laughed and went back into the bedroom.

Kit rolled her eyes in the direction of Joe before she joked, "God, what did you do to him, Julianna? He's right, though. He'll never meet another woman like you."

"Oh, please. They probably say that to everyone. *Amazing?* I *like* it! All right, quick! Let me see your nails." Julianna grabbed Kit's hands.

After a quick inspection, she shouted, "Oh, my God, your nails are *sooo jacked* up! Yes, yes, we can do a quickie on your hands and feet. Go get me a bucket of warm water. Now! If you want them done before the party." Kit whipped her platforms off and scurried into the kitchen.

Julianna noticed Bridget on the lounge chair, hurried over, and gave her the Italian kiss on both cheeks.

"Oh, God, *there* you are, Bridget! I didn't even see you with all the commotion with Igor—I mean, Greg! Hi, Sweetie, it's so good to see you!

Can you believe we're here and not in my salon? See, I'm doing the whole 'Italian kissing' thing. That's what my little driver taught me!" She winked, then looked down at Bridget's feet and tsked, "Ughh, and look at you, too—awful!"

"I know; I know; two days here and my feet are wrecked from wearing flip-flops all over and from the rocks on the beach!" Bridget moaned.

"Actually, I was talking about your … foot! What the hell happened? What's goin' on in this fuuu—" She stopped as she saw Joey peeking his head out the bedroom door. "What's going on in this … town? Why is everyone all jacked up? Thank God I'm here!"

She whipped out a miniature manicure set from her large shoulder bag. "Well, Christ, I'm not going near that! It looks like it hurts. I think we should wait before we do anything to your feet, or at least, *that* foot. Kit, hurry up!"

Kit scampered out with a bowl and a glass of prosecco. Julianna took one look at the oversized soup bowl and scowled. "*What is that?* How do you expect to soak your feet in that? It looks like a freakin' candy dish!"

"Sorry, I couldn't find a bucket. Will a glass of prosecco make it better?" Kit smiled sheepishly.

Julianna took the glass from her. "Yes, *of course.*" She sighed. "Well, we'll just have to soak one foot at a time, that's all. You know, I am good, but I'm not a miracle worker, Kit."

Natalie appeared and set two opened bottles of prosecco on the table. She poured herself a drink and stated, "It looks like we could all use a drink. I better go check on Madison and make sure she hasn't gone through and demolished all my makeup or your flatiron, Bridget."

"Send her out here. I'll take care of her!" Julianna half joked. "All right, now, let's get started on these feet of yours. And tell me about this crazy Fourth of July party you're having. I hope I have time to freshen up! So will there be any cute guys here tonight?" Julianna chattered as she scrubbed Kit's wet foot.

Kit looked at Bridget quickly, then at Julianna, and said, "Ummm, maybe—"

"What does *that* mean? Does this have to do with the freaky Italian guy with glasses that you like?" Julianna asked skeptically as she continued scrubbing.

Bridget snorted. She'd let Kit explain the Lassino situation herself. Gingerly, she pushed herself up out of the chair. She should probably go and get ready herself—although, for who or what, she didn't know. As she passed the green door, she thought she heard a rustling on the step and the sound of something coming into contact with the metal door.

"I think someone's at the door," Bridget spoke as she hobbled toward it.

"Well, maybe Tomaso has more alcohol to drop off." Kit shrugged.

Julianna took Kit's foot out of the bowl and placed it on a towel, then asked, "Ooooh, who's Tomaso? Is he cute? Can we like him?" Kit began filling Julianna in on their young friend who helped his father run the expensively swanky private section of the grand beach known as Bello Mare.

Bridget opened the door but found no one out there. Yet a plastic bag filled with something heavy was barely hanging from the brass door handle. *Somebody* had left *something*. That must have been the noise she had heard. Curious, she unfastened the bag from the door handle and looked inside it. In the dim alleyway, she thought she was seeing things. She opened the bag wider and looked more closely. Nope, she had been right. The Italian World Cup soccer team stared back at her from four large jars of Nutella. Was this some kind of joke? Who had left these? Bridget hopped off the step, her eyes darting around. She looked down the long stairway and thought she saw the back of someone turning the corner, and the someone was wearing Hawaiian board shorts.

Lorenzo, the grandson? Maybe her eyes were playing tricks on her in the dim light. The figure turned the corner and was gone from sight. Hmmm, if that was Lorenzo, that was certainly nice—yet totally unnecessary—of his grandfather to send him up to deliver the jars. Bridget was pleasantly baffled. She turned around and stepped back in through the apartment door. Kit looked up at her, smiled, and asked, "Who was out there?"

Bridget shrugged, held up the bag, and laughed. "No one. But good news: we've got backup Nutella!"

Chapter 9

"Bridget, another prosecco?" Joe called over his shoulder as he wandered into the kitchen.

"Sure," Bridget replied and nodded her head. Was she on her third or fourth? She wasn't sure. Well, at least she didn't have to drive—or walk, for that matter. She was pretty sure she wouldn't be moving too much from that lounge chair at all. And she could have a few more drinks, since she was not even close to being over her Weight Watchers points for the day. Of course, that was because she hadn't really eaten anything. What *could* she eat that would still leave room for alcohol on her points plan? The plump grape tomatoes and assortment of local crudite staring at her from the table would be a healthy choice. She *should* have some of that and maybe a piece of bread. Lord knew, she had certainly earned the right to eat and drink, since she'd sweated and suffered enough to get the food up here.

But no, she didn't feel like eating any of *that*. What could she have that was sweet, aside from Nutella, which she was staying far away from? Hmmm, marshmallows? For some unknown, yet probably alcohol-induced reason, that sounded good *and* it was low on the points value. Yes, that was it. They had enough of them for the s'mores they would *supposedly* be making for their *supposed* Italian guests. She didn't trust herself to get out of the chair and wasn't about to ask someone to get her a bag of marshmallows to tear into. She'd have to stick to prosecco for now. As long as she didn't try to get mobile, she'd be fine. In fact, she'd probably just end up sleeping out here on the patio anyway.

Holding two opened prosecco bottles, Joe stepped onto the patio and asked, "Anyone else ready for a drink?"

"Oh, me, me!" His wife giggled with a slight tipsiness. She held Joey on her lap, who sat drowsily slurping away on his thumb.

"Kit?" Joe asked as he began filling up the glasses on the table.

"Thanks, I think I'll wait a bit," she replied and smiled brightly.

Bridget watched her friend and thought her demeanor to be a bit forced. Kit excelled at being "happy," but Bridget knew better. It was now eleven, and the only people sitting on the balcony were Joe, Natalie, the kids, and themselves. Of course, Julianna should be done getting ready soon and would be out here to liven things up, but still …

It seemed to Bridget as if it was midnight. Of course, that was the American schoolteacher in her surfacing. She knew nothing got started in Italy until "late," but she still wondered whether anyone would show up at all. Maybe they were all heading to the disco instead. Would Lassino really blow off the party just to spite Kit? She had to admit that it was a definite possibility. If so, that would surely mean that Paolo wouldn't come either. She could give up on that one anyway.

Joe finished refilling Bridget's and Natalie's glasses, set the bottles down on the table, and asked, "So, how's the foot? Did my medical advice help at all?"

"Yes, I think you definitely missed your calling." Bridget raised her glass at him. It was true. She couldn't feel her foot at all. After putting on a pair of midnight-blue dress shorts and throwing a shrug over a James Perse tee, she'd squeezed her feet into the Twelfth Street platforms.

Bridget wasn't sure if the numbness in her foot was a good thing or not, but at least she couldn't feel any pain. And the dark blue-purple of her foot blended in so nicely with the purple straps of the platform. The fact that the swollen knot was protruding through and around the spaces of the straps was of no concern to her at all right now. At least she looked halfway decent and not too terribly handicapped.

Madison, who'd been sitting quietly in a corner of the patio listening to the adult banter, asked, "Can I have some prosecco?"

Joe smiled and shook his head. "No."

"But why can't I try it? We're in *Italy!*" whined Madison.

Joe ignored her plea, sat down on the balcony ledge, and stated, "There's Diet Coke, juice, and water in the fridge. Knock yourself out."

With a dramatic sigh, Madison got up and trudged across the patio and into the kitchen. The refrigerator door could be heard slamming open and shut, and then there was a banging of cupboards; Madison was clearly making her annoyance known to all.

Natalie spoke quietly, "Joe, can't she just have a sip? One sip's not going to do anything." Before Joe could answer, the refrigerator door slammed once more, followed by what sounded unmistakenly like bottles falling.

"I hope nothing in the fridge broke." Kit raised her eyebrows, a look of concern on her face.

Joe looked over at Natalie and said, "I would have thought about it, but she's being a little punk. Forget it! Madison, keep it up and you can forget about staying up for the party. Do you hear me?"

No reply came from the kitchen.

"Go in and see if anything's broken," Natalie said wearily.

Joe shook his head, got up, and said, "There better not be anything broken in there, or it's coming out of your allowance."

"Speaking of the party, I hate to say it, but I think we are the party," Bridget joked.

"I think you're right. Damn Lassino!" Kit grabbed the prosecco bottle and poured herself another glass.

"*Excuse me*, but *now* it's a party!" Julianna sang as she paraded onto the patio wearing a black, sleeveless, plunging minidress and a pair of four-inch, peep-toed, snakeskin stilettos.

"Refill me, pronto!" she sang as she reached into her dress and rear-ranged her visibly bountiful cleavage.

"Here." Kit motioned for her to bring her glass over. "You got ready fast! Why does it always take me so long?" Kit said in disbelief as she poured the prosecco.

"Well, I didn't want to miss anything! So where are all the men? If no one shows, do you want me to call my little driver, Greg?"

"Would he still be awake?" Bridget asked, thinking of his age and the fact that anyone might need a good night's sleep after carrying Julianna's mountain of luggage.

"Oh, he'll be awake if I call!" Julianna snorted and took a hefty sip.

"No offense to *Greg*, but I'd say we're not *that* desperate yet," Kit said, although a bit unconvincingly.

Julianna looked at her, smirked, and said, "Really? Well, girls, I love you both— oh, and you too, Natalie, even though I just met you—but I didn't come all the way to Italy to sit here on the patio so we could stare at each other all night! If no one shows up in the next hour, we're hitting the disco, end of story." She adjusted her short hemline before precariously perching herself upon one of the patio chairs.

Kit leaned back against her chair and sighed. "I don't feel like going to the disco. I'll just stay here."

Julianna snorted and asked contemptuously, "Why? So, you can sit around here moping over some creepy guy who hasn't shown up? What's up his ass, anyway?"

Kit shrugged darkly and sputtered, "Oh, I don't know. He's just … so … bizarre!"

Julianna scowled, picked up a fluorescent Twinkie from the assorted plates on the table, and answered, "Uh-huh. Well, maybe he heard you were serving weird food. What *is* all this crap? Twinkies and peanut butter and jelly? Italians aren't gonna eat this shit!"

"Well, they might!" Kit pouted. "It's *American* food for the *Fourth of July!* They should at least try it!"

Julianna jokingly persisted. "Tell me, or *dimmi*, as my little Italian driver would say, do *you* eat any of this stuff?"

Kit thought. She hadn't eaten a Twinkie since about the third grade, and the only time she ever ate peanut butter was when her refrigerator and cupboards were completely bare. Dejectedly, she admitted, "No," then quickly added, "but I do like s'mores! And you tell me, who wouldn't like s'mores? Oh, well, it doesn't matter, since probably nobody will come now because of Lassino! I wonder where he is."

"Please—he's probably at the disco. *That's* why we should all go. Don't waste good cleavage, Kit! Go let him see what he's missing, or better yet, go find someone else at the disco!" Julianna banged her hand on the table to make her point. "That's what I'd do!"

"No, no," Kit shook her head and frowned.

"Well, I'm telling you," Julianna insisted raspily, "the only way to get over a man is to get under a new one! So, girl, you go work that disco! Isn't that right, Bridget?" She looked over at Bridget expectantly.

Bridget, who'd been about to drain her glass, set it down with a per-turbed look upon her face. She wouldn't know anything about getting under *any* new men. To her, it seemed she'd been lucky enough to escape the evil clutches of one, only to repel all others! She looked over at Kit, who seemed irritated and to be giving her a look that said, *You can't seriously agree with her?*

"Ummm ..." Bridget stalled.

Julianna rolled her eyes. "Jesus, I forgot, I'm asking the two nuns! Well, I know what I speak of, and I'm right. Bridget, you'll go to the disco with me." She pointed matter-of-factly at Bridget. "Your foot's kinda jacked, but you can walk on it, can't you, Sweetie?"

Bridget raised her eyebrows, tilted her head, and answered, "Sure." She couldn't feel her foot anyway. As a matter of fact, she felt pretty good, and she didn't look *that* hideous. In fact, she looked better than nonhideous. She had a decent tan, and for some reason, the humidity hadn't turned her hair Chia Pet-like either. It was still flatiron-straight. And, she resolved, she definitely hadn't gained back all her weight, *yet*.

Yes, she'd go to the disco. She might even run into Paolo. Bridget imagined their meeting: her glowing tan would bring out her white teeth and blue eyes. Her hair (despite the fro-inducing humidity) would be perfectly stick-straight, and for some unknown reason, she'd look super svelte and modelesque, so much so that nobody would even notice her limp and Frankenstein-sized foot. Paolo would be shocked and overwhelmed by how cute she was for an old(er) woman, and maybe they'd dance, and then ... wait a minute ... Bridget stopped herself as she realized it was the alcohol making her delusional. She was pretty buzzed and should not be overtaken with foolish notions, which might certainly get her into danger later. But, yes, of course, she'd still go to the disco.

"Can I go to the disco?" Madison padded after Joe back onto the patio. Joe looked back at her and shook his head. "You're too *young*."

Madison complained, "That's what you say about everything! Why can't—"

Attempting to diffuse the impending shouting match, Julianna cut in, practically shouting at Madison, "I *love* your halter top! Where'd you get that?"

Momentarily distracted from her martyrdom, Madison sat on the balcony ledge, smiled, and gushed, "Forever 21!"

"I knew it! That's my *favorite* store! Hey, what size are you?" Julianna squealed.

Natalie squinted at Madison. "Hey, wait a minute, that's my top! *Madison!*"

Madison sulked and defended herself. "Well, you never wear it anymore!"

"Yeah, because I haven't been able to *find* it!" Natalie called out.

"Hon, let's get the kids to bed," Joe interrupted as he lifted a sleeping Joey from Natalie's arms.

Natalie pushed herself up and out of the lounge chair. As she wheeled Gina away in her stroller, she spoke over her shoulder at Madison. "We're gonna have a little talk later on about getting into my stuff, all right?"

"Fine, okay." Madison rolled her eyes. She looked pleadingly at the girls and moaned, "I'm not allowed to do anything!"

"How old *are* you?" Julianna asked.

"Thirteen," Madison answered glumly as she turned away to look out over the balcony.

Julianna's eyes popped and she whispered to the girls, "*Fuucckk!* I thought she was *way* older. Damn, that's trouble, all right!"

"No kidding," Kit agreed, and she got up from her chair to bring an empty prosecco bottle back to the kitchen.

Julianna clucked her tongue and shook her head, and then added sadly, "Reminds me of my little sister."

She noticed that Madison had turned her head back toward them and was once again listening, so she put her hand up to her mouth and turned toward Bridget so Madison couldn't see her. Out of the side of her mouth, she mumbled, "Yeah, she ended up pregnant at sixteen!"

Bridget cringed and whispered, "Don't tell Joe and Natalie that!"

"Well, maybe I *should* tell them, otherwise, they may end up raising her *and* her baby!"

"Good point," Bridget replied, somewhat soberly. The apartment door vibrated loudly as someone pounded upon it.

"Kit, someone's here!" Bridget shouted.

"*Thank God!*" Julianna moaned and pushed up her boobs with both hands.

Kit walked to the door, stopped in front of it, and smoothed her hair down. She then quickly adjusted her cleavage, ran a finger over her teeth to eliminate the possibility of unwanted lip gloss, and turned around to give the girls an excited smile.

Julianna hissed, "Jesus, hurry and open the door before whoever's out there leaves!" Kit quickly opened the door and enthusiastically cried, "Ciao!"

"Ciao, Kit!" Tomaso shouted back as he stepped inside and embraced Kit. A chorus of "Ciao!" followed from behind him. Standing behind Tomaso was the town's most flamboyantly gay boutique owner, Giorgio, flanked on one side by his Louis Vuitton satchel and his dog Memo (another town diva in his rhinetsone-studded collar), and on the other side, his stout architect, Roberto.

"Oh, come in, come in!" Kit gestured. "Giorgio! I am so happy you are here! Ciao, Roberto!" Kit toothily gushed.

Giorgio looked Kit over and cried excitedly, "Ahhh, Kit, you are *bellisima*! The quintessential Italian woman!" He handed her a bottle Veuve Clicquot champagne and added, "Here, this is for you. I am so glad you make a party and invite us! And we also brought Luca. You remember Luca? He is a cousin of Lassino and Paolo." Luca, related to Lassino and Paolo, as was half of the small town, nodded and smiled shyly from under his curly, dark hair.

"Yes, yes, of course!" Kit smiled. Before she could ask where Lassino was, Julianna raspily interrupted. "*Kit*, aren't you going to introduce us to your friends?"

"Yes, of course!" Kit called over her shoulder. She turned to the Italians and then back toward the rest to make the introductions. She waved her hands and said, "Tomaso, Giorgio, Roberto, and Luca, my Italian friends, meet my American friends! That's Julianna," Bridget watched the men smile warmly at Julianna as they looked her over, their eyes doing an obvious double-take on her cleavage. She heard Roberto utter in a low growl, "*Mama mia!*"

Julianna giggled flirtatiously. "So nice to meet you all!"

"And Bridget—you remember *Bridget*." Kit paused and waited expectantly for some kind of overwhelming acknowledgment of her friend from the Italians. Instead, they smiled with vaguely disinterested recognition. Bridget grinned anyway and waved, despite the mortifying fact that, once again, no one in this town seemed to have a clue as to whom she was. However, being a few drinks in somewhat deadened the extreme awkwardness that would have normally overcome her.

Kit continued on obliviously. "... and Joe and Natalie and their *niece*, Madison." She hastily added, "She's thirteen!"

As if super-gay Giorgio would be interested in the slightest, Bridget thought dryly. Still, though, she guessed it couldn't hurt to make Madison's age known to the others. Introductions complete, Tomaso turned to Kit, patted his chest proudly, and asked, "So, do you like my shirt? Is it okay for your Fourth of July party?"

In contrast to Giorgio with his black T-shirt and signature white-linen pants, and Luca and Roberto in their jeans and pastel-colored polos, Tomaso looked as if he'd come straight from the beachfront where he worked. He wore his usual pair of slouchy shorts with sandals; his windshieldlike sunglasses sat atop his slicked-back, ponytailed hair. His T-shirts usually displayed some type of tasteless (and usually sexual) message that ranged from "Every garden needs a good ho," to "Spring Break Daytona—Party Till You Puke!" Tonight's shirt had a somewhat American theme to it, Kit guessed. A line ran down the middle of the shirt; one side read "Good Bush" with a picture of a woman's nether regions underneath. The other side read "Bad Bush," over a picture of a jovial-looking George W. Bush.

Kit squealed, "You are so funny!"

"I like this guy. What can I get you all to drink?" Joe asked.

"Wine, please," Giorgio answered and batted his eyelashes coyly at Joe.

"Right, I'll go get that. Anyone want something else to drink?" Joe asked quickly.

"I'll have a beer. I know you have some, since I did the shopping for Kit!" Tomaso joked.

"You and I are going to get along just fine," Joe answered back as Tomaso followed him into the kitchen, leaving a disappointed Giorgio pouting.

The guests dispersed and seated themselves around the candlelit patio, then began chatting and admiring the twinkling, bobbing lights on the black water far below them. Kit beamed as she set a platter of peanut butter and jelly sandwiches down on the table and then ran back to the kitchen to bring out some more prosecco. She rummaged through the multitude of bottles in the fridge, grabbed a couple, and whirled around to find Lassino standing in the open doorway, staring at her.

"Hello." He wrinkled his brow and squinted seriously at her. He had shown up after all! And there he was, leaning against the doorway, in his faded jeans, a navy-blue polo offsetting his just-as-dark-blue eyes. His wavy, blond hair was slightly gelled, which gave it a casual, damp look, as if he'd just stepped out of the shower. Of course, he probably had done just that, Kit thought, since he took about three showers a day.

However odd he was at times—or most of the time—Kit conceded that she was completely under his spell. That was it. Tonight, she was going to stay at Lassino's, and she wouldn't take no for an answer. She wouldn't be sleeping in his old T-shirt and Umbro soccer shorts, either.

Her heart involuntarily skipped a beat. She smiled and exclaimed, "Hi! What are you doing here?"

"Well, you are very rude!" Lassino sputtered jokingly. "You invited me! Do you not remember *anything*?"

"Yes, I remember. It's just that I thought you weren't coming. You know, you're so *beesy* all the time!" Kit imitated him.

"Yes, well, of course, I am. Mario and I are late. We have restaurants to run, you know!"

Kit watched Lassino walk around the kitchen, carefully inspecting all the cabinets and kitchen appliances. He walked down the hallway and nosily poked his head in and out of every room. He entered the kitchen again, shrugged his shoulders and gave a half scowl, and admitted, "It's a nice place. How much are you paying for it?"

"Eleven hundred euros per week. Is that a good price?" Kit asked hopefully.

Lassino grunted in his cavemanlike voice. "How long are you staying? Huh! You must be rich."

He looked away, folded his arms across his chest, and then looked back at her to add, "I think I like you even better now!" To show he was joking, he smiled, then gave Kit a cross between a hair tossling and a noogie. Why couldn't he ever be normal and just kiss her? Kit removed his hand from her hair before he could wreck it any more. He then leaned in and kissed her passionately. Ahhh, that was better. Kit sighed.

Before she could even think about kissing him back, he barked, "Well, are you going to stand there, or are you going to pour your guests some prosecco? Oh, my God!" And with that, he turned and left the kitchen to join the others on the patio.

Kit looked around the patio happily. She was surrounded by some of her oldest and dearest friends. And now she actually had some real friends in *Positano*. She could hardly believe it, but it was true. They wouldn't have shown up if they didn't consider her a friend.

This little seaside town *was* a magical place. Here were her two completely juxtaposed worlds, the San Francisco Bay Area and Positano, mingling peacefully on one patio, and it was if they'd all known each other for ages. This was proof.

Natalie sat chatting animatedly about art and interior design with Roberto and Luca. Australian Rachel sat smoking and chatting with Giorgio and Julianna. Thankfully, Rachel wasn't on a rant about Paolo, who supposedly wasn't speaking to her right now. Giorgio busily described his new clothing line ("I tell the people at the factory, not so many buttons on the front of the dresses. My clients don't like that!") as he continuously reached for his bottle of olive oil in his Louis Vuitton satchel. He rubbed a little on his hands, grabbed Julianna's petite hand, and shouted, "Now, we make a massage!"

Julianna squealed, "Oh, my God! I'll never be able to look at olive oil the same way again!"

Mario, on Julianna's other side, grabbed her free hand and whispered something, no doubt naughty, into her ear as Julianna cackled wickedly. Madison sat on the other side of Mario and watched him and Giorgio with rapt attention. Kit half expected her, and wouldn't put it past the thirteen year old, to ask for a hand massage, too.

Although she'd made it very clear to Lassino and Mario how young Madison was, Kit could swear that Madison seemed to be flirting with Mario. Kit watched her smile at him constantly and inch her patio chair closer to him, until she was practically leaning on him. And was she imagining things, or did Madison's halter top appear to be showing some noticeable boobage? Had the kid stuffed her bra, or were they really that voluptuous? Kit would have been a bit worried normally, but she felt that Julianna had already worked her charms on Mario, and there was no way she was going to lose an Italian to an overdeveloped thirteen-year-old.

Of course, Mario would never in a million years try anything like that, but it was still comforting to know that Julianna had that situation under control. Indeed, there did seem to be some kind of competition going on between Madison and Julianna. For every inch that Madison scooted closer to Mario, Julianna would arch her eyebrows and, without even looking, pull Mario by the hand closer to her—so close that before long, his hand was resting on her thigh—any farther and he'd probably be sitting on her lap.

Thankfully, Madison should be going to bed soon. It was close to three a.m., and Kit felt that people would start taking off soon. And then, once everyone went to bed, she could leave with Lassino. Kit felt goose bumps on her arms as she snuck a peek at Lassino, who sat beside her.

Aside from him gagging on and then spitting out the peanut butter and jelly sandwich she had forced him to try earlier ("Disgusting, Kit! What did I do to deserve that?"), he had remained fairly quiet tonight and intently listened in on all the various conversations that were occurring. She wondered what he was thinking. Was he sorry he had come to the party, or was he happy to see her? Kit briefly worried about Lassino being possibly attracted to Julianna. She pushed the negative thought out of her head. This was no time for fluctuating self-esteem. Italians were so uncannily perceptive that they could smell something like that from miles away. There would be no second-guessing tonight. She was going to go home with him—just as soon as everyone either left or went to bed. And she wished they'd hurry.

She tried to casually look at Lassino's watch without being too obvious. *Would* he take her home with him? Kit tried to keep the wondering and self-doubt out of her head, but she couldn't help it. She'd waited so long— approximately 365 days, give or take! She just had to spend the night with him. Oh, God, she needed to think about something else and quick. At least the party had been a success, even though the Italians didn't quite get the food and her reasons for how it tied in with the patriotic celebration. Maybe if she'd used Nutella, instead, for the s'mores …

Kit glanced down at her camera in her lap, picked it up, and scanned the patio for any photographic opportunities. And there had been many already. Joe and Tomaso had hit it off, trying to one-up each other on the beer drinking and limoncello shots. They continually slapped each other on the back and talked politics.

Bridget lay back in her lounge chair, her eyes at half-mast, amusedly listening to the international-political dialogue between the two new friends. Kit knew it was only a matter of time before Bridget passed out. But at least she hadn't been in one of her dark, self-deprecating moods tonight, lamenting over how it was so typical that none of the Italians ever remembered *her*, how she couldn't exercise and was so fat, yada,yada, yada.

Yes, the state of Bridget's mood really could have gone either way tonight, what with her odd foot injury (how *did* Bridget manage to do these things to herself?), her slightly excessive drinking (but hey, with the exception of Madison—whom Kit had been watching like a hawk all evening—*everyone* here was quite toasted), and the disappointment of Paolo not showing up, most likely due to the surprise arrival of Australian Rachel, whom, according to Lassino, Paolo was avoiding like the plague. As soon as Rachel walked in, she noticed Lassino hurriedly texting—a sure sign that he was warning Paolo not to come. Darn, Kit hadn't really thought that Rachel would *actually* show up. She was always such a regular at Solo Tu and the disco, so how could Kit have known?

At any rate, Kit was proud of Bridget for handling it all quite well. Maybe this would be a kind of turning point for her. Kit just hoped she wasn't too hungover tomorrow, since they had to pack and catch an afternoon train from Salerno to Scalea for the wedding. She hoped she herself wasn't too badly hungover, either. Kit didn't usually let this happen, but this evening, she'd lost count of her prosecco intake.

As Kit wondered how she could suggest helping Bridget off to bed without annoying her, she overheard Tomaso drunkenly slur to Bridget, "You are famous in all of Positano!" Kit smiled at Tomaso's accent, which made the word *famous* came out sounding like "fah-mose."

To which Bridget slurred back, "*Really ...*"

"Yes, yes, you are, Breegeet!" Tomaso insisted. Ha, Kit thought. See, she was right. It was all in Bridget's head. As usual, *everybody* loved her, but she chose to ignore it and act overly paranoid instead. Now she wouldn't have to listen to Bridget sarcastically complain about it anymore. Kit grabbed her camera. This would be a great shot, she thought, as Tomaso proclaimed, yet again, "No, no, you are famous!" He paused dramatically before adding, "Because you are the friend of Kit!"

Kit's face fell as she watched Bridget bite her lip. Oh, that was just *great*. But instead of looking upset, Bridget merely smiled, laughed, and said, "And on that note, *buona notte!*" She leveraged herself up out of the chair, then waved at everyone and no one in particular.

"Night, Sweetie! Don't wait up! I'm in good hands here!" Julianna called huskily.

Giorgio waved to Bridget cheerily, then resumed the hand massage he had been giving Julianna, who giggled and pulled Mario closer. Rachel nodded at Bridget as she puffed away on yet another cigarette, while Madison looked on enviously. "Night, Bridget," Madison called sullenly, while keeping her eyes on the smoking Aussie.

Before Bridget could even disappear into the kitchen, the green door was flung open, which caused everyone to stop and stare at the darkened doorway. Carrie pushed Jared in, then slammed the door shut. Carrie looked at the surprised faces staring up at them and said, "Oh, yeah ... the Fourth of July party ... oops."

"Hi, happy Fourth to you, too!" Kit shouted. She was *so* over Carrie, but thankfully, the prosecco was keeping her even more pleasant than usual.

Lassino joked, "It's the fifth of July now—you're a little late!" Carrie pointedly ignored the remark as Kit jumped up to make the introductions again. She pointed to everyone around the patio. "Carrie, that's Tomaso, Giorgio, and you know Rachel, Luca, and Roberto ... and you know all the rest."

Carrie absently nodded in their direction. "Yes, ciao, ciao, uh-huh, yes, ciao."

Kit continued on. "Sorry, we're pretty much out of prosecco. But here, have a Twinkie and join the party!"

Carrie was still breathing heavily, and she panted, "Umm, thanks ... I'll pass. Kit, could I talk to you—in the kitchen?" Kit looked at Carrie's tense face and then at Jared, who shrugged back at her. *What now?* Kit thought. Her stomach involuntarily rumbled. In addition to her irritable bowel syndrome that plagued her, she was sure she had a stress-related ulcer as well. And she could feel the stress coming on.

Kit said, "Oh, sure."

"Jesus, *who* is that?" Julianna mumbled a little too loudly as she sat up straighter and stuck her chest out and made direct eye contact with Jared. Jared, whose female radar was always in effect, flashed his dazzling-white smile and swaggered over to give his personal greeting to Julianna. All the women on the patio (including Bridget, who hadn't been able to drag herself away) inadvertently fixated on the closest thing to a male supermodel they'd ever be seeing walking across the patio toward Julianna. The men, too, stared, a look of awe combined with obvious annoyance on their faces—all except Giorgio, who sat mesmerized, like a young schoolgirl gazing upon a crush.

"Huh, don't you think we look alike?" Lassino nodded in the direction of Jared before grunting at Kit.

She tore her eyes away from the Jared's brawny figure and said, "Uh, no."

Lassino looked a bit hurt and Kit hastily added, "Well, you both have blonde hair ..."

Before the beefy heartthrob could reach Julianna, who sat with bated breath, Carrie snapped, "*Jared!*" and jerked her head toward the kitchen.

"Oh ... yeah, sorry." He looked back somberly at Carrie, who appeared annoyed at him as well as at everyone else. "Nice to meet you. I'm Jared," he rattled in the vicinity of Julianna. He turned around and headed toward the kitchen, but not before swiping a couple of Twinkies off the table. Kit hurried behind them, with Lassino following her. Bridget retired to her room, and the party on the patio continued.

Kit set her prosecco glass down on the counter, and Kit asked with concern, "What's going on? Is everything all right?"

As Jared determinedly ripped open one of the Twinkies, Carrie shrieked dramatically, "Well, I've been absolutely traumatized tonight!"

Kit raised her eyebrows in alarm. "Oh, my God—what happened? Where were you?"

Carrie wiped the sweat drops from her forehead and answered with a heaving sigh, "At the disco."

Incredulously, Kit asked, "At the *disco?*" *At the disco?* It wasn't *that* scary of a place, although, on some occasions, she knew Bridget might beg to differ. What could've happened?

Lassino scowled and scratched his head as if thinking some deep thought, "Well, it *is* gay night at the disco."

Jared swallowed the last bite of his first Twinkie and piped in, "Gay night? Man, I never would've known! There were hot chicks *everywhere* tonight!"

"Hmm, *really?*" Lassino suddenly came alive with interest. Jared opened his eyes wide, whistled low, and said, "Uhhh, hell yeaahhh!"

Kit rolled her eyes and chuckled. "*Oh, God.*"

Attempting to be nonchalant, Lassino added, "Of course, nobody gay ever goes, except Giorgio. And he's here!"

Carrie stamped her foot impatiently and shouted, "Can we *please* get back to me?"

Kit bit her lip and said seriously, "Yes, yes, of course. Tell us."

"Well, for starters, my purse got stolen at the disco!" Carrie threw her hands up in the air. Before anyone had a chance to speak, Carrie whined,

"All I did was lay it down on the bar while I was dancing! Can you believe it! I never thought I'd be a victim of crime in *this* town! And of course, the bartender and the bouncers were of no help whatsoever!" She placed her hand on her heaving chest. Jared grimaced slightly, shook his head, and then shoved the second Twinkie into his mouth.

As much as she hated to feel bad for Carrie with her obnoxious drama, Kit did. Having your purse stolen in a foreign country had to rank up there with ... well, she couldn't think of anything comparable at the moment, but with something very, very, very bad. Kit thought of all the things she crammed into even the tiniest of her clutches: her cheap little digital camera, her phone, some cover-up, three to four different types of lip gloss, a few hairbands, and all her ... *money. Money. Oh, nooo.* Kit seriously hoped that Carrie's ATM card hadn't been in her purse, because if all her money was in her wallet and her ATM card was too, then ...

"I'm really sorry, Kit, but I just can't pay you now. All my money and my ATM card were in my wallet!" Carrie sobbed.

Kit closed her mouth, which she realized had been hanging open. This was so completely typical. Carrie hadn't paid for one single thing except her stupid miniature pizza a couple of nights ago, and now she would skip out on paying her share for the apartment. Kit felt terrible to even think it, but she wondered whether Carrie was telling the truth. She decided she wasn't about to let her off so easily.

"Well, are you sure you brought it to the disco? Maybe you left it at Jared's or in the back room?" Kit suggested hopefully.

"Of course, I had it! Why does this have to happen to *me*?" Carrie shrilly shrieked again. Lassino winced, plugged one of his ears with a finger, and took a sip of his drink. Jared coughed uncomfortably and added, "'Scuse me, I'm gonna get another Twinkie. Good stuff."

Kit racked her brain. The purse—or just the wallet—would be long gone, especially on a weekend, when people from Naples and neighboring towns from all over came to the popular dance club. What a minute, she had an idea, though ...

"Don't worry, Carrie. We can call and cancel your ATM card and you can get some money wired over, no problem. Then you'll be set for the rest of your stay."

Carrie snorted. "Oh, I'm not staying here any longer! Not only was my purse stolen, but I had my life threatened tonight as well! I'm going home!"

Lassino gave Kit a questioning look. Kit asked, "Are you serious? Who?"

"Luigi, that's who! He cornered Jared and me when we were leaving and threatened to kill us both for what we did to him behind his back!"

"Luigi?" Kit said in disbelief.

"Luigi? Which Luigi?" Lassino squinted. There was a plethora of Luigis in the town.

Kit explained, "*You know*, the one who delivers the fish and bottled water."

Lassino gave the Italian face-shrug and said, "Oh, yes, that Luigi is *pazzo*, crazy."

Carrie wailed, "Oh, my God, I knew it! I've got to get out of here!"

"Are you sure you heard him right? Was he speaking in English or Italian?" Kit asked, stalling for time.

"Kit, I took eight years of Italian. I know what the hell he said! He said how dare I use him and then sleep with an American in *his* town! And then he said he could kill both of us!"

"*Could* kill or *would* kill you?" Kit tried to reason.

Carrie stared at her in mock horror before rolling her eyes.

Kit backpedaled. "Well, I mean, it could've been a misunderstanding. Jared, did Luigi threaten you guys?" Kit asked as Jared walked back into the kitchen with a couple more Twinkies.

"The little crazy guy wearing the huge medallion? He came up and spit at my feet and then started ranting about something, but I have no idea. I know some Italian, but he was speaking way too fast for me. It was probably nothing." Jared tossed his head, dismissing the situation.

"Oh, really? Well, maybe you'd like to know that he specifically said he and his friends are going to personally cut off your balls!" Carrie spat out vitrolically as she stood with her hands on her hips.

Jared choked and then cleared his throat. "Maybe you should start packing. Yeah, or maybe it's about time for me to get back to L.A."

Carrie snickered bitterly. "Yeah, that's what I thought you'd say! I'd just love to know how Luigi found out about me and Jared!"

Lassino turned around, grabbed a pair of binoculars that stood on the shelf under the kitchen window, and said sarcastically, "You're living in a small town where everyone has a pair of binoculars in their house. What do you expect?" He tried squinting into the binoculars and, obviously unable to see anything, handed them off to Kit.

"I'm packing. I need to get the hell out of this godforsaken town! This is the absolute *worst* vacation I've ever been on! Jared, I'll be right back!" Carrie fumed as she swept out of the room.

Kit placed one hand over her eyes, sighed, and said, "Yes, it was a pleasure having you here, too." She never thought she'd want to leave Positano, but maybe getting out of town for a few days would be good. Thank God they were leaving for Scalea tomorrow. They would all relax and enjoy Diana and Leo's wedding. And Kit wouldn't have to worry about taking care of everyone else. No missing luggage, no crazy Italians threatening lives, no *anything*.

That is, until the next round of visitors showed up. Well, she was sure the other girls she worked with would be fine. There would be a group of them, and they'd be able to hang out together. They wouldn't expect her to be their personal event planner, would they? Kit didn't know them too well, but they seemed to all be really nice and *normal* girls. No drama at all, but they were young and … very *cute*. It was ridiculous of her to feel threatened. All of the girls had heard her crazy stories of her loony Italian romance with Lassino. None of them would take him seriously or touch him at all, for that matter. No, Kit wasn't worried about her co-workers. Lassino, on the other hand, well … she knew she was being ridiculously territorial and perhaps a tad jealous, but she'd kill Lassino if he hit on any of them! He wouldn't do that, would he? Kit's stomach rumbled again loudly. She glanced at Lassino and Jared who were both looking at her, a bit sympathetically too.

Jared spoke up uneasily. "Well, uh, I think I'm, uh, gonna take off. I think maybe it's better if I'm not seen with Carrie, if you know what I mean."

"You're going to leave her here? Without even saying good-bye? How's she going to get to the airport?" Carrie was annoying, but Jared was implicated in this whole thing too, since they'd practically been inseparable for the last couple of days. Plus, now Kit would be stuck having to cough up more money for a taxi. Oh, that was kind of bitchy of her, Kit thought remorsefully. She'd just have to suck it up as another unexpected travel expense. More and more of these seemed to be occurring.

Jared backed out through the kitchen door and onto the patio, and he groveled, "Uh, yeah, I am. Look, uh, just tell Carrie to … text me! Maybe I'll see her at the airport!" He turned to the rest of the party and spoke quickly. "Uh, ciao!" He closed the green door quickly behind him.

"Where's he going so fast?' Julianna called disappointedly from Mario's lap.

Kit replied dryly, "Home." She suddenly wished everyone else would take the hint as well.

"Well," Julianna answered, "too bad! Hey, why do you have binoculars?"

Kit sighed and answered, "Ask Lassino."

"Grazie! Buona notte!" Kit stood in the doorway and watched Giorgio and his entourage raucously traipse up the steps, Memo scampering ahead of them.

"Call me when you get back from Scalea!" Rachel yelled from the top of the steps, her cigarette glowing in the dark. Kit nodded and breathed a sigh of relief that Lassino hadn't left with them. He sat next to Mario, handed him a s'more, and mischievously said, "Mario, Kit wants you to try this!"

Mario took one and suspiciously sniffed it. "*Che cosa?* What is this?" Julianna grabbed it, broke it in half, and began suggestively feeding it to him. Mario choked, his face turning red.

"Oh, shit!" Julianna whacked him hard on the back, sending s'more bits flying.

"No more! Please!" Mario wheezed and then cleared his throat. He stood up and said, "Thank you, Kit. It was a wonderful party. I question the food, though. You Americans, are just so … American!" he joked as he shook his head.

"Well, thank you. I'll take that as a compliment, Mario!" Kit stated proudly. Mario put his arms around Kit, gave her the Italian kiss, and caressed her back (a little too long, Kit thought); his hands finally rested near her butt. She pulled away and looked at Lassino, who sat there, expressionless. Why would Mario, Lassino's best friend, do that, when he knew that she was with Lassino? Kit frantically wondered. Before she could think any more, Julianna grabbed Mario's arm and purred, "*Come on*, Mario. Are we gonna go for that walk down to the beach?"

He turned to Julianna, wiggled his bobble-head, and answered, "*Certo*, Bella. Are you ready?"

"Gimme me one minute, while I go freshen up!" Julianna called over her shoulder as she hurried down the hall to the bathroom.

Joe and Natalie stood in the doorway to their room. Natalie called, "Night, everyone! Kit, leave all the glasses and everything. We'll help with them in the morning." Joe looked over at Madison, who sat in the corner of the patio trying to blend in so she wouldn't miss anything, and said, "Come on, Maddie, bedtime. It's late."

"I'm not tired. I'm gonna go with Julianna and Mario," answered Madison matter-of-factly.

Mario raised his eyebrows with a slight look of panic, as Joe started to say, "No—"

"No, you're not, Sweetheart! Come on, Mario. I'm ready!" Julianna breezed back onto the patio, grabbed Mario's hand, and intertwined her fingers with his.

With a look of relief on his face, Mario called, "Buona notte!" as he pulled Julianna toward the door.

"Ciao! Night, everyone! Don't worry, Kit, I'll be all packed and ready to go tomorrow!" Julianna called as she stepped out the door. Madison sat glowering at the open doorway, a look of sheer pissiness on her face.

"Madison, come on. *Now*," Joe ordered. Madison stood up and walked silently past Lassino and Kit and in through the doorway. Joe rolled his eyes and put his arm around Natalie's shoulders, and then they turned and shut the door behind them. Kit shook her head and flopped down next to Lassino. Lassino shook his head and uttered, "She does not look thirteen."

"Don't get any ideas!" cried Kit with exasperation.

"Please, what do you think I am?" Lassino spoke disgustedly.

Kit didn't know anymore. She guessed he would leave now, too. Carrie charged onto the patio with her rolling suitcase in tow and stopped short in front of Lassino and Kit. Disingenuously, she apologized, "I'm really sorry about this, Kit, but I just can't stay when I feel my life is in danger! I'll get the money to you when you get home, I promise!"

Kit waved her off with a feeble, "Sure."

Carrie looked around in a sudden panic and asked, "Where's Jared?"

Great, now she would have to explain that to Carrie that she had been abandoned by Jared. Kit mumbled, "Uh, he left. He said he'd probably see you at the airport and to text him."

Carrie's eyes teared up as she blithered pathetically, "Oh, my God! I can't believe it. That asshole!" She sniffed and wiped her eyes.

"I'm sorry," said Kit wholeheartedly. What a mess. Once again, she felt like maybe, somehow, this was all her fault. If she hadn't gone out and invited all these extra people ... but no, she had absolutely no control over the *guys* in this town. Too bad she hadn't had this revelation any sooner. Lassino spoke up.

"Don't worry, I'll call Tino. He'll send a driver for you."

Lassino got on his cell, quickly called Tino, and spoke to him in his rapid Italian. Kit watched Lassino with gratefulness. He *was* so good. He hung up the phone, looked up, and said, "If you go right up the steps, the driver will be there. Don't worry about paying. It's all taken care of."

Carrie whimpered dramatically, "Thank you, Lassino, and ciao. Bye, Kit. I'll have the money ready for you when you get back." She reached over and awkwardly hugged Kit.

"All right, Carrie. Have a safe trip back. Hey, wait, I just thought of something. How are you going to pay to change your ticket if you have no credit cards?" Kit asked worriedly. Carrie certainly couldn't expect Lassino to pay for that.

Carrie stood in the doorway and looked at Kit as if she were an idiot. "Well, I'd never bring *all* my credit cards out with me! Thank God, I still have my mom's platinum check card. I'll just use that!" And with that, she left.

Kit fumed inwardly. If she didn't work with Carrie, she'd probably never see or hear from her again, Kit thought irritably. Of course, with the way things were going, Kit was sure she'd return to find out that Carrie had quit her teaching job at their school and had gone into hiding under the witness protection program, never to be seen or heard of again. Kit and Bridget would never see that money. As irritated as Kit felt, she'd have to vent later. She didn't want Lassino to hear her bitch over money, when he apparently thought she was made out of it.

She looked wearily over at Lassino, stared at him, and pointedly asked, "So, are you leaving too?"

He smiled and answered flippantly, "Of course."

Kit thought it was now or never. She walked over to where he was sitting and bent over him so her face was inches away from his. At least with his blindness, he'd be able to read her lips. She stated seriously, "I'm not waiting any longer, Lassino. You're taking me with you to your place." And with that, she kissed him, almost defiantly.

He looked at her just as seriously, and to her surprise, he answered, "All right, Amor. *Andiamo.*"

Chapter 10

Kit lay blissfully back against the barrage of pillows. Not only were Lassino's sheets undoubtedly a luxurious thread count of 600-plus, she was actually *here* in his bed being happily ravaged for the umpteenth time. How long had she gone without this? Too ridiculously long of a time. She thought she might definitely have made up for it in the last hour, though.

Lassino was taking a quick breather and laughed into her ear, "I thought you were tired."

When Lassino had turned on the TV and asked if she wanted to watch a *Friends* rerun, she'd walked right past him and into the bedroom, saying she was too tired to watch anything. *Friends?* Right now? And a rerun to boot? Please. Well, Kit *was* exhausted. Playing hostess, as well as trying to decipher the cryptic Positano male code, had turned out to be a little more than she had bargained for. If she and Lassino had watched any TV at all, she really would have fallen asleep, and that was not what she had come here for.

"I *was* tired. It was a long day, with the party planning and Carrie's drama." Kit smiled demurely at him. In the dim light, Kit could see Lassino smirk at her, as he grunted, "Yes, you are too *tired* ... to do anything to *me*, and you make me do all the work! You are very selfish!"

As he kissed her neck, Kit gasped in mock surprise. "Me? Selfish? I am nothing but nice to you all the time! You should be doing whatever I want you to do, with the way you treat me!"

Lassino chuckled and quipped, "Oh, are you going to break my balls now? Tired? Ha! Not only are you a bad liar, but you are rude *and* selfish!"

Once again, Kit wondered, why did she have to be attracted to such an immature weirdo? Well, this wasn't the time to ponder over that. She wasn't going to let him ruin this with his crazy ranting. Before Lassino could say anything else, Kit bit her lip gently and cooed, "Lassino, well, maybe I am being a little selfish. It's just been *so* long, and I'm really happy to be here, and you are *very* good at … *this*." Lassino quickly took his head out of her neck to squint interestedly at her. Kit cheesily raised her eyebrows at him. Aha, it had worked—although, in reality, she wasn't just saying that to appease him. Kit meant every word of what she'd just said.

"I am?" he asked, a surprised grin on his face. For a moment, Lassino looked so vulnerable and slightly unsure of himself. It was so refreshing and so *cute*. Kit had known all along, most of his craziness was just an act. She ran her hands through his Kerastassed tresses, and said, "Yes."

"Ha! I knew I was the best!" Lassino shouted. Kit grimaced. Well, so much for his humble insecurities. That was okay; she didn't like her men like that anyway. Besides, he was slowly inching his mouth down her torso again. With all his lunacy, Kit would let it go right now. She was content with letting Lassino do what he wanted with her as long as he kept doing it. She curled her toes and sighed contentedly. She was going to sleep in after this. They could all catch a later train to Scalea. Besides, she hadn't even packed her bag yet. She arched her back and drew her breath in sharply as she closed her eyes.

Wait a minute; *what* was *that*? No, no, not *now*. Ughh, it was her cell phone ringing. Kit knew it was hers, because Lassino's cell had some stupid Bryan Adams ringtone. Who would ever have thought he'd be into cheesy love songs of the '80s and '90s? Kit squeezed her eyes tightly shut and did her best to ignore the repetitive ringing. It was four thirty in the morning. Who the hell could be calling right now, at this particular moment? It absolutely had to be a wrong number.

"Are you going to answer your phone?" Lassino's muffled voice came from underneath the covers.

She answered and groaned, "No, nobody would ever be calling me at this time."

"What about Ronnie?" Lassino's voice came from what seemed a galaxy far away.

"Who?" Kit asked as her phone continued to annoyingly ring.

"Your *boyfriend*, Ronnie. Isn't that his name?"

Did he always have to make a dig about Johnny? Oh, like she was the *only* one to have had a fling last summer? Lassino, of all people, should talk! However, the old saying, "*Helloo, pot calling the kettle black!*" probably wouldn't translate quite well right now.

Kit sighed. "His name is *Johnny*, and he wouldn't be calling me at this time or *ever*, since I broke up with him a year ago. I already told you that!" And with that, the irksome phone ringing ended. Gosh, Kit thought worriedly, she hoped it *hadn't* been Johnny. It couldn't have been, could it? But that would be so typical for him to dial her when she was in the middle of ... *this*. But maybe he was in Italy somewhere and was in trouble (his Italian was pretty horrible—maybe he'd accidentally insulted someone!) and he had gotten her cell number from her mom (of course) and ... Kit's muscles tensed and she felt her stomach start churning. Oh no, this was not the time for her intestinal problems to kick in.

Lassino popped his head out from under the covers. He gently laid a hand upon one of her thighs and smiled. "Relax, Kit. I was only joking, amor." He threw the covers over his head and began kissing her right below her navel. Kit exhaled. And then Lassino's phone rang.

From under the covers, she heard him utter, "*Son of a beach!*" He threw the covers off and fumbled around in the direction of his nightstand. Kit knew Lassino would answer it. Maybe it was Monica or some other international love interest. Or maybe it was ...

"It's Natalie. She wants to talk to you," he said and thrust the phone at her. Natalie? Oh no, this couldn't be good. Kit sat up and bobbled the phone as she tried to pull the covers up and under her armpits.

"Natalie? Is everything all right?" *Is everything all right?* This was fast becoming one of Kit's most overly used expressions, she thought pensively.

"Kit!" Natalie's voice sounded frantic. "Madison's missing!"

Kit stared at the bedspread in utter bewilderment. "*What?* What do you mean *missing?*"

"I got up to go to the bathroom, and she wasn't in her bed or anywhere in the apartment. Her little backpack is gone, and she went through my purse! I found it out on the kitchen table with everything all over the place, and all the money in my wallet is gone and so is her passport!" Natalie exhaled loudly into the phone as if she was trying to catch her breath.

Kit's eyes were wide. "Oh, my God! I'll be right there!" She looked over at Lassino, who was staring at her with a look of perplexity. Before Kit could hang up, Natalie sobbed, "Kit, I am so sorry! Joe and I just didn't know what to do! Oh, my God, where could she be?"

Kit was quick to answer. "Nat, it's okay. I'm glad you called me. That's what I'm here for. This is a small town. We'll find her, okay? All right, I'm leaving right now, bye." Kit could still hear Natalie's sniffles as she hung up.

"What happened? Who are you going to find?" Lassino asked as he turned on the lamp on the nightstand.

Kit swung her legs out of the bed and grabbed her bra from the floor, then answered tersely, "Madison. She ran away."

Skeptically, Lassino asked, "What do you mean she ran away? Ran away where?"

Kit fastened her bra and then fumbled around looking for her pants. She didn't have time to explain. Who knew where Madison was at this moment? She hoped she was still in Positano. Kit answered impatiently, "I *mean*, she's gone! She *ran* away. Her backpack's gone and so is her passport *and* Natalie's money from her purse!"

Lassino was incredulous. "Why would she run away?"

Kit sighed and closed her eyes. Apparently, no one ever ran away in Positano. And if they did, they'd never get too far, what with the whole binoculars-in-every-home thing and intrusive town grapevine. Well, hopefully, this would work to their advantage in the search for Madison.

Kit opened her eyes, and her voice cracked as she shouted, "I don't know why she'd run away, Lassino! She's a messed-up little girl with a lot of problems, okay? Look, I can't stand around explaining it right now. I need to get back to the apartment to help find her!"

Lassino shrugged as if to say, *Okay, okay* and put his glasses on. Then he quickly grabbed a T-shirt off a chair and earnestly said, "I will call Tino and Tomaso. I'll drop you off. You should wait at the apartment with Natalie while we go out and look for her."

Kit blinked at him through teary eyes and whispered, "Okay."

◆　　◆　　◆

"Mommy, where's Madison?" Joey asked innocently as he climbed onto Natalie's lap.

Wearily, Natalie spoke. "I don't know, Sweetie. Daddy and the boys are out looking for her."

They all sat around the patio staring at Kit's cell phone, which sat on the glass table amid the burned-out tea lights and the leftover Twinkies. It was now eleven thirty in the morning, and Madison had yet to turn up.

After calling Tomaso and Tino, Lassino and his friends had scoured the beachfront restaurants and bars and had done a once-over at the disco, asking everyone if they remembered seeing a girl matching Madison's description. The only lead they had so far was that Madison had been spotted approximately around four a.m. on the beach with some males, whom, according to the locals, were *not* from Positano.

While Kit was glad they had uncovered that bit of information, she felt a certain amount of foreboding dread. On Saturday nights, the disco swarmed with people who'd driven in from miles around, including the huge metropolis of Naples. If Madison had taken off with people from Naples, they might never find her again. The city itself was monstrous in size and population, not to mention dangerous for anyone, let alone a mere thirteen-year-old. The more time went by, the more risk of Madison getting farther away.

Kit knew Madison to be a little more street smart and, ahem, "worldly" than other girls her age, but how long would she be able to fend for herself in another country? Kit involuntarily shuddered. What if Madison was in Naples at this moment being unwittingly sucked into a life of drugs and prostitution under the Camorra? Kit's eyes teared up for the bazillionth time that morning. She just felt so awful for poor Natalie, who *so* did not need this. This was yet another thing that wasn't supposed to have happened.

Kit sighed. Now she was going to have to miss Diana and Leo's wedding, too. She and Bridget and Julianna were supposed to be on a train to Scalea in an hour and a half. Bridget and Julianna were already packed, but Kit hadn't been able to put herself to that task. In her mind, leaving for Scalea was just not an option. There was no way she could leave Natalie and Joe if Madison was still missing. Kit knew Positano and the people better than they did and would be able to lend her help somehow, if not at least for some emotional support.

Besides, Kit knew herself as well. She wouldn't be able to concentrate on enjoying the wedding at all, not if she was distracted by the drama they'd left behind in Positano. Yes, the girls would just have to go without her. Kit hated to disappoint Diana, but she'd understand. At least, she hoped so. If not, she'd have another person to add to her ever-growing list of disgruntled friends/acquaintances/co-workers.

The sound of Joey's serious little voice interrupted Kit's thoughts and the silence that had enveloped the whole patio. "Mommy, is Madison in trouble?'

Natalie rubbed her eyes, looked down at Joey, and said, "Yes, yes, she is." She covered Joey's ears, looked at the girls, and added in a low voice, "And if she does turn up, she better be dead, because I'm going to kill her!"

Although they all sympathized with Natalie to the utmost, no one quite knew how to respond to the comment, and once again, they all fell silent and stared off in different directions. The glittery Mylar stars waved slightly in the warm breeze. Somewhere far above the apartment came the obnoxious crowing of the town rooster. Kit and Bridget had long become to accustomed to its incessant strangled-sounding crowing regardless of what time it was. Bridget snorted as Julianna scowled and asked, "What is up with the freaky roosters around here?"

"Another town mystery. They're crazy. You know, kind of like the men around here," Kit sarcastically replied.

Bridget cleared her throat and said, "Aside from the rooster, it's so quiet; how about a little music?"

"Sure," Kit answered. "Just keep it a little low, in case Lassino calls with some news."

Bridget nodded, put her good foot down first, and then carefully stood. Exhausted from the long night and from talk of the runaway, they all solemnly stared at Bridget's eggplant-colored foot, which actually looked slightly less mutant this morning. Bridget noted the girls' rapt attention to her foot, raised her eyebrows and picked up a few of the defunct tea lights, and then added, "I'm going to start cleaning, too. The kitchen reeks of alcohol."

Kit called after her, "Oh, Bridget, just leave it. It'll get done later." Especially if she was going to stay behind with Natalie and Joe, Kit thought wryly. She'd need something to do to pass the time. But oh, how she dreaded telling the girls she wouldn't be leaving with them.

"No, no. It's okay. I'd rather be doing something than sitting around waiting for your cell to ring. Let's just hope the smell of alcohol doesn't make me completely vomit!" They all chuckled. After their marathon drinking,

Bridget had gone to bed and remained passed out, almost corpselike, through all the early-morning drama. Used to waking up early, no matter how late she was up the previous evening or how many drinks it had entailed, she had been surprised to find everyone up *before* her, and it was only seven! She was soon informed that none of them had actually slept at all due to the disastrous turn of events.

From the kitchen, the sounds of bottles being dumped into the garbage mingled with Madonna's disco-infused "Get Together" coming from the iPod speakers: "It's all an illusion; there's too much confusion …"

Kit sighed and then asked dryly, "Too much confusion. Gee, do ya think Madonna's been to Positano?"

Natalie winced, looked desperately at Kit and Julianna, and exclaimed, "I didn't mean what I said about Madison being dead and all. I'm just so worried and so … angry with her!"

"Natalie, we know. It's okay," Kit sympathized as she patted her hand gently.

Julianna pulled a few bobby pins out of her hair and stabbed them back in her updo, then declared, "Well, I wouldn't blame you for killing her! The same thing happened with my little sister. She went missing for two weeks, and we didn't know where she was. It was about five years ago. You might remember. It was on the news and everything."

She paused dramatically, and Kit asked, "What happened? Where was she?"

Julianna continued. "Oh, we found out she was staying with some friends and totally partying it up, drinking, doing God knows what, just having a great old time, while we were all worried sick about her, the little shit!"

"Oh, that's awful. So what ended up happening?" Natalie was plainly stricken.

"My mom and I dragged her ass out of that house and took her back home," Julianna answered matter-of-factly. "And then we all found out she was pregnant, and that took care of that! Having a baby put a dent in her wild streak! Well, for a while, at least." Julianna pursed her glossily lacquered lips.

Natalie shook her head, placed Joey on the floor, and said, "Go play, honey, and maybe we'll go to the beach later on."

Joey wandered to a far corner of the patio and rummaged through his toys. Natalie looked at the girls and cried, "I know we set limits for Madison that she doesn't like, but she needs them. We have been so good to her. Why would she do something like this?"

"Natalie, she's just being a stupid, selfish kid. She didn't get her way when you told her she couldn't try the prosecco or go to the disco, and she's being a little brat to get back at you. I know she's been through a lot with her mom, but it's not an excuse anymore!" Kit fumed.

Julianna nodded her head in agreement. "Yeah, Natalie, she's a scheming little bitch! Sorry, I know she's your niece and all, but I saw the wickedness in her last night! I tell you, I know what I saw!" She continued in her crackly voice, "I'm not lying when I say that the little tramp was totally trying to go after Mario, and I wasn't about to let that happen!" Julianna pounded the table with her fist, which sent Twinkies flying. "You know, when she wanted to go out with me and Mario, and I said no, go to bed! I mean, I was nice then, but I'm not gonna be nice now!"

Natalie gasped, horrified. "Oh, God, I can't believe this! But ... but ... Mario's in his thirties!"

"It's true. I was watching her the whole time, Nat. I'm telling you, Madison needs help. It's so completely inappropriate for a thirteen-year-old to be flirting with a thirty-four-year-old," Kit stated in disgust.

"Well, that's why I made sure that Mario took that walk with me to the beach. I *had* to get him away from *her*," Julianna chimed in.

Kit raised her eyebrows with a smile. "Are you telling me if Madison hadn't been trying to hone in on him, you *wouldn't* have left with him?"

Julianna cackled coyly, "Oh, I still would've gone with him! His teeth and hair are a little jacked, but if he fixes his grill and puts some gel in his hair, he's not too bad, girls!"

Bridget poked her head out of the kitchen, waved a dishrag at them, and called, "Well, I bet Madison is planning on staying in hiding, or wherever she is, until you and Joe leave. Then as soon as you're gone, she'll show up at the apartment and expect to hang out with us for the rest of the trip!"

"Do you think ..." Natalie's voice trailed off.

Kit spat out, "Well, you can be sure that I'm going to be waiting here to beat her little ass, the inconsiderate little ... little ..."

Julianna finished Kit's sentence for her. "Oh, for God's sake, just say it, Kit: the little bitch!"

"Well … yeah!" conceded Kit.

"I'm telling you," Julianna said and pointed at Natalie, "that girl needs to go to boot camp. You know, one of my clients had to do that with her son. Some big, black man came in the middle of the night and kidnapped him for boot camp!"

"Oh, yeah, I saw that guy on Oprah!" Kit said as she picked Gina up.

Natalie put her head in her hands and murmured, "Oh, God, you're probably right. I can't take this anymore. At least now Joe knows what the situation with Madison is really like."

Kit's cell phone rang, and they all stared at it with startled looks on their faces.

"Here, give the baby to me while you get the phone!" Julianna jumped up and took Gina from Kit's arms. Bridget came out onto the patio, and Natalie sat on the edge of her chair as Kit grabbed it off the table.

"Hello?" she tentatively answered.

Lassino spoke rapidly. "No one has seen Madison. We have to talked to *everyone!*" Kit knew he wasn't exaggerating, either. Lassino, Tino, and Tomaso were probably three of the best people to tap into the Positano grapevine, and they had done so nonstop for the last six hours. Lassino didn't wait for Kit to respond. "Tino, he has to get to his shop, and Tomaso has to be down at the beach, so I am going to take Joe to the *carbinieri,* okay?"

"To the *police?* To make a report already?" Kit turned and walked over to the balcony, so as to avoid the look of sheer alarm that would be written all over Natalie's face.

"Yes, he has to make a report! She's missing! Look, the carbinieri may need to get involved, and they will want to ask Joe questions about Madison, why she would run away, all that sort of thing," explained Lassino impatiently.

"And then what? Lassino, they're all supposed to leave in a few days!" Kit turned around and found six pairs of eyes fixated on her. She shrugged at the girls as Lassino grumbled on, "And then, we're going to probably have to go to Naples to make a report with the police there." He heard Kit inhale sharply and then added more calmly, "It's just a formality, probably won't be necessary, but I'll need to go to help translate for Joe."

She couldn't believe this was happening. Kit looked out over the balcony and stared at the violet-hued water until it became blurry. "Kit! Are you still there?" screamed Lassino.

"Yes, yes! Okay, just tell me what I can do to help. I want to do something, anything," she pleaded.

"Tell me, what time do you need a car to pick you and the girls up today?" Why he was asking this *now*, Kit had no idea. She frowned and answered, "In about an hour, but I'm not going. I just can't, not while all this is going on. The girls can go without me."

Kit watched as Bridget's eyes grew wide and Julianna shouted, "Kit, you can't miss Diana's wedding!"

Natalie added sternly, "Kit, please don't miss the wedding on account of us. I'd feel terrible!"

Kit plugged her free ear with two fingers and turned back out toward the water as Lassino ranted into her other ear, "Don't be stupid!"

Great, now he was going to yell at her. She wished she wasn't so used to his weird caveman speech impediment. Then his insults would just roll right off her. Unfortunately, she was quite capable of deciphering what he was saying, and how dare he! Kit's stomach tightened in response.

"Stop yelling at me! Why is *that* being stupid?" Kit shouted back as she angrily yanked down one of the dangling silver stars. His voice echoed in her ear, "How can you be a teacher and be so dumb? Look, you wanted to help, so I am telling you … leave Positano!"

He was crazy. Why did he have to be so mean to her? "What? How is *that* going to help?"

Lassino muttered in Italian—fortunately, she assumed, in words she hadn't learned in her Italian classes. He fumed, "What are you gonna do? There is *nothing* more you can possibly do to help! Go to your friend's wedding!"

Kit stammered, "But … but …"

"Kit," Lassino spoke slowly and in a much gentler voice, "I guarantee Madison is probably asleep in someone's house right now. She'll have to get up sooner or later and come out, and someone will see her."

Kit sniffed and wiped her eyes. "But what if she doesn't? What if we can't find her?"

Lassino replied coolly, "Then I suggest Natalie leave with the kids as scheduled, and Joe should stay here. We'll all be here to help out." He paused and then added, "And then, if you feel like you need to come back to help Joe, then come back."

"Okay," Kit mumbled weakly, her anger subsiding for now. It was no use arguing with Lassino. You never could win. Plus, everyone would agree with him, she just knew it. They'd all gang up on her and make her feel like she was selfish to miss Diana's wedding, when all she was trying to do more than anything was help. That's *all* she'd wanted to do this whole trip—for everyone. Oh, to heck with it. Maybe she *should* leave before anything else happened.

"Good. Tino will send a driver to pick you up at the top of the stairs in *one* hour. And *don't* be late!" There was an abrupt dial tone in Kit's ear, which signaled that Lassino was done with the coversation. Kit turned around to face her friends.

Natalie asked slowly, "What did Lassino say to do?"

"Are you staying here?" Bridget questioned anxiously.

"You *cannot* miss the wedding because of some little bimbo!" Julianna cried as she shook her head vehemently. She turned and added apologetically to Natalie, "Sorry, Natalie."

"No offense taken. *Please*, Kit. Tell me you're going to Scalea," Natalie pleaded.

Kit thought if ever there was a time when she needed to put on her happy face, it was now. She would just have to keep telling herself that everything was going to work out fine. Plus, she really was so tired of everyone being irritated with her. If she gave in this time, everyone would be happy. She wouldn't be, of course, but nobody seemed too worried about that. Kit determined that until Madison was found (and hopefully alive and well), her anxiousness would have its way with her, so she might as well brace herself. Gee, she couldn't *wait* to get to Scalea, where she'd be popping her Rolaids nonstop and running to the bathroom every five minutes. The last thing she wanted to do in Italy was spend her precious time stuck in a bathroom! Well, at least there'd be a bidet.

And more importantly, she'd be there for Diana, who really needed some love from her compatriots. It appeared, from Diana's last e-mail, that having your wedding in Italy wasn't so much fun when you weren't actually from there and your mother-in-law to-be was calling all the shots. Kit would have to channel her worry into helping Diana get through this.

Kit smiled brightly and said, "Well, I've been told in no uncertain terms that there's nothing more I can do to help. Lassino is sure Madison is here somewhere and will show up. So, in the meantime, Natalie, just be ready to leave as planned. And I am going to throw my bag together, because the driver will be here in an hour to pick us all up."

Before she'd have to listen to anyone's comments, Kit rushed past them. She had no idea what she was going to pack, but that was definitely going to have to wait, as she beelined it to the bathroom.

+   +   +

Bridget leaned her head against the train window. Even in the somewhat air-conditioned car, it was the nearest and coldest thing she could find to lay her throbbing head and flushed face against. It didn't quite give the same comforting sensation as did lying face-down on a cool, tiled floor (preferably in close proximity to a toilet), but it would have to do. How much longer to Scalea? They'd been jostling along for at least two and a half hours, so they should be there soon, she fervently hoped. Nevertheless, she should start praying anyway. Her two most popular mantras were asking for forgiveness for the evils of excessive drinking and pleading to escape from having to turn her lovely Marc Jacobs satchel into a glorified barf bag. Bridget breathed in and out, short, shallow breaths. The other girls were sitting across from her, and she heard Julianna loudly whisper to Kit, "Is Bridget all right? She doesn't look so good!"

Bridget kept her eyes closed and pretended to be asleep. The last thing she wanted to do was chitchat over the embarrassing fact that she was thirty-four and had managed, quite well, thank you, to get so ripped the night before that she actually felt extremely ill right now. Quite a feat since she hadn't harbored such vomitous feelings since frequenting SAE bar nights in college. Why did *she* appear to be the only one feeling like total crap? Everyone else had been drinking a lot, too. At least she had thought so.

Up until their hasty departure, which had been inevitably caused by Kit's rendevouz with the bathroom and last-ditch packing, Bridget had felt better than all right. Once again, she had surprised herself by staying up until 3:00 a.m. and still waking up after only four hours of sleep. She guessed she hadn't had much time to pay attention to the toxic state of her poor body. Lack of real sleep, as well as being immediately consumed, like everyone else, with the whole runaway situation, and then throwing herself into the total post-party cleanup had most definitely taken her mind off of herself. With all the morning commotion, she couldn't remember if she'd even eaten. Oh, yes, there'd been that hasty spoonful of Nutella and a warm Coca-Cola Light. Bridget ruefully assessed that teaming *that* concoction with the smell of dishwashing liquid and stale alcohol wasn't the best cure for a hangover. However, she'd made it—they'd all finally made it—upstairs to meet their driver.

"Oohh, I wonder if Greg's gonna drive us? How do I look?' Julianna had called as they approached the last few steps of the narrow staircase. The lack of material on the thigh-high, strapless, white terry-cloth sundress, coupled with Julianna's signature high-heeled cork wedges, caused Kit to exclaim, "I'm not gonna lie. It definitely shows off your *assets*. You better make sure no men are walking behind you when you take the stairs in that sundress."

Julianna stopped, turned around, and admitted slyly, "Girl, if you got it, flaunt it! Don't tell anyone, but this isn't a sundress. It's actually a beach cover-up."

Kit laughed. "Why am I not surprised?"

Julianna cried, "Come on, it's Italy! If you can't get away with wearing this here, you ain't never gonna wear it."

Bridget trudged behind Kit and dragged her bag after her. She believed that Julianna could most likely get away with wearing something like that anywhere. She certainly didn't need Italy's permission to do so. At the top of the staircase, they stepped onto the curb and were relieved to find that the driver Tino sent had not been deterred by their tardiness. Bridget, used to waiting around for Kit, sometimes for a good hour or so, was amazed that they were only a mere twenty minutes behind schedule. Actually, according to Italian standards, this was probably considered punctual. Still, she was grateful that the driver was there and that they wouldn't have to bother Tino once again.

The tall, swarthy driver leaned against the standard black Mercedes used by the local taxi companies, in a white, short-sleeved oxford and navy dress pants, and looked up from the sunglasses he was buffing on his shirt. De-sunglassed, he appeared momentarily blinded by the sight of Julianna in her short, white dress and Kit in her teensy, red bikini top and denim miniskirt, thus causing him to stop short and blink a few times. Kit and Bridget blinked back. It was none other than oily-headed, furry-chested Vinnie, who worked at the restaurant they always passed on their way down the hill. He smiled a yellow smile at them and hurriedly grabbed their bags from them.

"So, do you know my friend Greg?" Bridget heard Julianna's raspy voice chirp as she lifted her case up and onto the sidewalk. Julianna turned back to the girls and whispered, "Girls, who wants to call shotgun?"

When neither of the girls answered right away, she said excitedly, "Oh, well, then, I guess I'll have to sit next to him." Julianna raised her eyebrows a few times.

Bridget rolled her suitcase over to Vinnie, who was already sweating in his attempt to position the other cumbersome pieces in the trunk. She crawled into the backseat and immediately descended into nauseousness. She had not escaped from the dreaded delayed hangover. The car wasn't even moving yet, either, so she couldn't claim it was carsickness. Exhausted and disgusted with herself for once again overdoing it, Bridget's mood quickly turned dark and gloomy. She was done communicating with anyone, and she lapsed into a silence that she would keep the duration of the car and train trip to Calabria.

Bridget sighed a little too loudly and laid her head back as Julianna, up in the front seat, coquettishly interrrogated Vinnie. "So, Vinnie, are you from Positano? Really? Oh, you lived in New York for a while? Hmmm … sooo, what do ya think of American women?" and so on.

Bridget remained silent as she watched the driver's eyes in the rearview mirror constantly watching Kit in the backseat. Another man checking out Kit. That was par for the course. Did they always have to be so obvious, though? She slunk lower in her seat and tried to tune out the incessant talking as the car came to a slow stop behind the Positano city bus. Bridget glanced out the window and watched people clamber off the bus. She stared blankly at the crooked old women carrying plastic-bagged groceries in one arm, their Prada purses draped over their other arm, and mothers leading their small children off for a leisurely day at the beach. Then came the tons of tourists, who no doubt hadn't yet realized how small the town really was and that they were were better off just walking the hill or risking the stairs.

Bridget was suddenly appreciative that although Positano would always have an undescribable, beguiling quality to it, a chaotic randomness, it was still a comfortable place for her. She could wander around quite aimlessly without looking or feeling like a complete tourista transplant.

She smiled slightly, in spite of herself, and felt a twinge of pity as she watched a guy in a visor and Ray-Bans pull out a map from his backpack. A *map* of Positano? Of course, she knew they existed, but she'd never used one. The town was so small that even Bridget, with her lack of navigational skills, could practically have a bag over her head and still be able to find her way around. Could you really get lost when all roads, staircases, and alleys eventually led to the beach or up the hill and out of town? Well, she did recall a time when she and Kit hadn't known where Lassino's restaurant was. All along, it had only been right across the street from their hotel. They'd sure come along way since then.

Bridget paid curious attention as the guy with the map scratched his head and sat against his wheeled suitcase, and then looked, rather confusedly, up and down the street as people bustled around him. Where was the poor guy from? The map was a dead giveaway that he was a visitor, but so was his very un-Positanolike ensemble. Bridget critically scanned his get-up: running shoes with white sport socks, khaki cargo shorts, a T-shirt sporting something about Spokane. What was someone from *Spokane* doing here on the Amalfi Coast? She could only imagine he was *from* there, since Spokane seemed unlikely to be a hot vacationing spot from which to purchase souvenir tees. Bridget had never been anywhere near Spokane. She'd only heard about it from Kit. Because of its small, hick-town feel, Kit was forever calling it Spokeyville or Spookyville or something like that after her trips to visit Johnny. Probably the only person Bridget knew from Spokane was Johnny. Ha! *Johnny* in Positano? Never.

At the thought of that, Bridget shook her head vehemently, as if she had some kind of tick. She snuck a look at the supposed Spokie on the curb across from her car window. From behind her super-dark glasses, Bridget thought that *now* that she was actually scrutinizing him, it certainly *looked* like Johnny. Wait, uh-oh. Actually, it *was* Johnny. Noooo, it couldn't be! But he was waving wildly at her, with a huge smile on his face, as if he knew her and had, perhaps, dated her best friend. She was hallucinating from dehydration, no? She yanked her glasses up and gawked. It *was* Johnny. She looked quickly at Kit, who for some reason was busily quizzing Vinnie about Italian holidays and asked him, "So, do you have the Easter Bunny here in Italy?'

What the hell was Kit talking about? Bridget swiveled her head to look out the window to find that Johnny was walking toward the Mercedes!

Bridget turned back to Kit and opened her mouth to say something but then closed it, unsure of what to do. Did Kit need something like *this* right now? The tour bus in front of them pulled over to the side, and Vinnie changed gears and shot out and around the bus, which caused a few pedestrians to scramble back onto the sidewalks. He answered Kit's question. "We do not have Easter Bunny here. We have a rat."

A rat? Bridget was temporarily confused by both Johnny being here in Positano and the scary notion of an Easter *rat.*

She quickly turned around to look out the back window. Johnny stood limply waving, becoming smaller as the car drove on, veering up Via C. Colombo. Bridget gave a pathetic little half-wave back, then turned around and pulled her sunglasses down. She'd wait until they were a ways out of Positano and her hangover had passed to tell Kit.

◆　　◆　　◆

And here they were on the train, three hours later, and Bridget felt no better. She clearly was not up for speaking right now, as the probability of projectile vomiting was very possible. Breaking the news to Kit would have to be further postponed until they were safely in Scalea.

Bridget knelt down in the pew carefully. The wedding Mass of Leo and Diana was coming to a close. Communuion had just ended, and without much of a warning. The girls had waited and waited for the rows ahead of them to head up for Communion, but hardly anyone did. Bridget shrugged at Kit and scooted past the people in their pew to make her way up aisle. By the time she and Kit had gotten out of the pew, the priest already packed up the Blessed Sacrament in the tabernacle and closed it, which left Bridget and Kit standing awkwardly in the aisle. Sheepishly, they again climbed over the stoic-looking Italians and conceded to the obligatory post-Communion kneeling.

Well, if she couldn't receive Communion, she had better at least kneel down and pray. Bridget could name a few things she'd like to pray for and about anyway. First, she'd thank God that Madison had been found and was all right. No sooner had they arrived in Scalea, than Kit had gotten a call from Lassino saying the police had found Madison sleeping on a chaise on Fornillo Beach. The details of her whereabouts from the evening before were still a mystery, but no harm had come to her, and that included her bitchy attitude. Apparently, she was as sulky and defiant as ever.

After talking to Lassino, Kit called Natalie and advised her, "I'm telling you, Nat, you and Joe better sleep with your bed across the door for the next few nights! Make sure she's on that plane with you!"

They'd been on pins and needles the next three days, expecting to get another call from the Positano Runaway Patrol, but none had come. They exhaled as they realized that meant that the family'd made it safely onto the SFO-bound plane and that Positano would be spared from further unnecessary American drama.

Bridget's second prayer was brief as well. She hoped her mom, sister, and grandma were all right. She really must call to check in. Things had been so bizarre, and no one had wanted to tie up the cell phone the last few days. She hoped the house wasn't in a total state of disarray. She'd remind Annie to check the cushions of her mom's chair for unauthorized hidden snacks.

Last, Bridget asked for a little divine assistance in what to do regarding the Johnny sighting. She still hadn't told Kit. There just never seemed to be the right time. Since they'd gotten to Scalea, they'd either been consoling Diana through her traumatic pre-wedding jitters, or they'd been preoccupied with the drama back in Positano. Kit either had the phone practically attached to her ear, or, well … or … Kit had been spending considerable time in the bathroom. Her irritable bowel syndrome had certainly been kicked up a few notches. Bridget knew the stress Kit was feeling must be pretty bad, since even with her problematic stomach, she almost never had issues with the food in Italy.

What was Johnny doing in Italy? Bridget remembered Kit leaving that phone message about Johnny being here, but she hadn't thought much of it. Of course, why *couldn't* he come to Italy if he wanted to? It wasn't like Kit and Bridget owned the country. But why Positano, of all places? The mere mention of the town would hit a nerve with Johnny. Besides, he and Kit hadn't even spoken for months. How would he know *when* they'd be there and where to find them? It's not like Kit had sent an e-mail to him with their travel itinerary. Bridget knew Kit was prone to zealously overextending herself, but would she really have invited Johnny to Positano, thinking he wouldn't show up, when after all, he was totally still in love with her? Yes, of course she would. *Oh, Kit.*

Even so, Bridget was plagued with uncertainty. Kit was so totally on edge that this would completely unhinge her for sure. Still, Bridget didn't want to be dishonest. Should she tell her later on at the reception, after everyone had a few drinks? Or should she just assume that Johnny would probably be gone by the time they got back to Positano?

Nobody ever stayed in Positano for as long as *they* did. He was sure to be long gone by then, right? Then Bridget would tell Kit about how she'd randomly seen Johnny, and they'd have a good chuckle. Yes, she'd wait to tell Kit. Bridget finished off her prayers with an "Amen" and blessed herself, oblivious to the fact that she had, for once, forgotten to mention anything about her weight in her prayers.

Kit stood at the edge of the stone patio amid all the wedding guests, adjusted her Nikon lens, and snapped away as Diana and Leo cut into the wedding cake, a tower of intricately designed, cream-colored balls of marzipan. With each snap of her high-powered digital camera, people standing nearby looked at her curiously, wondering if she was the actual wedding photographer. Kit clicked backward to check how the pictures were, and she was pleased to find that they were better than good. The lighting, the angles, the spontaneity of the shots were perfect, if she did say so herself. Maybe if she got sick of the whole teaching gig—and she was getting pretty darn close—she could fall back on photography. You could probably make a lot of money being a wedding photographer in Italy. Definitely something to think about.

Julianna took a sip of her champagne and seductively smiled at one of the groomsmen as he passed by, his athletically honed posterior complemented by perfectly fitting, navy-blue pinstriped pants, accompanied by an undoubtedly expensive navy shirt and dotted silk tie. As soon as he was out of earshot, she hissed, "Kit, gimme your camera; gimme your camera! I'm gonna take a picture of his butt!"

She grabbed Kit's camera before she could answer, and she click-clacked across the patio, a whirlwind in her stilettos and short, body-hugging, netted tank dress. Kit sighed, turned to Bridget, and said, "Doesn't Diana look beautiful?"

Bridget smiled and sighed as well. "She's beautiful *anyway*, but tonight she looks amazing! I'm glad the makeup thing worked out."

Two hours before the wedding, Diana had showed up at their hotel room, hysterical and in tears. "Oh, my God! The woman Leo's mother booked for my makeup showed up with absolute *crap*! The mascara she brought was like, circa 1970! Oh, my God, what am I going to do? There's no time to find anyone else! That *woman* is trying to sabotage me on my wedding day!"

"Yes, yes, I have stuff," Bridget had called and then run off in search of her makeup bag. After rummaging through the black hole of a kit, Diana left with an assortment of MAC shadows and some lip liner, as well as a tinted Dior gloss and mascara.

Kit agreed, "Yeah, Bridge, way to come through in the clutch!"

Julianna came up from behind, put one hand on each of the girls' shoulders, and exclaimed, "Oh, I just met my new boyfriend! He's a cyclist! For real, he's won a bunch of races! That's it, girls, we're taking up cycling when we get home! I want a butt like that!"

The pinstriped cyclist walked up, stood behind Julianna, and laid a hand on her lower back. In a low voice, he murmured, "May I get you something to drink?"

"Si!" she answered wickedly and allowed him to lead her away.

"Well, she wanted a butt like that; looks like she's going to get one!" Bridget joked.

"Here, would you mind taking some pictures? I think I need a refill. I don't want an empty glass the next time they make a toast," Kit said. She wasn't normally too superstitious, but for some reason, Kit felt compelled to adhere to the Italian toasting rules: look everyone you toast in the eye, or risk seven years of bad sex (who needed that?); and, for some reason, having an empty glass or water in your glass for a toast was just asking for bad luck as well. Kit decided that with all that had happened thus far, she wasn't about to tempt fate. "Sure," answered Bridget as she took the hefty camera from her.

Kit cut across the parqueted dance floor and wove through the dining tables, all adorned in crisp, white tablecloths and topped with flickering candelabras festooned with candles placed strategically amidst a dazzling spray of fuschia dahlias, white peonies, and pink ranuncula.

She stopped at their table, set her empty flute on the table, and began searching through her petite, but cramped, white-sequined clutch. Not only was it time for a champagne refill, but also for another glossy coat of shimmery lip-plumper. While she was sifting through the contents of her bag, her cell phone lit up and vibrated excitedly. Tempted to pretend she didn't see or hear it, Kit closed her eyes and sighed. She should answer it, she supposed. *Please do not let it be anything bad*, she pleaded. She grabbed it and looked at the number. It was Natalie.

What could have happened now? Kit racked her brain and wondered if it were at all possible for Madison to have pulled any more appalling she-nanigans before they'd reached home. Really, what else was there for her to do? Hijack the plane and demand to be brought back to Italy? Seduce a flight attendant and get inducted into the infamous mile-high club? Well, *that* one didn't seem too far-off a notion. Kit tried to erase that disturbing mental picture and decided to answer the phone before her imagination got the best of her.

"Natalie, hi!" Kit shouted into the phone, just as the DJ started up with the traditional Italian music and couples drifted out onto the dance floor.

"Kit! Hi, are you at the wedding?" came Natalie's cheery voice from across the Atlantic.

"Yes, it was *so* beautiful, and the dancing's about to start, I think. So, you all made it back home all right?" Kit asked with some trepidation.

Natalie chuckled mirthfully. "Oh, yesss. We are all back, and Madison is under complete house arrest, until we can figure out what to do with her. But, on the up side, things are better than ever with Joe and me. I mean, it was a total fiasco, but at least he gets it now. It's definitely brought us closer."

Kit released her breath, which she had practically been holding, to say, "Oh, that's so good, Nat!"

"Yeah, anyway, I don't want to keep you, but I was wondering if you could pick up some kind of gift for Lassino, Tino, and Tomaso. I really want to thank them for all their help with … *everything*."

Kit knew just the thing. "Well, they're all clotheshorses, especially Lassino. How about a really nice shirt? I saw a men's store here with a phe-nomenal window display."

Natalie answered without hestitation. "Perfect, and spare no expenses, please! I will pay you back when you get home. I just feel so bad about the whole thing! We *so* completely upset their normal routine. They must think we're all crazy!"

"Oh, Natalie!" Kit exclaimed, "they loved you guys. They do think Madison is a little bizarre, though. They just don't get why she would ever run away."

"Well, gosh, I hope it's not the talk of the town for the rest of your stay. In fact, besides getting them *really* nice shirts, tell them my other gift to them is to *never* return to Positano! At least not with Madison. I'm sure they'll appreciate that even more!" Natalie laughed.

Kit answered, "I will relay the message! But seriously, I hope you do come back—but maybe just you and Joe. I hope this whole thing didn't sour you on Positano." Kit habitually wrinkled her forehead.

Natalie put Kit's fears to rest by answering warmly, "Not one bit. Positano was truly a godsend." She paused a moment and added, "I actually think it was the best thing that could've happened to us. Thanks, Kit!"

Chapter 11

How repulsively overjoyed and relieved Bridget had been when she discovered an air-conditioned fitness haven that was practically right next door to the apartment. They'd returned from Scalea a few days prior, and as soon as she had been able to throw her clothes and shoes into some semblance of order in her side of the wardrobe, she fretfully tugged on her running gear. Was she hallucinating, or were her normally overly baggy running shorts feeling a little more snug? Even her socks felt tighter. She prayed it was due to heavy water retention, the culprit being the excruciating heat. However, she also had the sneaking suspicion that the four-course meals that they'd succumbed to during their stay in Scalea, not to mention the eight-course wedding feast, were beginning to settle down for a nice little stay, unfortunately, on her ever-troubling midsection.

As she grabbed the lone handrail that uncharacteristically graced the short staircase leading up from the apartment, Bridget could hear Kit's faint voice calling accusingly from their patio, "Bridget, you're being ridiculous. You don't need the gym when we have the stairs!" Maybe so, but she wasn't taking any chances.

Bridget clambered up two uneven, crumbly steps at a time and soon reached the top of the staircase that thrust her out onto the curvy bend of their slice of Via Pasitea. She stopped a moment to catch her breath and stood with her hands on her hips; she looked up and was assaulted by "Sera" and her piercing eyes and searing scowl, ever-present at her neighborhood-watch command post. Unable to look away, Bridget stared back as Sera shook out a pair of jumbo-sized striped boxers and pinned them to the clothesline that ran along the front of her scalloped wrought-iron balcony. Did Sera have a *husband*? And did she assail and subdue him with her death stare too? Bridget wondered what man could stand up against those dark, dagger eyes that looked right through you. She involuntarily half-shrugged/

shuddered and called out, as was her routine whenever passing beneath Sera's lookout, "Sera!"

Without waiting, she hastened toward their four-star neighbor, Palazza Bianca. The navy-suited doorman held the thick, beveled-glass door open, and as Bridget stepped inside, she heard Sera shout smugly from her balcony, "*Giorno!*"

Buon Giorno? Bridget glanced down at her watch skeptically. Oops, it was only noon, or *mezzogiorno*. Wrong again. Bridget resolved witheringly that she was never going to win the time war with her surly neighbor. She'd have to put that aside, though, since she must now focus on her other nemesis: the treadmill/workout room.

To her good fortune, the hotel fitness room was open to anyone, for, of course, a small fee: fifteen euros a pop. What was that in dollars? Something ridiculous, when she could just run up and down the road here. Except she was totally averse to huffing and puffing out in the open. People would no doubt gawk and assume she was having some kind of spastic fit or asthma attack from the stairs or something. No, it would not do. So fifteen euros it would be. A small price to pay, though, really, for temporarily saving face and making amends with her points menu plan when she unabashedly went overboard with the eating and drinking.

She was not listening to Kit with her standard response, "Come on, Bridget, everything here is so much healthier. No extra preservatives or hormones—you don't need to spend every day at the gym! Come on, we walk the stairs at least two or three times a day!" Yes, maybe so, Bridget conceded, which was all fine and good, when you ate like a bird. Of course, she *had* read somewhere that birds really eat three times their weight. Could that be true? Well, the analogy fit perfectly then, anyway. Kit ate like a "bird" and never seemed to gain an ounce when they were on vacation.

It was really quite irritating, if Bridget could be totally honest. If all Kit had to do to maintain was walk the stairs (albeit, hundreds of them) a few times every day after all her gelato, pizza, and prosecco, then good for her. Bridget, however, wasn't Kit. With her luck, she'd have to spend two-thirds of her vacation trapped on the stairs of Positano, and while they were picturesquely quaint, and certainly an endearing town feature, this wasn't an appealing thought. Hitting the treadmill, in addition to walking the stairs, seemed a more viable option. And since hardly anyone besides obsessive-compulsive American tourists ever really worked out, she'd probably have the fitness room all to herself. At least, she was sincerely banking on it.

Bridget found herself, once again, climbing stairs, as she left the lobby behind and ascended the majestically winding staircase up two floors. She followed the arrows and padded along the hallways, which were lined with an assortment of white-and-cobalt-covered divans and mahogany writing secretaries. The walls displayed impressionistic watercolors and antique maps of the Amalfi Coast, and her Nike runners squeaking slightly on the cerulean tiled floor. The hallway abruptly came to an end, and Bridget read a sign that said *"Palestra* (Gym)."

She pushed the heavy wooden door in cautiously. She passed a small alcove that lead to the bathroom, surveyed the room, and breathed a happy sigh of relief. It was half what she expected and half what she'd hoped for. The small room was lined on one side with a few Stairmasters, exercise bikes, and weight benches. Facing them, across the room, were a few treadmills. At the far end of the room were glass double doors that looked down on the pool, its backdrop being the famed Positano landscape of tiered houses, the green and yellow majolica-tiled dome of the church, and the miles of azure water, dotted with an assortment of yachts and smaller boats.

Bridget opened the doors and took in the glorious view. The only thing that was missing was the air-conditioning. She was sweating already, and she hadn't even gotten on the treadmill. Bridget had seen some kind of box with a switch when she'd come in, but she wasn't about waste any time trying to figure out how to work it. It was going to be daunting enough figuring out how the treadmill worked in Italian. She hurriedly hopped onto the machine and straddled the sides while she began pushing buttons. A feeling of panic momentarily swept her, as she rushed to get it working. The sooner she began, the sooner she'd be done, and hopefully before any other guests—or, God forbid, townsfolk—came in and spotted her.

The treadmill started, and she lapsed into a hearty pace somewhere between a jog and a run. She would run for as long as she could. But she had to admit that forty minutes running straight was her limit, especially when she'd forgotten her iPod. Well, she'd just have to listen to the Italian radio station that was on and let her mind wander.

Halfway through her run, the sweat was once again pouring out of her like a fountain in the stiflingly hot room. She hadn't seen any folded towels by the door, and she feared that if she got off the treadmill to look for some, she'd never get back on. Best to stay put and make use of her T-shirt as a gym towel. Bridget tried to ignore the embarrassing sweat drops she could see falling onto the treadmill, as well as the twinge of pain she was beginning to feel in her right knee. If she had thought having an injured foot in this town was a nuisance, well, a bum knee was just as bad, if not worse. She pretended she was fine and focused on the blaring radio that played the number-one club favorite "World, Hold On." Just a little longer, and then she'd be at the beach.

A chilled glass of prosecco sounded better than good. And some cold, creamy gelato ... Bridget pictured the footed-glass dish filled with two of her favorites, stracciatella and nocelle, complete with one of those strawlike cookies and a little Italian toothpick flag. She seemed to be accumulating quite a collection of those little flags, but ... ummm.

No! She must stop thinking about prosecco and gelato! They were the reason she was doing time on the treadmill. She was just so ... hot. She should really think about cool, rehydrating water instead. Bridget wiped her moist forehead on her shoulder as best she could and wondered how much longer of this she'd be able to endure. It was truly awful to be spending your vacation on a treadmill. She was contemplating the evils of food and drink as well as why she couldn't ever eat and drink responsibly like everyone else she knew, when her thoughts were interrupted by the echoing sound of the gym door opening and closing. Bridget silently cursed whoever was about to foil her plan for working out unseen.

"Is this it, Kit? This is the *gym*? Oh, my God, it's so cute! Where's Bridget? Bridget, where are you? Are you here?" Bridget huffed away in relief when she heard Julianna's unmistakable voice.

"Hey, what are you guys doing here? I thought you were going to the beach," panted Bridget, unable to downplay her heavy breathing.

Kit patted her midsection sheepishly, which was outfitted in a form-fitting Nike running bra, and admitted, "Well, we were feeling kind of lethargic, so we thought a quick workout would make us feel better before hitting the beach." *Feel better?* Had they failed to notice how wiltingly bedraggled she looked, sucking wind on the treadmill? She was so out of breath that she could barely speak. Bridget decided she'd have to keep the chitchatting to a minimum in order to conserve her quickly depleting energy. Feel better? Oh yes, she would, as soon as the workout was over. And just the thought of taking a dip in the refreshingly cold water at the beach made her almost forget how much she loathed being in a bathing suit.

Before Bridget could wheeze a reply, Julianna added, "Yeah, Bridget, before we have our gelato and prosecco, we thought it'd be fun to have a little workout session together!" Julianna paused and raised her eyebrows as she watched Bridget's tomato-flushed face drip sweat onto the humming treadmill. "But, uh, I guess we have a little catching up to do. Damn, how long have you been here, an hour?"

"Twenty-five minutes," Bridget said and exhaled pathetically.

Julianna cringed and replied, "Jesus, I'm having premature hot flashes just looking at you! If we don't get the air conditioner working in here soon, Bridget, I'm sorry, but I'm not gonna be able to look at you while I'm working out. No offense."

Bridget grinned as best she could and shrugged. She wasn't completely offended, since she didn't want anyone looking at her while she worked out anyway. Weren't people supposed to look hideous when they exercised?

Bridget watched Julianna circle one of the exercise bikes across the room. Her head was tilted to one side, and she grabbed onto the handlebars and cautiously placed one stilettoed flip-flop onto a pedal and then flung her other tanned leg over to the other one. Both feet firmly planted on each pedal, she squatted backward and tried to find the seat of the bike. Whoever had ridden the bike before had been much taller, and the bike seat jutted into the small of Julianna's back. She scowled and hoisted herself up onto the seat, her already tiny miniskirt riding up to her crotch.

"Ooops," she mumbled and stepped back down onto the pedals. She took one manicured hand off a handlebar, tugged at her skirt, and then hopped back up onto the towering seat. Once again, her skirt boisterously hiked itself up and became reduced to the size of an oversized, low-slung belt. Doing her best to wrinkle her Botoxed eyebrows, Julianna unsuccessfully tried to pull it down while still sitting. It was obvious to Bridget that the skirt had a mind of its own (and a small one at that), and Julianna quickly gave up. She sat, her skirt practically around her stomach now, revealing her black, metal-studded bikini bottoms, her feet dangling so that the tips of her French-pedicured toes barely touched the pedals.

Bridget couldn't help but snort. At least she wasn't the only one who looked ridiculous.

Julianna heard her snort and caught Bridget's eye, and then she called over the music, "*What?*"

Bridget found herself almost able to speak. "Are you serious about working out in *that?*"

"Of course," Julianna smiled assuredly, then added, "well, I'm not to going to work out like *you!* I mean, these shoes aren't made for the treadmill!" And with that, she made a downward sweeping motion toward her Barbielike, clear-plastic heels.

Bridget laughed and replied, "Well, they're not exactly spinning shoes, either. You're gonna hurt yourself!"

"Bridget, you're *too* funny! I was only going to do about five minutes of the bike and then just do some weights for a little toning. I mean, I've been taking that pole-dancing class for a while. I think I can give the cardio a rest here!" She stepped down onto the pedals, stood and began precariously pedaling away. "Hmm, too bad there's not a pole in here."

Pole dancing? "What?" Even in her exhaustion, Bridget managed to muster up some shocked horror. She then kicked the speed on the treadmill up a bit and latched her hands onto the handles while she continued running.

Julianna rolled her eyes and shouted, "Yes, *Grandma*, pole dancing! Great workout—you should try it, Bridget!"

"Right," Bridget coughed; a half laugh, half hyperventilation occurred.

Julianna looked at her sternly and quipped, "Well, you'd be having a lot more fun than you are on that freakin' machine right now! I mean, you *get* a workout, but you don't end up looking like … *that!*"

"Thanks, I'll keep that in mind." Bridget wiped her forehead with the back of her hand.

Julianna stopped mid-pedal and said thoughtfully, "Yeah, but you know, I think I'm gonna quit the class. All the girls in it are just there to learn how to be sexy for their boyfriends. And I don't need to learn how to be *that!*"

Bridget answered smirkily, "Oh, too bad; I don't have a boyfriend, so there's no need for me to take the class."

"Well, maybe you *would* have a boyfriend if you took the class!" snorted Julianna this time. With a dreamy smile on her face, she turned back to

Bridget and said, "Anyway, look, Bridget, I took the class, and I don't have a boyfriend either! And it's fun! But you know what? I don't need a pole-dancing class to teach me how to be sexy. I already am! *You*, on the other hand, could use a class like that! Look at you! On that fuckin'—sorry, Kit, I know you don't like it when I swear—but on that *fuckin' treadmill*, and you don't even need it!"

Bridget took a hand off the treadmill bar to swat in Julianna's direction. "Hellooo, I need to be on the treadmill after all that wedding eating!"

"Oh *whatever*, we *all* ate! *And* drank our fair share, but I'll be damned if I'm gonna spend my hard-earned vacation in Italy on a treadmill, in a fuckin' hot room! Kit! Have you figured out that air-conditioning thingy over there, yet?" Julianna furiously fanned herself, while Bridget ignored her and continued her stagger-a-thon.

"Fine! Don't take the pole-dancing class, but stopping running around in such baggy clothes!" spat Julianna.

"Excuse me; these are my workout clothes!" Bridget was incredulous.

"I mean *all* the time! You could stand to show off those boobs and that butt of yours a little more. Who the hell are you saving it for?"

"Nobody! Besides, I can't pull stuff off like you and Kit, it's just … not me!" Bridget stated.

Julianna hopped off the bike and stood in front of Bridget's treadmill and said, "You're too hard on yourself. Look at me today. I've got *jacked*-up hair." She stuck a finger into the rat's nest piled on top of her head. Then she pointed to her stomach and added, "And I've got a total dickie-do!" Then, to thoroughly make her point, she arched her eyebrows and bugged her eyes out and shouting, "And worst of all, my Botox is totally wearing out and I desperately need a refill! So there!"

With slight hesitation, Bridget asked, "I'm afraid to ask, but what's a *dickie-do?*"

Julianna raspily explained, "Oh, my gay friend, Hermes, calls it his dickie-do." She pointed to her stomach. She noted Bridget's blank look and added, "It's just a nickname. You know, his stomach is so big that he can't see his di—"

"Got it." Bridget chuckled. "You do not have a dickie-do!"

"Well, I don't have a dickie-doo like *Hermes* does." Julianna giggled. "But I get a little poochy too. See!" and with that, she unzipped her miniskirt, yanked it down, and stood in her bikini bottoms. She tapped her tanned—and as far as Bridget could see, quite toned—stomach and said, "See, I get it too, Bridget! So just stop worrying. You're beautiful! Men don't want a rail anyway! Embrace who you are!"

Well, she would if she could get her arms around herself, Bridget thought wryly. Okay, she was being slightly dramatic. She wasn't obese or anywhere near it, but people just didn't understand.

Kit walked over from the far corner of the room, glanced at Julianna's skirt around her ankles, and quipped, "Uh, you can put your skirt back on, since I figured out how to work the air conditioning!" A sudden blast of arctic air shot out from above them. Kit positioned herself on the treadmill next to Bridget and said with a confused look, "Bridget, why didn't you turn on the air conditioning? You look like you're about to pass out!"

Bridget lied, "I don't know; I didn't see it there." She wasn't about to admit that she had purposely chosen to not figure it out so that she could get a head start on her workout before anyone else came in. Well, at least the only people to have interrupted her workout were her friends.

At that, the door slammed open and shut and in strolled Lassino, outfitted in his soccer shorts, a World Cup T-shirt, and an obnoxiously fluorescent blue-and-green pair of Nike Shox. He nonchalantly nodded at Kit. "Oh? You are back already from Scalea?" Then he squinted at Bridget and added with some concern, "Bridget, here, take this. *Please.*" He removed the small, white towel that had been draped around his neck, walked over, and hung it on the treadmill handle. He turned around and stopped short when he noticed Julianna bending down to pick up her teeny skirt.

"Please, you don't have to put that on for me! Kit, why don't you work out in your bikini?" He smirked naughtily and hopped upon an exercise bike.

Kit rolling her eyes and grinned, and then suddenly pushed "stop" and jumped off the treadmill. She headed toward the weights, and sidestepped Julianna, who was now daintily lifting a long, metal rod that contained a loose, ten-pound disk at each end.

Bridget, chagrined at how truly scary she must look, given that fact that Lassino could tell, even with his subpar eyesight, nonetheless gratefully swiped the towel from the bar and wiped herself off. She watched as Lassino pedaled away and unabashedly stared at Kit. Kit briefly scanned the weight rack and picked up two tens. She placed one foot forward, raised her arms behind her slightly, and began a round of tricep kickbacks.

Lassino immediately got off the bike and made his way over to the weight rack and asked, "So, Kit, what are you doing today?"

Kit raised her head slightly to him, smiled, and said, "Going to the beach. And you?"

"You're doing that wrong." Lassino ignored Kit's question.

"What?" Kit asked cautiously as she kept her eyes focused forward and continued her round of tricep work.

"That exercise! That's not how you do it!" He shook his head disdainfully and waggled a finger at Kit's closest arm.

"Yes, it is. I do these in a class at the gym all the time." Kit raised her eyebrows, although she was none too irritated.

Lassino stated bluntly, "Well, you are wrong." He reached around Kit, smiled and picked up a pair of weights, and then he began his own tricep kickbacks at a brisque pace.

Kit stopped herself and watched him a few moments before she said, "That's exactly what I was doing!" Unable to hide the amusement on her face, she then looked over at the girls and rolled her eyes exasperatedly.

"No, it's not," argued Lassino, his eyes on the floor ahead of him.

"Yes, I forgot: you know everything, and I know nothing," Kit sang and resumed her bent-over position.

"Ah, for once, you're right about something!" replied Lassino tartly. He set down his weights, stepped behind Kit, and said gruffly, "Look, I feel I must help you do this right, or you will hurt yourself!"

Kit straightened up, but before she could reply, Lassino placed his hands on her hips and commanded, "Bend over!" Bridget noted a slight bit of impishness run across Lassino's face. Julianna made exaggerated eye contact in the mirror with Bridget as she continued her barbell lifting.

One of his hands gravitated from her hip down to her rear, and Lassino latched onto Kit's opposite leg and spoke into her hair. "Now move this leg forward and keep it bent."

Out of the corner of her eye, Bridget observed, with surprise, that Kit let Lassino's hand guide her leg forward. She slightly bent her knee, then turned her head and asked, "Like this?"

Oh, come on, Kit, thought Bridget with amusement. She looked ahead at the wall mirror to see Julianna's reaction. Julianna continued, zombielike, with her bicep curls, while she furtively shot sideways glances at Lassino and Kit.

"Yes, that is good." Lassino's hand remained planted on Kit's butt. Kit extended her arm back and bent it at the elbow, then did a few repetitions while Lassino's hand overtly massaged her derriere.

"So, is this right?" Kit asked innocently. Lassino purred huskily, "Mmm-huh."

"Good, because that's exactly what I was doing!" Kit shouted and stopped mid-elbow bend.

Lassino laughed. "Yes, I know. I really just wanted to touch you!" Lassino gave Kit's rear a playful squeeze and then patted her breast with his other hand.

Bridget, embarrassed to be in the room at all, kept her eyes glued straight ahead to the mirror, wishing she were blind and deaf. She needn't have worried for long, though. The awkward silence was broken when the loose weights on Julianna's barbell slipped off and thunderously clattered to the floor. Julianna, who'd been glazed-over watching Lassino's demonstration, came to with a shocked, "Oops! Oh, my God, sorry!"

Lassino quickly took his hand away from Kit's bosom and called, "Mama mia! Is the floor all right?"

"Oh, my God! I'm *so* embarrassed!" Julianna chortled and put a hand to her lips, none too embarrassed at all, as she shimmied down to pick up the weights.

Lassino turned back to Kit and murmured, "I have to go get the pizza dough ready. Do you want to help?"

"I can help make the pizza dough?" squealed Kit excitedly. "Oh my gosh, yes! When?"

"Now—I must go now. I am very beesy, you know!"

Kit stammered, "But, I just got here—"

"Kit, I can not wait all day for you. If you want to help, you come now!" Lassino started for the door.

"Okay, okay! Julianna, Bridget, you want to come?" Kit hurriedly set the weights back on the shelf. Bridget shook her head no and uttered, "I'll see you down at the beach."

Julianna flung the dismantled barbell down and cried, "Oohh! I love pizza! Do you have any cute brothers, Lassino?"

"Ciao, Bridget." Lassino nodded in her direction and led the girls, who waved to Bridget, out of the weight room.

Before the door closed behind them, Bridget could hear Kit shout excitedly, "Oh, wait! We have to stop at the apartment so I can get my camera!" Bridget could hear Lassino grunt some type of irritable response. She smiled wanly and kicked the treadmill up a notch.

◆　　◆　　◆

Bridget propped herself up on an elbow and wiped her sopping décolleté with the top of her beach towel before she lethargically rolled over onto her back. In the mere fifteen minutes she'd been at the beach, she was completely enveloped in a layer of sweat. Between the treadmill, the stairs, and the beach, it seemed as if she was perpetually soggy in this town. Bridget hadn't thought it possible to perspire this much. Could she really have that much liquid in her body? Hopefully, it was all the toxins flowing out of her and she'd be a few pounds lighter by the time she left this rocky sauna of the Spiaggia Grande. That, or she'd be back for a late-afternoon bout with the treadmill. At least she knew how to work the air conditioner now.

"Bridget, I can't stand it any more! It's so freakin' hot! I gotta get into the water!" Julianna sat up and wiped a small pool of sweat from her taut stomach.

"I know; I think I'm going into a heat coma," Bridget agreed as she rubbed her chin on her shoulder. She wrinkled her nose and then added, "Eeww, I've definitely reached the threshold of stinkiness."

Julianna stood in front of Bridget's lounge chair, hands on her hips, resembling a miniature version of Mariah Carey, in her black-studded bikini, heels, and oversized, wrap-around Chanels. "Well, come on, let's hit the water!"

Hmmm, the water. Getting into the water would entail actually having to stand up and totter unattractively across the molten rocks in her bathing suit in front of the plethora of sunworshippers. She'd wait a little longer before she summoned up the gusto to go for it. Besides, she was so wet with sweat that she probably looked like she'd already been in the water. The only difference was that she most certainly did not appear refreshed.

"I'll be there in a minute. I don't feel like lugging myself out there just yet." Bridget waved her off before taking a swig of lukewarm water from her pint-sized bottle of San Pellegrino.

"I feel the same way, but I can't stand it any longer. So I'm gonna do what my mother always says: just suck it in and stick 'em out!" Julianna sucked in her stomach and jutted her boobs out. She waved backward at Bridget and shouted over her other shoulder, "See ya out there!"

Bridget enviously watched her petite, yet overexaggerated posture swagger across the rocks, kick off her heels, and wade out, until she was just a tiny head bobbing in the blue-green water. Bridget lay back upon her elbows and let her head roll over toward one shoulder as she briefly perused the crowded beach, then finally stared out at the water, until it was a glittering blur. She felt almost mesmerized by the lazy din of the beach: the lapping water, surrounding Italian chatter, and the "Coco bello, coco fresco!" man trying to sell his coconut from one end of the rocky strip of terrain to the other. Her hypnotic state was soon interrupted by a cacophony of splashing and gregarious yelling.

Bridget's eyes came into focus, and she turned her head toward the racket. A group of raucous teenage boys, waist-deep in the water, were zealously batting a beach ball back and forth, making sure to splash a nearby cluster of bikinied girls whenever possible, causing the girls to flirtatiously yell back at them in mock exasperation. Bridget watched the amusing interaction continue on for quite some time and concluded that this was definitely some kind of Italian mating ritual. Males purposely tried to get females' attention by irritating them in some way.

In response, the females countered with a few standard responses: boredom, disdain, or by completely ignoring them, all flavored with some hint of haughty amusement. This, in effect, drove the men completely wild, thus encouraging them to try even harder to annoy/win over their objects of enamourment. Although Bridget was sure this tussling game was a bit more complicated than all that, she felt she just might be onto something. She'd have to keep a watch on this and take notes in her travel journal, since she could foresee nothing much happening to *her* on this trip. She could at least hone her anthropological interests by studying the locals. And since the whole pole-dancing thing was not an option, maybe she could pick up a few tips this way instead. Yes, keen observation and in-depth note taking seemed way more up her alley, for sure. She sat up and reached into her beach tote to feel around for her journal.

Before she could locate it, something wet hit her in the leg with a slight sting. Startled, she looked up. It was the boys' beach ball. It had somehow, typically, managed to hit her even though she was a whole two rows of beach chairs away.

"*Scusa! Scusa!*" One of the dark-haired boys (assumedly the ball thrower) waved as the others snickered naughtily and jokingly slapped him upside the head. Bridget looked at the ball that had fallen to the side of her beach chair. Unfortunately, she was too far away to throw the ball to the boys. She'd have to actually get up and walk down toward the water to get it to them. Resignedly, she pulled herself up and of the chaise, pushed her feet into her flip-flops, and grabbed the ball. It was about time she got into the water anyway, and now, at least she had a legitimate prop to cover up her chest and stomach as she walked amid the sunbathers.

Barely reaching the water's edge, Bridget was met by the ball thrower, who had run up the rocky shore to retrtieve the ball. "Oh, here!" Bridget smiled slightly and held the ball out to him. The dark-haired, muscley youth smiled a fresh-faced grin and replied, "Ah, grazie, signorina! Scusa!" before taking the ball.

"Prego," Bridget answered. He smiled again, turned, and threw the ball back to his pals, who dogpiled each other trying to catch it. To avoid being in the line of fire again, Bridget began to walk a little further. A piercing whistle behind her caused her to turn around. The teenager stood there, staring at her, with his hands on his hips and his head cocked to the side. Had she just been whistled at as if she was a dog or better yet, a taxi, by some teen? She looked around skeptically. Perhaps he was summoning someone else? No, he stood staring at her and called, "Signorina! Signorina!"

With a puzzled look, Bridget answered, "Si?" What could the youth want?

He shrugged and asked, "You go to the disco tonight?" then flashed a knowing smile.

Bridget grinned in spite herself and shrugged back at him. Of course, she'd probably be there, but no need to be stalked by town minors. She picked up her flip-flops and hastened away as he hopefully shouted after her, "I see you there tonight, bella! My name is Marco! Remember me tonight!"

He *was* kind of cute. *No, no, no,* Bridget immediately scolded herself. There was cradle robbing, and then there was *cradle robbing*. No way. Paolo had been young enough. She wished she'd run into *him* tonight, but she hadn't seen him at all since they'd come back from Scalea. Maybe he was still hiding from crazy Kim? Bridget knew he couldn't stay away from the disco forever. He'd be missing out on all the new girls in town. She kept walking, till she was a safe distance away from anyone remotely male or teenaged.

Bridget waded out until she was waist high. She shielded her eyes aand looked about, and she spotted Julianna further out talking animatedly to some beefy-looking guy. She wouldn't intrude.

"Ciao!" a scratchy little voice called from beside her. Bridget looked to her right to find a chubby-cheeked boy laying stomach down on his inflatable raft. Surprised, Bridget smiled at the olive-skinned tike and answered, "Ciao!" He could be no more than four years of age. A slight breeze in the air seemed to have stirred up the water as well, and Bridget herself was getting jostled around a bit as the water bumped up against her body. How had he paddled out here all by himself? She looked around to see if any possible parents were in the vicinity. The closest people happened to be two teens sucking the faces off each other and some guy up ahead whose back was to her. Others were scattered about but were paying no attention to the little rafter.

Bridget looked at the tanned little body in a Speedo. She never thought she'd ever give the okay to a guy in a Speedo, but the kid was just too adorable, with his big, dark-fringed eyes and plump cheeks. Poor little thing, out here all by himself and on a raft! Did he even know how to swim? Reassured that there was no way he'd harass her about going to the disco, Bridget decided to help. After all, she was a teacher. Kids liked her. She asked kindly, "*Come stai?* Are you okay?"

The boy cried out loudly and answered ... well, Bridget had absolutely no idea what he had answered. All Bridget could catch from his fast-paced gibberish was *aiuto, acqua,* and *mama.* Help, water, and mom. This was most likely bad. Was his mom drowning? Where was Paolo when you needed him? Was the boy's mom lost somewhere out here in the water? Why hadn't she studied her Italian a little more? Of course, the kid was young, so maybe he wasn't even speaking proper Italian yet. All Bridget could think to ask was a none-too-helpful, "*Che?*"

Again, the boy shouted at her, but much louder, as if *that* was going to help her translate any better. Bridget sighed and replied sorrowfully, "Uh, sorry, uh, no lo so …"

Openly agitated, the boy slapped the water viciously with a dimpled hand, which caused Bridget to jerk her head back slightly in surprise. He then looked at her with what clearly appeared to be annoyance and began screaming at her again. This time, Bridget caught the words *Madonna, non hai capito, and idiota.*

Bridget cried back with just as much agitation, "I'm sorry; I *know* I don't understand you. Hey, did you just call me an *idiot?*"

The boy pounded the water a few times and started screaming again, making sure to include the word *idiot*, and then he pointed ahead of him. This was getting a little embarrassing. Other swimmers, including the teenage makeout artists, were turning around to stare at a four-year-old berate her, about what, she had no idea. Calmly, Bridget stared down the boy and said slowly, "Look, *mi scusa, come si chiama?*" Maybe asking him his name would buy her some time before he went ballistic again.

The boy actually growled at her, put his hand in the water like he was trying to paddle, and then looked at Bridget menacingly and slapped water at her! That did it. The kid was not cute. She was *trying* to help, and it wasn't her fault she didn't understand what he was saying. Even the *kids* here didn't like her. Bridget ferociously splashed water back at him.

Her adversary looked back at her, too stunned to speak. Bridget realized she had sunk to new levels, having a water fight with a puny four-year-old, but the little punk deserved it. Bridget sputtered as she received a hearty splash of water in her face again. Oh, she didn't feel guilty anymore. The kid was purposely egging her on. She splashed water back, and this time, a wave of water hit the boy's face, which caused him to shake his head, blink his eyes a few times at her, and then cough pathetically. He furrowed his eyebrows at her and scrunched up his face, and Bridget knew it was inevitable …

"Wahhhhhhh! Mama! *Waaaaa!*"

Oh, God, she had made an innocent little boy cry. Now people were really gawking at her, the cruel American lady in the one-piece.

"Oh, you're fine; you're fine! Right? Ughh, why me?" Bridget groaned. In a panic, she looked around and saw someone pushing through the water toward them. She squinted, and she recognized the tall, muscular figure, the long, straight nose, the dark hair—and yes, if she wasn't mistaken, she thought she detected a pair of Hawaiian swim trunks. It was Lorenzo, the shopkeeper's grandson! Oh, no. She hoped he hadn't witnessed her acting so completely immature. What if this was his child that she had waterlogged? Worse yet, he was going to be up close and see her in a bathing suit!

He reached the raft, nodded at her politely, and spoke to the boy. "Che cosa? Dimmi!"

The child stopped blubbering long enough to whine the same unintelligible phrase at Lorenzo. But of course, not being unintelligible to another native, Lorenzo nodded sympathetically and said, "Ahh!" He then grabbed onto the raft and started pushing it toward shore. Bridget followed behind awkwardly. Once they were about knee-deep, Lorenzo gave the raft one last shove toward the shore and stood there and watched as the boy paddled a bit, then hopped off and ran up the shore.

He turned around, smiled angelically at Lorenzo, and called, "Ciao, ciao, grazie!" Then he looked at Bridget, stuck out his tongue, picked up a rock, and hurled it at her! Had she not been so totally humiliated, Bridget would've laughed. Instead, she bit her lip and gave him her best teacher death stare. The boy cried out in alarm, "Mama! Mama!" and dashed up the rocks to where his mother, dripping from her swim, stood talking to another woman. Bridget wondered how the woman couldn't have noticed her son screaming. Weren't women supposed to have some kind of uncanny, innate sixth sense when it came to their children?

Bridget watched the child grab his mother at the kneecaps, while she patted him on the head and said, puzzled, "Damiano, che cosa?"

Bridget then realized Lorenzo was still standing next to her. She quickly glanced at him. He was staring at her with amusement and ... something else. Bridget wasn't sure what. Was it interest? Perhaps he was curious as to what kind of woman could provoke a small child into throwing a rock at her? Maybe he was intrigued by her chaste bathing suit selection? She nervously tugged at her neck to make sure that the green-haltered suit she was wearing was still tied snugly. This was no time for a wardrobe malfunction.

Bridget suddenly felt extremely self-conscious. She really disliked being laughed at. Well, he wasn't actually laughing, but his eyes gave him away. Yes, how to escape gracefully in the rocky water?

Bridget looked up at the green eyes that were still staring at her. Where had all her Italian gone? Couldn't she think of *anything* to say? He smiled and revealed straight, square teeth. Bridget felt herself unexpectedly exhale; she hoped, not too obviously. Good hair, good teeth …

"Ciao," she heard his deep voice say.

"Ciao," she answered quickly, lest she forget the one word she still remembered.

He turned toward her and was about to say something, when a female voice called from the rocks. "Lorenzo, Lorenzo!"

Bridget looked at the shore and saw a tall, busty brunette looking at them. Clad in a small, sequined bikini, hair piled atop her head, and large sunglasses shading her eyes, she held a young girl on her hip. She set down the girl, who came careening into the water and straight for Lorenzo.

With a look of delight on his face, he scooped her into his arms, threw her up into the air, and said, "Ahh, *piccola bambina!*"

The small girl, whom Bridget noticed had that dark, almost-black hair and green eyes identical to Lorenzo's, giggled and wrapped her arms around Lorenzo's neck as she kissed him and spoke childish Italian words into his ear. Well, that took care of that. He had a child. She should've known. Bridget scooted away and headed up the rocky bank to find her flip-flops.

◆　◆　◆

Kit stepped out onto the bustling sidewalk and grinned widely at nothing in particular. She never really needed a reason to smile. It just came naturally, but today, right now, she truly had a reason to beam. She held the square cardboard box up to her nose and deeply breathed in the divine aroma. *Pizza.* And she had made it herself. Well, kind of. Okay, actually, Lassino had only let her knead the dough for about thirty seconds before he pushed her out of the way and took over. But Kit knew what he was up to. She felt certain that Lassino had wanted her to see him in his culinary domain, where he was the boss and expert.

Covered with flour and sweat, he barked orders at everyone, including his sister and cousin. Yes, Kit thought perhaps it was better that she left the pizza-making to him and his crew. At least he couldn't scream at her for taking pictures! Now she could look back and remember the day that Lassino had shown her how real Italian pizza was made. She could possibly die and go to heaven. Of course, only after she had eaten the pizza. And Lassino had made it just the way she wanted it. After the dough was finished, he had asked her, "Well, Kit, what do you want on your pizza?"

What didn't she want? Kit loved it all. But she chose carefully. She would want to savor everything. Too much on top might detract the distinct tastes from one another. She furrowed her eyebrows thoughtfully and answered, "Tomato, basil, and mozzarella *di buffala*." Yes, it was a trifecta of perfection, if she did say so herself.

And for once, Lassino didn't argue with her. "Ah, okay, caprese style. Good choice," he'd said and shrugged in agreement, as if surprised that she was capable of making wise choices regarding food.

When the pizza was taken out of the oven, Lassino artfully arranged the ingredients on top and placed it in the box for her. Kit would have preferred to eat the specially made pizza there at the restaurant, but Lassino had placed the box brusquely into her hands and said quickly, "Well, I must go shower. I have a football game in an hour!"

Kit grinned back at him and spoke. "Lassino, thank you *so* much for letting me come today and watch. I am so … happy!"

He ushered her out of the kitchen, held the front door of the restaurant open for her, and exclaimed, "Don't get any ideas about coming here every day to help or … watch!" He shook his head sternly at her.

Kit was unable to hide her disappointment. How could he dangle this pizza-shaped carrot in front of her like that and then yank it away so cruelly? He knew how much fun it had been for her, and he had also enjoyed showing off for her. Lassino noted her crestfallen face, sighed, and said, "Look, you just can't be coming here when I have to work."

Her indignant curiosity got the best of her, and she demanded, "Why?"

"*Why? Why?* Why do I always have to give you a reason? *Because!* That's why!" Lassino looked impishly defiant.

Kit countered back, "Because *why?*" Two could be childish.

Lassino rolled his eyes and spoke slowly. "Because … you are too sexy." He pulled her into him and squeezed her butt gently. Kit looked at him as if to say, *Come on, puh-lease!*

But Lassino continued, "I mean it. I would have a hard time concentrating on my pizza dough!"

"But—" Kit didn't have time to start her sentence.

"And none of my workers here will be able to concentrate either!" Lassino nodded his head in the direction of the kitchen. An assortment of males, from the seventy-year-old cook to the middle-aged waiters and the teenage bus boys stood huddled in the doorway, cigarettes hanging out of most of their mouths, watching the two of them. "See what I mean? They should be working!"

Lassino yelled at them in Italian, and they all shuffled off into the kitchen calling, "Ciao, Kit!"

Kit was used to that kind of overt testosterone-y attention, but maybe Lassino was right. "All right," she reluctantly sighed.

Lassino kissed her passionately and then added, "You can come another time. I promise. Just not every day!" He gave her a swat on the butt and added, "I'll see you tonight!" and left her standing alone on the patio with her pizza box and camera.

Her momentary disappointment having passed, Kit now stood on the sidewalk. She would bring the pizza back to the apartment to save for later. It would be all she could do to not devour every crumb of it herself. *Her* pizza, made specially for *her* by Lassino. But she would wait till they were all in the apartment. Then she would unveil the beautiful masterpiece for Bridget and Julianna and they could enjoy it together.

Then again, maybe she'd have a little taste now while she walked up the hill. She was starving. For sure, she'd probably have it burned off by the time she was through with all the stairs! Kit carefully opened the box as she continued along the curvy road, careful to avoid being jostled by toweled tourists and locals heading home for their lunch break.

She was about to take her first bite of pizza when she heard her name being called. Kit looked across the road. A tall man, leaning lazily against his taxi, waved at her. Oh, no, somebody else who knew who she was. And with her her bad eyesight, she could barely make out his face. She'd have to cross the street to say hello. She'd also have to wait to eat her beloved slice of pizza. Kit quickly put it back into the box.

She crossed the road, and with her vision thankfully in tact again, Kit recognized Vinnie, of the local restaurant and who'd driven them to Scalea. "Vinnie! Ciao!" she chirped happily.

"Oh, I am honored you remember my name!" Vinnie placed a large, olive-skinned hand on his hairy chest and smiled a pleasant, if not slightly yellow, smile.

"Well, of course! You taught me about Italian holidays—like the Easter rat!" Kit cried dramatically and threw one hand into the air.

"Oh, very good! I am happy to teach you, and whenever you need to know something, you can ask me." He smiled and, Kit thought, stared just a little too long. He reached into the front pocket of his starched, white shirt and said, "So here, please, my card. You can call me!"

Kit took the card and replied, "Grazie, Vinnie! I will see you soon!" Why did he need to give her his card when she'd probably see him all over town? Of course, she wouldn't call him, but that was nice of him. As Kit began walking away, he called, "Wait, Kit, I will drive you! You are staying by Palazza Bianca, no?"

Did everyone in town know where they lived? She quickly stammered, "Uh, no. I mean, yes, yes, I live near there, but I'm going to walk, thanks!"

To her chagrin, Vinnie began following her, pleading, "But, Kit, please, you are carrying a lot. I will drive you. Free of charge, of course!"

Please, she was carrying her camera case and a small pizza box. Even these two items put together weighed about five times less than some of her clutches! She did not *want* to be driven. She wanted to walk ... *alone*, with just her pizza. And she wanted to eat that slice without being watched.

Although she had no problem eating, every now and again, the old self-consciousness came out when she had to eat in front of others, especially if she didn't know them well. Kit couldn't help but blame it on having a mouthful of braces for half of her high school years. She'd shudder with abnormal fear and shyness before every lunch period, worrying about getting food tangled in her hardware and possibly walking around school with remnants of her lunch showing up there as well. Her friends, Bridget included, were all kind and never said anything, but they couldn't help but look at her a little oddly when she held a hand over her mouth while she chewed ... everything, and at all times. Well, at least they never said anything about it to her.

While those days were long over, Kit was going to pass on the free ride, which she somehow felt would have certain strings attached. Besides, she wanted to eat her pizza slice by herself. Plus, Vinnie was kind of getting creepy and stalker-ish.

"Vinnie, you are very kind, and I appreciate your offer, but I would really rather walk," she said pleasantly but firmly. She then added quickly, lest he think her rude, "The walking's good exercise! So thank you! Bye, ciao! See you soon!" she called over her shoulder and swished away up the road before she could see the expression on his face.

Phew, now she just needed to go a little farther and she'd be on the staircase to the apartment where she could eat her slice in peace. In fact, now she was so hungry that she might even need to eat two. There! There were the dumpsters, which meant the staircase was right behind them! Just a few more feet. Oh, she couldn't wait any longer, and she ripped the box open and grabbed the slice. Ahh, this would be almost as good as sex! It would certainly be orgasmic, especially if she was thinking about Lassino while she ate this luscious treat.

Kit reached the bottom of the steps and stopped momentarily. She glanced around and concluded that no one was in a close proximity to viewing her, and she cautiously brought the quivering slice of pizza to her lips. It was still warm! Before she could put it in her mouth, though, a car horn honked blaringly behind her, scaring her so much so that she jerkily dropped the pizza. Kit gasped, horrified, and then exhaled in relief as she found that it had landed in the box and not on the ground. But now she was irritated. She sincerely hoped that Vinnie was not the one behind her in his cab. With warp speed, she hastily threw the rejected slice back into the box and turned around to see who had honked.

Sitting in a flashy, doorless, convertible black BMW sat a dark-haired gentleman. With his tanned skin and his black hair flecked with bits of gray, Kit thought he looked quite like George Clooney. She remembered Lassino introducing her to him at the disco. If she thought Lassino was a big-wig here, apparently this guy was bigger. It had something to do with the fact that his family owned three of the most expensive five-star hotels in the town as well as some restaurants, including one that was always featured on Oprah. Although Lassino didn't seem overly fond of him (whatever his name was), Kit remembered him to be quite jovial and fun to talk to. If only she could remember his name. All she could think of at the moment, though, was her poor pizza.

"Kit, ciao, bella! How are you?" He pulled up his Prada aviators and shined a perfectly white smile at her. The pizza would have to wait. That's what microwaves were for anyway, right? Kit approached the passenger side of the sleek vehicle and gave her standard toothy smile. She answered, "Ciao! How are you?"

"Very well, thank you." He nodded and reminded her graciously, "Fabio, we met at the disco."

Good, a name—yes, Fabio. "You are going somewhere?" he asked while quite obviously looking her up and down. Kit seriously wondered if the men here had X-ray vision. It was impossible, thank goodness, but their penetrating stares sure made you wonder.

"Oh, just heading home to drop some things off, and then I'll head back down to the beach," Kit replied cheerily. The tiniest of breezes wafted over her, and Kit was aware that she could actually smell Fabio's cologne from where she stood. Citrusy (well, people around here were fond of lemons), but spicy, too, with a hint of cloves or nutmeg? Ugghh, her stomach was starting to groan with impatience.

Fabio asked gallantly, "Please, allow me to drive you up the hill."

Kit hesitated. She *so* didn't want to accept a ride, especially from someone Lassino wasn't too keen on; however, she didn't want to appear rude. She stalled briefly and uttered, "Uhh …"

She looked forward; all she had to do was take the staircase—well, an incredibly long, grueling one—but she'd be fine. She would have to stand firm and just say no.

"Kit!" Kit turned around to see Vinnie, although a ways away, nonetheless, coming up the bend, almost jogging.

"Yes, I'd love a ride!" Kit said decisively and practically shotputted herself into the passenger seat. She recalled with relief that according to Lassino, Fabio had some type of French supermodel girlfriend. Good, she was assuredly safe catching a ride with him.

"Oh, your hands are full, let me help you with the seatbelt." Fabio looked at her without blinking.

Before Kit could answer that she was capable of belting herself, Fabio added, "Usually, I wouldn't bother, but with no car doors, I wouldn't want to lose you going around a bend!" And with that, he pulled the shoulder belt up and over Kit, his elbow rubbing against her left breast as he reached around her to click it into place. Kit waited for him to grin with embarrassment and perhaps add a "Scusa, so sorry!" But he didn't. Maybe she wasn't so safe after all.

Instead, Fabio nodded at her assuredly and said, "And we are off." He put the car into gear and hit the gas, and they glided away smoothly. Kit watched Vinnie's reflection grow smaller in the sideview mirror. She exhaled, if only slightly. Now if she could just get out of the car without being fondled again. Although, it had *probably* been an accident that Fabio had rubbed against her. Nobody would purposely do that, right? Opting not to chance another freak boob encounter, though, Kit set her hands on top of the pizza box, so she could beat him to the seatbelt, should the need arise.

"Thank you so much, Fabio. I live—"

"Ahh, yes, right next to Palazza Bianca," he interrupted. Kit guessed she needn't have bothered. She had forgotten that she was living the Italian version of *The Truman Show*.

"Yes, right," was all she could answer before blurting out pleasantly, "so, how is your girlfriend?" Past experience told her it was best to arm yourself with useful information right away.

"Girlfriend?" He frowned slightly. "Renee? No, no, we are not together right now." *Right now.* What did that mean? Not being together right now was pretty convenient, since it was the apex of tourist season! Kit nodded as Fabio switched gears to slow down behind a city bus that was unloading passengers.

He looked over at her and explained, "She is a model and goes back and forth between Milan and Paris, so it is a bit difficult. The only thing that really keeps us connected is our son."

"Oh! You have a son," Kit hoped she didn't sound surprised, but she hadn't expected a child in the picture.

Fabio laughed and replied, "You sound surprised! Yes, I have a three-year-old son, *and* I am not married. Marriage is not for everyone, you know."

It was Kit's turn to nod in agreement. Yes, of course, she knew that quite well. Or at least, marriage seemed to be destined for everyone *but* herself and ... perhaps, the men in Positano ...

Fabio ignored her embarrassment and asked in a meaningful voice, "And you? Such a beautiful woman like you is not married? I am assuming, of course."

Kit shrugged and grinned. "No, you are right. I'm not married."

He laughed. "Well, you are not married, but there is *someone*. Some man *here*." He glanced down at the pizza box sitting on Kit's lap that bore "*Le Segreto Giardino*" in big, black print and continued knowingly, "You are the girlfriend of Lassino, I know."

Kit hoped her tan hid the pink she felt her face becoming, and she replied, "Oh, I don't know …" her voice trailed off, as the car sped up again.

"You don't have to pretend. You have *something* with *someone*. Maybe that is the reason for your radiant smile." His dark eyes crinkled with amusement as the car came to an abrupt stop at the top of their staircase.

Kit answered sunnily and matter-of-factly, "I smile because I am a happy person." *Well, most of the time.*

Fabio turned to her, one hand over the steering wheel, and spoke. "Well, if you are happy, that is a wonderful thing for you and for everyone around you, because you have a very beautiful smile. I like it."

Suddenly feeling flustered, Kit fumbled around clumsily as she unfastened her seatbelt quickly and said, "Thank you, and thank you for the ride, Fabio." She scooted over and threw her legs out of the car.

Fabio pulled his aviators down and said, "You are always welcome. You know, I believe this is the third summer you have been in Positano, and you have never come to my restaurant! I am starting to take offense!"

Kit cried, "I'm sorry! My friends and I will come. I promise!"

Fabio smirked slightly and added, "I look forward to it, but of course, check with Lassino first! Although, a little friendly competition never hurt anybody in this town!"

Competition? Was he talking about the restaurant or … something else? Or was this just another confusing innuendo?

Fabio revved the car engine and shouted loudly, "So, Kit, have fun at the beach, but remember, for a beautiful woman like you, in Positano, the sharks are not in the water. They're *on* the beach!" He winked and the car raced forward, leaving Kit once again on the sidewalk with her pizza box and camera.

Sharks on the beach? Oh, definitely. And in the driver's seat of a doorless BMW, Kit chuckled to herself. She turned on her heel and clattered down the stairs to finally enjoy her long-awaited and *well-deserved* pizza.

Chapter 12

"You're just too good to be true-oo; can't take my eyes of of you-oo; you'd be like heaven to touch; I want to hold you so much!" The glistening, spikey-haired, heartthrob singer crooned the Frankie Valli hit into the microphone as he stood behind the white baby grand and effortlessly pounded the keys.

Another night, and here they were again in the cavernous, yet completely crowded, disco. Strangely enough, it somehow never seemed to get old. Bridget fretted lest she and the girls become known as the American club/booze hags. She wouldn't let herself worry about it for too long, though. It seemed as if everyone she ever ran into around town was here, just like last night and the night before. If she closed her eyes, spun herself around with her arm and index finger outstretched, she'd surely find that upon stopping and opening her eyes, she was pointing at someone she knew or recognized. Bridget scanned the club. Oh, yes, there were the obnoxiously loud newlyweds from New Jersey whom Tomaso had unfortunately seated in the lounge chairs next to her at the beach. They lustfully groped each other, oblivious to the dancing mosh pit they stood in the middle of. Bridget turned her head.

Well. There was the bespectacled guy who always passed her on his Vespa as she made her daily hike further up into the old neighborhood for her morning cappuccino. She wasn't quite sure why, but sometimes he honked at her as if he knew her. He was pretty cute without his helmet on, if she could get past the flimsy, pink-linen capris he was sporting.

She turning her head slightly and recoiled when she saw the older man who ran the butcher store. On their late afternoon treks up the hill, she and Kit sometimes stopped in to pick up some slices of prosciutto and cheese to tide them over until dinner. And here was the man who always helped them. His getup was quite different from the wife beater, apron, and white cap Bridget was used to seeing him in. His linen shirt, unbuttoned to his navel, showed off a chunky gold necklace and quite a furry chest. The shirt was then tucked into a pair of oh-so-tight green pants. Well, now, *there was* someone who quite possibly had bigger boobs than her, as well as a hefty muffintop. And as much as Bridget griped about her midsection, she felt thankful that at least she didn't look like she was carrying twins! Wasn't he a bit old to be lurking about here? Bridget was certainly going to have a difficult time looking at him the next time they went in for some meat and cheese. And, oh no, he was looking over. Bridget avoided eye contact and thought, who *wasn't* here? If Neighborhood Watch Lady and the devil-child from the beach showed up, she was out of here.

And of course, the other usuals were soaking up the sweaty atmosphere as well. Lassino wandered back and forth and around the bar, stopping to mumble into Kit's ear, and then passed by to the other end of the bar, squinting though his glasses at everyone. If you didn't know him, you'd think he was bestowing his best dirty look upon you, which he very well might have been! Mario stood beside Kit, flanked by Gay Giorgio, Luca, and Australian Rachel. Paolo stood at a far corner of the disco on the open-air staircase, smoking a cigarette and staring back and forth from Bridget to Rachel. Bridget knew this because she had caught him looking at her. He had smiled, his huge, white teeth gleaming across the strobe-lit dance floor. No sooner had Bridget waved back and thought, perhaps, she might walk over to say hi, than Rachel's bony hand had reached over and clamped onto her arm like a vise. "Bridget, come have a cigarette with me on the stairs over there!" She nodded in the direction of Paolo. *Oh. Awkward.* Bridget wondered if Rachel possibly knew about her and Paolo, since it seemed as if she possessed some sixth sense when it came to him. "No, thanks, Rachel. I'll just hold our spots here at the bar." Rachel lost no time in scooting away.

Yes, it was unfortunate that *everyone* certainly was here tonight. Since they'd come back from Scalea, Rachel had wanted to hang out with them almost every night. After Rachel's third frantic text that afternoon asking Kit where they were going to be for the evening, Kit had commented to Bridget, "She wants to know what we're doing tonight—again. Ughh, I don't know if I can deal with this anymore. I *really* like her, but I think she's hoping that with us hanging out with Lassino, she'll be able to have better access to Paolo. I just don't want to listen to her bad-mouthing him anymore. Paolo's our friend! We've known him a lot longer than she has. Ohhhh, my stomach! I hope I have some more Rolaids left!"

Bridget couldn't disagree with Kit's observation. She just hoped Paolo would know they didn't share Rachel's vitriolic feelings toward him. So instead of easily ignoring Kim's texts or fibbing about staying in, Kit had sent a message saying they'd be at the disco. And they actually had a reason to be here tonight, other than it being a mere Thursday night in July on the Amalfi Coast.

A new, albeit small, influx of guests had arrived at the apartment earlier that afternoon. Taking her up on her generous invitation, three of Kit's young, single, and just as blonde teaching co-workers had traveled around Europe and were ending their fast-and-furious trip with a couple of relaxing days in the beach town. Of course, no visit here was complete without a first-night disco initiation.

Bridget thought it quite lucky for the girls to be here this particular night. Not only were there the typical Euro club favorites pulsing nonstop, but it was also the local singer/piano player, Fabrizio's, night to come out and play American tunes before switching over to Italian favorites. The crowd, both Italian and foreign, loved it. Of course, it didn't hurt that everyone was about three, if not more, cocktails into their late night. And for the *women*, Fabrizio was not only heartstoppingly good-looking, with his his ink-black, Joan Jett-styled hair, chiseled cheekbones, and unbuttoned shirt (revealing a tanned and chiseled chest as well), but he had a voice that would absolutely melt you.

"I love you ba-ay-by! And if it's quite all right, I need you ba-ay-by to warm the lonely night; I love you bay-ay-by, trust in me when I say!" belted out Fabrizio; his dark eyes scanned the wild crowd that surrounded the piano.

Julianna sipped her prosecco and watched Fabrizio intently as she tapped Bridget with the back of her hand, *"Who is that? Fuucckk, he's hot! And his voice! Does American Idol take foreigners? Is there Italian Idol?"*

"I don't know," Bridget, about to take a sip, realized her glass was empty. How did that always happen? She set her glass on the bar and asked, "So, what about Mario? You don't think he's cute anymore?"

They both turned in time to hear Mario asking Kit, "So, Kit, organize Tiffany for me." He raised his eyebrows and nodded at Kit's co-worker, who, with the other two teachers on the packed dance floor, was singing boisterously along with Fabrizio. If Mario was attracted to Tiffany, it wasn't for her drunken singing, Bridget thought. She'd have to make the assumption that it was quite possibly the curly froth of uber-blonde hair, the black-and-white striped tube top, white skinny jeans that appeared to be painted on, and her teetering red pumps.

"*Organize* Tiffany? What does that mean, Mario?" Kit laughed.

Mario smiled slyly. "You know, *organize* her for me. Me; Teefanee, together, si?"

Kit replied knowingly, "Yes, I see." Lassino walked up, squinted at them through his Coke-bottle lenses, and walked away. Kit shrugged at Mario.

Mario asked, "I just have one question. Why does Teefanee close her eyes all the time? Every time I try to talk to her, her eyes are closed!"

"Maybe she doesn't want to look at your jacked-up teeth, Snaggletooth!" mumbled Julianna out of the side of her mouth.

Kit shouted over the music, "Well, because I think she's a little drunk!"

"Ahh!" Mario nodded his head. "I think I'll go dance!" He threw a smile over his shoulder as he hustled off into the densely packed dance floor.

Julianna looked at Kit and then at Bridget, and then she replied, "In answer to your question, Bridget, I am *over* Mario! No offense, Kit, I know she's a friend of yours, but why would he go for Tiffany?"

Kit glanced nervously between Bridget and Julianna. "She's not really a friend. I mean, I know all of them from work, but not that well. She's *really* nice. Uh, I don't know. Fresh meat? And she's drunk? Which reminds me, I better keep an eye on her and the others. And Lassino better not hit on any one of them. I'll kill him!" With that, she scuttled out into the throng, her metallic, brick-bracked Prada wedges illuminated in the bouncing neon lights.

Julianna turned back to Bridget, furrowed her dark brows, and stated, "I hope I'm not losing my touch! Did I come off as being insecure? Because that scares men away! What do you think, Bridget? Do you thinks Mario got COTS?"

"Cots?" Bridget really hoped it wasn't some type of sexually transmitted disease.

Julianna raspily explained quickly, "COTS—you know, Coming On Too Strong? Do you think I gave off the COTS to him?"

"Noo, you were only together for that one night, the Fourth of July party night, right?" Bridget really didn't know why Julianna would ask her for advice on men. *She* wasn't the one with the pole-dancing credential.

"Oh, you're right, but still …" Julianna's voice trailed off a little.

Bridget countered with a consoling, "Well … maybe he … likes girls who … don't wear bras!" *And who are eight to ten years younger,* she thought, but she kept that one to herself. She was feeling a little long in the tooth herself.

They watched Mario dance; he shimmied his leg around jerkily, as if he were having some sort of fit, while Tiffany jiggled in her tube top, eyes at half mast. Kit's white teeth shone fluorescently in the background as she laughingly swayed her hips. Bridget wondered how much help Kit would be as a dance floor chaperone when she would soon have to fend off her own maulers who were starting to crowd closer. She hoped she wouldn't be called out there for back-up.

Julianna looked on and stated with a short sigh, "So my boyfriend found someone else! Well, she's kind of trashy-looking, and dammit, I'm classy." She tugged at the thigh-high slit of her red halter dress and commented, "I knew I should've bought this dress a size smaller. Don'tcha think? By the way, do these platforms make me look like a trannie?"

Bridget shook her head and laughed. "No, you do not look like a trannie! Where'd you get the shoes, anyway? Are they Miu Miu?" She observed Julianna's tiny feet strapped into the five-inch, shiny, gold, beglittered platforms.

"Please; I got them at a sex shop." She saw the sudden look of distaste on Bridget's face, and she immediately added, "Well, *sorry*, Sister Mary Bridget, but you have to bring a *really* high pair of heels to the pole-dancing class!" She glanced toward the dance floor and said, "Yeah, that's right; Stripes out there is just fresh meat! She's nice and all, so Mario can have her. I'm gonna go talk to Piano Man! Order me another drink, will ya?"

"Sure. What are you going to say to him?" called Bridget.

Julianna raised her eyebrows seductively and answered, "I think I'll request a song!"

Bridget watched her sashay over to the edge of the piano until she was practically behind the keyboard playing along with Fabrizio. Oh, she'd have Piano Man's attention in no time. She could only imagine what Julianna would request. "Like a Virgin?" "The Thong Song?" Something suggestively over the top was entirely possible.

Bridget turned around and found that her coveted spot at the bar had been taken over by a man wearing hideous seersucker slacks. *Seersucker?* Now she'd seen it all. She thought only guys in J. Crew ads wore seersucker. Perhaps he was a tourist from, say, Cape Cod? Where was Kit with her camera when you needed it? Bridget tried to carefully stick her arm around the man to reach for her wallet on the bar. He looked down and saw her hand next to his glass, and then he turned around and stared at her, with a less-than-friendly look, Bridget thought. Oh, and it was that Vinnie who worked in the restaurant down from the apartment and who'd driven them to Scalea! Hopefully, he'd recognize her and realize she wasn't some total pickpocket and possibly let her in to get a drink.

"Hi, scusa," smiled Bridget. Vinnie nodded, no sign of recognition on his face, and turned back around. He'd be no help. Yes, what a shocker. Someone else around here who hadn't a clue who she was. She'd have to move a little further down and wait for an opportunity to squeeze up to the bar.

All in all, you couldn't ask for a better night at the disco—except for the fact that due to it being ladies' night, it was unbearably overcrowded. Forget about Julianna right now; would *she* ever get a drink? Bridget wished people would actually go home. She was starting to get a little irritated that everyone who walked past always chose to cut right in front of her. And being short in this dense crowd, she was naturally the perfect height to receive an elbow in the side or back, or if the person was really towering, in the head, as people pushed around her!

Maybe if she started outright scowling at people with her best teacher daggers, she'd scare them away. It worked with small children, she knew. Why not with slobbering drunk people who—"*Oww!* Shit!"—who plowed into you and slammed down on your toes (which happened to be exposed and peeked through your expensive satin, peep-toed Pedro Garcia's), with their full weight, thus, spilling their drink all over you. Bridget winced and bit her lip to keep from saying something rude. At least it hadn't been her Nutella foot.

"Duuude, sorry!" exclaimed a broad-shouldered, twenty-something guy. Outfitted in the typical collegiate Californian/Abercrombie & Fitch attire, he shook his shaggy, blond hair out of his eyes and scratched at his puka shells, then smiled lazily at Bridget. As if somehow, *that* would make her less than annoyed to have her $400 shoes trampled on. Bridget gave a terse smile. The blond looked down at Bridget's feet and said, "Killer shoes," and then, in true male-ADD form, added, "Damn, I spilled my drink!" And he lurched past Bridget and took the open space that should've been hers.

Bridget sighed and checked her clobbered toes for blood (there was just a tad), and more importantly, her shoes (lucky for him, they were intact), and she then wiped down the front of her black crepe Theory top. Whatever the drink was (some kind of vodka concoction), it had managed to hit a perfect bullseye through the small keyhole in her top and was now running down into her cleavage. She really did hate people right now, especially drunk collegiate Americans. Oh! There was an opening at the bar! She clutched her wallet and hastily moved through people, trying her hardest not to actually bulldoze bystanders out of her way. Yes, she was just mere steps away from nabbing not only a spot, but a desirous barstool as well, and one that would put her up and out of the way of perilous elbows, feet, and anything else that could possibly assault her.

From behind the baby grand came Fabrizio's voice: "*Why, this car is automatic; it's systematic; it's hyyyydromatic ... why, it's a greased lightning!*" "Grease Lightning." If there was ever a cheesy, nostalgic song she loved to dance to, it was this. Bridget couldn't believe she was listening to it played live in Italy! This was extremely wacky and exactly what she loved about this country. She quickly looked over at the dance floor. Julianna was on top of the piano shimmying like a go-go dancer in her dangerous heels. Kit was in middle of the crowd, leading everyone with her "Grease Lightning" dance moves, moving an outstretched arm back and forth, then up, then down, and across her chest, just like John Travolta. Bridget conceded that there probably wasn't a person who had seen *Grease* more than Kit.

"*Go, Grease Lightning, you're burning up a quarter mile; Grease Lightning, go, Grease Lightning!*"

Kit caught Bridget's eye and shouted, "Bridget, come out here and dance with us!"

Bridget was torn. She had a shot at a barstool. But they were playing "Grease Lightning." Okay, she'd just order her drink and then get out on the dance floor. How long could that take?

Too long. Her hestitation had cost her the bar space, and it was now occupied by a very statuesque girl, whom, surprisingly, was no one she recognized. Bridget sighed. She had no chance whatsoever at ever getting a drink in this place. There were worse things, she guessed, but why was she so invisible?

"Hey!" Bridget heard a voice somewhere near her, but she didn't pay much attention. Now that she'd lost the barstool, she was totally sucked into Fabrizio's rendition of "Grease Lightning."

"A palomino dashboard and duel muffler twins, oh yeah ..."

"Helloo!" Oh, the voice was actually being directed at her. She looked around the corner of the bar and right into the face of Lorenzo. He smiled and called, "If you come over this way, I'll get the bartender to get you a drink."

Bridget stood there, a tad confused. Lorenzo, and he spoke *English*, with only the slightest of an accent. Well, why was she shocked? Everyone here spoke English, and quite well. In fact, the only odd thing about it was that he kind of sounded like someone from *The Sopranos*. She had a feeling she was gaping at him as if he had two heads or something.

"Helloo?" Lorenzo waved amusedly. Bridget snapped out of it. She must focus and not pass up his kind offer to help. She smiled and squeezed past dancers and drinkers alike until she was beside him. He was taller than she realized, and broad-shouldered. He was dressed in a plain navy-blue T-shirt, loose Levi's, and a pair of leather flip-flops; his outfit was quite simple and laidback, by Italian male standards. To Bridget, though, it was a welcome relief after the gold-chained, foofy linen, seersucker pants and tight-clothing fashion offenders she'd been exposed to this evening.

Bridget couldn't pinpoint it, but while there was nothing much to the clothing, there was something more to him. Amid the frenzied clubbers in the pumping disco, Bridget noticed a casual, but certain calmness about his manner. That alone was unusual in this chaotic town. He *had* to be from here, but aside from being quite handsome, he clearly seemed atypical to all the basic town-male stereotypes. Who was this guy?

His green eyes crinkled slightly, and she noticed a slight dimple in his cheek when he spoke. "I've been watching you try to get a drink. Tough crowd tonight, huh?"

"Uh-huh," Bridget answered. She didn't know what else to say. She looked around cautiously, ready for his dark-haired wife to suddenly appear and accuse of her of hijacking her husband at the bar.

He pushed his dark hair back, gave her a half smile, and asked, "Prosecco?" Very observant. He *had* been watching her. Of course, she had an empty prosecco flute in her hand. Still, Bridget guessed she must've looked pretty pathetic if he'd decided to come to her aid.

"Thank you. Here's my drink card." Bridget held her card out to him. He waved her off and said, "Don't worry 'bout it. The bartender's my friend." He called the bartender over and spoke to him in Italian. Bridget gasped slightly when she recognized the bartender as one of Paolo's friends. Apparently, he recognized her too and winked at her playfully. Automatically, the "love on the rocks" night came flashing back to mind. Well, there'd be no repeat of that. Bridget hoped the bartender didn't think she was going down to the beach with a married man! She'd get her drink, thank Lorenzo, and be off.

Lorenzo handed Bridget a bubbling flute, grabbed his glass and raised it toward hers, and said, "By the way, I am Lorenzo. Salute."

They clinked glasses and Bridget replied with a nod, "Salute, and thank you. I'm Bridget." Yes, and now she'd be on her way.

Before she could make an exit, Lorenzo took a sip of his drink and asked, "So, Bridget, how long will you be in Positano? I'm guessing longer than the average tourist, since you're staying in an apartment."

He, like everyone else in town, knew she was staying in the apartment. Of course, she was pretty sure he had been the one who'd—

"By the way, how's your foot? Not the one that's bleeding, the other one?" Lorenzo asked earnestly, and then he added, as he gazed down at her feet, "I mean, it's gotta be okay if you're wearing heels like that!"

"So, it *was* you who left the Nutella!" Bridget concluded with a grin.

Lorenzo smiled and nodded his dark head at her. "Yeah, well, my grandfather felt pretty bad about you spending money on all that Nutella, and then you hurt your foot and had to walk all that way up to your apartment. He sent me out to try to help you, but you'd disappeared." He smiled and raised his eyebrows a few times.

Bridget cleared her throat. "I'm kind of a fast walker like that." She recalled speed- limping up those stairs, with her swollen, Nutella-stained foot, drenched with sweat, and thanked God for the power of adrenaline in helping her "disappear" so quickly. She hadn't been a pretty sight.

"My grandfather will be happy to know that your foot is okay. He feels kind of responsible for the accident."

Bridget felt terrible. "Oh, no! It's not *his* fault that I'm so totally clumsy!"

Lorenzo said, deadpan, "Yeah, that's what I told him."

Bridget paused. He didn't have to be that honest, did he? She already felt terrible about trashing the whole candy rack. Bridget tilted her head, unsure of what to say.

As if reading her mind, Lorenzo smiled warmly at her and said, "Hey, I'm kidding."

Bridget sighed. "No, you are quite right."

"Hey, anyone could singlehandedly knock over a whole candy and gum rack. In fact, it happens *all* the time."

"Okay, now I know you're just being very nice or just really sarcastic," Bridget chided.

"Now you're completely correct," Lorenzo teased back. He then added, "Still, though, we did move the gum rack so it's not sticking out so much."

"Then at least my clumsiness paid off, and I've saved countless others from injuring themselves!" Bridget raised her glass toward Lorenzo for another clink. They locked eyes, and she immediately looked away and took a quick swig, almost choking on the sparkling wine. Were they flirting? She didn't know, but she should finish her drink and leave soon. Where was his wife?

Bridget started to say, "So," just as Lorenzo said, "So!"

"Oh, you first," Bridget said and waved him on.

"*So,* who are you traveling with? By yourself?" Lorenzo asked, then nonchalantly added, "Or with your boyfriend?" He then quickly called to the bartender, "*Due, lo mismo, grazie!*" Bridget knew enough to understand he was ordering them another round. He looked back at her as he waited for an answer.

Bridget answered, "Oh, no, no. I'm just here with my friend, and we have some friends visiting us while we're staying here."

Lorenzo countered playfully, "*Friend?* Girlfriend or boyfriend?" Why did he want to know?

Bridget replied, "My girlfriend. I mean, not a *girlfriend*! I mean, my friend that I have known forever, since high school, that is a—"

"Girl? Yes, I get it." Lorenzo looked as if he was trying not to laugh at her. Why was she cursed with being so, so dorky?

Bridget smiled lamely. "Yes, anyway, we're both teachers and have the summers off, so—"

He interrupted dryly. "Oh, you are *teachers?* Yes, if I remember from the beach, you have quite a way with children. I'd love to see you in the classroom!"

Bridget sputtered, "Hey, I'm on vacation!"

"Yeah, well, thankfully for you, I was there." Lorenzo stared at her as he took a sip.

"Yes. So ... I'm traveling with my friend Kit. Do you know her?" Kit was always a good conversation starter, and mentioning her would no doubt divert attention away from having to talk about herself. Besides, Bridget was so used to people saying, "Oh, so you are traveling with Keet," or "How do you know Keet?" or "The bella Keet! Does she have a boyfriend?" Ten to one, all male conversations came back to the topic of her blonde friend. Bridget figured she might as well bring it up first and get it out of the way.

Strangely, Lorenzo shook his head no. Well, of course, he obviously *would* know once she described Kit. *Everybody* within a ten-mile radius of the town knew who she was! Bridget disagreed and said, "Oh, you *must* know Kit. Blonde, blue eyes, curvy, beautiful ..." She let her voice trail off when she noticed the obvious blank look on his face.

Oh, come on. He had to know who she was. Bridget pantomimed. "You know ... Kit!" She motioned with her fingers like they were twinkling lights, then shook her butt slightly, almost as if she was doing the chicken dance. Lorenzo opened his eyes widely and asked with a grin, "What does *this* mean?" And with that, he mimicked Bridget's interpretation of Kit. Bridget snorted. He looked ridiculous, but she realized that was exactly the way she had looked just a moment ago. "I *mean*, she's very ... um, what's the word? *Bubbly!* That's what I meant!"

"Ah, yes, of course, *bubbly*. How could I not have figured that out? No, I'm sorry, I don't know who she is. Should I?" Lorenzo looked perplexed.

Normally, Bridget would say, "Yes, unless you've been living under a rock or are blind, you most certainly would know who my best friend is!" However, maybe she had it all wrong this time. This was most unusual, though, and Bridget was at a loss for the right response. She spoke slowly. "Um, I don't know. I just figured most ... *people* around here know who she is."

Lorenzo shrugged and said, "Well, I don't tend to notice many people, you know, unless there's something that really makes them … stand out …" His lips curved up in a slight smile. Bridget felt her stomach lurch, yet not in an unpleasant way. He *was* flirting with her, wasn't he? And he was really handsome …

Lorenzo continued on, "You know, like buying a surplus of Nutella, trashing an old man's shop, and starting a water fight with a little kid … now those are things you don't see every day!" Okay, pheeeww, he was just kidding around. Still, she was going to change the subject—and fast.

"So, I have to say, your English is very good!" Bridget enthused, as if he was from some time-warped, third-world country.

"Thanks, it should be. I've been living in the States for ten years," Lorenzo replied. He continued on, "Well, I was born and raised here, but aside from the crazy tourist season, there's not much going on. My cousin lives in Florida and runs a restaurant, and he had a place for me there, so I just went. And never came back."

Ahhh, Florida. That could possibly explain the whole East Coast Tony Soprano-infused accent. Lorenzo shrugged. "People say America is too stressful and crazy and all that. But living here is not much different, to a certain extent. Pretty much from November to February, the whole town shuts down. There's nothing to do. Then from March on, it's complete chaos with tourism. And you have no choice; you gotta work nonstop, because that's your income for the rest of the year. Yeah, you work long hours, and then you *still* gotta find time to go out and pick up girls at the disco!" He smiled mischievously.

Bridget rolled her eyes. "Yes, very true." She then thought of Lassino with his restaurant, and Paolo and Giorgio with their boutiques, all open for long hours every day. Lorenzo was right. They still managed to be out every night and sometimes until the early hours of the morning, only to be back at work a few hours later! Bridget then added in agreement, "I don't know how they do it!"

"Ahh, that's just life here. Don't get me wrong. I love it here, and I miss my family a lot. But now, when I come back, I can enjoy my time with them and with my friends. And when I go to the disco, I don't gotta worry what time to get up the next day!"

Bridget smiled and nodded her head in agreement. Lorenzo titlted his head and looked at her and asked, "So, you never answered my question. *Do* you have a boyfriend?"

She was going to have to put a stop to this. She pointedly asked him, "So, is your *wife* from Positano too?"

A look of surprise passed Lorenzo's face and he answered, "Wife? I'm not married."

He wasn't married? Of course, you didn't have to be married to have a child. "Oh. I ... well, I just assumed you were since I saw you with that little girl at the—"

"My *niece* Carolina, my sister's daughter." *Yeesss!*

"Oh," was about all Bridget could comment.

Lorenzo drummed his fingers on the bar. "And in case you're wondering, Bridget, *no*, I don't have a girlfriend *here* or in Florida. So? Do you have a boyfriend here or at home?"

Bridget looked at him and answered sarcastically, "I know this will come as a complete shocker, but, no and no."

"Excellent. And by the way, it is a shocker." And he exhaled with a smile.

◆   ◆   ◆

Kit stood at the bar and held the cool champagne flute to her forehead. She could dance all night when Fabrizio played, but she was glad he was taking a break before starting his Italian set. The dance floor had become a sweltering sauna. She could handle her own sweat, but she was tired of having to constantly deflect clammy hands and bodies from coming into unwanted contact with her. If one more guy tried to grope or grind with her, well ... well, it was just so annoying after awhile! Aside from trying to shield Tiffany and the others from Mario's hilariously awful mating dance, she was just out there to have fun. She wasn't looking for a dance partner. But she guessed that if you were alone on the dance floor, you were pretty much fair game.

Usually, Bridget was her dance partner/bodyguard, but she hadn't even come out to dance to "Grease Lightning!" Strange, but Kit assumed it had to do with the tall, good-looking guy she was in animated conversation with. She wondered who he was. Maybe she should keep an eye on Bridget, as well, since she had a tendency to disappear if she became out of sorts.

Although, she sure was looking quite unusually peppy and upbeat tonight, Kit thought. Well, that was good. Still, she'd have to keep one eye on her co-workers and one eye on Bridget. Kit really wished she had a third eye so she could figure out where Lassino was as well, in addition to being on the lookout for creepy people who might approach. Speaking of … she'd noticed Vinnie lurking about, sneaking looks at her from across the dance floor. Bridget might have been right when she complained about the disco being quite dangerous at times.

Yes, where was Lassino? Although he was not one to turn to for protection here. As long as she'd known him, she'd never seen him set foot upon the dance floor. "I don't like to sweat!" he'd told her once when she pleaded with him to come out and dance. Kit had jokingly thought him to be a little obsessive-compulsive when it came to taking showers and primping, but maybe she wasn't too far off. She couldn't conceive how he ever played soccer in the stifling heat if he was averse to sweating, but what did she know? Maybe he just didn't want to dance with her.

Kit's only consolation was that she'd never seen him dancing with any other girl. His disco routine was such: wander around, chat with friends, glower at people behind his glasses, then lean against the bar with a bored look upon his face. And yes, he'd also watch her while she danced. And when it was time, he'd say, "Are you ready?" and pay for both their drink cards, and they'd head up to the parking garage to get his scooter.

Kit supposed it wasn't just his routine, but *their* routine, and she liked it. She could live here and do this all the time and be happy. She knew it. She felt it. There was just something about this place. Kit was positive she wasn't just imagining or romanticizing it. She felt connected to the town and the people here.

Going home to California was not something she looked forward to at all. Endless faculty meetings, pushy parents, a social scene that ended when her friends had to get home to their respective others and kids or when the bars pathetically shut down at the ungodly hour of one a.m. … and then there was her less-than-existent love life.

She sighed. She was in need of a life-altering change of direction. A summer here was not enough. What could she do here during the winter? Well, she could travel and then be back when everything opened up for tourist season. Maybe she could teach English to children or start some kind of day care! This could all work if she put her condo up for rent and found a long-term substitute. Her principal would be a bear about it, but he would probably support her decision, since he was a total throwback to the hippie, "go where the wind blows you," flower-power generation. It was her mother she dreaded dealing with.

Delia McNally would not understand. Always a tad bit more worried about her daughter's love life than her career, she'd lament, "Kit, what about Johnny? Why can't you settle down with him? He's such a nice boy!" Then Kit would actually have to break it to her that they hadn't been together for almost a year! And after that, Kit knew her mother's stress-related reflexes. She'd immediately go on a mad vacuuming spree of the whole house—she'd leave no corner, no hallway, no room untouched, and she'd vacuum them all two or three times over, no less. If and when Kit returned home for a visit, she'd also find that her mother had completely redecorated her room as well.

Although it was completely exasperating having a mother who dealt with unsavory realizations with overzealous dustbusting and redecorating, Kit admittedly wished she took after her. Instead, she had to be cursed with stomach and bowel problems that practically flared up if someone so much as looked at her crossed-eyed. In fact, she wasn't supposed to be drinking anything carbonated, and here she was, drinking prosecco. She reasoned it away by reminding herself that for some odd reason, food and beverages never aversely affected her when she was in Italy, thus, another worthy reason not to leave this country.

Unfortunately, though, a little voice inside her head reminded her that with all the stressful drama of the runaway and other issues, she wasn't even immune to intestinal problems here anymore. Well, she might have to watch the prosecco intake, but she wouldn't give it up. Besides, it was just so hot right now.

"You look like you are deep in thought," a voice purred into Kit's ear. Kit turned her head in surprise. Fabio stood next to her and leaned an elbow on the bar, his chin in his hand.

"Fabio, hi!" Kit smiled brightly. *At least it wasn't Vinnie.*

"Ah, there's that amazing smile." Fabio smiled back and ran his other hand through his closely shorn hair. "Having a good time?"

Kit nodded, "Yes, Fabrizio's a wonderful singer!" Then, as she finished her prosecco, she added, "But pheww, it's so hot tonight!"

Fabio fanned himself by pulling at his black button-up and said, "Yes. Let me get you a drink."

She'd accepted a ride from him, albeit to escape Vinnie, but Kit decided accepting a drink now might perhaps create some unnecessary expectations. Where *was* Lassino, anyway? She wished she didn't have to, but she'd better decline.

Why, oh, why, had she decided to wear the cream-colored Nolita button-up? She thought she'd be safe from the heat in the short-sleeved top. Granted, the heaviest thing about it was the delicate frill that ran vertically down the bustline. After all her profuse sweating, though, the fact that she was wearing something lightweight and sheer was problematic, since she now looked as if she'd been a participant in a wet T-shirt contest. The neon strobe lighting did not make matters any better. Who needed X-ray vision when you could gawk at women wearing damp, transluscent clothing at the disco!

"No drink? Kit, you are always so perfect!" Fabio threw up his hands grandly.

"What?" laughed Kit.

Fabio explained, "Always beautiful, always smiling, and never *drunk* like most of the girls and women in here!" He nodded his head in the direction of the other end of the bar. Kit fervently hoped he didn't happen to be pointing out Bridget. No, Bridget looked quite sober and was still engrossed with whatever her new friend was saying. Instead, the drunken examples Fabio alluded to were none other than her houseguests/co-workers. Tiffany, Marnie, and Kara were standing at the bar, shrieking and cackling, before slamming some kind of shot with two surfer-looking guys. Kit watched Tiffany sway and unsuccessfully try to adjust her tube top, which was becoming as half-mast as her eyes had been earlier.

Kit shrugged demurely while Fabio asked, "Aren't those your friends?"

"Yes, I teach with them," replied Kit. Although she was tired of being a babysitter, she did feel she had to make some kind of excuse for them. "Well, you know, they're young and on vacation."

Fabio replied matter-of-factly, "Maybe so, but it's too bad women don't realize that when they act like that, they make it all the more easy for the men here!"

Yes, one more reason to take it easy with the prosecco. Kit was thankful that Bridget was on pretty low-key behavior tonight, and she pointed out, "I'm not the only one who's not drunk. There's my best friend Bridget over there!"

Fabio gave the typical Italian face-shrug and answered, "Ah, yes, the dark-haired one. I always see her writing in a notebook."

Kit gushed proudly, "Bridget's a teacher too, but one day, with all she's written, she'll be a famous author for sure!"

Fabio chuckled and said, "Yes, well who wouldn't want to read about our town?" Then, changing the subject, he asked thoughtfully, "So, you are all teachers?"

Kit nodded and tried to scan the club for Lassino without appearing too obvious.

Fabio spoke slowly and stared right at Kit and said, "You know, I am looking for a nanny for my son. His mother is becoming very busy with her career in modeling, and we've decided to have him stay here with me. Do you know of anyone who might be interested?" He raised his eyebrows in a questioning way.

Kit thought a moment. Hmm, everyone she knew had her own career. She'd do it in a heartbeat, but if Fabio needed a nanny for the summer, well, the summer was practically over. Would she want to spend the rest of her vacation babysitting?

Kit answered, "Um, I can't really think of anyone that doesn't already have a job or that could get here right away to nanny for the rest of the summer."

"Well, my son will be staying with his mother until the end of August, so I wouldn't actually need anyone till then. I just really wanted to start looking now, for someone who would be right for the position."

Kit was sure she'd be able to help in some way. "I can send out an e-mail to all my friends and see if there's anyone interested." Kit suggested.

Fabio said, "Actually, I was thinking more of … *you*. Are you interested?"

Taken by surprise, Kit stammered, "Oh, well, I, um …"

"Have a job already. Yes, I know. Look, you are just what I am looking for." Fabio stopped momentarily before adding, "… for my son."

Kit began to protest, although with a smile on her lips. "But—"

Fabio cut her off. "Listen, let me finish, please. I will pay you as much as you already make. You will have a place to live here and a car to drive. When

I travel during the winter, you would come and look after Gian Franco for me. It would be perfect. You would be perfect! You are a teacher and can help my son learn English."

Kit was speechless. Hadn't she just been thinking that she needed some type of drastic life change? And here was the opportunity. She'd be making as much as ahe already was, which was not too shabby given her wealthy school district. She could travel, and yes, she'd be …

"And you'll be here with your love," Fabio added sincerely. How had he read her mind? Was she that transparent? Before she could say anything, Fabio added, "Yes, with your love, *Positano*. It is very obvious to me how you feel about our town. Oh, of course, Lassino is here too. But, perhaps, you'll find *someone else* while you're here." He smiled a bit suggestively. Oh, no, he couldn't be implying …

Kit tried unsuccessfully to protest, but Fabio intervened and said scornfully, "Oh, I know, you will pretend Lassino is not your boyfriend! Boyfriend? Lover? Well, whatever he is, he is not paying any attention to you. Why do you put up with that?" Kit began to fume at his bold statement, but then she realized it was true. Lassino's attentiveness was quite sporadic. And their passionate affair was confined to either explosive sex or to his childish displays of temper, when he wasn't straight-up teasing or ignoring her. She could deal with it most of the time, since she truly felt he was a kind and caring person, but sometimes the whole guessing-game got tiring.

Bridget wandered up and said, "Hi! I'm gonna leave now. Kit, this is Lorenzo; Lorenzo, this is Kit." She nodded at Kit then to the tall figure standing behind her.

"Ciao, Kit. Ciao, Fabio." Lorenzo nodded at both.

"Oh, you know each other?" Kit asked.

Fabio replied, "Of course; he's a local boy. Ciao, Lorenzo." He turned to Bridget and asked jokingly, "So, where is your notebook?"

Bridget replied dryly, "Well, I don't normally bring it to the disco. I like to keep my hands free."

"Oh," Fabio responded, while giving Kit a quick wink, "so you can hold your drink?"

"Actually, so I can protect myself on the dance floor," Bridget smirked in a flat voice.

Fabio agreed dramatically. "Yes, Positano can be dangerous—a town full of lies and deceit, but above all, love! Write that one down, Teacher! But we are not all dangerous men here, are we, Lorenzo? As a matter of fact, I was just trying to convince Kit to stay and work here."

Bridget raised her eyebrows and asked, "And what did Kit say to that?"

Kit grinned and replied, "I haven't said anything yet. I'm going to think about it, though."

"Ah, very good! You think about it and let me know." Fabio stared intently at Kit and then ran his hand over hers. "Don't think I will forget. Buona notte, Bridget, Lorenzo, *Kit*."

He took a last sip of his drink, set his glass down, and moved away from the trio. After taking a few steps, he turned around and flashed his bright smile and said, "Oh, and don't worry about trying to get a hold of me. I'll find you. After all, it's a small town, isn't it?"

They watched him back away a few more steps, then turn and wade through the dance-floor maze. The hulkish bouncer guarding the door nodded at him without even blinking as Fabio exited, bypassing all the patrons waiting in line to settle up their drink cards.

Bridget turned to Kit and asked warily, "What was that all about? No, no, wait, Fabio wants you to work for him in … *some* sort of capacity."

"Uh, yes, I'll tell you all about it, *later*," admitted Kit, not wanting to talk about it in front of Lorenzo. All she needed was for someone in this gossip-fueled town to get wind of it and for it to reach Lassino's ears. No telling how he'd react, but if he thought Kit was planning on staying longer than her original visit, he'd probably flee the country.

Kit changed the subject by asking pleasantly, "So, where are you off to?" Then she gave Bridget a sly look as if to say, *Is this guy safe?*

"Oh!" Bridget said excitedly, "I mentioned I was kind of hungry, and Lorenzo said he'd take me to some bakery that has really good cornetti."

Mmmmm, cornetti. That sounded so good. She loved the flaky, Nutella-filled pastries. And the cream-filled ones, too. Then there were the delicate, triangular berry tarts …

"Oh, I wanna …" Kit stopped herself mid-sentence from blurting out, "I wanna come too!" She realized that she had a habit of either inviting extra people along or inviting herslf along on other people's outings. Although, to her credit, most of the time, she really was invited by *others* to do things, since she just happened to be in the right place at the right time. However, this wasn't one of those times, so she'd better back off. Bridget had done well. This guy was really cute, seemed gentlemanly, and was *from* Positano. Whether that turned out to be an impediment remained to be seen.

Instead, Kit shouted, "I … I think that sounds like fun! I didn't know any of the bakeries were open now!"

Lorenzo laughed. "They're not. I have a friend who works in one. He should just about be done with the first round of pastries."

"A friend who's a bartender, a friend who works in a bakery … if you tell me you have a friend who owns a shoe store, you'll be my new best friend!" teased Bridget.

Lorenzo raised his eyebrows a few times at Bridget and grabbed her hand. "Shall we go? Hey, nice meeting you, Kit." He waited as Bridget asked Kit, "Where's Lassino?"

"No idea." Kit shrugged.

"Oh, that's right—you're Lassino's girlfriend." Lorenzo nodded in recognition.

Well, at least he hadn't called her his lover. Kit was tired of denying being his girfriend. Apparently, everyone in the town (excluding Lassino, of course) seemed to think she was, so she'd let it go.

Lorenzo chuckled and added, "Lassino, crazy guy! *Good* guy, but crazy!" He noted the grimace upon Kit's face and he spoke quickly, "But, hey, don't worry. Have you met his brothers? They're all crazier than him!"

"Well, that should make you feel better," Bridget joked.

"Oh, yes, good to know he's not the *most* insane person in the town!" laughed Kit.

"Sorry," Lorenzo shrugged. "Hey, good luck!"

"Thanks! Bridget, see you—well, I'd say tomorrow, but it's almost four thirty! So, guess I'll just see you back at the apartment." She gave her a kiss on the cheek and joked quietly, "And stay away from the beach or rocks!"

"Very funny," smirked Bridget. She saw that Lorenzo was chatting with another local, and she whispered, "He's cute! And really nice! And … seemingly *normal!*"

Kit smiled. "This is good! Have fun, be careful, and dammit, make sure you bring me back some cornetti, okay?"

"Okay! Ciao!" Kit watched Lorenzo gently place a tanned hand at the small of Bridget's back as he guided her around the dance floor. Kit sighed as she realized that once again, she was alone with her camera. Well, for the moment. Giorgio wandered up, playfully pouted, and said, "I cannot find a man here to dance with!"

"Giorgio, it *is* ladies' night!" Kit chuckled.

"Well, in Positano, ladies' night really means men's night! All the men come to see the women. So why I can't find someone to dance with? You know, just to *dance!*" He shook his head sorrowfully and batted his eyes.

Kit patted his hand and replied, "A handsome guy like you! You'll find someone."

Giorgio shrugged. "This town is just too small. Ahh, I do not want someone for *love*—just for the dancing ... and the sex!"

Kit asked, "So, how do *you* meet people? How do you find someone?"

Giorgio explained simply, "I just call and make an appointment."

"An *appointment?*"

Giorgio's eyes lit up. "Si, I call and make an *appointment*. And somebody come out and then, we, uh ..." He stopped and pretended to unzip his pants.

"Ohhhh, I see. *That* kind of appointment!" Kit smiled.

"And then *finito*, ciao, ciao! Everybody happy!" Giorgio cried and clapped his hands.

He continued, "But tonight, you come and dance with me, bella!"

Kit's eyes darted to dance floor and back before she answered, "Oh, I will. Where's Lassino?"

"Lassino? He left already! Ah, Kit, don't worry about Lassino! You come dance with all of us!"

Lassino had left without saying good-bye. Well, she *would* go and dance with Giorgio and all of Lassino's other friends. That was just what she'd do. She forbade herself to let anyone see how hurt she was.

"All right, let's go." Kit beamed. She held her camera in one hand while grabbing onto Giorgio's oustretched hand with her other, and she followed him to the dance floor.

Chapter 13

It was ten thirty the *next* evening, and Bridget had finally returned to the apartment from her cornetti excursion with Lorenzo. Kit and Julianna lounged on the candlelit patio and suspensefully waited for her. Bridget pushed the slightly ajar door open and poked her head in cautiously. Julianna called loudly from where she sat back, her legs kicked up upon the glass table, "Well, it's about time, my little friend!"

Bridget winced. She had hoped that everyone would be out already, but what was she thinking? It was only a mere ten-thirty. Now she'd have to endure a complete interrogation. Although nothing had happened, a lot had happened, if that made any sense. All Bridget really wanted to do was sit on the quiet balcony and write in her journal, so she wouldn't forget anything.

That would have to wait. Kit jumped up and twittered, "Jeez, we thought you were never coming back! Hold on! I see a white bag in your hand. Is that …? Say it's the cornetti!"

Bridget held the bag up, nodded, and said, "Yes, it's the cornetti."

Kit squealed, lunged forward, and snatched the bag out of Bridget's hand. She opened the bag, stuck her nose inside it, and shouted, "Yes! Ahhh, it smells so good. Uh! I'm having one right now! Ooooh, and you brought biscotti too!"

"You're *welcome*, and it's nice to see you too!" Bridget joked.

Kit stopped short, her eyes wide. "Sorry. How are you? We *were* worried about you. Um, is it okay if I have one of your cornetti?" she asked sheepishly.

Bridget rolled her eyes and answered, "*Yes*, Kit. I brought them for you!"

Kit grinned cheesily, "You're the best! Here, sit!" She pulled Bridget over to one of the chairs and fished around in the bag for a pastry before sitting down herself.

Julianna got down to business and demanded, "So, *where* have you been this whole time?"

"Well, after the cornetti, we went and got a cappuccino," Bridget stated blandly.

Kit tore a chunk of flaky pastry and popped it into her mouth. She placed a hand over her mouth, chewed, and then asked, "*And?*"

Bridget shrugged. "And … then he took me to his family's home, and I had lunch there. Oh, and dinner." Kit and Julianna exchanged raised eyebrows.

"Oh, my God, Bridget! You had lunch *and* dinner with his family? And then did you have sex?" Julianna shrieked in anticipation.

Kit interrupted, "Wait, wait, wait; go back to the food part! I want to hear *everything* you ate. Don't leave anything out! I can't believe you had *two home-cooked* meals with his family at their house!" Kit shook her head in stunned disbelief. In her opinion, that was like hitting the jackpot.

Julianna swatted a hand at Kit and said, "Oh, please, tell us about the food later. Let's hear about the sex! I mean, you were gone a *long* time. There must've been something going on between the eating!"

Well … not quite. Not quite sure if she was disappointed about that or not. No, she was decidedly all right with not much happening. Bridget shrugged. "There *was* no sex!"

Julianna's mouth dropped as she mouthed the word *what?*

Bridget explained, "Yes, sorry to disappoint you, but I *just* met the guy!"

"*So?*" Julianna snorted.

"Well, even if I had considered that an option, I certainly wouldn't have slept with him while his whole family was right in the next room! So where would that leave us? Having sex on his *scooter?*" Bridget joked.

Matter-of-factly, Julianna stated, "Well, why not? If sex on an ironing board is possible, then you can do it on a scooter!"

Kit turned and looked at Julianna in awe. "You've had *sex* on an *ironing board? What? How?* How is that possible?"

Julianna tilted her head at her with a look that said, *What do you think? Of course I did!* Then she replied, "Kit, *anything* is possible. Besides, I'm little."

Kit looked at Bridget, who appeared just as perplexed as she was as to how that particular activity could be carried out without the ironing board collapsing.

Kit persisted. "Well, yeah, you're tiny, but what about the guy? Was he on the ironing board too?"

Julianna sighed. "Nooo, he was *big*. He didn't need to! All he had to do was—" She positioned herself on the edge of the patio chair, ready to demonstrate.

"Okay, yeah, we get it. Excuse me; I'm getting a drink." Bridget got up and headed toward the kitchen.

Julianna rolled her eyes and said to Kit, "I'll explain it all later, so I don't upset *Grandma* in there!" She nodded in the direction of kitchen.

Bridget stuck her head out and called, "I heard that!"

"Bridget, I'm kidding. Okay, so you didn't have sex, but was it worth it?" Julianna shouted back.

Bridget returned to the patio with a bottle of prosecco and three glasses. A bashful smile spread across her face and she answered simply, "Yes, it was."

Kit clapped her hands giddily. "Yay! I knew it. Pop the cork, and start from the beginning—you know, at the cornetti part! We have a good hour before we have to go out."

◆　◆　◆

All right, so she'd decided to leave the disco with another guy she barely knew. Well, in fact, Bridget didn't know Lorenzo *at all*, really. *What was she thinking?* she wondered as he chivalrously paid for both their drink cards. Bridget noted with surprise that the scary bouncer actually smiled at Lorenzo and called good night to him as they left the steamy crowd behind.

Yes, what *was* she really thinking at this moment? That was precisely the same question she had asked herself last summer when she'd accepted Paolo's swim-party invitation. As she followed Lorenzo's tall frame down the stone steps, Bridget noted that she didn't have the same apprehension that she'd had with Paolo. Of course, there'd been a certain amount of dangerous excitement involved in leaving with him. She'd long ago admitted to herself that she'd been overtaken not only by her infatuation with Paolo, but in her somewhat false ignorance of what was to take place. While she hadn't really known for certain what was in store for her when she left the disco with Paolo, she couldn't play completely naive.

At the bottom of the steps, Bridget snuck a glance at the abandoned beach chairs and beyond them, at the rocky water's edge. A group of chattering clubbers were standing clustered there, laughing and smoking. She turned away quickly when she realized that one dark-haired guy with a very pronounced nose had happened to look over. She knew only one person here with a nose like *that*. Bridget quickly put her head down and hurried after Lorenzo; she wondered if Paolo had recognized her as well.

While Bridget felt a great deal of anticipatory wonder of what would transpire with Lorenzo, she felt no anxiety or premature guilt for whatever *might* occur. In fact, she ascertained that the most remorseful thing that could possibly happen was that she'd waste a day's worth of her Weight Watchers flex points on the delectably fattening cornetti she was about to consume.

Truth be told, not only did she *not* feel anxious around Lorenzo; she actually felt comfortable with him. For starters, they were the same age. In this town, that was a novelty in itself. How refreshing to find someone over the age of twenty-four to converse with, and at the disco, no less! For once, she didn't feel like she was absolutely ancient. She realized that she might look younger than she was, but the reality of it all was, she wasn't, and she could only fake it for so long on vacation.

And while the mortification of Lorenzo having already seen her in a bathing suit was still quite horrifying, it was a relief that it had occurred and he had *still* chosen to spend his evening talking to her. *Although*, her stomach *had* been covered up by the water that day. At any rate, his vision was seemingly intact; he wasn't fazed by her spare tire, and he seemed to appreciate her droll sarcasm. More importantly, Lorenzo was the first male she'd met in this country who didn't once tell her she looked so serious and then ask the question that always infuriated her to no end, "Why don't you smile more, like your friend, Kit?" As if *she* were an oddity because she didn't walk around constantly flashing her teeth at people! Yes, it was a comment that, undoubtedly, would immediately put her into a bitchy mood, thus making her become not just the serious friend of the toothy, blonde American, but the scary, irritated one as well. Well, Lorenzo never once commented on her serious nature, but then again, she had been smiling more than usual and had somehow been entertainingly witty, with a touch of her usual dorkiness. Bridget couldn't figure it out. Had Lorenzo caused her to feel so secure that she'd let her somber wall down enough to laugh like she did with the people who knew her best? Or was she acting that way simply *because* he was someone who *hadn't* labeled her right away as being the "serious one?" And, why, why did she always have to overanalyze everything?

Bridget wouldn't let this puzzlement impair the good time she was having. For once, she had been invited to do something on her own and not because she was the trusty sidekick of Kit. And *maybe* Lorenzo would kiss her, but ... well, she wouldn't think about that. If the time ever came, she'd deal with it then.

They strolled past the beachfront restaurants, which were lit only by the glowing cigarette tips of those huddled around the lonely tables. They left the beach and the tiled dome of Santa Maria Assunta behind as they wound their way up the uneven cobblestone path, passing darkened shop windows and the occasional lovers who lingered in the shadowy archways. Bridget wondered where the bakery was and if it would really be open.

And quite suddenly, they were standing in front of the local parking garage. Bridget had an uneasy feeling. Maybe Lorenzo had changed his mind and was going home and she'd be left in the parking garage again. This time, though, she wasn't staying a block away at the hotel. It was quite a long, arduous hike, and especially in heels at four thirty in the morning. She'd better act fast.

"So, see you ... soon!" Bridget smiled brightly and took a step back. Lorenzo gently grabbed her arm and asked with a confused look on his face, "Where are you going? I thought you wanted to go for some cornetti."

"Oh! Yes, sure, yes, I did. I just thought, well, we've passed all the shops, and here we are at the garage ... and I just assumed you'd be taking off." Bridget smiled lamely and shrugged. *Red alert, red alert! Complete Idiot Factor resurfacing at full throttle!*

Lorenzo clarified, "Well, I'm not taking you to a bakery here. We're going up to Montepertuso. My friend works in a bakery *there*."

Montepertuso. *Montepertuso?* That was ... *far*. Bridget remembered hearing about the good hiking to be done up the mountainside road to the next far-flung neighboring town—that is, if you were hard core enough to enjoy hiking in the awful heat, or hiking at all. She thought the stairs around here were quite enough, thank you. Of course, it was a short ride there if you took the bus or a … scooter. Yes, this would explain them being at the garage.

A flicker of excitement ran through Bridget. She was going to ride on the back of some Italian guy's scooter! The time she'd ridden, Italian-sandwich style, with Kit and Franco didn't count. She'd been scared to death anyway. Wait a minute, *her* on a *scooter?* Who was she kidding? She was just as petrified to ride one now, too. Maybe she could get out of this. What about that old helmet law around here? She never thought she'd be the one to use the lame excuse, but a desperate situation such as this called for resurrecting it.

Oh, but it really, *really* was a shame, though, since she was completely having fun and Lorenzo was … unbelievably charming in a nonplayerlike way, not to mention more than cute … but, yeah, she'd have to use that helmet thing as her escape plan. The whole "scooter in Italy with a handsome man" thing was extremely romantic, but it was just a cheesy movie cliché, wasn't it? Bridget decided she'd have to pass on it. There was that damn rooster crowing again anyway. She should get up the hill and get a few hours of sleep.

Before she had a chance to decline, though, Lorenzo removed the helmet that had been dangling from the handlebars, directed it at Bridget, and commanded, "Here, put this on."

Bridget nodded at him and said deliberately, "Oh. You want me to ride on the scooter with you? Wearing the helmet?'

Lorenzo raised his eyebrows, "Yes … that would be why I handed you the helmet. What's wrong? Is there a problem?" Oh, well, now she felt bad and like a complete idiot, since he looked a little disappointed. Or was that more a look of irritation?

She spoke quickly. "Oh, no, no! But I know about the helmet law here."

Lorenzo chuckled and replied, "What about it?"

Bridget heard herself babble, "You only have *one* helmet, and so I just *assumed* …" She stopped and waited for him to clue in to her law-abidingness. Lorenzo put his hands in prayer position, shook them at her, and replied, "What? You just *assumed* that I'd invite you to go for cornetti and then disinvite you because I somehow forgot I only have one helmet with me?" He stared at her, and it was his turn to wait for her to respond.

Maybe. Bridget stammered, "Um … well …, uh—"

Lorenzo didn't wait. "*Or you just assumed* that I'd changed my mind and was just going to be an ass and let you walk up the hill—in *those* shoes—because I only have one helmet?" Wow, this was embarrassing. How had he known? Bridget bit her lip uncomfortably.

He smiled slightly, which showed his dimple, and continued, "You certainly like to assume a lot, Bridget."

Apart from the Tony Soprano-like voice, she was duly impressed with his English. Still, she wouldn't let that cloud her reasoning.

She retorted sassily, "Well, I'd prefer to think of myself as smart, a thinker." *More like overly cautious and paranoid …*

"You're on vacation; stop thinking so much! What are you worried about?"

Where to begin? Bridget stared back at him skeptically. And then a loud, howling sound echoed in the garage. Bridget's eyes popped and her hands involuntarily flew to her midsection as she realized the scary noise had come from her stomach.

Lorenzo ignored her embarrassment and added, "Look, you said you were hungry—and *clearly*, you weren't lying—and I'm willing to risk the helmet law to take you for some cornetti. If you really don't want to come, okay, but I'm still going to drop you off, so you might as well take the helmet and get on. You decide: home or cornetti?"

He stood there patiently, arms folded, helmet in hand. His green eyes stared intensely at her and his bottom lip stuck out, as if he were daring her. It was then that her stomach decided to roar unhappily again.

Bridget took the helmet from him and said, "Cornetti."

Lorenzo smiled, rolled his eyes, and said, "*Bene*! Let's go." He climbed up on the scooter and turned the key in the ignition, while she put the helmet on and awkwardly tightened the strap. She was thankful that he wasn't watching her as she gingerly threw her leg over the seat and wrapped her arms around him. The scooter gave a small lurch, and they puttered out of the garage.

Lorenzo called over his shoulder to her, "Don't worry about the helmet thing. They're not *that* strict about it. And if we do get stopped, it's not a big deal since—"

"Oh, let me guess," Bridget called over the sputtering scooter, "you have a friend who's in the carbinieri!"

His head was still slightly turned to her, and he winked. "Actually, a cousin!"

"Of course! Oh, Jesus! Keep your eyes on the road! Please!" Bridget yelled into his back as they took a bend in the road so fast and close that she felt some of the hanging wall shrubbery graze her arm.

"I know how to drive these roads. I'm from here, remember?" he shouted, although Bridget noted amusement in his voice.

Bridget apologized and said worriedly, "Sorry. It's just kind of dark, you know. Are you *sure* you can see all right?"

Lorenzo pulled over to the side of the road, turned to her again, and stated, "Bridget, it's almost five in the morning and quite light, and I have twenty-twenty vision, so just relax, okay? I'm not going to let anything happen to you."

Bridget exhaled and repeated quietly, "Nothing's going to happen to me. Okay, okay, sorry." She'd have to keep up this mantra until they got to the bakery.

"Yes, nothing's going to happen to you," Lorenzo stated again. Then he revved the engine, and they shot off. He called out jokingly, "At least, nothing's gonna happen to you on the *scooter!*"

"What?" Bridget cried and clung tighter to him as they took another turn at full speed.

◆　　◆　　◆

"How's your stomach now?" Lorenzo asked.

Even more hideously poochy, no thanks to the scrumptious, still warm, Nutella-filled pastry that she'd eaten. But she supposed she'd better keep that comment to herself.

"Much better. That was *delicious*," Bridget replied and then exhaled.

Lorenzo smiled back at her, popped the last remnants of his third pastry into his mouth, and said, "You didn't eat very much. Why don't you have another?"

It was super-tempting. In fact, she'd love to take a bite (or three) out of one of the cream-filled croissants, not to mention a nibble from any one of the assorted glazed fruit tarts she'd picked out and that now filled the paper bag that sat between them on the stone bench. Across the quiet street, a waft of fresh bread and pastries drifted out from the bakery. Resisting another sampling was going to be tough.

"I'll wait till later. I could easily inhale a few more, and I promised I'd bring some back for Kit," Bridget conceded.

"You're not alone. I can't believe I just ate three!" Lorenzo lifted his T-shirt up slightly and rubbed his stomach. She'd already seen him without his shirt on at the beach, but Bridget couldn't help but take a peek at the little piece of tanned flesh that lay exposed.

She made herself look the other way; she wished she could do the same—well, not reveal her stomach, but rather, undo the button on her jeans, which were cutting into her abdomen right now. Clearly, a late dinner, drinks, and now pastries were not conducive to wearing skinny jeans.

Lorenzo's voice interrupted her inner monologue on her too-tight J Brands, and he spoke genuinely. "Bridget, I've had a really good time with you—*really*." Not sure about what to say, she stared at the ground intently.

"So, I'm thinking … that I'd like to continue this. If you don't mind, of course!" She looked up to find Lorenzo watching her inquisitively.

Bridget wished he'd clarify a little more. Continue what? Eating pastries? Worriedly, Bridget just knew that she'd cave into temptation if he asked another time whether she was still hungry. Her daily points were already shot to hell, of course, but no! No more pastries!

But maybe Lorenzo meant he wanted to continue the lengthy conversation they'd started a few hours back at the disco and had continued for the last hour and half on this stone bench. What hadn't they talked about? She'd learned that his father was retired and his mother still helped his grandfather in his shop. His sister, Carla, only a couple of years older than him, had become a widow when Carolina was only a baby. She lived next door to his parents and worked in a linen shop. And then there was his adventurous move to Florida ten years back, and the cousin's Italian restaurant that he helped run.

What had he learned about her? Much more than she'd ever been prone to share with a virtual stranger, let alone a man! The whole "being over thirty and living at home with your mother" scenario usually sent males running in the other direction. Bridget had found it best to be very vague about it. Where did she live? *Oh, I have a roommate, an older woman in her sixties. Oh, yeah, we get along grrreat!* It was ridiculous, though, and she had found it was better to be upfront right away about living with her mother. If people couldn't understand it, then to hell with them.

To be honest, after her tortuous relationship with her ex, she was not anywhere near looking to find someone. And it was a surefire way to weed out the assorted oddballs and players, but even the "nice, normal" guys seemed a bit weirded out by her living situation and awkwardly found excuses to be "off to the restroom" or to not call again. If Bridget ever did find someone she was halfway interested in, he was going to have to be very understanding about her living at home because of her mother's health conditions.

"Jeez, Bridget, I know I'm not in the greatest health, but you make me sound like I've got one foot in the grave! If you ever bring anybody home again, they'll be surprised if I'm not laid out in a coffin!" Okay, so maybe she played it up even more than necessary. All right, so he'd not only have to understand about her mom; he'd have to seriously appreciate the fact that she liked to dress *extremely well* and travel.

Lorenzo listened intently as she debriefed him on her mother's illness and the fact that she lived at home with her, all about her small and tight-knit family, the teaching in a Catholic school—minus her clothes-shopping addiction. To Bridget's shock, he didn't seem surprised or put off by any of it. In fact, he appeared quite interested, as if she was some kind of fascinating person. Jeez, if she talked any more, she'd probably spill the beans about going to therapy and Weight Watchers! What was left to chat about that wouldn't potentially scare him away? Of course, maybe she wanted to scare him away. She wasn't sure yet.

Lorenzo reached over, gently placed a hand on Bridget's shoulder, and said, "Yes, I'd like to continue this. But there's one thing I really need, and I think you'll agree." He paused and looked at her as if she should be reading his mind. Oh, oh, *uh-oh* ... was he going to kiss her? What if he meant that he wanted to have *sex*? And where? Not on the rocks when it was light outside! Or *here*? Oh, no! How did she get into these situations? Bridget tried to appear calm and nonchalant as Lorenzo asked playfully, "So, do you know what I am thinking, what I want—right now?"

"I ... don't know," Bridget said.

He paused before saying, "A *cappuccino!* That's what we need right now after those pastries! And then, of course, I'm sure brushing or flossing the teeth would be a good idea." He ruffled her hair.

"Oh, of course, a *cappuccino*. And where are we going for that?" asked Bridget.

"I know the perfect place. Come on; let's go." He jumped up from the bench and handed her the helmet.

"Oh, yay. The scooter again," Bridget called sarcastically after him, but he was already kick-starting the engine.

✦   ✦   ✦

The scooter wound its way down the jutting mountainside in the early grayness. Every once in a while, Bridget summoned the courage to peek out and look down at the ant-sized outline of Positano. She'd then just as quickly squeeze her eyes shut and thrust her head into Lorenzo's back again. But the quiet solitude of the massive mountain, and the fact that there were no other moving targets on the road at this early hour, served as the encouragement Bridget needed. By the time they were back in the slumbering beach town, heading down Via Pasitea to the fork in the road and then speeding up Via C. Colombo, she had completely forgotten her fear and was like a dog with her head thrust out a car window, enjoying the scenery and the cool air in her face. Maybe she could possibly get used to riding a scooter, if only between the hours of 4:00–6:00 a.m.!

Rounding a few more bends, they pulled over to the side of the road when they came to a wrought-iron gate. Lorenzo cut the motor and put the kickstand down. He unlocked the gate and then wheeled the scooter inside the metal cage. From where she stood, Bridget noticed a few other scooters lined up in the enclosed space. She unbuckled the strap of the helmet and handed it to Lorenzo.

"Grazie." Lorenzo took the helmet, hung it from one of the handlebars and motioned to the scooters behind him, and then said with a slight bow, "Our garage. All right, time for some cappuccino!"

And with that, he locked the gate, turned, and headed down a staircase till they reached a wooden door. Bridget trailed behind gingerly, as she had not intended to wear her four-inch heels for six hours straight. Lorenzo unlocked the door and quietly pushed it open. He smiled at her proudly and said, "Welcome to my home."

His home—yes, that's what she'd figured. She sincerely hoped they had their cappuccino and left before his family got up. The fact that she'd been out all night and into the morning was evident. Once the family caught a look at her in her disco attire (and it wasn't, by any means, risqué), they'd still be sure to think she was some kind of American hussy who'd seduced their son into bringing her home! And all she'd wanted was a pastry!

Actually, all she wanted right now was to take off her shoes and go to sleep (after she brushed her teeth). Well, she'd have to hurry him along so he could get her home. She hoped Lorenzo would drive her, because the apartment was so … lost in her thoughts, Bridget had wandered into the middle of the spacious patio and looked around, and then she stopped suddenly in wonder. To her left, carved into the stone wall, was a long bench. An aqua-tiled table stood in front of it with cushioned chairs at either end. Protruding out from the wall above the bench, and stretching out and over the table and chairs, was a trellis canopy, which had become a cascade of dripping morning glory and jasmine. The waist-high stone wall ran along the patio quite a ways. Past the weathered limestone patio lay a long stretch of emerald grass, decorated with a few cushioned chaises and some glass lanterns suspended from iron stakes. Huge terra cotta urns, overflowing with colorful flora, lined the grassy area, and a tangle of lemon trees and creeping bougainvillea occupied the far corner, the fuschia bougainvillea having attached itself to the side of the house. Bridget thought the patio and garden exhumed the typically exotic Positanese charm. But most impressive about it all was the stunning view it harbored.

It was the famed shot that had launched a thousand paintings and ten thousand more postcards. Light-hued houses stacked on top of each other like a precarious pyramid of blocks and overlooked the protected cove of the rocky Spiaggia Grande. Then there was the shallow, turquoise water, which gave way to a sparkling, sapphire shade the farther out one looked. In the distance, the three islets known as Li Galli, or "the Sirens," sat in the dark water. Forget about the limoncello, the ceramic tiles, the handmade sandals; the best souvenir you could take away from this coastline village was *this*, the completely astounding and unforgettable image. No matter how many times Bridget viewed it, from whatever angle, at whatever time, it always knocked her out.

"Wow," breathed Bridget simply.

"You like? It's not much, but this is where I grew up," Lorenzo spoke.

"*Not much?* It's incredible. What's not to like? The fact that you woke up to this view every day is amazing!" Bridget was shocked.

Lorenzo shrugged as he explained, "I guess when you have something right in front of you all the time, you kinda take it for granted. I appreciate it a lot more now that I'm gone. And of course, seeing Positano through someone else's eyes, someone like you, who's not from here, also makes me—what's the word? Ah, more *aware*! More aware of what we have here."

Bridget nodded her head in agreement as she stared at the mountainside. Even from this far vantage point, she could spot the large, white building that was Palazza Bianca. Somewhere right below that was the apartment. Uh, yes ... about getting back to the apartment ... it would be a torturous trek around the mountainside in these shoes if she had to walk. Bridget suddenly wondered if the girls were concerned about her whereabouts. She should get going, and soon. She swiveled around and found her nose pressed up against the wide, firm chest of Lorenzo. Bridget jumped in surprise. "Whoa, sorry! Didn't know you were right behind me!" She spoke quickly and then looked up at him.

Lorenzo took her chin in one hand and combed his other hand through Bridget's hair, and then said quietly, "Sorry, didn't mean to scare you."

"Um, that's okay." Bridget spoke to Lorenzo's chest. Her heart was beating fast, and her stomach was suddenly a nervous wreck. She prayed it wouldn't start talking again.

"Ay! I'm up here!" Lorenzo tilted his head down at her, his lips not far away from hers.

"Yes, hi," Bridget almost whispered as she looked into his green eyes. Was she sweating? She felt a little light-headed. Maybe she should've eaten another pastry, or maybe she was dehydrated! Oh, God, now her head was throbbing, and so were her feet. What was going on? Lorenzo gently grasped her face in his large hands and pulled her to him. He bent down slightly, brought her face to his, and kissed her. It was a soft, delicate kiss. No aggressive slobbering, thank God—just simple. Bridget felt herself relax a tad. Lorenzo then followed up with a succession of kneading pecks, before his lips moved below her ear and to her neck. Okay, now she was headed for trouble. Bridget unintentionally exhaled. Lorenzo removed his head from her neck and asked, "Are you okay?"

Bridget swallowed and answered, "Yeah, but, do you think we could sit?" She nodded at the nearest lounge chair.

"Yes, of course; the height difference doesn't bother me at all, but sure." He clasped her hand and started moving. She hadn't been referring to her lack of height, but no need to clarify at this moment. Oh, wait a minute, hadn't Paolo made some weird joke about never having sex on a beach chaise? Was that common knowledge with all the men in the town? Great, what if he thought she was implying she wanted to *do it* with him? It was just that her feet …

"I mean, my feet are absolutely killing me. I'm sorry, Lorenzo, what I mean is I need to sit and take my shoes off for a little bit."

"Oh, sure, sure, no problem." Lorenzo laid himself back against the cushy chaise and waited for her. Bridget sat at the edge and pulled her satin heels off. Ahhh, released from the tight shoes, Bridget sighed. She looked at her feet and then gasped. Her normally tiny ankles were so swollen that she could barely see the anklebones. Horrified, she noted that her feet now resembled two very large sausages that had been stuffed into her expensive shoes. Was there no justice for her in this town? And then there was the light-purple bruise on one foot and the dried blood on the other. Lovely. "Oh, no, my feet!" Bridget cried out.

"Wow, they're really swollen. You're probably just dehydrated, and the heat doesn't help, either. Here, sit back and put your feet up." Lorenzo patted the tiny spot left next to him. If he really thought she was going to fit in there next to him, he was crazy. If her feet were that swollen, then the rest of her must be as well!

Lorenzo held out his hand to her and said, "Come on."

Bridget scooted backward, her feet pulsing. She stuffed herself in snugly next to Lorenzo; his arm encircled her shoulders. Exhausted, Bridget leaned her head back and closed her eyes.

He whispered into her ear, "Still want that cappuccino?"

Bridget shook her head no and then opened her eyes slightly and said, "No, thanks. I should really get going. I'm exhausted. The last thing I want is to be kept awake."

"Well, thanks a lot!" Lorenzo joked.

"I didn't mean it like that! I just meant, I'm so tired, and it's probably time for me to go home. Seriously, Lorenzo," she said as she patted his hand, "at home, sadly, I'm usually in bed before ten—well, at least, on a school night!"

He chuckled. "I know; it's the same for me too. How about I get you a glass of water, and then I'll take you home?"

"Okay, thanks." Bridget accepted the offer, leaned back against the cushion, and closed her eyes heavily. By the time Lorenzo had returned, she was out cold.

♦ ♦ ♦

Bridget pried her heavy eyes open. She knew she had fallen asleep, but for how long? As her eyes adjusted to the brightness of her surroundings, Bridget uneasily squinted about and noted that it was quite sunny and warm out, which most likely meant she'd slept for at least an hour or two. Okay, so it was about eight or nine o'clock. She prayed that Lorenzo's family was a late-sleeping bunch—except that she could hear clanking sounds, like pots and pans being knocked around and such, and talking coming from the kitchen. She turned her head in that direction and was startled to find a pair of huge, green eyes watching her. Lorenzo's little niece, Carolina, stood there in Bridget's towering heels. She let out a loud yell, jumped out of Bridget's shoes, and ran from the grass and into the kitchen.

Bridget sat up quickly. She had to get out of there! Oh, but her feet were sore. And, of course, she had to go to the bathroom.

"Hey, you're awake! I was about to come out and check if you were still breathing! But Carolina came in to report that you were up." Lorenzo strolled out, and his niece scampered right behind him.

Bridget winced and asked, "How long have I been sleeping? A couple of hours?"

"It's almost one. I guess I really put you to sleep," Lorenzo chuckled.

Bridget's jaw dropped. "What! I never sleep that late!"

"Come on, you're on vacation! And I did keep you out quite late."

Bridget looked around anxiously. "But, I need to go, and your family … they must think I'm some drunk American bimbo who passed out in their backyard!"

"Look, you weren't drunk. You were tired. I told them that," Lorenzo stated.

"*Them?* Who's *them?*" asked Bridget warily.

"Oh, my parents, my sister, my grandfather. And of course, my niece."

Great, the whole freakin' family was here. Lorenzo tried pulling the pigtailed child out from behind his leg, which she had attached herself to. "Carolina, *dai!* Say hello to Bridget." He patted her head. With a timid smile on her face, she looked up at her uncle and then back at Bridget, and then quickly hid her head behind his leg again.

"As you can see, she's my little shadow. When I come home to visit, I gotta answer to her. If I'm not with her, she wants to know everything I've been doing—huh, Carolina?"

Carolina popped her head out quickly to look back and forth between Lorenzo and Bridget, eyeing Bridget cautiously.

"Great, how did she take your being out till all hours with me?" joked Bridget.

"Well, I told her I brought home a teacher to teach her English. She wasn't so sure until she saw your shoes," laughed Lorenzo.

"Well, maybe I'll come back another time." Bridget scooted to the edge of the chaise and stood up.

"Oh, you can't leave now. We're about to have lunch, and my mother has invited you to stay," Lorenzo said, with a sly smile on his lips.

"Oh, no, that's so … nice of her, but I don't think I should …" Bridget tried to think of some kind of excuse. But darn it, she was kind of hungry again, and she sure did need to use the bathroom.

Lorenzo took hold of her hand and said plainly, "You must stay, or my mother will be offended. Especially, after I told her you were a teacher … in a Catholic school." He dropped her hand and made the sign of the cross as he bowed his head at her.

Fantastic. She just hoped they wouldn't expect her to lead them in grace in Italian or something. She did not want to do this. Of course, insulting an Italian mother was not something she wanted to do, either. She'd already somehow annoyed Neighborhood Watch Lady, and then there was that kid from the beach. She'd probably better stay and not push her luck. Bridget never thought being a Catholic schoolteacher would ever make her that appealing, but what the heck?

"Well, I wouldn't want to insult your mother …" Bridget said and shrugged resignedly.

"I knew I'd get you to stay!" Lorenzo smiled and then added, "I hope you're hungry."

Of course she was hungry. She was in Italy, wasn't she?

◆ ◆ ◆

"Ready for a little dessert?" Lorenzo asked from across the table. *Yes.* No, no, she shouldn't. Bridget considered herself to have been extremely good in a Weight Watchery way. Although always very capable of it, she'd steered herself away from completely clearing her plate each time Lorenzo's mother brought out another tantalizing platter. She'd sampled it all with relish, though: melon and prosciutto, toasted bruschetta, creamy mushroom risotto, fried zucchini, and a crisp white wine. For once, Bridget felt glad that she had a stomach like a vacuumous pit. She felt sorry for Kit, who loved food so much but repeatedly suffered afterward from intestinal repercussions. Perhaps that was how she always seemed to stay so thin. Yet, it was quite a price to pay. Yes, Bridget's ironclad stomach was a blessing and a curse in itself, she guessed. *Of course* she had room for dessert, but she didn't want to ruin the contentment her stomach felt right now. Plus, all the food and the afternoon heat were causing her to feel drowsy *again*. She really should get back to the apartment. She could feel her stomach bulging uncomfortably over the top of her jeans. That cemented it. There'd be no dessert for her.

Bridget looked at Lorenzo and then at his mother, who, with the rest of the family, waited with curious and expectant faces for her answer. "Please tell your mother everything was wonderful, but I just can't eat another thing."

"You sure? Okay." Lorenzo quickly relayed Bridget's answer. Bridget watched everyone stare at Lorenzo. Complete silence engulfed the table as everyone then gaped suspiciously at Bridget, who felt nervous stirrings in her stomach begin. And then a combustion of noise erupted as everyone, from Grandpa to Mom to Lorenzo's sister, looked back and forth from Bridget to Lorenzo and began chattering loudly and gesticulating wildly.

"What, what's the matter? Oh, no, are they mad?" Bridget spoke quickly.

Lorenzo shushed the table and replied, "No, they just can't believe you're not having dessert. And my mother is very worried that you don't eat enough. She thinks you could use a little more meat on you." Well, *that* was the first time she'd ever heard that said in regards to her.

"It's just … I'm just full. Really, I am, that's all." Bridget tried to diffuse the situation. Once again, Lorenzo translated. His mother threw up her hands and sighed, then despairingly clucked a few times, as the rest of the table joined in, regarding the horror of Bridget passing on dessert. Carolina gazed at Bridget with an utterly perplexed look. It appeared that this was bad, very bad. Bridget hated to end the lovely time she'd had on a note like this. Everyone had been so kind, first inquiring about her Nutella foot, and then continually fawning over the *maestra Cattolica*, as if she had a direct hotline to the pope. Bridget could only pick up a word or two here and there, but enough to get the gist of what was going on around her. And now she'd gone and ruined it all by declining dessert. Still, she was really baffled by how these people could eat so much and all be so slim. Anyone who ate three hefty meals a day like this would surely end up on a show like *The Biggest Loser*.

Lorenzo's father, who'd been silent the whole lunch, rolled his eyes and left the table.

"Where's he going? Oh, no, did I make him mad too?" Bridget asked Lorenzo.

"Relax, my dad couldn't care less. He's going for a cigarette!" Lorenzo smiled. He added, "Look, I don't care if you have dessert or not either, although I'd love to postpone taking you home a little longer, since you fell asleep on me." He winked at her. Bridget blushed slightly as Lorenzo's mother spoke rapidly again in the direction of the two of them.

"No, no." Lorenzo waved his mother off.

She looked over her glasses at Bridget and asked, in a doubtful voice, "No?"

Bridget answered almost as doubtfully, "Grazie, no."

Lorenzo nearly shouted incredulously, "*Mama*—no!"

She ignored Lorenzo and looked pitifully at Bridget again, and then she asked dejectedly, "*No?*"

This was just awful. The poor little woman looked as if she was about to cry. Dammit! Bridget gave up. There was only so much temptation she could resist, anyway. She sighed and said with a smile, "Okay, si."

"*Si?*" An immediate change of expression appeared on the woman's face. Jubilant relief now replaced shocked disappointment.

"Si," Bridget repeated. Lorenzo's mother lightly backhanded her son on the arm and said, with a smug look on her thin face, "*Si!* Brava, Bridgeet!" as if to say, *Ha! I knew all along that she really wanted dessert!* The rest of the table chanted joyously as well, "*Bene! Brava!*" as if she had just made the best decision of her life. Well, it wouldn't be the worst decision she'd ever made. She'd wait and see.

•   •   •

All right, so she didn't regret her decision at all. In fact, she and her stomach had miraculously caught their second wind. And the lemon sorbet, which was so light, washed down with a dainty little glass of limón crema (the creamy, and kinder, gentler cousin to limoncello), had perked her up a bit. She now sat with her chin propped in her hand and diligently concentrated on the fast-paced table conversation. They talked to each other and they talked to her, asking her many questions, as Lorenzo translated. "My sister wants to know how you get your teeth so white." Crest White Strips were definitely not in her rudimentary, equivalent-to-a-three-year-old's Italian vocabulary. Well, she couldn't feel that bad. With the exception of Lorenzo's grandfather, no one else had a firm grasp on English, and they didn't seem to mind her limited Italian. Still, Bridget was nevertheless aware of her need to continue her study of the Italian language.

Eventually, table conversation tapered off as afternoon shadows crept over the patio. Carolina was carried off to take a nap, Grandfather headed back to open up the market, and Lorenzo's mother busily cleared away plates and glasses. When Bridget tried to assist, she had been kindly but firmly shooed back onto the patio. Lorenzo motioned to the snug little place next to him on the chaise. Once again, she scrunched herself in beside him, and the crook of his arm waited to rest upon her shoulders. And again, she leaned her head into his broad shoulder and breathed in the smell of his T-shirt, the smell of him. He was probably going to kiss her again. He had been coyly hinting at it all throughout the leisurely lunch, as he squeezed her hand under the table and smiled at her. Her frantic qualms were put to rest. He was snoring. Bridget lifted her head from his chest and saw that his head was tilted back, his mouth slightly open. Relieved, but surprised to feel slightly disappointed, she laid her head back down. She closed her eyes and let herself drift off too.

◆   ◆   ◆

This time, when she awoke, it was dark; the only light emanated from the glowing boats on the water, the twinkling town lights, and the kitchen behind them. Bridget sat up and sniffed. Delicious aromas were drifting out from the kitchen. Was it time for dinner already? As if on cue, her stomach groaned in anticipatory glee. This whole eating/narcolepsy/eating again thing was getting to be ridiculous. Beside her, Lorenzo stretched his arms out above them and and grumbled groggily, "Well. Looks like we timed it right. Smells like dinner's just about ready. Hope you're hungry *again.*"

And, much to his mother's joy, Bridget found she was more than hungry. She was actually famished. Powerless to her stomach, she had healthy helpings of everything. Mrs. Reginella scuttered about, passing and collecting platters, but always with a watchful eye on Bridget. At one point, as Bridget shoveled another delicious morsel into her mouth, she swore she caught the petite woman gazing at her with what seemed like happy pride, as if Bridget were her very own eating protégé. *When this girl first came to me (this morning), she was pitiful! A bag of bones, I tell you! Barely ate! Wouldn't have known decent food if it came up and bit her! And now, now, look at her! I knew she had it in her!*

Bridget didn't turn any of it away. There was salad, smoked mozzarella, and pasta, and now she was ready to take on the heaping plate of meat that was placed before her. She took a forkful and placed it in her mouth. Mmmm. The texture was quite like chicken, but the taste was slightly gamey, not too gamey, just a bit. What was it? Whatever it was, it was very good. Lorenzo smiled, patted her on the back, and said, "Well, I'm glad you seem to have gotten your appetite back!"

Bridget stuck her fork into another piece of meat and answered, "Must be the … fresh air." She placed the juicy meat into her mouth and began to chew, as Lorenzo asked, a bit anxiously, "So, you like the meat?" *Why was he looking at her like that?*

She shook her head yes, then pushed the meat to one side of her mouth and asked, "Why? What is it?" Everyone else was eating it. Was she *not* supposed to like it?

Lorenzo answered, "It's *coniglio.*" *Coniglio?* Of course, that would be the *one* Italian food word she didn't know. Bridget shrugged to show her ignorance.

Lorenzo scoffed and said, "I thought you said you took Italian!"

"Well, I guess it must be the one thing I've never ordered off the menu. I'm wondering now if there's a reason for that." She made sure to keep the wadded-up meat in her cheek. She was not swallowing until she found out what it was.

He repeated, "*Coniglio,*" and then scrunched up his nose and began twitching it up and down. "You know, Bugs Bunny?"

Oh, so he was twitching his nose to look like a ... *rabbit.* Oh, no, she was eating rabbit. Oh, no. She swallowed hard and tried to rid herself of the countless images of fluffy bunnies hopping through grassy meadows that flooded her mind. She fought to control the surge of gagging she felt coming on.

Although he sported an amused look upon his face, Lorenzo spoke calmly. "Bridget, ten seconds ago, when you didn't know it was rabbit, you thought it was delicious. You're fine." He patted her hand. *She was fine.* Was she? Bridget focused on Lorenzo's face and then on the beautiful platters of food scattered across sthe table. Then she looked around and noticed that everyone was staring at her. Okay, he was right. It was delicious. As long as she didn't think of furry cottontails or anything remotely related to the Easter Bunny. She swallowed her food, smiled, and said, "Don't worry, I'm fine. I'm fine!"

From across the table, Mrs. Reginella said worriedly, "S'okay?" She nodded at Bridget.

Lorenzo nodded and said, "Si, s'okay. Brava, Bridget!"

After dinner, dessert, and espressos were finished, they were up and ready to leave. Amid the hugs and the strict instructions from Mrs. Reginella (Lorenzo thus translated) that she was welcome to come back anytime and was expected to do so, she found herself back on the scooter, during the peak of evening town traffic. Bridget now remembered why she absolutely could not ride on these death-trap-type transports. With every jagged turn in the road, with every herky-jerky stop behind a car or scooter, she crushed the bag of cornetti into Lorenzo's chest as she held onto him with a viselike grip. If the revelation that she had unwittingly eaten Bugs Bunny had been a shock to the system, a scooter ride around town at this particular time was enough to make her actually sick to her stomach. She would *never* be an adrenaline-craving, extreme-sports junkie. That was clear. This counted as that, didn't it? It was too bad. If she and Lorenzo were to spend any more time together at all, they were going to have to confine it to walking about the town or to meeting up between the hours between one and six a.m.! That was all there was to it!

She now stood on the curb, wobbly-legged, holding the helmet in one hand and the pathetically crushed bag in her other. Bridget held up the bag and said, "Thanks for the cornetti!"

Lorenzo leaned against the seat of the scooter and shrugged. "Well, I don't usually use the old cornetti ploy to lure girls back home, but you mentioned you were hungry, so I just decided to go with it." They stood looking at each other for a few moments. Bridget broke eye contact as a whizzing scooter jetted past them noisily. She hoped it was no one she knew, seeing her in her clothes from last night. Lorenzo looked down at his watch and joked, "So, meet you at the disco in about three hours?"

Bridget chuckled and answered, "I don't think I could make it tonight. I'm worn out from all the eating and sleeping! What about you? Will you go?" She hoped not. What if he met someone else? Maybe she *should* go ...

"Naw, besides, my mother wouldn't stand for me bringing another girl home, after having brought a Catholic schoolteacher." He made an exaggerated sign of the cross. Phewwww. No need to go to the disco tonight.

"Yes, I am *so* holy," Bridget agreed sarcastically.

Lorenzo tilted his head sideways at her and said earnestly, "But, I do want to see you again. Are you going to the beach tomorrow?"

Of course—what else would they do?—but ... *go to the beach? Together?* Having him see her when she was fully hidden in the water was one thing. How was she going to mask her boobs and stomach when she was sprawled out on the beach chaise? She guessed she could just lie on her stomach the whole time. No, she'd have to roll over eventually. Or ... she could find out exactly what time he would be there and make sure she was in the water *before* he showed up. Then she'd just stay in the water the whole time, until he left! Who was she kidding? She was becoming more insane by the minute.

Resignedly, Bridget answered, "Yep, the usual plan is to get to the beach by one; although, after all that eating, I'm not looking forward to exposing my spare tire." She patted her stomach. Ack! Why had *that* come out of her mouth? Well, he was going to see it anyway. He might as well be prepared.

Lorenzo looked at her quizzically and said, "Please; you're fine." He stepped closer and lowered his head toward hers. Bridget happened to look over his shoulder for a split second and involuntarily slunk backward. There was "Sera" hanging out watching them on her terrace behind them! There was no privacy in this town, was there?

"What's wrong now?" sighed Lorenzo.

Bridget explained in a hushed tone, "Well, don't look, but we have an audience behind us. It's this lady that's always on her balcony, watching people. She makes me nervous!"

"Who?" Lorenzo spun around.

"I said don't look!" Bridget spat out of the side of her mouth. She watched nervously as Lorenzo laughed at the woman, yelled some words to her, and turned back around. Sera cackled a response back, waved a hand at him, and walked off the terrace.

Bridget was incredulous. "How'd you do that? What'd you say?"

"She's my aunt." Lorenzo watched Bridget's eyes widen before adding, "I asked if she was still spying on everyone and told her that you were my new American girlfriend and to be nice!"

"*That's* your *aunt*? Well, great, because I know for a fact that she does *not* like me!"

"She doesn't like anyone, so don't worry 'bout it!" Before Bridget could make anymore protestations, Lorenzo swooped her into him and planted a long kiss on her lips. A kiss, Bridget was surprised, that went on for much longer than she had expected, given the fact that his cranky old aunt was lurking nearby.

Lorenzo stepped back, licked his bottom lip a bit wickedly, and said, "Well, I finally got *that* kiss I was waiting for, and now I can go. I'll find you at the beach tomorrow, okay? So don't try to go missing because of your flat tire!" He quickly threw a hand out and patted her stomach. Bridget, out of instinct, immediately swatted his hand away. Ughhh, he had touched her stomach. *Nobody* touched her stomach!

In annoyance, she sputtered, "It's *spare tire*, not flat tire. And nobody touches my ... tire!" Infuriatingly, he laughed at her, hopped on his scooter, and kick-started it with a jump.

"Whatever. Looks flat to me. Ciao, Santa Bridget!" She rolled her eyes at him. He winked twice and motored off, calling up to the balcony as he passed, "Ciao, Zia Antonia!"

"Ciao, Renzo!" she heard the woman call back faintly. *Antonia?* That was her name? Bridget looked up at the shadowy balcony and thought she detected the dim outline of Lorenzo's aunt peeking out her doorway. Bridget did a quick about-face and hurried down the steps.

+ + +

Kit gushed, "Yay! I love it! I *like* this Lorenzo guy! Oh, I hope you go back to his place to eat again. And by the way, the cornetti tastes just fine!" She wiped a few crumbs from her cheek.

Julianna agreed. "Yeah, he does sound *cute*, despite the no-sex part. Are you *sure* you're not leaving anything out of the story?" She arched her eyebrows at Bridget.

Kit snorted, "Did it sound like she left anything out! Oh, my gosh! The kitchen at Lassino's closes in fifteen minutes, and we told the other girls we'd meet them there for dinner. Shoot—well, we're going to be late. I hope someone in the kitchen takes pity and serves us some food!"

Bridget held up the bag and said, "Well, there's always cornetti!"

"Good thing. Listen, I know you already ate, but do you feel like joining us?" Kit headed off toward the kitchen.

Bridget answered, "Thanks, but I think I'll stay in tonight." She watched Kit hustle out of the kitchen and down the darkened hallway. Then, as she poked her nose into the bag of crumbly biscotti shards, she sniffed and shook her head in quick disbelief as she thought she just might be getting hungry again.

Chapter 14

Bridget hastily punctuated the end of her sentence, set the pen down in the middle of the journal, and clapped it shut. There was no telling if she'd even be able to read the mini-novel she'd just scrawled since she'd been scribbling so fast. Trying to write on the beach was just as bad as trying to read on the beach. The super-dark, oversized sunglasses she wore were so good at shielding her eyes from the sun that she could barely see what she was writing. There'd be no spellcheck here. The blistering Italian heat caused the pen to eventually start slipping around in her sweaty fingers, which made her hold onto it all the more tightly, so now she had a lovely cramp in her index finger.

She'd much prefer to sit on the (somewhat) cooler apartment terrace with a glass of prosecco at her side while she leisurely wrote or to linger alone with her thoughts and her journal over a panino in the little café at the top of their hill. But that just hadn't been possible since she had met Lorenzo. And she wasn't complaining. It was just that since they'd formally met that evening, she hadn't had much time to herself, let alone to write in her journal. Although she doubted it was possible to forget, Bridget felt a furious need to write. Because it seemed that the longer she waited, the more noteworthy things continued occurring, which made the task seem even more daunting, as if it were a dreaded term paper or a stack of bills to pay.

So, she'd finally succumbed and crammed a week's worth of writing into her little journal, all in the half hour that Lorenzo had been lounging about in the water, chatting with people. Every time she'd look up to see where his tall, tanned figure was, he'd wave and gesture for her to come join him. She'd wave back with a smile and then promptly continue her writing, as if oblivious to the stifling heat and the fact that a gorgeous man was waiting for her in the water.

Hot out here? Who, me? Never! In fact, I hardly ever sweat. I know; how lucky am I? Oh, and that studly, six-foot, hunky brunette with the piercing green eyes and beautiful teeth, beckoning to me? Oh, please, I barely noticed! Ha! It was all too surreal, which made it all the more imperative that she record it.

Bridget wiped the sweat off her lip and tucked her journal under her chaise. She was done (for the time being), and she guessed it was better to have an overabundance to write about than nothing at all. This was *so* not her life.

Kit's friends from work had left a couple days earlier, the biggest drama surrounding them being the obscene amount of dirty towels they left piled up on the bathroom floor each day. The ladies at the laundromat had looked upon Kit and Bridget with utter scorn when they'd dragged their hulking loads in for a third time. "Oh, for Pete's sake! It's a laundromat! People are going to bring in dirty laundry! You'd think they'd be happy to have our business!" Kit had uncharacteristically fumed when they left. Bridget nodded her head in agreement. She'd never be able to fully figure out the Italians. "Maybe the towels looked … too dirty?"

"Oh, please! I'll tell you one thing, Bridget, after Julianna leaves, I'm glad that it's just us until Marren gets here. I can't take doing any more laundry, especially when it's not even mine! Shoot—I forgot to bring my stuff in! Great! Now I'm gonna have to go back."

Shortly thereafter, they once again stood at the top of the steps with Julianna, while Gregorio hustled about and arranged her multitude of luggage in the trunk.

"Oh, girlies, I can't believe I'm leaving!" Julianna pulled Kit in tightly for a hug. "Thanks so much! Wish I could stay longer, but I've got a salon to run." She stepped back from Kit and added, "Now, Kit, I don't care what you say, but the men here are crazy, so watch yourself." As Kit opened her mouth to respond, Julianna cut her off and said, "Seriously, Kit, I know you want to be friends with everyone, but be careful, because they'll fuck you over. *This,*" she paused dramatically to whirl her index finger around, "is not real life!"

Kit rolled her eyes and said, "They're not all like that here, Julianna."

She turned toward Bridget and threw her arms around her, and then she shouted, "Oh, yes they are! Except maybe Bridget's guy—what's his name, Larry? Now he's a real man! Bridget, tell Larry, if you don't want him, I'll take him!"

"I will relay the message." Bridget chuckled into Julianna's teased mane of hair.

"Of course, Larry *is* from here, and they're all messed up, so you'd better be on the lookout too! In other words, just keep doing what you're *not* doing!"

"What you mean?" Bridget asked.

Julianna cackled and then snorted. "Well, you're *not* sleeping with him and it seems to be working for you, so there you go!"

"You know, that's his aunt up there; you might want to keep it down." Bridget nodded in the direction of the opposite side of the street.

They all turned their heads. "Sera" flicked her eyes shamelessly back and forth from the clothes she was hanging on the line to the three of them.

Julianna grimaced slightly and turned back to Bridget and Kit.

"See? She scares me," Bridget whispered out of the side of her mouth.

Kit shrugged. "Oh, she's probably some sweet, harmless old lady. Maybe she's lonely and that's why she's always out on her balcony, watching everyone."

"Maybe she looks so pissed off all the time 'cause she knows what the men are like in this town! I'll bet that's what her problem is. Maybe her husband is one of the creepy lurkers at the disco. You know, I've seen some old guys there!" Julianna rasped.

Harmless, my foot, Bridget thought. One look from her and you'd be turned to stone. She'd side with Julianna's opinion on this one.

Kit sighed and said, "I really *doubt* that. Anyway, I'm sorry that you were so thoroughly disgusted by the men in this town. I hope you're not scared away from coming here again."

Julianna raised her eyebrows and threw her head back with a laugh. "*Please;* the men in this town don't scare me at all. Don't get me wrong, they are *all* jacked-up here, but I had a fucking great time!" Julianna noted the quizzical look on Kit's face and added, "You know why?" She paused for emphasis. "I had a great time because I *know* what the men are like here and I ... don't ... *care!* That's the problem with you two, little Miss 'Everything's So Wonderful Here—I Want to Be in Love' and little Miss Sister Mary Bridget! You two *care;* that's what your problem is. I just came to have a good time, and I did! And I don't give a shit about what they think of me in this town!"

Kit sputtered, "We came to have fun! We're having fun!"

Julianna smirked. "You are, huh? You run around worrying about whether everyone here likes you all the time and about that asshole four-eyes who plays hot-and-cold with you. Yeah, that sounds like fun!"

Bridget bit her lip and looked down as Julianna suddenly looked her way, pointed an accusing finger at her, and said, "And *you!*"

"What? I didn't say a word!" Bridget held up her hands.

Julianna ignored her and spat, "And *you*—well, you actually seem like you're having fun, which is good! You need to have fun, Bridget! But Jesus! You don't need to overanalyze everything! So stop worrying and *stop* talking about your weight or that freakin' spare tire you hallucinate that you have—unless you're *trying* to drive what's-his-face away! For once, would you just *work it?*" She threw up her hands and shouted, "Oh, my God, what am I going to do with you two? Gotta go; I've kept Greg waiting long enough! I expect to see you at the salon. I know your nails will be all nasty-looking by the time you get home. Love you!"

She hoisted her bulky leather satchel over her shoulder and hopped into the front seat.

"Sorry, Greg! I'm all yours now. *Andiamo!*" Bridget and Kit stared at Julianna's tiny hand waving out the window to them as the sleek Mercedez pulled away and rounded the bend in the road.

Kit sighed again, turned a tired face toward Bridget, and asked wearily, "Is she right? I mean, about me? And about the men here?"

Bridget hesitated slightly. "Ummm ... yeah, she's probably right. Well, who doesn't want people to like them? You *are* a people pleaser. But maybe, sometimes, you overextend yourself trying to make everyone happy. And then you're exhausted or feel bad when things go wrong that aren't even your fault. Just give yourself a break sometimes. Know that you've done the best you could and that there are always going to be some people you can't please."

Kit's eyes welled up and she squeaked, "I know, but I just wanted everyone to have a good time here."

"And they all did—*in their own way*. And if they didn't, that's not because of you! Okay?" Bridget threw an arm around her.

"Okay, but what about the men here? Julianna is not right about that, too! Is she?"

"Yeah, probably—I mean, to a certain extent," Bridget answered matter-of-factly. "I think they're all great, but they're still *guys*. Aside from living in this amazing paradise and carrying man-purses, in a way, they're not much different from the men at home! In fact, they're so used to the vacation mentality of 'no strings attached' that, in essence, they're the typical noncommittal guys, times ten!"

Kit sniffed. "Yeah, maybe. I mean, I know that a lot of them are like that. But not *all* of our friends are like that!"

Bridget laughed. "Yes, the ones with girlfriends are harmless. So, that would eliminate about two of the male population here!"

Bridget noted the defeated look upon Kit's face and added ruefully, "Hey, I'm only joking. Look, I have *no* clue. If I've learned anything at all by now, it's that I know *nothing* about men *anywhere*! At home or here!"

"Well, you don't need to worry about Lorenzo. He so completely adores you. Bridget, I really think you may have found the best guy in Positano! Listen to Julianna and don't overanalyze too much. She's definitely right about that."

The best guy in the town? It'd only been a couple of weeks. Lorenzo was leaving soon, and her remaining time here was dwindling away as well. Bridget wondered, how could you be sure about anything when you were on a whirlwind vacation? She'd have to analyze the situation quite a bit more …

Right, *not* overanalyze things? It was a nice thought and superbly expert advice, and, of course, Bridget wasn't following it one bit. It was preposterously impossible for her make light of any situation, unless it involved her "throwing away money" (and she used that term loosely) on a kick-ass pair of shoes or some decent jeans. She was a neurotic worrier by nature. The slightest hint of a troubling qualm or dilemma of some sort would send her into a habitual gnawing of her nails, until all that was left was a row of jagged stubs on each hand.

In fact, Bridget thought she more than quite possibly met all the qualifications for someone having obsessive-compulsive disorder. Or was she just overly dramatic about, oh, say, *everything*? Oh, and that was just one more thing for her to agonize over! Could it be worse? Possibly. At least she wasn't schizophrenic or bipolar. Well, she didn't think she was … hmm, a definite topic to address on her next visit to therapy.

So, no, despite Julianna's orders, Bridget had not stopped beating everything to absolute death in her mind. But, she proudly ascertained that she had been a hell of a lot better than usual. Well, here she was on the beach for the sixth day in a row, with Lorenzo, and in a bathing suit! Quite clearly, wasn't that was proof enough? On the best of days, Bridget detested being in a suit around anyone. At best, she could handle being among friends and of course, around strangers she'd never see again. But parading around in a bathing suit—and in the company of a *love interest*—was taking it to another level of sheer hell.

Yet, something told her to get over it, and she'd managed, *ever* so slightly, to let go and meet Lorenzo at the beach that first time. From then on, there had been no turning back. While Lorenzo had a laid-back calm to him, he was also quite persistent. "Come on, you've been sitting there way too long. Come into the water with me," he'd said and laid a hand on her shoulder.

"I'll go in later." Bridget had rolled over onto her stomach. She was not about to get up and wander in and out among the beautiful sunworshippers. Besides, she'd just eaten a caprese panino and couldn't even suck her stomach in. Oblivious to this, Lorenzo countered with, "You'll get heat stroke. Come on, let's go in now."

To which Bridget replied into her soggy beach towel, "I don't want to go in now. You go." She was *not* getting up right now. It had taken all she could muster to show up at the beach again and let him see her in full bathing-suit glory. He was just going to have to go in without her.

"You absolutely need to get into the water. Now. Because I can't wait anymore." He stood over her, hands on his hips. *Hmmm, usually, people just left her alone. Well, she wasn't going in.*

Bridget looked up at Lorenzo and answered cheekily, "That's why you shouldn't wait. You should go in *without* me. Because I'm not getting in right now. Later, I promise!" And she threw her head down again quickly. *There, that was that.*

Lorenzo was silent a moment before he said, "Are you always this stubborn?"

"No." Bridget gave a tight smile.

With that, she turned her head to the other side. Silence. Good, she had scared him into the water. Wait a minute—bad. What if she'd scared him off the beach? Oh, now she felt remorseful. She really liked him, which was so unusual. The overanalyzing just wasn't going to cease, but she was really trying to curb the remarks about her weight—well, at least, in front of Lorenzo. What was she supposed to do, send him telepathic messages? *Yes, you see, I'm freakin' hot as hell and would really like to go into the water, but I have a huge gas bubble in my stomach from inhaling my sandwich, and, at this moment in time, it's just not possible for me to suck my stomach in at all while staggering across thousand-degree rocks to actually get to the water!* Sure, wasn't it obvious? No, of course not, and Lorenzo couldn't be expected to be a mind reader, but boy, it'd be so much easier.

Bridget sighed and pushed herself up to a sitting position. She shaded her eyes with a hand and looked around for Lorenzo.

A voice behind her caused her to jump slightly. "No, I'm still here, Bridget. And now you're really gonna be annoyed with me, because you're going in the water!" And with that, he picked her up, cradled her like a ginormous infant, and headed down the rocky shore.

"*Put ... me ... down ... now,*" Bridget hissed through clenched teeth. This was absolutely mortifying. Everyone was staring at them!

"Oh, I'm gonna put you down!" He chuckled and splashed into the water until it was chest-high to him. Lorenzo stopped and dropped a glaring Bridget into the water. She let the cool water wash over her. It felt so good, but she wasn't going to tell *him* that, since he had pissed her off. She popped her head above the water and began paddling off.

"Hey, where are you going?" Lorenzo called.

Bridget turned around mid-paddle. "To somewhere I can stand without the water being over my head!" Lorenzo waded out to where Bridget stood. He stood behind her, wrapped his arms around her shoulders, and asked, "You're mad at me, huh?"

No, I love being in my bathing suit and then being totally humiliated in front of a crowd of people at the beach!

Bridget exhaled and said, "I was *going* to come out here. You didn't have to do *that!*"

"No, you weren't, but I knew you *wanted* to, so—sorry." *Was he a mind reader?*

"Anyway, we're out here now, so let's enjoy it."

He scooped her up into his arms again. Well, at least she was weightless in the water. But, oh, if he thought that getting all romantic in the water right now was going to work with her, he was ... so damn ... right ... and ... *gorgeous.* Bridget momentarily lost her train of thought. "What? You're mad? What are you thinking?" Lorenzo stared back at her.

Isn't it totally obvious? I really want to kiss you right now! "I'm thinking that you're really quite bossy!" Bridget answered instead.

"Hey, I gotta beat the teacher at her own game." He smiled slyly and moved in to kiss her as he said, "But just remember, I'm not one of your students. It's not gonna work with me."

She held onto him tightly and murmured, "We'll see about that."

Lorenzo had promised that he'd never embarrass her like that again. Bridget wasn't taking any chances. From then on, she made sure she was the first one of them in the water. Oh, well, at least she was keeping herself cool. No, he didn't let her get away with much, from her hestitation to her self-depracating humor. For all her show of toughness, Lorenzo had won. But there were ceratin things that Bridget would never concede to.

On their second day at the beach, he'd asked her, "So, when am I going to see you in your bikini?"

Bridget looked at him as if he was deranged, snorted, and said, "You're not. I don't own a bikini."

Lorenzo rolled over on his side and looked at her, flabbergasted. "What? Oh, come on! You're joking!" He laughed until he saw that Bridget wasn't. "Oh, you're *not* joking."

"No. The last time I wore a bikini, I was about three years old." And even then, she'd had a gut, if she remembered correctly from the family photo album.

"It's not gonna happen, so you should just forget about that." She ignored his gaping mouth, pushed her sunglasses up the bridge of her nose, and adjusted the back of her chaise.

Lorenzo stated, "Well, I don't know why not. You should wear one."

"Well, I'm not going to."

"Well, you should."

"Well, I'm not." *Would he just drop it?*

"Why, though? Is this about your flat tire?" Of course it was. And it was *spare* tire, not *flat* tire! Why was he being so stupid? But she couldn't *say* that, since the new Bridget wasn't allowed to talk about her spare tire in front of Lorenzo.

"Look, it's just not a good look for me. It never was and it never will be, and I'm quite fine with that. I know my limitations."

"Let's see, it's been, what, thirty years or so? I think it's time you tried one on again!" He smiled at her.

"I think this is an argument you're not going to win." Bridget smiled back at him sweetly.

"I'm going to buy you one, and you're gonna wear it," Lorenzo announced and raised his eyebrows at her.

"No, you're not, and no, I wouldn't."

"Oh, I am. A little tiny one!"

"Don't waste your money. You wanna buy me something, there's a really cute pair of sandals I've had my eye on at Da'Stella. Buy me those. A little pricey, but at least I'd *wear* them."

Lorenzo chuckled and grabbed Bridget's hand. "You're not going to let me win this one, are you?"

Bridget shook her head no.

"You know," Lorenzo added, "I really don't think you have anything against wearing a bikini. You just enjoy disagreeing with me!"

Bridget sighed in annoyance. "No, I don't!"

Lorenzo rolled his eyes. "You just did it again!"

Bridget laughed. She squeezed his hand and said, "Well, only because you're wrong and I'm right."

She'd put her foot down on the bathing-suit issue, but that didn't mean she didn't fret about wearing her one-piece. In fact, after a week of missing the neighboring hotel gym to meet Lorenzo on the beach, Bridget had broken out her last-resort swimsuit. She'd spied it among the multitude of bathing suits at Nordstrom. The rich shade of chocolate would be a nice change from her typical black. And when she'd spotted a tag hanging off it that read, "Miracle Suit—Guaranteed to make you look ten pounds lighter!" it was a done deal.

She'd felt a bit flabbier than usual this morning, and she'd shimmied into the suit, which felt like she was getting into a wet suit. Miracle suit, indeed! The miracle was that she could get herself into it! Bridget had taken a look in the mirror and been pleasantly shocked. She was completely sucked in and looked actually pretty svelte. It was a one-piece, but it was no granny suit. While it was low-cut and showed off some of her tanned and bountiful cleavage, it also completely pushed her chest up and in. Bridget was never in favor of showing off her chest, but she couldn't argue with a miraculous suit that somehow helped her chest defy all gravity.

Lorenzo took one glimpse at her at the beach that day and had whistled, "Nice! I take it back. You don't need the bikini!"

And that was where she had left off in her journal. She reached for the bound notebook and patted it protectively. Lorenzo trudged up the rocks and shook his hair out over her, like a dog after a bath.

"There, now you're cooled off. I would've made you come in, but I saw you writing. You writing a book or something?" He grabbed his towel and wiped his chest.

Bridget shrugged. "Maybe." It was mainly just for her own pure enjoyment. One day, she'd hopefully reread it and have much to laugh about. Besides, who'd ever believe all the stuff she'd written about?

"Am I in it?" He grinned as he arranged his towel back down on the chaise.

Bridget shrugged nonchalantly and said, "Maybe." He'd definitely be the protagonist's love interest …

Lorenzo placed his hands behind his head and added, "Well, don't put me in it, unless you use my real name."

"Why? Don't you want to remain anonymous?" Bridget asked.

"Nope. I'm not ashamed of myself. Nothing scandalous has happened with me and you—yet!" He grinned at her impishly. True, nothing bookworthy so far in regards to that … Bridget changed the subject. "So, what time should I be ready tonight?'

Lorenzo had invited her to join him and his family for dinner. Afterward, they were to hit a friend's beach party on the Fornillo Beach side. Bridget was excited to spend time with Lorenzo's family, although she expected to miss out on a lot of the conversation. She'd bring her pocket dictionary. And the party was a welcome change from the crowded disco and … running into Paolo. Paolo didn't party on the Fornillo side; Bridget was pretty sure of that.

Aside from their bickering like an old married couple, Bridget was completely attracted to everything about Lorenzo. So much so that she'd almost forgotten the whole "love on the rocks" scenario and her perennial crush on Paolo. Until something weird had happened last night at the disco.

Bridget and Kit had just made their way off the dance floor to where Lorenzo stood chatting with Australian Rachel and Lassino. The Aussie had met up with Kit (they all assumed) in an effort to be around, should Paolo show up. Lassino's presence, as his cousin and a best friend, assuredly meant Paolo would be there. Kit and Bridget wanted no part of the awkwardness of the Rachel-Paolo situation. She ranted if she couldn't get a hold of him or see him. When and if they met up, a fight would inevitably ensue, with Paolo taking off and Rachel slandering him mercilessly in front of anyone within earshot. Kit would cry out in consternation, "I'm tired of listening to her talk about him that way! Paolo is a friend of ours. Doesn't she know that?"

"Well, maybe they'll be fine tonight, or maybe he won't be out," Bridget suggested, as they both took a sip of their drinks. Bridget had a strange feeling that she didn't want to Paolo to show up, and it had nothing to do with his feud with Rachel. How could she explain it? *She didn't want Paolo to see her with Lorenzo.* Although it was certain that he knew from Lassino that she'd spent most of the past week with him. Why would Paolo care, anyway? And why on earth should *she* worry or care about it? Their short, almost nonexistent history was long over. She was being so silly.

As was ever indicative of just the way things just always seemed to be timed there, Paolo then walked in. Bridget's stomach flip-flopped. Oh, no. She wanted to disappear, to suddenly be swallowed up into the bar behind her. No, she wanted Lorenzo to disappear. No, she … oh, she just didn't know.

She watched Rachel lean back, her elbows on the bar and her chest thrust forward. Bridget followed Rachel's darting eyes as they tracked Paolo's every movement. Lassino and Lorenzo chatted obliviously among themselves and the other males at the bar. Kit turned herself toward Bridget and said, "I can't watch another Italian-style Jerry Springer episode."

Paolo's white-linen shirt and white teeth flouerscently glowed as he wove his way through people, smiling and calling things to them as he walked by. Bridget covertly watched as Paolo's eyes scanned ahead to the bar. As he realized Rachel was there, a terse look came over his face. Almost immediately, the expression disappeared and he approached the bar with one of his wide, dazzling smiles. As he reached Rachel, he nodded at her and quickly walked past. Rachel gave a tight smile and watched him with narrowed eyes. Just as quickly, she turned to chat with Giorgio.

Paolo spoke a few words to Lassino and greeted Lorenzo, and then to Bridget's horror, he looked directly over to her, caught her eyes, and then looked back at Lorenzo. She had no idea if Lorenzo had seen the scandalized look upon her face, because she had instantly looked away.

"What's going on? I can't look," Kit asked.

"Um, nothing. He's talking to the guys," Bridget mumbled. Kit turned around to find Paolo right behind her.

"Paolo! Ciao!" She grinned.

He cheerily bestowed the Italian double-kiss on Kit's cheeks, smiled, and said, "Hello, Kit! Nice to see you!"

Then he nodded at Bridget and added in a less jovial tone, "Hello, Bridget."

Bridget felt like a deflated balloon. She knew she was overanalytical and hypersensitive at times, but she hadn't misread Paolo's flatness. She immediately tuned out the chattering between him and Kit. She wanted to leave.

"Okay, I'll talk to you later!" Paolo said to Kit and curtly nodded to Bridget before he walked to the other end of the bar.

"Is he mad at me? I think he's mad at me," Bridget commented.

"What are you talking about?" Kit asked.

"Why is it 'nice to see you,' but not me?" Bridget questioned.

Kit answered matter-of-factly, "I'm sure he meant both of us." *Right.*

Kit saw Bridget's scrunched-up eyebrows and added, "You're imagining things. Or maybe he thinks you're mad at him. You know, they pick up on things like that."

Yes, don't we all; and anyway, why would he think she was mad at him? Bridget knew she wasn't imagining things.

Before she could argue, a tall blur of blonde pushed by them. Bridget and Kit watched the back of Rachel heading in the direction of Paolo.

Kit exhaled and said, "Oh, here we go."

They watched as Rachel approached Paolo, baring her teeth. Oh wait, no, she was smiling. Paolo grinned back, it seemed almost in relief.

"Thank God," Kit mumbled. Bridget looked away. Why was she upset? This was ridiculous. She suddenly felt claustrophobic, as if the disco was closing in on her, as if Lorenzo was closing in on her. She didn't want a *boyfriend* on vacation, which was what the whole town undoubtedly assumed Lorenzo was to her. Bridget suddenly and desperately wished she hadn't met him. No, she didn't mean that, did she? And if *only* she'd never met Paolo either! This was supposed to be just her and her friends on a girls' vacation! So, what had happened? A summer romance in a foreign country? Please, get real. It was surely a waste of time. But she admittedly really liked Lorenzo. And while she'd known Paolo longer, Bridget certainly felt like she knew Lorenzo much better.

Yet, was it possible that she still liked Paolo more? She felt so conflicted. Bridget was upset with herself for once again pining over someone who wasn't the slightest bit interested in her. And who happened to be a good bit younger than her, to boot! She was icked-out by everything—by Lorenzo, by Paolo and Rachel, by herself! She had to leave. Could she sneak away without being noticed?

"Want another drink?" Lorenzo put an arm around her.

"No, thanks," Bridget said with almost a sigh. Now was her chance to escape. "I actually think I might leave. I'm not feeling well. But if you want to stay, you should," she added.

"Oh, okay. No, no, let me finish my drink, and then we'll go. I'll be right back," Lorenzo said with a concerned face. Ughh, now she felt like even more of a rat. Bridget snuck a look back at Rachel and Paolo. It appeared the pleasantries were over. There was no way to hear with the thumping music, but it was clear by the irritated looks on their faces and by the punctuational hand gestures that things had headed south pretty fast. Rachel turned on her heel and practically ran by them as she said tearily, "Bye, girls, I'm leaving. I can't be here tonight!" Bridget and Kit looked at each other with raised brows.

"Oh, no. Should I go see if she's all right?" Kit asked hesitatingly.

"I don't know. Do you really want to put yourself in the middle of that?" asked Bridget.

"You're right. I'll text her later." Kit sighed and walked over to Lassino.

Paolo hurried up, stopped at Bridget, and shook his head in the direction of Rachel. He rolled his eyes and said somberly, "Bridget, ciao." He walked past her a few steps, then stopped and turned around. He grabbed her hand and held it tightly. Caught completely off-guard, Bridget had no other response but to let him. Paolo stared at her with serious eyes, as if he intended to say something to her. Instead, he ran his thumb gently over the inside of her palm before he dropped it and walked away. As he passed the others, he said his good-byes and headed off. Bridget quickly looked over at Lorenzo. Had he seen them holding hands? No, his back was to her. She watched Paolo's white-linen shirt disappear past the bouncer and out the door. Where was he going now, to find Rachel? Why the cold shoulder, then the hand caress and lingering stare?

✦ ✦ ✦

What had happened last night? She had left the disco mystified and still couldn't figure it out now on the beach.

From his chaise, Lorenzo asked, "Do you think you're up for going out tonight? I don't want to be the cause of you getting sick, *Maestrina!*" He winked at her playfully.

Now he even had an endearing nickname for her: *Maestrina,* "little teacher." Damn him. He really *was* sweet. And she was *such* a stupidhead. That was it. She *did* like him. Whatever had she been thinking last night? And that weird handholding thing with Paolo? Well, maybe she'd been hallucinating. She was prone to exaggerating things in her mind. Bridget decided to try to forget about it and concentrate on Lorenzo. It was *so* on again. Definitely. Maybe. Well, she'd see.

Bridget answered assuredly, "Oh, yeah, I feel much better today." For sure, she'd be safe with Lorenzo's family and at the beach party tonight. It was that damn disco she needed to stay out of!

"Okay, then. Be ready by eight thirty." Lorenzo then added playfully, "So, you never told me if you had a boyfriend here in Positano." Bridget responded by pulling her sunglasses down the bridge of her nose to roll her eyes at him. She then turned over onto her stomach and quickly tucked her journal safely into her beach tote. *Seriously?*

✦ ✦ ✦

Kit leaned back on her elbows and rested her head to one shoulder, while she stared at the rippling water. She could lie on the beach here every day and never get sick of it. She tried not to think about how little time she had left before she had to return home, but it was difficult. Two and a half weeks, five hours, twelve minutes, and … but, aside from her, who was counting? Of course, she didn't *have to* go home. Well, "have to" depended on what you meant. Technically, she *should*. She had family missing her, a job in a very wealthy school district waiting for her, and a fresh batch of overly precocious incoming first-graders, along with their demanding parents, expecting her to be back come the end of August.

When you looked at it that way, it was tough to refute. She sighed as she thought about having so little time left, and yet, there was still so much she wanted to do while she was here. The list was endless, like: catch a day trip to the island of Ischia; take in one of the outdoor concerts up in Ravello; do a little shopping in Sorrento; oh, and have Tino get a driver to take her around Naples. Her one night there with Johnny had somewhat sullied her Neapolitan experience. Kit wanted to remember the city fondly, not as the place where she'd unwittingly led Johnny across the globe for a post-breakup-breakup. Kit cringed as she recalled the ugly evening and Johnny's confusion and anger. She supposed her penance would be to always feel wretchedly about it, while knowing there would never be anything she could do to make amends for the awkward situation.

Worse than that, though, she worried that maybe her penance was that after all this, she'd end up alone! Was she destined to flit about endlessly among all the marrieds and people with significant others? No matter how crammed her social calendar was, and it was overflowing with extracurricular activities, there was always something askew or missing. Kit wondered, if she ever just stood still to catch her breath for a moment, would she find what she was looking for? Or rather, would it find her? She was too scared to take that risk. What if she took a breather and it was all for nothing? The thought of sitting around—or, God forbid, staying home for a summer— was unfathomable. It was a "risk" she wasn't willing to take.

Her eyes welled up suddenly, and she quickly wiped them with the back of her hand. Kit decided she wasn't going to be able to deal with much more of this. As she thought back on all this summer's drama, she told herself again that she'd never meant for any of this to happen. She'd never meant for Carrie to have her life supposedly threatened by her ex-Positanese boyfriend, the fish/water guy. Just like she'd never meant for Natalie and Joe to go through the added stress of dealing with Madison running away while on vacation in another country! Or to have scandalized the town with the whole bizarre situation, as well as exhausting her friends here by having them search around the clock for the notorious, missing Americana. And people *still* came up to ask her at the disco or the beach to ask, "Why did your friend run away? I don't understand. What was the problem with her?" As much as the Italians loved a good scandal, it was still a tough one to explain.

Yes, Kit truly had the best of intentions, but for some unknown reason, things tended to go awry. So much so, that now whenever she approached Tino's ceramic shop, he'd call out, "Mama mia! Here comes my problem!" Of course, Kit laughed, because she knew he was only joking, but still. And who knew what else might transpire here in the next couple weeks ... or longer, if she indeed decided to stay?

How could she right any of those situations? She couldn't. Well, at least she could avenge or semierase the memory of the Naples fiasco by returning again for day of sightseeing and ... pizza. Right, she'd go back to Naples. Yes, the only problem was trying to motivate yourself to do anything other than nothing much! However, Kit felt the best days were never planned ahead of time anyway. There was no timetable here, no rushing to beat the clock, which was good, since she was never on time. Life just happened, and unlike at home, she did not need to overschedule things.

All she had to do was walk through the town to the beach or on the way back from it. Social opportunities availed themselves at every curve in the road. If someone invited her to chat over an espresso, she would. When Lassino's cousin Linda happened to ask if she'd like to tag along to Sorrento while she picked up fashionable trinkets for her tiny store, she happily jumped at the chance. And then of course, when she might feel the need to stop for a glass of wine to cool herself off on the walk up the hill, she'd no doubt run into another town friend, and another animated and leisurely conversation would ensue. The timing of it was all in the *untimeliness* of it! Kit savored it with the realization that when an opportunity presented itself, you just took it.

And that was how she was looking at Fabio's job offer. It had come at just the right time indeed. Now she didn't feel quite so trapped into return-ing to her life back home. Although, she had a slight inkling that working for Fabio might turn into another sort of entrapment, if she wasn't wary. For all her sunshiny naivete, Kit was not some stupid blonde. Every sly in-nuendo Fabio threw her way did not go unnoticed or misunderstood. The trick was to just smile (men seemed to like that) and throw your head back, then giggle a bit and make them think you weren't ruffled in the slightest. It had worked thus far. Men might find her attractive and friendly, but they never got much farther than a toothy smile and an animated conversation with her. Once they realized that, they'd let her be; they'd walk away and scratch their heads in bewilderment.

However, Fabio had not been deterred. She'd bumped into him a couple more times around town, and the offer was always charmingly presented again. He was just "desperate" to find someone decent, a kind person, who spoke English and was good with children. And then he'd gallantly throw in, "And she must have lovely, golden hair and a beautiful smile like yours! Yes, I think *you* should take this job!" And of course, the job benefits were still the same: her own car, living quarters, a hefty paycheck, and opportunity to travel. If only there was a no-groping clause in the contract! She'd assured him, "I'm thinking about it; I really am.

He'd then add as an aside, "I'm not offering this up to everyone, you know." No, she didn't think so. Surely, being the *only* job candidate should wield a lot of power and bargaining room, no? Unless, the only "bargaining room" she'd have would be the one she'd be expected to share with him! In that case, it was hopeless, and she might as well pack her suitcases (all five of them, plus her two carry-ons) now because she'd be headed home. And she just couldn't. Not now, and not especially since she and Lassino were getting along so well. Well, *she* always got along with him, no matter what state of mood he was in. It was just—now, he was being more than kind and caring. And although she was content, Kit couldn't help wondering how long it would last.

No, she could make this nanny thing work. Regardless of her feelings for Lassino, the job held its intrigue for her. Fabio would have to realize that she wouldn't be treated as his personal plaything. Because, truthfully, Kit didn't do anything that she didn't want to do. And she wasn't about to demean herslf just so she could extend her stay in Positano! She was going to find a way to make this work. And then she was going to have to find some kind of long-term sub ... ughh, she'd worry about that later. Kit readjusted her small, red bikini top, lowered herself back down into her chaise, and closed her eyes.

She let the powerful heat envelop her, and she temporarily dozed off, only to be woken by a shadowy coolness that had fallen over her. While it was a nice break from the scorching heat, she was irked, since she'd arrived later than usual today and had missed some prime sun time. She hoped these were not rain clouds. She opened her eyes to check and was visually assaulted by a bulging, white Speedo attached to two hairy legs standing directly over her. The legs and Speedo were attached to Vinnie, who just happened to somehow be wherever she was. Why wasn't he at the restaurant, innocently heckling the female passerby, like he usually did? She'd never thought about it, but of course, restaurant maitre-d's were entitled to taking breaks too. But there *really* should be some age cutoff to Speedo-wearing. If Kit had it her way, no one over the age of seven would be allowed near them! Ughh, and *white* Speedos, too! This was more than wrong.

Bridget would have a fit. Good thing she wasn't here for the trauma. Actually, Kit desperately wished her friend were here, since she had a feeling Vinnie was looking for a beach buddy. Oh, how she'd have preferred the rain clouds to this! How unfortunate that she didn't have her sunglasses on. Then she would at least be able to fake not seeing him, as if she were asleep.

However, it was too late. She'd already made the unintentional, yet inevitable eye contact with him. Kit hoped her face hadn't given away her repulsion. Vinnie gave a look of surprise, as if he had accidentally stumbled upon a long-lost friend, and said excitedly, "Oh, Kit, ciao! I was walking by, and thought it might be you, but I wasn't sure!" *Right.* He'd been scouring the beach for her, no doubt, and probably with a pair of high-powered binoculars.

"Ciao, Vinnie. How are you?" Kit asked; she was doing her best but was finding it difficult to muster a bit of her typical sunniness. Why couldn't people just leave her alone?

"Oh, wonderful, *now.* May I?" He nodded at the empty beach chiase next to her. Kit cursed herself for asking for two chaises. She'd known all along Bridget would be off with Lorenzo today. What had she been thinking? Kit hesitatingly replied, "Uh, sure, my friend will be here soon, though ..."

"Oh, yes, your friend, what's her name again?" Vinnie asked blandly while he unfurled his towel with a flourish.

"Bridget," Kit replied tersely. Could people *really* not remember who Bridget was around here? I mean, they were practically joined at the hip! Kit was beginning to think Bridget wasn't exaggerating about this phenomenon and could actually feel some of her annoyance. Although, the annoyance may have also been due to the hairy Speedo'd man infringing upon her sun time …

Vinnie arranged himself, in all his lumpy Speedo'd glory, and then pulled his Versace wraparounds down over his eyes and answered, "Yes, yes, Bridget, the quiet one. Doesn't she have a boyfriend now? Lorenzo?"

Kit tried unsuccessfully to avert her eyes from the pervasive white crotch. But it was like turning away from the Mona Lisa; wherever you were, it followed your every move. Kit threw a hand into her leather backpack and hastily yanked out her sunglasses. She practically took an eye out while she shoved them onto her face, and she answered, "They've only known each other a couple of weeks." There, now at least she couldn't get caught so obviously staring at *it*.

"Yes, well, even a couple of short week in Positano can seem like a life-time. Many things can happen in a week, you know." He smiled suggestively at her.

Vinnie added, "I'd love to keep you company—that is, until your friend gets here." He flipped the top of his tanning oil open and squeezed some into his hand. Kit seethed. He knew very well that Bridget most likely wouldn't show up. In fact, Kit wondered if he'd actually seen her friend and Lorenzo together on the Fornillo side and had made his way over here. Maybe she was being a little paranoid, but she couldn't help it.

Kit responded with a tight smile. Before she could think of anything else to say, Vinnie thrust the bottle of tanning oil at her and said, "Would you mind rubbing some on my back?"

Oh, no, no, *no*. Kit was disgusted and completely thrown off as to what to say. She stalled for time and wildly looked around for something, some-one to save her. Kit squinted at the figures wandering up and down the stony beach. As soon as she got home (whenever that was), she was going right in for the LASIK eye surgery! Wait, there appeared to be a somewhat familiar figure. Dark hair pulled back in a ponytail, windshield-type sunglasses … could it be Tomaso? Kit fervently prayed it was. The figure came closer and fortunately for Kit, into better focus. The mystery figure wore a T-shirt that read "Sex Therapist: First Session Free." A suggestive T-shirt like that could only mean that yes, it was Tomaso!

Kit ignored Vinnie's request and called out with a wave, "Tomaso! Tomaso, ciao!"

Tomaso spotted Kit and walked over, his typical lopsided grin spread over his face.

"Kit, ciao. Ciao, Vinnie."

Kit patted her lounge chair and said, "Tomaso, sit! Please, I haven't seen you in a while! Talk to me. How are you?"

Tomaso sat beside her and answered with a shrug, "Oh, I am busy. July, August is the worst time here. The Italian tourists—they drive me crazy. Always, they complain about everything being too expensive! Americans— they don't complain. They just pay. But Italians and the French, *Madonna*! I tell, them, you don't like it, go lay on the rocks over there!" He jerked his head in the direction of the roped-off section down the beach that was free, due to the fact there were no beach chairs, umbrellas, or drink service.

Kit clucked her tongue sympathetically, relieved that for once, Americans weren't the obnoxious culprits. "So, what are you doing tonight?" she asked pleasantly.

"I think I go to a party on the beach at Fornillo. You should come," answered Tomaso.

"Oh, I think Bridget is going with Lorenzo," Kit replied.

"Bridget, that's right. She has a boyfriend now," Tomaso answered in recognition.

Kit laughed. "They just met! I don't know if you can say he's her boyfriend!"

Tomaso gave the Italian face-shrug and said, "*Allora ...*"

Vinnie cut in sarcastically. "Well, if I were her, I would've picked someone much better-looking!" Unfortunately, Vinnie hadn't magically disappeared, like Kit had hoped. She rarely detested people, but she was really beginning to abhor him. He had some nerve! Lorenzo was ten times better looking than him. In fact, Lorenzo was gorgeous, *and* he was nice, *and* he most certainly didn't wear a disgusting Speedo and stalk people on the beach!

"I love Lorenzo. He's *soo* nice!" Kit overly gushed on purpose. She noted a look of irritation upon Vinnie's face. Good, maybe he'd leave soon. Instead, though, Tomaso stood up and said, "Well, I better go back up to the front. I see people waiting for beach chairs. Damn Italians! I must go! See you tonight, Kit?" he called over his shoulder.

"Okay, see you tonight, Tomaso!" Darn, she'd hoped he'd stay long enough to scare Vinnie away. Now what was she going to do?

Vinnie rubbed some oil onto his chest and asked nonchalantly, "So, you are a good friend of Tomaso?"

"Yes, Tomaso's a very good friend. I have known him for three years—well, since I started coming here!" Kit said enthusiastically.

Vinnie nodded and said with a smile, "Ah, you have many friends here. Everybody loves Kit!" Changing the subject, he asked hopefully, "So, you go to Fornillo tonight?"

"Uh, I think so. It sounds like fun." Now that Vinnie thought she was going to Fornillo, of course, she had no intention of being caught anywhere near there, but Kit wasn't about to tell him that. At least that'd throw Vinnie off her trail for a while.

From behind her came a low, familiar voice. "I should've known I'd find you at the beach!" Two hands gently landed on her shoulders, and Kit felt someone kiss her cheek. Kit noted a disdainful look upon Vinnie's face as he pulled his sunglasses off and narrowed his eyes slightly at whoever was behind her, and she couldn't help feeling slightly relieved. Maybe this person could help get rid of Vinnie. Kit looked up and into the handsomely chiseled face of Fabio. Someone was seriously messing with her. If Lassino showed up now, well … then she'd know the town really was bugged! At least she enjoyed Fabio's company, and he wasn't wearing a dreaded Speedo, but a pair of ultra-expensive shades and long swim trunks.

He set his satchel down and spoke to Kit as if Vinnie wasn't there. "I'm going for a swim. Would you like to join me?"

Without hesitation or a second glance at Vinnie, Kit answered, "Yes, I'd love to!"

"Very good, after you," Fabio answered suavely. Kit jumped up, slightly adjusted her bikini bottom and top, and hustled down the rocks toward the water. Was she being rude to Vinnie? She felt guilty, but he was so creepy! Not to mention, he couldn't take a hint. She said a silent prayer that Vinnie wouldn't follow them into the water.

Kit teetered over the rocks until she was waist-high. Her back to the shore, she faced the bobbing boats ahead and sank down until the cool water covered her shoulders. Ah, she felt she could finally exhale.

"I hope I didn't interrupt anything back there," Fabio's voice breathed into Kit's ear. She whirled around quickly. So much for exhaling. From one hairy situation to the next; lately, Kit couldn't shake the constant feeling of having to be on-guard.

"No, you didn't interrupt anything at all. I have a chair saved for Bridget, and Vinnie just kind of sat there," Kit explained as she treaded away slightly.

"So," Fabio began and treaded closer to her.

"So!" Kit answered with a bright smile. He was going to ask her about the nanny position. She just knew it. If only she could come to a full-fledged decision. Why was she hovering so? She was so not a ... *hoverer.* In fact, Kit found she was apt to jump into most things a little too impulsively.

"*So?*" Fabio treaded closer still and arched his eyebrows at her. Kit retreated once again. At this rate, she'd soon end up past the safety buoys!

"I know what you are going to ask, Fabio. No. No, I haven't decided yet about the job. But I promise, I will soon! It's a lot to think about."

Fabio gave a half smile and said, "Ah, maybe you are thinking too much. Kit, I think you *know* what you want. So why don't you do what it is that you want to do?" He waited for her to answer.

She knew what she wanted? Did she? Kit thought she did. She *wanted* to stay here. That was certain. She had friends here. No matter what Lassino might say, his friends liked her, and she absolutely adored them. He was just trying to be difficult. Was the town not big enough for the two of them? Of course, it wasn't just the two of them, was it? There would probably always be some girl from Brazil, another from England, a few from Australia ...

But, Kit would not concede that she might be mistaken about the relationship between the two of them. She knew what she felt was real. But it was as if Lassino was always testing her to see how much she could take. For all of her intuitiveness, Kit felt it impossible to predict how Lassino would react if she took the nanny position with Fabio. Everything might be fine, or everything might, well, *suck.* Lassino could be livid that she was staying and invading his space, or maybe he'd be infuriated with the thought of her working in such close quarters with Fabio! Or he might not care at all and just be surprisingly happy to have her there longer. Maybe if she were here when tourist season ended, their relationship could take a more normal course. That was Kit's most-fervent wish. How could she know, though? It could be the best thing to happen to her, or it could be completely and utterly disastrous. She needed more time to decide.

Obviously unable to answer, Kit smiled plainly and hoped that Fabio would let the subject die. Instead, he continued to stare intently at her and uttered sympathetically, "You are so closed."

"What?" Kit asked. *Closed?* What did he mean by that?

Fabio explained seriously, "You smile all the time, but there is sadness in your eyes."

She didn't like where this conversation was heading, because it was true. She did smile all the time, maybe too much; although, what was the harm in doing that? While the sensational grinning may overcompensate for what she might be really feeling at times, for the most part, she was a happy person. Just not lately. Still, Kit felt she'd done a pretty good job of masking her feelings of unhappiness or disappointment. Why were Italians always so uncannily perceptive? Kit decided she couldn't pass off another smile in place of an answer.

"Yes, I know. I am truly happy for each day. But there's something about Positano that always tugs at my heart. I guess that when I'm here, it just makes it all the more clear how much I love it and that I'm going to have to leave it. Well, until I come back next summer," Kit explained. In actuality, her sadness was caused by much more than simply this. Perhaps being in Positano just seemed to magnify the void she felt her life at home had become.

"Yes, but you don't have to leave now. You can have what you want, all that you've wanted. And maybe more," Fabio uttered insistantly. Where were the horns and the pitchfork right about now? Kit felt like she like she was conversing with the devil.

She stammered, "I ... I just ... need some more time to figure some things out, Fabio."

"You know, I can help you make a decision. I can help you with this sadness you feel," Fabio stated confidently.

A slight breeze rippled across the water, and Kit felt a batch of goose bumps spring up on her arms. It was not that cold, but Kit forebodingly felt that the goose bumps had nothing to do with the water temperature, but rather, with whatever Fabio was about to propose.

She let him continue. "Just one night with me, and I will help you." Despite the slight grin on his lips, Fabio's voice was serious.

What did he mean? Was he talking about sex? No! *No?*

Kit instinctively cried out, "No, no way!"

A cockeyed grin spread across Fabio's face and he playfully asked, "Why do you automatically assume that this is about sex?"

They were mind readers here. Of course this was about sex, wasn't it? Please, what were they going to do for that one night? Make lasagna, play tombola or bocce?

Kit arched her eyebrows and said, "Come on, what are you talking about, Fabio?"

Fabio shrugged, as if it was all very clear-cut and simple to understand and answered, "One night with me—no sex, we just talk. I will help you figure your life out."

He had to think she was stupid. The whole thing was so absurd that it was almost funny.

Kit bantered back, "Well, why can't we '*talk*' during the day?"

Fabio explained nonchalantly, "Night is different."

Seriously? Seriously.

"No, thanks." Kit grinned back at him as she began wading back toward the shore.

Fabio reached out and grabbed her arm gently, and he argued, "Kit, we are adults. You are not married; I am not married …" Aha! It *was* about sex! Kit suddenly felt very alone and disheartened. Why did it always have to come down to this, to sex? Why couldn't she be right about the people—actually, right about the *men* here? Kit refused to believe that Julianna had one up on her on this, but this whole conversation had certainly seemed to prove her friend's point. But Julianna just couldn't be right about *all* of them …

Kit smiled wanly at him and stated firmly, "No, Fabio. I really like you, but no. I'm sorry, but this conversation just helped me make my decision. *No.*"

"Even if there was no Lassino?" Fabio asked pointedly.

Kit shook her head and pulled away. She forced herself to smile brightly and called over her shoulder, "Ciao, Fabio. See you around. Thanks for the swim!"

"You'll change your mind, Kit!" he called after her.

Kit sighed with disappointment. That was that. Her vacation would soon be over.

Chapter 15

They left behind the crowded parking garage, which was brimming with sporty Fiats, white tour shuttle vans, mini half-trucks that served as the town porters for the hard-to-reach lodgings, and rows of colorful scooters. Bridget had tried heading out the main entrance that led to the bustling crossroads square, but she felt her hand being tugged backward by Lorenzo. Instead, he nodded mysteriously to what appeared to be some dimly lit tunnel at the far end of the garage and said only, "This way."

Bridget decided to forgo questioning him as to why they weren't taking the main road that wound down to the beach. She assumed she'd get Lorenzo's standard reply, "Stop worrying, Bridget. I'm *from* here, remember!" Besides, she was more than happy to be off the scooter and on terra firma once again. She was just *never* going to get used to riding that thing when other people were out and about. People who clearly were nonchalant about whether they lived or died, given the fact that they cut you off at a moment's notice *while* holding a conversation on their cell as well as turning around to chat with the person on the back of their scooter while they drove! And then there were the dogs in this town. Did they have death wishes too? Bridget noticed that for the most part, they were usually sprawled out at the bottom of steps, boredly watching the passing foot traffic. And then there were the Kamikazi-type who dodged in and out of traffic without warning. If you were so lucky as to miss hitting one, you might find it chasing after you in pursuit. This had been the cause of Bridget's terror this evening.

"Dog, dog, *dog*! There's a dog! Oh, my God, we're gonna hit it!" Bridget had cried through clenched teeth into Lorenzo's back.

"Don't worry; we missed him," Lorenzo said all too calmly. The scooter slowed down behind a stalling town bus.

"Oh, thank God. Why do they *do* that? *What* is the matter with the animals in this town?" Bridget wailed. The scooter jutted forward, and

Bridget turned her head back to see that the scrawny little mutt was sprinting after them. It might've been her imagination, but was it baring its teeth at her as well?

"And *now*, the dog is chasing us! Can't this thing go any faster?" Bridget practically shouted into Lorenzo's ear.

"*Madonna*, now you want me to drive faster! Make up your mind, would you?" Lorenzo jokingly chastised her. He glanced in his sideview mirror and said, "Hey, I think that's my aunt's dog!"

"Of course, I forgot you're related to half the town. Why not the dogs, too? Oh—your aunt that hates me—that's *her* dog? That figures!"

At any rate, they'd made it to the garage and without the dog escort. And now they were in some dark and spooky tunnel that was lit only by torches. Bridget guessed it could be considered mildly romantic in a *Count of Monte Cristo*-type way, given the eerie echoing of dripping water, the pungent odor that pervaded, and the fact that she could've sworn she'd seen the shadow of a rat running alongside the rounded brick wall. If she spotted any tally marks etched upon the wall as well, she was turning around and heading back with or without Lorenzo. She really needed to get over these imaginative horror/death scenarios, didn't she? There must be some explanation for all this. Where was the beach, though? She never thought she'd actually be hoping to see those rocky shores.

Bridget spoke up and joked, "Well, this is a side of Positano I've never seen before."

"Not many tourists do, but I think you're no longer a tourist here, so, here's a shortcut we use. I'm surprised you're not holding your nose because of the smell," Lorenzo said.

"Didn't want to break the romantic mood." Bridget shrugged sarcastically.

"Oh, good." Lorenzo raised his eyebrows seductively at her. "I thought for sure that rat back there would've upset you!"

Bridget hastened her step and mumbled, "I knew that was a rat back there!"

"Look around; where there's garbage, there's gonna be rats," Lorenzo replied and stopped. Bridget halted and squinted her eyes into the dimness. She didn't know how she'd missed them, but along the wall on both sides were garbage cans, each having the name of a different restaurant or shop.

She'd never thought about Positano's sanitation system before, but the garbage had to go somewhere. And here it was.

"Oh, there's Segreto Giardino." Bridget pointed at a can across the way.

"Right, so, next time you see Lassino, you can say you know him very well, since you've seen his garbage can."

"Too bad Kit's not here." Bridget giggled until she caught sight of a tail scampering through the darkness and off behind Lassino's trash bin.

"Ahh, there's another rat. Where is the beach?" Bridget dragged Lorenzo forward.

"Relax. Look, see? We're here."

The tunnel abruptly came to an end; it opened up to the other side of the Spiaggia Grande. The pier, normally crowded in the day with people either embarking upon a ferry for a day excursion or returning from one of the same, stood before them, empty and still, as people trekked past it and up the sloping path. Bridget knew they were following the walkway that wound itself up and over to Fornillo Beach.

"Was that so bad, Maestrina?" Lorenzo threw an arm around her shoulder as he lightly pulled her toward the Fornillo overpass.

"Aside from the smell and the rats, it was lovely," countered Bridget.

They walked along the sporadically lit path in companionable silence and every so often passed a fellow pedestrian. For the most part, they had the path to themselves. Bridget couldn't help but work herself up into a slight tizzy speculating about whether there really was an actual beach party. What if there wasn't? Was she prepared for another love session on the rocks? She stopped herself mid-obsess mode when she realized that if there was no beach party, she actually … didn't care. Lorenzo made her feel completely at ease. For starters, with him, she didn't worry about her age. She knew she was *only* thirty-four, for Pete's sake, but at any rate, that seemed ancient here! She didn't worry about her weight (as neurotically much) … and, she just … really, *really* liked him.

Was it possible she was in love? No! That would be crazy. And nearly unfathomable, since Fathead Seamus had depleted her of all self-esteem, confidence, and even the interest in trying out love again! Which was fine with her, because she didn't want any part of love. She was still stinging. But she could hang out with and enjoy Lorenzo. The thought of Paolo momentarily pushed itself into Bridget's head, but she shooed it away. What could she and Paolo ever have in common, besides a love of Prada and the rocks on the beach? *Right* ... nothing. Bridget nearly chuckled. There was no contest. Lorenzo had already won. Bridget realized she was breathing a tad bit harder than ususal. It was only a slight slope, but embarrassingly enough, she was starting to perspire and breathe heavily. She hoped Lorenzo hadn't noticed, but he'd been awfully quiet. Bridget suddenly wondered what he might be thinking.

"So, I'm thinking about changing my plane ticket to stay longer." Lorenzo spoke deliberately. *Huh? How did he do that?* Well, now she knew what he was thinking.

"*Here?* Stay *here* longer?" Bridget gave him a quick, sideways glance while pointing toward the stairs beneath their feet.

Lorenzo raised his eyebrows at her quizzically. "Yes, *here.* Positano. You know, where I'm from, where my family lives, where we are right now? Where else?"

So that had been a dumb thing to ask. It had just shot so unexpectedly out of her mouth. She hadn't been thinking. But perhaps, maybe, she was thinking too much, for suddenly, her mind had sprung into obsessive-crazy mode. *Why* was he thinking of staying longer? Bridget wanted Lorenzo to stay, but she wanted him to go. If he was staying because of her, well, then, this whole thing was getting too serious for her. He was liking her too much! When did that ever happen? But still. They'd only known each other for two weeks! Of course—no, no, she shouldn't flatter herself in assuming so. Lorenzo did have family here. Who wouldn't want to stay here longer to visit family? She would stop herself from letting her mind jump to conclusions again. Ha! Stay here because of her? Please.

Bridget looked over at Lorenzo and said, sheepishly, "Sorry, I meant, 'Oh! Staying longer!'" She then added quickly, "I guess your family will be very, very glad."

"Oh, for sure. I don't get to visit very often. It would be great to have more time with them. Yes, of course, my family will be very ... glad."

See? This was a family thing. Bridget exhaled slightly with relief. Yet, she felt a little let down. Didn't he want to stay longer for her *at all*? Oh, she *knew* it. He didn't like her that much at all! And, well, *why?* Bridget decided that like all the typical men here, this was probably just some wanton summer fling for Lorenzo. And it hadn't even gotten to the wanton part!

What exactly did *wanton* mean, anyway? Her mind was meandering *again*. At least it was diverting her from the uphill trek in the semidarkness. For someone who *so* did not want to care, Bridget was vexed to find that she evidently did. Dammit.

They continued their silent walk until they reached a staircase that, thankfully, only led down. The rocky beach of Fornillo lay below; the inky water lapped rhythmically upon the shore. Although it was really one long, continuous shore, broken up only by the formidable cliff that jutted into it, compared to the Spiaggia Grande side, Fornillo was humble and much less glitzy in comparison to its counterpart—not to mention, a whole lot cheaper. A smattering of platform boardwalk, flanked by umbrella'd tables and unassuming eateries, occupied a large section of the beach. A row of outhouse-type bathrooms stood behind the boardwalk, as if guarding it. Being a little farther from the center of the town, Fornillo seemed, in Bridget's eyes, like the ever, slightly less popular younger sibling. It never received the attention that the ostentatiously glamorous Spiaggia Grande did, the latter tauting its rich and famous people sightings as well as its pricey restaurants and beach-chair services. Bridget thought if she and Kit were smart with their money, they'd spend their beach days at Fornillo, where the chairs were half the price of what Tomaso charged them, even with the "Kit-Positano Discount" he gave them. With Kit's megawatt smile and her bodaciously filled bikini, they'd score beach chairs for practically nothing on this side!

While Fornillo was just as crowded during the day as the other side of the beach, it bustled in a quiet manner. Having been there a couple times with Lorenzo, Bridget realized she quite enjoyed being far from the watchful eyes of almost everyone she ran into at the disco and various other places about town. Although, that also meant she wouldn't have nearly as good people watching of her own, either. Yet, for a tiny amount of time, she felt she was incognito. Of course, there was no telling who was out on a balcony somewhere with binoculars. All in all, there was nothing over the top about Fornillo, and that was just the way it intended itself to be.

Tonight, however, Fornillo was dressed up. White lights lit the eaves of the boardwalk's lengthy canopy, and blue and green lighting emanated from the darkened recesses of where the tables and chairs were. Music and voices mingled up into the night air. There was definitely a party going on. Bridget chided herself. Not *every* male here was out to lure women to the beach in order to seduce them. She thought she might be just a tad bit disappointed, but then she thought better of it. This would be fun, and no clothes would leave her body in the process. Bridget quickly said a prayer of thanks that there'd be no sign of Paolo here, either.

Lorenzo cleared his throat and asked in a somewhat earnest voice, "So, I guess what I really want to know is, will *you* be glad if I stay longer?"

Why did he keep doing this to her, catching her off guard? Just when she was set on assuming that he just couldn't be that interested, he'd throw out a comment like *that* and prove her assumptions to be, once again, totally wrong. Yet, despite her confusion, Bridget was instantly happy. And then, just as quickly, she felt perturbed, since she decided that she didn't want him to stay, either. Clearly, there was something the matter with her.

"Well, *yes*, sure, I am." Bridget hoped she sounded just as earnest. It was *true* that she wanted him to stay. It was just that she wanted him to leave, too, but Lorenzo didn't need to know that.

"Um, huh. Yeah, I could tell." Lorenzo chuckled sarcastically. "I don' know 'bout you, Bridget. I don' wanna stay and cramp your style, you know, in case you got a boyfriend here." Oh, no. What did he know? This was silly. She didn't have a boyfriend here!

He smiled devilishly and left her at the top of the stairs as he began the descent.

"I do *not* have a boyfriend here!" Bridget called and hurried after him. Why would he even say something like that? Unless he knew about Paolo. But Paolo had never been a boyfriend.

Lorenzo continued his downward climb and called over his shoulder playfully, "It's no big deal, Bridget. I mean, come on, you've been here, how many times? You must've had a boyfriend."

"Three times, and no, I've never had a boyfriend here!" she called out defensively. It was pretty pathetic. She really had to be about the only one to come to this romantic idyll and not leave with a boyfriend of some sort!

Lorenzo continued, "You mean, you're gonna tell me that no guy ever brought you down to the beach some night for a little *romance* on the beach chairs?"

"I hardly think bringing someone down to the beach chairs qualifies you as a boyfriend!" Bridget shouted. "Would you slow down?"

Lorenzo stopped abruptly, which caused Bridget to ram into him.

"Sorry," her muffled voice spoke into his back.

"Once again, you're avoiding the question." Lorenzo turned around and looked down at her with a slight grin on his face. Of course, she was avoiding the question.

"I have *never* had a boyfriend here. Okay?" Bridget looked at him without blinking. Well, it was true. She'd been down on the rocks, but she'd never had a boyfriend. What a hussy.

"Okay, if that's your story, I'll go along with it," Lorenzo said smugly as he took her hand in his.

Bridget jerked her hand out of his and said impatiently, "What do you mean *story*? There is no story. I have *no* story!"

"Maestrina, *everybody* has a story. And the ones who swear the most about *not* having one, usually have the best." Lorenzo winked at her. Bridget realized her mouth was agape. What could she say? *Yeah*, she had a story. But he didn't need to know all of it, did he? At least, not right now. Bridget opened her mouth to say something and then closed it.

Lorenzo grabbed a hold of her hand and said, "Finally, you're not gonna disagree with me! Right, so, come on; let's go." Bridget found it quite annoying how Italian men thought they knew everything. It was even more irritating that they usually were right about this. At least, at home, men really didn't have a clue. However, she just couldn't let Lorenzo have the last word on this.

"Go down to the *beach* with some guy? Oh, please," Bridget mumbled, but loud enough for Lorenzo to hear.

"Aha, I knew you couldn't stay quiet for long! You should calm down. You're really getting a little too upset about this, Bridget," Lorenzo teased.

"I am not upset!" Bridget huffed and sounded, much to her irritation, quite upset.

"Right," replied Lorenzo as they reached the bottom of the stairs.

"I have never had a boyfriend here, and the whole 'going to the beach' thing—I don't even like being on the beach in a bathing suit!"

"Yes, I know," laughed Lorenzo drolly.

Bridget babbled on, "The beach chairs! Not all American girls are drunken bimbos, either, you know!" No need for him to know about her being a bimbo. Well, in her defense, 99 percent of the time, she was practically a nun.

"You're a grown woman. You're on vacation. Stuff like that happens. Whatever you did—but of course, you didn't do *anything*," he rolled his eyes and continued, "I don't care. I just asked because if I decide to stay, I'd like to spend time with you, but not if you've got something going on with some other *boy* here." *Boy?* He so *had* to know.

Bridget answered with a sigh, "Lorenzo, I don't have *anything* going on with *anyone* here." And at this point in time, that much was true. And she could forsee nothing else happening, anyway.

"All right, then. We'll have to do something about you not having a *boyfriend* in Positano this summer." He raised his eyebrows at her.

"Define *boyfriend*," Bridget joked dryly. She then added, "Because if you think that you're going to take me down to the beach to become my boyfriend, it's gonna take a little bit more than that. You know, like throw in that really hot pair of sandals—you know, I've had my eye on a pair …" She winked at him.

"What are you implying, Maestrina?"

"Absolutely nothing. Besides, I've heard those beach chairs are a bad idea—"

"Yeah. Not good for sex," Lorenzo joked as Bridget simultaneously said, "Too dangerous for sex."

Why had she said *that?* She was just joking, but now he would think she knew because she'd *done it* on a beach chair!

They stared at each other. Bridget stammered, "I mean, uh—"

Lorenzo smiled and said, "Yes, I thought that I'd be the one to fill you in on the beach chairs. Now I know, whoever he was, he was definitely a Positano boy!"

✦　✦　✦

Kit stood at the top of the steps that led to Ristorante Segreto Giardino. She looked down upon the broad stone patio spread out like a relief map before her, illuminated by glimmering white lights and candles. Behind it, the actual restaurant stood, the only activity within it being conducted in the kitchen or at the cash register. Nobody ever ate inside the restaurant during the summer. While the food was delicious, the ambience of the lush, extending patio lent itself to the whole dining experience of Segreto Giardino.

As usual, the many tables dispersed throughout the wide terrace were all filled tonight. Although Lassino had actually asked her to come to the restaurant for dinner tonight, Kit probably would have shown up anyway. Bridget had gone to Lorenzo's for dinner and was off to Fornillo afterward. Kit was elated with Bridget's recent good fortune in meeting Lorenzo. If she ever thought she was intuitive, she really had a good feeling about this local boy. And of all her dear friends, Kit felt that Bridget was really deserving of some good luck. Still, she couldn't help feeling a little forlorn. With all their houseguests momentarily gone, until Marren arrived in a few days, the apartment felt quite empty and, dare she say, sad. While Kit was glad that for the time being, the drama was over, everything was just so *quiet*.

Although, she presumed that Lassino, Tino, and the rest of the town were probably heaving a collective sigh of relief over this. Positano welcomed and appreciated their tourists. After all, their livelihood depended upon them. It was one thing to cater to town visitors at the beach or in hotels, stores, or restaurants. However, tracking down luggage that had gone MIA, as well as missing *people*, and continuously comping dinner, drinks, and aiport shuttling, was going above and beyond the call to hospitable duty.

Yet, everyone continued to graciously look out for them. In Kit's eyes, this elevated the town and endeared its inhabitants to her even more. People here took care of family and friends. This was a good sign. Perhaps they really did consider her a friend, and maybe she could live here on her own. Still, Kit couldn't help but hope she and her friends hadn't worn out their welcome. Here, they'd never tell her, of course.

Lassino, on the other hand, was less diplomatic. "When are you leaving?" He'd scratch his head and squint at her behind his thick glasses.

"I've told you a million times, in August!" Kit would answer.

"Well, August is almost here. You better start packing!" Lassino would sputter back.

To which Kit would roll her eyes. This repetitive conversation had grown into somewhat of a joke between them, although Kit suspected that Lassino was serious in his quest to find out the actual length of her stay. Whether he was hopeful to have her remain here longer, or anxious to be rid of her, well, that fluctuated upon the day. Little did he know how close she'd come to accepting Fabio's job offer. Kit cringed slightly as she thought about the fact that the whole nanny position had only been a type of ruse.

No matter how good-looking and debonair Fabio was, Kit just couldn't fathom the idea. It simply was not an option. And now staying on past August wasn't, either.

Well, she'd just push back her departure as long as she could. She really wanted to stay for the big holiday in mid-August, *Ferragosto*. It was a national holiday celebrated with the parading of a revered statue of Mary throughout towns, fireworks, bands, and more. Kit had to see it and be part of it. This could probably send Lassino over the edge, but she didn't care. It was one of the many things on her Positano to-do list that she actually planned to get around to doing.

She wondered what she'd do about a place to stay. They'd only booked the apartment until August 6. With Bridget and Marren leaving together on the sixth, she wasn't going to be able to afford paying for the extra week on her own. There *was* a back storage room at Tino's ceramic shop. Kit had joked with Tino about sleeping there in exchange for dusting all the ceramics in the shop on a daily basis. If she couldn't find someplace cheap, she wondered if Tino would take pity on her and actually take her up on the dusting offer! Something would have to happen soon, and Kit was sure it would.

All she needed to worry about tonight was getting a seat on the patio. It looked as if all the tables were full. This evening, Lassino was quite "beesy." He might work in the kitchen during the day, but at night, he worked the patio, greeting people, seating them, and moving from table to table chatting with friends and diners alike. Every once in a while, he'd shout something at one of the passing waiters.

Kit grasped the metal banister and carefully made her way down the two flights, until she was standing in the center of the patio. Waiters whizzed by her and called out, "Ciao, Kit!"

Lassino spotted her, excused himself from the table of diners he'd been talking to, and swiftly approached. He gave her a quick peck on each cheek and said gruffly, "You're late! You'll have to eat inside!" and then stormed off. She wasn't *that* late, Kit thought disappointedly. She looked around and suddenly spotted Tino and his girlfriend at a table a few feet away. A gleam of hope sprang up in Kit. Tino was a friend! But he was with his girlfriend. And it was one thing when the guys were all sitting around, but if one of the girlfriends was present, you never just plunked yourself down. You waited to be invited. At least, that's what Kit's observations had led her to believe. The last thing she wanted to do was offend the women here, when she'd yet to even come close to befriending any of them.

As if on cue, Tino looked up, and upon seeing her, he called out, "Kit!" while motioning for her to come to the table. What luck! Well, Kit conceded that luck probably didn't have much to do with it, since her lone figure, standing perplexed amid a sea of tables, probably had somewhat drawn his attention. She didn't mind. Maybe they'd invite her to sit with them.

Kit strolled across the patio till she reached the table where Tino and Antonella sat. She'd never met Antonella before, most likely due to the fact that she and Tino lived together, and therefore, being practically married, they didn't frequent the disco. Lassino joked that Antonella was very jealous and kept his best friend on a short leash, but Kit wondered if it were true to some extent. Aside from their saucy style and friendly, but no-nonsense attitudes, Kit had yet to really get to know any of their male friends' female counterparts.

It wasn't for lack of wanting to, though. Kit marveled over so many things about these amazing women. For instance, how did they so effortlessly climb up and down the multitude of stairs or even ride a Vespa in their stiletto sandals? How did they get away wearing those see-through linen tops or pants without looking totally slutty? Why was their skin always a healthy glow, despite their age and the abundance of sunbathing? And most importantly, how did they deal with the men in this town? Especially during tourist season? Kit wondered if the tightly knit local women ever got tired and resentful of the way the men flocked to the multudinous vacationing females.

Who really had the upper hand in this town—the women or the men? Or was there just some kind of understanding between them? Kit knew there *were* people who actually lived here and had boyfriends or girlfriends. Tino was a sure example. And there *were* obviously people here who were married. She didn't really know any of them personally, but still, it was *possible*. There were so many things she could learn from the Positanese women. And there was an endless list of questions she'd love to ask them, as well, provided the situation was right.

While she and Bridget joked about the necessity of handrails around here, it seemed they'd get a lot more use out of a women's handbook! If only such a thing existed! However, the next best thing would be to have a female friend here. Kit hoped Antonella didn't despise her in all her American glory already.

Tino stood up, smiled, and asked, "Kit, are you eating dinner here tonight?'

"Hi, Tino! Well, I was going to eat out here, but I've been told I'm too late and will have to eat inside." Kit smiled. She then quickly looked at Antonella and said, "Hello, I am Kit!"

"*Piacere*, nice to meet you. I am Antonella," the dark-haired girl smiled sincerely, then gently backhanded Tino's arm in mock annoyance. Oh, no, Kit worried, had she somehow irritated Anotnella?

Tino shrugged back at Antonella and said, "*Ay, che?*" He turned a sheepish grin toward Kit and apologized. "Sorry, my girlfriend, Antonella."

Kit smiled at Tino and then at Antonella. "Well, I figured she was your girlfriend!"

"Please, sit, have dinner with us." He pulled a chair out for her.

Before answering, Kit looked for some type of facial cue from Antonella. Any type of seriousness or blank expression and she would gently decline. But, to her relief, Antonella smiled pleasantly at Kit and added, "Please, join us." Yes, she was saved! She would be able to eat on the patio, and she was making new friends.

◆   ◆   ◆

She was having a great time. In fact, Kit thought she might be in heaven. Once Lassino got past his initial annoyance over her sitting and sharing a meal with his friends, while he worked—"Kit, don't you have any of your own friends?" "Excuse me, Tino invited me to eat with them!"—he returned to his charmingly jokey self. And not only that; he also made sure their meal wanted for nothing.

While they sipped on glasses of delectable brunello, a white-shirted waiter delivered their salads. Crisp romaine, garnished with juicy tomatoes and olives and covered lightly in velvety olive oil, started them off. But the best part of the salad, Kit thought, was that instead of croutons, it was garnished with bits of crispy, chopped-up pizza dough. Antonella stared at the salads set before them, looked up at Kit, and stated matter-of-factly, "Lassino never makes this salad. This is for you."

Kit smiled bashfully but said, "This is so good! I can't wait to see what he sends out for dinner!"

She looked around quickly to see if she could spot Lassino through the big, glass windows of the restaurant. He stood in the kitchen speaking to the chefs. While his mouth moved constantly and his hands gestured wildly, he continually peeked out the corner of his eye toward the patio. Kit wondered how it was possible for someone with such bad eyesight to always be able to keep such an eye on everyone and everything around him. Maybe the whole vision problem was a front.

And then there was *dinner.* If Kit thought that Lassino's thoughtfully delicious salad had been a masterpiece worthy of her praises, she was mistaken. For she clearly was not prepared for what Lassino sent out next. She thought she'd sampled every mouth-watering food, every local delicacy in her travels here. Of all the creamy gnocchi, of all the fresh seafood, of all the sumptuous cheeses (that she was never supposed to eat) ... this meal defied them all, *all* food, and *all* meals that she'd savored in Italy. There was pure irony in the fact that it was something so seemingly un-Italian-like. In shocking contrast, according to Kit, the meal was so completely ... *American*—the only difference being in execution and, she hated to admit, superiority. She had no problem admitting that Italians did a lot of things better than anybody else. When it came to food, whether it was produce, pasta al dente, cappuccinos, or even the Nutella manufactured here, Italy had no competition. But this dish was taking it to a new level.

"Oh, it's steak!" Kit nearly squealed in surprise when the waiter set the plate before her. The thick slab of of meat, dripping with some sort of red sauce, practically dwarfed the plate. To the side of the meat lay what appeared to be creamy mashed potatoes, as well as a side of long, crispy fries. How had she ever missed seeing this on the menu? Then again, it wouldn't be something she'd typically be perusing the menu for. Kit wasn't complaining, though.

"Filet mignon in a red-wine reduction sauce," the waiter pleasantly corrected her, before he headed off to another table. And it was the best meat she'd ever eaten. Kit knew she was prone to constantly declaring Italy to have the best this and the best that, but she was not exaggerating this time. She savored each velvety morsel slowly and deliberately. After every few bites, Kit stopped and and took a breather and patted her stomach, before she returned, again, to her feast, while Tino and Antonella looked on in mild amusement. The waiter, mistakenly thinking Kit to be finished, came to the table several times and asked, "You are done, Kit?"

It would be a sin to not finish this. She must pace herself. Plus, Italians thought bizarrely of Americans and their whole doggy-bag disposition anyway. She smiled and held up her hand. "Oh, no, no, I'm just taking my time."

"*Bene.*" The waiter smiled in appreciation before hurrying back to report to the kitchen.

Tino took a sip of his wine. He set it down and pushed himself away from the table, and then he said, "Excuse me," and walked off in the direction of the kitchen entrance.

Antonella explained, "The television is inside. He's going to check the football."

"Oh, that's right, World Cup," Kit replied and nodded in understanding. World Cup fever abounded, and the country watched with bated breath; excitement mounted with each Italian victory. Kit pierced another piece of juicy meat and looked around. The patio was pretty much dormant, except for a few straggling diners in a far-off corner, and the waiters busied themselves about the empty patio, clearing the tables of glasses and tablecloths.

Uh-oh, she hadn't realized she'd been eating that slowly. Kit looked at Antonella anxiously. Dinner conversation had been pleasant, but nothing too much more than common questions about what she did for a living, what California was like, and where else she'd traveled in Italy. No real dirt had been unearthed in regards to surviving in Positano while avoiding potential insanity in the process. But, of course, what was she expecting, if Tino was sitting at the table? Although, certainly, Tino defied the typical male prototype here. The conversation probably wouldn't apply to him at all. However, Kit wondered if Antonella had had enough of superficial chat and was ready for a speedy exit as well.

Kit spoke hastily. "I'm sorry, Antonella. I didn't realize I was eating so slowly! If you are ready to leave, please, go ahead."

Antonella waved her off. "No problem, Kit. I don't mind to sit to talk with you." She then rolled her eyes slightly and grinned. "Tino is crazy about the football! So, I can sit and have a cigarette."

Kit smiled and said, "Oh, good," and popped the forkful into her mouth. While she was relieved that Antonella didn't mind keeping her company,

Kit wondered what they might talk about now that Tino was no longer there to steer the conversation. She was pretty adept at keeping conversations afloat, but there was a line that crossed from genuine interest to being intrusive. The men here never seemed to mind all her questions; in fact, they acted quite flattered, but Kit wasn't so sure about the women. Well, if anything, at least she was getting a foot in the door with a local female. How awkward could the conversation be?

"So, you have been to Positano many times," Antonella stated while cupping her hands over her lighter and inhaling.

Kit nodded her head in affirmation. Antonella exhaled a cloud of smoke and continued. "And you and Lassino are ... what are you?" She looked at Kit with a nonchalant type of interest.

Kit involuntarily coughed her steak up a bit before composing herself. Well, now, she needn't have worried about what topic to bring up, had she? Kit hadn't planned to have a candid conversation about Lassino, but apparently, this was where the conversation was now headed, unless she could deflect it somehow. She watched Antonella take another long drag of her cigarette while staring back at her expectantly. She wasn't getting out of this one.

Well, all she could do, Kit thought, was be honest. It was funny how at home, she realized she was quite secretive about her amorous experiences, even with the closest of friends. It'd taken her four years after the fact to divulge even to Bridget that she'd slept with a high school boyfriend! And of course, she'd taken her time informing her mother about Johnny ... and all her other boyfriends before. She just didn't want to be judged. And she was always being judged by people. Maybe she was paranoid, but Kit really didn't think so.

Strangely, here, she felt she could be quite honest, without the typical repercussions. And how could anyone, especially, Lassino, be upset with her for that? Ten to one, she wouldn't be stating anything that everybody didn't somehow know already anyway. The Italians were pretty attuned to basically *everything*. In a small town, what else was there to do but observe everyone and everything they did, anyway? And with binoculars.

Still, Kit hoped Lassino stayed in the kitchen, far out of earshot. Antonella waited for Kit's response, a slight smile upon her lips. It was an amused smile, yet kind, and Kit felt better as she noted that perhaps she was unnecessarily obsessing about what the people around here thought of her.

Kit chose her words carefully and said, "Well, I've known Lassino for a few years." *And I'm scared that I may be in love with this crazy man! I want to quit my job and live here and ... and ...* She paused; she hoped that Antonella would somehow read her mind (like all the men around here seemed to be able to do) and not expect her to continue. Antonella tilted her head and then nodded it in understanding before she took a puff of her cigarette. Oh, good, she was going to let the conversation drop.

Antonella exhaled, shrugged, and stated matter-of-factly, "So, you are in love with Lassino."

The women here were, indeed, mind readers too.

Flustered, Kit stammered, "Well, I ... I think Lassino is *such* a good person. I care about him ... very much ..." There, that was enough, she'd said it. She just couldn't bring herself to utter the words *I'm in love with him.* Besides, what did she know? Could she be in love with him? Well, unfortunately, yes, it was more than quite a possibility ... but it was just that ...

"But there is a problem; there is ... *something.* You are unsure of something?" Antonella queried with a look of bland concern. *God, how did they do that?* Was it that obvious?

Kit sighed in resignation. "Well, I *think* I understand Lassino and how he feels about me, and then he does something to confuse me and I don't understand him at all!" Kit shrugged and chuckled.

Antonella laughed dryly in return and said, "Neither does anybody else! Lassino, he is ... strange sometimes. I don't know why he is like this. Maybe he has a problem with women; maybe he hates his mother? I don't know." Antonella shrugged and opened her eyes widely before she continued. "He is a good person. He is generous, but Lassino is *not* a good boyfriend."

Those were not the words of encouragement Kit had been hoping to hear. In fact, those were the very words that she had been afraid she *would* hear! In disappointed response, her stomach immediately felt queasy, and a low rumbling began down there. Other than her stomach voicing its concerns, Kit had no response for Antonella, except to sigh again.

So Antonella continued on, as if Kit needed further proof and explanation, "Lassino, he wants *this* from one girl, and *this* from another girl! He thinks you come here only for him, so he can treat you this way."

Kit felt a wave of indignation. It wasn't true! At least, not completely true. If anything, she was in love with the town, first and foremost. Of course, in her wildest dreams (and she didn't think they were too wild), Kit really wanted Lassino to be in love with her. And sometimes, in her heart, she felt and she knew that he was. But no, being here was not *all* about Lassino. It had been about herself and her quest for a dramatic life change of some sort. That just happened to be in a town where she had a love interest—so, yes, this really was about her, and what she needed and wanted out of life. But did Lassino really think that she was here only for him? Probably. Had it happened with other girls before? Had Monica been the same way? And if he thought this about her, did the rest of the town? The very idea of being perceived as a pathetic pushover was more than Kit could stand.

"Well, he's wrong!" Kit felt the need to obligatorily cry out. No need for anyone to know that it was a little more than partly true.

"Good, forget about Lassino! Don't come to Positano for him. Come for yourself." Antonella smiled cheekily and then stamped out her cigarette in the ceramic ashtray.

Kit smiled triumphantly. She had. And she would again. To hell with Lassino and his absurd craziness! Oh, but she still wanted him. Damn him! Why did he have to be such a, such a ... well, a jackass? And a really cute one, too.

"Antonella! I just don't understand how the women do it here!" Kit called out in exasperation.

"What do you mean?" Antonella asked.

Kit replied, "Well, how do you understand the men here? They're so confusing!"

Antonella laughed and took a sip of wine. "What is there to understand, Kit? They are *men*. Men are simple, and when they are not, don't try to understand them!"

Baffled, Kit protested, "But you! You are so lucky! You have Tino and he is soo ... just soo ... good! He's the best here!"

Antonella rolled her eyes and smirked. "Huh! You and your friends think Tino is the best! Ha! Tino is a man, like all the rest here! He is not perfect!"

Kit stared at her in horrified disappointment. *No, not Tino too!*

Antonella patted Kit's hand and said simply, "Kit, we women think we need a man to be happy, but we don't. I don't *need* Tino! But I love him, and I want him, and he the same for me. We are not perfect, but we are happy.

A man will not make a woman happy; a woman will not make a man happy; a man will not make a ... *man* happy, whatever, if they are not first happy with themselves. Maybe Lassino does not like himself? Maybe you are not happy with yourself? I do not know. But look to yourself first."

"I'm trying! Why is it so hard?" Kit cringed and stabbed the last piece of meat left on her plate.

Antonella shrugged and changed the subject slightly by asking, "Why you always come to Lassino's to eat? Tomorrow, you and your friend come to dinner with me and some of my friends. Leave Lassino to himself, and he will follow."

Would he? Kit thought not, but at least she had plans with some real Positano friends—and females, no less! A good sign, a sure sign that she could make it here. She'd gotten this invitation on her own, without any help from Lassino!

"I'd love to have dinner with you and your friends! I will tell Bridget," Kit beamed.

"Yes, yes, of course. Besides, maybe you will find you like one of my friends." Antonella smiled coyly. Oh, were there going to be men there? Kit did not want to be set up with anyone. Well, she'd risk it to go out with some females around here. At least she'd pretty much have an evening free of being "accidentally" groped on the disco floor or from being quizzed about whether her breasts were real or fake.

The sound of sandaled feet bounding down the metal stairs seemed to echo slightly throughout the quiet patio. Kit and Antonella looked toward the staircase and saw that it was Paolo.

He spotted them and approached the table smiling widely, the typical cigarette dangling casually from his lips. He removed the cigarette from his mouth with his thumb and forefinger, exhaled over his shoulder, and placed a light kiss upon each of them.

"Good evening! You are alone tonight, Kit?" he asked with interest.

Kit replied, "No. I am with Antonella! She and Tino were nice enough to let me eat with them."

Paolo chuckled and responded, "No, I mean, you are not with *Bridget*."

She was about to explain where Bridget was, but she stopped herself from telling Paolo that her best friend was out with Lorenzo. In addition to Bridget demanding that her romance with Paolo was a thing to be forgotten, she still kept lamenting over the fact that Paolo "hated her" this summer and was being weird around her. Not only that, but Kit had not failed to notice that whenever Bridget went out with Lorenzo, she seemed to avoid places where Paolo would for sure be. Kit ascertained that even with as complicated as Bridget was, it was not difficult to see what was going on. All this could mean only one thing. Her friend was still interested in Paolo. Or she was just very confused, because Bridget really seemed to like Lorenzo. Kit marveled at how at ease Bridget seemed when she was with Lorenzo, how happy, how unabashed, how … how … unlike her usual self!

Well, actually, Kit thought this was her friend's true self finally being exposed. Finally someone besides her friends was getting to see the real Bridget. Kit just hoped that Bridget didn't blow it all by pushing Lorenzo away and pining after one of the town's biggest Casanovas. Undeniably sweet, kind, and lovable, Paolo still had an amorous rap sheet about as long as his arm. And then there was the whole love/hate saga with Australian Rachel. Bridget *so* did not need to get caught up in that!

So, Kit figured the fit Bridget would throw should she divulge her actual whereabouts to Paolo, and instead, she answered vaguely, "I think Bridget went to a party on Fornillo."

Paolo nodded knowingly and then asked, "So, what do you do tomorrow, Kit?"

Kit shrugged. Go to the beach? Definitely. Clean the apartment since Marren would be here soon? She guessed she *should*. She had a pile of two weeks' worth of clothes lying in a heap in the corner of the bedroom. Of course, she could tidy up another day …

"Tomorrow, most of us have the day off. We are planning to go out on my boat. Would you like to join us? Antonella is coming." Antonella smiled and nodded in agreement.

Would she like to join them? On a boat, all day, sailing around the gorgeous Amalfi Coast? Um, *yesss*!

She would try to contain herself, though. "Yes, sure!" Oh, God, she could feel herself doing her inevitable head-bobbing thing. Well, it happened when she got super-excited about something. So much for trying to act low-key. She couldn't help but sing inside her head, *I'm goin' on a boat trip; I'm goin' on a boat trip!*

Oblivious to her head-bobbling, Paolo explained, "Good, it is very fun, very relaxing. We take the boat out, swim, stop for lunch."

"Great, what time?' Kit asked before thinking. It was silly to inquire, since Italians weren't big on the whole planning ahead/picking specific times thing.

Paolo shrugged. "In the morning sometime. Meet down at the bottom of the steps at the beach."

Morning? What did that mean? Early morning? Late morning? Which steps? The ones at the bottom of the church or at the other end of the promenade? What if she went to the wrong set of steps? What if she got there too late? She was always late, even by Italian standards ... but this boat trip was something she did not want to miss!

As if innately sensing her worry, Antonella added, "Kit, give me your mobile number and I will send you a message. I will give you my number too."

"Oh, okay, perfect." Kit couldn't help but flash her toothiest of grins. Lassino always thought she was hanging around to be near him, but now she actually had plans of her own! And with his cousin and friends!

Paolo added, "Very good. Lassino and I and everyone else will just meet you there."

Wait, Lassino was going? Kit was torn between excitement and deflation.

"Oh, will this be all right with Lassino that I am going?" Kit asked wryly.

"Of course," Paolo said simply.

"Kit, don't worry about Lassino. We are inviting you!" Antonella exclaimed.

"All right then, if Lassino tries to say I invited myself, you're both my witnesses!"

Antonella rolled her eyes. "Lassino, la *principessa* da Positano! Madonna!"

Paolo paused and said almost hesitatingly, "Oh, and tell Bridget too."

Bridget? Yes, yes, sure, sure, she'd tell her. Not that it would make much difference. Hmm, Kit wondered, which bikini would she wear tomorrow? Should she wear her hair up or down? What sandals? Her head was spinning already.

Before she forgot herself completely, Kit gushed appreciatively, "Thank you so much for inviting me!"

"You are welcome." Paolo paused before he casually threw out, "And Bridget, too, if she can come."

There he was, mentioning Bridget's name *again*. This was interesting, very interesting. It was too bad, since she knew for a fact that Bridget would *never* go on the boat trip. Anything that entailed being in a bathing suit for a prolonged period of time in front of Italian men would be instantly vetoed. Too bad, since Kit clearly sensed that something was definitely up. Was Paolo still interested in Bridget? She thought so. Never again would Kit listen to Bridget complain about her dreary love prospects.

Paolo stood, waiting for Kit to say something.

She quickly uttered, "Um, sure, I don't know what Bridget's plans are for tomorrow, but I'll make sure to tell her."

"Good, good." Paolo smiled, almost in relief. "Okay, ciao, regazze!" He nodded and hustled off and in through the entryway to the kitchen.

"*Allora*, Kit," Antonella said smugly, "a boat trip tomorrow and dinner tomorrow night. You don't need Lassino."

And Kit agreed that perhaps Antonella was right.

◆　◆　◆

They sat side by side, in a far-off corner of the boardwalk platform. Bridget leaned back against the canvas chair and took a sip of her granite-style mojito. The slushy drink gave quick relief as it made its icy-cold way down her throat. It was still so warm outside that she was sweating just sitting here watching the locals and their random guests cavorting in the shadows. She poured back the last of the slush and received an instant brain freeze. "Ahhh!" Bridget squeezed her eyes shut tightly while she placed a balled-up fist to her forehead.

"What's the matter?" Lorenzo asked.

"Ughh, brain freeze, brain freeze!" Bridget said through clenched teeth.

"Don't drink it that fast," he replied with a smirk.

With her eyes still clamped shut, Bridget answered, "Yeah, I know, but it's so … damn hot! And seriously, there cannot be any alcohol in this. It's like drinking tasty water! Oh, make the pain stop!" She thrust her forehead into her curled-up palm again.

"Well, just watch out with those. You may be small, but I don't want to be carrying you back up that hill!" Lorenzo laughed.

"Okay, okay, don't worry; I'll be fine." Bridget shooed Lorenzo off.

"You want another one?" Lorenzo smiled, ready to push himself up from his chair.

"Yes, of course." Bridget fanned herself, and then added, "I'll get them. It's my turn. You sit."

"Whatever you say, Maestrina," he called from his chair.

She set out and carefully weaved in and out among dancers and those lounging about smoking. Bridget reached the small bar, leaned against it, and looked back across the fluorescent darkness. Through the crowded dance-floor silhouettes, she could just barely see the back of Lorenzo, his broad shoulders resting back against his chair. She inhaled and exhaled. She would take her time getting the drinks. She needed a few moments to think about the conversation they'd just had. Besides, it would take awhile before she could get someone's attention behind the bar.

"Hello!" A voice from somewhere above her spoke. Bridget squinted up. She was surprised to find Vinnie smiling down at her. She felt her eyes involuntarily caught between staring at his oiled-back hair and his light-pink polo with the collar turned up, which seemed to glow iridescently in the disco lighting. Bridget quickly smiled, unsure of what he wanted, since he'd ignored her the last time she'd run into him.

"You are Bridget, right?" he asked pleasantly.

"Yes, hello, Vinnie," Bridget said.

"Oh, you remember my name?" he asked, as if he was quite shocked.

"You did drive us to Salerno last week to catch the train. And I've seen you at the disco." *Ogling my friend like a perv,* she felt like adding.

"Oh, yes, yes, of course. May I get you a drink?" he asked gallantly. Bridget wondered if he was a bit drunk. Even in the dark, his eyes appeared glazed, and if not for the Italian accent, she might think his speech a tad slurred. She wondered if he'd been hitting the mojito granitas too. Something to consider before placing her order.

"No, thank you. I'm ordering for myself and someone else." She most certainly did not want him buying her a drink. He had a slightly weird vibe about him. What if he slipped some kind of Italian roofie into her drink and dragged her off, behind Lorenzo's back? And what was up with the tight, white pants?

"Oh, is Kit here with you?" he asked almost too quickly, as his eyes darted out and about over the crowd before them. He quickly ran a hand through his hair before wiping a few beads of sweat from his brow.

Just as quickly, Bridget answered, "No, Kit's not here." She then added, "I'm not sure what she's doing tonight."

With a nonchalant Italian face-shrug, Vinnie replied, "Huh, too bad. So, I can buy you a drink?"

Creep. "Oh, no, no thanks …" But he had already sauntered off to a table full of girls.

Kit wasn't exaggerating. Vinnie was a total lurky, stalker. There was actually something sinister about him and the way he stared at people, or in the case of Bridget, *over* her so he could stare at other people. Bridget was glad she wasn't the object of his obsession, and she suddenly felt sorry for her best friend. While she was usually quite unsympathetic to Kit complaining about all the unwanted attention she received, Bridget really felt for her friend this time. It had to get old, especially when you had the town weirdos interested in you as well. Bridget was thankful that she didn't have that problem. She was practically invisible. No worries about anyone in this town being in love with her, let alone stalking her! Well, there was Lorenzo. If the conversation they'd just had was any indication, Lorenzo's feelings for her were far more serious than she had thought possible, but of course, not in the icky, stalkery way. Bridget didn't know if she was happy with this or not. It seemed a bit unreal, not to mention that it was in the most unlikely of places (Italy!) for *her*, of *all* people, to find herself in this type of romantic dilemma! And it *was* a dilemma. Of course, she was the only one who seemed to be having issues.

"I don't know; what do you think of all this?" she'd asked Kit and Julianna a few days earlier.

"What do you mean?" Kit had eyed her skeptically.

"I mean, I think Lorenzo *likes* me. I mean, I *think* so."

"Let's see. He calls you, makes a point to see you every day or night, takes you to his home for meals with the family … and given the fact that he *doesn't* hide from you, or act like he doesn't see you when you enter the same room as him, *or* send you odd, cryptic texts that you can barely understand, like *some* people I know, I'd say this is very good. Come on, Bridget, it's so very *obvious*," Kit had stated in exasperation.

"Yeahhh … trruuueee. But don't you think this is kind of *weird*? Of all the women that come here, that *live* here, why me?"

Kit shouted, "*Why not*? Jeez, Bridget, why can't you just accept that Lorenzo likes you, and why shouldn't he? I really wish Marren were here to knock some sense into you. I can't do this anymore!" Kit threw her hands up.

Julianna rasped, "Well, I'll do it for the both of you! Look, as far as the men here go, you have actually found a *real* man, Bridget! Not one of these playboys who likes to dick people around! Oh, don't roll your eyes, Kit! You just said so yourself!"

"I was making reference to someone in particular, Julianna, not the whole male population here!" Kit shook her head with a smile.

Julianna looked back at Bridget and continued, "Whatever. So, sweetie, if you don't want Lorenzo, you just point him in my direction, cause I'd definitely like to hit some of that!"

Kit ignored Julianna and burst out, "Just please, please, Bridget, don't blow it! Sorry, what I *mean* is, I think you're onto something good here. And I know you're a little skittish because of Seamus and all, but don't let yourself get frightened away. Just breathe in and out, and promise me you'll take it one day at a time. Please! Sorry."

"Okay, okay," Bridget had promised, and she had. Until know. She was having trouble inhaling and exhaling without her stomach going into panic mode or protruding in a quite unflattering way. She longed for Kit and her supply of Rolaids, or maybe some type of girdle.

"Will me coming to California help you make a decision about me?" Lorenzo had just asked her, as they sat against their chairs, the tips of their fingers hooked together, dangling between them. She'd taken a quick sip of her drink to avoid having to answer. Lorenzo continued, "I've never been. My cousin's been talking about finding another place to open a restaurant. Why not California? You need a good Italian restaurant where you live?"

Noo! She and the girls *already* had a good Italian restaurant: La Bella Vita. There could be no other competition. She'd feel like a traitor gallivanting between the two.

However, this had nothing to do with La Bella Vita. It had everything to do with the fact that a man she'd only known a couple of weeks was willing to move across the country for her! There would be way too much pressure involved trying to make the whole situation work out, thus, ensuring total failure and let-down.

A little internal voice spoke up and said, *Well, maybe it will work. Maybe,* she answered back reluctantly. *But don't be silly!* She just couldn't have Lorenzo move himself and everything he had to Suburbianna for *her.* When things went awry, it wasn't like he could just pack up and move back to Florida. Well, maybe he'd be able to find someone new. Everyone knew the ratio of single women to available, straight, noncreepy men in the Bay Area was completely lopsided. A hot Italian import like Lorenzo would be swooped up immediately, if not by some pretty young thing, then by some cougar-type. He'd be set. But maybe she didn't want him finding anyone else. A wave of jealousy flickered through Bridget. No, he'd just have to move back to Florida. Wait, what was she thinking?

Then an uneasy thought popped into Bridget's head. Maybe Lorenzo was looking for a *green card.* Why hadn't she ever thought of that before? Bridget was instantly disappointed. How could he do that to her? Wait, would Lorenzo be the type to do that? She was getting ahead of herself, but she'd already been swindled by a foreigner before. Bridget was not about go through that whole hellish scenario of humiliation and heartbreak again. Hadn't she learned anything? She just wouldn't risk herself.

"Hey, Maestrina, *Bridget.*" He waved a hand in front of her and stared at her with those big, green eyes. "What do you think?"

"What?" she asked blankly. He'd lost her way back at the Italian-restaurant part.

"Well, I was just saying how I was coming to California because I'm in love with you and was planning on marrying you," he said with a gleam in his eye.

Bridget could feel her eyebrows going into their scrunched-up squint.

Lorenzo laughed. "Relax! Good thing I *didn't* profess my love, since you were somewhere else! And don't worry. I'm not after you for a green card. I've already been married." *What?*

"What? You were *married?*" she asked, as if he'd just stated he'd been to Mars. He'd been married? *Who? Who* had he been married to? There went her whole green-card theory.

Lorenzo stopped chuckling to answer, "Yes, in Florida."

"What happened? Who was she?" Bridget blurted out with genuine interest.

Lorenzo sighed. "She was a friend of my cousin, and we became friends. Just friends, that's all. My work visa was about to expire and I knew I didn't want to come back here. So, we made a deal to help each other out. I wanted to stay, and she needed help paying her mortgage. It worked. We were friends, and we thought maybe it could turn into something more over time." His voice trailed off.

Bridget interjected, "But ..."

"But ... it didn't. You can't make yourself feel a certain way. You either feel it or you don't." Lorenzo shrugged.

"How long?"

"Almost five years," Lorenzo answered.

Five years. "Well, did you two ever ... you know ..." Bridget fumbled for the words to say.

"Did we ever have *sex*? Bridget, come on!" Lorenzo placed his hands in prayer position and shook them at her.

Bridget shrugged. "Well, you *just* said you were only friends, that you didn't feel *that* way about each other!"

"We were married for *five years*. Of course, we had sex!" Lorenzo laughed at her.

"All the time?" Bridget couldn't let this one go. Well, she had to know. Plus, it was diverting her from talk of him coming to California.

Lorenzo rolled his eyes. "I know I'm Italian, but who has sex *all* the time? Does anybody?"

"Well, I don't know; *I've* never been married!" Bridget shouted back.

Lorenzo patiently explained, "Yes, we had sex. I guess we thought maybe it would change things, make us feel like a real married couple. After awhile, we just stopped. And one day, she came home and told me she'd met someone else. She'd been seeing him for over a year, and she was in love. And that was the end of it."

Poor Lorenzo. Who in their right mind could resist falling in love with him? *She* could, of course, and she was going to have to, but ... "Were you upset?"

"Yeah, I was upset, but not because I was in love with her. We were good friends. She should have just been honest and told me, instead of going behind my back. I know we weren't in love, but I still respected that fact that we were married. She should've just told me, and we could've ended it a lot sooner instead of wasting all that extra time, that's all."

Bridget was silent a moment before she asked, "Was she cute?"

Lorenzo threw his head back and laughed out loud. "Mamma mia! No, she wasn't *cute*."

Phewww.

Lorenzo nodded thoughtfully. "She was beautiful." *Damn.*

"But I *still* wasn't in love with her. As good of friends as we were, we didn't have that other connection, you know? Look, I didn't feel … well, I guess, the way I feel with you."

Whoa, hold up. Wait a minute. What was he saying? Time to change the subject once again.

"And you haven't had a girlfriend since? I find that hard to believe, Lorenzo!" she joked.

"Of course, I've had other girlfriends. I didn't become a hermit! But like I said, I just haven't met anyone that I've felt that way about. Until about, say, two weeks ago." He looked at her squarely. "You know, like I was trying to tell you, but you always seem to change the subject."

"Oh, please, I don't know what you're talking about." Bridget sipped her drink and looked away uncomfortably. Why was he always able to call her out on things?

"Change the subject, disagree with me, whatever. I've almost figured you out, Maestrina. So, like I was saying, I want to come to California. What do you think?"

"Well, I mean, for how long?" Bridget cleared her throat.

"I don't know, for however long it takes," Lorenzo stated matter-of-factly. He then added, "Unless you want to come and stay in Florida."

"No, thanks. Aren't there hurricanes there?" Bridget said in horror.

Lorenzo guffawed. "Like once a year, maybe! Not every day!"

"I'll stick to the California earthquakes," declared Bridget. With her luck, the one hurricane of the year would strike as soon as she touched the ground there.

"I guess that settles it. I'm coming to California." Lorenzo reached over and stroked her cheek. She said nothing.

Lorenzo stared at her. "What are you thinking?"

Nothing and everything. So she answered safely, "Nothing."

"Nothing. *Nothing?*" He stared at her expectantly.

How could she put into words what she didn't quite know how to even explain? It was just easier for her to say "nothing" or to say, "I don't know." So she did.

"You don't know? You don't know? Bridget, you gotta *know something!*" He looked away and then back at her, and he tilted his head sideways, as if to get a better read on her.

And that was when she'd chugged her drink back and gotten her brain freeze. She couldn't have timed it better if she'd tried. But she knew Lorenzo would ask her again. And her elusiveness was bound to tire him at some point. Maybe he'd just give up on her. She wanted him to, and then she so hoped he didn't. *Please, don't be a quitter, like all the rest.*

Having finally gotten her drink order, Bridget turned and surveyed the small, open-air dance floor behind her. She couldn't stall here at the bar any longer. She had to get back to Lorenzo. She held the two brimming plastic cups close to her and decided that in no uncertain terms was she going to successfully make it across the dance floor without being throttled or spilling one or both of the drinks. All pathways appeared to be booby-trapped. The dance floor reverberated with a techno version of Michael Jackson's "Billie Jean." Arms were flailing, hips swaying. She thought she witnessed someone in the dancing mob attempting a very weak moonwalk. As much as it was all very entertaining, drunk, gyrating dancers were very unpredictable and thus, unsafe to be around in the drink-ferrying process. Then there were the dancing smokers, thrashing about with cigarettes barely hanging out of their mouths. And don't forget about the numerous guys who randomly threw out a hand or arm to corral you into dancing way too close with them as you passed by.

Bridget wondered how anyone could possibly escape these discos without some type of mauling or catastrophe befalling them. Bridget decided she couldn't stand there all night waiting for a pathway to clear for her. There appeared to be a tiny space between a smoker who was clumsily hopping around and someone having some kind of convulsions on the floor. Bridget gasped in horror at the convulsing guy in the tight jeans. Why were people standing around clapping for the poor fellow instead of helping him? She stopped herself short when she realized he was just performing a very spastic rendition of the centipede. If she could just get past him and the smoker, she'd reach the outskirts of the dance floor and be out of peril. There *was* a couple going at it on the edge over there, but they'd pose no threat to her safe passage. The two were liplocked so tightly that they appeared almost to be one person; the man's hands moved back and forth between squeezing his companion's butt to moving his hands up and down her back. What was happening underneath the long, dark tendrils covering her back was unknown.

Bridget took a breath and scooched her way through the dancers. As she approached the kissers and was just about in the clear, she felt something clip her heel unexpectedly. It was the wild centipeder, who, when coming back into contact with the floor, had also come into contact with her heel. Bridget caught herself quickly. She was still up and on her feet, but one of her hands lurched forward, sending her slushy beverage flying, projectile-style, out of one of the cups and onto the backs of the make-out couple. *Oh, dear.* How could one person be so clumsy? But this time, it really wasn't her fault.

"Scusa, sorry!" Bridget cried as the dark-haired girl spun around to glower down at her. Over her shoulder, her boyfriend's eyes stared back at her. Bridget barely looked at him and said to the girl again, "*So sorry*, excuse me!" as she tried to slink past. No need for dirty looks, thought Bridget. Couldn't she see the idiot doing the centipede behind her? He was practically taking people out left and right on the dance floor.

"Bridget?" Oh, what now? It was an American accent calling to her. She turned. It was the girl's boyfriend, staring at her with a smile, a smile that she recognized.

"Johnny?" Johnny was here, *still*, in Positano?

"Bridget! It *is* you! I thought so!" His blue eyes and white teeth glowed in the disco lighting. He sidestepped his gawking brunette friend and grabbed Bridget in a bear hug.

Then he held her at arm's length and grinned. "It's so good to see you. I'm enjoying the locals," he nodded sheepishly at the girl behind him, "but it's nice to run into an actual friend from home!"

"Yes! Although, you seem to be assimilating quite nicely, I'd say." Bridget raised her eyebrows knowingly at him. She nodded at the girl. "From Positano?" She'd never seen her here before, but maybe she was a Fornillo-side girl most of the time.

"*Venezia. Piacere*, I am Laura," the girl purred huskily and spread her full lips into a wide smile.

"Bridget; piacere." She smiled back.

Johnny interrupted. "After I left here, I flew to Venice and ended up meeting Laura. She'd never been to Positano, so I said I'd show her around. I mean, Positano's not that big. There's not too much to the place, right? So, I've been her tour guide." He turned and planted a passionate kiss on Laura's lips.

Not much to the place? How little he really knew, but perhaps that was a good thing. The aggressive kissing continued. Bridget wasn't quite sure what to do. Stay and wait to say good-bye, or sneak away? Bridget reached for her skinny drink straw, missed her mouth, and almost picked her nose with it.

She moved her cup away quickly before anyone could detect the near nose-picking. It didn't seem to matter, though. Johnny and Laura were oblivious to anyone and anything. Bridget stood around and tried to appear engrossed in sucking her drink dry, but she couldn't help but sneak sideways glances at Johnny. His light-brown, closely shorn head was now a golden, grown-out crewcut. A bit of a scruff on his face did nothing to deter from his tan and, paired up with the fluorescent lighting, only accentuated his blue eyes and white teeth.

And the body ... Bridget tried to keep her eyes to Johnny's face, but she couldn't help but sneak a peek at the rest of him. All Bridget had ever heard Kit complain about was how skinny Johnny was. It was impossible to believe she had been speaking about the same person that stood here now. The long, but solid frame, clad in a snug, white tee and loose-fitting jeans, practically enveloped Laura's statuesque body, and his well-defined arms encircled her. While he was still an all-American boy, right down to his flip-flops, he was oozing a type of raw sex appeal, enhanced even more by his clean-cut, boy-man looks.

Wow. Johnny's time in Italy had obviously done him some good. Bridget was amazed by his apparent transformation—not only in looks, but seemingly in attitude as well. He seemed so alive, so carefree, so *manly*. Not anything like what she'd expected. But what *had* she expected? Bridget wasn't quite sure, but something more along the lines of a driveling mouse of a broken guy who'd followed Kit to Italy in search of a hopeful reunion. She was glad she'd been mistaken. At least life went on for the poor fellows, post-Kit. This in no way meant she loved her best friend any less; she just couldn't help but feel bad for the well-intentioned guys who were often left in the dust. Maybe with all her own romantic mishaps, she related to them on some innate level.

With the make-out session in full swing, and with no apparent end in sight, Bridget snuck off. A formal good-bye probably wasn't necessary since, according to Johnny, "There was nothing much to Positano." They'd be running into each other again soon enough. And Bridget actually looked forward to it. How Kit would feel was another story. She headed back to the bar to replace the drinks that had disappeared.

◆　◆　◆

"So, Johnny is still in love with Kit," Lorenzo commented as they left the scooter behind and headed around the curve toward the apartment. Bridget had been right about running into Johnny again. No sooner had she sat down next to Lorenzo, than a voice boomed behind them, "There you are! Bridget, always trying to sneak off! Hey, who's your friend here?"

For the next three hours, Johnny had insisted on buying drinks for an assortment of different reasons: to make up for the one that had been accidentally rocket-launched out of Bridget's hand, for old times' sake, for "compatriots in Italy!" and then almost tearfully, "For Kit—I'd never be here in Italy if it weren't for her!" to which Lorenzo and Bridget couldn't help but notice Laura's puzzled scowl. As a result of the numerous mojito toasts, Bridget was quite tipsy, which made her even more disagreeable.

"He is *not* sssstill in love with *Kit!*" she half-slurred as she tried to overenunciate.

"You didn't hear him toast her four different times?" laughed Lorenzo.

Bridget rolled her eyes. "Did you see who he's with? And he was all over Laura all night! He's done with Kit."

Lorenzo stated, "Laura's just a diversion; trust me."

Bridget rolled her eyes again and proceeded to stub her toe on the curb, which caused her to fly forward. Lorenzo grabbed onto her arm in time to keep her from doing a face-plant on the uneven pavement. Bridget looked at him in sheepish annoyance. "Ouch."

"Maestrina, you're drunk," sang Lorenzo.

Bridget hated being tipsy and then being called on it. "I am not … *that* bad," she said stubbornly.

"You tried sticking your plastic holy card of the pope into the ATM machine. You're drunk!" He laughed again.

Well, it *would* have been a miracle if any money had come out. Bridget winced at having conducted such sacrilege. She *was* drunk. She stepped up onto the sidewalk curb so she could be a little taller and placed her hands on Lorenzo's shoulders to steady herself.

"So." Lorenzo winked at her.

"So," she answered back before giving a small hiccup. "Oops, 'scuse me."

"So, we're gonna take a break this week? You okay with that?' he asked uncertainly.

This was so crazy. They'd only known each other for two weeks, but they had spent so much time together that she felt like they'd been together for two *years*. And now they were going to "take a break." Lorenzo was going to be changing his plane ticket to stay longer anyway, so why not? It was obvious that their discussion had spooked Bridget. And Johnny's bizarre reappearance had interrupted their conversation, therefore putting Bridget's decision-making on a momentary hiatus.

"I think you need a little time to yourself, Maestrina. You gotta figure out some things."

Bridget looked at him and he added, "Hey, we still got time. Vacation's not over yet."

Lorenzo was right. She needed some time. A week's worth? At the end of the week, would she have magically figured herself out? It seemed an impossible task. Now that she thought about it, a week seemed like an *awfully* long time … look at all that had happened in just two weeks! Maybe she only needed a couple of days …

He pulled her close and kissed her below the ear. She snuggled her head into his neck. They stood like that for a few minutes. He kissed her neck and then spoke into it. "Okay, I better go."

Bridget pulled her head up from his shoulder and asked, "You're not going to stay?" Maybe it was the mojitos talking, but Bridget didn't want Lorenzo to leave.

"I thought you wanted to take a break." He grinned at her.

Bridget countered, "Yess, but I thought we were starting tomorrow."

She was practically throwing herself at him! At least for her, this was as close to throwing herself at someone as she got. Would he *not* take the invitation? Mortification at her forwardness was setting in and quickly sobering her up.

"*Errrr-errrr-errrr-errrrrrrrrrrrrrooooooo!*"

Well, that and the earsplitting cry of one of the town roosters clearing its throat.

Lorenzo looked at her and smiled. "It *is* tomorrow."

"Okay," she answered, somewhat dejectedly. Oh, my God, she was actually pouting.

Lorenzo kissed her and asked, "Hey, you're not mad at me?'

Bridget sighed. "No, I'm not mad." Dammit, she could feel her lower lip sticking out.

Lorenzo tilted his head sideways. "You're not gonna disappear on me?'

"Disappear? In this town? I think that's impossible," Bridget said drolly.

"All right, good." Lorenzo leaned in and kissed her several times. He backed away, squeezed her hand, and said, "*Allora*, Maestrina. I'll talk to you later."

"Okay." She watched the back of him walk up the street and around the bend.

"I'll talk to you later." That was a phrase she despised. When a guy casually threw that out, it could mean anything: I'll talk to you in five minutes, two days, three weeks, a year, the twelfth of never! "I'll talk to you later"—what did Lorenzo mean by that? It was so ambiguous. It was all good and fine for *her* to be the ambiguous one, but she didn't do well when the ambiguity was aimed at her.

Bridget sighed a bit despondently. What if she *never* heard from Lorenzo again? *Get a grip*, Bridget thought. But, what if? She guessed it was possible to somewhat *disappear* or keep yourself out of sight around here if you really wanted to. Would Lorenzo do that? Had she messed things up with her blundering indecisiveness? Here it came. Now she'd start all over with a new set of worries.

"Ciao," she called out to the empty street. She headed down the stairs and thought that she quite possibly missed Lorenzo already.

Chapter 16

Bridget sat at the kitchen table and listened to Kit's recap of the night before.

"And then Paolo *and* Antonella invited us to come on Paolo's boat! Can you believe it?" Kit poured herself a glass of water while she waited for Bridget's response. Bridget had wondered why Kit was up so unusually early, but now it was clear: there was some boat trip involved that she was not about to miss. Bridget sat quietly and waited for Kit to continue with further details.

"And I have to tell you, Paolo asked more than once if I'd make sure to invite you to come," Kit informed her. And ... *bingo* on the details.

Bridget pretended to ignore the mention of Paolo and asked, "And when is this boat trip?"

"Today, sometime late morning, I'm pretty sure. Look, I knew you wouldn't want to go, but I didn't want to say anything last night, so I just said I'd let you know."

"I'll go," Bridget stated matter-of-factly. What else was she going to do? She and Lorenzo were "taking a break" and Lorenzo had said he'd "talk to her later," which inevitably meant "Ciao!" and not in the *hello* sense of the word. As of this minute, he was probably down at the beach cavorting with hot, bikini-clad girls. What the hell, she'd go on this boat trip. It would be better than sitting around wondering what he was doing and why he wasn't calling her.

"Wait, what? You want to go?" Kit appeared slightly stunned.

Bridget sighed. "Sure ... sounds like fun."

"Okay ... people are probably going to be wearing bathing suits, you know. I mean, you should wear your suit. We might all go swimming," Kit stated, a little worried.

"Well, I assumed everyone would be wearing bathing suits, Kit. It is a boat trip, and we *are* on the Amalfi Coast. I mean, wasn't the bikini invented around here? Nobody does anything around here without a bathing suit, right?" Bridget joked.

Kit bumbled, "Well, I don't know. I just didn't think you'd … what's Lorenzo doing today?"

"I don't know. We're taking a break," said Bridget, trying to sound upbeat. She didn't know why she was beginning to feel irritated.

Kit scrunched her eyebrows in perplexity. "Taking a break? I thought people only did that when they'd been together a long time."

"Yeah, I know. But I gotta tell you, two weeks in this town is a long time," Bridget answered with a sigh.

"Good point. All right, this is good! We're gonna have so much fun! Everyone will be *so* excited that you're coming!" Kit smiled.

Bridget doubted that anyone would notice she was even on the boat once they got a look at Kit in her bikini, but that was fine. Kit noted the absent look on Bridget's face and asked, "Are you okay? With the break?"

Bridget shrugged. "Umm, yeah. I guess so. Lorenzo thinks I need time to figure things out, and he's probably right."

Kit raised her eyebrows a few times. "Maybe this boat trip'll help you do that."

"Yeah, maybe," Bridget agreed.

"Do you think they left without us? You don't think they somehow missed seeing us, do you?" Kit balanced her new Prada shades atop her head and apprehensively glanced around the crowded beachfront café where they sat and waited. She downed her second espresso quickly and began drumming her fingers nervously on the table.

Bridget couldn't imagine missing Paolo's nose anywhere, but she hadn't really been looking for him. It was Lorenzo she was scanning the crowd for, although she wasn't sure whether sighting him would send her running straight to him or into hiding under a table.

"I don't know. What time did Antonella say?" asked Bridget absently.

Kit spoke. "Well, she called and said ten, and then Lassino called and said eleven instead. But, I never know whether I'm translating his English correctly! Knowing him, though, he probably gave me a phony time!" Her fingers continued to incessantly drum, staccatolike, against the tabletop.

Bridget reached out and clamped a hand down upon Kit's fingers and said, "I think one cup of espresso is quite enough for you."

Kit winced. "Sorry. I just ... *really* want to go on this boat trip. It means a lot since someone, besides Lassino, invited us."

"Invited *you*," corrected Bridget. "I do appreciate you including me, though," she added quickly.

"*Us, us*, Bridget. They *do* like you! And they know what good friends we are. It's inconceivable to them to not include both of us, you know; we're like family," Kit explained with slight irritation. This was no time for Bridget's silly insecurities. She was starting to feel her own surfacing and it was about all she could do to keep them in check.

Right, exactly, it was inconceivable to invite Kit without me, Bridget thought. She wasn't sure whether she wanted to be known as the charity case of Kit, invited simply by default. Most people would think her overly sensitive or very insecure, and no doubt she admitted she was. But she knew this wasn't *all* in her head. If she had traveled alone to Positano two years ago, would she have met Lassino, Paolo, and the whole lot of them here? She doubted it.

However, Bridget realized that Kit was never going to understand the whole second-choice/sidekick part that she played to her. And if she did, well, it wasn't in her nature to acknowledge it. Forever looking on the bright side, she typically refused to see people and situations in a negative light. Cynics thought Kit to be naïve or quite unrealistic, and sometimes Bridget agreed with them. Yet, maybe this was how Kit shielded herself from disappointment: by refusing to dwell on ugliness or sadness. See only good, and therefore, that's all that exists.

In sharp contrast, Bridget's means of survival were quite the opposite. Go in with *no* expectations, and you were sure to avoid disappointment when things inevitably didn't pan out. And then there was also the old standby: bailing out before the other person involved beat you to it. As much as Bridget wished she could have even an ounce of Kit's positive thinking, whenever she ignored her instinctive "fight or flight" pattern, she ended up getting dumped on. So maybe it was better this way. She and her best friend were polar opposites, but it worked. They balanced each other out. And how often would she be able to say she'd been invited to cruise the Amalfi with a bunch of Italians? Kit deserved the credit for this. So, whether or not Bridget wanted to ride Kit's coattails, she was there, and she might as well enjoy the ride.

Bridget pushed herself away from the table and said, "I'm gonna run to the bathroom."

She noted the startled look on Kit's face and hastily added, "I'll be *right* back. Don't worry. I'm sure they haven't left without us. I mean, why would they do that, when they invited us?"

Well, Lassino was capable of anything, Bridget thought, as she wove her way through the tables. Although, knowing that Kit was bringing Bridget, Lassino would not dare leave them behind. It was one thing to toy with Kit, but Lassino would never do it to her. For some odd reason, while everyone else in the town treated Kit like a princess, Lassino played a hot-and-cold guessing game with her. And while most people around here regarded Bridget as simply the "lucky" best friend, *if* they even remembered who she was, Lassino always seemed to look out for her, as if she were the younger sister who needed extraspecial protection. It was a very strange reversal, indeed. Bridget did not doubt that Lassino liked her, but she did wonder if maybe at times, it was a bit of a show, just to spite Kit. There was no other way to explain it but that he was just so odd like that.

Bridget agreed that Lassino did have feelings for Kit. Of course, they ran the gamut of annoyance to infatuation to lust to friendship. But certainly, there was *something*, some kind of sexual friction, going on between them. What Bridget couldn't understand was why and how Kit continued to take what Lassino doled out to her, when at home and abroad, she could have her pick of men. Whatever the payoff was, it must be enough. Bridget couldn't imagine dealing with those constant ups and downs without becoming completely loony. Perhaps Kit didn't actually come by her sunny obliviousness naturally. Was it possible that it was prescribed? Bridget thought that would explain perfectly how she was able to deal with things so cheerily all the time, but of course, she knew Kit too well to know that it wasn't true.

While Bridget was off, Kit stared at her cell phone, which was lying on the table in front of her. Had she misunderstood Lassino? She thought back to their quick conversation earlier. Yes, she was sure he'd mumbled in his super-fast accent, "Be there at uhh-looen. Don' be late. Ciao!"

Maybe "uhh-looen" was really noon? Or was "uh-looen" an Italian word? Kit snorted out loud. This was so ridiculous! Lassino had said eleven. And according to her cell phone, it was eleven forty-five right now. Unless they were going by typical Italian time, this was not good.

The phone rang, which caused Kit to jump unexpectedly in her seat. Kit picked it up and recognized Lassino's number. She prayed he wasn't calling from Capri or somewhere else far along the coast.

"Pronto!" she called cheerfully into the phone.

"Ciao, where are you?" he grunted quickly.

"We're *here*, sitting at the café at the bottom of the steps." Kit spoke just as fast.

"You're late!" Lassino commented.

"*You're* late! You said eleven, and it's eleven forty-five right now!" Kit's stomach lurched. Oh, she could feel the espresso acidically inching its way back up her throat. How did he reduce her to a bunch of jittery nerves in a millisecond?

Lassino mumbled something in Italian. "What?" Kit asked in annoyance.

"We're leaving! You are not ready; forget about coming!"

What was he talking about? "Excuse me, we've been *here*, where you told us to wait, for forty-five minutes!" Kit shouted. She then added, "*Where* are you?"

Lassino shouted back, "We just got on the boat!"

What did he mean, they just got on the boat? "You're *on* the *boat?*" Kit asked succinctly, trying desperately to keep the panic out of her voice.

Lassino huffed, "We can't wait around for you all the time, Kit. We're leaving. I will talk to you later." The dial tone rang in her ear, and she fumed. *Wait for her?* Okay, so she was usually late, but that had never been a problem in this country. In fact, her chronic tardiness was one particular idiosynchrosy of hers that enabled her to fit in so well here. And for once, she'd actually been on time, even early! Lassino was insane. No, he was bipolar, not to mention rude, immature, idiotic, and just … super-*mean*. Kit inhaled and exhaled shakily as she tried to postpone the tears that would inevitably come. She quickly pulled her sunglasses down over her eyes. Bridget headed toward her and stopped at the table.

"Ready?" Bridget asked expectantly.

"Ready for what? They already left," Kit answered flatly.

"Are you sure? They wouldn't do *that* … would they?" Bridget asked, her eyebrows raised.

"Lassino just called to tell me *we* were late and that they were already on the boat! I can't believe him. Why does he have to ruin everything for me? What did I ever do to him? God, he's such a jackass!" spat out Kit bitterly.

"Okay, calm down," soothed Bridget.

Kit shouted, "I'm not going to calm down! I put up with a lot from him, but this time, I'm really pissed! Don't screw with me and my Amalfi boat trip!"

The phone rang. Kit swiped it from the table. "It's *him*. What the hell does he want now? Yeah, probably to gloat that I'm *not* there!"

Bridget shrugged. This was going to be a long day. They were both used to Bridget and her moody depression. But Kit in a foul mood? It so seldom happened, Bridget wasn't sure how to respond.

Kit clicked the answer button on the phone and said in exasperation, "Yes?"

Lassino replied earnestly, "Kit, are you and Bridget coming? Everyone's here, and we're waiting for you."

"And how are we supposed to do that, since you're already on the boat?" snapped Kit. Once again, there was a sudden dial tone in her ear.

"He just hung up on me *again*, Bridget." Kit paused and then stated, "I *hate* him."

And why was Bridget smiling at her now? What was she so happy about? Probably because she'd escaped being seen in a bathing suit today. Well, she didn't find this funny at all.

"Why don't you turn around," Bridget said.

Kit whirled around in her chair and found Lassino looking down at her from underneath a white-straw fedora. He smiled wickedly at her and bent down to kiss her cheek.

"You hate me?" he asked with a grin.

"Yes," Kit said, but she couldn't help but flash her signature white smile. Damn him! She should've known he was up to one of his little pranks. But Lassino better not mistake her smile for complete forgiveness. She was still livid … for the time being.

Lassino shrugged. "How very rude!" He kissed her again, and then looked up and explained, "Sorry we are late. It's all Paolo's fault. He took much too long getting ready."

He nodded in the direction of the cappuccino bar where Paolo, Antonella, and a host of their friends stood crowded around. Although hidden behind her oversized Dolce & Gabbana shades, Bridget felt she now had a legitimate excuse to check out Paolo. Paolo lounged casually against the counter, clad in a pair of long swim trunks and black flip-flops, no doubt of the Prada variety. His smooth chest was barely covered by a white linen shirt (of the typical Moda Positano variety), unbuttoned to the navel and rolled up at the elbows. A beach towel draped over one shoulder and silver aviators perched upon his nose accessorized his look. Paolo glanced over and smiled. His illuminatingly white teeth seemed to scream "Bling!" which made Bridget glad she was safely behind her dark glasses.

They left money on the table and followed Lassino.

"You're late because of Paolo? He's in a pair of *swim trunks!*" Kit laughed.

"Ha! You laugh, but do you know how many pairs of swim trunks and linen shirts he has?" Lassino replied with a smirk.

"Besides, I think he was nervous because Bridget was coming." He chuckled and tried winking through his thick glasses at Bridget. Or maybe he was just squinting.

Bridget, in turn, smirked back at him. Well, if Paolo's closet was anything like what she'd heard Lassino's was like, it was possible he had gotten lost in it. But the thought of Paolo, a-twitter because *she* was coming was just so, so, not possible. Oh, just another one of Lassino's silly jokes. What a kidder he was. He was kidding, wasn't he? Now *she* was feeling slightly a-twitter. Maybe it was a mistake for her to have come.

Kit stood on the tiny deck at the front of the boat. What was the front of the boat called again? Starboard or port? Oh, she couldn't remember. Not that it mattered much to her. She didn't even know what kind of boat this was. It wasn't a yacht. She knew enough from seeing the many luxury boats and cruisers floating out beyond the buoys off of Spiaggia Grande. It wasn't a sailboat, because there were no sails and it had a motor. But it was much bigger than the typical speedboat. It had a tiny top deck that you reached by climbing a short ladder, and the back part of the boat had built-in side benches and a sort of deck that a few people could lay on. And then there was this triangular front part, just beyond the helm, enclosed by the metal handrail that ran along it, big enough for about two people to lie about. Kit honestly didn't care what kind of boat she was on. She just loved being out here, under the hot sun, the boat gently swaying upon the glistening turquoise water.

The only disturbing part about this boat trip was that it just made her fall even more woozily in love with this lifestyle. How great to have every Tuesday off (albeit, you worked doggedly until Tuesday), but to have a day off, and not only that, to spend it gathered with all your best friends on a boat! Kit couldn't remember the last time she and all her close friends had even been in the same room for more than five minutes, and without someone's screaming kids. Well, there had been a few weddings in the last year and the monthly book club she and Bridget shared with their high school friends, but even so. Did Lassino realize how lucky he was to be surrounded by his friends like this? Some might claim the town was claustrophobic and nosy, but at least there was an innate sense of family, of camaraderie, even among the people you couldn't stand.

Kit wanted that feeling of belonging so very badly. And she just didn't feel like she belonged back home. She was very proud of where she came from, no mistake about it. She was one of the most staunchly patriotic people she knew. You'd never find her without a hand over her heart for The Pledge, "The Star-Spangled Banner," or any other all-American song, and that included even when she watched sporting events on television! She even got misty-eyed with pride when she read her students anything about George Washington or Abraham Lincoln. And she could recite the preamble of the Constitution without blinking an eye. Of course, so could anyone her age who'd grown up watching *Schoolhouse Rock!*, but still. She loved anything and everything American: peanut butter and jelly sandwiches, baseball, hot dogs, tacky *American Idol*, and crappy light beer! And this list could go on and on. So why wasn't she happy living at home?

She had a wonderful family that loved her, that was for sure. And she loved her parents—her dad with his supportive, yet quiet, keep-to-himself ways, and her mother, even though she incessantly drove her crazy. They just did not get along. She sympathized with her father, who kept to himself. Kit loved her mother—but at times, she felt she was just so domineering. It didn't make it any better that all her friends thought her mother was practically Mother Teresa.

"Let me get this straight. You stayed overnight at your parents' and your mom did all your laundry *and* ironed your clothes? *And* she washed your car and cleaned the inside of it? While you were asleep?" Bridget had said incredulously once.

"Ughhh, yes," Kit had answered in disgust. "Isn't that so annoying?"

"My mom can barely get out of the car, let alone wash my clothes, and I just paid forty bucks to have that done, so, no, I don't find that to be annoying," answered Bridget.

"Well, I didn't *ask* her to do that! Just like I didn't ask her to repaint my room or reorganize my closet, or bake cookies for my class! She's just soo—"

"Thoughtful?" Bridget commented in bewildered amusement.

"*Overbearing* and *needy* were the words I was about to use." Kit rolled her eyes.

Bridget added, "Well, moms love to do stuff like that. If it makes her feel good trying to make you happy, then why can't you just give her that?"

"Whatever. And she's not making me happy. She's irritating me! No one is *that* nice without wanting something in return! She just does all that stuff to try to get on my good side and try to get information out of me, like *who* I'm dating, *why* I'm *not* married, *when* she'll ever be a grandmother! Please, I see right through her!" Kit had responded in annoyance.

"So," Bridget remarked thoughtfully, "you're saying that everyone who is more than nice and thoughtful and goes above and beyond the *normal* call to help others, is really just full of shit?"

"No ... I didn't say *that*," Kit said uncomfortably.

"Well, you did, in so many words," retorted Bridget.

"Well, I didn't mean *everyone* ..." Kit's voice trailed off.

"Oh, well, that's good, since I know *someone* who's a lot like your mom. You know, someone who's always helping others, kind of a do-gooder, with the best of intentions, of course." Bridget smiled and looked pointedly at Kit.

"What?" Kit looked blankly at her. Then a wave of recognition passed over her face, followed by a dark scowl. "Oh, please, don't *even* compare me to her. I'm nothing like my mother!" Kit said in contempt.

Bridget opened her mouth, but Kit continued vehemently, "I'm not some person who just butts in everywhere, trying to take over and steal the spotlight under the guise of helping when really I'm totally infringing upon people's lives! That's so unfair, Bridget!" Kit glared at her.

"I didn't say any of those things, Kit. You did. Don't try to put words in my mouth," Bridget had answered. She loved her friend, but she could feel the whole martyr routine coming on.

Kit spoke up. "So what do you really *think*, Bridget? Am I a phony do-gooder who sticks her nose where it doesn't belong?" Kit's voice was bitter, but her face held a look of earnest fear.

"Is this a rhetorical question?" Bridget asked warily.

Kit sighed in annoyance. "*No.*"

Bridget would have preferred to remain silent. But once Kit was focused on something, it was like trying to take a bone away from a starving dog. Not possible. And there was no point even trying to argue your side with her; no matter how logical, how foolproof, how right you actually might be, you weren't going to win with her. Yes, for being one of the most upbeat, cheerful people she knew, Kit could, at times, be one of the most obstinate as well.

Instead, Bridget said tiredly, "Look, this whole conversation started out about your mother, and you turned it into an attack on you! All I was saying was that I think your mother is a lovely person and you happen to share some of her wonderful qualities. Why do you have such a problem with that?"

"Oh, yeah, wonderful qualities that apparently make me so annoying to other people!" fumed Kit.

"Oh, dear God, everyone loves you!" said Bridget.

Kit recanted, "Fine. But I still resent being compared to Delia McNally."

"Fine. You're nothing like her. I must've been thinking of someone else," shouted Bridget, causing Kit to smile slightly and giggle in spite of herself.

Indeed, *like* her mother? All right, Kit conceded that *maybe*, sometimes, she went a bit over the top. But she never meant to turn anything into a three-ringed circus. Or to become the center of attention! It just seemed to happen, by some cosmic force, some weird alignment of the planets, some … *something*. She didn't know.

So, she'd accept the positive things Bridget had said about her mother. It wasn't so bad to go all out on showering people with kindness. And Kit (somewhat) appreciated Bridget's pragmatic stab at being tactful with her. Except for that "martyr" comment. She loved Bridget to death, but her friend had it wrong about that whole martyr thing.

It wasn't fair. And what was she supposed to do? Apologize for who she was? Apologize for caring about others and trying to help them when they needed it? If she were *wrong*, she would be the first to apologize. But she wouldn't apologize for being herself. That would be like saying she was going to undergo some massive personality change to fit what everyone else thought she should be. People were just wrong and judgmental. Kit felt so misunderstood, but that was nothing unusual as of late. All she could do was rise above people's misconceptions about her. She knew the truth about who she really was, even if everyone couldn't see it.

That's why she was *here* in Italy … on a boat, sailing around the Amalfi. It seemed ironic, a paradox, that she had to go to another country to feel appreciated and accepted. Was that good or bad? She had mixed feelings about it, but she knew for sure that there was something to be said for *that*, for this country, for her. Kit flung her towel out upon the small deck and nestled herself onto it for a little nap.

✦   ✦   ✦

"Okay, smile, you two!" Kit sat across the crowded table, poised with her hulkish camera. Paolo leaned his arm over the back of Bridget's chair and asked in her ear, "Is this okay … to take a picture with you?"

It was only a *picture*. Paolo made it sound like he was asking to do something indecent with her, although, Bridget had her suspicions. There was a definite crackly, charged chemistry in the air, as if they were on the brink of *something*. Everywhere she was, Paolo happened to be, as if keeping an eye on her, or as if he was actually *trying* to get close to her in some capacity. Of course, they *were* on a somewhat-small boat. You'd be hard-pressed to become invisible. But it wasn't just on the boat … it was even in the water …

About the water … Bridget had held out hope that once everyone caught sight of Kit up close in her bikini, she'd be home-free to scoot off and become one with the boat, left alone with her morbid, agonizing thoughts about Lorenzo and what he might be up to, as well as her obsessive paranoia over how atrocious she looked in her Miracle Suit and how bizarre the Italians would think she was once they caught sight of her in the scandalously chaste one-piece.

However, that was not to be. When Paolo cut the motor and announced that they would stop for a short swim, Bridget immediately panicked. Oh, how she hated getting declothed in front of people. It wasn't as if she was about to perform a striptease, since she had her suit on underneath, but she still felt so self-conscious, as if all eyes were upon her. Why was everyone else so perfect-looking? And why did she have to look like … well, like herself? There could be no worse body combo of being short with boobs, a slight gut, and what she called her "drumstick" legs—skinny calves that led up into meatier thighs. It was so unfair!

Bridget decided there were only two options at the moment. It was unfortunate that liposuction wasn't one of them. She could wait until everyone else was in the water before pulling her clothes off and getting in. No, no, then she'd have to climb down the little ladder, with everyone watching. And with her luck, she'd probably slip or pull some kind of Don Knotts-like maneuver and draw even more attention to herself.

Her best shot was to get out of her clothes as quickly as possible, while everyone was doubly blinded by Kit's smile and her perky boobs, and stealthily hightail it down the ladder and into the water.

Bridget waited patiently. Soon enough, the guys began ogling Kit and asking her the usual questions about the authenticity of her bosom, while the girls rolled their eyes and laughed. Although, Bridget thought, they, too, looked to be a bit in awe of Kit's amazing physique. With all attention diverted, this was her chance! Bridget successfully pulled her clothes off with warplike speed and, just as quickly, shimmied down the ladder and into the water.

As she tread water, she watched the beautifully tanned crowd on board, and now she worried about how she was going to get back on the boat. Getting into the water had been nothing! Whatever had she been worried about? Getting out of the water gracefully, while you were soaking wet, making sure you were all tucked and sucked into your suit, was going to be no easy task. And she really needed to go to the bathroom again. That cappuccino and bottle of water had not been a good idea. How long until they got to the restaurant Paolo was taking them to? As she bobbed in the water, she looked up in time to see Lassino sneak up behind Kit and push her off the little wooden platform that was attached to the bottom of the ladder. He then proceeded to pick up Antonella and toss her into the water as well. Kit's head popped up from the blue water and she sputtered, "Lassino! My sunglasses! I just bought those!" Her arms flailed around in front of her in search of the glasses.

From the top deck of the boat, Paolo called, "Don't worry, Kit!" He grabbed something at his feet and hopped up onto the edge of the boat. Without hesitation, he plunged into the water. Once in, he swam to the deck. He grabbed onto it with one hand and pulled his other hand out of the water to reveal what had been in it: a pair of swim goggles. He quickly donned the goggles and dove underwater like a duck. Within moments, he resurfaced, triumphantly holding Kit's dripping Pradas.

"Here, Kit!" he said excitedly. "I'll put them on the deck."

"Oh, thank you, Paolo!" she called out and then gave a Lassino a dirty look.

"What?" Lassino shrugged mischievously from the bottom deck.

"Next time you want to push me in, make sure I *don't* have my sunglasses on!" Kit called back as she treaded water in the direction of Bridget. She doggy paddled up to Bridget and breathed, "I didn't even see you get in the water, Bridget."

"Yes, that was the whole point," Bridget said as she uncomfortably treaded water next to her. Being jostled around in the bobbing water was not conducive to a full bladder. She didn't know how much longer she could stand it. How was she going to suck her stomach in while getting out of the boat without squeezing her bladder and causing herself to have an accident? Could this get any worse?

Kit rolled her eyes at Bridget. Then she looked over her shoulder and laughed. "Can you believe him? He's so immature!" The girls looked over in time to watch as Lassino tried to "pants" Franco.

"Well, I always knew there'd come a day when wearing a one-piece would be beneficial. Ohhh!" moaned Bridget.

"What's the matter?" Kit turned back to Bridget.

Bridget explained, "I'm in desperate need of a restroom. What was I thinking when I had that second bottle of water?"

Kit smiled. "Just use the restroom here."

There was a bathroom here? On the boat? How had she missed it?

"I gotta get back to the boat, then." Bridget began paddling in its direction.

"There's no bathroom on the boat," called Kit.

"What?" she stopped mid-paddle.

"Just use the *restroom* out *here*," Kit said and raised her eyebrows a few times.

Why hadn't she thought of that before? Actually, she *had*, but she would never want to admit it. Bridget was forever scarred regarding the idea of peeing in water since an incident at summer camp, when the lifeguard had warned them all that the chlorine in the pool would turn pee orange—so anyone considering using the pool as their personal bathroom should think twice about whether they wanted a cloud of orange following them around while swimming. They'd all sat listening, horrified, but completely awestruck. Could chlorine really do that? Nobody wanted to find out.

However, all camp session long, Bridget and the rest of the campers had been on the lookout for any signs of orange trailing behind someone, but to no avail. Either everyone else was too scared to risk it, or their counselors had lied to them. They'd never know, and no one was going to admit peeing in the pool to test the theory. Needless to say ... this wasn't the summer camp pool. *Thank God.* Probably worse things had happened in this water, but she'd try not to think about them.

Kit interrupted her as she reminisced. "Just swim over there. No one's going to know, and no one's going to care. Lassino told me everyone does it anyway."

God bless Lassino! As much as Bridget hated the thought of polluting the beautiful, seemingly pristine water, a bladder was a precious commodity.

"Right. I'm off to the bathroom," Bridget said cheerily and began paddling further out.

"Okay, I'll see you in a few," Kit called as she swam in the opposite direction.

Once she'd paddled to an appropriately safe distance, Bridget stopped herself so that she could turn and face the boat. She was far enough away, yet close enough to make it back to the boat quickly. Bridget didn't want anyone near, but she wanted to keep the boat in her sight. No need to risk being overlooked and left behind as she peed in the water. Maybe she should have grabbed one of those life vests she'd noticed on deck ... really, what had ever possessed her to come today?

She'd better hurry and go. And Bridget did, feeling a sense of euphoric release. Literally. Ahh, now maybe she could actually enjoy herself. Even getting back on the boat didn't seem like such an embarrassing chore, now that her bladder was back to its normal size.

She looked about her, at the mesmerizing blue water. As she listened to the sounds of splashing and laughter coming from the other side of the boat, she was strangely overtaken with a sense of joyful exhilaration. She thought, *I'm so glad I came. Who cares what people think of me in my lame one-piece? Who cares if Lorenzo has probably forgotten all about me? Who cares if I had a half of jar of Nutella for breakfast this morning, and I have no more available Weight Watchers points for the day? Just … enjoy being here! Just …*

Shit, something had touched her foot! What the *hell* had that been? A wave of fear ran through her. Of course, it was just a fish, right? It was improbable that it was anything else, like, say, an eel, water snake, or a *shark*. Bridget instantly rued the day she'd ever watched *Jaws*. Even at age eight, she'd known it was a terrible mistake to watch that awful movie. Sharks weren't attracted to the smell of pee, were they? She was freaking herself out for nothing, she was sure. It was nothing. But her heart was still pounding wildly. She would just slowly start swimming back, calmly, with no sudden movements. She definitely should *not* have come today. She was *so* not a boat-trip person. She said a quick prayer that maybe it was some kind of seaweed or algae, even though she was quite sure she'd never seen any of that, even on the beach.

Oh, my God! There it was again, brushing up against her foot! Another second later, something yanked her toe. Bridget screamed shrilly and instinctively kicked her leg back; she hit something hard. Something dark was surfacing, a flurry of bubbles surrounding whatever it was. Popping up out of the water was a dark head of hair, attached to pair of goggles strapped atop a large nose.

"Paolo?" Oh, thank God, it was him! *Oh, no, it was him!* Where had he come from? How had she not seen him coming? And had he watched her peeing through his goggles? Had he gotten a full frontal view of how big her boobs and stomach were, too? Bridget was aghast.

Paolo pulled his goggles up. He tread water and winced as he held his nose. So that's what she had kicked. That'd teach him to sneak up on people in the water. He smiled sheepishly and said, "Hi, Bridget."

Bridget asked, "Your nose, is it okay?"

Still holding his nose, Paolo waved her off with the other hand and said, "It's okay. I shouldn't have scared you."

Bridget asked with phony nonchalance, "So, where did you come from?" Best to investigate now and see if he'd caught her relieving herself.

"Oh, back from the other side of the boat." He pointed to the opposite end of it.

The innocent look on his face gave no indication whatsoever whether he'd seen anything.

When she remained silent, Paolo asked, "Why?" He paused and put a hand to the top of his forhead, like a shark's fin. "Did you think I was *Free Willy?*" It came out sounding like "Free Weely." In spite of her near-mortification, Bridget laughed.

"You mean *Jaws*. Uh, I didn't know what you were. But I'm glad it was only you!" she said, and she truly meant that.

Paolo smiled and treaded closer. She wished she'd kept her sunglasses on. The sunlight reflecting off the water and his big, white teeth were blinding. And against his tan skin, his pale-blue eyes were almost hypnotic. Bridget needed to get back to the boat before she sunk.

"Yes, *only* me," he repeated slowly. Bridget then watched Paolo's lips move as if in slow motion, as he asked, "So where is Lorenzo today?'

At the mention of Lorenzo, Bridget came out of her semicatatonic state, shrugged, and said simply, "I don't know."

"But you are with Lorenzo, no?" Paolo asked in earnestness.

Well, she wasn't *with* him today. Of course, Bridget knew what Paolo was getting at, but she still asked, "What do you mean?"

"Well, everybody is talking about your new boyfriend." He shrugged, if that was possible to do while treading water.

Everybody was talking about her? Please, even if they were, it was because she was Kit's friend. And didn't they have anything better to talk about? What did they need to talk about her and her nonexistent love life for? But that little annoying voice that kept resurfacing lately spoke up and suddenly said, *Excuse me, your love life is no longer nonexistent. Why do you keep trying to downplay it?*

This voice was so irksome. *Lorenzo is not my boyfriend! Besides, what if I don't want a boyfriend? And even if I did want Lorenzo, he doesn't want me. We're on a break, for God's sake. Who does that when they've only just been seeing each other? It's completely over.*

The voice was not deterred. *He did it because of you, moron! Not because he doesn't want to see you. You're the one with the problems. He* wants *you to want to be with him—duh! But you've got to make the decision yourself.*

Oh, shut up, you big know-it-all! Bridget yelled silently inside her head. To her relief, the voice remained quiet. But she knew it wouldn't stay that way for long and at the moment was probably rolling its eyes and making faces at her. She ignored it and answered Paolo in a somewhat defiant voice, "Lorenzo's not my boyfriend."

"Oh, hmm, I see," Paolo said, with a slight smile on his lips. He then looked at her pointedly. Oh, she could see the wheels turning in his head. He inched closer in the water to her.

Bridget felt a sharp pang of guilt. She was such a Judas. Why had she said that about Lorenzo? But he *wasn't* her boyfriend! But in so many words, she knew he wanted to be her boyfriend, didn't she? But this was too scary for Bridget. She didn't want to allow herself to like him enough to give him a chance. And to make things worse, she was still so uncontrollably captivated by Paolo. These two factors were at odds with each other, conspiring against her and causing her utter confusion.

Paolo moved closer still. She could almost feel his breath on her face, and he was chewing something minty. Aside from it being broad daylight, their close proximity to each other in the water inevitably felt more than slightly reminiscent of a *certain* night they'd shared last summer. Alarmed, Bridget decided that she could not let Paolo kiss her right now. There wasn't even the buoy rope to hold onto! Definite danger.

She did the backstroke and moved away slightly; then she called out with a smile, "Come on, race you back to the boat!" Without looking back, she turned over and broke into her fast-paced crawl. She didn't stop until she'd reached the boat platform.

Bridget had tried to keep her distance, to find some unobtrusive spot to sit once they were back on the boat, but oddly, the Italian girls kept talking to her. Why and how her teeth were so white proved to be a popular topic of conversation. All the while, Paolo kept stealing sly glances at her. That is, when he wasn't leaving the steering of the boat to Lassino or Franco to come and sit next to her.

Prosecco was poured all around, and Bridget felt herself loosen up a bit, although, she did feel a little twitch of apprehension that they were all drinking and … boating. Could you get a BUI in Italy? Of course, even with the slight breeze, the water was tranquil, and the boys knew what they were doing, but still. Lassino had to practically hold things up to the lenses of his glasses to be able to see them. Should *he* be left to steer the boat? Thankfully, they were far past Li Galli, the trio of rocks known as the mythical Sirens, whom, according to ancient folklore, had lured many a sailor to their crashing doom. Bridget sipped her prosecco and let it soothe her. She was overreacting a bit, as usual. Even Lassino, with his lack of clear vision, couldn't miss Li Galli, or Chicken Island, as he jokingly called the islets. Yes, they'd be fine. This was a routine outing on the boat for them.

Yet, Bridget wondered how routine it was for Paolo and Lassino to invite visiting females aboard for a day trip on the love boat. She and Kit were probably not the first, nor would they be the last. Ah, well. She'd have to say that being invited on a boat trip that included Italian girls and other friends, had possibly, if only slightly, elevated them to another realm in the sphere of Positano life. Was it possible that she and Kit were no longer considered as merely tourists/disco conquests? Bridget hoped so. Of course, that had no impact on the overt flirting (on the part of Paolo) and double entendres (on the part of Lassino) going on.

And here they were, at lunch. The boat docked in a small cove. Two tanned, smiley youths dressed only in shorts and sandals waited for them at the dock and helped all the girls jump from the boat to the platform. When they'd all clambored off, they followed the short walkway leading up to the restaurant. A balding, bespectacled waiter in black pants and a white polo sat them at a long table on the awning-shaded terrace that overlooked the emerald cove. Aside from a few other diners, it appeared that they were to have the terrace to themselves. They seated themselves in the rattan chairs around the table, and Paolo waited until Bridget sat down.

Paulo settled himself in next to Bridget at the end of the table and spoke rapidly to the waiter. Within minutes, four ice buckets filled with bottles of prosecco appeared. The prosecco was inspected, sampled, and deemed favorable by Paolo. Glasses were filled and they sipped, amidst the typical toast of "Salute!" Soon after, bread baskets and large, overflowing antipasti platters arrived and were strategically placed around the table.

"Bridget?" Paolo held the serving spoon and fork above the platter and nodded at her.

"Oh, thank you," she said as she moved her appetizer plate closer. If Bridget even so much as lifted her hand to reach for her glass (prosecco or water) or even glanced in the direction of the array of food on the table,

Paolo beat her to it by grabbing the bottle of prosecco or the water pitcher, or reaching for the antipasti to serve her. Bridget decided that while she enjoyed being waited on, it was a little unnerving having Paolo watch her every move in anticipation.

Besides, Bridget didn't think she could eat or drink as fast as Paolo was trying to serve her. While very sweet, it was a little much, but what to do? To distract herself from his bright eyes, which were practically boring a hole into the side of her head, she kept shoveling in the assorted cheeses, eggplant, and prosciutto and melon, until she noticed her small plate was wiped clean. This led Paolo to refill her plate again. If this kept up, they'd have to roll her off the dock and onto the boat. When he attempted to load up her plate for a third time, Bridget held up her hand and said, "Please, no more for right now, Paolo!"

"No more? Okay." He put the serving utensils down. Then he winked at her and added, "That's right, I forgot, you once told me that it's not so good to swim on a full stomach."

"Right," Bridget said, dying that Paolo had cited her from their "love on the rocks" evening.

Paolo replied, "You have to go swimming again, since I'm taking you to a special spot on our way back."

More parading around in a bathing suit—would the torture never end? And where was he taking them? And she hoped he meant all of them and not just her. Before she could ask, it was then that Kit, who'd been busy snapping pictures of the others, turned to them and asked them to smile.

Was it all right to take a picture with her? A picture, yes. However, she did not want to risk getting into the water with him again. "Come on you two, say ... *formaggio!*" Kit called out.

Paulo threw his arm over her shoulders, leaned in even closer, and sang, "Formaggio!" as Kit took their picture.

"Oh, that was cute. Okay, one more. Bridget, lean in a little," Kit said as she looked into her camera.

"Oh, a group picture!" an Australian accent called cheerily from behind Bridget and Paolo. Kit looked up from her camera suddenly. Hearing *that* voice and seeing the forced smile upon Kit's face, Bridget inadvertently tensed up, upon realizing exactly who was standing behind her and Paolo.

She laid a firm hand on both Bridget and Paolo's shoulders, which made them jump, and Rachel squatted down behind them and stuck her face in between theirs. She smiled widely and said through her clenched teeth, "Hiya! Perfect timing, wouldn't you say?"

Kit took a large sip from her wine glass. The prosecco flutes had been moved aside to make way for oversized wine goblets. The table was now littered with flutes, goblets, water glasses, and seafood platters. The Italian girls chatted among themselves at one end of the table. Gay Giorgio gesticulated in conversation with Lassino and Franco. Sitting next to him were others he'd brought, along with Rachel, on his boat: a business partner, Roberto, the architect restoring the villa he'd recently bought, along with his sister and another friend, Stefano, who happened to be a doctor. Whose doctor he was and what kind of doctor, Kit was unclear about. It appeared that Stefano didn't care as along as everyone knew he was a doctor of some sort.

Kit had other things to worry about. She sat beside Lassino and nervously watched Rachel on one side of Paolo and Bridget on the other. She'd forgotten the text Rachel had sent this morning asking what she was doing today. In the confusion over whether Lassino had left without them, it had truly slipped Kit's mind. Then again, Kit thought that perhaps that had been for the best, since she knew she couldn't invite Rachel along to torment Paolo, but she also didn't want to hurt her feelings by telling her who they were hanging out with. *Oops.*

Rachel was being quite pleasant, though. Of course, they'd all been distracted by the delicious food and wine that seemed to just keep coming. And Giorgio had been regaling them with fascinating stories of the latest Hollywood starlet who'd come into his boutique with her girlfriend to buy things. Not to be outdone, Stefano, the dapper doctor (could he really be a doctor? he was so good-looking), tried to one-up Giorgio with his hospital horror stories, or the tale of how he'd ended up with his arm in a sling (a yachting accident that involved some type of waverunner—or was it a wakeboard?).

The doctor was interesting and certainly nice to look at with his typical Italian tan and dark, brooding eyes underneath a lush head of black hair, but he seemed to like to hear himself talk. And he paid particular attention to whether Kit and Bridget were listening to him. Kit was too preoccupied with Rachel to give the doctor the due attention he was seeking. She was just glad that between the food and Giorgio and Stefano holding court, not much other conversation had taken place, which kept Rachel from questioning her.

Kit hoped any bad feelings Rachel may have had had passed. Rachel could just be so ... scary. She'd witnessed the Australian's fiery flare-ups and didn't know how she'd withstand one of them being directed at her.

As she held her glass and swirled the wine in it, Rachel asked, "So, I sent you a text this morning, Kit. I guess you didn't get it?" Her voice was sweetly nonchalant, her lips upturned in the slightest smile, but there was a definite accusing undertone.

Kit cleared her throat. Time to do a little damage control. While she felt a little flustered, Kit was also quite peeved. Why did she have to answer to Rachel? It was none of her business what they did without her! What was she supposed to say, though? Kit hated to lie, but she didn't want to be mean. Rachel was just too frightening. Kit was going to have to cave into her intimidation and fib a little. She looked across the table and saw Bridget's bugged-out eyes staring at her as if to say, *Psycho alert! Be careful how you answer!*

"My phone was in my bag, and Lassino had us in such a rush to be on time that I didn't even think to check it," Kit explained earnestly. There, that was a plausible answer. She'd been believable. Then Lassino grunted in her direction, "What? I heard my name."

Kit said, "I *said* you had us in a rush to be ready on time."

"I don't know what you are talking about. For once, you were early and I was late." He looked at her as if she was a loon and went back to his conversation with Giorgio and Franco.

Damn Lassino. Why couldn't he have crappy hearing too? It was like he had bionic hearing to overcompensate for his near-blindness. "Don't listen to him. He had us completely stressed out, thinking we were late!" Kit laughed lightly. She caught Bridget rolling her eyes upward and looking away. Paolo sat, amused, with his arm still draped, almost protectively, over the back of Bridget's chair. Kit assumed that at the moment, he didn't care whether Rachel's feelings were spared.

Had Rachel sniffed out the situation between her friend and Paolo? Nothing, per se, had happened today, but given Bridget and Paolo's past and all the flirtatious tension flying between them, it was only a matter of time.

Kit adored Paolo, but she wondered what was going on in Bridget's head. What about Lorenzo? He was, by far, much better for Bridget in every way. They were seemingly perfect for each other. Kit caught herself. What did she know? Look at her! She'd left Johnny for ... she glanced over at Lassino. Well, she'd left him for the *unknown,* so to speak. She guessed she wasn't the best judge of romantic character right now.

Rachel smiled drolly and pulled her cigarettes out of her linen beach bag. "Yes, well, I was texting to see if you wanted to come out on Giorgio's boat *with us*. But it all worked out, didn't it? I mean, what a *coincidence*." Surface-wise, Rachel gave off the appearance of being very easygoing, in her fun-loving Australian way, but she wasn't stupid. Kit detected the sarcasm underneath.

Rachel stood up, looking like a golden Amazon. Beneath her short, denim cut-offs, her long, tanned legs seemed to stretch for miles. Nothing but a small, leopard-print bikini top above revealed more endless, tautly tanned skin. She adjusting her blonde topknot, grabbed her lighter, and said, "I'm going for a smoke. Anyone care to join me?" She looked specifically at Bridget first and then Paolo.

"No, thanks," Bridget murmured and looked away.

Rachel ignored Bridget and stared pointedly at Paolo. "Paolo?"

He merely shook his head no. "Don't tell me you don't smoke anymore, Paolo! I have a hard time believing *that*." She spoke with exaggeration.

Once again, Paolo declined. "No, thank you. We need to get the check. Excuse me." He pushed himself out of his chair, and as he walked past Bridget's chair, he squeezed her shoulder twice. This did not go unnoticed by Rachel. Her eyes narrowed slightly, and she turned on her heel and walked away. Bridget opened her eyes wide and whispered to Kit, "What is Coocoo-Bananas doing here?"

"I don't know. I guess I should've answered her text," Kit whispered back as she threw her hands up.

"And *what* is Paolo doing—putting his arm around my chair and squeezing my shoulder? *Trying* to piss her off?" Bridget cried hoarsely.

Kit chuckled. "Probably! But he *does* like you, Bridget!"

Bridget rolled her eyes and answered, "Oh, yeah, I could tell, what with him using me as psycho bait! I'm telling you Kit, if Rachel gets on Paolo's boat, you better watch my back that I don't get thrown overboard!"

Kit laughed. "Please; she's not going to try getting onto Paolo's boat with us!"

Bridget tilted her head and stared at her in disbelief.

Kit sighed and said, "Okay, she'll probably jump aboard. Jeez, Bridget, what are you going to do?"

"Put a life vest on. I think I saw a few on deck." Bridget began biting a nail worriedly.

"Bridget!" Kit smiled and pulled her friend's hand away from her mouth. "I *mean*, what are you going to do about Paolo and Lorenzo?"

"Oh, *that*. Nothing. Nothing's going to happen, Kit. It's over with Lorenzo, and Paolo's just doing this to annoy Rachel," Bridget said matter-of-factly and shrugged.

Kit rolled her eyes in exasperation. "Would you please stop! You have two men vying for your affection!"

Bridget sighed. "Kit, this is *me* we are talking about. Things like this just don't happen to *me*."

Kit was incredulous. She forgot to whisper and replied loudly, "They do in Italy! Anything goes; it's like … like … Disneyland meets … Vegas!"

"Meets hell," added Bridget sarcastically. She then laughed and said, "I'm kidding. I'm just finding this all a bit surreal and confusing."

"It's okay to be confused. You don't need to know right now, anyway. In the end, things will all be made clear, my child." Kit raised her eyebrows knowingly at her.

Paolo came up behind Bridget and propped his hands on her shoulders. "Everything is taken care of. Let's go."

Kit protested. "Oh, you paid already? But we wanted to give you money!"

Paolo shook his head, smiled, and said, "No, no. Lassino and I took care of everything. It's our pleasure. Ready?" He nodded his head sideways to look steadily at Bridget.

"Yes, *pronto*," Bridget replied.

"Good, we go!" Paolo grabbed Bridget's hand and walked off, dragging her behind him. Bridget quickly snatched her bag off the chair and shot Kit an alarmed look. Lassino came up behind Kit and patted her on the small of her back; he nodded at the exit, where the rest were headed. Kit smiled. She loved this country.

Well, Bridget had more than half-expected Rachel to stow away on Paolo's boat for the return trip, and she'd been right. However, had she known that Stefano, Giorgio's friend, would hop aboard as well, she might've decided to swim back to Positano. Having realized that Kit was beholden to Lassino, who couldn't keep his hands off her, that the Italian girls all taken, and that Rachel was obviously preoccupied with stalking Paolo, Bridget was left as the only available female aboard. Apparently Stefano hadn't gotten the town memo about her and Lorenzo … or her and Paolo. As soon as they set sail, he immediately honed in on Bridget and there was just no way to dodge him.

While the boat was not miniscule by any means, there were only so many places you could go. Antonella and her friend were on the front deck and Franco and Paolo were steering the boat. Bridget found herself left with the seat-bench on the back deck. Lassino, Kit, and Rachel sunbathed on the floor in front of her. Bridget hugged her knees into her chest. The plentiful food and drink and the warm late afternoon sun had put her into definite snooze mode. A nap was inevitable. Although, she wasn't in close proximity to the life vests, she felt somewhat safe from Rachel.

Aside from dodging Rachel's evil looks, it seemed to Bridget that the Aussie was back in better spirits, laughing and joking. Of course, whenever possible, she'd throw Paolo's name around like they were very close, and sneak looks at Bridget to see how she'd respond. Once again thankful that she'd splurged on the huge, dark glasses, Bridget pretended to see (and hear) nothing, despite Rachel lounging right in front of where she was sitting. At least if Rachel tried anything, Kit and Lassino would be her witnesses. Bridget laid her head upon her knees. *Somebody wake me when we hit Positano.*

"So, I hear you are a teacher," a deep, melodious voice said next to her. Bridget felt the strong urge to fake that she was asleep. She had dark glasses on. It wouldn't be that hard to pretend she was out. She could even throw in a little heavy breathing or a light snore. But she'd *just* put her head down. While Bridget thought she had some narcoleptic tendencies, falling asleep *that* fast would seem a little far-fetched. She was going to have to actually converse with Stefano.

At least he was no eyesore, Bridget thought. In fact, Stefano was roguishly handsome. He had the whole typical "Italian good looks" thing going on, if there was such a thing as the *typical* Italian: the black, slightly longish hair brushed back, big, dark, fringed eyes, gleaming white teeth underneath

a bit of dark stubble. His short-sleeved linen shirt was completely unbuttoned and showed off a tanned torso with just a tinge of chest hair. The
odd absence of chest hair (for such a dark guy) fiercely contrasted with
his abundantly hairy legs. Bridget wondered if he shaved his chest. It was
entirely possible.

He wore a chunky Rolex on one wrist, while his other arm rested in
a sling. The sling, unfortunately, did nothing to impair his ability to com-
municate verbally. Okay, Bridget knew she was being critical. Although
she had been seated at the other end of the table at lunch and hadn't been
paying too much attention to Stefano, what with worrying about Paolo
possibly mauling her in front of Rachel and/or Rachel jumping across the
table and attacking her Jerry Springer-style, she guessed he *seemed* to be
quite charming. However, she was just not in the mood to focus on being
social. Why couldn't he bother Kit, like every other man usually did? That
figured. Today was shaping up to be typically atypical.

Bridget threw out the most nonfake smile that she possibly could. "Yes,
I'm a teacher."

Stefano nodded as if she'd just said something quite moving and pro-
found and then asked, "And what do you teach?"

"I teach seven- and eight-year-olds, so pretty much everything," answered Bridget.

"Ah, so you teach English?" Stefano perked up with interest. Bridget
shook her head in affirmation.

"Maybe my English would be much better if I had a beautiful teacher
like you!" he flirted.

Oh, please.

"Oh, your English is just fine," she said and smiled back.

He shook his finger at her. "Teachers are not supposed to tell lies! Oh,
you flatter me. My English is very poor, very poor. I am embarrassed,"
Stefano protested humbly as he clutched his chest with his good arm. Behind
her dark glasses, Bridget felt herself roll her eyes. He didn't fool her with his
fake modesty. His English was almost as good as her own. Seriously.

Bridget hated to unnecessarily stroke his ego, but she felt inclined to
respond. "No, no. Your English is quite good—in fact, very, very good. I
mean it."

Stefano suddenly grabbed her hand, nearly causing Bridget to lose her

Catie Costa

balance and fall off the bench. *What was he doing?* He raised her hand to his lips and kissed it.

Then he looked up and spoke grandiosely. "Thank you, *Bella*. It is not every day that a beautiful teacher compliments me." Oh, no, she hoped he didn't take her comment as a come-on. Bridget tried gently prying her hand away, but his was like Velcro to the touch.

From under his dark lashes, his eyes seemed quite suggestive, and he spoke in his deep, throaty voice, "Yes, *beautiful* … and I respect the praise and opinion of a *magnificent* teacher, such as yourself. Such a compliment! I am honored!"

He was too much. As if she was some type of supermodel/Nobel Prize-winning teaching guru. She felt his grip loosen a bit and took the opportunity to slide her hand out of his. She joked, "*Now* you're flattering me!"

He parlayed, "It is not flattery, Bridget. I speak the truth. A good teacher is like a gift from heaven. The one that teaches …" he paused dramatically "… touches the souls of others." So, so corny, but maybe he'd redeemed himself (if only by the slightest margin) with the teacher adoration. And now, could she please get back to trying to nap?

"You are a good teacher, no?" he asked. Was she? That was debatable. It depended on the day of the week and whether PMS had struck.

"I have my good days and bad days. You know, *Kit's* a teacher too," Bridget offered. *Please go talk to Kit.* Bridget was hoping the telepathy would kick in any minute now.

"Yes, yes, Kit." Stefano looked over to where Kit and Lassino lounged, with sorrowful eyes, as if he pitied her and her choice in men (since it wasn't him).

He grabbed Bridget's hand again, sighed, and said, "Ah, and I can see you are humble too. I guess all teachers have a certain humility, as well. I find that very attractive, you know." He stared at her.

Changing the subject, Bridget asked, "So, what is it that you do, Stefano?"

He seemed to puff out his chest a bit before answering, "I am a doctor."

"Oh, what do you specialize in?" It might be good to know a doctor while over here. What if she and Kit had a recurrence of swollen ankles and heat rashes, like they'd had one summer before? Yes, knowing a doctor might come in handy.

"I'm a gynecologist," he said importantly. *A gynecologist? Eeww.*

"Oh," was all Bridget could muster, while she tried not to sound disgusted. Really, what could she say? It wasn't like he was a foot doctor and they could breezily discuss foot ailments—hammertoes, bunions, flat feet, neuropathy, and the like. A gynecologist? No, you couldn't really talk shop there. At least, Bridget wasn't about to discuss the female reproductive system with an Italian *male* gynecologist. There were male gynecologists all over the world, she knew. Why, though, did *she* have to be stuck talking to one on a boat, in the middle of the Tyrrhenian Sea? Really, she had the worst luck.

The doctor was not deterred by Bridget's lack of interest. He explained, "Yes, I deal with women's bodies, you know?"

"Yes, I *know,*" Bridget answered a bit snarkily. Yes, of course she knew. She was a woman, wasn't she? Every woman knew what a gynecologist was, not that she really wanted to. Going to the gynecologist was one of her least favorite things to do, besides trying on bathing suits.

Her hint at sarcasm had gone unnoticed, and Stefano continued, "Yes, the female body, so wonderful, so, so … *complex.* I enjoy my work." Oh, yes, *of course* he did. He was a *man.* And Italian.

Once again, Bridget found herself at a loss for words. Stefano continued, "So, if you need anything, have any *problems,* while you are here, please let me know. I will take care of you."

Bridget blurted out, "Oh, no, no, I'll be fine. I mean, I never ever get sick. Or have … *problems.* Thanks, though." Never mind that she'd rescheduled her latest pap smear about four times now. She'd rather go to the dentist and have all four wisdom teeth extracted again. She'd never consider going to a male gyno, unless he was older than the hills and practically blind. Call her old-fashioned. And please, don't give her that favorite quote that doctors were always heard spouting: "It's no big deal. If you've seen one body, you've seen 'em all!" She didn't believe that for one minute.

"You just let me know. Things sometimes happen when you are traveling …" he offered again. Bridget hoped that perhaps this signaled the end of the conversation, but nooo.

On and on Stefano continued with his knowledge and anecdotes of the wondrous female body, as well as his favorite childbirth/delivery-room stories. Not only did Bridget never want to go to the gynecologist again, she also now never wanted to have children, either. Alas, she was a captive audience, as he practically had her pinned to the bench, and they *were* out at sea. There was nowhere for her to go, and worse yet, she had to sit and listen to his gruesome stories, while the three sunbathers got to carefreely nap right in front of her. Bridget thought she might've seen a slight smile on Kit's face during one of the doctor's stories, but of course, if it were her, she'd fake sleep as well. Oh, why hadn't she? She really was too nice sometimes.

Bridget was beginning to tune Stefano out, nodding every now and then in what she thought were the appropriate pauses. And suddenly, miraculously, Stefano stopped talking. Perhaps he'd exhausted all his stories finally? Bridget stared out at the shimmering water and enjoyed hearing only the sound of it.

"Excuse me, Bridget." Stefano spoke almost urgently, interrupting the serenity of the moment.

"You know, we have been talking for quite some time, and I feel I know you." *Knew her?* Not quite, although she knew just about everything there was to know about him, except his shoe size.

He continued, "So, I feel it is all right to ask you to take off—"

"Take off what?" Bridget interrupted hastily.

"Why, take off your sunglasses," he answered sternly.

"I'm sorry?"

"Yes, your sunglasses. Hmm, Chanel, very nice, very nice. But, when I talk to someone, though, I want to see the eyes. Then I will really know them. You have had your glasses on the whole time we have talked," he explained, as if this was quite obvious and she was a complete dunce. Did this mean he was going to talk *some more?* Was that possible?

"I'm wearing glasses because the sun is bright." Bridget stated the obvious.

"Yes, of course, I understand. Please, humor me." And before she could protest, Stefano gently pulled her glasses off her head. Bridget immediately squinted in the light.

"Ah, mamma mia! Bellisima! Are they real?" Stefano asked in wonder.

"My eyes? Yes, they're real," Bridget answered, surprised. She had blue eyes, yes. There were tons of Italians with blue eyes, like Paolo, for instance. Where was he, anyway?

Stefano shook his head as if dumbfounded. "Wow! Very unusual, with your dark hair. Amazing!"

He crossed his arms and leaned back a bit, as if to get a better look at her. This was really uncomfortable, almost as bad as listening to his story about the exploding ovary he'd saved.

"Bellisima! But your mouth ... it does not move much. You do not talk," Stefano said.

Of course it hasn't moved. It hasn't had a chance to move, since you never shut up! Bridget thought.

"Yes ... your mouth, it does not talk, but your eyes speak, Bridget," he said smugly.

"Really?" Bridget felt impelled to ask. Stefano was quite amazing if he was able to actually see the "Get the hell away from me!" in her eyes right now.

"Your eyes, they tell me ..." he paused dramatically, which made Bridget feel like she was having her fortune read by some two-bit fortune-teller. Bridget grimaced and almost held her breath as she waited for his answer.

"Your eyes, they tell me there is a ... *seduction* about you." He over-emphasized and drew out the word *seduction*. Bridget stifled a snort by pretending she was coughing. Now she'd heard it all.

"You are a seductress!" he boomed with gusto. The three sunbathers jerked momentarily and then went back to their fake snoozing. Damn them.

"*Seductress?* Wow, I'm pretty sure that word has *never* been used to describe me," said Bridget drolly.

Stefano shook a finger at her and inched closer. "Oh, do not tease me with those haunting eyes—with those enchanting eyes, so blue, like the water in *La Grotta Azzurra!*" he cooed. Was Bridget imagining it, or with every compliment, did Stefano's Italian accent become more dramatically pronounced? The English was perfect, no doubt, but his accent had become overly exaggerated.

"What?" What was he talking about *now?* Bridget was not to be impressed with the whole over-the-top Romeo act.

"The Blue Grotto—you have heard of it?" he inquired, in a suddenly near-perfect English accent.

Oh, the *Blue Grotto.* Yes, yes, of course she had heard of it. Off the Isle of Capri (they must be near it) was the famed cavern of dazzling blue water, which had been on both her and Kit's to-do list for a couple of years. They always had the best of intentions to take day trips while they were here, but once in Positano, they just never seemed able to leave. Maybe it was the heat; maybe it was the prosecco; maybe it was the people. They never were sure, but leaving, for any reason, had become somewhat of a daunting task. "Day trip to Sorrento tomorrow? Be at the bus stop by nine a.m.? Sure."

And then when 9:00 a.m. rolled around the next day—and it did quickly, when you only got home from the disco around five or six a.m.—one of them was always apt to say, "Sorrento? I can't even think of getting up right now. Let's skip it today. We have the whole rest of the trip to go!"

And of course, the rest of the trip came and went, with them enslaved to the beach chairs and the late nights at the disco. Yes, they thought themselves quite lucky they'd even made it to Leo and Diana's wedding in Scalea! *The Blue Grotto? If only* … Bridget sighed wistfully.

"Well, that is where Paolo is taking us." *Oh.* Well, they could finally scratch something off that to-do list and be able to boast that they'd done something besides lie lazily on the beach! Hmm … was it possible they could get to Pompeii today too? And then maybe do some shopping in Sorrento? That might be pushing it a little.

Bridget reached her hand out and asked, "Perfect. May I have my glasses back now?"

◆　◆　◆

"We have to get into one if *those* little rowboats?" Bridget asked skeptically, to no one in particular. Paolo had stopped the boat a slight distance from the Blue Grotto. At least Bridget assumed it to be the famed destination, since she noticed a congregation of other boats bobbling about, as well as a few rowboats with gondoliers aboard. Passengers and gondoliers alike screamed back and forth at each other. Then the gondoliers screamed heatedly at each other. Then there was more screaming back to the passengers on the waiting boats. Hopefully just some normal Italian negotiating? It appeared that maybe all the gondoliers were in competition with each other for passengers, trying to outdo each other and still swindle some decent money out of the customers.

And then there was the smallish opening in the side of the rock cliff that led into the Blue Grotto itself. Bridget felt slightly nauseous as she realized that they would not only have to get into a rickety rowboat, but would also have to fit through that small opening in the rock. Bridget now understood where the old saying the "camel through the eye of a needle" came from! There was absolutely no way a boat, even such small rowboats, could fit through! This was ridiculous!

She tried thinking of a good excuse she could give in order to stay on the boat with Antonella and her friend, but there really was none. Besides, Paolo had casually mentioned that he'd planned the trip specifically with Bridget and Kit in mind, since they'd never been there. And apparently, the weather conditions were optimal for the trip into the cave: a clear, sunny day and a calm sea. Bridget willed her acute anxiety away. She wanted to see the famous tourist attraction, where diffused sunlight from a clear sky turned the water inside the cave into an amazing, crystal blue. She'd seen the pictures and postcards. The water looked mysteriously surreal, as if there was some sort of underwater lighting system creating the whole effect. And now she was actually going to see it for herself. All right, she was over it. Bridget just fervently hoped that whatever rowboat she wound up on did not also include Rachel or Stefano.

One of the screaming gondoliers approached the boat and began shouting at them all. Kit and Bridget raised eyebrows at each other. Rachel explained, "He's telling us it's going to be twelve euros a person." They watched as Lassino, Paolo, and Franco simultaneously yelled back at the small rowboat. The gondolier barked something in return.

"Okay, we're on for eleven euros a head, now," Rachel stated. Another rowboat and gondolier approached, and the same screaming match was held.

Rachel put a hand up in front of her mouth and uttered from behind it, "This guy will take us for ten euros a head, but no lower." More angry shouting, now between the two gondoliers, and then some rapid words in the direction of Paolo, who answered with a curt, "*Bene.*"

"They all stopped screaming. That means something good happened, right? What's going on, Rachel?" Kit asked anxiously.

"They're both going to offer us ten euros per person, since obviously, we can't all fit in one rowboat. Quite the businessmen, aren't they?" Rachel said in amusement.

With the exception of Antonella, who was staying behind with her friend, they all headed over to the ladder that led down the back of the boat. Bridget crowded close behind Kit; she hoped to ensure they were on the same rowboat.

Lassino jumped into the rowboat and held a hand out to Kit. Before Bridget could step forward, Franco beat her to it and in no time was in the rocking boat. Bridget waited for an outstretched hand. Instead, the surly gondolier held up a hand and shouted, "*Basta!*" and then began rowing away.

Rachel turned around and looked at Bridget, Stefano, and Paolo and said coyly, "I guess that leaves just the four of us."

"Apparently." Bridget tried to keep the annoyance out of her voice. Despite the Australian's ability to intimidate, she was starting to get on Bridget's nerves.

Bad-tempered gondolier #2 held out a hand stoically. Bridget grabbed it and tottered onto the gently swaying boat. "Grazie." She tried smiling at him, but he was already lending a hand to Rachel. Rachel hopped in, and the gondolier motioned for her to sit opposite Bridget. He then explained, "So the boat don't *teep* over."

There is potential for boat-"teeping"? Oh, fantastic, Bridget thought. Next in was Paolo, who seated himself beside Bridget, so close that he was practically on her lap, with his arm resting behind her. Bridget, sans her sunglasses, averted her eyes from Rachel, who she was sure was sending her telepathic death threats. Stefano gingerly got in, careful of his slung arm, and resignedly sat next to Rachel.

And they were off, sloshing through the water (did it seem a bit choppier all of a sudden?) till they reached the narrow, four-foot entrance in the cliff. They bobbed about behind the boat and held the other boats while they waited their turn for admittance. Bridget watched as their friends disappeared, seemingly swallowed up into the black vortex in the rock.

The gondolier spoke and motioned with his hand. "Everybody, down, please."

Bridget looked at Paolo. He explained, "The opening is not very high, so we all must lay down until we are are inside."

They were all supposed to lie down in a rowboat? Before Bridget could question the likelihood of that, Paolo pulled her to him and down into the middle of the boat. Rachel and Stefano followed. They were uncomfortably squeezed together; Bridget's face was pressed into Paolo's chest, and she hoped she wasn't crushing him. If she was, he didn't seem to mind. He rested his chin upon her forehead while they waited momentarily for the low water between the waves to usher them in.

Bridget thought that this could've been quite romantic, if she was actually interested in Paolo (but she wasn't, was she?) and not heartbroken over Lorenzo ditching her (and she was, wasn't she?) ... *and* if she didn't have Rachel and Stefano breathing down her neck ... *and* if she weren't worried that Paolo was being suffocated under her weight ... or that there might be a leak in the rowboat. She just knew she felt water seeping into the boat. And what if they got stuck in the cave? What if the waves suddenly grew ginormous and they were unable to get out? She hoped there weren't any bats in there either. She *hated* flying things. She didn't even like birds. She'd for sure have to keep her eyes closed, and then she'd miss the whole Blue Grotto! That would suck.

In dreaded anticipation, Bridget closed her eyes. But wait, they were moving forward! She opened an eye, and then the other one. Bridget held her breath; she expected a loud scraping sound, since they were sure to career against the sides of the rock going in, but it never came. She exhaled as the gondolier easily guided the boat in with a gilding *swoosh*. He then hurriedly grabbed onto a rope that was somehow attached to the wall and pulled them in a bit further. It all felt very Disneyland *Pirates of the Caribbean*. She inadvertently pushed herself up to get a look, and the others followed. She sat herself against the side of the boat and looked out in amazement. The cave was dark, indeed, but the water was lit-up to a brilliant, crystallike blue. It was absolutely unreal. How was the light from the mere opening of the cave able to illuminate the water like this?

"This is incredible," Bridget stated. "I can't believe the color of the water. I mean, how is it possible?"

Paolo shrugged. "As long as there is a lot of sun, it is like this. You can understand why so many people come to see. But for a long time, people wouldn't come here. They thought that ... how do you say ... ah, witches! Yes, they thought witches and monsters lived in the cave." He laughed.

No need to panic. She was in a *haunted* cave. *Freaky.* But kind of cool. Wasn't there a *Brady Bunch* episode similar to this? Oh, wait, that was the one when they were in Hawaii and found the cursed tiki necklace. Never mind. Even if the cave was cursed, what worse luck could she possibly have, anyway? You couldn't help but be intrigued by the creepy, romantic mythology of it all.

Still, Bridget asked, "Do people still think there are witches in here?"

Paolo smiled, and his white teeth glowed. "No, the mystery of the cave just made people superstitious. Now they don't care, because they can make money from it!"

Stefano added (Italian accent in full effect again), "La Grotta Azzurra is ancient. Antique statues were found here, which shows that the cave was well known, even to the Romans." Bridget had forgotten the doctor was on the boat with them. He'd actually been quiet for a record five minutes. Well, at least his comment was relevant to the conversation at hand and not anything at all to do with the female body. Although, if pressed, he'd no doubt tell them that the statues found in the grotto had been naked women or fertility goddesses or something.

He then added, "Some say that at one time, maybe even pirates used the cave as a hiding place for their treasure, since no one dared to come here."

"Very practical of them." Rachel spoke up with a laugh.

Bridget wondered if Kit was getting the same interesting historical tidbits about the Blue Grotto on her rowboat.

"Ohhhhh, *solo miiiioooo!*" The cave suddenly reverberated with deep, melodious singing. Kit's gondolier had dropped the surly act in favor of some live musical entertainment.

"And, of course, you will notice that the acoustics are marvelous," Stefano added.

Quite. Paolo and Stefano sang along boisterously, and Bridget could hear Lassino and Franco as well, from their rowboat. Amid the singing, a splash could be heard. It had come from the direction of Kit's rowboat. Someone had gone into the water! Had he or she fallen in? The four of them strained their eyes to see who it was. In a moment, Kit's head bobbed up. From however far away they were, Bridget could still see her friend's day-glow teeth. "The water's great! Come in!" she called to the others in the boat.

Rachel asked, "We can swim? Is that all right?"

The guide answered, "Is okay, but just for a few minutes."

Immediately, Rachel slithered out of her tiny cut-offs and threw herself over the side of the rowboat. Paolo looked at Bridget. "Want to swim?"

No, of course not! She was not giving Stefano an opportunity to see her in a bathing suit so she could swim in a haunted pirate cave. It was all good and fine to *look* at the gorgeous water, but she didn't need to get into it. The image of her trying to clumsily hoist herself up back over the side of the boat … well, that alone was enough to keep her from going in! It wouldn't be easy, and it most definitely would not be pretty. By the way, how deep *was* the water? Bridget couldn't help but wonder how many people had drowned in here. That settled it. She was staying put.

"Okay, I'll be right back," Paolo said as he swung his legs over the side of the boat and lowered himself into the water. He swam off in the direction of the other rowboat.

Bridget and Stefano were left with their silent gondolier. *Just stare out at the lovely water and make no eye contact with Stefano.* Bridget repeated the mantra to herself a few times, before Stefano's voice interrupted.

"You do not like to swim?' he asked, as if implying that she was staying on the boat for some other reason—like, say, because he was there.

"Oh, no, I like swimming. I'm just tired," Bridget answered. And she was, since he'd foiled her naptime. *And back to staring off at the water.*

"I love to swim, but unfortunately …" His voice trailed off and he shrugged and nodded toward his sling.

"Oh, of course," Bridget answered. She should really be nicer. Stefano hadn't actually done anything to her but keep her awake. He was probably harmless. Why did she have to get so paranoid about everything? Bridget actually felt a little sorry that he wasn't able to swim.

With innocent interest, she asked, "How much longer will you have to wear the sling?"

"Just a few more days. You know, Bridget, I am very strong, but when I get this off," Stefano motioned to his injured arm, "I will be even *stronger*." He looked pointedly at her. Even in the dimness, she could see the whites of his eyes aimed at her.

"Well, sure you will," she said and smiled brightly.

"No, I mean, I will be *stronger*." Stefano emphasized the word again.

"Yes, stronger, right, *forte*!" Bridget called out jokingly.

Stefano looked a little perplexed, and he used his good arm to brush back his dark hair before saying, "*Forte*, yes, very good. What I mean is, I will be able to do so much *more* than I can do now. *Stronger*, understand?"

Yesss. Yes, she got it, she thought. "Yes, right, *stronger.* I understand." Okay, he was starting to get a little bit annoying again. Time to cease conversation and go back to staring at the water.

Stefano looked at her in relief, and his lips parted slightly. He spoke huskily. "Ah, you understand what I mean when I say I will be able to do more?"

"Yes, you'll be able to swim, and, and ..." Bridget was at a loss for what else he'd be able to do with the use of both arms. Shoot hoops? Did they do that in Italy?

"Um ... you'll be able to ..."

"Make the sex, of course." Stefano chuckled, but in a way that meant he wasn't joking. Wait, *oh.* Oh, no. She was being punished for something, wasn't she? The cave *was* cursed by witches. Why else would she be placed in another creepy conversation with him? Unless (hopefully) he was implying that he wanted to "make the sex" just in general, and not with her.

"Understand?" He raised his eyebrows at her and smiled knowingly. It was "make the sex" with her, wasn't it? Of course, that would be her rotten luck. Maybe if she played dumb, he'd leave her alone.

"*Understand?*" Stefano asked again and winked coyly at her.

"No. I mean, yes. I mean, no. Uh, I'm not quite sure what you're getting at," she stammered. Why couldn't *their* gondolier bust out in song now? Why couldn't he come to her rescue, instead of standing there, statuelike?

"Oh, I am quite sure you know." He waggled a finger at her accusingly.

"I *really* don't, Stefano," countered Bridget as she looked anxiously out at the swimmers and willed Paolo and even Rachel to get back to the boat so they could get going.

"You, Bridget, are very good. You know *just* what you are doing to me." *Huh?*

Stefano moved across the rowboat and sat next to her.

"I think you're supposed to stay over there," Bridget said as she pointed to the opposite side, "otherwise the boat might tip over. Right? Excuse me, right? Tip over?" she called out to the gondolier, who ignored her. Fine, she'd move herself to the other side.

Bridget swiftly moved herself opposite Stefano.

Infuriatingly, he laughed at her and said, "You are like a *fox.* You know how to play the *game.*"

What was he talking about now? "Game? I don't know what you mean by *game*," answered Bridget tersely.

"The game! The game between man and woman! You act as if you are not interested in me …" *Um, that was because she wasn't interested in him.*

"But it is all a game! A game of seduction! You make me want you. You, Bridget, are the queen of seduction!" he cried passionately and was just about to move himself next to her, when she felt a splash of water on her neck. Bridget gasped at the feel of the cool water and swiveled her head around. Oh, her prayers were answered. For the second time that day, it was Paolo!

He grabbed onto the sides of the boat and pushed himself up. He tumbled in and dripped water all over her, but she didn't care. Bridget was just glad that she wasn't alone with Stefano anymore. The gondolier didn't count for a person. He had been no help whatsoever. Paolo settled in next to her. Despite the dimness of the cave, he cut a lovely profile, even with his nose. He sat there and water dripped down his smooth, cut chest and arms. He reached a hand up and ran it through his short hair as he tried to somewhat dry it. He then leaned back into the boat, slung an arm behind Bridget, and rested it on the side of the boat. He looked casually over at her and caught her staring. She was embarrassed to be caught like a deer in the headlights, but she couldn't turn away. It was alarming, how cute he was. Besides, she was afraid to glance around for fear she'd catch Stefano's eye and he'd start talking again.

Paolo stared back and smiled slightly, as if pleasantly surprised she'd been watching him. Time for her to look away. Bridget looked down at her lap. One side of her linen skirt was waterlogged from Paolo.

He scooted closer, put an arm around her, and said, "Your skirt is wet, sorry."

Oh, God, he was practically on top of her! But she didn't mind. But she should. But she liked him. But she *really* liked Lorenzo. She wished it *were* Lorenzo. She wondered if Lorenzo had tried calling her today. Probably not. Was she being fickle? Oh, she didn't know! But at least she was safe now from Stefano, who was like that pesky Pepe Le Pew cartoon character! Yes, she was relieved Paolo was next to her. Oh, no, he was kissing her! How had that happened? She was kissing him back! He'd started it. But she was definitely kissing him back. This was bad! But this was not *that* bad … this should stop … soon. Well, maybe just a little longer … okay, now, time to stop. Besides, truth be told, aside from the excitement of it all, something felt a bit off about it. It wasn't quite right. Because Paolo wasn't Lorenzo.

Bridget pulled away. Besides her skirt being wet, so was the rest of her now, including her face. She felt slightly embarrassesd to have succumbed to a PDA, even if they were in a dark cave. But of course, that sort of leant itself to some type of wild abandon, didn't it? Careful to avoid meeting Stefano's eyes, Bridget looked past him … and right into Rachel's.

◆   ◆   ◆

Kit flung another top to the clothes-littered floor. She was making a mess. A mess that she'd have to clean, too, since Marren was arriving tomorrow afternoon. Not that she wasn't completely delighted to see her friend—she just couldn't stand cleaning. Well, it'd have to wait. Tonight, she and Bridget were on Lassino and his friends' timetable. No snacks and prosecco while leisurely getting ready, no waltzing into Lassino's restaurant thirty minutes before the kitchen closed—no dillydallying of *any* sort. She'd actually been told so by Lassino, which was no shock, since he was always trying to tell her what to do. Although, unless it had to do with specific hair care products, she was learning to only half-listen.

Really, though, Kit didn't know *what* he was thinking. When they'd hopped off Paolo's boat and onto the dock in the marina grande, it was already eight o'clock! And they were expected to get up the hill, change, and be back down at the bottom of the steps to the beach by nine o'clock? The location of dinner had yet to be disclosed, but even Antonella had reiterated that they be there by nine o'clock, and Kit was prepared to listen to her, an actual *sane* person. She'd even agreed good-naturedly with Bridget's comment at the beginning of their uphill climb: "Now, Kit, I'm not trying to be a killjoy, but we *cannot*, under any circumstances, stop to say hello to everyone who knows and adores you. If you must, at any time, make eye contact, just wave and keep walking! An hour to get up the hill and get ready? I mean, that's even pushing it a little for me!"

And Bridget was speedy when it came to getting ready! If this was not enough time for her, well, then it was hardly enough time for Kit to get gorgeous enough. Kit hated to be rushed. She couldn't think straight, and she needed to look good tonight. After the wonderful day she'd had, the night could only get better; she just knew it. But deciding upon the right top, while seemingly of a trivial nature, was essential. Looking at the ever-growing pile of clothes on the floor didn't help her concentration either.

Ughhh, *cleaning.* Of course, the good thing was that Marren was hardly a neat freak by any means, but still, she *would* be a guest here. Hmm … maybe she could just shove the pile into a corner of the room. Marren would be sleeping in the other bedroom, anyway. But the muddle might irritate Bridget, who was, in fact, sharing a room with her. Bridget, the speed dresser, always impeccably and gorgeously groomed and ready at least a half an hour earlier than her, and who never left a mess, even if it was just to shove everything into her side of the closet. Kit sighed. It made her feel a bit inadequate at times, until she reminded herself that she just wasn't inclined that way, and she never would be. She marched to the timeless beat of her own cell-phone clock (and that, by the way, was even off a bit as well). Timeliness was not one of her character traits, but she did possess others that were just as positive, such as … responsibility (sigh), she thought gingerly.

Yes, of course she'd tidy up, for sure, but *tomorrow.* Procrastination happened to also be one of her suits, as well. She quickly checked her phone for the time. Only twenty minutes—and ten and a half of those minutes would be spent walking down the hill! That meant she still had to find a suitable top, flatiron her hair, and do her makeup! Maybe it had been pointless bringing as many clothes as she had. Clearly, it had not helped matters.

Kit stood, perplexed, in her tight, black skinny jeans and a push-up bra and glanced at herself in the huge, oval mirror that leaned against the wall on top of the bureau. She had a healthy, golden glow from the sun, just right, not too dark and not burned either. She'd worried a bit about burning since the red Cosa Bella bikini was relatively tiny, even by Italian bikini standards, and they'd pretty much been on or in the water all day, but she was fine. And the bikini had been worth wearing, just for the looks that Lassino gave her.

Okay, it *was* starting to get annoying that all the guys, even gay Giorgio, kept (albeit jokingly) asking if her boobs were real. However, she knew what they meant, and she wasn't trying to be the slightest bit narcissitic or conceited. They were simply implying that her chest looked pretty good, almost unnaturally so. Because, nobody asked people with saggy, dejected boobs, "Hey, are those sad things real?" or "Are they really that droopy?" Therefore, when referenced to herself, she'd take the "Are they real?" as a compliment, however juvenile and inappropriate.

Kit squinted slightly at the mirror. She knew her eyesight was bad, but she thought she detected the tiniest of pudges around her midsection. Nothing that anyone else would ever notice, but it was obvious to her, since she typically had nothing but a washboard- flat stomach. She patted her miniature pooch lightly and grinned. She loved eating. It made her happy. She also ate *when* she was happy. She didn't have that whole love/hate/guilt thing about eating that so many of her friends, like Bridget, did. It was *all* good. She rarely overdid it, of course, and that was the key. Well, she didn't overpartake of anything unless she was *here*, where her food allergies and bowel problems hardly seemed to exist.

She felt giddy with happiness and excitement. Kit was happy because, by and far, this had been the best day of the trip. After the trauma and drama, all the lost luggage, the lost *thirteen-year-old*, Diana's nightmare wedding ordeal, petulant houseguests, Fabio's loaded nanny offer, and, well, *Lassino, the absolute king of drama* ... today had made up for them all. The boat trip had been worth it, but it was more than the actual boat trip, itself. It was everything, every crazy, random element of the day.

Being out on the water, napping in the hot sun, next to Lassino, the to-die-for food, swimming in *the* Blue Grotto—it all been so extraordinary. But the best part had been the people. From no-nonsense, fun Antonella, to flamboyant Giorgio, to lovable Franco and charming Paolo ... Kit felt like she really had friends here. It was so refreshing to see them all outside of their shops and restaurants, and outside of the disco! Kit and Bridget had gotten a true glimpse of these people. Take away the hordes of tourists and the glitzy disco scene, and you had real people, real friends, like they had back home. And then there was Lassino, who, aside from his prank about leaving without them, had been so attentive and, spookily, sweet. And dare she say, even loving and boyfriendlike. But why was she shocked? Kit knew he possessed those qualities. It was just so nice having him shower them on her and all day.

It was difficult to put into words how she felt, other than happy. Although, *happy* was such an overused and diluted word, and Kit was far more than that. All day long, she'd been in a perpetual state of nervous, dizzy excitement. And tonight? She felt fortunate and appreciative that she was going to be included in the gregarious dinner party (and whatever else happened after dinner and the disco—sorry, but she couldn't help thinking about *that*). But, she digressed. What to wear? Kit stooped down and frantically rummaged through the pile on the floor, like a dog digging up something in the yard. Settling upon a violet-blue sleeveless top, she quickly threw it on. Knit, with a playful ruffle around the low neckline, it was just right. How had she missed it before? It was perfect and definitely depicted how she felt.

Her cell phone rang. Kit hoped it wasn't Lassino telling her they were late. They still had a good, well, eight minutes. Oh, boy. Hmm, it was some unknown Italian number. Kit had noticed that same number had called her phone a couple of times that day, but she'd been out of earshot and no one had left a message. She answered with a breathless, "Pronto!"

"Ciao, Kit?" a mild Italian accent asked.

"Yes?" Who was this? The voice was familiar, but she really didn't have time to chat.

"Kit, hi, it's Lorenzo. Is Bridget there?" Oh, Lorenzo, of course! Kit smiled. This should put a stop to Bridget's lamenting over their "break." She should be excited. Wait, or would she? *Something* had happened in the Blue Grotto. How anything could've happened while they were in the cave for a mere fifteen minutes was beyond her. Bridget had promised she'd tell her later, but later never came since they kept bumping into people they knew on their trek up the hill. Well, whatever it was, it couldn't be good and it had to involve Paolo and, obviously, Rachel too, since Bridget kept cryptically musing about whether anyone had ever been murdered in Positano. So then again, maybe Bridget would be happy to hear from Lorenzo. Kit didn't have time right now to try to figure it out. She needed to pass the phone off quickly before her hair turned into a huge cloud of frizz.

"Hi, Lorenzo! Sure, I'll get her for you." Kit hurried down the hall and onto the patio, where Bridget sat calmly in the dimness.

"Bridget, Lorenzo's on the phone," Kit walked toward her and held out the phone.

Bridget took it in surprise and said, "Thanks." She then did a double take on Kit.

Kit knew the look. It was the "What the hell have you been doing? Why aren't you ready by now?" look. She quickly waved her off. "I know, I know. I *just* have to do my hair quickly. And put my makeup on."

Bridget opened her mouth to say something and then closed it. Kit took the opportunity to continue. "It'll take ten minutes, ten minutes! Okay, maybe fifteen, I swear!" She headed off the patio and called over her shoulder, "Don't worry. We'll just catch a cab down the hill!"

Bridget shook her head. Well, in all fairness, expecting them both to ready in an hour and down at the bottom of the steps was a little ludicrous. Worrying wasn't going to do anything, and *Lorenzo* was on the phone! Bridget's stomach lurched with a happy nervousness. This was good, wasn't it? Unless he was calling to say that the break they were on had so far been very successful and he'd met someone much better-looking and that any more time apart was unnecessary since whatever they'd had going on was now over.

Oh, no, now she wished he wasn't on the phone. And she felt guilty about kissing Paolo, as well she should. It had been just so spur of the moment. And she had to admit, she'd been quite happy to blatantly go along with it just to get Stefano off her back. That was why she'd succumbed to Paolo's kisses, right? Well, there was more than a hint of truth to that, but if she had to really be honest … hell, she didn't have time to be honest about it right now. She'd beat herself up about later, for sure. The important thing was that kissing Paolo had worked. Stefano had barely spoken to her for the rest of the trip back to Positano. Of course, Rachel had picked that moment as well to get back onto the rowboat, and as a result, she had spent the rest of the return trip shooting icy death stares at Bridget and Paolo.

But, even more importantly than all that, Lorenzo was on the phone now. What *could* he be calling about? She didn't have time to fantasize about that either, seeing as how they were once again behind schedule.

"Lorenzo, hi," Bridget said into the phone; she tried to keep her voice steady, since she suddenly felt winded.

"*Maestrina, come stai?*" Lorenzo's deep voice answered jovially.

"*Bene, grazie. E tu?*" Bridget tried out a semidecent Italian accent.

"*Va bene!*" he answered warmly before he launched into a fast-paced Italian soliloquy. Lorenzo finished and waited for Bridget to speak. Ummmm …

"Sorry, you lost me back at 'va bene,'" she answered sheepishly.

"I said, my day was good. My mom and I took my niece to the beach." *Okay, that was good.* He'd been at the beach with his *mother and niece.* No chance of him flirting with hot, bikinied women when he was under the watchful eye of Signora Reginella and with his niece attached to his hip. Bridget was a little shocked at her obvious jealous glee that Lorenzo's flirting abilities had been thwarted. How hypocritical, when she'd let herself be shamelessly romanced on the high seas, not to mention in a cave as well!

Oh, she was terrible. Who did she think she was, someone in a Jackie Collins book? Not that she could claim much smut at all, really. A mere kiss or two was mild stuff in the Blue Grotto, according to their gondolier, who typically came back to life as soon as they were about to exit the cave and told them cryptically, "When *two* go into the cave, *three* leave."

Whatever that meant, she'd thought. All that mattered to Bridget was that five of them had gotten on this rowboat, and thankfully, five were leaving. Yes, in fact, she was quite grateful to still be in the puny boat, although, she could've done without Rachel or Stefano. Bridget's face must've given away her puzzlement, for Stefano took the opportunity to explain, "He means, when a *man* and *woman* come into the cave as two, they will leave as *three.* You know, *understand?* They will have a baby …" His voice trailed off, but he looked right at her, as if to make sure she comprehended and wasn't completely mentally incapacitated as to the ways of the world and what men and women might possibly get up to in watery circumstances.

"Thank you, yes, I understand." Did everything he *ever* talked about have to relate to sex?

But back to Lorenzo. He was on the phone and he'd been at the beach with his mom and niece. So was that all he'd called to tell her? Was she supposed to tell him all about her day? What would she say? *Yes, I had a lovely day myself, nothing too unusual, you know. Being constantly hit on by Italian gynecologists and making out with hot twenty-six-year-olds in the Blue Grotto is just a typical day for me.*

Before Bridget could say anything in response, Lorenzo asked, "So, did you miss me today?" He was joking, but Bridget detected a bit of earnest curiosity too.

She felt a pang of remorse, because, even though her attention had somewhat been diverted by other *things,* in reality, she had missed him. But *she* wasn't the one who'd suggested the break, now was she? What did he expect her to say? *Yes, I was absolutely crushed that you didn't want to see me today, since in case you hadn't already noticed, I have no self-confidence whatsoever, especially when it comes to men!* However, she needed to preserve a little dignity, a bit of self-protection.

She paused momentarily and then answered jokingly, "It hasn't even been twenty-four hours, Lorenzo!"

"Oh, I see how it is." He laughed.

"Why, did you miss me?" Bridget asked sarcastically.

"Nope, not at all," he said warmly. Aha! He *had* missed her.

"So what are you doing tonight?' Lorenzo asked a little too casually. Should she tell him she and Kit had dinner plans with Lassino and Paolo and friends? Well, why not? It was only dinner. Did she invite him? Did he already know, anyway? Bridget wasn't sure what the protocol here was. Everyone in town knew each other, but they all had their own social circles. Would it be improper to bring someone else to an already planned dinner? And, well, what about Paolo? Bridget stopped herself. Why was she even worrying, still, about Paolo?

Bridget decided on being truthful. "Kit and I are headed down the hill in a minute. We're going to dinner with Antonella and Lassino, and some other people." Okay, so she'd left out a few other key people that would be there ...

"Is your *boyfriend* going to be there?" Lorenzo joked, but was there a slight edge to his voice?

"I told you, I don't have a boyfriend," Bridget said plainly. Why was he being all weird now? She'd never, ever mentioned Paolo to him. Had somebody else?

"All right, Maestrina. So where you gonna be? Wanna meet up later?" Pheeww, he seemed to be over the alleged-boyfriend thing.

"We're going to some restaurant right next to the disco. I don't know what time we'll be done, though, seeing as how we're running a little late."

"Oh, I know the place. It's one of Fabio's restaurants. I'll meet you later, then. Hit the disco afterward?" he suggested.

"Okay, I'll see you there. But, wait a minute. I thought we were supposed to be on a break from each other," laughed Bridget.

He laughed slightly, then said, "Yeah, I know. How 'bout a little break from the break? Do you think you can handle that?"

"Oh, I *guess* so." Bridget sighed in mock resignation. *Yess! Of course she could. Could he?*

"All right, Maestrina, I'll see you then. Ciao."

"Ciao, Lorenzo," she answered and clicked the phone off. So, the break was over.

✦   ✦   ✦

They'd actually made it down the hill (via taxi) and had only been a mere ten minutes late. The miracle of their semitimely arrival was ultimately due to Kit deciding to forego a thorough blow-drying and flatironing of her hair.

Kit explained in resignation that it was just going to have to be an "au natural" night, yet she kept lamenting over the wildness of her hair. Bridget reminded her that she had a gorgeous tan and at least her clothes still fit quite nicely, unlike some people. Not to mention the fact that she also didn't have the added stress of having a death warrant on her head, issued by some disgruntled Aussie.

"God, I hope I'm not poisoned tonight. Why, why, does *she* have to come to dinner tonight, too?" Bridget had worried.

Well, Kit wouldn't argue with Bridget about scary Rachel. Although Bridget was prone to a bit of exaggeration at times, Kit was glad it wasn't her and felt bad about hoping that there would be no guilt by association. But, Rachel was a grown woman. Surely, she'd be over it by now.

And that aside, Kit had to admit that a bit of wavy hair, while in Italy, was a given but a small price to pay for the beautiful day they'd had and the evening they were about to enjoy. She would try to get over her hair issues.

"You know, the only one who'll probably comment on how bad my hair looks is Lassino!" Wow, but her hair was more than a bit wavy, wasn't it? It had somehow turned into a super-huge, blonde, glowing mane, which caused her to further whine, "Ughhh! My hair is awful! I look like a lion!" She slammed the heavy, green door behind her.

"You're fine. But hurry up, Mufasa, the cab's waiting!" Bridget had called down the stairs from the street.

When the taxi stopped in the "square," they jumped out and frantically made their way down the slippery cobblestone path till they hit the last flight of steps that led down to the beach promenade. Bridget was quite thankful she'd decided to wear some simple flip-flops, even though they didn't appear to make it any easier. She caught herself a few times before completely letting her feet slip out from under her on the uneven stones. She really might as well have worn some ridiculous heels.

Kit, however, had opted for ridiculously towering wooden platforms. She lagged a bit behind Bridget, and halfway down the stairs, she stopped suddenly and pulled off her shoes. There was no need to jeopardize the evening with a broken leg, although, she thought, she'd gladly overlook any pain and suffering tonight.

At the bottom of the steps stood all their boating companions from that day, everyone who'd been on Paolo's boat, as well as those who'd shown up later with Giorgio, plus a few more cousins and friends. All familiar faces.

"Oh, my God, look how many people ... and they're all waiting for us!" Bridget muttered over her shoulder to Kit as they hopped down the last couple of steps. As they did so, Paolo led the others in a round of applause, which caused the nearby diners on both sides of the stairs to look up in wonder.

"Hello," Bridget said shyly, close to mortification. She looked at the smiling, applauding group in puzzlement. "What?"

Antonella answered instead, "Brava, Bridget and Kit! Lassino told us we should leave and go eat, that he would wait since you'd be another hour or two!" She looked over at Lassino in mock exasperation. Lassino didn't reply, but he held his watch literally two inches away from his glasses and squinted at it. He dropped his wrist slightly and stared at Kit, then jerked his wrist up again to check his watch.

"Huh! How was I to know? She's always late!" He hurumphed and threw a thumb in Kit's direction. With a face-shrug, he gave a slight smile and said, "Well, let's go!" And off he shuffled, leaving the group behind. Kit quickly put her shoes back on, scampered after him, and called, "Where are we going?"

Lassino called over his shoulder, "Fabio's restaurant."

Fabio's restaurant? Kit was hit with excitement and nauseousness. Fabio's restaurant was pretty exclusive. It was exciting in the fact that it was well known for all the vacationing stars who dined there. And Kit could've sworn Oprah had featured it on one of her "best of the best"-type shows.

She couldn't believe she and Bridget would be eating there! She hoped for a star-spotting of any type. Not only was there that; also, the food was supposedly to die for. Hell, Oprah ought to know.

But, of course, Kit's excitement was dutifully tainted by a feeling of slight nausea. This was *Fabio's* restaurant. She hadn't run into him since she'd declined his nanny offer out in the water the other day. Would he be there tonight? Most likely. *What if* ... Kit pushed any unpleasant worry from her mind. Everything would be fine. She was with Lassino and a horde of his friends and family. Fabio would leave her well alone. She could be pleasant to him without any reverberations. She didn't dislike him at all. She just didn't want to sleep with him, and she'd made that clear. There'd be nothing to worry about. Nothing and no one, not even a delightfully charming playboy, would ruin Kit's evening.

◆   ◆   ◆

After shocking Lassino with their uncharacteristically timely arrival, they headed down the restaurant-lined beachfront until they reached Fabio's restaurant, which was aptly called Ristorante Fabio. Bridget wondered how she'd never noticed the place before. It remained one of those popular eateries on the way to the disco that was continually and overly occupied well into the night. Why had they never come here for dinner before? Fabio kept insisting he'd been waiting for them to come to one of his restaurants for the last three years. Bridget had a sneaking suspicion that he'd really meant he'd been waiting for Kit to show up, but that was no surprise.

Their avoidance of any of Fabio's dining locales was nothing personal, though. Their comfortable, go-to restaurants had already been established that fateful night three summers ago when Lassino had invited them to come to his restaurant. No, it didn't do to go anywhere else when one of them was smitten with a certain pizza chef, a chef who also had other close friends in the restaurant business. There was also the small fact that all of Fabio's places were more than a little out of their price range. Oprah's hailing of this beachfront establishment as one of her top-ten best picks in dining most certainly meant it was super-upscale, trendy, overcrowded, and overpriced. So besides Kit's crazed hair, the money issue had caused them a bit of a dilemma this evening as well. How much cash to bring?

The usual splitting the check in half with their Visa cards would not be applicable.

When Bridget had inquired about it, Kit had commented, "I don't know how much to bring, Bridget. I mean, I saw the bill from lunch, and it was eighty euros a person. And they paid for both of us!"

Bridget had gasped. She certainly didn't want them to think they expected to be paid for like that again. But based on where they were dining tonight, the meal was bound to cost a lot more than eighty euros! Bridget didn't want to fathom thinking about spending that much on a mere dinner. She wouldn't even be able to enjoy the meal, knowing she would undoubtably go over her Weight Watchers points for the week! In a perfect world, she would have taken up smoking effortlessly (like everyone else here) and therefore curbed her appetite, so that she was whittled down to a svelte, supermodel-esque physique (emaciated, gaunt—whatever, she wouldn't have minded) by the time she got on the plane for home.

However, nothing, thus far, had gone according to plan on this trip. And now she was going to spend even more money, money she could spend on something like, say, the sandals at Paolo's boutique she'd had her eye on. That was a lot of money for a pair of sandals, too—maybe letting the boys pay for one more meal wasn't such a bad idea …

No! Lassino and Paolo had been gracious enough already. As a result, they decided to err on the safe side, so they practically bankrupted the Bancomat (ATM) on their mad dash to get down to the beach.

Bridget wondered if Fabio would be here tonight or at one of his other restaurants. It would probably be better if he weren't here, for Kit's sake. His nanny offer to Kit had been less than altruistic. Bridget had been tempted to reprimand Kit with an, "I told you so. He's not looking to hire you for the nanny position. He's looking to hire you for some *other* positions!" How easy it would have been to chide her friend for her obliviousness to what she herself would've considered a complete come-on from the the very beginning. Yes, Bridget knew she was prone to compulsory cynical thoughts about, say, *everything*, but *come on*.

However, while Kit played her sunny, blonde card quite well, she was not stupid. In fact, Bridget knew better than most that her friend was very intuitive and even shrewd, if need be. Best to drop the subject. If you made too big a deal about any one of Kit's decisions to do or not do something, she was likely to do the opposite just to prove she could. And the last thing she needed was to get entangled with Fabio. Bridget again worried if he'd be here tonight. Everybody in town knew everything in milliseconds, what with them being a mere text (or a pair of binoculars) away from each other.

To her relief, it was not Fabio who stood out front greeting people, but some other Posi gentleman, another recognizable figure from the disco—or was it the beach, or the café by the apartment? Or all three? Who knew? Aside from his shaved head and funky Prada glasses, he could've doubled for sauve Fabio, clad in chic Armani pants, a crisp, white button-down, and expensive sandals. He greeted them warmly and led them straightaway to a long table. Apparently, he'd known their group was coming. Five square, white-clothed tables had been pushed together and occupied a very prominent position at the front of the restaurant, looking out upon the beach-walk promenade, which was clearly a place to see and be seen.

And now they were seated here, among the supposed rich and famous. Bridget wished she could enjoy the sultry glitz of it all, but she was awkwardly squeezed in between Paolo and Rachel. Bridget felt she was serving as the unfortunate buffer between the two, and who was going to be *her* buffer? At least, with Rachel *next* to her, Bridget wouldn't have to dodge her dirty looks all night. However, she was in the line of fire with Stefano, who sat across from her. While he'd been somewhat cooler toward her after she and Paolo had been attached at the lip, he continually stared at her, as if he were trying to figure her out—either that or undress her (gag!). It was unsettling and almost as unnerving as Paolo purposefully draping his arm around her and caressing her shoulder.

What was she supposed to do? This was all wrong! And Kit would be of no help. Seated at the end of the table, she seemed about a million miles away, so engrossed with Lassino, Giorgio, and the others next to her, that she was oblivious to Bridget's uncomfortable plight. If she could have, Bridget would have crawled under the table and headed straight for the disco to wait for Lorenzo. But that wasn't possible either, and she was starving again, anyway.

What was with this country that made her so hungry? She guessed she'd just have to stay and eat. And drink. There was no shortage of wine and prosecco being served. This could be troublesome, since the elegant antipasti platters were quite miniscule. Marinated olives and delicately sliced proscuitto with beautiful melon cubes were not cutting it. And who knew what was for dinner? No menus had been brought out. Somehow, amidst the table seating arrangements going on and despite the clamorous waiters and diners alike, Lassino managed to order for everyone. At this point, Bridget didn't care what it was. She'd eat it. Total starvation mode wasn't the ideal frame of mind to be in when trying to wisely dispense of your Weight Watchers food points, but she'd passed that point about the minute she'd stepped off the plane in Naples. Her stomach growled impatiently.

Thankfully, the crowded surrounding tables and the loud table banter made it impossible for anyone to hear her rumbling gurgles. Bridget would have to be content to sip away at her prosecco, hopeful to be left alone and out of any precarious conversations with Rachel, Stefano, or even Paolo, for that matter. He really needed to stop touching her. She nearly winced each time she felt his fingers drum softly against her shoulder.

There was no doubt that Paolo was a bonafide hunk in all sense of the word, the dreamiest of all Italian—*no,* make that all *male* standards (at least, twenty-six-year-old-male standards)—but it wasn't right. Well, he wasn't right for her, no matter how much she'd been enthralled by the idea of it all before. And now all she could think of was Lorenzo. What was wrong with her? What did she want? Who did she want? And when had she ever had choices? Something was wrong. And it also had to do with the fact that someone was touching her flip-flopped foot. Why was someone touching her foot? Her *foot* was being *touched. Right now.* By someone else's *foot.* Someone was touching her foot! *Who was it?*

✦   ✦   ✦

Kit stood up from her chair and scooted away from the table, swatting Lassino's hand away from her rear. She smiled back at him widely, and then looked to the rest of her corner of the table and then briefly at Bridget. Was she imagining it, or was Bridget making some kind of face at her? She couldn't be sure. She'd had a few glasses of prosecco and had started on a glass of wine, so a happy tipsiness had begun to settle over her, possibly impairing her (already impaired) vision as well. However, Bridget was the facial-queen extraordinaire. Besides her expressions of exaggerated boredom or surprise, there was the typical look of irritation, usually directed at her (for some unknown reason) or at some other unfortunate person in the vicinity, or else, there was her famous look of distress or warning (depending upon the situation), which either conveyed the messages of "Help me!" or "Watch out! This guy's a loon!"

Yes, she'd perfected her facial techniques to an almost Jim Carrey-like art form, often able to singlehandedly send any approaching or lingering men away with the slightest arch of her eyebrow. Kit had learned to pick and choose when to ignore Bridget's looks, as they sometimes lead to minor misunderstandings and altercations between them, and when all was said and done, was it really worth it? Besides, Kit hated to admit it (and usually didn't), but Bridget had become pretty adept at spotting playboy losers, what with dating Seamus for so long. She guessed she couldn't complain too much. It was like almost having her own personal bodyguard, wasn't it?

However, tonight was a different story. Neither of them needed protection. So, Kit decided she was going to pretend she didn't see Bridget's fake-tormented look of pain. Her best friend was quite overly dramatic at times. And what could be wrong now? There was no way Rachel could do absolutely anything to her. Bridget was in good hands; in fact, Paolo's hands were practically all over her. No one else would have a chance. Could she not just go with things and stick it out? Bridget might have a momentary freak-out, but in the end, she always conceded to have had a good time.

Yes, while Bridget was adept with the facial cues, Kit was highly proficient with playing things off as if everything was quite fine. Of course, there were some things she wouldn't ease up on. No, let it be known that she wasn't a pushover, by any means, for goodness sake! But for the most part, she was a true believer in living in the moment, and to do so, positive thoughts and energy were necessary. Sometimes overlooking negative feelings on the part of yourself or others was imperative. Well, as long as they were trivial. For instance, the face Bridget was making (if, indeed, Kit wasn't seeing double due to the alcohol) was most likely due to another one of her friend's negative thoughts about herself. Ten to one, it had to do with her weight, since she had such a ridiculous hang-up about it. Bridget was probably lamenting the fact that she'd had another prosecco and didn't have any more Weight Watchers points (or whatever they were called) left to eat dinner.

She'd spend all night being pissy and scaring away the Italians. No good could come of negativity like that. Kit would let her sort it out herself. Besides, Bridget could be scary when she was annoyed. As long as Bridget wasn't in mortal danger, Kit could easily pretend not to notice. Just like she pretended not to notice the looks she was getting from various men as she squeezed by the crowded tables in search of the bathroom. She wasn't even showing much cleavage tonight. It must be her ferocious blonde hair. Being in the sun had made it a little too blonde, even for her standards. In fact, she felt like she had a hat on, a hot, fluffy hat that she couldn't take off. Kit skirted past waiters carrying dizzying platters of entrees and finally found a removed alcove that was the entrance to the ladies' room. She put her hand on the doorknob but stopped short when she heard, "Well, to what do I owe the honor of having you in my restaurant tonight?"

Kit turned around. Dressed in a black T-shirt and expensive jeans, Fabio leaned against the wall behind her, with a knowing grin on his chiseled face.

"Oh, hi, Fabio." Kit noted the nervous catch in her voice. She didn't know why she was surprised. This was his restaurant, wasn't it? Gaining quick composure, she added, "Yes, I finally am here ..." her voice tapered off. She was unsure of what to say next—and she really needed to use the bathroom. She fought the urge to cross her legs.

"Yes, you are finally here. You came with Lassino," Fabio stated assuredly, but with a tinge of disdain.

"Yes, well, and Bridget, and Paolo, and Antonella, and many others," Kit explained, almost defensively. She rebuked herself silently. Why did she need to explain anything to Fabio, anyway?

He chuckled, showing off his perfectly white teeth. "Ah, very good. Thank you for bringing your friends; although, I'd be lying if I didn't say I'd prefer it was just you. Then you could receive my full attention." He spoke jokingly, but Kit felt it was no joke.

In spite of this, she kept it light and said, "Well, actually, *they* invited me to dinner. Besides, there's no way you'd be able to give me extra attention. It's so crowded here. You do a very good business!" Could he please leave now, so she could go to the bathroom? She was going to explode. Not to mention that in this heat, she felt like she was totally pitting out. She'd been in such a hurry to get out the door that she couldn't even remember if she'd put on deodorant.

"It's not always business, Kit." Fabio gazed at her, letting his dark eyes run up and down her frame.

"Right," she answered and turned toward the bathroom door again.

"You've got to have some fun, Kit. You've got to *live*." She knew how to live, Kit thought in disgust. She had been doing it all summer.

She sighed into the bathroom door, and then she turned and said brightly, "I always have fun. You don't have to worry about me, Fabio."

He stepped toward and said, "I don't believe you." He put one hand up against the bathroom door, leaned closer, and whispered, "Two hours with me, Baby. You will change your mind. I guarantee it. You will stay in Positano."

Not this again. *Really?* The whole "two hours with him" (at nighttime, *of course*) that was going to entail some kind of life-altering, mind-blowing sexual experience, so much so that she'd leave her lucrative job and ditch her family and friends to shack up with Fabio, until he tired of her and found some bimbo to replace her! Never mind that she'd possibly be more than willing to do that with Lassino—but that was beside the point! And it was totally a whole different situation with Lassino. Ha! The closest she'd get to nannying would be in dealing with *Lassino*, since he was so immature. That didn't sound too appealing, either. She and her bladder were not in the mood for this conversation right now.

Kit chuckled, shook her head, and whispered back, with a firm smile in place, "No, thank you. Excuse me." She tried reaching for the doorknob, but Fabio stood still, partially blocking it.

He stared at her, as if taken aback by her polite refusal. Then, almost as suddenly, he changed the subject by saying huskily, "Your hair is beautiful tonight."

What? Kit wished she were bald. This was ridiculous. He didn't get the answer he wanted, so Fabio thought he could woo her with a cheesy compliment? She stared at Fabio incredulously.

Mistaking her shocked look for some sort of request for more obsequeious complimenting, he growled, "You shine like the sun. Your hair is like a golden halo."

A golden halo? Please, more like a dead animal or (she hated to admit) a freakish Rip Taylor-type toupee, on top of her head! Enough was enough. Would kneeing Fabio in the groin be a little too harsh? Kit was quite tempted, given her desperate bladder. She was saved from making a decision, as the door was pulled open from the other side by someone coming out. Fabio stumbled slightly and then regained composure.

"Scusa, Madam," he said chivalrously and stepped backward, bowing. The woman gave him a dirty look and scooted past. As she did so, Kit seized this opportunity to jump into the bathroom. She shut the door quickly and locked it. If anyone else wanted to come in, they were just going to have to wait. Her only concern now was whether or not Fabio would be gone when she came back out.

✦ ✦ ✦

Bridget sat, tensely rigid, while the phantom massager had his way with her foot. At least, she assumed it belonged to one of the males at the table. Her eyes darted from Paolo, at her side, to Stefano across the table, along with some other fellows next to him, whose names she couldn't remember at the moment. The table was so close that her view of what was going on underneath was obstructed by the long, white tablecloth. She knew it should've been obvious as to who was doing this, but she couldn't tell from which direction the assaulting foot was coming. At times, it seemed to be creep out from where Paolo's feet would be, at other times, from somewhere across the table. The foot kept massaging the top of her foot and in between her toes, which might have been relaxing if she was reclined in the vibrating massage chair at the Vietnamese nail salon she went to for pedicures when Julianna was overbooked. Unfortunately, she wasn't enjoying this one bit. Bridget kept drawing her feet back, but the foot kept coming. She'd tried in vain to get her foot on top of it to push it away but was immediately squashed down by another foot, which she assumed to be its mate. Bridget felt like she was playing thumb war, but with her toes.

To compound things, Paolo's hand had left her shoulder, only to find its way to her thigh, where it began its own massage session. She tried swatting it away, but then he would grab onto her hand playfully before reaching for her knee or thigh again. Bridget mentally added new body parts to her growing list of off-limit regions: the paunchy stomach area was always a no-go, and she now never wanted the fleshy top portions of her "drumsticks" touched, nor did she desire her feet to ever be fondled (unless, of course, by her little Vietnamese friends).

She was beside herself with squirming agitation. Would the dinner never come? Surely, the distraction of food would put a halt to all this repellent foot-touching? Finally unable to stand it any longer, Bridget decided to take matters into her own hands—er, or feet, specifically. With all her might, she would kick the offending feet away, hopefully, hard enough to make the culprit cry out in pain, thus unveiling him in embarrassment. And then she'd be left alone with just Paolo's hand to pry away from her thigh. Bridget took a deep breath and kicked her foot forward so hard and with such swift force that the table was jolted suddenly, spilling several wine glasses. This produced a "What the bloody fuck?" from Rachel, as her glass was one of the disturbed few that spilled, as well as a loud thud and then a "Goddamnit!" as Bridget's foot slammed against the metal pole in the middle of the table.

All table conversation ceased as everyone turned to look at Bridget. Kit looked perplexed and asked, "Are you okay?"

No, she was *not* okay! Her foot had been mercilessly molested for the past fifteen minutes, and now she'd re-bruised her poor Nutella foot, and all in vain.

She blushed and muttered through clenched teeth, "I'm fine. Sorry, sorry, just trying to move my foot. I thought it … had fallen asleep."

Rachel smirked and said snarkily, "Oh, Bridget, stop trying to play footsies with Stefano over there. You passed on your chance with him this afternoon, now, didn't you?"

Bitch. She *would* say that. The others merely stared at her in slight confusion, as if she was the poor child with Tourette's Syndrome, then returned to their conversations. Paolo looked at her imploringly, his hand still planted firmly on her thigh, and exclaimed, "Ho, my Gad, are you all right?" Bridget winced as she tried to shift in her chair. She could feel a slight throb in her foot—nothing as bad as the Nutella avalanche, but it still smarted.

"Would you like me to look at it?" Stefano pushed his chair back and lifted the tablecloth as if he were about to crawl under the table. Oh, *now* he was a foot doctor? Like hell was she going to let him come anywhere near her lower body. She'd risk another pole-kicking if need be. From the corner of her eye, Bridget saw Rachel smile slightly. She clearly was enjoying Bridget's pain.

"No," Bridget panicked. "I'm fine, thank you," she tried adding calmly.

Stefano shrugged and sat back down.

"Sure you're okay?" Paolo squeezed Bridget's thigh (again) and then swung his arm back around her shoulder. Relieved his hand was off her thigh, Bridget now wondered what she could do about his arm being on her shoulder. If ever she was going into her antisocial mode, it was right now. She wanted her own space, away from wandering feet and hands. She needed to end this. Bridget took her hand and grabbed onto Paolo's, in an effort to swat-free her shoulder.

It was then that Rachel chirped loudly, "Hi, there, Lorenzo."

What? Lorenzo? Here, already? How funny. Right? For a moment, Bridget thought she'd heard Rachel say hello to *Lorenzo*, as if he was standing before them. But she had, hadn't she? Bridget looked up and across the table and found that Rachel was, indeed, correct. Dammit. Lorenzo stood there and stared at her and then Paolo, his bright-green eyes questioning under scowling eyebrows. Bridget suddenly remembered that Paolo still had his hand attached to her shoulder territorily, and worse, that her hand was on top of his, as if she was holding it there willingly, instead of trying to remove it. Bridget quickly pushed Paolo's hand off her shoulder, as if it was a pesky fly or mosquito. Paolo looked at her quizzically, as did Lorenzo. Bridget realized, whatever she did or said, it all looked pretty sketchy.

"Hi!" she squeaked as everyone at the table looked up and at Lorenzo.

"Ciao, Lorenzo." Paolo spoke first, and the rest of the table followed suit.

"Ciao." Lorenzo nodded back. He stood there, staring expectantly at Bridget, as the rest of the table went back to its lively chattering—all except Kit, who sat watching, a concerned look on her face. And of course, Rachel, who chose that moment to speak up, yet again. "I ran into Lorenzo on my way down the hill and told him to come to the restaurant. I mean, you were expecting him, right, Bridget? Although, it's too bad you didn't think to save him a seat." She looked pointedly at Bridget and then at Paolo.

Rachel had done this on purpose. She was such an evil bitch!

Bridget stammered, "Well, yeah, we were going to meet at the disco … I thought …" And her voice trailed off. She knew she sounded completely guilty, and she hadn't even done anything! Did she invite him to stay? There was no room at all at the table, and barely any room on any side of the table, as they were bunched in around other crowded diners, with hardly enough space left for the passing waiters. Would the Italians think it rude to invite another person? What did she do?

"Well, he's here now. Pull up a chair, Lorenzo. I mean, *I* don't mind if you join us!" Rachel sputtered grandly, then took a seductive swig from her wine glass.

She was going to kill the Aussie. The first Positano murder was going to be committed by her! She wasn't a violent person, and she'd never gotten into a fistfight, but Bridget was quite prepared to do so.

"And I don't mind that he's here, either!" Bridget said, her voice rising. Lorenzo looked at her with a searching gaze, as if he was trying to find out the truth about what was going on.

A waiter carrying a large tray bumped into Lorenzo and pushed him awkwardly into the back of Stefano's chair, which caused the doctor to spill wine down the front of his open shirt and onto his chest. Apparently, the food had finally arrived. "Scusa," the waiter said as he impatiently jostled his way around Lorenzo and tried to serve people their steaming plates. Stefano looked up at Lorenzo with distaste as he wiped the dribbling wine off his chin and chest with his good arm.

Lorenzo ignored him and looked at the food and then Bridget, then said awkwardly, "Oh, you haven't even eaten yet. I should ... I'm just ... gonna go. Yeah, I'm gonna go." He waited for Bridget to say something, but she was at a loss for words. What did she do? Nobody was speaking up. In fact, they acted like Lorenzo wasn't even there.

Taking her indecisive silence as a cue, Lorenzo added coolly, "Yeah, I'm gonna go. I'll just ... see you later." Without another look, Lorenzo stuck his hands in his pockets and gingerly made his way around the waiter, nodding at Kit on his way out.

Frantically, Bridget tried to stand up, but she was stuck between the shrubbery behind her and the table. She called out after him, "Okay, at the disco!" She wasn't sure if he heard her, since her words were immediately swallowed by the noisy din surrounding them. She watched him head out and down the boardwalk. She hoped he'd wait for her at the disco, but it didn't seem likely. If only she could get out of here and run after him and explain, but she was literally trapped, and the food had just come. Damn the food in this country! While the Italians were laid-back about a lot of things, mealtime was sacred. If she left the table now and didn't come back, she would surely be considered rude, as well as not right in the head.

Rachel lifted a forkful of steaming food to her lips and said with mock innocence, "That's too bad Lorenzo didn't want to stay."

Bridget was too stricken by her own self-loathing and mortification to speak. Why hadn't she said something, anything? She'd count the minutes till the meal was over.

Chapter 17

Really, the food was lovely—all four endlessly drawn-out courses of it. Who ate four courses and then dessert on top of that? *Come on.* But, yes, of course, it was heavenly, definitely worthy of Oprah's praises. Except, Bridget tasted none of it. Well, she actually lifted her fork to her lips several times, placed food in her mouth, and chewed it; thereby, she ingested food, so as not to arouse suspicion, but she tasted nothing. If she had been eating gravel, she wouldn't have known the difference. Her mind was elsewhere. Namely at the disco, where she fervently hoped Lorenzo was waiting, and patiently, during this marathon meal they were having. Bridget had stopped drinking, too. Although, it might've helped pass the time a bit, she was over it. Besides, if she drank any more, she'd probably cry. Drunken crying would interrupt the Italians' eating, and more precious time would be wasted.

When espresso and dessert finally arrived (beautiful, delicately sliced semifreddo set atop chocolate sauce, but she'd never know), everyone oo-hed and ahhed, but Bridget felt like standing up on her chair and shouting, "Hurry the fuck up, would you all? How can you people eat at a time like this?"

But she would've sounded insane since no one (except evil Rachel) knew the drama she was replaying in her mind. No one would've heard her anyway. The noise level at the table, and in general, had not ceased. Bridget heard the noise, but she didn't listen. In fact, she was making a conscious effort to not pay attention. If Rachel had turned to her and said, "I'm going to kill you now," Bridget would have looked at her blankly and said, "Sounds delightful. Thank you."

At least no one seemed to notice her lack of socializing. After all, she was deemed the "quiet" one by the Italians, anyway. At this point, striking up conversations with people or trying to butt into the myriad of random ones that were already going on, would just be pointless and, well, weird.

Only Paolo, from time to time, would look at her, a mix of concern and puppy-dog crush on his face. Finally, after course number four was cleared away and before dessert came out, he asked, "Are you okay, Bridget? You are not eating very much. Are you tie-red?"

Bridget smiled at him and said, "Yes, I think so." No, she wasn't tired at all. She was a ball of nervous agitation, tightly wound up and ready to snap at a moment's notice. Either that, or she was going to sob uncontrollably. Neither would be pretty. But she couldn't very well say that to Paolo, now could she? It was easier to just agree that she was "tie-red."

"When we are finished, I can take you home ... to my house. Or we can sit on the beach, if you do not want to go to the disco," Paolo said and grabbed her hand. Oh, no, not the hand-holding. Would the thigh-grabbing begin again too? Go to *his place* or to the *beach? The beach?* More like the rocks. She'd already fallen for that one. Bridget looked at Paolo, hopeful still that he might just be joking. There was a playful look on his face and a slight smile on his parted lips, but there was definitely intent in his eyes. Right, Italians did not joke about food, and they didn't joke about sex, either. However, Bridget admitted there was no denying that he was gorgeous, with those big, light-blue-turquoise eyes staring at her, that handsomely tanned face ... it would be very easy. Of course, the mood would be ruined when Rachel showed up and tried to kill them both. Well, Rachel would most likely just kill her. But still, that would suck. No, it was a no-go. Bridget wouldn't do it. Besides, she thought tearfully, he wasn't Lorenzo.

"Oh, I think I'll be fine to go to the disco," Bridget said. Out of the corner of her eye, she thought she detected Rachel's Jokerlike mouth turn up just a bit.

◆　◆　◆

The food had been far better than what Kit had expected. Not that she didn't expect to get anything but delicious food *anywhere* on the Amalfi coast, but Oprah's ratings kind of set the bar pretty high. Usually, these highly tauted places fell short by being overpriced and underfeeding you. Most of the time, you were just paying to be seen dining under the famous moniker. And while the latter was certainly true for Ristorante Fabio, this place, dare she say, was on par with the delectability she reserved for

Lassino's Ristorante Segreto Giardino. Yes, she dared say, but she wouldn't tell Lassino. He'd interrogate her endlessly about what she could possibly like about Ristorante Fabio and then would probably bar her from coming to *his* place to eat. Yes, of course, there was the whole Italian machismo thing, and in the restaurant business of a small town, everyone must seem like competition. She also would not tell Fabio how much she was enjoying herself here. He'd take any flattery from her as something suggestive. Thank God, he'd been gone when she peeked her head out of the bathroom.

It had all worked out, though. She'd made it back to the table un-scathed, bladder intact and back to its normal size, and had enjoyed *four* beautiful and delicious courses and then dessert. From the preliminary delicately diced sushi served in elegant martini glasses to the espresso paired with decadent semifreddo (and everything in between), Kit had savored each mouthful. She would remember it all. But just in case, she'd taken multiple pictures of each course.

"Are you going to eat or just take pictures?" Lassino grunted.

"I always eat. Here, hold up the martini glass, and I'll take a picture of you with the sushi," she'd countered. Kit was passionate about food and about her photography. She couldn't care less what anyone, even Lassino, thought about her crazily snapping away at the food. If you couldn't do this on vacation, then when could you?

And it was so pleasurable not being rushed through your meal. At home, speedy table turnover was the norm. The way people were rushed into wolfing their food down was criminal and enough to give you indigestion just watching them. And Kit had seen plenty of that while working at La Bella Vita, and that was even with true Italians running the place!

She was amazed that it was eleven thirty. They'd been there for two and a half hours and dessert had just been served, which was perfectly fine since no one showed up at the disco before midnight anyway. She could sit and listen to her Positano friends talk all night. In fact, Kit thought she'd much rather prefer to do that than go to the crowded disco, where you could barely hear anyone talk above the thumping music.

Kit wondered how Bridget was doing at her end of the table. She wasn't really at the end, but in between Rachel and Paolo (how unfortunate). She'd tried to catch Bridget's eye a few times throughout the evening but with no success. If she didn't know better, she'd think her friend was ignoring her, but Bridget wasn't talking to anyone. She appeared to be either really engrossed in something across the restaurant or she was simply staring off into space. This, no doubt, had to do with Lorenzo unexpectedly showing up way too early. Kit winced as she thought about the awkwardness of the scenario. She couldn't understand why Bridget hadn't invited Lorenzo to sit down with them. If it were her, she would have, but she did have a habit of inviting or overinviting people into any given situation, which had a tendency to get her into trouble at times. But even though Lorenzo had shown up sooner than necessary due to Rachel's inviting him, Kit felt Bridget really should've said something, at least offered him a seat. She just didn't understand Bridget sometimes. Kit hoped Bridget wasn't going to completely blow-off Lorenzo. She sighed and picked up her fork, ready to do some damage to her already melting semifreddo. Before she could get the fork to her mouth, she felt two hands squeeze her shoulders. She looked up and almost dropped her semifreddo. It was Fabio. Kit set her fork down with a noisy clink.

"How is everything?" Fabio addressed the table and then spoke again in Italian, no doubt reiterating what he had just said. The table combusted into a chorus of voices, "Grazie, Fabio, *tutto bene* ..."

Fabio spoke in Italian again. Kit tried to translate quickly in her head. Something about the prosecco being on the house ... she would've been able to concentrate better if she hadn't been distracted by Fabio squeezing her shoulders. He then took one hand and moved it up her neck and head, where it stopped and began fondling the side of her face. What the hell was he doing? Kit's stomach turned and rolled with a wave of nausea. And then, to her horror, she realized that no one was talking at the table. They were all staring at her. Even Bridget, who'd been practically catatonic all evening, was sitting up with wide eyes. They were gawking at her and at Fabio, who was now trying to run his hand through her lion's mane. Kit would've wrestled away from him, but Fabio's hand suddenly became ensnared in her crazy hair. He tried jerking it through smoothly, but to no avail. Ha, that'd teach him to tell her she had hair like a halo!

Ouch! Kit wanted his hand out of her hair and his hand off her shoulder, where it still lay possessively. Everyone at the table stared at Fabio as he continued talking while still attempting to untangle his hand from her hair. Kit sat in pain (due to the hair pulling) and embarrassment (due to

Fabio's sleazy touches). She snuck a look at Lassino, but his face held an unimpressed expression upon it. He was either unimpressed with Fabio or he was unimpressed with her. Or both. Did it matter? Wouldn't he help her? Wouldn't he stand up to Fabio's brazen show of disrespect? It was clear that Kit was with *Lassino*. She had only ever been with him while she was here. Lassino knew it. Everyone knew it. And Fabio knew it as well. Which was what made it all so unfathomable and disgusting. If Kit had been startled about people around here referring to her as Lassino's *amante*, what would they think of her now, with Fabio openly alluding to some kind of romantic understanding between them? She felt disgusted with Fabio and with herself. She practically felt violated and wanted to go home and shower off. And worse, she couldn't even eat now. *That* was pretty bad.

Fabio finished up whatever he was saying and then spoke in English. "Enjoy the rest of your evening." His other hand, finally free from her hat-hair, was placed back on her shoulder. He gave her shoulders another squeeze, turned, and left the table. The table was silent for a moment and then, just as suddenly, the talking resumed again as if nothing had happened. But Kit couldn't speak. She looked down at her melting semifreddo and felt tears come to her eyes. Why didn't someone just stamp a big scarlet *T* for *tramp* on her head? And she wasn't one, but everyone would think so now. And Lassino didn't even care. He hadn't even spoken up for her. Why?

"Eat your semifreddo before it's ruined," Lassino said, but not gruffly, like he usually did. Kit looked at him through her somewhat blurry eyes and saw that his face was not angry, but held more of a resigned look upon it.

Kit shook her head and said quietly, "I'm not hungry anymore."

Lassino shrugged at her and took a bite of his semifreddo.

◆　◆　◆

The check came, and Lassino waved off Bridget and Kit's attempts at flinging their wads of euros at him. But to Bridget's frustration, the deliverance of the bill didn't send everyone wildly stampeding from the table in a mad dash to the disco. Instead, it ushered in a relaxed smoking interlude, where those who indulged started passing around their cigarettes or lighters, while others (mostly the women) hit the restroom to freshen up. Bridget, stone-cold sober by now, would not be partaking in the smoking, and she didn't need to use the restroom, but she could sit there no longer. If she did, she might simultaneously combust right there on the spot. She had to get out of there. Bridget feigned like she was joining the girls and scooted out from the table. If she left, she knew for sure that Rachel would remain at the table, hopeful to get some type of conversation going with Paolo. Good, leave her to it. She only hoped that Paolo would not follow her out.

She hustled behind Kit and Antonella and whispered urgently, "I'm heading to the disco. I'll see you over there."

Kit nodded silently as Bridget practically sprinted through the restaurant. Bridget glanced quickly over her shoulder as she snuck out. No need to worry, though. The lively restaurant was still buzzing, distracting anyone from noticing her hasty departure. *Please let Lorenzo be there,* Bridget prayed. She would explain everything, if he was there, if he would listen.

Be there; be there; be there, she repeated inside her head as she swiftly made her way down the last few feet of the boardwalk. When she reached the bottom of the disco's stone staircase, Bridget hesitated. Did she climb the stairs and go in, or should she just go back to the apartment?

Go on, now. Go in! her little voice encouraged.

But her heart had begun to pound. Her mouth suddenly felt dry like sandpaper, and she was sweating. Well, she was sweating more than usual for her. *No, no, no. I'm just going to go back to the apartment.* Yes, the apartment was a much safer option. Her heart seemed to slow back down to its normal pace, as if in relief.

How old are you? Don't be an idiot! You're here. Get up those stairs! commanded the voice. How annoying this voice was once again being, Bridget thought. *But it's pointless! Pointless, I tell you! He's not even going to be there.*

It's not pointless at all! You don't know that he's not there. Go in and find out! the voice urged on peskily.

But, but ...

But, what?

But what if Lorenzo is annoyed with me? she whined to herself. *And worse, what if he won't even speak to me? Come on, a little sympathy here, please ...*

And why wouldn't he be annoyed with you? He shows up and there's Paolo, draped all over you, and you don't even invite him to sit down! How the hell is he supposed to feel?

Excuse me, I didn't plant Paolo's hand on my shoulder—or my thigh, for that matter!

The voice relented, if only slightly. *All right, fair enough, but you could've been a little more polite. What's the matter with you?*

She tried to reason with herself. *Look, I already feel bad enough! There was no room! Then he walked away. What was I supposed to do? Catapult myself over the table?*

Well, that would've been a nice gesture …

That's it. I'm leaving! He hates me now anyway! Bridget knew when she was beaten. She'd blown it. Why go in for more rejection? Because that was sure to happen once she found Lorenzo and tried to explain. Defeated, she turned away from the staircase.

The voice quickly reasoned, *Whoa, whoa, whoa! Lorenzo doesn't hate you. He probably thinks you hate him! That's why you need to apologize to him. And if he's still mad, at least you can say you tried. But you'll never know if you don't even go in.*

Bridget wavered. The voice had a point (or two). Dammit. *Fine, fine! I'll go into the damn disco! You know, you're really quite annoying and bossy.*

The voice answered smugly, *Of course I am. I'm you, aren't I? Come on, now, go for it!*

Bridget rolled her eyes at herself and sighed, and then she turned around with grim determination. When it came down to it, you just couldn't argue with your conscience, could you? Especially when it was Catholic. Oh, what a scourge it was.

Thankfully, there was no line to get in, being that it was only a mere midnight. By Positano standards, the night was quite young. It might be young, but Bridget sure hoped she wasn't too late. She flip-flopped noisily up the stone steps and tried to pump herself up for the daunting, humbling task at hand. She could *so* do this! How bad could talking to Lorenzo be? He liked her! At least, he used to like her. But, he might still like her! You couldn't just turn off your feelings for someone, could you? Maybe, Lorenzo even *loved* her. If you could love someone who acted like a complete dork most of the time. But that was an endearing quality about her, right? He *might* love her! If he didn't already hate her.

Did she love him? Honestly, Bridget really didn't know. The thought of her possibly loving, really loving, someone else again (someone that she wasn't related to) had never occurred to her. Anything was possible, of course, but … she was so far from there right now, she couldn't even fathom it. And now, if she began to, she'd be heading right back down the stairs. But she was definitely *in like*—*real* like, not superficial, meaningless, rebound like. This was good! She hadn't felt this way in quite a long time.

Surely, Lorenzo would at least listen while she explained that she was, well … not interested in Paolo (wait a minute now) … *at all.* This was amazing, an astounding revelation! Bridget smiled to herself. It had taken her all this—the mini-"break," the boat trip with annoying Stefano, the Blue Grotto, Paolo all over her—to figure out that it was Lorenzo she wanted! It wasn't too late! He wouldn't reject her, no! *Who wouldn't want you, Bridget?* she thought vehemently. *Well, let's not get carried away here …* a typical negative thought popped into her head, but was instantly silenced by a *Shhh! Don't interrupt yourself. You're on a roll! And you made it up the steps!*

It was true. She had reached the top of the staircase. Bridget felt as if the theme to Rocky should be blaring, so she could raise both arms in the air and do the Rocky shuffle. Instead, through the open door, Madonna's "Sorry" was pumping.

"I don't wanna hear; I don't wanna know; please don't say you're sorry …"

The exuberant feeling of victory began to wane slightly. She hoped this wasn't an omen of what was to come. She stepped inside and received her drink card. Adjusting her eyes to the dimness and the spinning strobes, she scanned the place. It wasn't obscenely packed yet, but it was crowded enough. She'd start at the bar first.

She sidestepped dancers and made her way to the end of the bar, and she immediately spotted lurky Vinnie at the other end. You couldn't miss his six-foot body stuffed into super-tight, red pants. Who wore red pants? *She might've had a pair in the '80s …* and his unbuttoned linen shirt, chest hair aplenty spilling out. Too bad he couldn't grease the chest hair back, like he did the hair on his head. Eeewww. She shuddered and quickly looked away to avoid any accidental eye contact. Thankfully, before averting her eyes, she'd already seen that Lorenzo was not at that end of the bar.

"Ciao, Bella!" said an American voice right next to her. Bridget turned to find a grinning Johnny standing beside her. Boy, Italy had been good for him, Bridget couldn't help but think again. The whole smolderingly hunky boy-next-door look had not been a figment of her imagination last night.

Bridget tried not to be too obvious as she gave him a sneaky once-over. She was quite distracted and almost dropped her clutch over the fact that he was wearing a pair of True Religions. A good ol' Spokanite boy wearing trendy jeans? Bridget guessed that these types of vacation-in-Italy fashion metamorphoses must occur all the time. Before she could detract herself any further by Johnny's extreme Italian makeover, she smiled and said, "Johnny! Hey! Enjoying Positano?"

"Love it. All I've done here is eat, drink, and lay on the beach. It's awesome!" He laughed.

"That's what you do here. Although, today, we did actually take a boat trip, and we visited the Blue Grotto," Bridget stated proudly.

"Oh, I've been meaning to look into going on one of those day tours," Johnny mused enthusiastically, and then he asked, "How do you get on one of those tours?"

"Oh, we didn't actually take a real tour. We went with some friends, Antonella, and Paolo, and Lass … ino. Yeah, and some others." Bridget hadn't meant to throw Lassino's name out in front of Johnny.

He shrugged. "It's okay, Bridget. I would've assumed he'd be there. Besides, I just ran into your friend a little while ago, and he told me you were all out to dinner next door anyway."

Her friend?

"My friend?" squeaked Bridget with nervous hope.

"Yeah, the one you were with last night down at the beach party. Lorenzo, right?" Johnny looked at her a bit strangely.

"Lorenzo!" Bridget almost shouted. "Yes, Lorenzo. Is he here?" she asked quickly and looked around.

"Yeah, he was here at the bar, and then he headed over there." Johnny pointed across the crowded dance floor to the other side of the club.

She jerked her head in the direction he was pointing. The dance floor was a jungle of sweaty, moving bodies. There was no way to tell if Lorenzo was on the other side of that vast moshness. Unless he was dancing in the middle … with *someone else*. Time to go.

But Johnny interrupted her thoughts when he said, "So … that sounds like a fun day. And you all had dinner together?"

Bridget had a feeling she knew where this conversation was headed, and she wanted to avoid it altogether. "Uh, yeah, it was a … nice day. Dinner was … nice … but kind of um … long, a lot of food," she added blandly, trying to downplay the day and evening. She stood there, unsure of what to say next.

"So, is everyone coming to the disco after dinner?" Johnny asked too casually.

Yes, Kit will be here. Bridget knew that was what Johnny was trying to find out. And Kit would be there. Well, she had been planning on coming. Of course, Fabio's strange appearance at the table and his overt fondling of Kit in front of everyone had seemingly put a damper on Kit's mood. But Bridget had noticed that when she'd hightailed it out of the restaurant, everyone else had still been quite geared-up to go to the disco, including unpredictable Lassino.

But she didn't have time to catch Johnny up to speed on the details of dinner or have a Dr. Phil-type conversation about Kit right now. She must get away and search for Lorenzo! What if he was helping some other girl get a drink at the bar? What if he took that girl on his scooter for cornetti? And then back to his house for cappuccino? And then they fell asleep and spent the next day together, and his mother really liked her and invited her to stay for dinner, and … Bridget replayed the night they'd met and their first couple of days spent together on fast-forward. And then warp speed. Oh, no, no, no! Take some other girl home? She couldn't let that happen!

She smiled at Johnny and began to say, "I'm gonna go," but he gently put a hand on her arm and asked, "Bridget, is Kit still with that guy? That … that—"

"Lassino?" Bridget asked as she looked into Johnny's concerned face.

"I was about to say Italian playboy, but, okay, Lassino. Believe me, that's not a name I'll ever forget," he answered dryly.

Lassino a playboy? He was an eccentric, enigmatic figure in the town, a handsome, well-connected pizza chef who loved fashion and food, was near-blind, and spoke so fast that even his own friends sometimes had a hard time understanding him. He was a Positano *male,* but a playboy? Bridget just didn't see it, but then again, maybe she should try to imagine Lassino through Johnny's eyes. Bridget conjured up every Italian male stereotype that existed and multiplied it by ten. Poor Johnny. In his mind, Lassino was probably some swarthy, slick-haired, Gucci-wearing, gold-chained, yacht-owning, Italian business mogul-love-God. Well, he'd be dead on with the Gucci part. But then again, when it came down to it, whether Lassino was dirt poor or a millionaire, to Johnny, it made no difference. Lassino was simply the man who had stolen Kit away from him. Of course, Lassino and Kit would beg to differ on the "stolen" part.

So, new Italian girlfriend from Venice or not, Johnny was still in love with Kit. The pained look on his face was proof enough. He stood there, waiting for an answer, but Bridget didn't think she quite had one, or at least one that made any sense. Her best friend's love life had become somewhat of a mysterious roulette game here—either that, or a bad game of craps.

"I don't know, Johnny," Bridget answered honestly. Then, seeing what appeared to be a flicker of hope wash over his face, Bridget quickly spoke up. "*Johnny.* Look, I really don't know what's going on with them or what's going to happen, but Kit is *with* Lassino right now. Okay?"

That was about all she could tell him. Bridget knew about as much as Kit knew, and that wasn't saying much. Kit barely knew what was going on from one day to the next! And what would happen when Kit walked into the disco tonight and was greeted by a True Religion-clad Johnny, his Venetian girlfriend in tow? What would happen when Johnny and Lassino finally met? Shit would surely hit the dance floor. And through it all, Kit would play it off somehow, as if it was no big deal at all. Until she got back to the apartment. Oh, boy. Bridget hoped she was long gone (with Lorenzo) by the time that happened. Which reminded her that she should be having some sort of conversation with Lorenzo right now. She had to find him first.

Johnny ran his hand through his hair, winced slightly, and said, "Maybe it was a mistake for me to come here. I just thought … shit, I don't know what I thought." He gave a rueful laugh.

Bridget knew. Johnny had flown around the world because he was in love with Kit. It was beautiful and tragic at the same time. She felt a pang as she wondered if anyone would ever love her enough to hop on a plane and follow her to Italy … or to California.

Bridget patted Johnny's arm and said, "Hey, I think it's great. And if anyone asks, you just tell them you came to Italy for a *vacation*. And I really hope you got one." Bridget looked at him knowingly.

Johnny smiled back at her in understanding. "That's right; I came here for a vacation! Hey, I know it's gonna sound like I'm just saying this, but no matter what happens, I am glad I came. This country is *incredible*. This town is … well, I can't even explain it! I can finally understand why you and Kit come here."

Supermodel-esque Laura came up and wrapped herself around Johnny. "Ciao, Bridget." She nodded sweetly before she ducked her head into Johnny's neck.

Johnny threw an arm around Laura and said, "Bridget was just telling me about the boat trips to Capri and the Blue Grotto. Maybe we should go on one tomorrow. What do you think?"

Laura nodded her approval. Now that Laura was here, Bridget thought she was safe to excuse herself.

"Well, I'm gonna see if I can find Lorenzo," she said and smiled at them.

Johnny reached a free hand out and said, "Thanks, Bridget." Bridget smiled over her shoulder and Johnny called out, "Hey, Bridget. Lorenzo—I like him!"

"Me, too!" she replied and began wading her way across the dance floor. This was no easy task. How to look, really look, for someone on the dance floor without making eye contact with any of the men looking for a female dance partner? Being on the short side, she found all she mostly saw was chest, and all kinds of it, at that. Ugh, if Lorenzo even knew what she was suffering through in an effort to find him! Bridget finally reached the other side of the dance floor and practically threw herself onto the "smoking" steps, the steps that led up to the bathrooms. Various people lounged about on the steps, talking, smoking, and taking in the cooler night air coming in through the large, open windows. Bridget climbed a few steps and surveyed the dance floor and club in front of her. He was not out there. She would have seen his tall frame hovering above the rest.

"Ciao, Bridget!" Suddenly, a body was approaching her from the steps below. Minus his windshield-type sunglasses, Bridget recognized pony-tailed Tomaso right away. She looked to see what his T-shirt would read tonight. The bright yellow tee said in big, bold letters: "F.B.I.," and underneath, in just slightly smaller print: "Female Body Inspector." Where did he find these shirts? Only in Positano would she find the hilarity and not the absurdity of it.

"Ciao, Tomaso! Nice shirt." She smirked at him.

"Oh, you like? Do you need some inspecting?" He jokingly raised his eyebrows at her.

She laughed, shook her head, and said, "Actually, I'm trying to find Lorenzo. Have you seen him?"

Tomaso raised his eyebrows in recognition. "Ah, Lorenzo! Si, I saw him, but he left already."

"What? How long ago?" Bridget asked in alarm.

Tomaso shrugged and turned his hands up slightly. "Uh, I don't know—"

Trying not to sound desperate, Bridget asked, "A long time ago, or a short time ago?"

She waited painfully as Tomaso scratched his head. "Hmmmm, *allora ... allora* ... maybe about ... ten minutes ago?"

Ten minutes ago? That wasn't too long, but it was long enough. If she left now, she might have a chance to catch him before he got back to the garage to get his scooter!

Before Tomaso could say anything else, Bridget hugged him hard and said, "Thank you, Tomaso! Ciao, grazie!" She waved at him as she bounded down the steps.

He grinned boyishly and then nodded after her with cocky suaveness as he called, "Of course, Bridget. Anytime; you just ask Tomaso ... the female body inspector!" He looked around and spotted a group of girls watching him amusedly. He winked at them and said, "Want to dance?"

Bridget heard not a thing. She was already making her way through the throes of the dance floor.

✦   ✦   ✦

The restaurant had emptied out, and the waiters were stacking chairs on top of empty tables. Their group, led by Giorgio, stamped out their cigarettes and began making their way toward the door. Kit looked around. Thankfully, Fabio was nowhere to be seen. She needed to speak to Lassino about what had happened at the table. She hadn't been able to talk, to eat her dessert, to concentrate on anything at all since Fabio had stopped by the table and made such a show of touching her. Kit cringed with shame and embarrassment. And anger—how dare he!

Kit lagged behind Lassino and gently tugged on his hand.

"Lassino, I need to talk to you."

He looked back and her, grabbed her hand, and led her toward the door. "Okay," he said.

"Wait, stop. Can I talk to you here, while the others go on ahead?" Kit asked hopefully. She really wasn't in the mood to argue with Lassino. She hoped he'd be patient and listen.

Lassino stopped and looked at her inquiringly. "What is it?"

Kit exhaled and blurted out, "I want to talk about what happened with Fabio. At the table." She held her breath as she waited for him to speak.

Lassino stared at her a few moments before he sighed with slight boredom and said, "Why?"

"Why? *Why?* Because I'm upset, that's why! I don't like what he did!" Kit's voice went up a bit.

Lassino shook his head calmly. "No, we're not talking about this right now."

She was not going to let him get out of discussing this with her. Kit needed Lassino to know that there was nothing going on between her and Fabio. She also was tired of guessing how Lassino felt about her.

"Why?" she demanded.

Lassino stared her down and sputtered, "Why? Why?" He tapped the side of his head and hissed, "I'm not going to talk with you about Fabio in his restaurant! You want to talk about it, okay. But not here! Understand? We'll talk about it later." He dropped her hand and began walking.

Kit stood there, limply, and watched him leave. Lassino reached the door, turned around, and said, "Come on."

Kit felt she didn't have much more energy for this. It was hard to be on guard all the time. On guard from inappropriate male advances (granted, they were harmless, most of the time), from stares, from whispers. And she was tired of always trying to decipher between the reality and the absurdity of this town. Unfortunately, most of the time, the two were intertwined.

Lassino walked back, put an arm around her, and whispered, "Come on, let's go. We'll talk about it at the disco."

She let him lead her outside.

◆　　◆　　◆

Bridget hit the bottom of the stone steps of the disco and took off, almost slipping as she hurried up the boardwalk and past Fabio's restaurant. She prayed that Paolo and the rest would not pick that moment to come outside and insist that she head back to the disco with them. The only one from their dinner party she spotted was Stefano. He was leaning against the wall outside talking to some poor girl who looked quite befuddled. From her light-blonde hair and fair skin, Bridget guessed she must be a tourist. As she rushed by, she heard Stefano say to the girl, in his thick accent, "You are like a *fox*. You know how to play the game!"

Bridget rolled her eyes and continued her fast pace. At the end of the beachwalk, she hurried up the steps and followed the familiar route that all the locals took, up the uneven cobblestone steps, past the angry cobbler's shop, around the bend, and up the bougainvillea-canopied walk. She wiped her brow and continued on, stopping only for a brief moment when she reached the window of Paolo's boutique. As she caught her breath, she paused to see if her sandals were in the window. No, just some linen ensemble. She picked up her pace again and raced on until she was in the middle of Mulini Square, where the cab drivers hung out and waited for those too tired, lazy, or drunk to make it up the hill after their night at the disco.

Bridget glanced around the square and walked past the lounging cabbies and on to the garage. She peeked her head in through the entrance. Even in the dimness, she could see that while there were a multitude of scooters, there was no Lorenzo. She had missed him. There was not much more she could do now but begin her walk back to the apartment.

◆   ◆   ◆

How on earth were they to have any sort of serious discussion in the disco? Kit thought irritably as they took their drink cards and pushed their way toward the bar. Unless you found yourself on one of the white couches in the far-off corners, you would be in the thick of the thumping music and crowd, barely able to hear the person next to you. Lassino, of course, knew that. That was it. He didn't want to talk. Kit prepared herself for Lassino to avoid talking, maybe even to avoid her once they reached the bar. And on top of that, in front of all his friends, she'd have to pretend like she was happy and enjoying herself, even though she was caught between feeling rage and being on the verge of tears. It would be exhausting and an ironically disappointing end to her best day here.

Kit began to hand her drink card over to the bartender, but Lassino put his hand on hers and shook his head. "Go sit over there, on the couch." He nodded toward the couch attached to the stone wall adjacent to the bar. "I'll bring the drinks."

She stared at him, not sure what to say. What this some kind of trick? Was Lassino going to use this as an opportunity to wander off and talk to friends, leaving her on the couch? Maybe once she'd turned her back, he'd shuffle right out the disco door, without so much as a squint back at her? Kit knew she was scrutinizing Lassino, her head cocked sideways, her eyebrows knit in a frown, as if she were trying to read his thoughts and anticipate his next move. Lassino noticed the perturbed look on her face as well and assured her, "As soon as I get the drinks, I'll be right there."

"Okay," she said resignedly and headed off to the couch. She settled herself in and leaned her head back tiredly against the uneven rocks of the wall. She closed her eyes and breathed in and out deeply to calm herself. Everything would be fine, she told herself, although, none too assuredly.

"Ah, the most beautiful girl in Positano! And alone? How can this be?"

Kit blinked her eyes open and found Vinnie smiling widely at her. Ugh, not now! Besides Fabio, Vinnie was the last person that she wanted to chat with at this moment—or *ever*. And it was disturbing that all Kit could still picture (too vividly) in her mind was him in his white Speedo, looming over her at the beach. Once again, she thought there should really be some kind of mandatory age limit for Speedo-wearing. The tight, red pants were not much of an improvement, either. She wasn't opposed to wearing red pants *herself*; in fact, she thought she might have a pair stashed away in her closet at home, but on a guy? Even in Italy, that was pushing it, Kit thought.

"Hello, Vinnie," Kit said a bit less cheerily than she had intended.

"You are without a drink. I will get you one," he said confidently.

"Oh, no, no, thank you," Kit replied hastily.

"Yes, yes, of course, I will," Vinnie ignored her. *Really?* Would anyone listen to her in this country when she said *no*? Next, he'd be telling her how lovely her hair looked tonight. She'd had it.

Before Kit could protest again, Vinnie turned around to leave, but he found Lassino standing behind him, a drink in each hand. Finally, someone to come to her rescue! Kit thought she'd love to kiss Lassino right then and there, she was so relieved.

"Scusa, Vinnie." He squinted at him and moved past, not waiting for Vinnie to respond. Kit watched Vinnie eye Lassino as he sat close to her and handed her the bubbling flute of prosecco. She detected the irritation on his face at being foiled. He nodded curtly at them, said "Ciao," and walked off. Lassino ignored Vinnie and raised his highball glass toward her flute and said, "Salute." They clinked glasses and sipped their drinks.

"So," Lassino stared at her through his thick lenses, "you want to talk, so *talk*." All right, two for two—he'd actually gotten the drinks and come back to her like he said he would, and now, he was initiating the conversation that she *so* thought he'd try to avoid. Kit felt like any minute now, Ashton Kutcher might pop out and tell her she'd been "punk'd." She almost didn't want to talk about the incident with Fabio anymore. She was just so tired and confused. But this was too important, and she was worn out from always pretending that nothing bothered her. Where did she even begin? Well, she'd just have to jump right in.

"I don't like what Fabio did at the table in front you and your friends and family. It was totally inappropriate. I hate that he was touching me, touching my hair like that, like, like we were … were …" Kit spluttered.

"*Lovers?*" Lassino guessed correctly, an amused look on his face. Why was he smirking? She found nothing funny about this. Somehow, this wasn't quite how she'd envisioned starting the conversation.

"Well, yes!" Kit closed her eyes tightly and shook her head in disgust as she said, "It was totally uncomfortable, and I'm so disgusted that I feel like I need to wash my hair!"

Lassino snorted and gave the obligatory Italian face-shrug. How could he be so cavalier?

"And you!" Kit's eyes bugged out. "*You!*" She pointed a finger at Lassino. "You didn't even do anything! You just sat there! Don't you even care? Aren't you even mad?"

Kit braced herelf for Lassino's outburst. He was sure to sputter wildly (and incoherently) and then stomp off. Instead, with a strange calmness, Lassino spoke succinctly. "Kit, I am not mad. I am not mad at you, and I am not mad at Fabio."

Not mad at her? Well, why would he be? She hadn't done anything! Not mad at Fabio? But he should be mad at Fabio! Why wasn't he infuriated with Fabio, like she was? Kit thought better and held her tongue. At least Lassino wasn't screaming illogically, and she felt as if he just might be on the verge of telling her something … something important, something that she needed to hear.

Lassino sighed and looked upward, as if trying to decide how to explain something very complicated to a small child. He looked back at her and said, "I will try to explain. Kit, I am not mad, because I know you. You could dance naked in a room full of men, and it would be okay."

Why would she ever dance naked in a room full of men? *Okay, stay calm; stay calm; just listen to what he's saying …*

He took her hand and said, "I mean, nothing would happen. I know you wouldn't go off with any of them, because that's not you. You are not like that."

She exhaled with a sudden relief. Lassino *did* understand her. He *did* know her. Of course, she wasn't like that. Kit felt the worry begin to dissipate. Lassino then added matter-of-factly, "Yes, I know you are not like that, but not *everyone* knows that."

Wait, what? So, did everyone else in the town assume she was some kind of, well, glorified … sexpot? Maybe she should've known that Lassino's compliment would come with some type of disclaimer.

"So what are you really saying, Lassino?" Kit asked with some trepidation.

"You let everyone touch you!" he said and shooed at hand at her, as if she should know. Yet, oddly enough, Lassino still showed no sign of jealousy or anger. However, Kit was once more furious.

"I do not!" she shouted indignantly.

Lassino said smugly, "What about Mario?" *Mario, his friend?* Oh. Mario, *right.* Kit winced as she remembered the night of the Fourth of July party when Mario had given her a hug and his hands rested dangerously and unnecessarily close to her butt. It had made her feel uncomfortable then, just as thinking about it now did. Kit had not asked for that and had not let it go any further. She now remembered Lassino watching her then, just like he had at the table tonight, without emotion. Then there were all the guys asking her if her boobs were real. Well, she'd laughed it off. What was she supposed to do? And Lassino had sat through it all, saying nothing.

She hated to admit it, but all these things did, in fact, bother her. So if they bothered her, why didn't they bother Lassino? Kit couldn't help but think that if it were Johnny, he wouldn't have stood for such things! Why had she thought of Johnny just now? This was a bad time for him to pop into her thoughts. She quickly shoved him out as she explained, "Mario shouldn't have done that. He shouldn't touch me like that!"

Lassino took a sip of his drink, shrugged, and said, "I know it doesn't mean anything to you, but everyone else—they don't know. You're too nice to everyone. You treat everyone the same!" He looked at her triumphantly, as if daring her to refute his point.

"But I'm just trying to be nice, that's all," Kit said incredulously. Since when was it wrong to be nice? And why did she suddenly feel like she was guilty of something? This was all wrong. This was not how she had planned for the conversation to go.

"Well, then, in my opinion, you're a little too nice. You don't have to be *so* nice to everyone!" Lassino's speech was rapidly returning to its all too feverish pace.

"What are you talking about? *How* am I *too* nice?"

"You don't have to smile at everyone!" Lassino countered simply. Ah, yes, *smiling*. As if that was the answer to all her problems in this town! Smiling was the *least* of her worries right now. She was just trying to avoid being inappropriately fondled and to have a conversation with any male that didn't involve the authenticity of her chest!

Kit wanted to shriek, but she spoke calmly." Listen, Lassino, I really don't see how *smiling* is being too nice to people. That's just ridiculous. Are you saying that no woman in this town can ever smile at a man?"

Lassino held up a finger. "Not when they look like *you!*" Oh, he was impossible! She didn't believe him.

He continued on, "You smile at everyone. When you smile at the men around here and treat them all the same, you give them the wrong idea. Then they think you might be interested, that they can touch you!"

"Smiling at people does not mean I want them to touch me. I do not treat people the same here—well, I do not treat the *men* here the same! I don't treat them like I treat you!"

"What does that mean?" he scoffed.

"You know what it means!" Kit said angrily. Was he really going to make her say it? He knew damn well that he was the only one in the town with whom she'd ever ...

"What, it means you don't sleep with them?" he asked coolly. Once again, she hated him.

"Well, it means a lot more to me than that! But thanks for cheapening it!" *Jackass!*

Lassino looked at her blankly and went on. "So you don't sleep with them, but you smile all the time at them and let them touch you. Make up your mind. Do you want them to do that or not?" Finally, *there* was the anger and jealousy—at least some sort of feeling—that Kit had been hoping to see from him. It was a pity that at this moment, she felt like grabbing one of his fancy Prada slides and beating him upside the head with it! In fact, besides her tumultuous stomach, her head was throbbing, but maybe that was because she felt she was beating her head against a wall when talking to Lassino.

"First of all, smiling at people does not give them permission to touch me inappropriately. And second, why don't you ever say anything if it bothers you? Why didn't you say anything to Fabio? Or to Mario? He's your friend! He shouldn't touch me like that!"

Lassino spoke slowly. "Kit, I do not say anything, I cannot say anything, because it's not my place to do so ... you are ... *not* my girlfriend." He squinted at her expectantly and then looked down at his drink.

Kit felt like the wind had been knocked out of her. There it was. He'd finally said the something important that she needed to hear. Of course, it wasn't what she wanted to hear at all. Okay, she knew that she wasn't his *girlfriend* in the technical sense of the word. She was here just for the summer, but they had a past. And it wasn't just a simple one-night stand. It hadn't even started out that way. She and Lassino had slowly worked their way up to their overnights. This relationship had spanned three summers, a bazillion transcontinental texts, just as many phone calls, even flowers on her birthday, dammit! And here she was now, and they *were* together, and everyone knew it. They had real feelings for each other. In the three years she'd been coming here, Kit knew she had absolutely not imagined it all. And now, she felt compelled to ask *the* question.

"Then what are we? What do people around this town think of us?" There, it was a question that she'd always wanted to ask, but she had been afraid to hear Lassino's answer.

He shrugged and gestured with his hands in prayer position. "We are lovers."

There was that word that she hated, especially when it was describing her. Could she argue with this one? Maybe it was no big deal here to be known as lovers, but it sounded so wrong (at least, in her Catholic mind). The thing was, there was no one else for her when she went home. There was Lassino *here*, and that was it. Didn't he get it? Didn't she deserve a better title than *lover*?

Lassino looked at her hurt face and asked in exasperation, "What? What's wrong with that? That's what we are! That's all we can be!"

"What do you mean, that's all we can be?" Kit questioned. Why was she was suddenly and miraculously able to understand every (normally unintelligible) mumbled word and grunt he made? It'd only taken three years. It figured that her ability to translate Lassino's English was kicking in during *this* discussion.

"Don't be stupid! I live here. You live in California. You come here in summer, and we are together ... most of the time ..." His voice trailed off slightly.

"What do you mean *most of the time?* Oh, that's right, I forgot, most of the time, but sometimes not, in case some other woman from abroad happens to show up!" Of course, Kit knew for a fact that there really had been no one else with Lassino this summer, which boded well for them. And maybe it explained why he played such a hot-and-cold game with her. He wanted her, but he wanted his space. He enjoyed having her here, but he knew she was leaving in August. It suddenly dawned on Kit. Why did she ever think that the men in Italy were any different from the men at home? They still jerked you around (if you let them).

Lassino shook his head and said, "You and me—it happens, it's possible, because you are *here*, in Positano. Me? I stay here and you leave, and then it stops." Was it really that simple for him?

Kit felt a boldness come over her. "Why does it have to stop? Come to California. Come and stay for a while. See how you like it there." It could work. California was sort of similar to Italy, wasn't it? They could try each other out over there. She would take care of him, and she wouldn't leave him to fend for himself, like he did with her here. Of course, the Bay Area was quite a bit bigger than Positano, but still.

Lassino looked at her as if she was insane. "Come to California? And do what?"

"*Live there* for a while. See if you like it. You could stay with me," Kit suggested.

"Live there? And do what? Sit on my ass all day while you are at work?" he said sarcastically.

"Well, there *are* things to do and places to see in California! You could even get a job, *work*. Work—you do know what that is, don't you?" Kit said just as sarcastically.

Lassino looked at her with disdain. "Work? Oh, come all the way from Italy to become a waiter in an Italian restaurant that doesn't even serve authentic Italian food?"

Actually, she'd been thinking more along the lines of him opening his own restaurant. His pizza and everything else they served at Segreto Giardino was superb. He could make it! And she could help out in the restaurant!

"Why would I do that? Listen, Kit. Here, in Positano, I am, how do you say? Uh, I am a beeg fish in a … small pond. I do well. I live well. I have everything I need here. *This* is my home," he said definitively.

Kit knew she should choose her words carefully, but she still felt compelled to say, "So, you will never leave Positano because everything is so easy for you here? That seems a bit lazy."

She knew the backlash was sure to come.

Lassino set his drink down angrily. "Lazy! Do you know how hard I work from March to November? I am—"

"Yes, *beesy* all the time, yes, I know! Yes, so beesy, playing soccer, shopping in Sorrento, hitting the disco, I mean where do you even find the time to fit in working?" Kit fired back.

"Don't talk to me about work! You come here on vacation and spend your money. All you know is the summer in Positano. If you tried to live here, you wouldn't last one extra month past tourist season!"

Was he calling her a mere tourist! Now, that was going too far! And if he were daring her to try living here, well, she'd do it! She could. She had friends here, and she'd get along without him. Of course, she didn't want to get along without him, but he was quite impossible.

"Don't tell me I couldn't live here. I have been! I could live here, and not just during the summer!" she shouted over the loud music.

Lassino rolled his eyes, crossed his arms, and then asked, "Yes, really? And what are you going to do here?"

What was she going to do here? What was she going to do here? What *was* she going to do here? Well, there were a million things she could do in Positano. She could ... teach English, or ... be a nanny! Well, she might be blackballed from any nanny positions since her refusal of Fabio's proposition ... never mind, she could be a photographer and make her own Positano postcards to sell! She could dust things in Tino's ceramic shop, and better yet, she could be a Positano tour guide for Americans! Yeah, and specialize in helping the *women* tourists who came here. She'd make sure they knew all the basic survival skills—from the "no handrails on the stairs" to the confusing males! Or ...

"I could find a job in no time. In fact, your cousin just said she'd hire me as a waitress at the restaurant." Kit smiled innocently. It *was* true; Angela had said she could work there should she decide to prolong her stay. Kit was tempted to accept since the nanny offer was kaput, but she thought better of it. Lassino would have a fit. Still, it wouldn't hurt to let him sweat a bit knowing that she had her own connections here.

Lassino's eyes bugged out. "At Segreto Giardino? *My* restaurant? Ha! Unbelievable ... we are done talking about this." He stood up.

"But—" Kit began.

Lasisno shook his head. "I'm not talking about this anymore." He walked off, squeezing through dancers till he reached his friends at the bar. He then looked back at her as if to say, *I'm here. Are you joining me?*

Kit glanced at him and looked away. She was irritated, to say the least, and needed to cool down. Or she might just leave instead. A walk on the beach by herself would help clear her head. Yes, she would do that as soon as she finished her prosecco. She'd barely touched it, and it would be sinful to leave a full glass. She closed her eyes, tilted her head back, and took a long sip. She probably shouldn't drink anymore since her stomach was acting up, but she was hot, she was distressed by the evening's events, and she'd already passed the tipsiness threshold. So what did it matter now, anyway?

"Kit!"

Kit opened her eyes mid-swig to find a handsome face staring down at her. It was a tanned, stubbled face, and bright-blue eyes peeked out from under blondish fringe. The mouth, drawn up in a wide smile, showed a set of white teeth, illuminated by the fluorescent lighting. This face was more than handsome. It was *gorgeous* and … unfamiliarly *familiar*. Wait, this was a face Kit knew all too well, or did she now? Were the dark lighting and her poor eyesight playing tricks on her? No, it was Johnny! Kit immediately choked on her prosecco.

"Oh, wow, are you all right?" Johnny sat next to her and pounded her on the back gently. Her eyes watering from choking, but when her wild sputtering was finally under control, Kit looked up at him and opened her mouth to say hello. Instead, to her horror, a hiccup-burp popped out. She immediately covered her mouth with her hand.

"Glad to see you, too." Johnny smiled in amusement.

"Sorry. How are you?" Kit mumbled from behind her hand.

"Great, great! I've been all over …" Johnny talked animatedly about his travels in Italy while Kit sat and pretended to enthusiastically listen. It's not that she didn't want to listen; she was just having a difficult time focusing. Johnny was so … well, she was completely thrown off, seeing him here, looking like … *that*. He was the same, yet so different. There was more of a manly worldliness about him. Could traveling really do that to a person? From her own personal experience, Kit knew better than to ask that question. The evidence was right before her. The sexy, grown-out hair, the tan, the simple linen shirt unbuttoned just enough, the … wait, *True Religion jeans*? And they didn't look completely ridiculous on him, either. What else would there be? A tattoo hidden away somewhere? Would he whip out a pack of cigarettes and start chain-smoking? Would he be able to dance with wild abandon, and with some sort of uncanny rhythm? Well, Kit admitted, after the jeans, nothing could possibly shock her.

Johnny stopped talking suddenly, paused, and then said, "What's the matter? You're staring at my pants. Did I spill something on them?"

Oh, dear. Had she been that obvious with her perusal of his pants? Apparently. Kit quickly looked up and expected Johnny's typical, eager-to-please look to be plastered on his face. But there wasn't an eager look on his face at all. It was more of a playful look. A look that said, *I'm joking. Whatever; I couldn't care less.* How … unlike Johnny. What was happening here? Something in the universe was out of whack. But maybe it was her?

Kit cleared her throat. "Oh, no." She laughed. "I was noticing your jeans. I … like them!" she answered overenthusiastically.

"Thanks, a friend helped me pick them out."

Kit nodded. She wanted to look away, and under normal circumstances, she would have, but she just couldn't help but stare, dumbstruck, at Johnny. "Kit, you look like you're seeing a ghost. Do I look *that* different?" Johnny laughed at her.

Kit felt like she *was* seeing a ghost—the ghost of boyfriends past, to be exact. Or she was having an out-of-body experience. Johnny was almost glowing, everything about him, his teeth, his white shirt, his blond (when had it become so blond?) hair, his glistening skin—surely, the disco lighting was responsible for this ethereal concoction, but ...

Kit hesitated and stammered slightly, "No, no! I am just, um, surprised to see you, that's all. Here, in Positano ... in the disco." She laughed awkwardly.

"Yeah, I guess it is a bit strange. Bridget didn't tell you I ran into her last night?"

Nooo. Kit wondered how Bridget could've possibly forgotten that small bombshell, unless she had been drinking a lot and didn't remember. Entirely possible.

"Oh, well, she probably meant to tell me, but we were in such a rush to get going this morning, it probably just slipped her mind," offered Kit.

"Yeah, I heard you went on a boat trip today ... with Lassino ... and your friends," Johnny said purposefully. Kit wondered, had Johnny been waiting for an opportune moment to utter Lassino's name? It had hung like a thick shadow over them for so long anyway.

As if he'd been eavesdropping on the conversation and waiting for his name to be spoken, Lassino appeared, squinting at them both. He set another flute down in front of Kit and said, "Giorgio sends this over for you." The one time she wished Lassino would avoid her, and here he was. Kit's stomach lurched as Lassino looked hard through his glasses at her. She felt her heart pounding in her ears as she then watched Lassino and Johnny silently size each other up. Lassino, being practically blind, could in no way look someone over casually. His full-on visual assault was met by Johnny's cool stare. The scary thing was, Kit knew that they both realized who the other was.

It was Lassino who spoke first. "Are you going to introduce me, Kit?"

Kit snapped out of her catatonic state to answer. "Of course. Lassino, this is Johnny. Johnny, this is Lassino." She held her breath as she waited for something awful to happen. If Lassino said something provoking about their relationship, Johnny was sure to stand up, if not to defend her honor, then his own male ego. And some sort of fisticuffs would certainly ensue. Lassino would be pummeled, what with not being able to see and hating to break a sweat.

"Nice to meet you. Welcome to Positano," Lassino said genuinely.

"Thanks, nice to meet you too," Johnny replied—not overly friendly, but politely.

Okay, so no fisticuffs yet ... it was only a matter of time.

Lassino asked with interest, "So, where are you staying?" *All of a sudden, he was into making pleasant conversation?*

"Oh, past La Sirenuse at ..." and this launched them into a lengthy conversation about Positano and what to do while there, even about Johnny coming to Lassino's restaurant for dinner some night! Um, was Kit the only one who felt completely awkward? Which was worse, having Johnny and Lassino come to blows, or having them become buddies? The friendly chit-chat would have continued, had a tall figure not emerged from somewhere and sidled up to them. The woman was definitely Italian. Kit could tell by the glossy, olive skin, the high cheekbones and full lips, the long, dark locks, and, well, by the clothes. She wore a tight, white, cropped tank top that showed off ample cleavage and a flat, tan stomach. Her white, drawstring linen pants glowed in the disco lighting, which made it obvious that she had on something lacy underneath. She wore gladiator sandals and sported a tattoo of a star on her inside wrist. Kit didn't recognize her from Positano. Did this girl know Lassino? Lassino's blatant gawking (more so than his usual gawking) told Kit that he did not recognize this girl.

"Scusa," she said huskily and gave the group a slight smile. She then sat down next to Johnny and wrapped her arms around him.

Johnny spoke up. "This is Laura. Laura, this is Kit, and this is Lassino."

Lassino said hello, then glanced at Johnny with an admiring look that said, *Well done, man!*

It dawned on Kit that this must be the "friend" who had helped Johnny pick out his jeans. So, apparently Johnny had met someone while traveling. Which was good, *great*, of course. And why wouldn't Johnny interest someone who looked like *that*? Kit felt she should be happy for Johnny. And let's not forget that *he* had traveled across the globe for her and *she* had shot down any hopes for a romantic reunion. So why couldn't he travel Italy and meet someone else? But did this someone have to look like an uber-Italian version of Angelina Jolie, ala *Lara Croft, Tomb Raider?* Why couldn't she be short, squat, and wearing tacky clothes? Kit found herself thinking begrudgingly. That was when she remembered her Mufasa/fright-wig hair. Oh, dear God, how embarrassing! Of all nights to have out-of-control hair! She was mortified, but there was nothing she could do but smile.

"Piacere." Kit smiled pleasantly, while she tried to nonchalantly smooth down her hair. "Where in Italy are you from?" she asked. If the girl answered Naples, Kit would just die.

"Venice," she answered, and Kit noted that even this Laura's *voice* oozed sexiness. Oh, and *of course,* she hailed from Venice, the city of unadulterated romance. That figured. Kit hoped for Johnny's sake that he hadn't been reeled in by some con-artist gypsy masquerading as a bona fide Italian. Johnny really was too nice. Kit suddenly felt very protective. It was her fault he was here, and she should probably make sure Johnny was not being taken advantage of. This was just a friendly sense of obligation she was feeling, right? No, this was the alcohol … that and having really bad hair tonight. All this, combined with the last few hours, had made her feel old, and tired, and so unattractive—American. She'd be over it by tomorrow, but she really needed to get out of here.

Johnny explained, "I was eating in a little café off of San Marco Square and Laura was working there. We got to talking, and she said she'd take me around Venice on her day off. So she did. And then I told her I'd show here around Positano, and here we are!" He smiled as Laura cuddled against him.

All right, so maybe she was an authentic Venetian and not some crafty swindler. But wait, Johnny, show *her* Positano? Johnny'd never been there before! Kit knew she'd endlessly talked about Positano in front of Johnny and to Johnny, but did he really think that qualified him as a legitimate tour guide?

"*Really?*" Kit asked. She hadn't meant it to, but it had come out skeptically.

Johnny looked at her squarely. "Yeah, I was here a couple of weeks ago, before I worked my way up north."

"You were *here?* In *Positano?*" Kit asked, mystified. How had she not run into him? Had he been casing her about the town, unbeknownst to her?

Johnny looked her questioningly. "Yes, I was *here*. *You* suggested that I try it out for myself, remember? So I did. Maybe you were at that wedding?"

Kit ignored Lassino's raised eyebrows. Oh, yes, yes, of course. She'd told him in Naples that he was welcome to check out Positano (on his own), since she didn't feel comfortable with playing tour guide for him. Of course, she hoped he'd forsake Positano for the rest of Italy …

Johnny in Positano (twice) … Johnny with a Venetian hottie, Johnny in trendy clothes, Lassino chatting with Johnny, and don't even get her started about the whole Fabio thing or her discussion with Lassino … this was all starting to hurt Kit's head and her poor stomach.

Thankfully, Laura whispered into Johnny's neck. It was close and sensual, and very awkward for Kit, who looked away. Lassino continued staring with interested amusement.

"Excuse us. We're gonna go dance. Lassino, it was nice to meet you." Johnny extended his hand.

"My pleasure. See you at the restaurant," Lassino said earnestly.

Kit and Lassino watched Laura lead Johnny by the hand out into the crowd, where they were immediately swallowed up into the dancing abyss. She was glad. Kit didn't want to witness anything else. What was wrong with her? She did not want to be back together with Johnny. They were over. They'd been over a year ago. But it was more than a little "in her face" to see him here with a beautiful woman. She didn't want or need to see that. Not after the night she'd been having. Once again, maybe this was part of her punishment?

"So, did you know he was coming to Positano?" Lassino asked bluntly.

Kit rolled her eyes. "*No, I didn't know.*" She wasn't about to tell him that Johnny had (innocently) shared a room with her in Naples due to that damn e-mail she'd sent out!

Lassino shrugged. "He's very nice. Why don't you want to go out with him anymore?"

Was he freakin' kidding? Kit felt like screaming, *Because I'm in … I want to go out with you*" Wasn't it obvious? Lassino had to be joking. Of course, one never could tell the fine line between his joking and his seriousness.

Kit eyed him with scrutiny and said tersely, "I *know* Johnny's *nice*. But I'm not in love with him, and I didn't want to waste any more of his time. I just couldn't be who he wanted me to be."

Lassino nodded his head in quiet understanding. He looked like he was about to say something when a group of people made their way to the couches, calling, "Ciao, Lassino!" Perhaps more cousins? Lassino was related to half the town. They plunked themselves next to Lassino, and Kit watched them animatedly talk in Italian. She was too tired to try and translate the fast-paced dialect. And Lassino didn't think to try including her. Kit was glad for the excuse to leave. She took a last sip of her prosecco and pushed herself up from the couch. No one seemed to notice. All night, she'd been a beacon with her unruly blonde hair, and now she was invisible. This was a good thing, though, because this would enable her to slip out quietly. Not having had to pay for any drinks, she handed her card over to the bouncer and was given a quick nod to pass.

She stood on the top step overlooking the beach chairs on the rocky shore. That was where she was headed. She was feeling better already, out of the claustrophobic heat. She'd walk the beach and find a lounge chair to sit on for a while before heading back to the apartment. Kit was glad for some time to herself. She needed to digest everything about the evening and come to some sort of conclusion about what she was going to do. No one would bother her out on the beach. It was unfortunate that she was unaware of a certain someone in the shadows watching her exit.

✦   ✦   ✦

Dangling her platforms from one hand, Kit stepped off the wooden walkway and into the sand. She trudged her way along the rocky shore. Once the pulsating music spilling out of the disco and the huddles of chattering people outside were nothing but faint background noise, Kit settled on a beach chair. She laid back and listened to the water as it calmly rolled back and forth to the shore. The evening had thrown her off so completely. She was never at a loss as to what she wanted to do. Even if she had no actual plans in the works, Kit never worried too much about it. Something interesting came along, and you went with it. But tonight … everything was so muddled.

What did she do next? No offense to her friends, but when Bridget and Marren got on that plane home next week, she did not want to be with them. Leaving with them in August had never been her intention anyway.

But maybe all that had transpired this evening was a sign that she should go. She just didn't know anymore. Her usually perceptive intuition seemed to have disappeared, rendering her confused and quite helpless. Kit wished for some miraculous sign to point her in whatever direction she was supposed to go. *Come on, give me some sign. Please, any kind of sign …*

Kit glanced down the beach and warily watched as a tall figure in red pants headed her way.

Among the late-night beach revelers, she heard a voice call out, "Vinnie …"

It *was* him! Had he seen her on the beach chair? He appeared to look in her direction, but he heard his name called, and he turned to talk to the group. This wasn't exactly the sign she'd been looking for, but it was definitely Kit's cue to leave the beach, and in a hurry. She grabbed her shoes, sprang from the lounge chair, and hustled up the sand. Once on the boardwalk, she momentarily hesitated as she tried to decide if wearing her shoes would impede a quick escape. She didn't have time for the shoes. Plus, with the heat and drinking, she no longer had any semblance of ankles. Forget the shoes.

Kit picked up her pace, looking over her shoulder every few seconds. Vinnie was still talking to his group of friends, but he turned and looked down the beach. His head swiveled and he seemed to gawk at the boardwalk, as if trying to spot her. Kit was relieved that so many other people were out. She could hopefully blend in, although, Kit briefly thought that life might be easier if she was a brunette. Her hair, even on its best-behaving days, acted like some type of spotlight, drawing attention. She'd never minded, until tonight, when her mane had seemed to take on a life of its own.

She just needed to get to Mulini Square and up the hill a bit. Once past the square, she'd forgo walking the main road and pick one of the many staircases to make her ascent. It would be extremely exhausting, but it would keep her safe from Vinnie, as he'd have no idea which set of stairs she'd taken.

Kit pattered up the steps, leaving the people and brightly lit beachfront restaurants behind. She nodded reverently and made a sign of the cross as she hastened past the darkened church of Santa Maria Assunta. She took another fork in the uphill path and wiped the sweat from her upper lip as she walked the cobblestone path between the darkened shops. She marveled at the silence and stillness of it now, as compared to how crowd-infested and nearly impossible it was to travel along during the scorching daylight hours. She slowed down a bit to catch her breath. She had one more bend on the way, and then she'd be past the last little stretch of shops. She was being silly, of course. She was in Positano! Kit had never felt unsafe here … before tonight. Not that she necessarily considered herself in grave peril, but there was a strong sense of uneasiness that Kit couldn't seem to shake.

She took a few steps and nearly bumped into two teens that had just rounded the bend. Kit involuntarily gasped, her heart pounding wildly. She had been so lost in thought that she hadn't even heard them approaching.

"Scusa!" They spoke loudly, then stopped to look her over. Kit's hand instinctively flew to her chest and she fiddled with the ruffle on her low-cut top. Why did she suddenly feel as if she was naked?

"Scusa," Kit croaked. What was the matter with her? She was fine. The two boys could be no more than sixteen or seventeen. Sporting tight-fitting T-shirts and jeans, asymmetrically cut hair gelled and spiked forward, they were definitely en route to the disco.

"Disco?" the taller of the youths asked her and nodded his head in the direction she had just come from. The other leered at her, almost suggestively, and then stared at her chest. Oh, she knew she hadn't been imagining things!

"No, no. Buona notte," Kit said quickly and took a step past them.

The boys shrugged and continued walking. Kit walked a few steps, then turned around. She squinted her eyes in the dimness and waited until the teens had disappeared down the hill. She looked down and realized that she was clutching her shoes, one in each hand, heels turned out as if they were pistols. This was ridiculous. She was completely paranoid.

Put the shoes on or keep them off? It was truly a no-win situation. Shoving her swollen feet into the platforms and limping up the hill at a snail's pace would be tortuous. Walking barefoot was not optimal, either. By the time she got to the apartment, her feet would be just as bad. Kit decided she'd sacrifice her bare feet. And besides, while she hoped not, her shoes might better serve her being in her hands. With her shoe-weapons in hand, she moved on and kept her eyes to the ground, in an effort to avoid glass and such.

She continued and rounded the bend, her eyes keenly focused upon the uneven ground beneath her. So far, so good, for someone with sub-par eyesight. Although her vision was bad, her hearing was good. Kit stopped and listened. Wait, somewhere, a ways behind her, she was sure she detected the sound of running feet. She hastened her pace, as the footsteps got louder and apparently, closer. Someone was running up the pathway that she was on! Kit began a fast walk that turned into a jog. The footsteps were almost on top of her! Wait a minute. This was stupid. Whoever it was, was not after *her*! Kit would not let herself be afraid. She would turn around and stare down this person until he—*or she*—passed. Kit stopped short and turned around, ready for whomever it was to run on past her.

The person stopped. It was Vinnie, panting, in his hideous red pants. Okay, she *was* afraid.

Should she start sprinting or remain calm? Kit clutched her shoes tightly, ready to jab at him with her deadly heels.

"Kit!" Vinnie stopped and bent over his knees, breathing hard. He straightened up and said, "Kit, it is you. I didn't know if I'd be able to catch you."

He smiled his yellow smile before wiping his brow. Oh, please, he'd probably planted a homing device on her at the disco, Kit thought with scorn. Though she was frightened, her irritation was kicking in and taking over, giving her some added courage.

She stared at him, for once, unable to smile. "Hello, Vinnie."

"Hello, Kit. Let me walk with you." He smiled again. Kit didn't think he was drunk, but there was something slightly askew about Vinnie. Something creepy and weird, aside from the whole stalker bit. She began to walk on and said, "I'm on my way home."

He joined in her fast walk and answered, "I will walk with you." *Yes, of course he would.* Kit didn't answer. Maybe if she didn't talk, he'd grow bored and leave her alone.

But no. "I saw you leave the beach, and I had to find you. There are things I must say to you."

Kit quickly glanced at him out of the corner of her eye. What was he possibly going to say to her? That he remembered every single outfit she'd worn since she'd gotten to Positano? Freaky, but not unfathomable. Really, whatever it was, Kit was sure she didn't want to hear it. Kit continued walking. Vinnie was sure to speak anyway.

From behind her, his hand reached out and grabbed her arm, jolting her backward. Kit stopped and clutched her platforms tighter. Vinnie spoke dramatically as he declared, "Kit, you know, I am in love with you!"

Kit wanted to laugh at the ridiculousness of it, but she was actually quite fearful. There was a crazed wildness in Vinnie's eyes that had nothing to do with love. It was dark, and he had almost-black eyes, but were his pupils dilated too?

"What? No, no," Kit sputtered and pulled her arm away from Vinnie. She backed away, fists up and shoes pointing outward, as if they were a force field around her.

"You do not love me." Vinnie stared at her blankly. And then, with a menacing sneer, he spat out, "You do not love me!"

He took a step forward. If he tried to touch her at all, she would impale him with her Loeffler Randalls! She didn't care how expensive they'd been. Kit inched backward. Where were all the other people who should be heading up the hill? She couldn't be the only one leaving the disco a little early.

Vinnie muttered something Italian in a low voice. Kit strained to hear and translate, but she stopped when Vinnie began shouting out loud. He was a lunatic! Kit thought Lassino was crazy at times, but never like this, like someone possessed!

"People have been telling you about me, haven't they? That is why you do not love me!"

No, but she wished they had told her about his apparent mood swings, or possibly the mood-altering drugs he might be on.

"I don't know what you're talking about," Kit said calmly, while backing away slowly.

With a low growl, Vinnie sneered. "Yes … they … have … I know you have heard about me being married." What was he talking about? She knew absolutely nothing about him, aside from him working at the restaurant and for the taxi service and having a hideous taste in bathing suits and other such clothing garments.

Kit tried to interject, "No, Vinnie, no—"

"People have told you I am a drug dealer, too! Haven't they?" Vinnie shrieked and then cackled wickedly.

Whoa, if possible, this had just gotten even weirder. She was going to be killed by an insane taxi driver, and one wearing tight, red pants, on the worst night of her hair's life! Kit's only consolation was that she'd die in the town she was in love with. Oh, God, she had to get to Mulini Square quickly!

"Haven't they?" Vinnie screamed, when Kit didn't answer.

Kit shook her head, gulped, and said, "No, no, Vinnie! No one has said anything to me!"

"Don't lie for them! I know you have heard these things from people here!" He reached out and grabbed Kit's arm again.

"No, Vinnie, I—" Kit began frantically.

"No, I know they have, but these things are … not true." His voice tapered off. He looked up at her with pleading eyes. At that moment, Kit thought that perhaps Vinnie was not a drug dealer but was truly on drugs. He was completely paranoid, and more so than she was.

Kit spoke up firmly. "No, Vinnie. *No one* has talked to me. I don't know what you are talking about. I honestly don't. Now, please, excuse me, but I need to get home." She yanked her arm away and began jogging up the cobblestone path.

In a second, he was next to her, panting. "Let me drive you home." Like she would ever step foot in a car with him again. Kit fought the urge to snort. Besides, no need to make Vinnie any more exacerbated.

"No, I'd prefer to walk. *By myself.*" Kit kept her eyes ahead and continued her uphill sprint.

"No, let me take you! I can drive you, Kit," he argued, while he panted hard next to her.

Enough already. "Listen, I don't want to drive. I want to walk!" Oh, thank God, she was finally in the square. The last short curve of the walk had seemed like miles! A dozen taxi drivers lounged against their cabs, smoking and chatting. They looked up at her in interest.

For a third time, Vinnie grabbed Kit's arm, more forcefully than before, and said angrily, "Why do you do this to me?"

A scooter pulled out of the garage, and a horn tooted. Kit and Vinnie looked over to see Tomaso smiling across the square. Walking up the hill was no longer an option. Tomaso was her chance for escape. And she knew for a fact that she didn't have to worry about him trying to put the moves on her.

Kit jerked her arm free and ran toward Tomaso. She shouted, "Tomaso, hi! Can I have a ride up the hill?"

"Of course!" He smiled toothily.

Without a glance backward, Kit hopped on the scooter, threw her arms around Tomaso, and left Mulini Square and scary Vinnie behind.

◆ ◆ ◆

They had spent most of the morning on the patio reliving each other's evenings. It was now almost noon.

Kit had just finished her random tale of personal trauma. She said in tearful frustration, "I swear to God, Bridget, I seriously think they all get together and have a town meeting to decide how they can screw with me."

Bridget shook her head sympathetically. She couldn't argue, since it did, in fact, seem like it. Bridget thought of her nonexistent lovelife—she hadn't even been able to *locate* Lorenzo last night—and her situation paled in comparison to Kit's harrowing evening dealing with the love square of Fabio/Lassino/Johnny/Vinnie!

Bridget usually felt herself to be cursed, but maybe Kit was actually the unlucky one. Too much of anything was never good. And in the case of her best friend, being too good-looking and vivacious had attracted far too much male attention and led to some scary situations. Bridget decided to stick to too much eating, drinking, and shopping any day, rather than deal with the whole scary male/love thing.

"And you know what else, Bridget? The scary thing is, someone referred to me as Lassino's lover the other day ... and I agreed! What is happening to me in this town?" Kit wailed, interrupting Bridget's gloomy thoughts.

"Well, it doesn't seem to bother anyone around here," Bridget commented dryly.

"But it bothers me! What have I become? I don't welcome any of that! I really don't." Kit waited for Bridget to concur with her.

"I don't! *What?* Do I?" Kit looked cautiously at Bridget.

"I wouldn't normally agree with much of what Lassino tells you, but he does have a small point," Bridget said carefully.

Kit burst out, "I do not try to lead people on!"

"No, of course not. But I'm telling you, when you smile at *certain* people here, they think it's an open invitation to at least come talk to you. I can say this because *no one* bothers me in this town. People around here may not think I'm as friendly as you, but at least I'm not getting stalked on my way home from the disco."

Kit pursed her lips in annoyance. "Smiling at people isn't a crime."

"I know that. Just be aware that *some* people may take it the wrong way," Bridget added.

"That's an understatement," Kit said wryly. She then added accusingly, "So, what are you going to do about Lorenzo?"

Bridget looked at Kit as if she had two heads. "*Nothing.* There's nothing I can do. He obviously doesn't want to see me. Even though, I might add, *technically*, I didn't even do anything! He showed up too early, and it just *looked* really bad!"

Kit shrugged, but she didn't say anything.

It was now Bridget's turn to ask, "*What?*" She then sighed and said, "It was bad, wasn't it? Do you think I was mean to Lorenzo?"

Kit answered honestly. "Well, kind of. I mean, I know you weren't trying to be mean, but it was just so obvious that he came to see you, and you didn't even offer him a seat."

Bridget cringed. It *had* been quite bad, worse than bad. "I wasn't trying to be mean. I just didn't know what to do! The whole thing caught me off-guard. I feel so awful." Bridget threw her hand to her forehead.

"I know you do. Why don't you call him? You have his number," Kit suggested simply.

"Why? So he can hang up on me?" Bridget peeked out from under hand.

Kit rolled her eyes. "No, so you can apologize. Lorenzo's not going to hang up on you. And if he does, he's not the person I think he is. Remember what I said, Bridget. You may have found the best guy here!"

Bridget rolled her eyes in return. A far-off rooster crowed. "Oh, shut up!" Kit shouted out. "I do not find the roosters here charming anymore. You know, kind of like the men!" She stood up and sighed, "I have to clean before Marren gets here. She sent me a text saying she'll be here around four or so, so I guess I can't put it off any longer."

Bridget settled back into the lounge chair and gazed blankly over the balcony and out to the shimmery water, unsure about what to do. From the hallway, Kit yelled, "Go call him!"

Call Lorenzo? Should she? Bridget couldn't lie to herself. As much as she'd love to spare herself the humiliation, she knew she owed him an apology and an explanation. And then if Lorenzo wanted to hang up on her, so be it.

She lugged herself off the chair and across the patio to the kitchen and pulled the piece of paper with Lorenzo's number off the refrigerator. She stared at it until it became a blur. What would she say, that is, *if* he decided to speak to her?

From the back bedroom came Kit's voice. "You're awfully quiet out there! I hope you're dialing his number right now!"

"Give a person some time to rehearse what they're going to say!" Bridget yelled back.

Kit poked her head into the kitchen. "What do you need to rehearse? Um, hi, Lorenzo. I'm really sorry about not inviting you to sit down at the table last night. I became momentarily insane due to the intense heat here and the vat of prosecco I ingested all day long, but my senses have come back to me now, so please, please accept my apology. What? You forgive me and are in love with me? Oh, and want to marry me? Why, yes, I accept! Buh-bye!" Kit smiled cheesily.

Bridget smirked. "Yes, I'm sure that's exactly how the conversation's going to go."

Kit shook her head. "You're thinking about things too much. Just call. You'll come up with the right things to say."

"I will, if you go back to cleaning and don't eavesdrop on me," Bridget said as she picked up Kit's cell from the kitchen table.

"It's not that I want to eavesdrop. I just really don't want to clean. Fine, I'll go. Good luck!" Kit sighed and left the kitchen. The door to the bedroom closed and the Go-Go's' "Vacation" cheerily began playing from Kit's iPod.

Kit was right. Too much rehearsing and she'd just end up talking herself out of calling. Bridget quickly dialed the number and waited while it rang.

"Pronto," Mrs. Reginella's voice answered.

"Pronto. Uh … is Lorenzo there?" Bridget asked hesitantly. Mrs. Reginella didn't speak English, but she'd be able to tell who Bridget was asking for.

"Ah, un momento," Mrs. Reginella answered. Bridget waited, her mouth dry and stomach turning, and considered hanging up. Did they have *69 in Italy?

As Mrs. Reginella had said, a few moments later, Lorenzo's voice spoke. "Hello?"

"Hi, it's Bridget." Was her voice suddenly higher, like she'd inhaled some helium?

"Hi, Bridget," Lorenzo answered. No trace of overt anger or disgust in his voice. This was a good sign. No need for small talk, though. Bridget decided to err on the safe side by launching right into her explanation/ apology before he could hang up.

She blurted into the phone, "I'm really sorry about last night. I *really* didn't know you were coming to the restaurant. I would've saved you a place. It was totally rude of me, I know. I went to the disco to try to find you and apologize, but you were already gone. I'm so, so sorry." She was now out of breath. She waited for an abrupt dial tone in her ear.

"It's okay," Lorenzo said easily.

Oh, God, he hated her, didn't he? Wait, what had Lorenzo just said? *It was okay?*

"It's *not* okay. I feel terrible," Bridget argued.

Lorenzo laughed. "Maestrina, you never want to agree with me, do you? Look, it's okay; forget about it."

Before she could further prove his point by disagreeing with him some more, Lorenzo asked, "I'm heading to the beach. Wanna meet in the square at Spiaggia Grande?"

He was letting her off too easily. She didn't deserve it …

"Okay," she said simply.

"All right, see you in an hour?"

"Okay." She was suddenly relegated to speaking in monosyllables.

"Good, see you then, Maestrina. Ciao."

"Ciao," she replied, and she hung up, slightly stunned. She was being given another chance? For once, Bridget wouldn't argue.

✦   ✦   ✦

In a total role reversal, Kit stood on her side of the room, which was all tidied up now, clothes put away, bureau cleared off. Of course, everything was smashed into the drawers and shoved into her half of the closet, but never mind; it was clean, and it had taken her a record twenty minutes. She watched, open-mouthed, as Bridget practically tore the closet door off its hinges while she flung things out of the wardrobe and onto the bed.

"What, what are you looking for?" Kit asked quizzically, as she worriedly eyed the lump of jeans and other assorted clothes Bridget pulled out. She knew Bridget hated being in a bathing suit, but a full-on ensemble like this was ridiculous.

"My eyelet cover-up. Where is it? Where is it?" Bridget breathed, while strewing more clothes on top of the growing pile.

"It's hanging on the balcony." Kit pointed to the open door off their room.

"Right, right, right," mumbled Bridget absently as she scratched her head.

Kit stared at Bridget in amusement and asked, "What's the matter? You look confused, perplexed, dazed … you're acting like me when I try to get ready. What's happening here?"

Bridget exhaled and said in a panicky voice, "I don't know which bathing suit to wear. Which bathing suit do I wear? Help!"

"You only brought two, Bridget."

"I know! But which one? Kit, please!" Bridget practically shrieked.

"Okay, okay, the brown one. I like that one," Kit answered quickly.

Bridget stared at her suspiciously. "*The Miracle Suit?* Because I look fat? I look fat. Oh, shit, I look fat! Being stuck on that damn boat yesterday with no exercise! Be honest; you totally think I look fat!"

Kit held up her hand. "Oh, my God, would you stop? You do not look fat at all! I only said the Miracle Suit because it makes your boobs look *really* good. I mean, your cleavage is absolutely amazing in that suit! The other suit kind of smashes you down." Kit made a face that showed her distaste with the latter suit.

Bridget shook her head. "Right, I'll wear the smasher one instead. Where is it?"

"No! Do not wear that one! I will not let you leave the apartment. Listen, I know about bathing suits. Trust me on this. You *must* wear the *brown* one. I repeat—"

"Okay, okay, Jesus, where is it, before I change my mind?" cried Bridget.

"It's on the balcony with your cover-up. Here, here, let me get them. You're in no condition to be on the balcony. You might throw yourself over." Kit hurried onto the small overhang and grabbed the cover-up and suit from the iron terrace. She threw them at Bridget and commanded, "Now get ready!"

"Okay. Are you coming to the beach?" Bridget asked hopefully.

Kit shook her head. "No. After last night, I don't feel much like seeing anyone. I think I'll lay low. I mean, I'll go out tonight once Marren gets in and settled ... just, would you get ready? Don't make Lorenzo wait anymore!"

"Okay, thanks." Bridget smiled sheepishly as Kit left the room.

As she walked down the hallway, Kit mused in satisfaction, "Must be love if she's taking fashion tips from me."

◆　　◆　　◆

She was dripping with sweat already. And she was five minutes behind schedule. This was so unlike her, Bridget thought. Lorenzo's easy forgiveness and beach invitation had completely flustered her, and she'd gone into panic mode trying to get ready.

But she'd taken Kit's advice and worn the brown Miracle Suit. When it came to swimsuits, Kit did know that of which she spoke—not that she'd *ever* know what a Miracle Suit was really all about. She'd thrown the white eyelet cover-up and some silver flip-flops on, pulled her hair back in a high, tight ponytail, threw her oversized glasses on, along with some lip gloss, and she was out the door. That fact that it had taken almost a whole forty-five minutes and the help of Kit to decide on this minimalist outfit was quite worrisome to her (and Kit). Bridget was never late, and she always had her outfit planned about a day or so in advance! This was frightening, to say the least.

Now she was just past Mulini Square and practically hugging the wall of the tobacco shop, since a huge city bus had taken up half the street and part of the sidewalk as it unloaded a barrage of people. The bus took off, leaving a cloud of black exhaust in its wake. She scooted through tourists loaded with shopping bags, mothers dragging their children by the hands, zipping scooters, and slow-moving cars. Yet every time Bridget tried to push ahead or around someone, another aimless person or clump of people would stop right in front of her. This was quite normal here, and Bridget usually didn't care, since time didn't really seem to matter. But today, she was on borrowed time! She needed to get off this human obstacle course.

And now, another problem: she must pass Paolo's shop. She prayed he was inside with his back turned to the front window or that he was on an early lunch break. As she approached his store, the crowded thoroughfare slowed to an almost complete stop, like a backed-up freeway. What was going on now? People were talking animatedly and straining their heads to see something near Da'Stella. Ah, yes. Bridget recognized the aging rocker in the cowboy hat with his new girlfriend—the new girlfriend who had supposedly (if the tabloids were correct) stolen him away from his Hollywood wife who also happened to be her (now former best friend. They were holding hands and had just gone into Da'Stella as everyone gawked. As much as Italians were cool and sophisticated, they still loved a good star sighting, especially if it involved Americans, Hollywood, and scandal. Paolo was no stranger to high-profile customers, Da'Stella being frequented by many a famous tourist passing through. And luckily, if he was in the shop right now, there wasn't a chance he'd notice her in the cattlelike foot traffic passing by.

Bridget aggressively pushed herself through the throng. The masses thinned as soon as she rounded the bend and passed Santa Maria Assunta. She stood at the top of the steps that overlooked the Spiaggia Grande Square. She stared hard, looking for Lorenzo. Like any other day in Positano, a man in a rumpled straw hat stood in the middle of the crowded square, painting at an easel, while people were milling about, heading in and out of restaurants, walking down the promenade, lounging about the grand staircase.

There he was. At the edge of the cement square stood Lorenzo, tall, with a beach towel slung over one shoulder and his arms crossed. She wouldn't be able to miss him for many reasons: this easygoing, self-assured stance, the brunette hair pushed back behind his ears, the strong, tanned arms, and well, he was wearing another pair of Hawaiian board shorts. She watched him, in his wraparound shades, look about the square. His head turned toward the staircase. He seemed to be scanning it, step by step, over the bodies walking it, or those sitting on its many steps.

After a moment or two, his head cocked to the side, and Bridget knew Lorenzo's eyes had finally reached the top of the steps where she stood. She fought the urge to wave frantically like a complete dork. He gave her a nod and smile—an ever-so-slight, "not sure if he was annoyed or happy to see her" smile, but a smile all the same. Should she try to read into this already? Okay, so he wasn't dramatically rushing the stairs with open arms, hurdling people to get to her, but he was here, and having laid eyes upon her, he hadn't run the other way. For the second time in the last hour, Bridget wasn't about to complain or second-guess things. That was all she needed. She made her way down the steps.

◆　　◆　　◆

They were standing chest-high in the water, gently rocking to and fro as the afternoon current rolled against them. Lorenzo grabbed Bridget's hand, and he pulled her against him. She stood with her feet on top of his. Since they'd gotten to the beach, they hadn't talked much or joked like they usually did. Normally, Bridget wouldn't have thought much about it, but after last night, she worried if things were all right between them.

Lorenzo said into the top of her head, "So, Bridget, was our break long enough for you, or too short?"

She lifted her head to look at him and to check to see if he was joking. If he was joking, his face gave no indication.

"I think it was long enough," she answered quietly. And she meant it, too. She put her head back down into his chest.

Lorenzo rubbed her back and said, "I guess I didn't give you much time to miss me."

Technically, *no*, but she had. How did she explain that one? She remained quiet.

Lorenzo cleared his throat. "You're not saying anything. Does that mean I'm right?"

"No, I *did* miss you, Lorenzo," Bridget answered. What was he getting at? She thought she might know.

He raised his eyebrows at her and asked, "How was the boat trip?" There was a bite to the question. *Yes, yes, of course, that stupid boat trip she never should've gone on!*

"It was fine. It was fun," she answered lightly with a shrug. *Don't ask about Paolo …*

"So, how was your *boyfriend?* He was on the boat with you, wasn't he?" He stared at her, as if daring her to disagree.

Bridget stared back. "I don't have a boyfriend." *Not this again.*

Lorenzo laughed. "Really? Well, your boyfriend from last year. The one you went … *skinny-dipping* with?"

Skinny-dipping? As if she'd ever do that willingly. The memory of her bra almost floating off into the dark, watery oblivion last year caused her to cringe at the mere thought. That had been a close one. The closest she'd ever get to skinny-dipping. Skinny-dipping indeed! Besides, it was on the rocks where the clothes had come off …

Bridget snorted. "I didn't go skinny-dipping! And Paolo—I'm assuming you're talking about him—is not my boyfriend!"

Lorenzo shrugged. "Whatever, I already know all about it."

Bridget spoke sharply. "Then why are you asking me, if you already know all about it?"

How did he know about last year? Rachel would've been Bridget's first guess as to who had ratted her out about Paolo, but then she remembered that Rachel didn't know about the "rocks."

Lorenzo dropped his hands and looked at her dead-on. "Then let me ask you this: Did you kiss Paolo on the boat yesterday?"

Bridget froze. Damn the Aussie. Rachel had to be behind this one. How did she answer? Well, did Lorenzo mean on Paolo's boat or in the rowboat? Should she ask for specification of an actual location of supposed kissing? No, that would imply guilt, which she did, in fact, harbor. Of course, she hadn't meant for any of that to happen!

"I did not kiss Paolo on the boat," Bridget stated matter-of-factly; she felt like such a Bill Clinton. Lorenzo looked at her skeptically, his head tilted to the side, as if he was trying to bore a hole into her head to read her thoughts. Bridget felt like she was about to throw up. She couldn't lie. She was very bad at it anyway. She would just tell the truth, not to make herself feel better, but because she should. The whole thing was pretty innocent and light-hearted. The Blue Grotto, trying to escape the freaky gynecologist, Paolo picking that moment to kiss her—who wouldn't think the scenario was comical? Anyone would, except Lorenzo. He might definitely not see the humor in it.

Bridget swallowed. "Well … not on his boat, but kind of in the rowboat in the Blue Grotto …"

"Aww, Madonna! Wawawawawa!" The rest of whatever Lorenzo was shouting was lost on her. She really wished she'd practiced her Italian more. Bridget thought she'd at least like to know what he was calling her right now.

Bridget slapped the water hard a few times to get his attention. "Lorenzo! Lorenzo!"

He stopped and looked at her angrily.

She shouted, "Can I just explain? The whole thing was awful! I got stuck talking to Giorgio's doctor-gynecologist friend for half the boat trip—which was horrible in itself—and then I end up being on the rowboat with him and Paolo and Rachel, who, by the way, already wanted to kill me. Then Paolo and Rachel went swimming, and as soon as they did, the guy starts totally hitting on me. And then Paolo showed up and saved me."

It was the lamest explanation ever. But the thing was, it was true.

Lorenzo boomed sarcastically, "Well, I'm sorry that you have so many men throwing themselves at you, Bridget. Yes, I guess it must be awful. I suppose I should be grateful that you've spent the last two weeks with me at all!"

Bridget felt her voice get higher. "Okay, so now, you're being a total jerk. I didn't *ask* for some creepy gynecologist to bother me all day, and I didn't know that I was going to end up trapped on a rowboat in the Blue Grotto with *him and Paolo*, or that Paolo was going to kiss me! And, by the way, shit like this *never* happens to me!"

"Whatever," Lorenzo said in disdain. He turned and began swimming out to the roped buoy.

Whatever? The word itself didn't hurt so much as the way Lorenzo had said it. That stung.

But it also infuriated her. Well, she wasn't going to hang out in the water waiting for him to come back and yell at her. Bridget swam ashore and flung herself face-down on her beach chaise. Despite the constant bombardment of thoughts of self-pity, remorse, and anger, Bridget managed to completely doze off.

She awoke, sweating, and grabbed for her watch. Only half an hour had gone by. She looked over at the empty beach chair next to her. Lorenzo's towel and flip-flops were still there. Bridget turned over and sat up. She shaded her eyes and looked out, but she couldn't spot him in the water amid the bobbing swimmers. Where was he? She'd been hyper-paranoid about Lorenzo off cavorting with bikinied women yesterday, but certainly, today, her worry was well founded. Bikinied women or not, she guessed he'd have to come back for his stuff sometime. At least, she hoped so.

Then she saw him, further down the beach. He swam to shore and stood up, and then he headed toward the beach chairs. Bridget grabbed her dark glasses, threw them on, and flipped over, then fumbled through her beach bag for her paperback. The last thing she wanted was for him to think she'd been watching for him. For all she knew, Lorenzo might just grab his things and take off without so much as a good-bye.

She heard the crunching of the gravelly rocks as Lorenzo approached. Out of the corner of her eye, she saw him towel off. But instead of drying himself and leaving, he laid his towel back on the chaise and lay down on it, hands behind his head. Bridget could feel Lorenzo look over at her, but she pretended to read her book with interest. What could she say to him, anyway? Bridget thought there was probably nothing she could say that would make him understand what had happened. She didn't even fully understand! If only she hadn't gone on the boat trip. If only she'd not gone into the Blue Grotto—the damn place *was* cursed by witches. If only, if only!

Minutes lagged on, with Bridget intently staring at the same page, not reading at all, just lost in thought. Would Lorenzo ever say anything? What was the point of them being at the beach together?

A small pebble hit her in the arm. Did he just throw a rock at her? How juvenile. Humph. Bridget flipped to the next page—never mind that she hadn't read one word of the last page—and pretended she hadn't been pelted by a scorching rock.

Lorenzo rolled onto an elbow and said, "That's either a really good book, or you're ignoring me."

"I'm not ignoring you," Bridget lied and turned another page without looking at Lorenzo. Another burning rock hit her arm, harder this time. *Ow.*

"You gonna ignore me throwing rocks at you?" Lorenzo said with a sly smile on his face.

"If you would like to speak to me, you could just say so instead of throwing things at me. Or is that a Positano thing?" Bridget said, still without looking at him.

"Oh, now you're mad at me, Maestrina?" Oh, he'd called her his pet name for her. That was a good sign! But she was still pissed at him. Oh, sure, it was fine for him to be mad at her, but she wasn't allowed to be upset with him! How typically male of him! Of course, she *was* the one in the wrong, but still, Lorenzo really didn't realize how bad she felt about everything.

"I'm not mad. You're the one who swam off in a huff." Bridget finally turned her face in his direction.

Lorenzo sighed. "Fine. You're right. I *was* mad, Bridget. But can you blame me? Look, I know I'm not your boyfriend, but we just spent two incredible—at least, to me they were—weeks together, and you went off and kissed some guy like it was nothing. What the hell am I supposed to think?"

Oh, how dare he suggest that she just went off and did that like it was nothing!

"Look, Lorenzo, you're the one who suggested that we take a break! For all I knew, it was over between us!" Bridget stated.

Lorenzo sat up and pointed at her. "I suggested the break because of you. I tell you I want to come see you in California, and that was absolutely the wrong thing to say to you, apparently. I ask you how you feel about everything, about us, and it's always 'I don't know'—can't make up your mind about anything! So I say 'let's take a break,' not really wanting to, and you agree. And then you go off on the boat trip and kiss Paolo!"

Bridget sat up and pulled her chaise closer to Lorenzo's. She hoped no one around them was listening. She hissed at him, "I am sorry! When you dropped me off, it just seemed like *you* wanted the break, and then Kit told me we were invited on this boat trip. I just thought it would be better to go than to sit around wondering if you were off with some … other girl at the beach." Her voice trailed off. She was mortified. She sounded like such a … girl. A jealous girl, too.

"You were jealous? So you kissed Paolo because you thought I'd be off with some other girl?" Lorenzo looked at her questioningly.

"Nooo! It just happened! And it was nice and all," Lorenzo stuck his chin out and looked at her sharply, but Bridget continued on, "but it was just all wrong! And you showed up at dinner and everything looked really bad, and I … I'm sorry." She looked down. She was glad she had her dark glasses on. If not, Lorenzo would've seen her eyes tearing up, and she didn't let anyone ever see her cry. Oh, but she'd really made a mess of things. Bridget pretended she had something in her eye and carefully lifted her glasses to quickly wipe under her eye, then pulled her glasses back down.

"So …" Lorenzo began. Great, what was he going to say now? "Is that other guy really a gynecologist?" He looked at her with interest. Of *all* the things he could say or ask right now, Lorenzo wanted to know whether

Stefano was really a gynecologist? Bridget was actually thankful for an interlude in the seriousness.

"Yes, he is. If you'd like to know anything about childbirth, the female reproductive system, women's bodies, or any other *female* ailments, ask away, since I learned about them *all*," Bridget said dryly. "Ew, it was like my worst nightmare. Well, *one* of my worst nightmares." She shuddered.

Lorenzo got up and pushed his chair closer, so that it was touching Bridget's. He plunked himself down and scooted next to her.

"I think I'd like to see more—I mean, uh, *hear* more about the female body." Lorenzo chuckled and threw an arm around her. What was he doing putting his arm around her? Wasn't he mad? Maybe he'd caught on that she was crying and felt sorry for her?

Bridget said, "Look, it's okay. I know you're mad. You don't have to do ... this," and she tapped his hand that lay around her shoulder.

"Stop thinking the worst all the time. I know I don't have to put my arm around you. I want to. Just like I don't have to kiss you either, but I'm going to."

They kissed. It seemed like forever and it seemed like a millisecond. Lorenzo said quietly, "Let's not worry about what happened. We only have a short time left here anyway."

Bridget shook her head in affirmation. She was glad they had at least another week.

"Listen, want to go to dinner tonight? Just the two of us?" he asked.

Dinner? Just the two of them? Like a ...

"Like a *date*?" Bridget blurted out in surprise.

"Yeah, you and me, on a *date*. Yeah, I'll come and pick you up at the apartment," he answered.

Bridget hesitated slightly. She wanted to go on a date, in Italy, with an Italian guy ... that she just might be in love with ... maybe, well, you never knew. But Marren was getting in this afternoon, and the plan was to take her out tonight. Maybe Marren would be too tired to go out, Bridget couldn't help but think hopefully. No, Marren was 100 percent Irish. Which meant, she was just about born ready to go out under any circumstance. Well, Bridget reasoned, she and Lorenzo could come and meet them at the disco after dinner. She had to go on this date. No, not *had* to. She wanted to. She was going to.

"Okay?" Lorenzo asked.

"I would love to," Bridget answered.

"All right, it's a date then," said Lorenzo. *Yes, it was.*

◆   ◆   ◆

"If you stop at every sandal shop on the way home, I'll be at your place to pick you up before you are!" Lorenzo joked.

"This is only the second place I've stopped! And I'm not going in. I just want to look at my sandals," said Bridget.

She had attempted to stop in at the angry cobbler's shop to get her foot measured for a pair of his custom-made sandals, but so had half the beach. One look and Bridget could see that the surly shopkeeper was more irritated than pleased with the overwhelming beach business that had been thrust upon him. She'd come back another day for some of his dismissive scowls and hopefully a pair of sandals.

She had been quite prepared to pass Da'Stella without so much as a glance. She and Lorenzo were okay now, but running into Paolo still had its potential for awkwardness. She'd rather avoid the situation. However, just as they were walking past the front window, Bridget involuntarily took a peek, and *there they were.* Calling to her, like one of the infamous Sirens, was *her* pair of sandals. They were black—no shock there. They had a flat, sculpted bottom, almost like a Birkenstock, but these were no hippie shoes. The black-suede toe grip came up and over the front of the foot and was encrusted with a thick band of black Swarovski crystals. It came up high and attached around the ankle with two straps. It was a hot urban take on the simple gladiators that women in the Mediterranean had been wearing for years. They were casually sexy … and they were *black*! Bridget couldn't see the price tag, but she knew they were also *molto caro.* But they were *black*! They'd go with *anything* … so mesmerized was she by the sandals, she'd even forgotten to check if Paolo was inside the shop. Bridget glanced quickly and saw only an assistant inside, most likely one of his many cousins.

"*Those* are the sandals you been talking about?" Lorenzo looked at them skeptically.

"Uh-huh." Bridget nodded her head while staring at the store window.

"They're just *black* sandals," Lorenzo stated, as if that was detrimental to her owning such a pair.

Bridget looked at him with shock. "They are not *just* black sandals! And you call yourself Italian? Lorenzo, you've been in the US for too long."

Lorenzo rolled his eyes. "Da'Stella? Probably pretty expensive too. You'd do better to buy a bikini here, Bridget. Now that'd be worth your money!"

Bridget sighed in exasperation and walked on.

Lorenzo followed after her. "Aren't you going to try them on?"

"Another time, since you're worried about me being late. Let's just hope they don't run out of size 37."

They reached the square where Via Pasitea and Via C. Colombo met, and they separated. Lorenzo turned to her and said, "I'd give you a ride up the hill, but I have some things to pick up for the shop for my grandfather. I'll be at the apartment by nine thirty to get you." He kissed her and sauntered off past the tobacco shop. Bridget watched Lorenzo disappear up the crowded sidewalk. For a moment, she considered heading back down to Paolo's to try on the sandals, but she quickly changed her mind. Marren would be at the apartment soon, and who knew when Paolo would show up back at Da'Stella. She turned and headed up the hill.

Chapter 18

Bridget stood on tiptoe in an effort to get a full-length glimpse of herself in the oval mirror that was set precariously atop the bureau in their room. She had on her black, four-inch, lace-up espadrilles. Unfortunately, being slight in stature, she could still only view from about her knee upward. Yet the white Inhabit scoop tee, the long, black-linen Nolita skirt, and the heels gave her the appearance of being somewhat statuesque. Not bad, she conceded, hoping that the mirror wasn't playing one of those funhouse tricks on her eyes. Her hair was blown dry and flat-ironed—the first time she'd given in to doing so this week. Who knew how long the straightness would last in the heat, but it looked good now. Her signature Dior Blackout mascara was magnificently, well, black and elongated her thick lashes. She had her lip gloss, camera, etc., in her small clutch. And … she was nervous. What would she and Lorenzo talk about tonight? Would they talk about what was going to happen with them? They still had a week left. But only a week! While it felt like it was an eternity here, it also felt like it was nothing.

What would happen when they left Positano? Would they talk about *that*? Bridget decided she could now handle the topic without multiple drinks or incurring brain-freezes. And what was to progress *after* they left the disco? Again, Bridget's mind was muddled with all sorts of different scenarios. And all of them involved the possibility of not having any clothes on. Shameful, she knew, and so unlike her, since she totally abhorred peeling off any of her layers. However, Lorenzo was quite free to take off as much as he'd like. She'd seen him without his shirt on. With a rock-solid body like that, he had nothing to worry about anyway. The rest of him had to look just as well honed. Her stomach involuntarily jumped. Yes, she was ready for her date with Lorenzo.

Bridget turned off the light in the room and walked the dim hallway. When she'd left the patio about an hour ago to take a shower and get ready,

Kit had been preparing a platter of various crostini and fresh produce in anticipation of Marren's arrival. Marren had sent word that her train, en route to Naples from Rome, was delayed due to a cow stepping on the tracks. Now, though, as she walked through the double doors that led from the kitchen to the patio, Bridget spotted two figures sitting at the candlelit table. An open bottle of prosecco and two glasses sat between them. Marren had arrived.

"You're here! Welcome!" Bridget called out gleefully.

Marren got up and hugged Bridget. "*Finally!* I can't believe I'm actually here!" She then stood back and looked Bridget up and down. "Look at you. You know, you didn't have to dress up for me!"

Bridget shrugged and smiled guiltily. "Um, I have to go on a date."

Marren raised her eyebrows and looked at Kit, who exclaimed, "No, no, she is very happy to be going on this date! And, in actuality, it is *imperative* that she go on this date!"

"Oh, this is the guy. *The guy.* The cute, nice guy we like. Oh, yes, by all means, you should go on this date! We have the whole week to spend together, Bridge." Marren smiled.

Bridget added hastily, "But, we can come out and meet you at the disco afterward, for sure!"

Kit cut in. "You know, we might not even go out anyway. It's not a big deal, if you feel too tired, Marren."

Marren's head swiveled around, and she gave Kit an incredulous stare. "*I'm* goin' out tonight."

Kit explained lamely, "Oh, well, you said you were exhausted since you didn't sleep at all on the plane or the train, so I just thought …" Her voice trailed off.

Marren nodded and said excitedly, "I *am* exhausted. I'm still going out. Kit, it's my first night in Italy. This'll be like my first real night of my new freedom!"

Bridget interrupted, "What do you mean new *freedom?*"

Marren shrugged and said blandly, "Oh, Liam and I broke up last week."

"What? What happened?" Bridget's eyes bugged out. Marren and Liam had been dating for six years, ever since he stepped off the plane from Ireland and wound up in the same Irish pub she frequented every Friday after work.

"What happened was he went out for a pint with the boys after work and didn't come home *or call me* for *four days*."

"Oh, my God ..." Kit exclaimed and covered her mouth with her hand.

Marren waved her off and said, "*Yeah*, said he had just really needed to do some thinking about us."

"Yeah, lemme guess, he had to do that in Dooley's Pub," muttered Kit in disgust.

Marren looked at her and said sharply, "Kit, does it *really matter* where?"

"Right, sorry," said Kit meekly.

Marren continued on. "Anyway, he came back and said it was nothing but just a little *break*."

Bridget rolled her eyes and moaned, "I *hate* that *stupid* word."

"Yeah, well, *he* called it a little break. I called it: pack your shit up and be out of the apartment by the time I'm back from Italy. So, here I am! And I will be going out and I will most likely be drinking heavily ... all week. I can cry later."

Kit and Bridget exchanged worried looks, which were not unnoticed by Marren, and she said reassuringly, "Do not worry, girls. I will be *no* drama at all. I just want to lay on the beach, drink, eat occasionally, and meet cute boys. *And* ... I am so looking forward to meeting all these people you've been talking about. Especially, what's his name? Your guy, Kit ..."

"Lassino," Kit mumbled with a scowl on her face.

Marren looked at her quizzically.

"There was a little bit of drama last night ... *again*," Bridget explained, trying to head off the discussion.

"Great, as long as it doesn't involve me, I'm good," Marren said dryly before taking a sip of her prosecco. She then added, "Look, Kit, if you don't want to go out, it's fine. I'm a big girl. I'm sure I can maneuver my way down to the disco and back up here, no problem."

Kit sighed forlornly. "No, no. I'll go out ..."

"Thanks; you sound really enthusiastic. I thought you were the poster child for this town. Show a little excitement for someone who's never been here before," Marren chided jokingly.

Kit laughed and explained, "It's just that last night ... well, it was ... a *night*. But I will go out. We have snacks here, so we can eat, get ready, and then maybe have dessert down by the beach before hitting the disco. I'd normally take you to Lassino's restaurant, but I just can't handle seeing him tonight!"

"Perfect. As long as I get to meet the infamous Lassino before I leave. He sounds hilarious," said Marren.

Kit rolled her eyes and poured some more prosecco. "Yeah, hilarious. He's a complete pain in my ass!"

"Oh, he can't be that bad. I'm sure I'll get along just fine with him," Marren said mirthfully. Bridget bit her lip and raised her eyebrows at Marren.

"I'm sure you will, since he seems to get along with everyone except me!" said Kit bitterly. She then added, "You don't even know the half of it!"

From the center of the glass table, Kit's cell phone buzzed once. She picked it up, pressed a few keys, and looked up and said, "It's from Rachel ... again. She's been texting me all day. She wants to hang out tonight."

Marren watched Bridget and Kit give each other looks. She asked, "Why do you both look scared?"

Bridget answered, "Because we are."

Marren asked, "*Who* is this person?"

Kit explained quickly, "She's an Australian who works here and she had a thing going on with Paolo, but it's been over—well, at least Paolo doesn't want anything to do with her anymore—and then Rachel thought something was going on between Bridget and Paolo, and she tried to sabotage Bridget and Lorenzo, and, well ... she's just a very angry person!" Kit exhaled, then asked, "So, should I invite her to come to dessert with us?"

Marren looked at Kit and then at Bridget. "I'm sorry—you just told me she's angry and scary, and she tried to ruin things between Bridget and Lorenzo. Why are you considering inviting her to come out with us?"

"I know she's been kind of *hostile,* but she can be very nice, and I feel sorry for her. She's really feeling bad about the whole Paolo thing," Kit sympathized. She turned to Marren and asked tentatively, "So do you mind if I tell her to come meet us?"

Marren shrugged. "I'm already irritated by her, but sure. What the hell? Nobody knows me in this town anyway, so I really don't give a shit."

"Boy, I kinda wish I was going to dessert with you guys now!" Bridget declared.

Marren grabbed her carry-on and pulled her suitcase toward the door that led straight into her room. "I'm gonna go get ready. Have fun, Bridget. This is exciting! I'll make sure Kit catches me up to speed on everything before we head out."

✦   ✦   ✦

The evening thus far had been flawless. If someone had asked Bridget what the so-called perfect date should entail, she would have described it like this: guy shows up at pre-planned, said time to pick girl up. Does not merely toot scooter horn from the street, but actually parks scooter, comes in, sits for a drink, and makes lively conversation with girl's best friends. Girl's best friends now adore him (even more) and are slightly jealous of girl's good fortune, but still happy for her nonetheless. After charming friends with his effortless wit and easy banter, they depart. Opens door for girl. Friends sigh wistfully as couple leaves. On way up stairs, guy stops girl to tell her how lovely she looks and (even better) how lovely and wonderful she actually *is*. Kisses girl, but doesn't ruin her makeup job. Girl thinks he just might be a keeper. Has even been thoughtful enough to bring an extra helmet for her, since walking is out of the question, as they will have to drive up mountain to romantic neighboring town for dinner and even if eating close by, girl is known to wear ridiculously impractical heels when going out (i.e., they would still have to drive). He does, however, concede to her that her shoe collection is pretty hot. She now decides he's definitely a keeper.

Dinner is delicious, but girl is not paying much attention to food. Guy has decided he wants to sit right next to her at the table and not across from her. Wants to be closer to her. Kisses her often. Has arm over her shoulder like a (gasp!) boyfriend would. They sit and watch late sunset from a restaurant balcony in Montepertuso, chatting endlessly about life in general. He admits he wants to open his own restaurant. Someday, she'd like to do some kind of freelance travel writing. She definitely has the meticulous travels diaries to do so.

Although guy and girl have not yet spoken about what is to become of them once leaving Positano, they are very much comfortable. They are enjoying each other. Girl once again thinks that this is how all dates should be. Realizes, of course, *Italian* boy and being in a foreign country probably might have a little bit to do with it all. But … *no*. Girl then concludes that even if she were with said guy in any god-awful situation, say, on a ferris wheel or at a monster-truck show, she'd still have a good time. He's just so *right*. Girl freaks out momentarily at this realization, but quickly comes to. Dessert has arrived.

The waiter set the panna cotta on the table before them. It looked delicious. Surely, it would be delicious, not that she was the least bit hungry. But, what the hell? What did it matter now, anyway? For once, she wasn't going to obsess about eating, and she actually didn't care. Why spoil a good evening with neurotic thoughts? Besides, Lorenzo thought she was lovely and wonderful. *No, really*, he'd told her that and more than once and not just this evening. It was enough to go to a girl's head. Although Bridget didn't like to admit it, like most females, she was a sucker for a compliment from a male admirer, as long as it was sincere. And while Lorenzo teased her a lot, Bridget knew he was for real. That was one of the many things she liked about him. In fact, it made him quite different from most of the men she got mixed-up with. Lorenzo actually meant the things that he said.

Lorenzo waited for her to take a bite first before he dipped his fork into the caramel-glazed custard. After he'd taken his turn with the panna cotta, Bridget looked at him and asked, "So, what are you doing tomorrow?" She grabbed a spoon and used it to scoop up some of the thick pool of caramel. So much for not eating the dessert. She savored the sugary taste in her mouth, until she realized Lorenzo wasn't saying anything. She looked up at him. He had set his fork down and was looking at her hard. He glanced down at the table and then inhaled and exhaled quickly.

Bridget's heart thumped quite suddenly. He was about to tell her something, wasn't he? Yes, woman's intuition clearly was telling her so. That, and there was an obvious anxious look on his face ... what could it be? A nervous feeling came over her. Maybe he was going to tell her he loved her? Surprisingly, she hoped so. What would she do, though? What would she say? Bridget decided quite suddenly that she would tell him that she loved him too, because she did. Wait a minute; she was in love with Lorenzo. She could admit it. As strange as it was ... *she was actually in love!* Instantly, she felt like dry heaving as she waited expectantly for Lorenzo to speak.

But he looked at her with a pained expression on his face and said quietly, "Maestrina, I'm ... I'm leaving tomorrow."

Wh-hat?

Bridget knew her mouth was slightly open, but she remained silent. Lorenzo was going home. Why? He had been talking about staying an extra week for the past two weeks! What had happened to change his mind?

He explained quickly. "I don't want to, but I couldn't change my plane ticket, and I talked to my cousin and he needs me back at the restaurant anyway. I'm … sorry." Lorenzo reached out and took hold of her hand. What should she say? She bit her lip anxiously, then looked at him and said simply, "Um, okay."

"Okay?" Lorenzo looked at her as if he didn't believe her.

Bridget felt defensive. "Well, yes. What am I supposed to say? If you have to go, you have to go," she justified. But she felt angry and let down. It was happening again—the whole "being disappointed by a guy" thing. Yet, she didn't know whether to feel sorry for herself and be angry with Lorenzo or to feel angry with herself. Was this all because of … well, she knew she had to ask.

She looked at Lorenzo's serious face and his furrowed forehead and said, "This is because of what happened in the Blue Grotto, isn't it? Don't lie to me. I know you're still mad."

Lorenzo rolled his eyes, threw up his hand, and said, "Yes, Bridget, you're right. I am still mad about that. But that's not why I'm leaving. It was just too hard to change the plane ticket, and it's really busy at the restaurant right now. My cousin needs me."

Bullshit! People changed their flights all the time! He was *so* lying. She was being thrown over again … she couldn't believe this! She remained silent for a moment and then asked plaintively, "Why did you wait until now to tell me? Why didn't you tell me at the beach today?"

Lorenzo looked at her a moment before he said, "I didn't tell you at the beach because I didn't want you to come to dinner with me tonight just because you knew I was leaving. I just wanted to … see if you'd be willing without feeling like you had to. To see how you felt."

Bridget raised her eyebrows in shock and asked, "You were testing *me*, like to see if *I really* liked *you?* Look, Lorenzo, I explained to you what happened on the boat trip!"

Lorenzo interrupted. "Yeah, I know you did. And I understand. I know it didn't mean anything, but you are a very difficult person to read, Bridget! Do you know why you don't have a boyfriend? Because I do. You don't have one because you don't want one!" He sat back and folded his arms across his chest.

Bridget stared down at the half-eaten plate of panna cotta. She really wanted to argue with him on this one, but sadly, she admitted that Lorenzo was right. Bridget thought back on the countless guys who'd shown interest in her and she'd blown them off because she found numerous "flaws" with them. She'd blacklisted many a decent guy before they could even have a chance with her. Then there were the ones that *were* truly flawed. Of course, these guys were the ones she'd fallen head over heels for, the ones who were so completely in no shape at all for real relationships and who inevitably ended up disappointing her. She'd grown so accustomed to this cyclical pattern of haphazard relationships, and then so used to using the excuse that love just wasn't in the plans for her. But of course, maybe she was just too scared to try. And now, she'd found Lorenzo, and she kept holding him at bay. How much could one guy take?

Lorenzo said, "I'm just being honest. You have a lot of things to figure out, I think. So, you know, maybe it's good that I have to leave." He shrugged and sighed.

"Yeah … maybe," she answered in resignation. She would not cry. She would absolutely *not cry*.

"So, you still want to go to the disco? Or do you want me to take you home instead?" he asked.

Take her home? And leave her there alone to wallow in self-pity and despair that she'd blown it once again? Normally, she'd say yes. But not tonight. No, they had at least a few more hours left. She'd try not to ruin that short time.

"Of course I want to go to the disco. It's your last night here." She hoped her smile wasn't too weak and that her eyes were not too watery. "Unless *you* want to go home," she added.

Lorenzo shook his head, smiled, and said, "No, let's go to the disco."

◆   ◆   ◆

Kit, Marren, and Rachel sat at Mario's beachfront restaurant. They had finished the zabaglione that Kit insisted they have since it was "the best I've ever had! I'm not kidding!" For most of the time they'd been there, Mario had seated himself right next to Marren and quizzed her on her life. "So, Mahr-ren, are you a teacher too?" He flirted while sucking on his cigarette.

"No, I work in clothing store." Marren had smiled and took another sip of the second round of complimentary limoncello that Mario had brought out to them. She then gave Kit a sneaky sideways glance that Kit read as saying, *He's not my type.*

Kit was already prepared to head off Mario when he asked her to "organize Marren" for him. That request was sure to come once her friend was out of earshot. Luckily, Marren was tough. In fact, with her tendency for abrupt curtness, she made Bridget look like Pollyanna. While Mario would probably ignore Kit and try to go for it with Marren anyway, Kit knew he wasn't going to get very far. No, she wasn't worried about Marren at all.

While's Mario's presence at the table was entertaining, to say the least ("Mahr-ren, can somebody be in love with someone else if they haven't had sex with them? What do you think?"), it was also a relief. Rachel could no longer dominate the female conversation with her lamentations over Paolo and their lost love. Kit was just glad the Aussie hadn't started spewing profanities and vendettas, since last night she had seemed so overtly angry over the situation. In fact, Rachel was being quite pleasant, especially, Kit noticed, when she'd found out that Bridget was out on a date with Lorenzo.

"Oh, that's lovely. I'm glad they worked things out!" Rachel had uttered, as if she had forgotten she was the one who had caused the near breakup in the first place. Marren had rolled her eyes at Kit and taken another swig of her limoncello. With their second shots of limoncello finished, Mario headed off to the kitchen. As soon as Mario left, Rachel looked at her watch and said, "Well, shall we head to the disco, girls?"

Kit was trying to postpone hitting the disco for as long as she could, since she feared running into Vinnie, Johnny, or Fabio. Before she could give an answer, Mario appeared and set three more shots of limoncello, along with three dainty espressos down in front of them, which caused Rachel to utter, "I guess *not.*"

Kit ignored her. She would never turn away free limoncello and espresso, and besides, Lassino had just walked down the stairs and was standing in front of their table, staring at them. She had been hoping to avoid him as well after his disappointing revelation that she was *not* his girlfriend, but now that Lassino was here, Kit felt happy excitement. She just couldn't help it.

"Hello, Kit. Is this your friend?" Lassino nodded in Marren's direction.

Kit made the introductions and Lassino pulled up a chair and sat next to Kit.

"Why didn't you bring Marren to the restaurant tonight? You always bring your friends to my restaurant on their first night," he asked with concern.

Kit waved him off. "Marren got in late, and we decided to eat at home." She really didn't want to go into it all now with him. … Yeah, the public humiliation with Fabio, the resurrection of Johnny, the run-in with Vinnie … it *was* a bit much.

Lassino turned to Marren and said, "She is mad at me. Kit is always mad at me!" He smiled mischievously.

Kit rolled her eyes and conceded, "Actually, I just didn't want to run into *anyone* … especially *Vinnie*." Lassino looked at her questioningly, and Kit couldn't help but proceed to tell him about Vinnie chasing her down and his crazed paranoia. After she had finished her tale, Lassino looked at her and said smugly, "He *is* married."

"What?" Kit shouted. Lassino gave the face-shrug and then added, "Yes, of course. And he sells drugs and does a lot, too."

Both Marren and Kit shouted, "*What?*"

Lassino answered matter-of-factly, with the Italian facial shrug, "Yes, but he's a good boy."

Rachel, bored, puffed away on her cigarette. Marren snorted in amusement, and Kit cried out indignantly, "Well, I don't think so! He scared me! It was scary! *He* is scary! Why isn't he at home with his wife, anyway?"

Lassino shrugged again. Rachel stood up and said, "I'm heading off to the disco. Are you coming, Kit?"

Before Kit could answer, Rachel called out to some girls in the square and walked off to talk with them. Kit looked at Marren. Marren said, "Whatever's fine." That was the answer Kit had been hoping for. She'd much rather sit and talk with Lassino a while longer, and the longer, the better. They watched Rachel head down the walkway with her friends. She then turned around abruptly and shouted, "Kit, are you coming?" Kit hesitated as Lassino looked at her.

Rachel shouted again in a loud, irritated voice, *"Kit, are you coming or not?"*

Marren said harshly, "What the hell is her rush? Isn't the disco built into the side of a fuckin' rock? I mean, it's not going anywhere!"

Lassino chuckled. "She is probably hoping to find Paolo. Shall we go?"

Kit looked over to where Rachel stood waiting, her hands on her hips. "Be right there!" she called.

◆　◆　◆

They left Lorenzo's scooter parked up on the sidewalk. Before starting the climb down the stairs, Bridget looked up and over her shoulder at the empty balcony across the street.

"Sera" wasn't even on her stoop tonight, keeping a glaring eye on everyone's comings and goings. But why should Bridget be surprised? Ever since Lorenzo had told her that he was leaving tomorrow (instead of telling her that he was *in love with her*, like he was supposed to), everything seemed out of kilt.

The disco, of course, was its usual intensely hot, crowded self. But Bridget felt like she was in an episode of *The Twilight Zone*. If the DJ had happened the play the show's theme music (duh nuh nuh nuh nuh nuh nuh), she wouldn't have thought twice about it. For starters, the first person she laid eyes on when she and Lorenzo made it to the bar was Kit, who was standing next to Lassino, who was conversing—in a way she'd never seen him chatting in the disco before—with Johnny! *Johnny*, Kit's ex-boyfriend, who'd once said he'd never set foot in Italy, who'd once gone ballistic at the mere mention of Lassino's name—stood comfortably next to his nemesis while Kit smiled and laughed at whatever they were saying. Odd, to say the least.

Laura, Johnny's Venetian girlfriend, was nowhere to be seen. Apparently, she'd had some bad mozzarella while on their day trip to Capri and was laid-up in the hotel room. Bridget hadn't thought it possible to have any type of bad cheese in Italy, but who knew? Nothing was as it seemed anymore.

While chitchatting with the trio, Rachel, like the she-devil she was, materialized out of nowhere and planted a hand on both Lorenzo's and Bridget's shoulders. Bridget involuntarily inhaled sharply. Smiling her wide, Jokerlike smile, Rachel patted them and said sweetly, "Hi, guys! Heard you were off having a lovely dinner!" Both Bridget and Lorenzo stared at her almost suspensefully. Bridget, in particular, was waiting for the snide remark or threatening snarl that was sure to come out of her mouth next. But Rachel just continued smiling and said, "I'm off for a smoke. See you in a bit!" Lorenzo shrugged at Bridget and ordered their drinks.

By the time Bridget had downed two rounds of prosecco, she thought for sure she'd be in better spirits, but she was so wrong. When Marren dragged her out onto the crowded dance floor, she felt she had feet made of lead, a veritable Frankenstein, clomping about, with no sense of rhythm whatsoever, and *that* never happened. Bridget felt grateful for the tattooed, earringed, muscley K-Fed look-alike in the wife beater and straw fedora who had glided into their small dance space and commandeered Marren as his dance partner. Marren didn't seem to mind, either.

Bridget pushed herself out of the crowd. She didn't have time to waste on the dance floor when her time with Lorenzo was running out. They'd already been at the disco for two hours and had barely talked, due to the extremely loud music and quite possibly (Bridget felt) the awkwardness now between them. She was feeling quite rejected and upset, and if she could admit, even indignant! He was feeling remorseful (well, possibly), or perhaps, just feeling over the whole thing, over *her*!

But once she reached his side, Lorenzo turned to her and said, "Well, I'm gonna say good-bye to everyone, and then I better take you home. I gotta pack and be up early." She was deflated, but Bridget wasn't about to argue. It was over, wasn't it? Better not to drag things out.

"You guys are leaving?" Kit asked in surprise.

"Yeah, Lorenzo's leaving *tomorrow*. He's gotta get packed," Bridget said.

"What? He's leaving? Positano?" Kit screamed in an effort to make herself heard over the music.

Bridget winced and nodded. "Yeeesss."

"*Why?* Are you okay?" Kit asked with concern.

"I'm fine," Bridget said and walked toward the door to wait for Lorenzo, who was shaking hands with his bartender friends. Lorenzo walked over, and Bridget scanned the dance floor quickly looking for Marren. In a dance-off with K-Fed, with a circle gathered around them, she didn't notice them leave. Bridget was glad someone was having fun.

◆   ◆   ◆

Bridget pushed open the unlocked green door. It seemed like it was just yesterday when she had opened that same door to find a plastic bag full of Nutella swinging precariously from the door handle. The bag that *Lorenzo* had delivered. Why couldn't he have gone to the wrong apartment with the Nutella? Why did *she* have to be at the disco *that* night trying (unsuccessfully) to get a drink at the bar? And why did *he* have to spot her and help her get a drink? Why had *any* of it happened? What was the purpose—just to trick her into having her heart broken again? What a cruel thing to have happen to her here.

Bridget sighed and said, trying to sound pleasant, "Well, have a safe trip."

Lorenzo looked slightly hurt. *"Have a safe trip?* Can't I come in?"

"Oh, sorry, you said you needed to get home ..." Bridget replied lamely. *He wanted to come in? Why?* Her interest was definitely piqued.

"Well, I do need to get home, but I want to get your address, phone number, e-mail ... you know ... I don't want you dropping off the face of the earth on me," he said and smiled warmly.

Oh, *that*. He wanted her *address*. That was all. *Right*, like they were really going to keep in contact, like some kids who had met at summer camp. *Please.*

She answered, "Sure," and led him in. The patio was dark, and she fumbled around until she found the light switch by the door. She found her travel journal on the table and tore a blank page from the back, and then went into the kitchen in search of a pen. She spotted one on the counter, grabbed it, and whirled around—right into Lorenzo.

"Oh!" she exclaimed. She had thought he was still on the patio. She scooted around him, found a pen and began jotting her information down. She finished and handed the pen to Lorenzo, who was staring at her intently. What was he looking at?

He took the pen and quickly wrote on the paper. When he had finished, he tore it in half and looked at what she'd written. He asked, "Sure this is the right address and all? Not fake?" *As if he would really contact her ever, once he left Positano ...*

Bridget rolled her eyes and smiled. "Yes, it's the right address and number."

"I guess I'll find out," he smiled, folded the piece of paper, and placed it in his front jean pocket. There was an awkward silence as they stood looking at each other. Bridget wondered, what did one say in a situation like this? *Nice meeting you! Take care now! See ya next summer?* No, too trivial and somewhat flippant. How about *I'm so sorry I was an idiot. Don't go, please! I love you?* A tad on the desperate side, but far closer to the truth. She'd never be able to say it now. It was too late. Lorenzo was leaving. If he loved her, wouldn't he stay? Bridget felt painfully uncomfortable and looked down, deciding to take great interest in the tiled floor.

"Bridget," Lorenzo said.

"Yes?" she answered, still staring at the floor.

"What are you thinking? And please, don't tell me you don't know," he said seriously.

What was she thinking? What *wasn't* she thinking? There was so much, but she just couldn't say any of it. She fought the urge to utter her old standard, "I don't know." She knew that she must say *something*, though.

She heard herself blurt out, "Do you think the last two weeks were a mistake?" There, that was something.

Lorenzo asked, "Do you?"

"I asked you first," she said quickly. She needed some kind of confirmation from him to know that whatever had gone on hadn't been for nothing, that it was more than a silly vacation fling.

Lorenzo shook his head. "No, I don't think any of it was a mistake. *Do you?*" There was a worried look on his face.

"No, I don't," she answered.

Lorenzo looked relieved and smiled. "At least you found something to agree with me on."

Bridget ignored his attempt to make light of the situation and asked, "But ... so, what do you think? What does this mean?" She didn't know what he would say, but either way, she needed clarification before he left.

"What do I think about us?" Lorenzo shrugged simply before he said, "I don't know. I guess we both go back to our lives at home. And then ... let's just see what happens."

See what happens? Bridget knew enough to know that this was definite code for *nothing is going to happen, but I don't want you to hate me, so I'm going to pretend like there's a chance ...*

"Right," she answered with a confidence she didn't feel. She didn't want to keep him any longer. Bridget headed past him, out onto the patio, and stood waiting by the door.

Lorenzo followed. He stopped at the door, turned to her, and said, "I'm very bad at good-byes, so I'm not gonna say it."

Bridget stood there, mute. Did "Ciao!" count as good-bye since it was in another language? What to say? Standing there in silence was just about unbearable.

"Maestrina, come here." Lorenzo reached his arms out, encircled her waist, and pulled her to him. He held her to him firmly. There was nothing for her to do but to hold onto him just as tightly, so she did. But wasn't he even going to kiss her?

Lorenzo bent his head down close to her face. She could feel his breath. His face came closer until his lips were on hers, softly, and then forcefully. And there was nothing she could do, again, but kiss him back. It felt innocent. It felt passionate. It was powerfully frantic and urgent. It was wonderful and it was awful—awful only in the sense that this signified the end. Although, Bridget wondered when the kissing *would* end. Lorenzo had her clasped to him, as he leaned back against the door. Bridget hoped no one decided to come home right at this moment. How much longer could they go on like this before something else happened? And then, finally, Lorenzo pulled his lips from hers and said, "I should go. I better go. Okay?" He dropped his hands from her back and grabbed onto her hands. Bridget stared at him.

Lorenzo said, "Bridget, I want to stay with you tonight, but I just can't."

"Why?" Bridget blurted out.

Lorenzo ran a hand through his dark and sighed. "I can't because I think I know you better than you think I do. If I stayed with you tonight, if we were together, you would think it was because I was leaving in the morning."

"No—" began Bridget, but Lorenzo interrupted and said, "Yes, Bridget. You know I am right. I have to go."

He probably was, but she didn't care. She just wanted to hold onto him for a little bit longer. Once he walked out the green door, she knew that was the end of it.

"Okay," Bridget sighed and took a step away from him. "Have a safe trip," she added and truly meant it.

"Thanks," he whispered. "Enjoy the rest of your time in Positano, Maestrina." Lorenzo grabbed her face and kissed her again. He glanced quickly back at her, opened the door, and left. Bridget poked her head out and watched him ascend the dark staircase. She wondered if it would seem too pathetic to run after him, grab onto one of his legs, and scream, "Take me with you!" Yes, probably.

She closed the door and leaned against it with a thud. She inhaled and exhaled choppily. Well, that took care of that. Bridget didn't know what to feel. She felt exhilaration (he had kissed her, hadn't he?) but extreme sadness (he had left her, hadn't he?). She was in the depths of despair (no, no, he'd gotten it all wrong! She did love him!), yet crazed with relief (God, that had been close!). She was hopeful (*Let's see what happens* ... something could happen!), but she felt hopeless (it was unlikely she'd ever hear from him again, let alone see him). It never would've worked out, anyway. Lorenzo was right. It was better this way. Yes, thank God, she had escaped the clutches of love again. She walked into the kitchen and picked up the scrap of paper with Lorenzo's e-mail and address. She quickly crumpled it and flung it back onto the counter and walked back to the bedroom. She closed the door, threw herself face-down into her pillow, and wept uncontrollably.

◆　◆　◆

Bridget lifted her head from the pillow. She had no idea what time it was. The room was bright, too bright, and the messed-up roosters were crowing, but that was no indication of the time, since they did that twenty-four hours a day. She felt hungover. Her mouth was dry (no doubt from sleeping with it open), and her throbbing head felt like it had been held in a vise. She wasn't hungover, though. Oh, she only wished that was the reason for the pain! But no—it was because she had cried herself into a deathlike sleep coma because Lorenzo had deserted her. He hadn't deserted *per se*, but he'd left Positano to return to Florida. She'd never see him again. The term *desertion* was certainly applicable.

Bridget pushed herself up and looked at the other side of the king-sized bed. It hadn't been touched. Kit obviously had stayed the night with Lassino. She trudged over to the door that led to the small balcony off their bedroom. She pushed it open and immediately shrunk back; she threw a hand over her eyes, like a vampire. The light and heat were intense, and Bridget backed away. As she passed the bureau, she glanced at herself in the tipsy mirror. There she stood, dejected, in her rumpled clothes that she'd slept in, including her espadrilles.

But the clothes weren't the worst of it. Her hair was completely furry on one side, almost like there was a tumbleweed sticking out of her head, while the other side was matted down. Upon closer inspection, Bridget saw a huge, jagged crease down the side of her cheek from being face-planted into the pillow. Her eyes were black-rimmed from her mascara running—not that she could even really see her eyes. They were practically swollen shut from the crying. Forget about Lorenzo; just the sight of her now was enough to start another round of sobbing! Bridget couldn't look at herself anymore. It was too painful a reminder of last night. And quite frankly, it was very scary as well. She bent down to unlace her shoes, and blood rushed to her head. She kicked them violently across the room and left the bedroom. This day sucked already. She hoped it was half-over.

As she staggered past Marren's room, she peeked her head in the slightly cracked door. A limp hand dangled from the side of the bed. Thankfully, it was Marren's hand and not that of some random male. Bridget didn't think she could stand the sight of any males in close proximity to her, anyway. With a man or not, at least her friend had made it home safely.

Making it to the kitchen, she decided she was in dire need of caffeine— yes, a cappuccino! But that wasn't going to happen, since she didn't know how to make cappuccino and she certainly wasn't leaving the apartment to get one looking like a victim of domestic violence. A chilled glass of prosecco would suffice instead. The whole bottle would actually be better, but she'd start with a glass. The two empty prosecco bottles on the counter did not bode well for that.

Bridget opened the fridge and found a plate with four green olives and two slices of mozzarella. As she had suspected, there was no prosecco and no bottled water either. However, there were three Coca-Cola Lites (as Diet Coke was so called in Italy). One, she was going to guzzle, and the other two, well, they were going to serve as ice packs for her eyes, since she knew for a fact there was no ice in the freezer (since ice was like the Holy Grail here and was only doled out in restaurants).

What to eat? She was starving, of course. Couldn't she be one of those people whose depression made her lose her appetite, so she could drop a few pounds? Of course not. She did not want the four pathetic olives and a couple slices of mozzarella. That would have been almost too healthy. No! On the counter was one of the many Nutella jars that sported the Italian World Cup soccer team logo. Next to it sat an opened bag of marshmallows, left over from the Fourth of July party. Marshmallows couldn't go bad, could they? Food poisoning seemed unlikely, but she'd take her chances. What did she care now, anyway? Yes, she was in full self-pity, depression mode.

She scooped up the three Diet Cokes, the Nutella, and the bag of marshmallows, and walked out onto the patio. As she made her way to the lounge chairs that sidled up to the balcony ledge, she tripped over something. Dammit! She looked down and saw a sand-covered, gold flip-flop on the tile floor. She kicked it out of the way and plunked herself down into one of the reclining lounge chairs. She cracked open one of the cans and took a hefty swig. Ahhh ... she burped and opened the Nutella jar. She grabbed some marshmallows and dipped them into the creamy, chocolate-hazelnut spread. Bridget shoved them into her mouth and chewed. *Delicious.* Everything would taste so much better if covered in Nutella. *Nutella ...* she sniffed as she thought of Lorenzo finding the apartment and secretly leaving the replacement Nutella jars on the doorstep.

And now ... she'd never see him again. She could no longer eat Nutella without thinking of Lorenzo. Dammit! She would never eat Nutella again at all! Perhaps, that was a good thing, considering Weight Watchers had no doubt assigned a very high points value to Nutella. She put the top back on the jar. Tears filled her eyes. When Bridget couldn't see through the blur anymore, she blinked and let the tears stream down her face. Then she lay back and placed a cold Diet Coke on each eye.

◆　　◆　　◆

The door from Marren's room to the balcony creaked open.

"Good morning," Marren said in a groggy voice. From under her Diet Coke cans, Bridget replied, "Morning, although, I'm pretty sure it's sometime in the afternoon."

A rooster crowed far off. "But ... *what?*" Marren asked, confused.

"Ignore the roosters. They're … just like that here," Bridget said blandly while trying to keep the cans balanced on her eyes.

"Why do you have a Diet Coke can on each eye? And what the hell happened to your hair?" Bridget could hear the amusement in Marren's voice.

Bridget sighed before explaining, "Lorenzo is on a plane right now back to Florida, and I'm never going to see or hear from him again. I completely cried myself to sleep; therefore, I look like I have elephantitis of the face … and I'm not quite sure what happened to my hair."

Marren said sympathetically, "Aww, I'm sorry, sweetie. But are you really sure you're not gonna hear from him? You never know …"

Bridget held up a hand to halt Marren and said, "No, no, I *know*. Let's talk about something else before I start crying again."

"Okay, but you're gonna have to give up one of those Diet Cokes, because I am *hungover* and I know there's nothing to drink here, because we drank it all," Marren said and sat in the lounge chair next to Bridget.

Bridget handed her a can and said, "Let's hear about your fun night."

Marren opened the can and took a long swig before she said, "Uh … well, I, uh … left the disco and went down to the beach with some random guy—in fact, some guy whose name I can't even remember and who I probably wouldn't be able to pick out of a lineup!"

"Was it K-Fed?" Bridget asked in interest.

"What?" Marren laughed.

Bridget snapped her fingers a couple of times. "You know, the guy who looked like Kevin Federline, the one you were dancing with, with the straw fedora …"

"Ah, yes, K-Fed. He paid for all our drinks and we took off. Yes, it was him … on the beach …" Marren's voice drifted off.

Bridget sat up. "Did you have *love* on the rocks?"

Marren said sheepishly, "No, it was *love* on a beach chair. Nice, huh?"

Bridget waved her off. "You're on vacation. Take the advice you would give me—who cares? Big deal!"

"Yeah, except he was married," Marren said and looked sideways at Bridget. Before Bridget could open her mouth, Marren exclaimed in disgust, "The jerk decides to tell me *after* we're all done that he has a wife and two kids, but his wife is an absolute mess, as if that made it all right. Oh, God!" Marren shook her head and pinched the bridge of her nose.

"Was he Italian? From Positano?" Bridget asked in disbelief.

Marren looked at her and winced. "I don't even know. I can't even remember if he had an accent! In fact, once we got to the beach, it all went a little fuzzy. But believe me, I snapped to as soon as he said he had a wife. I took off without even saying good-bye!"

Bridget looked worried. "Maybe you were drugged!"

"*I wish*. Bridget, I would know the difference. I was extremely *drunk*—all the prosecco, the limoncello, then more prosecco ... it was bad. *And* I lost my flip-flop!" Marren cried out.

Bridget pointed across the patio. "Oh, it's over there."

"No, I lost the matching one. I left so fast, I couldn't look for the other one. Then I had to climb five thousand freakin' stairs at five in the morning, in one flip-flop! I had no idea where I was even going. All I knew was I *had* to keep climbing till I found the green door with Kit's stupid bubbles-doorstop!"

Bridget bit her lip to keep from giggling.

Marren looked at her sharply and said, "Are you laughing? I was practically in tears, you know. Dammit, those were my favorite flip-flops!"

"Sorry. We'll get angry cobbler man to make you a new pair. Up the hill in *one* flip-flop at five in the morning. That's *great*. Welcome to Positano!" Bridget said mirthfully.

"Shut up; look at your hair!" Marren shrieked and pointed at her.

They looked at each other and broke into laughter. After Marren had wiped the tears away, she said, "It is kinda funny, huh? Well, not the K-Fed part, but the flip-flop ..."

Bridget nodded.

"Feel better about Lorenzo, now?" Marren asked hopefully.

"Well, maybe just a tad." Bridget pinched her two fingers together to show a smidge.

Marren grinned and said, "Good, but don't expect me to go losing any more shoes for you!"

◆　◆　◆

Kit was in a good mood. Well, a "better than her usual good mood" mood. To be quite frank, she actually didn't have to even fake her good spirits, like she'd been doing as of late. While she'd been very happy that Marren had finally arrived, she had still been quite hesitant about leaving the apartment. Her hopes that her friend would be too exhausted to venture out on the town had been for naught. Marren was always up for going out. Kit wondered why she had ever thought that forty-eight hours of traveling and sleep deprivation would have made any difference. And anyway, her determination to be a good hostess and tour guide wouldn't allow her to wallow any more. Besides, she couldn't stay holed up in the apartment for much longer. That would just draw more attention to her, which apparently was something she didn't need any more of.

But she'd purposely boycotted Lassino's restaurant in favor of having dessert at Mario's instead. Surprisingly, everything had gone well from there on. Mario was his usual flirty, gracious self, minus trying to grab her (thanks to Marren being there); Rachel was in a less foul mood (who really knew why); and Lassino had showed up, and of his own accord, he had pleasantly accompanied them to the disco.

Kit conceded that once they hit the disco, things had certainly had the potential to go awry. But strangely enough, they didn't. Kit had cringed as she spotted Johnny heading their way while they waited for their drinks. She remembered feeling surprised once again to find that he looked just as good as he had the night before. Hadn't she ever noticed his good looks? Of course she had, but she supposed she had been too preoccupied with other things. And truly, there really was something more to him here that she was finally able to see.

Maybe Positano was a magical place. And what's more, she had actually enjoyed talking to Johnny and watching Lassino and Johnny get along so well. It was a scenario she'd never expected: her ex-boyfriend and the man who'd supposedly stolen (or maybe *lured* was a better choice of words) her away were having drinks together and talking about American football in the disco in Positano! Kit finally felt comfortable with Johnny being here. They were grown-ups, and they could be friends. Johnny even had a beautiful Italian girlfriend. It was too bad Laura had gotten food poisoning. Kit would've loved to have chatted with her a bit more, now that she was having a better hair night.

Everything had gone better than expected. Even when Vinnie showed up later on, he kept clear of her. At one point, it appeared as if he was making his way directly toward her, but he was suddenly held up on the crowded dance floor. And then, magically, he made a detour to the other end of the bar, where the only thing he did was stare pointedly at Kit. Well, she could handle that, as she was used to that sort of thing happening. The only slightly disconcerting moments of the evening were the announcement of the surprising news that Lorenzo was leaving the next day and Marren's disappearance from the disco. There was nothing Kit could do about those two things happening. She worried momentarily about Marren, but she felt that despite Vinnie and Rachel, Positano was a very safe place for a single female. Marren would be fine.

And when Lassino had asked her if she was ready to go home, she was secretly ecstatic. "Home" meant going to his place to spend the night. She hated to leave Johnny alone at the disco, especially when he'd been trying to tell her something. The music had been thunderously loud, and Johnny had shouted something that included, "Laura! ... love! ... " and then the rest had been lost in the music. Kit had stared at him, perplexed, and tried to figure out what he was saying. Johnny was in love with Laura and wanted to tell her? That could only be it. The eager look on his face told her he wasn't mad at her, so perhaps he wanted her blessing or for her to know that after everything between them, they were finally okay? Kit had smiled, shook her head and said, "Okay" and waved at him, as she grabbed onto Lassino's hand and headed out the door. Everything had a way of working out in the end.

Yes, it did. Lassino had taken her back to his place and, well, she didn't need to go into details, but he was very attentive to ... all of her. Whenever she stayed over, he always was. That, she could never complain about when referring to Lassino. Kit hadn't expected such full force from him, since she'd only been over just a few nights before. But Lassino acted as if he hadn't seen her since last summer. And Kit had to admit, she relished his exuberant interest. He even spoke sweet Italian nothings into her ear— nothing with "Ti amo" in it, but there was a lot of "Amor-this" and "Amor-that," which she liked just as well.

His benevolent and affectionate behavior didn't vanish when late morning rolled around, either. Instead, Lassino drove the two of them down to the restaurant and let her help him start the pizzas. She'd stayed all day, chatting with the waiters and taking pictures of Lassino while he prepped and joked with the staff.

Late afternoon came around quite suddenly, it seemed, and Lassino packed up a pizza, hot out of the brick oven, for her to take back up to the girls for a pre-dinner snack. Not only that, but he'd packed a couple of bottles of prosecco in a plastic bag for her too, and said he'd call her later. Yes, all that, and she wasn't accosted once by any lurky people on her way up the hill. She'd made it up the hill and the arduous steps so fast that when she pushed open the green door, she realized in surprise that the pizza was actually still hot. Someone *was* looking out for her today.

"Hello? Anybody home?" Kit called out as she pushed the door closed with her foot.

"Hey," a voice called from the corner of the balcony. Kit looked over and saw Marren sprawled out on one lounge chair, a folded washcloth covering her eyes. Marren lifted her hand to wave before she fumbled around for one of the marshmallows strewn about. She located one, plunged it into the open Nutella jar on her lap, and then popped it in her mouth. Bridget laid on the chair next to her, like a corpse, a can of Diet Coke teetering over one eye. Kit scrunched her eyebrows questioningly.

"Um, are you two all right?" Kit asked hesitantly while setting the pizza down on the table.

"*No.* Is that food I smell? We're starving," Bridget called out and sniffed the air. She removed the Diet Coke from her face and sat up eagerly.

Kit involuntarily stared at Bridget's head, specifically the tumbleweed side, as she answered brightly, "Uh, yes, pizza! Lassino's treat!"

Bridget explained, "I know, I know, the hair; it's all Lorenzo's fault."

Kit stared at Bridget and her hair incredulously and said, "Lorenzo did that to your hair?"

Bridget closed her eyes and threw herself back down against the chaise. "Yes … in a *manner of speaking.*"

Kit winced,."Oh, God, sorry, that's right. He left … what happened?"

"I think … maybe we should talk about something *else.*" Marren took the cloth off her eyes and shook her head at Kit.

"Oh, okay. Well, what about you? I looked for you before we left, but you had disappeared. Were you off with K-Fed?" Kit asked excitedly. When Marren didn't answer, Kit shrieked, "Did you have … oh, you did!"

Bridget snorted, and Marren smirked and said, "Again, maybe we should talk about something *else.*"

"Oh, come on, tell! Lassino and all the guys think you really went off with the actual

K-Fed. Seriously, I think you just went up a notch in their books," Kit cried out.

"Really? How nice," Marren said sarcastically. "He was not K-Fed! I mean, I would know. Wouldn't I?" she asked unsurely.

Kit laughed. "I'm kidding. But he did really look like him. Didn't you think so?"

Marren shrugged and looked at Kit and then Bridget helplessly.

"You don't remember what he looked like? But, but—" Kit started.

"Look, just because I slept with him doesn't mean I remember what he looked like!" sputtered Marren. She then added, "That sounded bad. Oh, are those bottles of prosecco there? Kit, you're a star!"

Kit hopped up from her chair and grinned widely. "Oh, yes, yes! Here, let me get glasses and some plates! You guys just sit right there! Don't move!" She scurried off into the kitchen.

Marren looked at Bridget and said, "Well, someone's in a chipper mood. I mean, even more chipper than usual. I don't know if I can handle all that right now on one patio." She looked at the Nutella-covered marshmallow in her hand and moaned, "Why am I eating Nutella and marshmallows?"

Kit reemerged with three glasses and answered with no contest, "Because it's good." She popped the prosecco cork and poured three very full glasses.

◆   ◆   ◆

The week had flown by, though not due to any dramatic excitement. Nothing about their Positano routine had changed in the least bit. They managed to get down to the beach by one (at the very earliest, or at the very latest—it depended), and they ate a lazy, late afternoon lunch at "their table" at one of the front and center beach restaurants. They slept and sweated some more on the beach, then meandered up the hill, making various pit-stops along the way to either shop and/or sip a beverage or two at an outdoor café. Back at the apartment, they took their time getting ready and moseyed out to to dinner (almost always to Lassino's or Solo Tu) around ten or ten thirty. They finished off the evening at the disco. And then they started all over again. To most people, it might seem an extremely frivolous and care-free existence, but make no mistake; the girls set daily goals for themselves, that is, besides that one about getting to the beach by one.

Bridget: "I'm gonna drink a lot of water today. I feel bloated. Oh, yeah, and mail my postcards."

Marren: "I'm definitely going to get some new sandals. How late does angry cobbler guy stay open?"

Kit: "I need to go to Tino's and buy a wedding gift for Diana and Leo."

While they were not the loftiest of aspirations, they clung to them fiercely, so that by the end of the week, when none had been accomplished, it had become their own personal joke. Yes, everything was routine in its enjoyable nothingness. It was alarming how easy it was to do nothing. But they would savor every moment. Especially since once they left and returned home, they would be like veritable hamsters running on their own personal wheels again.

The only thing that had changed for Bridget was that Lorenzo wasn't there. However, she thought about him constantly and wondered what he was doing back in Florida. Was he thinking about her at all? As a result, she did manage to add the teensiest of something new to her daily routine that week. After returning from the beach, while the girls were getting ready, Bridget would steal away to their hotel neighbor, Palazza Bianca, to use the Internet. She insistently told herself that she would be better for cleaning out all the junk mail from her mailbox instead of having to sift through hundreds once she got home. But really, she was checking to see if there was any word from Lorenzo. There wasn't. A week had gone by, and there had been no word at all. For all she knew, the whole thing with Lorenzo could've been a figment of her imagination. A little glimmer of hope remained that maybe when she got home, there'd be a message waiting on her cell phone, but her utterly disap-pointed and dejected psyche readily and repeatedly squashed it into oblivion.

And hard as it was to believe, they were leaving tomorrow. That is, she and Marren were leaving tomorrow for sure. Kit had yet to specify whether she would be on the flight with them. Bridget supposed that since things had been going rather well this week with Lassino, it would just be Marren and herself departing from Naples. She would not be surprised in the least, either.

Bridget chided herself for wasting five euros a day on the Internet and decided it would be ridiculous to do so again. Instead, she called home. Which was what she should've been doing on a more regular basis, anyway.

Her mother, of course, was thrilled to hear from her, which made Bridget feel quite guilty for not calling more often. After filling Bridget in on the news at home, Mrs. Moretti chirped, "Well, I'm so glad you girls have been having a good time!" She then added, as Bridget knew she would, "But I'm glad you're coming home. I was afraid you might stay this time. So, meet any *nice* people?"

Ahh, yes, "nice people." That was Mom-speak for, *Did you meet any eligible males?* Her mother might've been deathly afraid of Bridget falling in love with an Italian and moving there, but she was still a mother—a mother who would forever be hopeful that her over-thirty daughter had finally found someone, and someone who was most likely to be a Catholic too.

"Everyone here is very *nice*, Mom." Bridget chuckled. The Lorenzo story was just too long to go into while on Kit's cell phone bill. And still too painful a disappointment.

Her mother sighed. "Okay, well, that's good. Oh, a couple of packages came for you from Italy. Did you *buy* something?" There was a slight wariness in her voice. Besides Bridget's socializing and adult-beverage intake, her shopping sprees also tended to cause her mother acute concern.

Boxes? Oh, yes, the boxes. Bridget had forgotten that she and Kit had actually gotten something done early in the week.

"We had Tino send some stuff home for us, so we wouldn't have to carry it in on our suitcases, some clothes and stuff." And a few ceramic platters, a ton of bottles of limoncello, a watercolor painting of Positano, a pair or two of Prada sandals (well, they'd been on sale)—no need to alarm her mother. Besides, most of what she had bought were gifts for friends … well, they could be (not the sandals, however).

Bridget added hastily, "Just leave them in the garage. I'll unpack them when I get home."

"Okay, honey. I love you. Have a safe trip and remember," Bridget mouthed the words silently as her mother said them, "*don't drink too much.* Annie will be there to pick you up."

Bridget ignored the "drinking too much" part and answered, "Love you too, Mom. See you tomorrow."

❖   ❖   ❖

"How's your stomach?" Bridget asked Kit as they sat in one of the candlelit corners of Segreto Giardino's dining terrace. The three of them had just about finished off the special pizza Lassino had sent out as an appetizer. They oohed and aahed over the fresh basil, mozzarella, and tomato, and Kit tried not to beam too much about the pizza being in the shape of a heart. It was too cute. You'd only make a pizza that way for someone if you liked her, right? Well, she thought so. She'd made the girls snap a few pictures of her and the pizza.

No, her stomach was fine, *for now*. It was the last three mornings that it had wreaked havoc on her and caused her to hole up in one of the bathrooms, hunched over the toilet. Kit was hoping she had some strange Italian strain of the flu bug, but for now, she'd blame it on her irritable bowel syndrome. Although, it wasn't her bowels bothering her. It was definitely only her stomach. Along with her testy bowels, Bridget and Marren knew how delicate her stomach was and how easily it went out of whack if she didn't follow certain dietary cautions. But in Italy, she usually threw her food cautions to the wind, and it had never really been a problem. Of course, maybe she had thrown some *other cautions* to the wind, as well …

She was a couple weeks overdue for her … well, *you know*. Of course, Kit was quite aware that traveling in different time zones, as well as eating differently, could certainly mess up a person's cycle. But this whole morning sickness … well, she had many friends who'd gone through it. But, she just *couldn't* be … Kit couldn't even utter the words to herself, lest they come true. Although, what would happen if she was? She knew she wanted a family. She wouldn't think twice about living in Positano. She certainly knew how she felt about Lassino. But how would Lassino feel? He'd been so loving and sweet this whole week. In fact, he had invited her to stay with him, should she decide to stay longer.

Kit thought she was hearing things when he said to her one morning, "So, where are you going to stay, if you stay longer?"

Kit had answered, "I don't know. I guess at one of the hotels." She hadn't even started looking to see if there were vacancies in any. Well, any that might be in her price range.

And he'd surprised her by actually saying, "No, you stay at my place."

"Really?" Kit had asked in shock. This was something she hadn't expected from Lassino. She was so used to having him quiz her on when she was getting out of town.

He squinted at her and said simply, "Yes, really. Unless you don't want to."

"No! That would be great. I'd love to. Thank you!" Kit had gushed in appreciation. That was the green light she needed to prolong her stay.

Lassino had shrugged. "No problem. I will have someone come and pick up your luggage the day you have to be out of the apartment."

It was one thing to invite her to stay at his place for a while longer. It would be a whole other thing for Lassino to find out he might be a father—and to make it worse, she couldn't even try to so much as look at one of those *tests* at the pharmacy. In fact, Kit thought they weren't even out on the shelves. She'd have to shamefully ask someone behind the counter. And then everyone in town would know that she was worried about being … well, *you know*.

So for now, she was just going to try to not think about it and pretend like she wasn't. Heck, she didn't know for sure anyway! She was just a person with a messed-up stomach; that was all.

"Oh, I'm feeling better," Kit said with a smile as she grabbed the last (and her third, or was it fourth?) piece of the beautiful, heart-shaped pizza.

"You must be, since your appetite sure is back!" Marren said. Oh, God, did Marren know? Jeez, she must be inhaling food in front of them like a, like a person who was … Kit conceded she *was* ravenous. Could it be? She took a quick swig of her white wine to settle her nerves. Wait, maybe she shouldn't be drinking! She set the wine glass and the piece of pizza down suddenly.

"Oh! I'm sorry, do either of you want this piece? I guess I kinda pigged out!" Kit said fretfully.

Marren answered with a smile, "Relax, I just said that because you haven't eaten all day."

Kit smiled what she hoped was a natural smile. God, she was paranoid. She was fine. She was fine. Still, she *was* absolutely starving. She *would* take the last piece of pizza.

From across the table, Bridget asked, "Okay, Kit, so what's the verdict? Are you coming home with us, or are you staying?"

Kit held the pizza mid-air and sighed with a slight blush.

"You're staying. That's what we figured," Marren cut in before Kit could say a word.

"But are you gonna be all right for a place to stay?" questioned Bridget.

"*Actually* ..." Kit said with suspense, "Lassino invited me to stay with *him.*"

"Does he know you're *really* staying, or does he think you're just saying that?" Bridget mused skeptically.

"Thanks a lot!" Kit cried with a laugh. She knew exactly what Bridget was getting at, and she'd even wondered the same thing herself.

Bridget stammered, "Well, you know how he is! Just ... have a back-up plan; otherwise, you may be sleeping on the beach!"

Kit nodded, "I know, I know. But girls, I'm telling you, he means it. I just know."

"Good, and cheers to Lassino." Marren raised her glass, and the others followed.

"I mean, think about it. Something is in the air. This whole week has been great—well, better than great! Do you realize we have had no drama whatsoever?" Kit cried as she set her glass down dramatically.

"That's because I'm here," answered Marren with a droll smile.

"She's got a point," added Bridget.

Kit explained excitedly, "No, no, you're not drama at all. What I mean is, no *other* drama involving anyone else has happened! I haven't heard from Rachel at all. Vinnie hasn't been anywhere near me, and Lassino and I are totally getting along!"

Marren raised her eyebrows and said knowingly, "It's because *I'm* here, Kit."

Kit and Bridget looked at Marren questioningly.

She waited a moment and then said, "Well, you know my first night here? After all that alcohol, well, I might've said a *few* things to—"

"To who?" Bridget asked with raised eyebrows and wide eyes.

"Uh, to Rachel. I think I basically told her to stop using Kit to get to Paolo. I told her that her paranoia had almost ruined you (pointing to Bridget) and Lorenzo and was totally uncalled for. Then I told her that being a psycho bitch wasn't going to get Paolo back. In fact, I told her she looked ridiculous and that she might do better finding someone closer to her own age." Marren winced ever so slightly.

Kit and Bridget both gasped. Kit asked incredulously, "Was she mad?"

"I don't know; I walked away, but she hasn't been bothering you anymore, has she?" Marren asked.

"Nooo. But what about Vinnie? You didn't say anything to him! Did you?" Kit said.

Marren shrugged sheepishly. "Guilty again. I saw him making his way toward you, and I stopped him."

"Oh, my God," Bridget uttered. "This is great."

Marren continued, pointed at Kit, and said, "I said something basically to the effect of him being a freak and that he had completely scared you out of your mind. That you couldn't even feel safe walking home any more. *And* that he if he ever tried something like that in the US, he'd have a restraining order slapped on him for harassment! I probably never should've had those three limoncello shots, should I?"

"No, no, I'm glad you did," Kit said in awe.

Kit added, "And here I thought Lassino had gone all chivalrous and told Vinnie off to protect me. And all along it was you!"

Marren smiled and said devilishly, "Come on; friends do that. And don't *ever* mess with the Irish!"

◆　　◆　　◆

"Hey, you know, I think we're on the same flight tomorrow!" Johnny exclaimed after Bridget told him what time they had to leave for their early-afternoon flight. Leaving Segreto Giardino, they had run into Johnny walking to the disco, and he had happily joined them. He admitted he was glad for a little company since Laura, unable to recover from her food poisoning, had decided to leave Positano the day before to return to Venice.

Though the disco was almost stretched to its usual heavy capacity, they'd all been able to take over a few of the coveted white couches that ran along the cavernous walls. Kit sat between Antonella and Mario. On the other side of Mario sat Marren. Mario was still trying to unsuccessfully finagle something between the two of them. Apparently, her supposed tryst with *the* K-Fed had made her all the more appealing, not only to the hot-blooded males, but also to the hot-blooded *gay* males. Giorgio sat on her other side with some of his entourage and quizzed her about their beach-chair escapade.

He queried breathlessly, "Thees Kee-Fed—you make the sex with heem. What was he like? Beeg and strong?"

Marren shook her head and admitted, "It really was not K-Fed. Just some guy … sorry to disappoint you."

Giorgio waved her off and said giddily, "Tell us anyway!"

Bridget thought the only ones who were missing right now from the usual crew were Lassino, who would be there as soon as the restaurant had closed, and *Paolo*. Bridget hadn't seen him since the dinner at Fabio's. And she'd never gone back to Da'Stella to try on the sandals. She turned to Johnny, who sat next to her, keeping her company.

"Tino's sending a driver to pick us up. Want to split the cost of the driver? We can swing by your hotel to pick you up, if you want," Bridget suggested.

"Will there be enough room? I don't have much, but I know Kit, alone, packs a lot!" he joked.

"Actually, there should be plenty of room," Bridget said. "Kit's not leaving tomorrow. She's staying an extra couple of weeks."

"Oh," Johnny said in surprise. "Where's she going to stay? Don't you all have to be out of the apartment?"

"She's going to stay with Lassino," Bridget said without even thinking. She looked quickly at Johnny and immediately felt awful. His face had become serious. Well, how could she have known? Johnny'd shown up in Positano with a girlfriend, and even weirder than that, he and Lassino had seemingly hit it off. Bridget had assumed, like everyone else, that Kit and Johnny had finally moved forward. Maybe not? She hoped she was wrong.

Johnny's face lightened and he said, "Yeah, that'd be great. Swing by, and I'll be ready to go."

"Sure," Bridget affirmed. She took a peek at Johnny out of the corner of her eye and wondered whether she should ask him about his thoughts on him and Kit, but there was no delicate way to go about that. Not that she wanted to counsel him on her best friend. Besides, she was about as helpful solving other people's love problems as she was her own! She kept quiet. Marren approached with Mario and Giorgio right behind her.

"We're dancing. Care to join us?"

Kit called out, "I will!" She stood up and dragged Antonello from the couch as well.

"I will too," chimed in Johnny.

"I'll stay here and guard your purses," Bridget said. She felt like sitting this one out. She watched their trail weave out and into the bobbing crowd. She didn't know how much longer she'd last. Despite her two-hour doze at the beach, she felt tired and was preoccupied with her suitcase that wouldn't quite close all the way. Bridget watched the door and thought how easy it would be to just sneak out and head back. Then Lassino's bespectacled face appeared at the door. And behind him stood Paolo with a tall, busty girl. In fact, she had a good two or three inches on him, but possibly it was due to her lace-up platforms. Bridget hoped they wouldn't see her on the couch and would pass straight to the bar. Lassino, in all his blindness, though, did see her and shuffled over.

"Hello. Where are they?" he motioned to the purses and drinks that littered the couches and tables where she sat.

"Dancing." Bridget pointed toward the dance floor.

Lassino shrugged and said, "I'll be back," and walked to the bar.

Bridget waited for Paolo to inevitably saunter by and stop to chat. Instead, holding onto his date's hand, he led her protectively through the crowd. As he approached the couches, he looked over, smiled, and waved, and kept going till he reached Lassino at the bar. Bridget wasn't sure if she'd rather Paolo pretend not to see her or to carelessly flit by like that. She then realized that *she* might've been *that girl* trailing Paolo into the disco tonight. Well, a week ago, she would've been that girl. It now seemed a million years ago.

It dawned on her, though, that she didn't want to be *that* girl anymore. In fact, she wasn't really a girl now, was she? But that was okay. Vacationing, especially *here*, had always conjured up feeling the need to be young and beautiful. And instead of truly enjoying vacation, Bridget spent most of the time stressing out over how many calories/points she'd used up, how many wrinkles were sprouting up on her face, and if men (practically half her age) on the beach had been gawking at her cellulite! What was the point of vacationing, then?

Bridget suddenly felt so much older and wiser, and in a good way. Well, she hadn't wasted the *whole* vacation lamenting over her flaws. She had fallen in love. It was a shame that she had realized it too late, but it was something. Now she knew she was ready for it. Should it *ever* reappear in her life again, she'd be prepared. And that was when Bridget realized that unlike last summer, when she'd dreaded stepping foot on the plane to leave, this year it was okay. She would miss Positano like she always did, but she was ready to go home.

+ + +

Kit pushed her way through the pulsing, sweaty bodies, until she reached an empty corner of the dance floor. She glanced back at where her friends were. A circle had formed around Marren, with various people jumping in and out to try some moves with her, Mario and Giorgio included. Apparently, word had caught on that Marren was the girl who had danced and romanced K-Fed. Everyone wanted to see her dance floor, maneuvering. K-Fed in Positano? Kit didn't believe it. She's seen other big stars here, but she doubted that Mr. Britney Spears strayed far from Vegas's Tao or the greater Los Angeles area. But let the Positano people think what they wanted. It did no harm. She wished she could take her own advice. Kit noted that Johnny wasn't in the dance circle anymore. She wiped her forehead and looked toward the bar. Lassino was talking with some friends and looking sideways at everyone who passed.

From behind her, someone gently touched her elbow. "Hey, Kit." She turned her head to find Johnny standing beside her, which explained where he'd gone.

"Hey." She smiled. She could feel the somewhat cooler air filtering in from the open door. It felt good.

Johnny looked down at her and said, "So, I hear you're staying longer."

Kit nodded her head yes.

"Where are you staying?" Johnny asked nonchalantly, but there was a bit of discord in his voice. Kit had the eerie feeling that Johnny already knew where she was staying. Anxious already, Kit understood that this wasn't going to be a pleasant conversation.

She said, just as nonchalantly, while looking out at the dance floor, "I'm staying with Lassino. He was nice enough to offer his place." There was silence from Johnny. Kit hoped that this signaled the end of this chat.

Johnny cleared his throat. "I'm leaving tomorrow."

"I know," she answered. *What was his point?*

He shook his head and said, "You should be on that plane with us. Kit, *what* are you *doing?*"

Kit sighed in exasperation. "What do you mean, *what am I doing?* I am staying longer in Positano!"

Johnny said seriously, "I mean, what are you doing with *Lassino?*"
What?

Kit sputtered, "Lassino's not the only reason I'm staying in Positano, Johnny. I like it here, and I do have other friends in this town!" She was getting angry. Why couldn't he just let go of them?

Johnny rolled his eyes, crossed his arms, and said, "Right, right. You're gonna stand there and tell me that your staying in Positano has nothing to do with Lassino?"

It had *something* to do with Lassino—well, a lot to do with him—but not *everything*, like Johnny was so implying. "You're being stupid," Kit countered defensively.

"I'm not the one being stupid. Look, I think Lassino's a nice guy. I actually do. But he's never going to treat you the way you want to be treated, the way you *should* be treated."

Kit snapped, "How do you know what I want and how I want to be treated?"

Johnny shouted, "Jesus, because I was your boyfriend, that's how I know! If you think this guy is going to bend over backward for you, you're wrong."

They both looked to the bar to see Lassino surrounded by a gaggle of scantily clad girls. Granted, some of them were his cousins, but still it looked bad, Kit thought.

Kit began to walk away. Johnny called out, "He doesn't love you, Kit."

Amazing how clear she heard those words in the crowded disco. And what the hell did Johnny know? Who did he think he was?

Kit spun around. "You don't know anything. And let's not point fingers, Mister 'show up with your hot Venetian girlfriend and flaunt it in everyone's face!'" She hadn't meant to sound jealous, but Kit realized that was how it sounded.

"Oh, that's nice coming from *you!* Laura was not my girlfriend, not that it's any of your business anymore. But just to let you know, she didn't leave Positano because of food poisoning. She left because I told her I was still in love with you." Johnny stared at her.

Kit felt she was going to be sick, legitimately sick. This wasn't happening, was it? *Why* was this happening? He was still in love with her? How could this be? Had she known this all along? Hadn't she seen it in his face, heard it in his voice, when they were in Naples?

"Come home, Kit. There's someone there who really loves you and is gonna be there for you. This place isn't real life. *This* isn't reality," Johnny argued.

"This is a very real place for a lot of people, and don't insult the people who actually live here!" Kit spoke.

"Fine, this is real for them. But even for them, it's like a fuckin' reality show! *This* is not *our* reality!" He motioned between the two of them. Why did she feel like she was having the same conversation she'd had with Julianna?

Kit said with scorn, "Don't try to put me in the same category with you, Johnny. We're different."

"We're not so different, Kit. We're really not," Johnny said gently.

Oh, yes they were. But a small seed of doubt had been planted.

"Have a safe trip back," Kit said tersely and headed toward the bar.

❖   ❖   ❖

Bridget had eventually been dragged off the couch by Mario and pushed into the dance-floor spectacle that was transpiring around Marren. For every sweaty guy (and they were all guys) that jumped in and tried to either grind with Marren or throw down some break-dancing moves, Bridget would hop in, sidestep the male dancer, and bust out with one of her own maneuvers, calling Marren out. Marren, in turn, responded with her own variation. It went back and forth like that until finally, it was just the two of them, the men dispersing, having realized they could never infiltrate that small circle (Mario and Giorgio, of course, had stayed for the show).

They called it quits around 3:00 a.m. and found Kit to say good-bye.

Bridget hugged Kit and said, "Okay, call me and let me know how everything's going. And be careful! And—"

"Don't even pull your mom's line about not drinking too much!" Kit laughed.

"Close, but no. I was going to give you another one of her favorites: make sure you come home. And don't do anything to embarrass the family! Ha ha!" Bridget said.

"Well, it's probably too late for that." Kit smiled sheepishly. *Little did they know,* she thought. "I'll call and give you updates, I promise."

"Thanks for everything, Kit. It was wonderful. *Just* what I needed, and with or without K-Fed!" Marren winked and hugged Kit. She then took her new flip-flops out of one hand and threw them on the floor to slip her feet into.

She raised her eyebrows and added, "Don't wanna lose those!"

"Talk to you soon!" Kit called after them. She watched the surly bouncer nod Bridget and Marren out the door. As her friends disappeared down the steps, Kit wondered if she should be leaving with them. It was too late now. She wouldn't think about it.

✦　✦　✦

Kit stood at the sink in Lassino's bathroom and stared at herself in the mirror. Usually, he'd get out a pair of shorts and a T-shirt for her to wear, not that they stayed on her for long, but she'd headed straight to the bathroom, her stomach once again finding an inopportune time to start acting up. She hoped it didn't pull anything tomorrow morning. Kit picked up one of the tubes of fancy facial cleanser Lassino kept on the glass stand next to the sink. She was grateful that Lassino was so attuned to personal hygiene and beauty regimens. He *was* Italian, though. Knowing him, it wasn't too farfetched to think that he'd bought them for himself. Then again, Kit wondered if he had purchased these with her in mind or for some other female guests. Johnny and his annoying little spiel on Lassino and the unrealness of Positano immediately replayed in her head.

He doesn't love you, Kit. He doesn't love you, Kit. He doesn't love you, Kit.

"Shut up," Kit mumbled irritably at the mirror, as if it was Johnny. She squeezed the tube so hard that gel shot out all over the sink, making a disgusting, fartlike sound in the process. She sighing and wiped some into her hands. As she worked up a sudsy lather under the warm water, Kit wondered again if she'd made the right decision to stay behind.

✦　✦　✦

When Kit finally emerged from the bathroom, exfoliated, rinsed, moisturized, flossed, and mouth-rinsed, she found Lassino reclined on the bed in his briefs, looking at pictures on her hefty Nikon digital camera. She hadn't brought it out the last few evenings, giving the camera and everyone else a break from her nonstop snapping, but she had decided to drag it along for the girls' last night in Positano.

She climbed across the bed and sat next to Lassino. He held the camera literally an inch away from his glass frames as he clicked through the pictures and occasionally snorted in amusement. Kit didn't even bother to ask for a T-shirt. She was exhausted and lay back against the pillows to close her eyes.

Just as Kit's breathing had reached its peaceful, sleeplike rhythm, just as she was drifting off into a REM-like state, Lassino spoke up. "When was this taken?"

Kit thought she might be dreaming that Lassino was speaking to her until she heard his voice again and he more urgently asked, "Kit! When was this?"

She slowly opened her eyes and tried to focus on him in her drowsiness. Lassino was holding the camera out at her, practically in her face, a perplexed look upon his.

Kit slowly pushed herself up and took the camera from Lassino. She rubbed her eyes and forced them to take in the picture. There she and Johnny sat, smiling. A table, complete with a red-checkered tablecloth, dripping candles, a pizza, and a bottle of wine, sat between them. *When had that been taken?* Kit wondered. Oh, yes, she remembered. That had been their night in Naples. *What a night.* They had sort of been having a good time, as much as Kit could after the shock of Johnny showing up in Naples! Yes, the picture had definitely been taken *before* she'd told Johnny *not* to come to Positano, which had caused him to go ballistic and then crazy with the Chianti.

An easy picture to explain, really. Hadn't she told Lassino that Johnny had shown up in Naples? Kit could've sworn she had. But wait a minute. The thought of Johnny actually showing up in Positano after the conversation they'd had that evening had seemed so unlikely, and the whole situation had been so totally innocent, that Kit had simply thought there was no need to even mention it. The angry, questioning look on Lassino's face right now suggested that maybe she had been wrong. Well, she could explain.

"Oh, that was in Naples. Didn't I tell you that Johnny showed up in Naples?" Kit said easily, as if it were completely normal for her ex-boyfriend to show up unexpectedly on her hotel room doorstep halfway around the world.

"*In Napoli? This* summer? Before you came to Positano?" Lassino asked, conveying that he did not see the normalcy of it.

Kit nodded. "Well, yes. He found out where I was staying and just showed up. I had *no* idea, and there he was. So we just went to dinner, and that was … it." And that *was* it.

So why was Lassino looking at her like she was withholding important information?

"Why did he just show up?" asked Lassino as he folded his arms.

Hmm, how to explain this? Kit would leave out the part where she'd included Johnny on the e-mail sent to friends who should come visit them in Italy …

Kit took her time answering. "Johnny wanted to … see Italy and found out where I was staying. Then at dinner, it became clear that he hadn't just come to Italy to travel. He wanted to … get back together." Kit inhaled and exhaled quickly and then said, "But I told him it was over and *not* to come to Positano! I never knew he was going to come here! I never knew he was going to come to Italy!"

Lassino squinted and asked, "And that was it? After dinner, he just left and went off by himself in Napoli?"

"Well, *noo*. He was staying at the same hotel …" Kit's voice trailed off. This was definitely a bad time to tell him that Johnny had passed out in her room—on top of her bed.

"Did you sleep with him?" shot out of Lassino's mouth. Good Lord, was he kidding?

"No!" Kit shouted indignantly. However, she couldn't lie. Kit had never lied to Lassino before, and she wouldn't now. She wasn't wrong. She hadn't done anything. The truth could not hurt her.

"He did stay in my room," Kit said and watched Lassino's eyes bulge behind his thick lenses. She said quickly, "He hadn't even booked a room at the hotel. He'd thought he'd be staying with me, and he was so drunk that he passed out in my bed!"

Lassino was incredulous. "*In your bed?*"

Kit stammered nervously, "I mean ... I mean, *on* my bed, *on* my bed! Not *in* my bed! On my bed, with all his clothes *on*! And I had all my clothes on!" Oh, no, this wasn't going as she had hoped.

Lassino spoke rapidly in his grunty, caveman Italian. Kit assumed he was swearing at her or about her. He stopped for a moment to scream, "Johnny is in love with you, and you let him sleep in your bed! You still have feelings for him! You slept with him!" He began ranting in warplike speed Italian again.

Kit tried to calm him down. "He was passed out! Look, I don't normally try to have sex with someone who's comatose!"

Lassino glared at her and yelled, "Stop *bullsheetting* me!"

This was so asinine! He was so insane!

"Oh, I wouldn't *dare* try to bullshit the king of bullshit!" Kit screamed back. She had had enough of this.

Lassino paused to acknowledge her retort. Then he stood up and pointed to the door.

"You cannot stay here. You've lied to me. I cannot have someone who has lied to me stay here!"

"You are crazy! I have never lied to you, ever, since the very beginning!" Kit spat out.

Lassino shrugged and said, "Get out! I cannot have someone who has lied to me stay here!" He was demented, never mind that he was wrong. She hadn't done anything. Kit began crying. She couldn't help it. She stood up, grabbed her camera and wallet, and walked out of the bedroom and toward the front door. Lassino followed along after her, as if he was a bouncer escorting an unwanted patron out of a club.

Once again, he spoke disdainfully. "You have lied to me. I cannot let someone who lies to me sleep here!"

"Thanks, I heard you the first two times." Kit wiped her face and opened the front door. He was so full of shit. He was trying to get rid of her, because Johnny was right, Lassino didn't love her.

Lassino then added, as if everything was fine, "Do you want me drop you off at your place?"

Kit turned and looked at him with disgust and anger. "No, I cannot accept rides from people who accuse me of *lying*!"

She was dying inside, but she would hold her head up high ... and walk that god-awful curvy, dangerous road, *in heels*, for as long as it took her to get to the other side of the mountain and the apartment. Damn him.

"Fine! Do not expect to hear from me again!" he shouted after her childishly.

"Good. *Fuck you, jackass*," Kit said under her breath.

◆　　◆　　◆

Bridget and Marren had only had about two hours of sleep when Kit finally reappeared at the apartment. Bridget really wasn't even asleep yet. Instead, she lay in bed mentally running through the check-off list in her head and, hearing the door open, she became alarmed. She'd woken Marren and made her tiptoe down the hallway with her to see who the early-morning intruder might be.

Kit sat, weeping silently on one of the lounge chairs. After she had explained the showdown that she'd had with Lassino and that she would, indeed, be leaving with them, the girls had tried, albeit unsuccessfully, to cheer her up.

Kit waved them off, wiped her eyes, and said tearfully, "Lassino is going to regret it one day … he will. Even germs know when they're dying! Even … even cockroaches know when they've eaten Raid!"

"Are you planning on poisoning him?" Bridget asked with a smile before adding, "Not that he wouldn't deserve it this time."

Kit spoke through her sniffles. "I just meant metaphorically. All evil must come to an end! Every flea-bitten, mangy, rabies-carrying, dirty dog will have his day! And Lassino will! He will regret treating me this way!" Kit practically shook her fist in the air.

"That's the spirit! Just please don't go looking for 'I Will Survive' on your iPod right now," Marren said.

Kit smiled weakly and turned to Bridget. "Bridget, you were right. I needed to have a back-up plan."

Bridget sighed. "I didn't want to be right, though. At least this happened while we were still here."

Kit nodded and then scowled. "Ugh, and Johnny'll be happy that he can gloat now!"

"Yeah, about Johnny … um … well, he's driving *with us* to the airport," Bridget said.

"Oh, yes, well, why the hell not?" Kit snorted in disgust and walked off the patio.

"I think she took that well. Good night, er ... good morning, er, whatever. I'm going back to bed," Marren said and headed off into her room.

In the morning—well, later in the *same* morning—the three of them were racing around the apartment, on and off the balcony, scurrying in and out of rooms, nearly colliding with each other as they cleared things off tables, threw things out, and shoved items into their bulging suitcases. You know, all the things you did when you'd overslept and had to be ready for the driver who was arriving in, say, fifteen minutes. Bridget felt like she was running on pure adrenaline. She was actually looking forward to the plane ride, where she might be able to get a little shut-eye, and maybe even without the aid of her beloved Ambien.

"Where's my flip-flop? Has anyone seen my flip-flop?" Marren shouted hysterically from her room.

Before the girls could answer, she called out, "Found it! Was under the bed!"

Kit opened the front door and yelled, "I'm taking the trash bags down to the dumpster, and then I'm gonna drop the keys off to Olivia." She left the door open behind her.

Bridget decided to start bringing the bags up to the street. She clumsily dragged Big Blue out the door and up the two flights, till she was on street level. Sweating already, she leaned against the suitcase for a moment to catch her breath. Sera was hanging laundry on her balcony. She glanced down at Bridget, without her usual death glare, but with a nonchalance that she reserved for those she was accustomed to seeing—those that *belonged* here on *her* street. Then she looked away and went back to her laundry-hanging. Well, wasn't that something? Bridget almost waved at her but decided not to push it.

A scooter whipped around the bend, honked twice, and then slowed to a stop at the curb in front of her. Clad in a black polo shirt (collar upturned), white cargo shorts, and his sandals, Paolo pulled off his helmet and smiled his wide, toothy grin at her.

"Bridget, hello! So you are leaving today?"

Bridget smiled and nodded.

Paolo looked at her a bit shyly and then said, "I am sorry we did not get to talk last night, but, uh—"

"It's okay; I understand." Bridget waved her hand and smiled.

"I thought maybe I would see you in my shop ..." Paolo's voice teetered off.

Bridget explained, "I meant to come in and buy those sandals, but I just never got around to it." Yet another thing she'd somehow not found the time to do this week.

Paolo shrugged easily. "Ah, well, someone bought the last pair of size thirty-seven anyway."

Bridget said ruefully, "I guess it just wasn't meant to be."

Paolo looked at her, winked, and then said meaningfully, "No, I guess it just wasn't meant to be."

She blushed and looked away. *No, they had not been meant to be ...*

Paolo then hopped off his scooter, reached over, and pulled Bridget in for an Italian double-kiss. He then grabbed her face, kissed her on the lips, and whispered, "Ciao, beautiful girl."

In surprise, Bridget watched Paolo get back onto the scooter. He threw his helmet on, revved the motor, and scooted away from the curb. He shouted over his shoulder, "Ciao, Bella! See you next summer!"

Bridget waved then turned around in time to see a large, black Mercedes pull up. Their driver was here, and thankfully, he wasn't Vinnie. She wondered briefly where Vinnie been all week long. She said hello and left the driver to awkwardly fumble with Big Blue while she ran downstairs to get more luggage.

"Okay, all set. Is the driver here?" Marren stood in the middle of the patio surrounded by the rest of their luggage and extra carry-ons.

"Yep, he's up there. Is Kit back?" Bridget asked as she grabbed her gold tote and another wheelie.

"Yeah, she's in the bathroom, *again*. I hope she's okay on the flight," Marren muttered as she stacked a few smaller bags on top of her large suitcase. "See you up there." She wheeled around Kit's luggage and out the door.

Bridget took one last look around the patio, out over the shingled rooftops that sloped down below the apartment and then out to the sea that stretched out so brilliantly. Who would be renting the apartment next? A brief feeling of sadness took hold of Bridget. She quickly reminded herself that it would all still be here next summer when she came back. That is, *if* she decided to return. There could never be another summer like the one she and Kit had just experienced. She'd wait and see.

Bridget paused at the door. Did she have everything? Passport, wallet, camera? Yes, yes, yes. Her address book? Yes. Wait, she'd almost forgotten Lorenzo's address! She'd left it crumpled up on the kitchen counter. She'd probably never hear from him, and she would most likely never get in touch with him. Yet, it made her feel slightly better knowing that if she *wanted to*, she *could* get a hold of him. Bridget hurried into the kitchen and checked the counter where she'd thrown it that night, but it was spotless. She looked wildly around the kitchen at the counters, the table, under the table, all over the floor, but after their crazed early morning cleaning, *there was nothing.*

No!

"Kit!" Bridget yelled.

"I'm coming! I'm ready!" Kit flew into the kitchen.

"Kit, did you see a small, crumpled paper on the counter, by the sink?" Bridget asked quickly, her heart thumping in anticipation.

"Yeah, I threw it out with all the other junk on the counter. Why? Oh, no … was there something on it?" Kit asked cautiously.

Bridget closed her eyes and shook her head. "Lorenzo's address, phone number, e-mail …"

"Oh, no. Sorry. I *didn't know.*" Kit spoke plaintively, and Bridget recognized the defensive tendency that was about to surface, which always did when Kit felt accused.

Bridget said hastily, "It's my fault. It's my fault. How the hell were you supposed to know? I crumpled the paper up."

"I can run down and check the dumpster. The garbage bags are right on top," Kit suggested hopefully.

Although it was slightly tempting, Bridget dismissed the idea of her friend running down the two hundred-plus stairs to rummage through the dumpster. Clearly, this was a sign that she and Lorenzo weren't supposed to be. It was time to let it go.

Bridget answered, "No, no, you're *not* going through the garbage! The driver's here. We gotta get going." She left through the green door and headed up the steps.

✦   ✦   ✦

Bridget opened her eyes and put her Rosary beads back into the pocket of her lightweight cardigan. They had survived takeoff. Of course, she wouldn't feel safe until they turned the seat belt sign off, but they were successfully airborne. She and the girls sat in a row of three. They'd kindly let Bridget have the window seat since she was so short that the neck rest always hit her uncomfortably. She needed something to lean against or she'd risk a crick in her neck.

Marren said, "I'll take the middle seat. As soon as I have a glass of wine, I'll be asleep anyway. Besides, Kit, you and your stomach need the aisle seat."

"Are you drinking already?" Kit asked with a laugh.

Marren replied without hesitation, "Yes."

"Well, it is the afternoon. We'd be having a prosecco in Positano right now, anyway," Kit said as she looked down the aisle to see if the drink cart was anywhere in sight. She turned back around and stopped suddenly. The woman across the aisle was reading an Italian magazine. Nothing notable about that. It was what was on the cover of the magazine that made her gawk. Kit hit Marren with her arm and whispered, "Marren, Bridget, look at the magazine that lady is reading!"

"What?" Marren peeked over Kit's shoulder. "Kit, I can't read Italian."

Bridget craned her neck to get a better look as Kit hissed excitedly, "You don't need to know Italian—look!"

Marren read out loud, "Britney, K-Fed, something, something, Capri, something, something and … Positano. *Positano?*" She glanced quickly at Kit and then Bridget with a startled look on her face.

Underneath the exclamatory phrases was a picture of a very ripped and tattooed K-Fed cavorting with some blonde (*not* Britney) on a Capri beach, and then a somewhat grainier picture of him in a fedora dancing with another nameless woman. The woman could only be seen from the back. But she appeared to have auburn hair and the same distinctively striped Sonia Rykiel halter that Marren had worn …

"*Oh. My. God!*" Kit shrieked and then covered her mouth quickly as a few heads turned. A hunky flight attendant stopped and asked with concern, "Is everything all right, miss?"

"Yes, yes, sorry," Kit squeaked. Marren turned toward Kit with her mouth agape. The flight attendant smiled and moved down the aisle.

"Oh, stop. *No way,*" said Bridget in amused shock. Marren stared again at the woman across the aisle with wide eyes and said, "Kit, ask her if you can have that magazine when she's done with it."

✦   ✦   ✦

A week had already gone by since they'd returned from Positano. Kit had immediately booked a flight to New York to visit some friends. Unable to convince Bridget into coming along, she'd taken off two days later. When she'd get back was anyone's guess—roughly a day before school started, no doubt. Bridget suspected that was Kit's way of dealing with her stressful departure from Positano—diversion through more travel.

Bridget stayed home, adjusted to the time change (and subpar food), and tried to retain that relaxed Italian attitude she annually acquired in Positano of refusing to rush about, that, "Don't worry about it. It'll get done" mantra. It had worked so far. She hadn't even gone into her classroom yet to start fixing it up. Of course, that was probably just pure procrastination. But ... it *would* get done.

Yet, every day, she did think about Positano, She would comment to herself, "Ten days ago at this time, we were on the beach, talking to Tomaso," or "Two weeks ago, Lorenzo and I were at the Fornillo beach party ..." She was finding it difficult to erase the jutting cliffside town and Lorenzo from her mind just yet.

Maybe that was why today, she was finally going to open the box they'd had shipped from Positano. The huge box had sat in the center of the garage, causing her mother to complain and ask when she'd ever be able to park the car inside again. Bridget slit the top of the box open and then lifted out, undid all the bubble wrapping, and examined the assortment of items she'd had Tino pack: ceramic picture frames, a platter, a bunch of limoncello and limon crema, a plethora of Baci candy (she'd figured only two Weight Watchers points per candy), her new Pradas, the watercolor, and ... the stash of Nutella in the commemorative Italian World Cup jars. *Oh, the Nutella ...*

Bridget winced and looked down. It was then that she realized that there was a second box, much smaller, hidden behind the large one she had just unpacked. She racked her brain trying to remember what else she possibly might've bought. She was pretty sure the rest had been able to fit into her suitcase. She sat down on the treadmill to open it. Inside, she found what looked to be a shoebox. Bridget lifted the lid and gasped. It was *her* pair of sandals from Da'Stella. There they sat in all their black suede, gorgeous, Swarovski-blinged glory. Had Paolo sent them to her? She lifted the sandals out of the box with childish glee. They were lovely; she turned them over to check, and they were, indeed, her size. Delighted, but slightly puzzled, Bridget was speechless. Not that there was anyone with her in the garage she could talk to anyway … maybe there was a card, a bill, even, some sort of explanation. She peeked in the shoe and the box and noticed that there was something else, something black in there as well. Bridget lifted it out and found that there were also actually two smaller things … *a black bikini top and the matching bottom.* She stared at them incredulously. Wait a minute. This package was not from Paolo. It was from Lorenzo!

Bridget threw the bikini next to her on the treadmill and grabbed the box. There was a small envelope that had "Bridget" written on it. With a pounding heart, she shakily tore it open and read.

> *Dear Maestrina,*
>
> *Hope you are not mad at me for sending the bikini. Much more sensible than the sandals, I think. But you'll never agree with me and will probably never wear it. That's why I bought the sandals too. It may be a long shot, but I hope to see you wearing them* both *in Positano. Or maybe much sooner than that? I will let you decide.*
>
> *Love,*
>
> *Lorenzo*

Bridget read the note a few more times. He hadn't said he loved her, but it did say "Love, Lorenzo." *And he hoped to see her! Who cared if it was in a bikini? This wasn't over yet! They weren't over yet!* She'd see him in Positano … or maybe *here* … or maybe in *Florida!* Bridget grabbed the note, the sandals, and the bikini and danced around wildly. No, it was not over yet, not by a long shot.

Epilogue

They gathered in the upstairs dining room at La Bella Vita to celebrate the one-year anniversary of Diana and Leo's wedding in Calabria. Diana and Leo had opted not to take any trips to celebrate the event, since Diana was expecting their baby within the month. Instead, they'd planned a small party with close friends. The girls were all on-hand to celebrate. As food was served, drinks poured, and the wedding album (that Kit had made with her photos) passed around, it was difficult for any of them to believe that a whole year had passed. So much had happened ...

Marren had returned to an empty apartment. Liam had, indeed, taken her threat seriously. He and all his belongings were gone by the time she got back from Positano. However, Marren found one thing Liam had left behind: a note profuse with his love and sorrow, with an engagement ring attached to it. Marren accepted but still insisted that during the engagement Liam get his own place while she found a new roommate. They'd sorted through a lot, and it hadn't been easy. Now that a year had passed, all in all, things were going better than ever between Marren and Liam, although, he did find her sudden fascination with Britney and K-Fed a bit odd at times. He would live with it, though.

They were working on a wedding date within the next year, possibly in Ireland with a Positano honeymoon. Marren felt that Positano had come at just the right time for her and Liam. She would forever be grateful for that much-needed trip, even if it had involved K-Fed. Luckily, the sandals and limoncello were the only souvenirs she'd brought back from the Amalfi Coast, unlike one of her other friends, who now had a *baby*.

Kit sat at one end of the table and contentedly cradled the baby in her arms. His eyes were closed, and his mouth moved and made tiny sucking sounds. She wondered what babies dreamt about. Did this little one dream about gelato, and prosecco, fresh basil and mozzarella, the hundreds of stairs with no handrails, the pyramid-shaped town built into the side of a mountain, the rocky beach? Could babies somehow know and have an affinity for the place where they'd been conceived? When this baby grew up, would he have a predisposition for all those things? And someday, would he want to travel around the world to meet his father?

"Damn, Kit, you're a natural! Look at little Gianni, asleep like that!" Julianna cooed.

Kit smiled and rocked the baby some more. She *was* a natural. She could do this. And someday, Kit hoped she would. As soon as they'd gotten back from Positano, her body appeared to resume its normal functions. Her cycle returned with a vengeance, and her irritable bowel syndrome kept up its steady pace. Now, besides dairy and anything acidic or carbonated, she had gluten products to add to her list of food allergies. Kit still couldn't explain the whole morning sickness that had overcome her in Positano. Perhaps her nerves had gotten the best of her, or maybe she had created the psychosomatic symptoms because she'd really wanted to start a new life in Positano. Whatever the cause, Kit admitted that given what had transpired with Lassino, it was more than just as well that she hadn't been, well, *you know.*

Ahh, Lassino, her Italian jackass. After spewing that she'd never hear from him again, he began sending her amusing texts every other month asking if she was still mad at him and whether she was returning to Positano the following summer. Kit ignored his question about whether she was still mad (what an idiot—of course she was), and she kept her replies lighthearted and noncommittal. When she finally mentioned that yes, she was coming back to Positano, he immediately sent a text saying she could stay with him. Kit had laughed at how absurd the offer was after he'd thrown her out so easily last August. She told him thank you, but she already had a place to stay. And she did.

The apartment was not for rent this summer and would've been a silly and expensive choice anyway, since she was traveling solo. But Antonella had offered her a room, and Kit had taken her up on it. The situation was perfect and low-maintenance. Kit was going to enjoy not having to play hostess around the clock. In addition, this summer, her physical and emotional safety would remain intact. In other words, she would not have to deal with stalkers, romance with a crazed pizza chef, or ex-boyfriends. Antonella had informed Kit that Vinnie had left his wife and run off with Rachel to her native Australia and Fabio had ended up wedding his supermodel girlfriend, as well as hiring a blonde nanny who suspiciously resembled Kit.

Yes, Kit could cross those worries off her list. And she was completely done with Lassino. He was nothing more than that ever-annoying friend. She couldn't completely hate him, but she'd never take him seriously—or romantically—again. And of course, Johnny wouldn't be there either, professing his love for her. Although, the timing this year would've have been much better for that. However, they hadn't spoken since Positano. Kit felt that this time, she'd finally driven away Johnny for good. It was possible that she'd thrown out the truest love she'd ever received. But there could be no regrets. She could only go forward and be optimisitic for the future, no matter how unrealistic people might think she was sometimes. So, Kit might not have a man in her life right now, but she had *something*. She had family and friends, and she had … Positano.

"Here, Kit, let me take him. It's almost time to feed him." Kit was transported from her thoughts of Positano and back to the party. She handed the sleeping baby to his mother, Julianna.

"Oh, sweet little boy. Are you gonna wake up now?" Julianna whispered in her raspy voice and stroked the baby's face with her small, manicured hand. The whole table stopped to watch her.

"Shit! Can you guys believe I have a baby?" squealed Julianna as she looked up at them.

A solid *no* resounded across the table. Julianna laughed. "I know, me either! Well, sometimes you're given a precious little gift like this, and you just gotta take it. Isn't that right, Gianni? You're my precious little angel, aren't you?" She rocked the baby back and forth.

"I'll tell you one thing. I am glad I'm not pregnant any more. I couldn't stand not being able to highlight my hair or get Botox!" she said to the girls.

They watched her in awe. You'd never have known she'd been pregnant at all. She was back in her tight, size-two jeans, her push-up bras, and stilettos. In fact, Julianna told them that she had more guys asking her out now that she had a baby than in her pre-pregnancy days. She was truly what the Italian men coined her: *"amazing!"*

As for Italian men, Julianna had yet to reveal who the father was. She would only say, "The father lives in Italy. He's not gonna be interested in helping me out with the baby. So I don't even know if I'm gonna tell him. What good's he gonna do?"

Kit had questioned, "But don't you want Gianni to know who his father is? And … who is the father? Come on, tell us!"

Although the girls pestered her to no end about whether it was Mario, from the night they'd gone down to the beach together, Julianna simply replied that she'd let them know after she let the baby's father know ... if she ever did. Yes, the father could certainly be Mario. But there had been *someone else* in Positano. Julianna decided she'd have to wait till the baby got older—perhaps he'd exhibit some of his father's distinct looks. Until then, she was content to raise him as a single mother. Women all over the world did it, and she would, too.

What good would a father who lived in another country be to her son? And anyway, her traveling days were over for the time being. She had a beautiful four-month old son and a booming business to run. Kit could go back to that jacked-up town, Positano, without her. Julianna couldn't imagine what Kit was thinking in returning, but Kit was a bit messed-up. Julianna had tried to warn her, but some people just had to learn the hard way. No, Julianna decided she wouldn't be going back to Positano, unless it was to introduce her son to his father.

And Bridget ... her life had changed dramatically in its own way. For starters, she'd learned to save money, because now she had to pay rent. She'd moved in with Marren for the term of her engagement, which gave her at least about another year and a half before she had to look for another place to live.

Of course, she still worried nonstop about her mother being on her own, but she was only ten minutes away. In fact, she thought she might be home more now than when she had lived there! Bridget would miss heading to Positano with Kit this year, but she couldn't go. She had a guest coming for a month-long visit: *Lorenzo.* After all, it was his turn again, since she'd gone to Florida for Memorial Day weekend.

Yes, after finding Lorenzo's care package in the garage, Bridget had been ecstatic, although short of sending out a private investigator, she was unsure about how to find him. She didn't have to worry for too long. Lorenzo called her a week later, concerned whether she'd received the package and concerned about *her.* And so they began again, on American soil, but thousands of miles apart. Bridget was a little skeptical since, on a good day, she had trouble dating anyone within a five-minute radius—and here Lorenzo was, across the country! And yet, they were still together. Bridget was forever surprised at how things managed to work out, if you just let them.

About the Author

Catie Costa lives in the San Francisco Bay Area. This is her first novel.